Pediatric and Adolescent Gynecology

Pediatric and Adolescent Gynecology

Third Edition

S. Jean Herriot Emans, M.D.
Associate Professor of Pediatrics, Harvard Medical School;
Associate Chief, Division of Adolescent/Young Adult Medicine,
The Children's Hospital, Boston

Donald Peter Goldstein, M.D.
Assistant Clinical Professor of Obstetrics and Gynecology,
Harvard Medical School; Attending Surgeon, The Children's Hospital;
Attending Obstetrician/Gynecologist, Brigham and Women's Hospital, Boston

Little, Brown and Company
Boston/Toronto/London

Contents

16. Teenage Pregnancy   505

17. Sexual Abuse   539

18. Legal Issues in Pediatric and Adolescent Gynecology   569
    Richard Bourne

19. Sex Education   581
    Robert P. Masland, Jr.

    Appendixes

    1. Instruction Sheet for Taking 28-Day Contraceptive Pills   587

    2. Informed Consent for Oral Contraceptives   589

    3. Patient Handout for Calcium Intake   591

    4. Sexual Abuse Protocol of the State of California   593

    5. Sexuality: Additional Information Sources   599

    Index   605

Contributing Authors

Richard Bourne, J.D., Ph.D.
Associate Professor, Department of Sociology, Northeastern
University; Attorney, Office of the General Counsel,
The Children's Hospital, Boston

Robert P. Masland, Jr., M.D.
Associate Professor of Pediatrics, Harvard Medical School;
Chief, Division of Adolescent/Young Adult Medicine,
The Children's Hospital, Boston

Preface

Over the past few years, many pediatricians, obstetrician-gynecologists, family practitioners, and nurses have expressed an interest in a simplified approach to the common gynecologic problems of children and adolescents. Problems such as the differential diagnosis of ambiguous genitalia, vulvovaginitis, precocious development, and sexual abuse arise in the care of infants and children. Dysmenorrhea, irregular periods, sexually transmitted diseases, and pregnancy represent common presenting complaints of adolescents.

Many gynecologic problems can be diagnosed on the basis of the history and the physical examination, including rectoabdominal palpation. Over the past decade, more pediatric practitioners have become comfortable doing vaginal examinations to meet the increasing medical needs of the sexually active adolescent. A step-by-step description of the routine examination of the child and adolescent is covered in Chapter 1. It is hoped that physicians in practice and residents in pediatrics and family practice will become proficient in medical gynecology. Many gynecologists are unfamiliar with the techniques of examining small children who have vulvovaginitis or are victims of sexual abuse as well as methods for approaching the young adolescent with delayed puberty or amenorrhea. A positive, nontraumatic examination will help these girls seek future care.

In Chapter 4, the physiology of puberty is reviewed as a background to the assessment of the child with signs of sexual precocity (Chap. 5) and to the evaluation of the common menstrual problems of the adolescent (Chaps. 6 and 7). The importance of growth charts is underscored throughout these sections, as they often provide a clue to the differential diagnosis. The patient can benefit from ongoing dialogue among gynecologists and medical physicians and nurses to give the best care in areas of contraception, pregnancy, and sexual abuse. Psychosocial issues involved in the provision of medical care are discussed in every section.

In general, the discussion focuses on the most common diagnoses rather than rare conditions that the generalist is less likely to encounter. Additional references are listed at the end of each chapter for the physician or nurse interested in more extensive reading on a particular subject. Treatment regimens included in each section are intended as suggestions, not as the only method of therapy, especially since treatments in many areas are rapidly changing.

Our third edition has been expanded to include the gynecologic problems seen in our clinics over the past 8 years since the publication of the second edition. Special interests have included the evaluation of pelvic pain, congenital anomalies of the uterus and vagina, oligo-menorrhea and hirsutism, treatment of estrogen deficiency states, vaginitis, contraceptive compliance, sexual abuse, and sexuality. Chapters have been updated, and new sections have been added on human papillomavirus, acquired immunodeficiency syndrome (AIDS), *Chlamydia trachomatis*, and sexual abuse. The controversies and use of the colposcope in the evaluation of the sexually abused girl are discussed. Color plates of normal and abnormal genital anatomy have been added. The 1990s could not be addressed without the addition of a chapter on legal issues in pediatric and adolescent gynecology.

As authors, we want to stimulate the physician to become knowledgeable and proficient in the gynecologic care of the child and the adolescent. Working together for the past 15 years, we established a comprehensive program for gynecologic service and teaching at The Children's Hospital, utilizing two nurse counsellors and a Fellow in the Gynecology Clinic and a nurse practitioner and Fellows in the Adolescent Clinic in addition to valuable full-time staff physicians. Both clinics have benefitted from being able to offer primary care. We are grateful to the gynecologists, pediatricians, family physicians, and nurses who have referred many patients to our clinics. Sometimes we have been puzzled; we hope we have usually been able to provide a diagnosis and effective medical/surgical therapy. The year 1988 saw a transition at The Children's Hospital when Donald Peter Goldstein, M.D., retired as Chief of Gynecology after 15 years to devote more time to private practice; Dr. Marian Craighill has continued the strong tradition of service to children and adolescents.

The dialogue between medical and surgical specialties to provide excellent care to pediatric patients with gynecologic problems culminated in 1986 in Washington, D.C., when the North American Society for Pediatric and Adolescent Gynecology (NASPAG) was established with Dr. Alvin Goldfarb as President. The sharing of ideas, research, techniques, and protocols at annual meetings and informally among members, as well as the creation of a new journal devoted to adolescent gynecology, *Adolescent and Pediatric Gynecology*, has been of significant importance for the future of this field. Establishment of ties to the American Academy of Pediatrics, American College of Obstetricians and Gynecologists, and Society for Adolescent Medicine has furthered the mission of NASPAG.

We are indebted to the many people who have helped in the preparation of this and previous editions: Joan Mansfield, M.D.; Samir Najjar, M.D.; Jan Paradise, M.D.; Marian Craighill, M.D.; John F. Crigler, Jr., M.D.; Richard Bourne, J.D., Ph.D.; Stuart Bauer, M.D.; Jane Share, M.D.; Rita Teele, M.D.; Elizabeth Woods, M.D., M.P.H.; Joan Wenning, M.D.; Odette Pinsonneault, M.D.; Jacques Mailloux,

M.D.; Trina Anglin, M.D.; Susan Pokorny, M.D.; Kenneth Welch, M.D.; Mary Aruda, R.N., P.N.P.; Beverly Hector-Smith, R.N.C., M.S.; Elinor Wolfson, R.N.; Susan Ogle, R.N., P.N.P.; and Mary McCann. Our special thanks go to Ann Davis, M.D., for her extraordinary help in reading the entire manuscript and her many suggestions; Robert Masland, Jr., M.D., for his encouragement of this undertaking and his authorship of the chapter on sex education; Hardy Hendren, M.D., and David Nathan, M.D., for their support and understanding of the need for the Division of Gynecology at The Children's Hospital; Dottie MacDonald, R.N., and Ann Barrett-Dodwell, R.N., M.S.N., for the encouragement of the role of nurses in our program; Laurette Langlois and Beth Ingraham for artistic contributions; Jim Koefler for his much appreciated help with photography and preparation of the various figures; The Children's Hospital Media Services Department; Miriam Geller for tireless searching of the medical literature; and Annette Luongo for her invaluable assistance in preparing this manuscript.

We dedicate this book to our families who have lived through stacks of references and manuscripts and to all the friends of the Division of Gynecology.

S.J.H.E.
D.P.G.

Pediatric and Adolescent Gynecology

1. Office Evaluation of the Child and Adolescent

OFFICE EVALUATION OF THE INFANT AND CHILD

The traditional avoidance of the female external genitalia has sometimes prevented parents and physicians from dealing with the total health care of the young girl. Although gynecologic problems are not common among young girls, the physician should always include inspection of the external genitalia and palpation of the breast as part of the routine physical examination. If the child accepts a brief look at her genitalia as part of the normal physical examination, she is less likely to feel embarrassed or upset by the same examination when she reaches adolescence. In addition, the physician may note smegma or feces in the labial folds, indicating inadequate perineal hygiene. Careful instruction to the parents and child during the examination may prevent the later occurrence of a nonspecific vulvovaginitis. The presence of a cyst, clitoromegaly, early signs of puberty, *Candida* vulvitis, or an abnormality of the hymen may be a clue to other problems. Errors in diagnosis often stem from lack of simple inspection.

A healthy dialogue between parents and children on issues of sexuality should begin during the prepubertal years. Parents should be encouraged to answer the questions of their young children with simple facts and correct terminology. Appendix 5 contains a list of pamphlets that may help parents become more comfortable talking with their children about sex. Physicians should become knowledgeable about the books available at the local library and select appropriate pamphlets for the office.

Obtaining the History

Vaginal discharge or bleeding, pruritis, signs of sexual development, or an allegation of sexual abuse should prompt a more thorough evaluation. The nature of the history obviously depends on the presenting complaint. If the problem is vaginitis, questions should focus on perineal hygiene, antibiotic therapy, recent infections in the patient or other members of the family, and the possibility of sexual molestation. Behavioral changes and somatic symptoms such as abdominal pain, headaches, and enuresis may suggest abuse. Information on the caretaker should always be elicited. If the problem is vaginal bleeding, the history should include recent growth and development, signs of puberty, use of hormone creams or tablets (including maternal exposure), trauma, and a previous finding of foreign bodies in the vagina. Although the history is usually obtained chiefly from a parent, the child should be asked questions not only about genital complaints but also about toys or school to put her at ease. Eye contact should be maintained with the child, and it should be stressed that she is an important part of the team. Questions focusing on what has bothered the child (such as itching or discharge) can help the child understand why the examination is important. She should be given the opportunity to ask questions. This time promotes the understanding that the physician is acting in her best interests.

GYNECOLOGIC EXAMINATION

The gynecologic examination should be carefully explained in advance to the parent and the child. It is extremely important to tell the parent that the size of the vaginal opening is quite variable and that the examination will in no way alter the hymen. Often a diagram showing the introitus is helpful because many parents still believe that the virginal introitus is totally covered by the hymen (Fig. 1-1).

Both parent and child should be told that instruments will be used that are specially designed for little girls. The otoscope or hand lens to be used for external examination should be shown to the child with an emphasis that the physician will use these instruments "to look." If a colposcope will be used for a sexual abuse evaluation, the child should have a chance to look at the instrument, turn on and off the light, and view fingers or jewelry through the binocular eyepieces to feel comfortable with the examination.

The child can then be offered the choice of gown color and whether she wishes to have her parent lift her onto the table or climb "up the big stairs." In our clinic the parent typically stays in the room to talk with the young child and assist in the examination. Although the father, mother, both parents, or a relative may accompany the child for the assessment, the mother most commonly plays an active role during the examination. The older child should be asked whom she prefers in or out during the examination. Most children and many young adolescents prefer their mothers in the room; almost all mid to late adolescents prefer their mothers out of the examining room.

The majority of children are comfortable on the examining tables with mother (or father) sitting close by or holding a hand. Some girls are quite fearful, especially if they have been previously sexually abused or had a painful genital examination. In this case, the mother (or the caretaker bringing the child) can sit on the table in a semi-reclined position with her feet in stirrups and have the child's legs straddle her thighs. The use of a hand mirror has been found helpful by Pokorny to help the child relax and become an active participant in the examination. If the physician is confident and relaxed, the patient usually responds with cooperation. An abrupt or hurried approach will precipitate anxiety and resistance in the child. Sometimes it is necessary to leave the room and return when the patient feels ready.

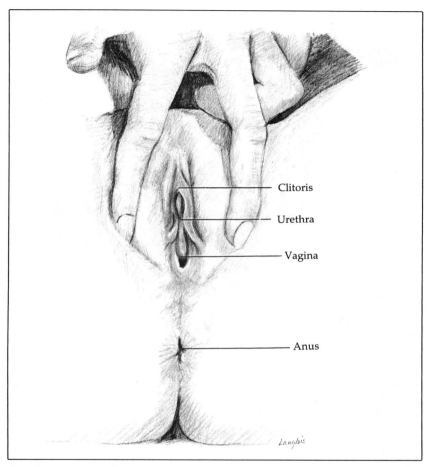

Figure 1-1. External genitalia of the prepubertal child.

The examination of any child having gynecologic complaints should include a general pediatric assessment of the child's weight/height, head and neck, heart, lungs, and abdomen. The abdominal examination is often easier if the child places her hands on the examiner's hand; she is then less likely to tense her muscles or complain of being "tickled." The inguinal areas should be carefully palpated for a hernia or gonad; occasionally, an inguinal gonad is the testis of an undiagnosed male pseudohermaphrodite. The breasts should be carefully inspected and palpated. The increasing diameter of the areola or a unilateral tender breast bud is often the first sign of puberty.

The gynecologic examination of the child includes inspection of the external genitalia, visualization of the vagina and cervix, and rectoabdominal palpation. This examination is usually possible without an-

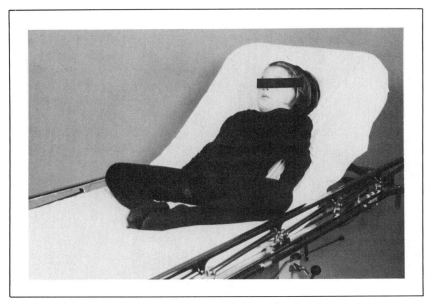

Figure 1-2. Positioning the prepubertal child in the frog-leg position (can be flat or with the head of the examining table raised). (Courtesy of Dr. Trina Anglin, Cleveland, Ohio.)

esthesia if the child has not been traumatized by previous examinations and if the physician proceeds slowly. The child should be explicitly told that "the exam will not hurt." The young child should be examined supine with her knees apart and feet touching in the frog-leg position or in the lithotomy position with the use of adjustable stirrups (Figs. 1-2 to 1-5). As the external genitalia are inspected, the young child may be less anxious if she assists the physician by holding the labia apart. The physician should note the presence of pubic hair, size of the clitoris, type of hymen, signs of estrogenization of the vaginal introitus, and perineal hygiene. Friability of the posterior forchette as the labia are separated can occur in children with vulvitis and/or history of sexual abuse [1]. If the hymenal orifice is still not visible, the labia can be gently gripped and pulled forward (traction maneuver) to view the anterior vagina (Fig. 1-6). The average size of the normal clitoral glans in the premenarcheal child is 3 mm in length and 3 mm in transverse diameter [2]. The vaginal mucosa of the prepubertal child appears thin and red in contrast with the moist, dull pink, estrogenized mucosa of the pubertal child. Frequently the perihymenal tissue is erythematous. The vaginal introitus will often gape open if the child is asked to take a deep breath or cough; if not, the labia should be gently pulled downward and laterally.

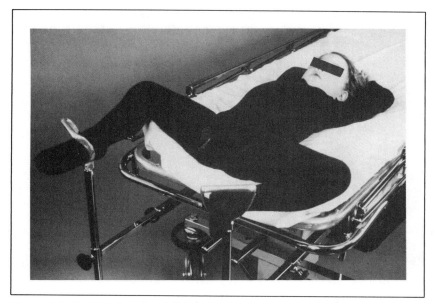

Figure 1-3. Positioning the child in the lithotomy position with the use of stirrups. (Courtesy of Dr. Trina Anglin, Cleveland, Ohio.)

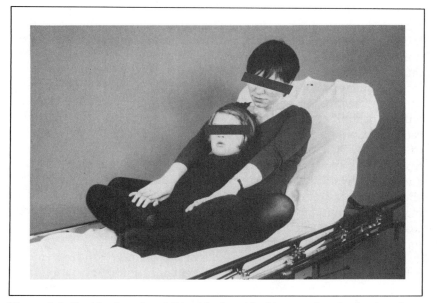

Figure 1-4. Positioning the child with the aid of her mother in the frog-leg position. (Courtesy of Dr. Trina Anglin, Cleveland, Ohio.)

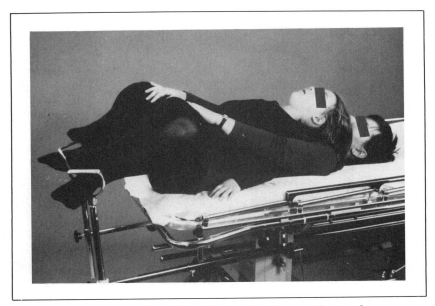

Figure 1-5. Positioning the child with the aid of her mother in the lithotomy position. (Courtesy of Dr. Trina Anglin, Cleveland, Ohio.)

The type of hymen should be noted (Figs. 1-7 and 1-8; see also color plates) using a hand lens or the light and magnification of an otoscope (without a speculum). Hymens can be classified as posterior rim (or crescent), annular, or redundant [3]. The edges of the redundant hymen and the orifice are often difficult to visualize. Congenital abnormalities of the hymen are not uncommon, especially microperforate and septate hymens (Figs. 1-9 to 1-13). The presence of an opening in a microperforate hymen may be difficult to establish without using the technique shown in Figure 1-14 and sometimes probing with a nasopharyngeal Calgiswab* moistened with saline or small catheter. Congenital absence of the hymen has not been documented to occur [4, 5]. Acquired abnormalities of the hymen usually result from sexual abuse and rarely from accidental trauma (see Chaps. 3 and 17). Physicians seeing girls for annual physical examinations should be encouraged to visualize the genitalia and the hymen and to make a drawing in the office notes of its type. Knowledge of a change from previously noted anatomy could provide an important clue to ongoing sexual abuse.

The significance of measurements of the diameter of the hymenal orifice is controversial. The transverse and anterior-posterior measurements are influenced by age, relaxation of the child, method of

*Spectrum Laboratories, 1100 Rankin Rd., Houston, TX 77073.

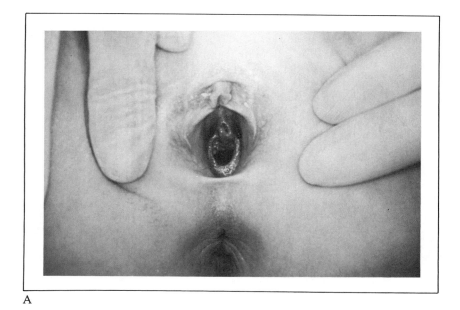

A

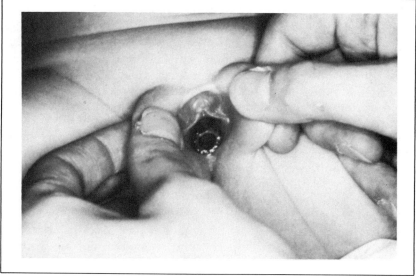

B

Figure 1-6. Examination of the vulva, hymen, and anterior vagina by gentle lateral retraction (A) and gentle gripping of the labia and pulling anteriorly (B).

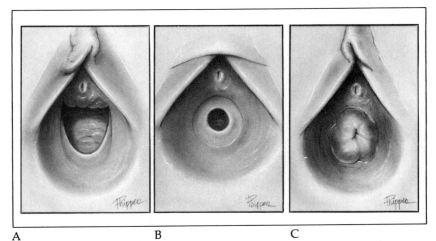

A   B   C

Figure 1-7. Types of hymen in prepubertal girls. A. Posterior rim or crescentic hymen. B. Circumferential or annular hymen. C. Fimbriated or
redundant hymen. (From SF Pokorny, Configuration of the prepubertal
hymen. Am J Obstet Gynecol 1987; 157:950. By permission.)

examination and measurement, and type of hymen. The older the
child and the more relaxed, the larger the opening. The opening is
larger with retraction on the labia and in the knee-chest position than
with gentle separation alone in the supine position. The orifice of a
posterior rim hymen will appear larger than the opening of a redundant hymen. Because the hymen is distensible, vaginal penetration
can have occurred even though the measurement is only 5 mm. In
cases of sexual abuse, we measure both anterior-posterior and transverse dimensions using a Tine test 5-cm ruler. Some colposcopes
have the markings in the eyepiece, and direct measurement can be
done during the examination. More data on normal children are
needed, but our study of 3- to 6-year-old girls found a mean transverse measurement of 2.9 ± 1.3 mm (range 1–6 mm) and mean
anterior-posterior measurement of 3.3 ± 1.5 mm (range 1–7 mm) [1].
A good rule of thumb is 1 mm for each year of age as the upper limits
of normal (i.e., 8 mm for an 8-year-old), remembering all the caveats
of changes with relaxation and position. Abnormal measurements in
the prepubertal child are often 10 to 15 mm. The finding of a large
hymenal orifice may be consistent with a history of sexual abuse but
should only be considered a part of the evaluation, not the absolute
criteria.

The anus and labia should always be examined for cleanliness,
excoriations, and erythema. Perianal excoriation is often a clue to the
presence of pinworm infestation.

Once the external genitalia have been carefully examined, the physician should proceed with visualization of the vagina. In girls more

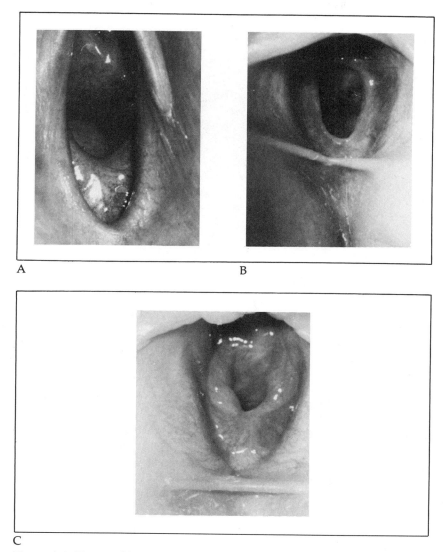

Figure 1-8. Types of hymen, photographed through a colposcope.
A. Crescentic hymen. B. Annular hymen. C. Redundant hymen with
crescent appearance after retraction.

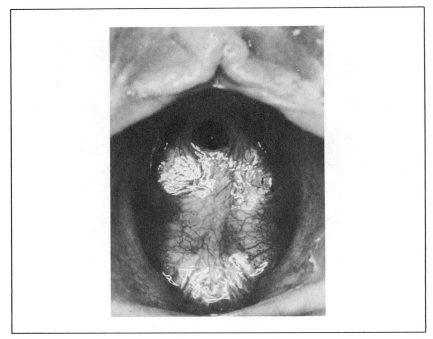

Figure 1-9. Microperforate hymen.

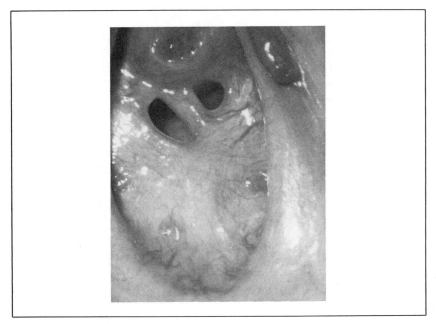

Figure 1-10. Microperforate septate hymen.

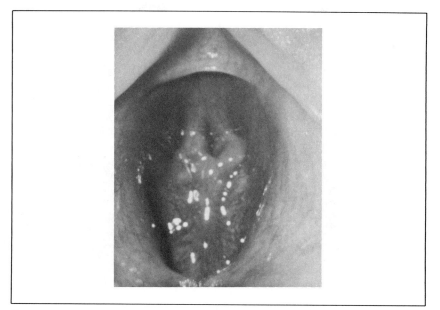

Figure 1-11. Imperforate hymen.

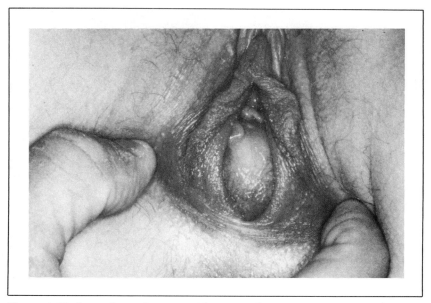

Figure 1-12. Imperforate hymen with mucocolpos.

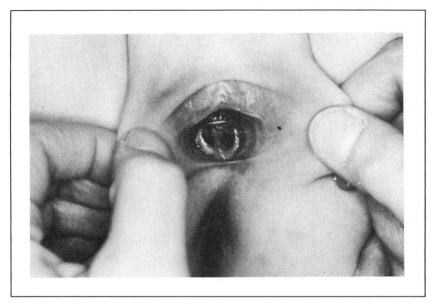

Figure 1-13. Septate vagina.

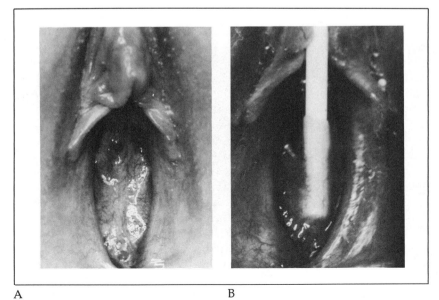

A

B

Figure 1-14. Microperforate hymen. A. Opening difficult to visualize.
B. Opening gently probed.

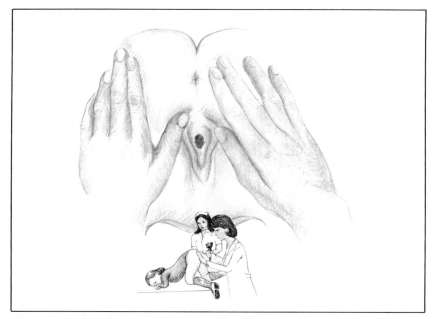

Figure 1-15. Examination of the prepubertal child in the knee-chest position.

than 2 years old, the knee-chest position provides a particularly good view of the vagina and cervix without instrumentation [6, 7]. The patient is told that she should "lie on her tummy with her bottom in the air." She is reassured that the examiner plans to "take a look at her bottom" but "will not put anything inside her." In the knee-chest position (also used for sigmoidoscopy in older patients), the child rests her head to one side on her folded arms and supports her weight on bent knees (6–8 inches apart). With her buttocks held up in the air, she is encouraged to let her spine and stomach "sag downward." A pillow can be placed under her abdomen. An assistant or mother helps to hold the buttocks apart, pressing laterally and slightly upward. As the child takes deep breaths, the vaginal orifice falls open for examination (Fig. 1-15). In 80 to 90 percent of prepubertal girls, an ordinary otoscope head (without a speculum) provides the magnification and light necessary to visualize the cervix. Clearly the child's anxiety will be allayed if she is again shown the otoscope light and her full confidence is gained before this part of the examination. A running conversation of small talk about school, toys, and siblings often diverts the child's attention and helps her maintain this position for several minutes without moving or objecting. Since the vagina of the prepubertal child is quite short, the presence of a foreign body or a lesion is often easily ascertained.

An alternative method of visualization is the use of a small vagino-scope, cystoscope, hysteroscope, or flexible fiberoptic scope with wa-ter insufflation of the vagina [8]. The child is examined supine with her knees held apart. An excellent step-by-step method of inserting the vaginoscope in the young child has been introduced by Dr. Cap-raro of Buffalo [9]. The child is first allowed to touch the instrument and is told that it feels "slippery, funny, and cool." The instrument is then placed against her inner thigh and the same words are repeated. Next, the instrument is placed against her labia, again with words, "This feels slippery, funny, and cool." As the vaginoscope is inserted through the hymen, the examiner repeats the words and presses the child's buttocks firmly with the other hand to divert her attention. Application of viscous xylocaine to the introitus makes insertion easier. Good visualization of the cervix and vagina is thus possible without general anesthesia. Since it is unlikely that the general physi-cian will have a vaginoscope or cystoscope in the office, examination with a narrow veterinary otoscope speculum with the child in the supine (lithotomy) position can be helpful [10]. In addition, a narrow vaginal speculum can only rarely be useful in examining the older child if insertion does not cause pain or trauma. For anesthesia exami-nations, a nasal speculum with light source can be used (Fig. 1-16).

If vaginal discharge is present, samples should be obtained for culture, Gram stain, and saline and potassium hydroxide (KOH) preparations (see p. 33–34). Usually, the child prefers to lie on her back with her knees apart with feet together or in stirrups so that she can watch the procedure without becoming excessively anxious. The child should be allowed to feel a cotton-tipped applicator, Calgiswab, eyedropper, or catheter on her skin before insertion of a sterile device into her vagina. For example, a cotton-tipped applicator can be gently stroked over the back of her hand to allow her to feel it as "soft," "it tickles." For the prepubertal child, we usually use a nasopharyngeal Calgiswab moistened with nonbacteriostatic saline (Fig. 1-17A). This can be inserted into the vagina painlessly by avoiding touching the hymenal edges. The child can be asked to cough as the examiner inserts the swab. This action distracts the child and makes the hymen gape open. Several Calgiswabs can be obtained in rapid succession without discomfort. If indicated, the *Chlamydia* culture can be ob-tained by using a male urethral swab, gently inserting through the hymen, and scraping the lateral vaginal wall. If multiple samples are needed as in a rape evaluation, a soft plastic eyedropper (such as a Clinitest* or Medi[†] sterile clinic dropper) or a glass eyedropper with

*Ames Co., Division of Miles Laboratories, Elkhart, IN 46514.
†Medi, Inc., 27 Maple Ave., Holbrook, MA 02343.

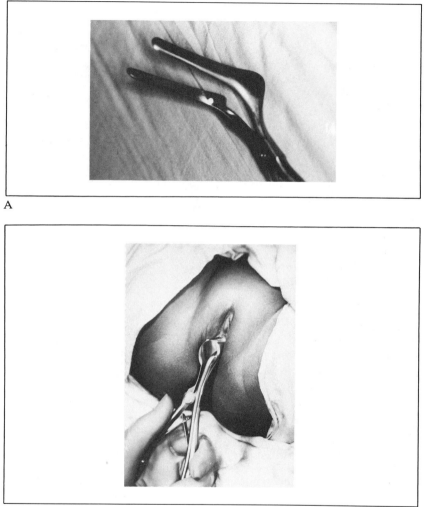

A

B

Figure 1-16. Anesthesia examination using a Killian nasal speculum with fiberoptic light (can be obtained through Codman and Shurtleff, Inc. Pacella Dr, Randolph, MA).

4 to 5 cm of intravenous plastic tubing attached [11], can be gently inserted through the hymen to aspirate secretions.

Another method for obtaining samples has been suggested by Pokorny and Stormer [12] using a modified syringe and urethral catheter (Fig. 1-17B). The proximal 4-inch end of an intravenous butterfly catheter is inserted into the 4-inch end piece of a No. 12 bladder catheter, and a syringe is attached. The catheter is slid into the

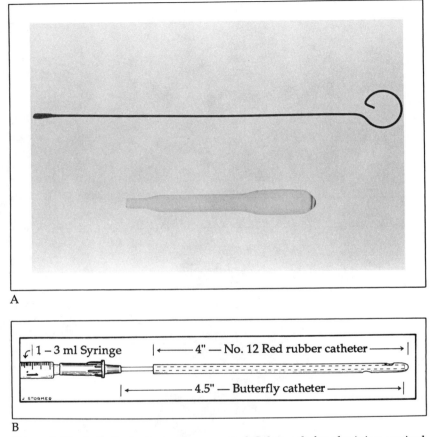

A

B

Figure 1-17. A. Soft plastic eyedropper and Calgiswab for obtaining vaginal specimens in the prepubertal girl. B. Assembled catheter-within-a-catheter, for obtaining specimens from a prepubertal child. (From SF Pokorny and LVN Stormer, Atraumatic removal of secretions from the prepubertal vagina. Am J Obstet Gynecol 1987; 156:581. By permission.)

vagina, similar to catheterizing the bladder. One half to one milliliter of sterile saline is injected into the vagina and aspirated.

A culture for *Neisseria gonorrhoeae* should be done on modified Thayer-Martin-Jembec media* at the time of the examination. Cultures for other organisms are done by placing the moistened Calgiswab into a transport Culturette II with medium.[†] The bacteriology laboratory should plate the swab in the standard genitourinary media, which usually include blood agar, MacConkey, and chocolate

*Scott Laboratories, Fiskeville, RI 02823.
†Marion Scientific, Kansas City, MO 64114.

media. The laboratory should be notified that the Thayer-Martin media being processed is from the vagina of a *prepubertal* child so that if a *Neisseria* species grows, it is properly and unequivocally identified as *N. gonorrhoeae* for medicolegal purposes. The Centers for Disease Control (CDC) reported that 14 of 40 bacterial isolates from children less than 15 years of age identified as *N. gonorrhoeae* during 1983 to 1984 proved to be other *Neisseria* species including *N. lactamica, N. meningitidis, N. cinerea,* and *Branhamella catarrhalis* [13, 14]. Cultures for *Chlamydia trachomatis* are recommended rather than indirect tests and slide immunofluorescent tests in the prepubertal child because of the possibility of false-positive tests [15] and the association of this organism with sexual abuse (see Chaps. 3 and 17). A Biggy agar* culture (for patients who complain of itching or have suspected yeast infection) can be incubated and read in the office (see p. 35).

After the samples are obtained, a gentle rectoabdominal examination is done with the patient in stirrups or supine with her legs apart. For bimanual palpation, the examiner places the index or little finger of one hand into the rectum and the other hand on the abdomen. The child can be reassured that this examination will feel similar to having her temperature taken rectally. Except in the newborn period when the uterus is enlarged secondary to maternal estrogen, the rectal examination in the prepubertal child reveals only the small "button" of the cervix. Since the ovaries are not palpable, adnexal masses should alert the physician to the possibility of a cyst or tumor. At the end of the rectal examination as the rectal finger is removed, the vagina should be gently "milked" to promote passage of polypoid tumors or discharge.

After assessing a patient's chief complaint and results of the examination, the physician should spend time with the parents and child discussing diagnosis, mode of therapy, and necessity of follow-up. Praising the young child for her cooperation and "bravery" helps establish the important doctor-patient relationship for future examinations.

OFFICE EVALUATION OF THE ADOLESCENT
The evaluation of the adolescent requires additional technical skills, including speculum examination of the vagina and rectal-vaginal-abdominal palpation. More importantly, the physician needs the interpersonal skills, sensitivity, and time to establish a primary relationship with the adolescent herself. The doctor must be willing to see the teenager alone and listen to her concerns. For example, the patient with oligomenorrhea may return each visit with the same question, "Why am I not normal?" Listening to her describe her feelings is just

*Scott Laboratories, Fiskeville, RI 02823.

as important as drawing diagrams of the hypothalamic-ovarian axis. The statement, "Your pelvic exam is normal," answers few questions for the adolescent.

It is helpful to discuss the special needs of adolescents with the pubescent girl when she reaches her eleventh or twelfth birthday. The parents also need to hear that adolescents require special time to discuss concerns about peer relations, school, family, drugs, alcohol, and sexuality. Visits for the well teenager should be on at least an annual basis; a patient with medical or psychosocial concerns should obviously be seen more frequently. Parents should be included as much as possible in important medical decisions, but the need for the adolescent to have medical privacy should be respected. Parents should be encouraged to call in advance of an appointment if they have special concerns since an adolescent may sometimes be strikingly nonverbal about troubling issues at home or in school. At the same time, parents may need help communicating more effectively with their adolescent.

Consider the body changes involved in the development of the prepubertal latency-age girl of 10 years as she changes into the sexually mature woman of 20; these changes underscore the many issues that arise in the medical care of adolescent girls. The appearance of pubic hair and breast development, over which the girl has no control, can be quite distressing. The fact that these changes occur at the same rate within her peer group may offer some reassurance; to be early or late can provoke considerable anxiety. A 12-year-old girl who looks 16 may be confronted with heterosexual demands that she is unable to cope with; a 16-year-old girl who looks 10 may be embarrassed to undress in physical education class or to interact with her peer group. Since the young adolescent has many fantasies about her body and its changes, she may ask the same questions at each visit. The older teenager is intellectually more capable of coping with a diagnosis and the physical examination. The physician must, therefore, be sensitive to the different needs of each patient.

Obtaining the History
The source of the medical history depends on the medical setting and the age of the patient. The older adolescent tends to seek gynecologic care on her own initiative. In a clinic setting, the mother (and father) may be seen by the physician first to ascertain the nature of the chief complaint, as well as the past medical history, school problems, and psychosocial adjustment. Most of the visit should be devoted to seeing the teenager alone, since her presenting complaint is quite often different from her mother's concerns. In the setting of private practice, the mother may make the appointment by telephone, and then the teenager may appear alone for the examination.

GYNECOLOGICAL HISTORY SHEET

USE PLATE OR PRINT

M.R. No. ______ DATE ______
PT. NAME ______
PARENT ______
ADDRESS ______
DATE OF BIRTH ______ B.C. No. ______
M.A. No. ______
DIV ______ CLIN. ______ P.P. DR. ______

REFERRED BY: ______ AGE: ______

MENSTRUAL HISTORY

MENARCHE ______
CYCLE ______ DURATION ______ AMT. ______
DYSMENORRHEA ______
INTERMENSTRUAL BLEEDING ______
LMP ______ PMP ______ WKS LMP ______

GYNECOLOGIC HISTORY

LAST PELVIC ______
LAST PAP ______
PREGNANCY TEST ______ RESULTS ______
DYSPAREUNIA ______
POST-COITAL BLEEDING ______
VAGINAL DISCHARGE ______
V.D. ______
MATERNAL STILBESTEROL ______

OBSTETRIC HISTORY

GRAVIDA ______ PARA ______
INDUCED ABS. ______ SPONT. ABS. ______
NO. OF LIVING CHILDREN ______
DATE OF LAST DELIVERY ______
NORMAL ______ C-SECT. ______

CONTRACEPTIVE HISTORY

TYPE ______
DURATION ______
PROBLEMS ______

MEDICAL HISTORY

ANEMIA ______
HEART DISEASE ______
LUNG DISEASE ______
LIVER DISEASE ______
KIDNEY DISEASE ______
HYPERTENSION ______
MIGRAINE HEADACHES ______
THROMBOPHLEBITIS ______
EPILEPSY ______
DIABETES ______
ASTHMA ______
BREAST DISEASE ______
CANCER ______
PSYCHIATRIC CARE ______
SICKLE CELL ______
ALLERGIES ______
CURRENT MEDS. ______
HOSPITALIZATIONS ______
SERIOUS ILLNESSES ______

MAY WE CONTACT YOU AT HOME? ☐ YES ☐ NO
IF NOT, WHERE? ______

THE CHILDREN'S HOSPITAL MEDICAL CENTER, BOSTON, MASSACHUSETTS 02115

16421 01 5C 6-74

Figure 1-18. Gynecologic history sheet. The Children's Hospital, Boston.

The history sheet shown in Figure 1-18 is currently used in our gynecology clinic. As it indicates, the general medical history is quite relevant to the evaluation of gynecologic problems. A history of in utero exposure to diethylstilbestrol (DES) should be recorded in all patients; fortunately this medication was not prescribed during pregnancy after the early 1970s. The implications of DES and the special examination of the DES-exposed adolescent are discussed in Chapter 12. The routine visit with the adolescent should always include a carefully taken menstrual history and a straightforward question about sexual relations and birth control, such as, "Do you need birth control?" The physician's approach toward confidentiality should be explicitly stated because few teenagers will volunteer a need for birth control. Asking about peer group behaviors may also be helpful in obtaining information about the adolescent patient seemingly reluctant to discuss her own sexual behavior. Asking "Do you have friends who have been pregnant? Do you have friends who have been sexually active?" can give clues to the patient's peer influences. An adolescent's sexual and drug-taking behavior frequently is similar to that of her friends. Other good questions might be, "If you make a decision to have sexual relations, would you know how to protect yourself from pregnancy?" Or, "If you had a girl friend who didn't want to get pregnant, could you help her?" If she says, "Yes," ask, "How?" Such discussions require skillful handling, since repeatedly offering birth control advice may push a young woman into premature sexual relations that she may regret. Frequently, pointing out that one third of adolescents have not had intercourse by their nineteenth birthday reassures the patient who would like to remain virginal but believes that all her friends are sexually active.

It is not uncommon to find that a 13- or 14-year-old girl with school problems, mother-daughter conflict, and a history of running away is involved in unprotected intercourse as part of her "acting out." She also may have been previously sexually molested. In the adolescent mind, intercourse is rarely associated with pregnancy and motherhood. The older teenager of 16 or 17 years of age is more likely to consider the consequences of her actions; but, nevertheless, she too may fail to obtain birth control. The physician may feel in an ethical bind: To encourage birth control implies approval; to deny birth control may result in an unwanted pregnancy. Although the physician may have strong opinions regarding the morality of premarital intercourse, defining the issues under discussion and identifying alternatives may direct the adolescent to an acceptable solution. Concerned medical care that is sensitive to the patient's needs will hopefully assist her in the development of a healthy body image and responsible sexuality.

GYNECOLOGIC EXAMINATION

Once the history is obtained and the problems identified, the patient should be given a thorough explanation of a pelvic examination. The use of diagrams or a pelvic plastic model is helpful. For first examination, the feelings of the adolescent should be acknowledged. A statement such as "some girls I see are worried about pain or embarrassment" helps establish good patient-doctor communication. Adequate drapes and gowns and allowing the adolescent to control the tempo of the examination will alleviate her concerns. The patient should then be given a gown and asked to remove all her clothes, including brassiere and underpants. If she is covered appropriately and approached in a relaxed manner, resistance is unlikely. The presence of a female nurse in the room is often reassuring, especially if the physician is a man. The young adolescent may request that her mother stay with her during a pelvic examination. Most patients prefer the mother to stay in the waiting room. The patient's wishes should be respected. The general physical examination of a teenage girl should always include a breast examination, inspection of the genitalia, and a careful notation of the Tanner stages of breast and pubic hair development (see Chap. 4). Demonstrating self-examination of the breast of the patient as one actually performs the breast examination (see Chap. 14) often puts the young woman at ease. Physicians and patients occasionally ask why it is necessary to look at the genitalia. There are a number of reasons: *Candida* vulvitis may be the first sign of diabetes; an imperforate hymen may be the cause of adominal pain or primary amenorrhea; a cyst or clitoromegaly may be found unexpectedly. The actual examination frequently initiates questions that the teenager was embarrassed to ask, such as queries about a vaginal discharge, a lump, or irregular periods.

When is a pelvic examination indicated? A bimanual rectoabdominal examination (in the lithotomy position) should be performed on any teenager with gynecologic complaints or unexplained abdominal pain. A vaginal examination is important to assess irregular bleeding, severe dysmenorrhea, vaginal discharge, in utero exposure to DES, sexually transmitted diseases, and amenorrhea. Sexually active patients should have a routine vaginal examination every 6 to 12 months; a patient who is not sexually active can begin routine annual examinations at any age that she feels comfortable with initiating gynecologic care, hopefully at least by the age of 17 or 18 years. Contrary to popular belief, rarely is a patient unable to be fully cooperative during a pelvic examination if she has received a careful explanation about the procedure and its importance in evaluating her individual problem.

The pelvic examination is done with the patient in the lithotomy position with the use of stirrups. A mirror can be offered to the patient. The external genitalia are inspected first; type of hymenal opening, estrogenization of the vaginal mucosa, distribution of the pubic hair, and the size of the clitoris are assessed. The pubic hair should be inspected for pediculosis pubis if itching is present. The inguinal areas should be palpated for evidence of lymphadenopathy. The estrogenized vagina has a moist or thickened, dull pink mucosa in contrast to the thin, red mucosa of the prepubertal child. The normal clitoral glans is 2 to 4 mm in width; a width of 10 mm is

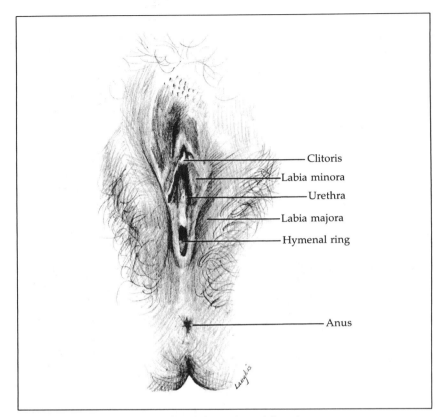

Figure 1-19. External genitalia of the pubertal female.

considered significant virilization. The normal anatomy is illustrated in Figure 1-19. The hymen in the adolescent girl is estrogenized and thickened. Minor changes due to sexual abuse or minor trauma that might have been easily seen in the thin unestrogenized hymen of the prepubertal child may be impossible to visualize in the estrogenized adolescent. Because the hymen is elastic, tampons can be inserted by most adolescents without tearing the hymen. The hymenal opening in the virginal adolescent is usually large enough to allow insertion of a finger for palpation or a small speculum. An adolescent who has been sexually active may have a hymen without any obvious trauma or may have old or new lacerations of the hymen (down to the base of the hymen) or myrtiform caruncles (small bumps of residual hymen along the lower edge). In the examination of the sexually abused adolescent, the hymenal ring can be carefully examined by running a saline-moistened cotton-tipped applicator around the edges. As noted in the section on the prepubertal child, different configurations of hymens may be seen in the adolescent (Fig. 1-20). A simple hy-

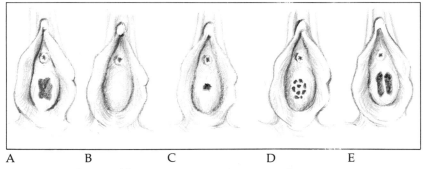

A   B   C   D   E

Figure 1-20. Types of hymen. A. Normal. B. Imperforate. C. Microperforate. D. Cribiform. E. Septate.

menotomy is required for type B at the time of diagnosis and in types C, D, and E prior to tampon use or intercourse. The septal band may be excised in the office; it may also break at the time of tampon removal or with coitus. It is important for the adolescent with type C, D, or E to be aware of her anatomy so she is not traumatized with her difficulty to use tampons or have intercourse. The timing of intervention should be decided by the patient after discussion with her physician.

To avoid surprising the patient, a manual or speculum examination should be preceded by a statement such as, "I'm now going to touch your bottom," or, "I'm now going to place this cool metal speculum in your vagina." In the virginal teenager, a slow, one-finger examination will demonstrate the size of the introitus and the location of the cervix, which allows subsequent easy insertion of the speculum. It is helpful to warm the speculum and then touch it to the patient's thigh to allow her to feel its "cool metal" quality. The speculum should be inserted posteriorly with a downward direction to avoid the urethra. Applying pressure to the inner thigh at the same time as the speculum or finger is inserted into the vagina is helpful. If the hymenal opening is small, a Huffman speculum ($\frac{1}{2} \times 4\frac{1}{4}$ inches)* is used to expose the cervix. A latex glove with the tip cut off can be slipped over the narrow speculum to keep the vaginal walls from collapsing in the virginal girl [8]. In the sexually active teenager, a Pederson ($\frac{7}{8} \times 4\frac{1}{2}$ inches)† or occasionally (in the postpartum adolescent) a Graves ($1\frac{3}{8} \times 3\frac{3}{4}$ inches) speculum is appropriate. A child's speculum ($\frac{5}{8} \times 3$ inches or $\frac{7}{8} \times 3$ inches) is rarely ever useful because of inadequate length and excessive width (Figs. 1-21 and 1-22).

*GL 34 Huffman-Graves Adolescent Vaginal Speculum is available from V. Mueller, 1500 Waukegan Rd, McGaw Park, IL 60085.
†GL 31 (same address as above).

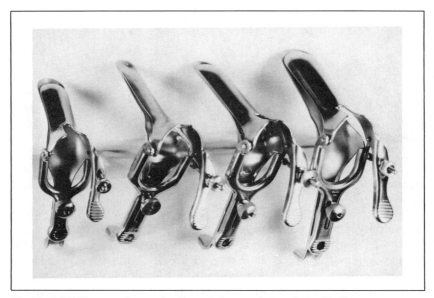

Figure 1-21. Types of specula (from left to right): infant, Huffman, Pederson, and Graves.

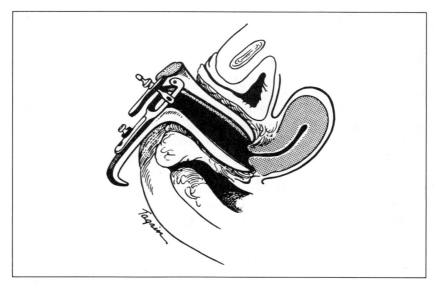

Figure 1-22. Speculum examination of the cervix. (From T Green, *Gynecology: Essentials of Clinical Practice* [3rd ed.]. Boston: Little, Brown, 1977. By permission.)

The stratified squamous epithelium of the cervix is usually a homogeneous dull pink color; however, in many adolescents an erythematous area surrounding the os is noted. The so-called ectropion is the presence of endocervical columnar epithelium on the cervix. The squamocolumnar junction, instead of being inside the endocervical canal, is visible on the portio of the cervix; it does not represent a disease process. However, a very large ectropion, especially if columnar epithelium extends onto the anterior vaginal wall or if the cervix has an abnormal shape, should make the clinician suspicious of in utero DES exposure in the girl born before 1974. Large ectropions in older adolescents who have not been exposed to DES may be associated with discharge and the presence of Nabothian cysts. Mucopurulent discharge from the endocervix and ectropion characterizes chronic cervicitis and is typical of infections with gonorrhea, *Chlamydia*, or herpes, or a combination of these. Small pinpoint hemorrhagic spots on the cervix ("strawberry cervix") can be seen with *Trichomonas* infection. The character of any discharge present should be noted (see Chap. 9). Samples for the Papanicolaou smear, cultures, and saline and KOH preparations are taken with the speculum in place; the techniques are described in the section Diagnostic Tests (see p. 27). After visualization of the vagina and cervix, the speculum is removed, and the uterus and adnexa are carefully palpated with one or two fingers in the vagina and the other hand on the abdomen (Fig. 1-23) [16]. Normal ovaries are usually less than 3 cm and are rubbery. The adolescent may complain of discomfort with palpation.

A rectal-vaginal-abdominal examination performed with the index finger in the vagina, the middle finger in the rectum, and the other hand on the abdomen permits palpation of a retroverted uterus and assessment of mobility of the adnexa and uterus (Fig. 1-24). The uterosacral ligaments should be palpated carefully in patients with pain or dysmenorrhea since tenderness is often found in patients with endometriosis (see Chap. 8). The patient is usually less anxious if she is told in advance that the rectal examination may seem disturbing because of the sensation that she is "moving her bowels" or "going to the bathroom." Allaying this fear usually elicits better relaxation and cooperation.

In patients with a tight hymen, a simple bimanual rectoabdominal examination with the index finger pushing the cervix upward allows palpation of the uterus and adnexa. In a relaxed patient, a negative examination rules out the possibility that there are large ovarian masses or uterine enlargement.

After the examination is concluded and the patient has dressed, the physician should sit down and discuss in detail the patient's complaint and what was found on examination. It is essential that the adolescent be treated as an adult capable of understanding the expla-

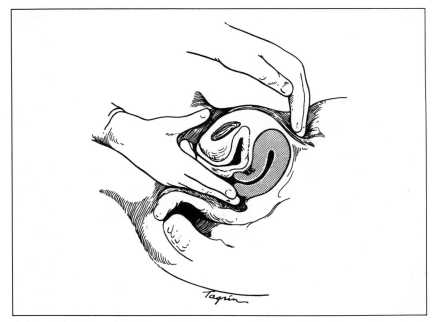

Figure 1-23. Bimanual abdominovaginal palpation of the uterus. (From T Green, *Gynecology: Essentials of Clinical Practice* [3rd ed.]. Boston: Little, Brown, 1977. By permission.)

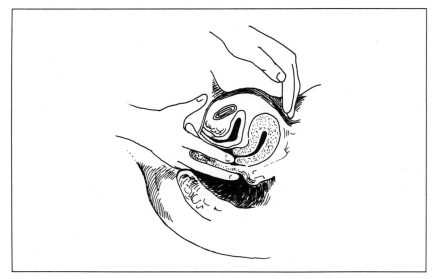

Figure 1-24. Bidigital rectovaginal examination. (Adapted from T Green, *Gynecology: Essentials of Clinical Practice* [3rd ed.]. Boston: Little, Brown, 1977. By permission.)

nation. If her parent has accompanied her, the patient should be asked whether she would like to tell her parent the findings herself or whether she would prefer to have the physician discuss the diagnosis in her presence. It is extremely important for the patient to know that the doctor and her parent will not have a "secret" about her and that confidential information will not be divulged to her parent.

DIAGNOSTIC TESTS

PAPANICOLAOU SMEAR

A Papanicolaou (Pap) smear should be taken on young women who have a speculum examination. Cervical dysplasia and, rarely, carcinoma in situ can occur during adolescence, especially in adolescents who become sexually active with multiple partners shortly after menarche or who have been exposed to human papillomavirus (HPV) [17–23].

Recent research has found that abnormal Pap smears are strongly associated with the finding of HPV DNA in vaginal washings and cervical biopsies. Follow-up of patients showing HPV on Pap smear have shown a high prevalence of dysplasia and carcinoma in situ. Certain types of HPV including types 16, 18, 31, and 33 have been particularly oncogenic in contrast to types 6 and 11 (usually associated with condyloma accuminata), which appear to have a low risk of dysplasia (see Chap. 11). Cofactors such as tobacco use, herpes, and vaginitis may promote oncogenesis [24]. Adolescents may be at particular risk because of the immature cervix and the normal process of squamous metaplasia. Most centers have noted an increase in abnormal Pap smears in the past decade in adolescent and young adult women, and many special cervical clinics have been initiated or expanded. It should be remembered that Pap smears may have a false-negative rate of 10 to 30 percent. Thus high-risk individuals, such as the teenager with multiple partners or sexually transmitted diseases (STDs), should be screened more frequently than annually. An abnormal growth on the cervix (regardless of Pap smear results) should be assessed with colposcopy and biopsy (as indicated).

For accurate cytologic diagnosis, the collection of the sample must be representative of normal and abnormal cell populations and must include the squamo-columnar junction and the endocervix.

The procedure is as follows. With the speculum in place, an Ayer spatula is rotated with pressure around the cervix in a circular motion, and the collected material is spread thinly on a slide, applying both sides of the spatula. In addition, an endocervical specimen should be obtained by using a cytobrush, glass pipette, or saline-moistened cotton-tipped applicator. The cytobrush is preferable to the Q-Tip; either of these should be inserted into the os and twirled, and then the sample should be rolled onto a glass slide. The slides from the exocervix and endocervix should be fixed immediately, either by using a spray fixative or by placing the slides in a bottle of Pap fixative (95% ethyl alcohol). The use of frosted slides allows the examiner to mark the name of the patient and "endo" (endocervix) or "exo" (exocervix) on the slide before starting the examination. The laboratory should be provided essential history such as last menstrual period, use of oral contraceptives, presence of an intrauterine device, and prior abnormal Pap smear or treatment for dysplasia.

Physicians are encouraged to follow the collection and fixation methods that are standard in their community. They should communicate with their cytologist regarding the classification system used. Physicians should note whether the cytologist thought that the smear was adequate and whether endocervical cells were present.

In the past, the most widely used Papanicolaou system classified smears as I to V as noted below.

Class
I. Negative
II. Benign atypia
IIR. Atypical cells
III. Dysplasia
IV. Suspicious for tumor cells, probably carcinoma in situ
V. Definite tumor cells

However, II can include inflammation and/or atypia. Atypia is variously defined by different laboratories; true atypia (not just inflammation) and koilocytosis are risk factors for cervical intraepithelial neoplasia (CIN) [25, 26]. Occasional laboratories have used a I to IV classification with II indicating mild dysplasia, a condition requiring colposcopy and assessment.

In response to the variable systems, a group of consultants, cytopathologists, and representatives of a variety of medical specialties were convened at the National Institute of Health in Bethesda, Maryland, in December 1988. The new system has been published [27] and is abbreviated below.

Statement on Specimen Adequacy
General categorization
Within normal limits
Other: see descriptive diagnosis, further action recommended

DESCRIPTIVE DIAGNOSES
Infection
Reactive and reparative changes

Epithelial cell abnormalities
  Squamous cell
    Atypical squamous cells
    Squamous intraepithelial lesion
      Low grade
        cellular changes with HPV
        mild dysplasia/CIN 1
      High grade
        moderate dysplasia/CIN 2
        severe dysplasia/CIN 3
        carcinoma in situ/CIN 3
    Squamous cell carcinoma
    Glandular cell
      abnormalities
      adenocarcinoma
Nonepithelial malignant neoplasm
Hormonal evaluation (applies to vaginal smears only)
Other

Patients with true atypia, koilocytosis, cervical intraepithelial neoplasia, or carcinoma require further evaluation and treatment (see
Chap. 11). Schiller's iodine stain and colposcopy (visualization of the
cervix with a 15× power binocular microscope) allow the gynecologist to take appropriate biopsies. The squamous cervical and vaginal
epithelial cells take up the stain, producing a brown color, whereas
the columnar epithelium of the endocervix and abnormal areas do not
take up the stain (Fig. 1-25). Newer methods such as cervigrams for
evaluating the cervix are under investigation.

VAGINAL SMEAR FOR ESTROGENIZATION
In the presence of inflammation, a vaginal smear is useful for evaluating the patient's hormonal status. This smear is best obtained by
inserting a speculum and then scraping the side wall of the upper
vagina with a wooden tongue depressor or cotton-tipped applicator
moistened with saline. The smear can also be obtained without using
a speculum by inserting a moistened cotton-tipped applicator or in a
small child a moistened Calgiswab into the vaginal introitus and
scraping the upper lateral side wall. The cells obtained are rolled onto
a glass slide, and the slide is placed immediately in Pap fixative. The
cytologist reads the smear by the number of parabasal, intermediate,
and superficial cells. The greater the estrogen effect, the more
superficial cells there are. The patient with little or no estrogen, such
as the prepubertal child or the adolescent with amenorrhea secondary
to anorexia nervosa, will have predominantly parabasal cells. The

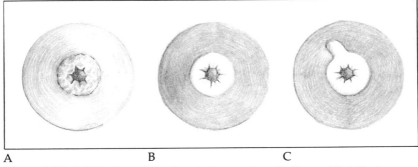

A   B   C

Figure 1-25. Schiller's test. A. Cervical ectropion. B. Normal Schiller's stain. C. Abnormal Schiller's stain. (Adapted from T Green, *Gynecology: Essentials of Clinical Practice* [3rd ed.]. Boston: Little, Brown, 1977. By permission.)

relationship between the percent of superficial cells and the level of estrogenization can be characterized as follows:

Less than 5 percent	Poor estrogen effect
5 to 10 percent	Slight estrogen effect
10 to 30 percent	Moderate estrogen effect
Greater than 30 percent	Marked estrogen effect

The smear can be correlated with the clinical situation (Table 1-1).

The maturation index reports the number of cells as a ratio of Parabasal: Intermediate: Superficial. In interpretation, the clinician should remember that the vaginal epithelium is influenced by estrogens, androgens, progestins, and adrenal hormones and that differ-

Table 1-1. Percentage of Parabasal, Intermediate, and Superficial Cells in the Vaginal Smear

State	Parabasal	Intermediate	Superficial
Childhood	60–90	10–20	0–3
Early puberty	30	50	20
Stage 5 puberty			
Proliferative phase	0	70	30
Secretory phase	0	80–95	5–20
Pregnancy	0	95	5
Anorexia nervosa (depends on			
clinical status)	75	25	0
Isosexual precocity	20	50	30
Premature thelarche	60	30	5–10
Premature adrenarche	60–90	10–20	0–3

ent patients respond differently to the same level. A preponderance of intermediate cells does not make a diagnosis in the absence of clinical information; thus a similar maturation index could be seen associated with pregnancy, the luteal phase of the cycle, secondary amenorrhea, or long-term administration of a low-dose estrogenic preparation.

A scoring system has also proved useful if combined with clinical information, especially in the follow-up of girls evaluated and treated for precocious puberty. The original system proposed by Meisels gave a 1.0 for superficial cyanophilic cells, 0.6 for large intermediate cells, 0.5 for small intermediate cells, and 0 for parabasal cells [28]. The points are multiplied by the percentage of that type of cell. A score of 90 to 100 is seen in hyperestrogenic patients, 31 to 55 in hypoestrogenic patients, 60 to 70 in newborns, 50 to 60 in pubertal girls, and 0 to 30 in prepubertal girls. Meisels has subsequently modified the system to give 1 point to superficial cells, 0.5 to intermediate cells, and 0 to parabasal cells.

Some clinicians find it extremely useful to perform the assessment of the vaginal smear at the time of the examination. A stain can be formulated by combining 83 ml of light green (5% aqueous solution) with 17 ml of eosin Y (1% aqueous solution). A saline-moistened cotton-tipped applicator is used to obtain the vaginal sample and is then placed in a test tube with 2 ml of saline and 3 drops of the stain. The tube is gently shaken, and a large drop is applied to a slide and covered with a coverslip for examination under a microscope [29].

Since the epithelial cells in urine show the same hormonal changes, the urine of a prepubertal child can be collected for a urocytogram. The first morning urine specimen is centrifuged, and the sediment is spread on a slide. The cytologist records the percentage of superficial, intermediate, and parabasal cells. Two methods for collection and staining are described by Lencioni [30] and Preeyasombat [31].

CERVICAL MUCUS
An examination of the cervical mucus is another method of evaluating a patient's estrogen status. The cervix is gently swabbed with a large cotton-tipped applicator, and a small sample of cervical mucus is obtained with a long forceps or saline-moistened Q-Tip. Profuse, clear, elastic mucus is seen in the preovulatory period and at ovulation. The elastic quality decreases rapidly following ovulation. Thick, sticky mucus is characteristic of the secretory phase of the cycle (see Chap. 4).

The mucus is spread on a glass slide and allowed to air dry for 5 minutes. Under the microscope, beautiful ferning patterns will be seen in the smear taken from the late proliferative phase of the cycle (Fig. 1-26). Ferning does not occur in the presence of progesterone.

32

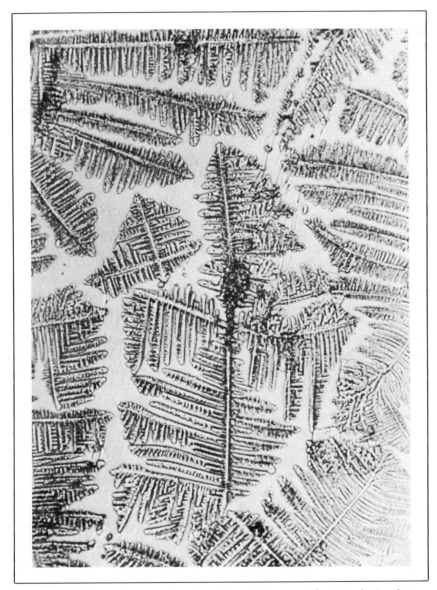

Figure 1-26. Microscopic evaluation of cervical mucus; ferning during late proliferative phase of the normal menstrual cycle.

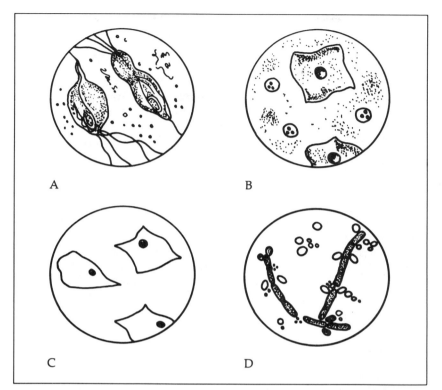

Figure 1-27. Fresh vaginal smears. A. *Trichomonas*. B. Clue cells of bacterial vaginosis. C. Leukorrhea. D. *Candida*. A, B, and C are saline preparations; D is a KOH preparation.

WET PREPARATIONS

The so-called wet preparations are useful in defining the etiology of a vaginal discharge. In the prepubertal child, the discharge is collected with a saline-moistened Calgiswab or an eyedropper. In adolescents, a cotton-tipped applicator is inserted into the vaginal pool with the speculum in place. The applicator is mixed first with one drop of saline on a glass slide and then with one drop of 10% KOH on another slide. A coverslip is then applied, and the slides are examined under the microscope (low and high dry power) (Fig. 1-27; see also Figs. 9-2 and 9-3). On the saline slide, trichomonads appear as lively, flagellated organisms, slightly larger than a white blood cell. A saline preparation of bacterial vaginosis (previously termed nonspecific vaginitis or *Gardnerella vaginalis* associated vaginitis) typically shows many refractile bacteria within large epithelial cells (so-called clue cells) and rare leukocytes; mixing this discharge with 10% KOH may liberate an aminelike odor (a positive "whiff test"). In contrast, physiologic leukorrhea is characterized by numerous epithelial cells without evidence of inflammation. On the KOH slide, the presence of budding pseudohyphae and yeast forms is evidence of *Candida* vaginitis (Fig. 1-27D).

pH
The pH of the prepubertal vagina is neutral. In contrast, the pH of the vagina of the pubertal adolescent is acid (< 4.5). A higher than normal pH (> 4.5) occurs with bacterial vaginosis and *Trichomonas* vaginitis. Testing vaginal secretions with pH paper can be very helpful in diagnosing vaginal discharge (see Chap. 9).

GRAM STAIN
In symptomatic gonorrhea, a Gram stain of a vaginal or cervical discharge may reveal polymorphonuclear leukocytes and gram-negative intracellular diplococci. Although a positive Gram stain is highly suggestive of gonorrhea, only a positive culture is conclusive evidence of this diagnosis in females. The Gram stain may also show an increased number of polymorphonuclear leukocytes in chlamydial infections (see Chap. 10) as well as *Trichomonas* and herpetic cervical infections.

CULTURES
Sexually active teenage girls should have screening tests for sexually transmitted infections, including *N. gonorrhoeae* and *C. trachomatis*. For gonorrhea, a cotton-tipped applicator is inserted into the cervical os and then streaked directly onto Transgrow, Modified Thayer-Martin-Jembec, or Thayer-Martin media. The use of plain Thayer-Martin plates requires immediate transportation of the culture to a bacteriology laboratory and incubation under increased carbon dioxide tension. Transgrow and Jembec are transport media and can actually be mailed to a laboratory. The Jembec media, with a small carbon dioxide generating tablet inserted into a well in the plastic case, is easy to use and reliable; the media can be transported after an incubation of 24 to 48 hours or processed in the office. In patients seen for a test of cure, a rectal culture for gonorrhea can also be done, since the recovery rate is thus increased by approximately 5 percent.

For *C. trachomatis*, endocervical samples can be screened by using cultures, direct immunofluorescent smears (MicroTrak), enzyme immunoassays, or DNA probes (see Chap. 10). The culture is preferable but still expensive in many settings. The direct immunofluorescent smear has a sensitivity of 60 to 93 percent compared to culture; in contrast, the enzyme immunoassay (Chlamydiazyme) has a sensitivity of 82 to 93 percent. Both have the highest predictive value in a population with a high prevalence of infection. Prepubertal children should have cultures done because of the medicolegal implications related to sexual abuse (see Chap. 3). Enzyme immunoassays and sensitive DNA probes are likely to be further improved. Because adolescents are at high risk of acquiring this infection, screening is indicated every 6 to 12 months and with any change in sexual partners.

Biggy agar medium is helpful in confirming the presence of a *Candida* vaginitis if the KOH preparation is negative. A sample of the discharge is streaked on the medium, and the tube is incubated at 35°C. The appearance of brown colonies 3 to 7 days later is a positive test for yeast; however, a positive culture suggests but does not prove infection, since *Candida* may be part of the normal flora.

Cultures for *Trichomonas* are significantly more sensitive than the "wet prep" but are not generally available. Monoclonal antibody tests look promising (see Chap. 9).

Aerobic cultures of the vagina are useful in the diagnosis and treatment of vaginitis in prepubertal girls in which respiratory pathogens such as group A β streptococci may play a major role, but such cultures are rarely indicated in the diagnosis of vaginal discharge in the adolescent. Normal flora is discussed in Chaps. 3 and 9.

PROGESTERONE TEST

The patient is given medroxyprogesterone (Provera), 10 mg orally twice a day for 5 days or 10 mg once a day for 10 days, or progesterone-in-oil, 50 to 100 mg intramuscularly. If the patient has an estrogen-primed endometrium and is not pregnant, she will have a period 3 to 10 days later. Progesterone given orally or intramuscularly is used as a diagnostic test for the evaluation of primary and secondary amenorrhea (see Chap. 6), never as a pregnancy test.

PREGNANCY TESTS

A number of highly sensitive, rapid pregnancy tests are available. Qualitative kits used on urine samples are the most practical for office use [32, 33, 34]. The newer kits use specific monoclonal antibodies to human chorionic gonadotropin (HCG) and enzyme-linked immunoassay techniques (ELISA). For example, the detection limit of Tandem ICON HCG (Hybritech) kits are 20 and 50 mIU/ml; the kits are not affected by blood or protein and have a built-in control (Fig. 1-28). In studies of ectopic pregnancies, 26/27 and 95/95 ectopic pregnancies were detected by ICON [35, 36]. Very low levels of HCG (10–50 mIU/ml), especially in a urine with low specific gravity (< 1.015), may be missed. A modified method using 20 drops of urine instead of 5 drops can be used in such exceptional clinical circumstances. Testpack (Abbott) offers similar advantages. Because of sensitivity of this type of kit, detection of early pregnancies and ectopic pregnancies is significantly enhanced. Pregnancy tests should always be correlated with clinical information and examination (Table 1-2).

Figure 1-28. ICON office pregnancy test. The presence of the center dot is a positive test; the dot on the outer circle is the positive control.

Blood tests can be qualitative or quantitative in measuring HCG. For example, Tandem ICON can be used on serum to determine a positive or negative pregnancy test. Quantitative HCG levels are important in the diagnosis of ectopic pregnancy and some miscarriages and for the follow-up of molar pregnancies and choriocarcinomas. Because not all laboratories use the same units or methodology in reporting HCG levels, sequential measures in a patient should use the same laboratories. Two international systems for HCG can be reported: the newer International Reference Preparation (IRP) or the

Table 1-2. HCG Levels in Normal Intrauterine Pregnancy

Time Postconception	Expected β-HCG (mIU/ml)
1 week	5–50
2 weeks	40–1000
3 weeks	100–5000
4 weeks	600–10000
5–6 weeks	1500–100,000
7–8 weeks	16,000–200,000
2–3 months	12,000–300,000
2nd trimester	24,000–55,000
3rd trimester	6000–48,000

older Second International Standard (second IS), which is roughly half of the IRP levels. Although urine HCG can also be quantitated, blood measurements are preferred for serial measures. Serum HCG generally doubles approximately every 2.3 days at 5 to 8 weeks of gestation and can be used to assess the normal progression of an early pregnancy.

A useful chart has been developed by Robert Romera [37] and published by the Dade Division of Baxter Health Care, Cambridge, Massachusetts (originally Travenol-Genentech). Once the initial β-HCG is at least 100 mIU/ml (IRP), another assay is performed 1 to 10 days later (preferably 2–3 days later), and the percentage increase is compared. At 2 days, the percentage rise above baseline is 66 percent, at 3 days 114 percent, at 4 days 176 percent, and at 5 days 225 percent in normal early gestation. For example, an HCG value of 440 mIU/ml at baseline and 820 mIU/ml 2 days later would be an 86 percent increase over baseline (i.e., normal). Clinical assessment is important along with ultrasound because 6 to 15 percent of normal intrauterine pregnancies will have abnormal HCG increases and 13 percent of ectopic pregnancies will initially show a normal increase in HCG. HCG peaks between 10 and 14 weeks of pregnancy. Depending on the radiologist and type of scanner, abdominal ultrasonography of the uterus can detect an intrauterine gestation with an HCG level above 6000 mIU/ml (IRP). Transvaginal sonography has detected pregnancy even earlier at 1500 mIU/ml [38, 39]. Fossum [38] reported finding a gestational sac at 34.8 ± 2.2 days from last menstrual period (LMP), at which time HCG was 1398 ± 155 mIU/ml (IRP) and 914 ± 106 mIU/ml (second IS); a fetal pole at 40.3 ± 3.4 days from LMP, with HCG 5113 ± 298 (IRP) or 3783 ± 683 mIU/ml (second IS); and fetal heartbeat at 46.9 ± 6.0 days from LMP, with HCG 17,208 ± 3772 mIU/ml (IRP) or 13,178 ± 2898 mIU/ml (second IS).

Over-the-counter pregnancy tests have improved significantly, and most use monoclonal antibody technology, which yields sensitive and specific results at the time of or shortly after a missed period. However, adolescents may misread the instructions and the results and should thus be encouraged to use primarily office and laboratory tests and confirm the results of at-home tests with a medical assessment (and repeat office test).

BUCCAL SMEAR
A buccal smear is obtained by having the patient rinse her mouth with water and then scraping the buccal mucosa with a tongue depressor. The material is streaked on a glass slide, which is immediately placed in a 3:1 methanol–acetic acid solution or Pap fixative. The cytologist looks for the presence of Barr bodies. In the normal female, the chromatin-positive material represents the second X chromo-

some. Since laboratories vary in their normal counts, a control smear must always be run concurrently. Some laboratories report counts for the normal female in the range of 10 to 35 percent; others report 19 to 49 percent. A patient with no Barr bodies is 45,X or 46,XY; a patient with a low count may be a mosaic (e.g., 45,X/46,XX, 46,XX/XY). The presence of two Barr bodies per cell indicates XXX or XXXY. In addition, the size of the chromatin mass can be evaluated by an experienced technician. A small Barr body may signify a deletion of part of the X chromosome; a large Barr body may represent an isochromosome for the long arm of the X chromosome.

Incubating the buccal smear or peripheral blood with quinacrine dye allows demonstration of the Y chromosome by fluorescence.

Some centers now prefer to use only blood karyotypes.

BONE AGE

The bone age is determined by comparing x-ray films of the patient's wrist and hand (carpal and phalangeal ossification centers) with the standards in Greulich and Pyle [40] or applying the Tanner-Whitehouse method [41]. An x-ray film of the iliac crest can be used in a similar way. At puberty, the epiphysis along the iliac crest undergoes ossification. During adolescence, the ossification progresses from the lateral to the medial part, and fusion occurs at 21 to 23 years of age.

Growth hormone and thyroid deficiencies, glucocorticoid excess, delayed puberty, and malnutrition result in delayed maturation; androgens produce an advanced bone age. In the absence of sex steroids (for example, sexual infantilism associated with Turner syndrome), the bone age will not advance beyond 13 years.

ULTRASONOGRAPHY

Ultrasonography of the pelvis has become an extremely useful technique for evaluating gynecologic problems such as ovarian cysts and tumors, pelvic inflammatory disease, pregnancy, and pelvic anomalies [42–45]. Since an ill-defined adnexal mass found in an adolescent may represent a congenital abnormality of the müllerian system, ultrasonography should also include views of the kidneys. Renal agenesis often accompanies müllerian duplications in which one side of the vagina is atretic and obstructed with resultant hematocolpos. Although ultrasonography is an extremely helpful technique, false-positive findings do occur, such as when bowel gas is read as an ovarian cyst.

The uterus can usually be identified in the prepubertal child, with measurements of 2.0 to 3.3 cm in length and 0.5 to 1.0 cm in width. The fundus and cervix are the same size. With puberty, the fundus increases in size; the postpubertal uterus is 5 to 8 cm in length, and the fundus is 1.6 to 3.0 cm in width. In the prepubertal girl, the

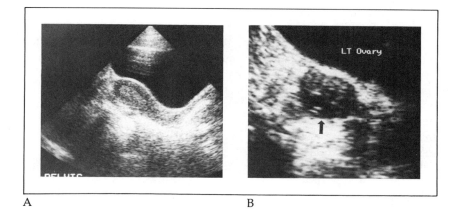

A   B

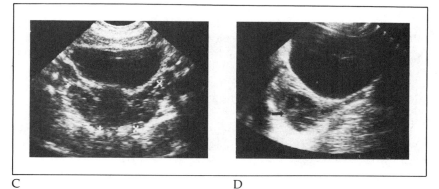

C   D

Figure 1-29. Pelvic ultrasounds. A. Normal uterus. B. Normal ovary.
C. Polycystic ovary syndrome (the enlarged ovaries are shown between the
two + and two X markings). D. Hemorrhagic ovarian cyst. (From J Share
and R Teele, Ultrasonography in adolescent gynecology, Clin Practice
Gynecol [in press]. By permission of Elsevier Science Publishing.)

ovaries are usually less than 1 cm^3 in volume (0.13–0.9 cm^3) (Fig. 1-
29A and B). In the pubertal girl, the ovaries are 1.8 to 5.7 cm^3, with a
mean of 4 cm^3 [45]. The average reproductive ovary varies from 2.5 to
5 cm in length, 1.5 to 3.0 cm in width, and 0.7 to 1.5 cm in thickness.
Prepubertal girls can have follicles up to 7 mm in diameter. Stanhope
and associates [46] have reported a progressive increase in the proportion of normal girls over age 8½ years with more than six follicles
in each ovary ("megalocystic ovaries"). Small cysts (1 to 3 cm) of ovarian follicles and corpus or thecal luteum occur normally in adolescent
girls. In fact, girls in early and midpuberty may have enlarged ovaries
with multiple small "cysts" that are normal. Small amounts of fluid in
the cul-de-sac may be seen in normal girls with ovulation. Fluid may
also occur with bleeding or infection.

Ultrasonography is useful when bimanual examination is difficult, when a mass is felt, and to define anatomy in patients with amenorrhea. Patients with gonadal dysgenesis should have their renal status assessed by ultrasonography. Patients thought to have uterine agenesis can also be assessed by this technique; the absence of the uterus can be confirmed, the presence of normal ovaries established in Mayer-Rokitansky-Kuster-Hauser syndrome, and the kidneys examined. In patients with androgen insensitivity, the testes may sometimes be visualized as soft tissue densities behind the bladder or in the inguinal areas.

Ultrasonography is very useful in defining uterine anomalies with or without obstruction. In the assessment of müllerian abnormalities, the kidneys should be scanned to look for unilateral agenesis, horseshoe kidneys, and crossed fused ectopia. Skeletal anomalies also occur commonly in patients with müllerian anomalies and include abnormalities of segmentation and rudimentary and wedge vertebrae.

Conversely, patients with cervical spine anomalies or congenital scoliosis, or both, should have ultrasonography to screen for renal and pelvic anomalies in midpuberty prior to menarche. A renal screen can be done much earlier, but pelvic screening is easier in the pubertal child. The girl with unilateral renal agenesis should have ultrasonography and gynecologic assessment prior to menarche.

Uterine hypoplasia as well as ovarian failure often occur in patients treated with pelvic radiation therapy for childhood malignancies. Uterine leiomyomas are rare in adolescents; ultrasound may show uterine enlargement and alteration in texture and contour.

Pregnancy and the abnormalities including ectopic pregnancy, miscarriage, and trophoblastic disease may require the aid of ultrasonography. An intrauterine gestational sac should optimally be visible on abdominal ultrasound with HCG levels above 6000 mIU/ml (IRP) (see p. 37). It should be noted that since different laboratories use different methodology and units for testing, the literature on ultrasonography and HCG levels is confusing, and practitioners need to consult with their own laboratories. Ectopic pregnancies may be visualized by pelvic ultrasonography, but often the findings in ectopic pregnancy are nonspecific and overlap with those caused by an ovarian mass or infection. Dating of pregnancies is also very useful in adolescents who may not be able to give an accurate last menstrual period (LMP).

Ovarian enlargement and pelvic pain are often evaluated with the use of ultrasonography [47–51]. Patients with polycystic ovaries may have normal sized or enlarged ovaries with multiple cysts and a thickened capsule [52, 53] (Fig. 1-29C). Simple ovarian cysts are very common in adolescents, usually 3 to 6 cm in diameter, unilocular, and without internal debris; these often resolve spontaneously. Septated ovarian cysts may be a simple cyst, cystadenofibroma, cystadenosis, or a teratoma. Adnexal masses that are solid or have mixed solid and cystic parts may be a hemorrhagic ovarian cyst (Fig. 1-29D), ovarian torsion, ectopic pregnancy, tubo-ovarian abscess, ovarian tumor, or periappendicular abscess. Hemorrhagic ovarian cysts have quite variable findings depending on when they are scanned; most are heterogenous with mixed solid and cystic areas, which may become more cystic as the clot resorbs. The ultrasound of ovarian torsion is also variable; the classic finding is that of a large solid mass with peripheral follicular cysts. With pelvic inflammatory disease, the edema and loss of anatomic planes may produce a disorganized pattern and adnexal enlargement [42, 54]. Ovarian tumors with a cystic component may be easier to visualize than solid teratomas, which can be obscured by bowel gas. An x ray of the abdomen may help identify fat, calcifications, or teeth in these tumors.

It should be noted that some solid tumors such as dermoid tumors may be palpable and yet not be visualized by ultrasonography. Thus, physical examination is extremely important in adolescents with pelvic pain.

Transvaginal ultrasonography is now being used increasingly in the evaluation of intrauterine and ectopic pregnancy, spontaneous and incomplete abortion (see Chap. 16), pelvic masses, pelvic inflammatory disease, and uterine abnormalities. Gross anatomic fetal malformations such as anencephaly have been detected in the first trimester. The pseudogestational sac that occurs in 6 to 10 percent of ectopic pregnancies is more easily recognized using this technique [38, 39], and transvaginal ultrasound may detect a noncystic adnexal mass. Signs of abnormal early gestation include irregular decidua, pathologic double ring, subchorionic bleeding, degenerative changes of fetal pole and yolk sac, and absence of fetal heart beat. Tubo-ovarian disease can also be assessed and the actual tube examined in greater detail with both pelvic inflammatory disease and ectopic pregnancy.

CT scans and, more recently, magnetic resonance imaging (MRI) have become important additional tests when ultrasound has not yielded sufficient diagnostic information with pelvic pathology. MRI has advantages over CT because of the lack of radiation and risk of allergic reactions caused by contrast media and the greater tissue definition. However, MRI also has disadvantages because of the high cost and long imaging times [55].

OVULATION DETECTION METHODS

A number of methods have been used for detecting the occurrence of ovulation. Most are utilized primarily in the evaluation and treatment of infertility patients. In some cases of older adolescents with conditions such as oligomenorrhea or Turner syndrome with normal

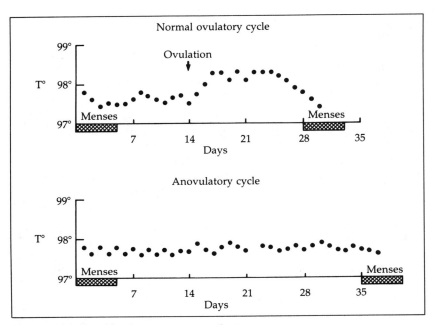

Figure 1-30. Basal body temperature charts.

gonadotropin levels, the physician may wish to establish whether ovulatory cycles are occurring. Methods include measurement of basal body temperature charts, serum progesterone levels during the luteal phase, luteinizing hormone (LH) testing, ultrasonography, and endometrial sampling.

For basal body temperature charts, the patient is instructed to take her temperature every morning as soon as she awakens. For accurate recording, a basal body thermometer is kept at the bedside, and the patient is told "not to go to the bathroom" or "even wiggle" before the temperature is taken. The temperature is recorded on a special chart. The typical ovulatory and anovulatory cycles are shown in Figure 1-30. Basal body temperature charts are useful if the patient shows a classic pattern, but some ovulatory patients may not be able to demonstrate a biphasic chart, may have an illness during the recording, or may fail to use the proper methodology. The use of basal body temperatures during the placebo week of oral contraceptives can also be helpful in managing girls with lack of withdrawal flow; for example, a low temperature of 97°F is consistent with pill amenorrhea, not pregnancy (see Chap. 15).

Home kits are now available for LH testing of urine to detect the midcycle rise [56]. These kits, which use monoclonal antibody technology, are helpful in infertility patients, since the time from the detected surge to ovulation is typically around 12 to 24 hours. However, as is noted in Chapter 4, the presence of an LH surge in an adolescent may not be evidence of normal ovulation and a normal luteal phase. Similarly, a random serum progesterone may be suggestive but not definitive evidence of a normal luteal phase. Endometrial sampling, even with the new small instruments (e.g., Pipelle endometrial suction curette), can be difficult for the physican to perform in the virginal patient and uncomfortable for the adolescent.

Clearly the use of any of these tests necessitates discussion with the patient of the problems and likely benefits from the results.

REFERENCES
1. Emans SJ, Wood ER, Flagg NT, et al. Genital findings in sexually abused symptomatic and asymptomatic girls. Pediatrics 1087; 79:778.
2. Huffman JW, Dewhurst CJ, and Capraro VJ. *The Gynecology of Childhood and Adolescence.* Philadelphia: Saunders, 1981.
3. Pokorny SF. Configuration of the prepubertal hymen. Am J Obstet Gynecol 1987; 157:950.
4. Jenny C, Kuhns MLD, and Arakawa F. Hymens in newborn female infants. Pediatrics 1987; 80:399.
5. Mor N, and Merlob P. Congenital absence of the hymen only a rumor? Pediatrics 1988; 82:679.
6. Emans SJ, and Goldstein DP. The gynecologic examination of the prepubertal child with vulvovaginitis: Use of the knee-chest position. Pediatrics 1980; 65:758.
7. Emans SJ. Vulvovaginitis in the child and adolescent. Pediatrics in Review 1986; 8:12.
8. Pokorny SF. Tricks, tips, and tests (abstract). North American Society for Pediatric and Adolescent Gynecology (NASPAG), October 1988.
9. Capraro V. Gynecologic examination in children and adolescents. Pediatr Clin North Am 1972; 19:511.
10. Billmire ME, Farrell MK, and Dine MS. A simplified procedure for pediatric vaginal examination: Use of veterinary otoscope specula. Pediatrics 1980; 65:823.
11. Capraro V, and Capraro E. Vaginal aspirate studies in children. Obstet Gynecol 1971; 37:462.
12. Pokorny SF, and Stormer J. Atraumatic removal of secretions from the prepubertal vagina. Am J Obstet Gynecol 1987; 156:581.
13. Alexander ER. Misidentification of sexually transmitted organisms in children: medicolegal implications. Pediatr Infect Dis 1988; 7:1.
14. Whittington WL, Rice RJ, Biddle JW, et al. Incorrect identification of *Neisseria gonorrhoeae* from infants and children. Pediatr Infect Dis 1988; 7:3.
15. Hammerschlag MR, Rettig PJ, and Shields ME. False positive result with the use of Chlamydia antigen detection tests in the evaluation of suspected sexual abuse in children. Pediatr Infect Dis 1988; 7:11.
16. Green T. *Gynecology: Essentials of clinical practice* (3rd ed.). Boston: Little, Brown, 1977.
17. Martinez J, Smith R, Farmer M, et al. High prevalence of genital tract papillomavirus infection in female adolescents. Pediatrics 1988; 82:604.
18. Delke IM, Veridiano NP, Russell, S, et al. Brief clinical and laboratory observations. Abnormal cervical cytology in adolescents. J Pediatr 1981; 98:985.

19. Fields C, Restivo RM, and Brown MC. Experiences in mass Papanicolaou screening and cytologic observation in teenage girls. Am J Obstet Gynecol 1976; 124:730.
20. Hein K, Schreiber K, Cohen MI, et al. Cervical cytology: The need for routine screening in the sexually active adolescent. J Pediatr 1977; 91:123.
21. Crum CP, Ikenberg H, Richart RM, et al. Human papillomavirus type 16 and early cervical neoplasia. N Engl J Med 1984; 310:880.
22. Lancaster WD, Castellano C, Santos C, et al. Human papillomavirus deoxyribonucleic acid in cervical carcinoma from primary and metastatic sites. Am J Obstet Gynecol 1986; 154:115.
23. Macnab JCM, Walkinshaw SA, Cordiner JW, et al. Human papillomavirus in clinically and histologically normal tissue of patients with genital cancer. N Engl J Med 1986; 315:1052.
24. Hellberg D, Nilsson S, Haley NJ, et al. Smoking and cervical intraepithelial neoplasia: Nicotine and cotinine in serum and cervical mucus in smokers and nonsmokers. J Obstet Gynecol 1988; 158:910.
25. Mittal KR, Miller HK, and Lowell DM. Koilocytosis preceding squamous cell carcinoma in situ of uterine cervix. Am J Clin Pathol 1987; 87:243.
26. Noumoff JS. Atypia in cervical cytology as a risk factor for intraepithelial neoplasia. Am J Obstet Gynecol 1987; 156:628.
27. National Cancer Institute Workshop. The 1988 Bethesda system for reporting cervical/vaginal cytological diagnoses. JAMA 1989; 262:931.
28. Meisels A. Computed cytohormonal findings in 3,307 healthy women. Acta Cytol 1965; 9:328.
29. Rakoff AE. Hormonal cytology in gynecology. Clin Obstet Gynecol 1961; 4:1045.
30. Lencioni LJ, and Staffieri J. Urocytogram diagnosis of sexual precocity. Acta Cytol (Baltimore) 1969; 13:302.
31. Preeyasombat C, and Kenny F. Urocytogram in normal children and various abnormal conditions. Pediatrics 1966; 38:436.
32. Delfert DM, Rea MR, Kissler G, et al. Criteria for evaluating nonquantitative assays: application to serum choriogonadotropin. Clin Chem 1987; 33:150.
33. Gelletlie R, and Nielsen JB. Evaluation and comparison of commercially available pregnancy tests based on monoclonal antibodies to human choriogonadotropin. Clin Chem 1986; 32:2166.
34. Bandi ZL, Schoen I, and Delara M. Enzyme-linked immunosorbent urine pregnancy tests. Am J Clin Pathol 1987; 87:236.
35. Cartwright PS, Victory DG, Moore RA, et al. Performance of a new enzyme-linked immunoassay urine pregnancy test for the detection of ectopic gestation. Ann Emer Med 1986; 15:1198.
36. Norman RJ, Buck RH, Rom L, et al. Blood or urine measurement of human chorionic gonadotropin for detection of ectopic pregnancy? A comparative study of quantitative and qualitative methods in both fluids. Obstet Gynecol 1988; 71:315.
37. Abnormal pregnancy detection: using serial quantitative β-hCG percent increase. Travenol-Genentech Diagnostics, Cambridge, MA, 1984.
38. Fossum GT, Davajan V, and Kletzky OA. Early detection of pregnancy with transvaginal ultrasound. Fertil Steril 1988; 49:788.
39. Timor-Tritsch I, and Rottem S. High-frequency transvaginal sonography: New diagnostic boon. Contemporary Ob/Gyn April 1988; 111.
40. Greulich WW, and Pyle S. Radiographic Atlas of Skeletal Development of the Hand and Wrist. Stanford, CA: Stanford University Press, 1959.

41. Tanner JM, Whitehouse RH, Cameron N, et al. Assessment of skeletal maturity and prediction of adult height. (TW2 method). New York: Academic Press, 1983.
42. Share J, and Teele R. Ultrasonography in adolescent gynecology. Clin Practice Gynecol (in press).
43. Sanfilippo JS, and Lavery JP. The spectrum of ultrasound: antenatal to adolescent years. Semin in Reprod Endocrinol 1988; 6:45.
44. Salardi S, Orsini IF, Cacciari E, et al. Pelvic ultrasonography in premenarcheal girls: relation to puberty and sex hormone concentration. Arch Dis of Child 1985; 60:120.
45. Lippe BM, and Sample WF. Pelvic ultrasonography in pediatric and adolescent endocrine disorders. J Pediatr 1978; 92:897.
46. Stanhope R, Adams J, Jacobs HS, et al. Ovarian ultrasound assessment in normal children, idiopathic precocious puberty, and during low dose pulsatile gonadotropin releasing hormone treatment of hypogonadotrophic hypogonadism. Arch Dis Child 1985; 60:116.
47. Wu A, and Siegel MJ. Sonography of pelvic masses in children: Diagnostic predictability. AJR 1987; 148:1199.
48. Baltarowich OH, Kurtz AB, Pasto ME, et al. The spectrum of sonographic findings in hemorrhagic ovarian cysts. AJR 1987; 148:901.
49. Bass IS, Haller JO, Friedman AP, et al. The ultrasonographic appearance of the hemorrhagic ovarian cyst in adolescents. J Ultrasound Med 1984; 3:509.
50. Warner MA, Fleischer AC, Edell SL, et al. Uterine adnexal torsion: sonographic findings. Radiology 1985; 154:773.
51. Graif M, Shalev J, Strauss S, et al. Torsion of the ovary: sonographic features. AJR 1984; 143:1331.
52. Hann LH, Hall DH, McArdle CR, et al. Polycystic ovarian disease: sonographic spectrum. Radiology 1984; 150:531.
53. Yeh H-C, Futterweit W, and Thornton JC. Polycystic ovarian disease: US features in 104 patients. Radiology 1987; 163:111.
54. Swayne LC, Love MB, and Karasick SR. Pelvic inflammatory disease: sonographic-pathologic correlation. Radiology 1984; 151:751.
55. Council on Scientific Affairs. Report of the Panel on Magnetic Resonance Imaging. Magnetic resonance imaging of the abdomen and pelvis. JAMA 1989; 261:420.
56. Rebar RW. Practical appreciations of home diagnostic products: A symposium. J Reprod Med 1987; 32(9S):705.

SUGGESTED READING

Elkins TE, McNeeley SG, Rosen D, et al. A clinical observation of a program to accomplish pelvic exams in difficult-to-manage patients with mental retardation. Adolesc Pediatr Gynecol 1988; 1:195.

2. Ambiguous Genitalia in the Newborn

Although most clinicians will rarely see an infant with ambiguous genitalia at birth, the need to assess the situation as quickly as possible makes this subject essential for discussion. Any deviation from the normal appearance of male or female genitalia should prompt investigation, since apparent, but incomplete, male or female external genitals may be associated with the gonads and genotype of the opposite sex (e.g., the male with androgen insensitivity syndrome, and the markedly virilized female with congenital adrenocortical hyperplasia [CAH]). Even a slight doubt that arises in the initial newborn examination should be pursued systematically to prevent the possibility of later confusion. Bilateral cryptorchidism, unilateral cryptorchidism with incomplete scrotal fusion or hypospadias, labial fusion, or clitoromegaly requires evaluation.

DETERMINING SEX ASSIGNMENT

When the physician finds that an infant has ambiguous genitalia, the parents should be reassured that they have a healthy baby, but that because the external genital development is incomplete, tests are necessary to determine the sex. A straightforward explanation of the factors necessary for normal sexual development in utero may be helpful. Clearly, most parents will react with dismay and anxiety; they should be reassured that tests will show the cause of the problem and whether their baby is a girl or a boy. The possibility of an intersex disorder (hermaphroditism) should not be raised at this time. Speculation about possible sex assignment should be kept to a minimum; it is not helpful for the physician to say, "I think it's a girl," or "I think it's a boy." The parents should be told that within a few days, or at most 1 to 2 weeks, a definite answer will be possible. The physician should examine the baby in the presence of the parents and explain the common genital anlage for boys and girls. The concept of an "underdeveloped" male or "overdeveloped" female helps parents accept their baby's condition. Parents should be encouraged to use the names they had previously selected for a boy or girl, once gender is decided.

Although a diagnosis of the patient's condition requires knowledge of the genotype (karyotype), assignment of sex is based on other criteria as well. The first issue is fertility. The female with CAH may be virilized at birth, yet with normal ovaries and uterus she is potentially capable of bearing children. Thus, management, including surgery, must aim at female gender identity. When fertility is not possible, as with mixed gonadal dysgenesis (MGD) or male pseudo-hermaphroditism, decisions are based on surgical requirements for reconstruction of the external genitals. In general, surgical techniques are more suited to reduction of the size of the phallus/clitoris and, later, the creation of a vagina, than to the construction of a normal male phallus. Once the decision as to sex assignment is made, the physician should help the parents accept their infant as a normal male or a normal female [1]. As long as parental attitudes toward the child's sex remain unequivocal, the child usually assumes his or her gender role without difficulty, regardless of the genotype.

REVIEW OF EMBRYOGENESIS
Prior to the seventh week of gestation, the fetal gonads are sexually bipotential. Differentiation of the gonad to a testis requires testis determining factor (TDF). The differentiation to an ovary occurs in the absence of TDF. Both 46,XX and 45,X fetuses have oocytes, but in 45,X fetuses, oocyte atresia is accelerated in the second half of intrauterine life and in the prepubertal years. Ovarian determinant genes are responsible for oocyte maintenance and are necessary to prevent the accelerated atresia seen in 45,X individuals that results in "streak ovaries." Mapping of the X chromosome has led to the observation that certain deletions are responsible for short stature and varying degrees of menstrual function from primary amenorrhea to secondary amenorrhea to full fertility. Autosomes also play a role in normal ovarian differentiation. DNA probes are likely to help decide if patients with 45,X have a second cell line; for example, Y-linked fragments have been found in individuals previously thought to be 45,X [2].

Male internal and external genital development depends on a functioning testis. Female genital development occurs in the absence of a testis, so a patient with 46,XX (normal female) or 45,X (Turner syndrome) has a uterus, fallopian tubes, vagina, and female external genitalia. An outline of normal development is shown in Figures 2-1 and 2-2.

Between 6 and 8 weeks of gestation, the gonad differentiates into an ovary or testis. Recombinant DNA techniques have found a testis determining factor (TDF) on the short arm of the Y chromosome, separate from the H-Y antigen [3,4,5]. A hypothesized "TDF" has been found in individuals with previously unexplained male development, including 46,XX males [6] and 45,X/46,XY intersex patients.* It is important to remember that TDF is not on the distal long arm of the Y chromosome, which is responsible for "Y-fluorescence." The Y chromosome is also postulated to have genes or gene products for growth determinants and protection from gonadoblastomas. The

_____
*See Further Reading for new developments in TDF.

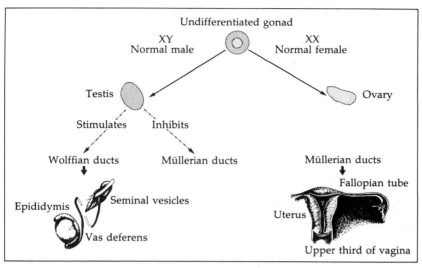

Figure 2-1. Internal genital differentiation in utero.

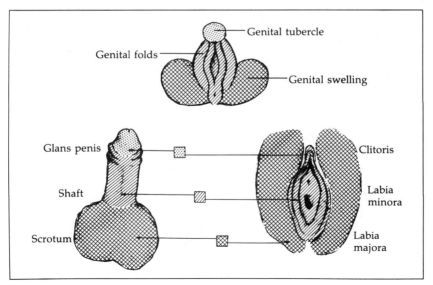

Figure 2-2. External genital differentiation in utero.

fetal testes produces two substances: müllerian inhibiting substance and testosterone. Müllerian inhibiting substance (MIS), a high-molecular-weight glycoprotein, is secreted by Sertoli cells and acts locally to prevent the development of the tubes, uterus, and upper vagina in a critical period between 8 and 14 weeks of gestation. Testosterone, secreted by the Leydig cells, is responsible for the development of the wolffian system (vas deferens, seminal vesicles, epididymis) and, via conversion to dihydrotestosterone, is responsible for the development of the normal male external genitalia. By the twelfth week of gestation, the genital tubercle has formed into the penis, and the genital swellings have fused to form the scrotum. Thus, if the testis is present but inadequate during the first 10 to 12 weeks of gestation, the internal genitalia may be a mixture of müllerian and wolffian structures, while the external genitalia are ambiguous (so-called dysgenetic male pseudohermaphroditism). If the testes function normally until the sixteenth week of gestation and then disappear, the internal and external genitalia will be male except for bilateral cryptorchidism and possible small phallus (so-called congenital anorchia).

The patient with MGD (e.g., a patient with 45,X/46,XY and a streak gonad on one side and a testis on the other) may have a mixture of müllerian and wolffian structures (e.g., a uterus, tubes, and perhaps a vas deferens) (see p. 207). Internal genitalia may be asymmetric because of the variable local action of müllerian inhibiting substance (MIS). The external genitalia are also often asymmetric due to an enlarged labioscrotal fold on the side of the testis. The gonads in MGD are dysgenetic, and generally the testis does not virilize the external genitalia completely. However, the testis is capable of producing androgen levels sufficient to cause unwanted virilization of the apparent female at puberty [7]. Approximately one half of patients with MGD have ambiguous genitalia at birth; 26 out of 36 patients in Federman's series [8] were raised as females.

True hermaphroditism occurs when both ovarian and testicular tissue are present. A testis may be present on one side and an ovary on the other side, or bilateral ovotestes may be present. A uterus (frequently hypoplastic or abnormal) is present in 90 percent of patients. Most patients have ambiguous genitalia, although approximately 7 percent have normal female genitalia and 2 percent have a penile urethra. In the past, most have been reared as males. At puberty, three fourths of the patients develop gynecomastia, and one half menstruate. Decision about sex assignment should be based on the internal and external genitalia, and all organs of the opposite sex should be removed once a decision is reached on the sex of the rearing. If the patient is to be reared as a male, the phallus must be adequate and the testis brought down into the scrotum. A 46,XX karyotype is present in about two thirds of patients, mosaicism (e.g., 46,XX/46,XY, 46,XY/47,XXY) in nearly one third, and 46,XY in one tenth. 46,XX true hermaphrodites have been reported to be H-Y antigen positive, a protein produced by the Y chromosome (near TDF) [9–11] suggesting that Y chromosomal material has been translocated to the X chromosome or to an autosome. In one 46,XX true hermaphrodite, the testicular portion of the testes was H-Y antigen positive and the ovarian portion H-Y antigen negative [10].

46,XY patients with androgen insensitivity (testicular feminization) usually appear to be normal females in the newborn period. Although their testes function normally, thereby inhibiting müllerian structures (no tubes, uterus, or upper vagina) and producing testosterone, the end-organs are unresponsive to androgens. Although testicular feminization represents one end of the spectrum of male pseudohermaphroditism, other patients with partial enzymatic blocks of androgen synthesis or variable sensitivity to normal levels of androgen may have ambiguous genitalia as neonates.

In the absence of testicular function and MIS, the müllerian ducts differentiate into the uterus, fallopian tubes, and upper one third of the vagina, and the genital tubercle, folds, and swellings form the normal female external genitalia. However, in the normal 46,XX female, the presence of androgen either from a fetal source (CAH) or a maternal source (certain drugs, maternal CAH, or a virilizing tumor) will alter the external but not the internal genitalia. Androgens, danazol, and synthetic progestins (in doses much higher than in oral contraceptive pills) given prior to the fourteenth week of gestation can cause labial fusion and clitoromegaly; such therapy after the fourteenth week is only capable of causing clitoromegaly.

Thus, from this brief review of embryogenesis, it is clear that many important disorders are responsible for ambiguous genitalia in the newborn period.

ASSESSMENT OF THE NEONATE
The initial evaluation of ambiguous genitalia in the neonate includes a careful history, physical examination, buccal smear, karyotype, and urinary and serum hormone analyses (Fig. 2-3) [1, 12–15]. Since the most common cause of ambiguous genitalia is CAH, serum sodium, potassium, and glucose levels should be monitored so that the diagnosis of impending adrenal insufficiency can be promptly made. It is often important to establish internal anatomy by cystoscopy, vaginoscopy, urogenital sinography, and ultrasonography. Laparoscopy or laparotomy and biopsy of the gonad are generally restricted to cases of suspected male pseudohermaphroditism, true hermaphroditism, and selected cases of nonadrenal female pseudohermaphroditism. Occasionally, a trial of human chorionic gonadotropin (HCG) or tes-

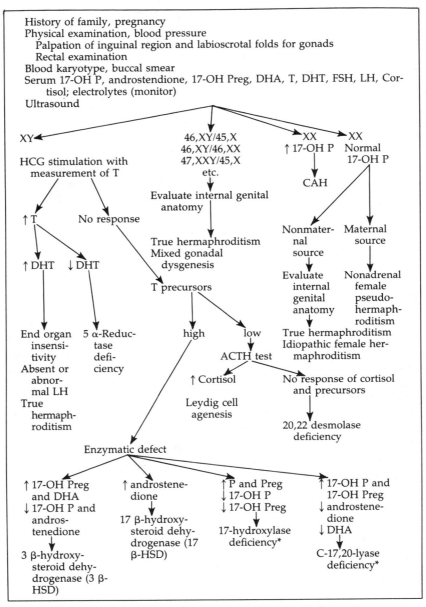

Figure 2-3. Evaluation of ambiguous genitalia in the newborn. P = progesterone; Preg = pregnenolone; 17-OH P = 17-hydroxyprogesterone; 17-OH Preg = 17-hydroxypregnenolone; DHA = dehydroepiandrosterone; T = testosterone; DHT = dihydrotestosterone; 3 β-HSD = 3 β-hydroxysteroid dehydrogenase; CAH = congenital adrenal hyperplasia; FSH = follicle-stimulating hormone; LH = luteinizing hormone; HCG = human chorionic gonadotropin; ACTH = adrenocorticotropic hormone. *These two deficiencies have the same gene, so either or both can be impaired.

tosterone is given to assess whether the male phallus is capable of responding normally before a final determination of sex assignment is made.

HISTORY

A careful history should be obtained from the parents regarding the following:

1. Other family members, especially siblings, with CAH. This diagnosis may be missed in males because the only physical sign is increased scrotal rugae and pigmentation. Thus, the history may reveal only a brother who died in early infancy of vomiting and dehydration (not recognized as secondary to adrenal insufficiency).
2. Aunts or other relatives with amenorrhea and infertility (suggestive of male pseudohermaphroditism).
3. Maternal ingestion of any drugs during pregnancy.
4. Maternal history of virilization or CAH.

PHYSICAL EXAMINATION

The physical examination of the infant should include measurement of the clitoris-penis and notation of the site of the urethral opening (perineal versus penile), fusion of the labioscrotal folds, and the presence of gonads in the scrotum or in the inguinal rings. Labioscrotal fusion may be suggested by finding an anogenital ratio in females (determined by anus to forchette [AF]/anus to base of clitoris [AC]) of greater than 0.5 which falls outside the 95 percent confidence limits [16]. A palpable gonad below the inguinal ligament is almost always a testis. Asymmetry of the labioscrotal folds with a unilateral gonad suggests mixed gonadal dysgenesis or true hermaphroditism. Hyperpigmentation of the labioscrotal folds would suggest congenital adrenal hyperplasia. A rectal examination should be done to assess the presence of a uterus. The uterus is often easily palpable at birth because of in utero stimulation by placental estrogen.

LABORATORY TESTS

The most important laboratory tests include a buccal smear with Y fluorescence, karyotype, and serum hormone levels. A buccal smear can be done immediately, although low counts are seen in the first 2 days of life. Few normal females have counts less than 5 percent, but many have counts lower than 20 percent; thus a mosaic may be missed. A repeat buccal smear on the third or fourth day of life is indicated if counts are borderline [17]. Staining with quinacrine dye will pick up the presence of a Y line in most patients. Increasingly centers are relying on the karyotype to aid in the diagnosis; results

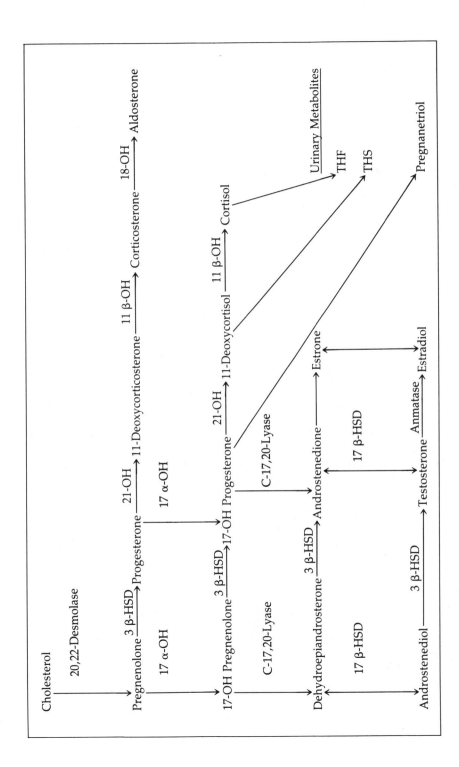

can be available in 2 to 3 days if the laboratory processes the blood as an emergency diagnosis. The availability of DNA probes to detect Y fragments on the X or an autosome should yield further information.

Although many centers used urinary collections in the past to make the diagnosis of CAH, serum tests of hormone levels have simplified the approach. In normal infants, the 17-hydroxyprogesterone level is elevated in cord blood but decreases to 100 to 200 ng/100 ml after 24 hours of life. This decrease may take longer in premature infants. The early-morning 17-hydroxyprogesterone is generally greater than 1000 ng/100 ml in 21-hydroxylase CAH. Androstenedione is also elevated; serum cortisol may be very low or at the lower range of normal. It is likely given the frequency of the CAH gene in the population (varying from 1:300 in Alaskan Eskimos to an average of 1:14,500 worldwide) that neonatal screening for 17-hydroxyprogesterone will aid in the early detection of cases. Other serum tests that may be useful in the diagnosis of the infant with ambiguous genitalia (Fig. 2–3) include follicle-stimulating hormone (FSH), luteinizing hormone (LH), testosterone, dehydroepiandrosterone (DHA), and 17-hydroxy-pregnenolone.

During the evaluation of the infant with suspected CAH, fluid and electrolyte balance must be carefully monitored. If a 24-hour urine is collected, a 17-ketosteroid excretion of less than 0.5 mg/24 hours excludes the diagnosis and greater than 3 mg/24 hours practically makes the diagnosis of CAH (with the rare exception of an adrenal tumor). However, normal females may excrete up to 2.0 mg/24 hours for the first 1 to 2 weeks of life; after that, 1.0 mg/24 hours is abnormal until adrenal androgens begin to rise at age 6 to 9 years. In Figure 2-4, the pathways of steroid biosynthesis are reviewed.

A sonogram can be very helpful to detect the location of gonads and the presence of a uterus.

THE XX NEWBORN WITH AMBIGUOUS GENITALIA
As is shown in Figure 2–3, the differential diagnosis of XX patients includes the following:

1. Congenital adrenocortical hyperplasia

Figure 2-4. Major pathways of steroid biosynthesis. 21-OH = 21-hydroxylase; 11 β-OH = 11 -hydroxylase; 18-OH = 18-hydroxylase; 3 β-HSD = 3 β-hydroxysteroid dehydrogenase; 17 βHSD = 17 β-hydroxysteroid dehydrogenase (17-ketosteroid reductase); 17 α-OH = 17 α-hydroxylase; C-17,20-Lyase also termed 17,20-Desmolase; THF = tetrahydrocortisol; THS = tetrahydrodeoxycortisol. The last three steps in aldosterone synthesis (11-hydroxylation, 18-hydroxylation, and 18-oxidation) are all catalyzed by the same P-450c11 enzyme.

2. Female pseudohermaphroditism
   a. Due to drugs
   b. Due to maternal CAH or a virilizing tumor
   c. Idiopathic
3. True hermaphroditism

CONGENITAL ANDRENOCORTICAL HYPERPLASIA

Congenital adrenocortical hyperplasia represents the most common cause of ambiguous genitalia in the XX newborn. Because of the variability in enzymatic block, ambiguity may range from labial fusion with or without slight clitoromegaly [18], to a "male phallus" with labial fusion and rugae on the labioscrotal folds. The enzyme most commonly involved is 21-hydroxylase. Because of inadequate cortisol synthesis, adrenocorticotropic hormone (ACTH) increases with resultant increased adrenal androgen production. Salt-losing is seen in about one half of patients with the 21-hydroxylase deficiency because of the severity of the deficiency with decreased aldosterone secretion and increased secretion of compounds that are aldosterone antagonists. Babies with more severe virilization tend to be salt-losers (Fig. 2-5). A deficiency of 11 β-hydroxylase is usually associated with hypertension and moderately increased urinary excretion of pregnanetriol and the metabolites of 11-deoxycortisol and deoxycorticosterone (Tetrahydro-S and Tetrahydro-DOC). A rare form of CAH, 3 β-hydroxysteroid dehydrogenase deficiency, results in severe adrenal insufficiency and increased ACTH levels; however, virilization is quite mild because the block is in the initial steps of hormone synthesis so that only the weak androgen (dehydroepiandrosterone) can be produced in excess.

The diagnosis of CAH should be made as soon as possible after birth because of the need to prevent dehydration, hyponatremia, and hyperkalemia with glucocorticoid and mineralocorticoid replacement. Serum samples and, if possible, urine collections should be done prior to treatment even on babies who probably have CAH, such as those who have a sibling with CAH. Since salt-losing usually does not occur until the second week of life, studies can be performed without significant risk during the first week while the baby's weight and electrolytes are closely monitored. Treatment can then be instituted pending return of the laboratory results. Hydrocortisone, 2.5 mg 3 times daily (or 13–25 mg/M^2/day), is the usual starting dosage. If salt-losing is documented by decreased serum sodium and increased serum potassium in the second week of life, salt (2–4 gm/day) should be added to the formula and a mineralocorticoid, fludrocortisone acetate (Florinef), 0.05 to 0.1 mg, should be given orally each day. Adjustment of the hydrocortisone dosage is made on the basis of growth parameters (length, weight, skeletal maturation) and serum 17-

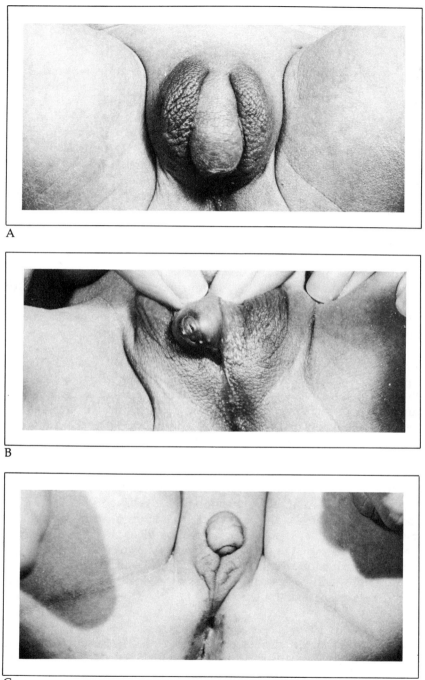

Figure 2-5. Two newborn females presenting with virilization and salt-losing congenital adrenocortical hyperplasia. A and B. Patient S.C.C. Patient M.T.

hydroxyprogesterone, Δ^4-androstenedione, dehydroepiandrosterone (DHA), DHA sulfate (DHAS), and (except in infant and adolescent males) testosterone, and urinary 17-ketosteroids and pregnanetriol. Therapy should aim to keep 17-hydroxyprogesterone levels well below 1000 ng/100 ml; levels less than 200 ng/100 ml in the morning usually indicate oversuppression. Patients in good control have normal Δ^4-androstenedione levels and DHAS levels below the normal range. However, DHAS levels are not sensitive for detecting overtreatment. Urinary 17-ketosteroids should be in the low normal range (for bone age). Measurement of plasma renin levels appears to be the most accurate way to determine the adequacy of mineralocorticoid replacement. Overtreatment with glucocorticoids results in growth retardation; undertreatment in acceleration of the bone age beyond the height age and virilization. The glucocorticoid dosage must be increased at times of stress, such as during illness and in the event of surgery. (See p. 205 for discussion of CAH.)

It should be emphasized that 46,XX persons with CAH are females and are potentially fertile. Thus, regardless of the appearance of the external genitalia, the sex assignment should be female. Surgery may be undertaken for (1) recession of the clitoris, (2) division of the labioscrotal folds, and (3) creation of an adequate vagina. Because the buried clitoris can respond with painful erections to high levels of androgens (which may occur with noncompliance during adolescence), recession is usually accompanied by partial corporectomy and preservation of the neurovascular bundle with reanastomosis of the glans. This procedure along with a vaginoplasty in infants whose vagina enters distal to the external urethral sphincter is usually carried out in the first 6 months of life. In patients with a high entry of the vagina into the urethra, vaginoplasty is delayed until 2 years of age [13]. A second vaginoplasty or the use of dilators may be needed during adolescence, the age determined by dialogue with the patient on their readiness to undertake operative and postoperative care. In cases in which surgical construction is necessary, postoperative use of dilators is usually necessary to keep the vagina patent until the patient has regular sexual relations.

OTHER DIAGNOSES OF XX NEONATES

If an infant is 46,XX and has no evidence of CAH, she either has a primary gonadal abnormality or has been exposed to exogenous hormones or a virilizing lesion in the mother. If the drug history is negative, the mother should have a careful physical examination and laboratory tests for hyperandrogenism. In the absence of a history of maternal virilization or maternal hormone ingestion, the infant should have an evaluation of internal genital anatomy to determine the gonadal cause of the ambiguous genitalia: true hermaphroditism or idiopathic female pseudohermaphroditism.

THE XY NEWBORN WITH AMBIGUOUS GENITALIA

The differential diagnosis of the infant who is XY includes the following:

1. Male pseudohermaphroditism
   a. Defects of testicular differentiation
   b. Deficient placental LH
   c. Leydig cell agenesis
   d. Defects in testosterone synthesis
   e. 5 α-Reductase deficiency
   f. Receptor defects
2. True hermaphroditism
3. Hypogonadotropic hypogonadism (Kallmann's syndrome)

Increased understanding of the differentiation of the fetal testis and the many steps involved in the development of the normal male has made it possible to diagnose more specifically the kind of XY syndrome the infant with ambiguous genitalia has (Fig. 2-6). The Y chromosome contains a testis determining factor (TDF). If TDF is not present in spite of an XY karyotype *or* if receptors for the gene product are not present, the infant has a female phenotype. The syndrome would be diagnosed during adolescence as pure XY gonadal dysgenesis or Swyer's syndrome (streak gonads, normal to tall stature; see p. 158) [20]. If the first step occurs normally but HCG is deficient because of a (postulated) placental insufficiency or inadequate LH, stimulation of testosterone secretion would be insufficient for complete masculinization (step 2). If the testis is unresponsive to HCG or LH, lacking normal Leydig cells or receptors (Leydig cell agenesis, step 3) [21, 22], the infant has abdominal testes, elevated LH, a female phenotype with short vagina, and absent uterus. Depending on when during fetal life the testicular regression occurred, patients will have phenotypes ranging from normal females to males with cryptorchidism [23].

A number of defects in testosterone synthesis (step 4) have been described, including deficiencies of 20,22-desmolase, 3 β-hydroxysteroid dehydrogenase, 17 α-hydroxylase, C-17,20-lyase (17,20-desmolase), and 17 β-hydroxysteroid dehydrogenase (17-ketosteroid reductase) [24]. The first three defects are also associated with adrenal insufficiency. Patients who have these deficiencies do not have müllerian structures, but the external genitalia is either female or ambiguous.

Failure to produce müllerian duct inhibitory substance (MIS) (step 5) or the lack of MIS receptors will cause persistence of müllerian structures and the presence of a uterus (hernia uteri inguinale) in a male who may have normal external genitalia or may have unilateral

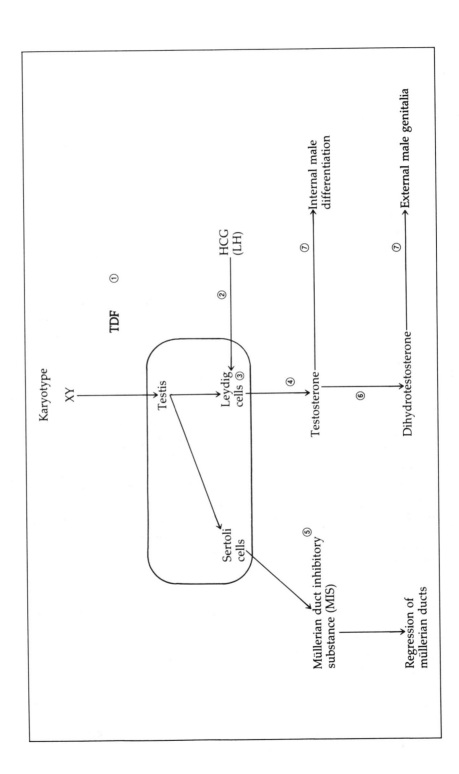

or bilateral cryptorchidism. The development of the wolffian ducts varies among individuals; few males are fertile [25].

The enzyme 5 α-reductase (step 6) is responsible for the conversion of testosterone to dihydrotestosterone, which results in male differentiation of the external genitalia. Patients with 5 α-reductase deficiency (so-called pseudovaginal perineoscrotal hypospadias), an autosomal recessive condition, have a cleft scrotum, hypospadias, and perineal invagination [5, 26]. In some families in the Caribbean, such individuals have been raised as females, but then because of masculine changes at puberty (descent of the testis, enlarging scrotum, and lengthening of the penis), they have taken on the male gender identity [27]. Imperato-McGinley and associates [28] have shown that infants with 5 α-reductase deficiency can be diagnosed by the finding of increased basal plasma testosterone to dihydrotestosterone ratios, especially after administration of HCG for 3 days, and by the finding of elevated urinary tetrahydrocortisol to 5 α-tetrahydrocortisol ratios (compared to age-matched controls). An iatrogenic block of 5 α-reductase may occur in the fetal hydantoin syndrome.

Ambiguous genitalia may also be caused by defects in receptor proteins or transcription mechanisms (step 7) [14]. Complete resistance to the action of testosterone results in the classic picture of testicular feminization (p. 198); the baby appears as a phenotypic female, although occasionally testes are noted early in life. Partial androgen insensitivity results in a spectrum of ambiguous genitalia syndromes at birth and during adolescence [29]; these include the Gilbert-Dreyfus, Reifenstein, Rosewater, Lubs syndromes. These patients have partial wolffian development, some pubic hair, and partial labioscrotal fusion. Recent research in androgen insensitivity has delineated a number of different syndromes, some with absence of receptors, some with abnormal receptor structure, and some with presumed postreceptor defects. Errors in testosterone biosynthesis may give a similar phenotype. The pattern of X-linked inheritance coupled with a high LH and testosterone level (especially before and after HCG stimulation) suggests androgen insensitivity [14].

Cytogenetic studies may be helpful in distinguishing between patients who have structural defects or dysgenetic testes and those who have structurally normal testes. Many patients in the former group have abnormal sex chromosomes with mosaicism; the patients in the latter group have a 46,XY karyotype. Biochemical studies can pinpoint a diagnosis. Retrograde contrast x-ray film studies, ultrasonog-

Figure 2-6. Development of the normal male. TDF = testis determining factor; HCG = human chorionic gonadotropin; LH = luteinizing hormone.

raphy, magnetic resonance imaging (MRI), and possibly laparoscopy or laparotomy are necessary to establish the final diagnosis and determine the particular syndrome present. If the patient has a micropenis and testes, sex assignment should be delayed until a 1- to 3-month course of intramuscular HCG, intramuscular testosterone enanthate, or topical testosterone cream is tried. If the response is good, a male gender assignment is made (Fig. 2-7). If the response is poor or if the male phallus is so small that the patient cannot possibly function in the male sexual role, a female identity should be chosen regardless of the genotype, since the phallus will not grow at puberty in patients with androgen insensitivity. Mean stretched penile length in normal males, plus/minus standard deviation, is 2.5 ± 0.4 cm for a 30-week newborn, 3.0 ± 0.4 cm for a 34-week newborn, 3.5 ± 0.4 cm for a full-term newborn, 3.9 ± 0.8 cm for a 0- to 5-month-old, and 4.3 ± 0.8 cm for a 6- to 12-month-old. Three monthly injections of testosterone enanthate, 25 to 50 mg intramuscularly, should produce lengthening of the penis by 2.0 ± 0.6 cm [30].

Choice of gender identity thus depends on the external genitalia and the possibility of future coital adequacy. When the sex assignment is definitively made, the gonads that conflict with the assignment should be electively removed. For example, the patient with MGD and 45,X/46,XY given a female sex assignment should have her testis removed to prevent virilization at puberty. Intra-abdominal testes should be removed prophylactically in patients with male pseudohermaphroditism and MGD, since there is a substantial risk of malignancy. In addition, it should be noted that all patients with genital abnormalities should have a careful search for associated anomalies, especially of the urinary tract.

HYPOSPADIAS AND CRYPTORCHIDISM

The incidence of hypospadias in newborn males ranges from 1 in 300 to 1 in 800. A familial tendency has been reported with this congenital defect; hypospadias is present in a second individual in 21 percent of families [31]. Although results of hormonal studies have been conflicting, it is likely that some patients have a mild form of male pseudohermaphroditism, including defects in androgen receptors or partial deficiency of 5 α-reductase. More severe forms of hypospadias, especially if accompanied by cryptorchidism (unilateral or bilateral), any defect in scrotal fusion, or a cervix palpable by rectal examination, necessitate a complete evaluation.

Cryptorchidism occurs in 2.7 percent of full-term newborn males and in 27 percent of premature infants. The incidence decreases to 0.8 percent by 1 year of age, the same percentage that occurs in adults. Thus descent is unlikely after age 1; this fact coupled with the potential for damage or tumors occurring in intra-abdominal testes has led

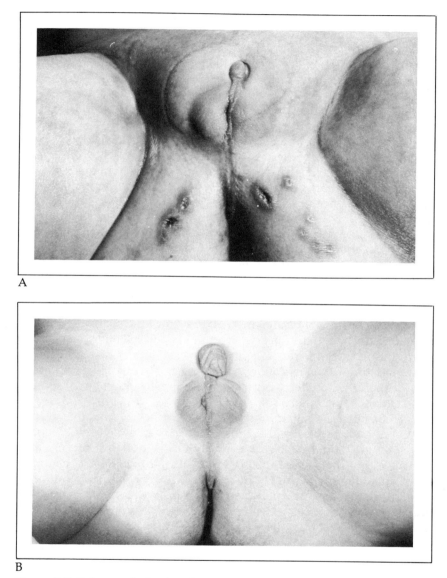

Figure 2-7. Infant male (patient M.F.) with Kallmann's syndrome. A. At 4 months of age. Note micropenis and undescended testes. Evaluation revealed an XY karyotype; at surgery the testes were brought down to the inguinal rings. B. M.F. at age 1 year. Penile size increased after a 3-month course of intramuscular HCG. Patient required repeat orchiopexy and HCG therapy to induce pubertal development.

to the recommendation that evaluation occur by 12 months of age [32, 33]. It should be noted that both the cryptorchid testis and the contralateral testis have an increased risk of cancer even with surgery. Cryptorchidism can occur with Kallmann's syndrome, with other hormonal deficiencies, with dysgenetic or "vanishing" testes, and with more than 40 congenital syndromes [32]. Thus intersex disorders, CAH, and defects in testosterone synthesis need to be considered in the infant with cryptorchidism.

If one testis is absent but the genitalia are otherwise completely normal, a rectal examination should be done to rule out the remote possibility that there is a cervix or large utricle and an intersex state. If a midline structure is not palpated, a pelvic ultrasound may demonstrate the presence of müllerian duct structures. If this is normal, no further workup is indicated. If both testes are missing, but the genitalia still appear to be that of a normal male, a buccal smear, karyotype, and hormone analysis should be done to rule out CAH. If the buccal smear is chromatin-negative or the karyotype is XY and the genitals adequate for male function, the infant should be raised as a male. Some of these patients may have bilateral undescended testes that are capable of function; others have congenital anorchia in which the testes presumably functioned at least until the sixteenth week of gestation and then disappeared. Serum LH and FSH may be elevated early in life in the latter patients, and testosterone does not rise in response to HCG stimulation, indicating the agonadal state; testosterone therapy at puberty is necessary for the development of secondary sexual characteristics.

MRI has been less helpful than hoped in the preoperative evaluation of cryptorchid testes. Laparoscopy has been quite useful in locating intra-abdominal testes or cord structures entering the inguinal canal, suggesting a descended but probably atropic organ. The use of hormonal therapy with HCG or gonadotropin-releasing hormone (GnRH) remains controversial; success rates are low with truly cryptorchid testes, in contrast to retractile testes, which usually descend with hormonal stimulation [34]. Whether surgery could be made easier by pretreatment of patients with GnRH is under study.

REFERENCES
1. Rock JA, and Katz E. Ambiguous genitalia. Semin Reprod Endocrinol 1987; 5:327.
2. Page DC, and de la Chapelle A. The paternal origin of X chromosomes in XX males determined using restriction fragment length polymorphism. Am J Hum Genet 1984; 36:565.
3. Simpson JL. Genetic control of sex determination. Semin Reprod Endocrinol 1987; 5:209.
4. Page DC, Mosher R, Simpson EM, et al. The sex-determining region of the human Y chromosome encodes a finger protein. Cell 1987; 51:1091.

5. Imperato-McGinley J. Disorders of Sexual Differentiation. In J.B. Wyngaarden and LH Smith, *Cecil Textbook of Medicine* (18th ed.). Philadelphia: Saunders, 1988.
6. Muller U, Latt SA, and Donlo T. Y-specific DNA sequences in male patients with 46,XX and 47,XXX karyotypes. Am J Med Genet 1987; 28:393.
7. Gantt PA, Byrd JR, and Greenblatt RB. A clinical and cytogenetic study of fifteen patients with 45X/46XY gonadal dysgenesis. Fertil Steril 1980; 34:216.
8. Federman D. *Abnormal Sexual Development*. Philadelphia: Saunders, 1968.
9. Wachtel SS, Koo GC, Breg WR, et al. Serologic detection of a Y-linked gene in XX males and XX true hermaphrodites. N Engl J Med 1976; 295:750.
10. Winters SJ, Wachtel SS, White BJ, et al. H-Y antigen mosaicism in the gonad of a 46XX true hermaphrodite. N Engl J Med 1979; 300:745.
11. Gerald PS. H-Y antigen. N Engl J Med 1979; 300:788.
12. Schlaff WD. Dysgenetic male pseudohermaphroditism. Semin Reprod Endocrinol 1987; 5:431.
13. Donahoe PK, and Crawford JD. Ambiguous genitalia in the newborn. In KJ Welch, C Ravitch, et al. (eds.), *Pediatric Surgery* (4th ed.). Chicago: Year Book, 1986.
14. Brown TR. Male pseudohermaphroditism: Defect in androgen-dependent target tissues. Semin Reprod Endocrinol 1987; 5:243.
15. Donohoue PA, and Berkovitz GD. Female pseudohermaphroditism. Semin Reprod Endocrinol 1987; 5:233.
16. Callegari C, Everett S, Ross M, et al. Anogenital ratio: Measure of fetal virilization in premature and full-term newborn infants. J Pediatr 1987; 111:240.
17. Smith DW, Marden PM, McDonald MJ, et al. Lower incidence of sex chromatin in buccal smears of newborn females. Pediatrics 1962; 30:707.
18. Marshall WN, and Lightner ES. Congenital adrenal hyperplasia presenting with posterior labial fusion without clitoromegaly. Pediatrics 1980; 66:312.
19. Hughes I, and Winter J. The applications of a serum 17-OH progesterone radioimmunoassay to the diagnosis and management of congenital adrenal hyperplasia. J Pediatr 1976; 88:766.
20. Espiner EA, Veale AM, Sands VE, et al. (eds.). *Congenital Adrenal Hyperplasia*. Baltimore: University Park Press, 1977.
21. Berthezine F, Forest MG, Grimaud JA, et al. Leydig-cell agenesis: A cause of male pseudohermaphroditism. N Engl J Med 1976;295:969.
22. Katz E, and Damewood MD. Male pseudohermaphroditism: Testicular response to human chorionic gonadotropin and luteinizing hormone (Leydig cell agenesis or hypoplasia). Semin Reprod Endocrinol 1987; 5:277.
23. Coulam CB. Testicular regression syndromes. Obstet Gynecol 1979; 53:44.
24. Givens JR, Wiser WL, Summitt RL, et al. Pseudohermaphroditism and deficient testicular 17-ketosteroid reductase. N Engl J Med 1974; 291:938.
25. Donahoe PK, Ito Y, Morikawa Y, et al. Müllerian inhibiting substance in human testes after birth. J Pediatr Surg 1977; 12:323.
26. Walsh PC, Madden JD, Harrod MJ, et al. Familial incomplete male pseudohermaphroditism, type 2. N Engl J Med 1974; 291:944.
27. Imperato-McGinley J, Peterson RE, Gautier T, et al. Androgen and the

evolution of male-gender identity among male pseudohermaphrodites with 5 α-reductase deficiency. N Engl J Med 1979; 300:1233.

28. Imperato-McGinley J, Gautier T, Pichardo M, et al. The diagnosis of a 5 α-reductase deficiency in infancy. J Clin Endocrinol Metab 1986; 63:1313.

29. Griffin JE, and WIlson JD. The syndromes of androgen resistance. N Engl J Med 1980; 302:196.

30. Villee, D. Endocrinology. In ME Avery and L First (eds.), *Pediatric Medicine*. Philadelphia: Williams & Wilkins, 1989.

31. Bauer SR, Retik AB, and Colodny AH. Genetic aspects of hypospadias. Urol Clin North Am 1981; 8:565.

32. Murphy AA, and Zacur HA. Unclassified forms of abnormal sexual development. Semin Reprod Endocrinol 1987; 5:295.

33. Colodny AH. Undescended testes: Is surgery necessary (editorial). N Engl J Med 1986; 314:510.

34. Rajfer J, Handelsman DJ, Swerdloff RS, et al. Hormonal therapy of cryptorchidism: A randomized, double-blind study comparing human chorionic gonadotropin and gonadotropin-releasing hormone. N Engl J Med 1986; 314:466.

FURTHER READING

Burgoyne PS. Thumbs down for zinc finger. Nature 1989; 342:860.

Palmer MS, Sinclair AH, Berta P, et al. Genetic evidence that ZFY is not the testis-determining factor. Nature 1989; 342:937.

Koopman P, Gubbay J, Collignon J, et al. ZFY gene expression patterns are not compatible with a primary role in mouse sex determination. Nature 1989; 342:940.

3. Vulvovaginal Problems in the Prepubertal Child

VULVOVAGINITIS

ETIOLOGY

In the newborn period, the vagina is well estrogenized from maternal hormones. As the hormone levels wane, the vagina becomes atrophic with a pH of 6.5 to 7.5. Because of poor hygiene, the proximity of the vagina and anus, the lack of protective hair and labial fat pads, and the lack of estrogenization, the vulvar skin is susceptible to irritation and is easily traumatized by medication and clothing. Vulvar inflammation—"vulvitis"—may occur alone or may be accompanied by a secondary vaginitis. A child may acquire a primary vaginal infection, and the discharge may cause maceration of the vulva and secondary vulvitis.

The etiology of vulvovaginal symptoms are listed in Table 3-1. "Nonspecific vulvovaginitis" accounts for 25 to 75 percent of diagnoses of vulvovaginitis of prepubertal girls seen in referral centers [1–5]. The vaginal culture typically grows normal flora (lactobacilli, diphtheroids, *Staphylococcus epidermidis,* or α-streptococci) or gram-negative enteric organisms (usually *Escherichia coli*).

Either a high hymenal opening that does not allow normal vaginal drainage or a gaping hymenal ring that allows easy contamination of the vagina can predispose to nonspecific vaginitis. In addition, girls typically urinate on the toilet with knees together, increasing the possibility of urine refluxing into the vagina. Especially in hot weather and in overweight girls, nonabsorbent nylon underpants, nylon tights, close-fitting blue jeans, and ballet leotards may result in maceration and infection similar to the diaper dermatitis seen in infants who wear infrequently changed cloth diapers or plastic-covered paper diapers. Bubble baths and harsh soaps may cause vulvitis and a secondary vaginitis. It is also possible that children susceptible to recurrent vulvovaginitis may have other factors that promote adherence of bacteria to epithelial cells. The role of toxigenic or invasive strains of *E. coli* and other enteric organisms such as *Campylobacter* has not been investigated.

The specific infections that occur in the prepubertal child are often respiratory, enteric, or sexually transmitted pathogens. The respiratory pathogens include group A β-hemolytic streptococci (*Streptococcus pyogenes*), *Streptococcus pneumoniae,* and *Neisseria meningitidis.* *Staphylococcus aureus, Branhamella catarrhalis,* and *Haemophilus influenzae* can occur as normal flora, but they also appear to be responsible for some cases of vaginitis [1, 6–10]. *S. aureus* can be associated with

Table 3-1. Etiology of Vulvovaginal Symptoms in the Prepubertal child

"Nonspecific" vulvovaginitis
Specific vulvovaginitis
  Respiratory pathogens
    Group A β-streptococcus (*Streptococcus pyogenes*)
    Streptococcus pneumoniae
    Neisseria meningitidis
    Branhamella catarrhalis
    Staphylococcus aureus
    Haemophilus influenzae
  Enteric
    Shigella
    Yersinia
    Other flora
  Sexually transmitted diseases
    Neisseria gonorrhoeae
    Chlamydia trachomatis
    Herpes simplex
    Trichomonas
    Condyloma accuminatum (human papillomavirus)
  Pinworms
  Foreign body
  Polyps, tumors
  Systemic illness: measles, chickenpox, scarlet fever, Stevens-Johnson syndrome, mononucleosis, Kawasaki disease
  Vulvar skin disease: lichen sclerosus, seborrhea, psoriasis, atopic dermatitis, scabies, contact dermatitis
  Trauma
  Psychosomatic vaginal complaints
  Miscellaneous: draining pelvic abscess, prolapsed urethra, ectopic ureter

impetiginous lesions on the vulva and on the buttocks. *Shigella* is the most common enteric pathogen. It can cause a mucopurulent, sometimes bloody discharge, which in one fourth or less of cases occurs in association with an episode of diarrhea [11]. *Yersinia* has also been reported to be associated with vaginitis [12].

Although *Candida* vulvovaginitis is common in pubertal girls, it is uncommon in prepubertal children unless the girl has recently finished a course of antibiotics, has diabetes mellitus, is still in diapers, or has other risk factors.

Sexually acquired vulvovaginal infections occurring in the prepubertal child include *Neisseria gonorrhoeae*, *Chlamydia trachomatis*, herpes simplex, *Trichomonas*, human papilloma virus (condyloma accuminata), and possibly *Gardnerella vaginalis*. It is clear that all children with *N. gonorrhoeae* vaginitis should be reported to local authorities that deal with child abuse so that adequate evaluation can be carried out [13, 14]. As noted on p. 17, confirmatory bacteriologic tests are crucial in prepubertal girls with a culture that appears to be positive for *N. gonorrhoeae* [15, 16]. It is not uncommon to find siblings with asymptomatic gonococcal infections. The perpetrator is often a family member who may be identified only by culturing the entire family.

The presence of *C. trachomatis* in the vagina in prepubertal children has been recently associated with a history of sexual abuse [17, 18]. Although some infants can be expected to acquire vaginal colonization with *C. trachomatis* at birth from a mother with endocervical infection, persistence for more than 12 to 24 months (rarely 36 months) is unlikely [19, 20] especially if the girl has been treated with antibiotics for upper respiratory infections or otitis media (e.g., erythromycin, trimethopim-sulfamethazole). Ingram and associates [17] reported that 10/124 sexually abused girls and 0/90 controls had a positive introital culture for *C. trachomatis*. *C. trachomatis* can occur as a coexisting infection in girls with *N. gonorrhoeae* [21]. How frequently *C. trachomatis* is responsible for signs of vaginitis is a subject of controversy.

Herpes simplex type 1 (oral-labial herpes) can cause simultaneous lesions in the mouth and vulva of young girls with a primary infection. Both types 1 and 2 can be acquired by abuse, although type 2 is more likely to be secondary to abuse. Recurrent lesions may occur with either type but are more likely with type 2 (see chap. 9).

Condyloma accuminata (venereal warts) are caused by human papillomavirus, usually type 6 or 11. Because the time from exposure to the virus to the occurrence of warts can take months, contact tracing may be difficult. Warts occurring in the first 1 to 2 years of life are usually acquired by the infant at the time of vaginal delivery. The more difficult and increasingly frequent problem is the care of the 5-year-old child with vaginal or anal warts. To rule out other sexually transmitted infections and sexual abuse in the child, the physician should evaluate the child carefully and thoroughly. Given the association of certain types of papillomavirus infection and cervical and vulvar neoplasia in adolescents and adult women, the long-term prognosis of this infection in prepubertal children is unknown but of obvious concern (see p. 86 and Chap. 11).

Trichomonas can be transmitted from the mother to the child at birth and rarely can cause a persistent urethritis and vaginitis after estrogen levels wane. This pathogen is rarely seen in the prepubertal child because the unestrogenized vagina is relatively resistant to infection. It occurs primarily in the pubescent sexually active teenager (see Chap. 9). Although *Trichomonas* can be spread by wet towels and washcloths, it is primarily a sexually transmitted infection.

The role of *G. vaginalis* in causing vaginitis in the child has been controversial. The isolation of *G. vaginalis* from the vagina of prepu-

Table 3-2. Aerobic and Facultatively Anaerobic Bacteria Isolated from Vaginal Cultures of 59 Girls, Ages 2 Months to 15 Years

Organisms	% of Patients with Positive Cultures
Diphtheroids	78
Staphylococcus epidermidis	73
α-Hemolytic streptococci	39
Lactobacilli	39
Nonhemolytic streptococci	34
Escherichia coli*	34
Klebsiella*	15
Gardnerella vaginalis	13.5
Group D streptococcus*	8.5
Staphylococcus aureus	7
Haemophilus influenzae	5
Pseudomonas aeruginosa	5
Proteus	5

Source: M. R. Hammerschlag, S. Albert, I. Rosner, et al., Microbiology of the vagina in children: Normal and potentially pathogenic organisms. *Pediatrics* 62:57, 1978. Copyright American Academy of Pediatrics, 1978.
*Predominantly in girls under 3 years of age.

bertal girls appears to be more likely in sexually abused girls (14.6%) than control patients (4.2%) or patients with genitourinary complaints (4.2%) [22]. However, Bartley and co-workers [22] did not find any association of this organism with vaginal erythema or discharge. Another entity, bacterial vaginosis, is characterized by alteration of the bacterial flora with the presence of increased concentrations of G. *vaginalis* and anaerobes. Bacterial vaginosis has been reported to occur in girls who presented with vaginal odor after an episode of rape; the diagnosis was made by the observation of clue cells on microscopic examination of the discharge and the presence of a characteristic amine odor on the "whiff test" (1 drop of discharge is mixed with 1 drop of 10% potassium hydroxide [KOH] on a slide). The diagnosis of bacterial vaginosis should not be made solely on the basis of finding a positive culture for G. *vaginalis* (see Chap. 9).

Data [23] on the normal flora of the vagina are shown in Table 3-2. Concern has been expressed about the application of these data to prepubertal girls because of the wide range of ages, including pubertal and prepubertal girls, and the small number of subjects examined in this inner city hospital study. Paradise [2, 24] has cultured 52 premenarcheal girls without genitourinary signs or symptoms (Table 3-3). These tables can be used to compare culture results obtained from symptomatic patients in clinical practice.

Table 3-3. Aerobic Bacteria and Yeasts Recovered from Vaginal Cultures of 52 Girls without Genitourinary Symptoms or Signs

Microorganisms Isolated	N (%)
Normal flora*	52 (100%)
β-Hemolytic streptococci (not group A or B)	2 (4%)
Escherichia coli	4 (8%)
Group B streptococcus	1 (2%)
Coagulase-positive staphylococcus	1 (2%)
Candida tropicalis or "yeast"†	2 (4%)

Source: J. Paradise. Unpublished data.
*Includes diphtheroids, α-hemolytic streptococci, and lactobacilli.
†If fewer than one-third of the colonies in a culture are yeasts, the laboratory does not identify their species.

Other causes of vulvovaginal complaints include vaginal foreign bodies, vaginal and cervical polyps and tumors, urethral prolapse, systemic illnesses (measles, chickenpox, scarlet fever, mononucleosis, Crohn's disease, Kawasaki disease [25]), anomalies (e.g., double vagina with a fistula, pelvic abscess or fistula, or ectopic ureter), and vulvar skin disease (seborrhea, psoriasis, atopic dermatitis, lichen sclerosus, scabies, contact dermatitis). A new entity that we have seen in our clinic and that has been recently reported is gelatin-like beads simulating "vaginal discharge" that result from superabsorbent disposable diapers [26, 27]. Occasionally, children have psychosomatic vaginal complaints of itching or tickling, which usually precipitate great concern from parents.

True vulvovaginitis should not be confused with physiologic leukorrhea. Newborns and pubescent girls often have copious secretions secondary to the effect of estrogen on the vaginal mucosa. In newborns, since maternal estrogen is responsible for the discharge, the leukorrhea disappears within 2 to 3 weeks after birth. The treatment of the pubertal child with leukorrhea is discussed in Chapter 9.

Obtaining the History

In the usual case of vulvovaginitis, the parent brings the patient to the physician with complaints of discharge, dysuria, pruritus, or redness. A complete history should be obtained prior to the examination. The physician should elicit the information on the quantity, duration, and type of discharge, perineal hygiene, recent use of medications or bubble baths, symptoms of anal pruritus (associated with pinworm infection), enuresis, history of atopic dermatitis and other allergies, and recent infections in the patient or family. A history of recent infections is important because, for example, a group A β-hemolytic streptococcal vaginitis, perianal cellulitis, or rarely proctocolitis may follow a streptococcal upper respiratory infection in the child or other family members. Overvigorous cleansing of the vulva in a girl with mild vaginal symptoms or odor can lead to significant vulvitis. Questions about caretakers that might give a clue to ongoing sexual abuse should be asked. The parent should be asked about behavioral changes, nightmares, fears, abdominal pain, headaches, and enuresis, all of which may suggest the possibility of abuse. The vaginal discharge may be copious and purulent, or it may be thin and mucoid.

The child should be included in the history taking by asking her what she has noticed. She should also be asked to demonstrate her motion of wiping. A child's scratching because of vulvar pruritus may cause conflict between parent and child. Compulsive masturbation may also cause vulvar irritation and erythema and guilty feelings for the child. The child should be asked both at the time of the history taking and later during the examination about the possibility of someone having touched her in the vaginal area.

The history may give a clue to the diagnosis. For example, a foul-smelling discharge may result from a foreign body (usually toilet paper), a necrotic tumor (rare), or vaginitis. Both *Shigella* and group A β-streptococcal infections can cause bleeding. An odorless, bloody discharge may occur following vulvar irritation (from scratching or masturbation), following trauma (from playground equipment, bicycle, or sexual abuse), with precocious puberty, from a foreign body, from vaginitis, from condyloma acuminatum or rarely from a tumor (adenocarcinoma, sarcoma botryoides) [28]. A greenish discharge is usually associated with a specific cause of the vaginitis such as *N. gonorrhoeae*, group A β-streptococci, or a foreign body. Itching and redness are usually nonspecific signs of irritation. A review of girls seen in the gynecology clinic of our hospital [1] found that a short duration of symptoms (less than 1 month) was associated more often with diagnoses of a specific nature, perhaps because the parent noted an abrupt change in the vulvovaginal area. Girls with nonspecific vaginitis often had symptoms dating for months or, in some cases, for years before clinical presentation. Nonetheless, even a long history of symptoms requires a careful examination.

PHYSICAL EXAMINATION
For children with symptoms of vulvitis, a brief history and external genital examination in the office and instructions to the parent on improved hygiene, avoidance of irritants, and/or treatment of pinworms is all that is needed. A similar approach can be taken for many little girls with vulvitis and minimal vaginal discharge. The only findings on external examination are usually a scanty mucoid dis-

charge and an erythematous introitus. The etiology is usually traced to poor perineal hygiene, which results in infection with a mixed bacterial flora. Cultures are unnecessary if the condition responds promptly to improved hygiene.

Any child with persistent, purulent, or recurrent vaginal discharge deserves a thorough gynecologic assessment. The physical examination of the prepubertal child is described in Chapter 1. To diagnose the etiology of the vaginal complaints, the physician should undertake a stepwise approach: (1) do a general physical examination; (2) inspect the perineum and vaginal introitus with the patient supine; (3) visualize the vagina and cervix with the patient in the knee-chest position; (4) obtain specimens for wet preparations, Gram stain, and cultures; and (5) do a rectal examination with the patient supine, knees apart, and feet together (or in stirrups). The observation of visible discharge at the time of the examination increases the likelihood that the vaginal culture will be positive for a specific pathogen [2]. If the knee-chest examination does not allow adequate visualization and the symptoms are significant or persistent, visualization can be accomplished in the cooperative child using a veterinary otoscope, hysteroscope, or cystoscope with the patient supine. Xylocaine ointment can be applied to the vulva prior to insertion. An examination under general anesthesia using a Killian nasal speculum or other instrument is sometimes necessary for complete assessment of the young child. It should be remembered that although visualization of the vagina and cervix is optimal and usually easily performed, this part of the examination can be deferred if mild symptoms of vulvovaginitis improve in 2 to 3 weeks of good perineal hygiene. The rectal examination is important in the examination of girls with persistent discharge, bleeding, or pelvic/abdominal pain. The rectal examination can bring out discharge not previously seen, can allow palpation of hard foreign bodies, and can detect abnormal masses.

LABORATORY TESTS
If the discharge is persistent or purulent at the initial office visit, Gram stain, wet preparations, and cultures should be done. As mentioned in Chapter 1, a soft plastic eyedropper, a glass eyedropper with plastic tubing attached, a small urethral catheter, or a nasopharyngeal Calgiswab moistened with nonbacteriostatic saline can be gently inserted through the hymenal opening to aspirate secretions. If no discharge is apparent, 1 or 2 drops of saline can be squeezed into the vagina with an eyedropper and then aspirated. The secretions are mixed first with 1 drop of saline on a glass slide and then with a drop of 10% KOH on another slide. A coverslip is applied, and the slides are examined under the microscope for Candida and

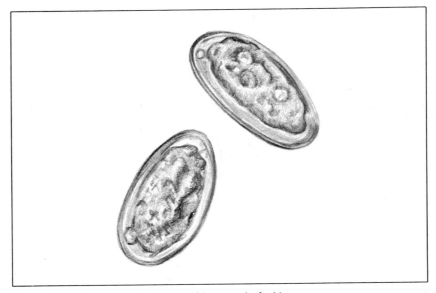

Figure 3-1. Pinworm eggs (*Enterobius vermicularis*).

trichomonads. A culture for *N. gonorrhoeae* is done on modified Thayer-Martin-Jembec media at the time of the examination. Cultures for other organisms are done by sending the cotton-tipped applicator or Calgiswab or small amount of aspirated secretions to the hospital bacteriology laboratory for plating on genitourinary media (blood, MacConkey, and chocolate media). The swab can be kept moist in a Culturette II transport tube in transit to the laboratory. A *Chlamydia* culture is generally obtained in girls with persistent symptoms and those with a history of sexual abuse. Since enzyme immunoassays and direct slide tests may yield false-positive tests and have not been studied in prepubertal girls, the medicolegal significance of a positive culture makes a *Chlamydia* culture the much preferred method of diagnosis in children [29, 30]. A Biggy agar culture done on patients with itching or suspected yeast infections is incubated in the office and observed for the growth of brown colonies 3 to 7 days later. Patients with vulvar or anal pruritus should be screened for pinworm infestation. Material is obtained (in the morning) by pressing the sticky side of a piece of cellophane tape against the perineal area. The tape is affixed to a slide and examined under the microscope for the characteristic eggs (Fig. 3-1). The parent should also check the child's anus late at night (with a flashlight) for adult pinworms. X rays of the pelvis looking for foreign bodies should be avoided since most are not radioopaque.

TREATMENT

As noted in the section Etiology, a "nonspecific" etiology is found in a substantial portion of prepubertal girls with vulvovaginal symptoms. The culture may grow gram-negative enteric organisms such as *E. coli* or normal flora. Ninety percent of children under 3 years of age in Hammerschlag's series were colonized with *E. coli* (see Table 3-2). Although gram-negative organisms are part of the normal flora and Hammerschlag and associates [23] reported an *E. coli* colonization rate of 15 percent in normal asymptomatic girls in this age group, we found that 47 percent of 3- to 10-year-old girls with nonspecific vaginitis had *E. coli* on culture [1]. These findings suggest that hygiene and contamination with bowel flora may play an important role in the persistence of symptoms [1].

Treatment of nonspecific vulvovaginitis should focus on improved hygiene (white cotton underpants, front-to-back wiping, loose-fitting skirt, no nylon tights or tight blue jeans), handwashing, and sitz baths. The child should be asked to urinate with her knees spread apart so the labia are separated and urinary reflux into the vagina is minimized. The vulvar skin of the prepubertal child is extremely sensitive to drying, chapping, and irritants (including heat, medications, and soaps).

The child should be instructed to sit in a tub of clear, warm (not hot) water for 10 to 15 minutes once or twice daily. At the end of the time interval, the child should be washed with a bland soap (such as Basis, unscented Dove, or Neutrogena) with little or preferably no soap applied to the vulva. No scrubbing of the vulva should be done. Hair should be shampooed over a sink or in the shower. If neither is possible, the shampooing should occur at the end of the bath and the child rinsed in clear water. A hand held sprayer is helpful. Bubble baths should be avoided since the irritant soap may exacerbate the symptoms. After a bath, the child should pat dry the vulva or air dry it with the legs spread apart; a hair dryer on cool setting can aid drying. Sleeper pajamas should not be used if possible, since the heat and poor air circulation frequently cause maceration of the vulva.

A small amount of A and D Ointment, Vaseline, or Desitin can be used to protect the vulvar skin. Different children appear to tolerate preparations variably, and it may be necessary to try several creams. Loose-fitting clothes such as skirts and knee socks or loose pants or shorts should be worn during the daytime. During the summer, girls should not spend long periods of time in a wet swimsuit; a change to a pair of shorts or a dry suit should be suggested.

If after 2 to 3 weeks the discharge of nonspecific vaginitis persists, the possibility of pinworms should be excluded, and a regimen of oral antibiotics (such as amoxicillin, amoxicillin-clavulanate (Augmentin), or a cephalosporin) may be given for 10 days. Some girls, in fact, have recurrent episodes of vulvar irritation and dysuria ("transient vulvitis"), which last for 12 to 24 hours and usually respond to tepid sitz baths and one or two applications of hydrocortisone cream 1%. These episodes are often triggered by irritants or a long period of time in tights, leotards, or sleeper pajamas.

Intravaginal medications are rarely indicated and may present difficulties with administration for parent and child. In some unusually persistent cases, irrigation of the vagina with a 1% Betadine solution using a syringe and a small infant feeding tube or urethral catheter may be helpful. This same technique can be used to apply intravaginal antifungal creams in the pubescent girl with *Candida* vaginitis who cannot use a vaginal applicator.

An easier, and often effective, approach in the child with persistent or frequently recurring symptoms in whom a specific etiology has been excluded is the prescription of a 2-month course of a small dose of an antibiotic at bedtime or even 3 nights a week, similar to suppression of urinary tract infections. Estrogen-containing creams, which thicken the epithelium making it more resistant to infection, can also be applied to the vulva but should be used only briefly (3–4 weeks at a time). The parent should not be given a refillable prescription, since systemic absorption of estrogen does occur. Hygiene needs to be stressed in all these girls, since the prescription of medication sometimes suggests to parents and child that the other measures can be discontinued.

Nonspecific vaginitis often recurs when the child develops an upper respiratory infection or uses poor hygiene. Obese girls with inadequate hygiene are particularly prone to recurrences. Occasionally a prepubertal girl with frequent recurrences of vaginitis has a minute high hymenal opening that impairs vaginal drainage; a hymenotomy done under general anesthesia is curative. Other causes of recurrent discharge, though rare, need to be considered, including a pelvic abscess and ectopic ureter. An ectopic ureter may cause daytime wetness, sometimes in quite minimal amounts. If the kidney is infected, purulent perineal discharge will result, and the patient may be initially diagnosed as having a "vaginal discharge." The ectopic ureter usually empties on the perineum adjacent to the normal urethra but may also open into the vagina, cervix, uterus, or urethra. The physician should look for a small drop of urine (or pus) adjacent to the urethra after the child drinks a large amount of a beverage such as a Coke. Ultrasonography of the kidneys may detect the double collecting system but also may miss the anomaly. An IVP is often more helpful; even if the double collecting system cannot be visualized because of poor function in the upper pole, the contour of the kidney is likely to provide the key to diagnosis. Other tests such as vaginoscopy and cystoscopy may be necessary to establish the diagnosis.

Recurrences may become a source of considerable anxiety for the parent, who may express fear that the child's future reproductive capacity will be harmed. In particular, the mother may have concerns about whether her own gynecologic problems of recurrent vaginitis, pelvic infection, or abnormal bleeding are hereditary or are related to the child's symptoms. The physician can offer important reassurance by performing an adequate physical examination, obtaining vaginal cultures, and outlining a treatment plan.

Specific causes of vulvovaginitis are listed in Table 3-1, and treatment is outlined in Table 3-4.

The treatment of group A β-streptococci and *S. pneumoniae* is oral penicillin. Perianal streptococcal infection may occur with a vaginal infection or alone and may require a longer treatment course of 14 to 21 days if symptoms recur. The finding of *N. gonorrhoeae* should prompt careful evaluation for sexual abuse. All contacts (extended family, babysitters) and siblings should be cultured. The patient should be examined for *C. trachomatis* as a co-infection and given appropriate treatment to cover both infections (see Table 3-4 and Chap. 10). Since sexual abuse often involves genital fondling, oral sex, or vulvar coitus rather than vaginal penetration in young girls, a physical examination of the external genitalia of many abused girls shows a normal vulva and hymen. Thus, a normal examination in the girl with *N. gonorrhoeae* or *C. trachomatis* should not be taken as evidence against sexual abuse (see Chap. 17). A history of prior antibiotic therapy that would be expected to eradicate *Chlamydia* transmitted at birth can help establish the likely timing of acquisition.

In contrast to the frequent occurrence of *Candida* vaginitis in the estrogenized pubescent (pre- or postmenarcheal) girl, the presence of this infection in the (toilet-trained) prepubertal girl who has not used recent systemic antibiotics should prompt laboratory tests to exclude diabetes mellitus. Topical antifungal creams to the external genitalia should be tried first and are usually successful. If not, the diagnosis should be reassessed and intravaginal antifungal therapy suggested. An intravaginal application can usually be accomplished by using a small urethral catheter attached to a syringe filled with an antifungal cream. Alternatively, 1 ml of nystatin (100,000 units/ml) can be instilled with a small eyedropper 3 times daily. Nystatin, 100,000 units orally 4 times daily, may be helpful, although efficacy studies in children are lacking.

Pinworms (*Enterobius vermicularis*) always need to be kept in mind as a specific cause of recurrent "nonspecific" vaginitis and are easily treated with a single dose of oral medication, repeated 2 weeks later.

Table 3-4. Treatment of Vulvovaginitis in the Prepubertal Child

Etiology	Treatment
Group A β-*streptococcus* (*Streptococcus pyogenes*) *Streptococcus pneumoniae*	Penicillin V potassium, 125–250 mg qid po × 10 days
Chlamydia trachomatis	Erythromycin, 50 mg/kg/day po × 10 days Children ≥ 8 years of age, doxycycline, 100 mg bid po × 7 days
Neisseria gonorrhoeae	Ceftriaxone, 125 mg IM. Patients who cannot tolerate ceftriaxone may be treated with Spectinomycin, 40 mg/kg IM once. Children ≥ 8 years of age should also be given doxycycline, 100 mg bid po × 7 days. Children > 45 kg are treated with adult regimens.
Candida	Topical nystatin (Mycostatin), miconazole, or clotrimazole cream
Shigella	Trimethoprim/sulfamethoxazole, 8 mg 40 mg/kg/day po × 7 days
Staphylococcus aureus	Cephalexin (Keflex), 25–50 mg/kg/day po × 7–10 days Dicloxacillin, 25 mg/kg/day po × 7–10 days Amoxicillin-clavulanate (Augmentin), 20–40 mg/kg/day (of the amoxicillin) po × 7–10 days
Haemophilus influenzae	Amoxicillin, 20–40 mg/kg/day po × 7 days
Trichomonas	Metronidazole (Flagyl), 125 mg (15 mg/kg/day) tid × 7–10 days
Pinworms (*Enterobius vermicularis*)	Mebendazole (Vermox), 1 chewable 100-mg tablet, repeated in 2 weeks

Mebendazole is not recommended for children under age 2 years. Family members may also need to be treated.

A purulent and/or bloody discharge is often the presenting complaint in a girl with a vaginal foreign body, most commonly toilet paper. The child should be questioned alone to determine if another child or adult placed the object in the vagina, since sexual abuse may be involved. If the child herself repeatedly places objects in her vagina, a thorough psychiatric assessment is necessary. Toilet paper in the bathroom can be replaced with Tucks pads to prevent accidental or purposeful shredding of toilet paper.

SUMMARY OF THERAPY FOR NONSPECIFIC VULVOVAGINITIS

General measures

1. Good perineal hygiene (including wiping from front to back after bowel movements).
2. Frequent changes of white cotton underpants to absorb discharge.
3. Avoidance of bubble baths, harsh soaps, and shampooing hair in bathtub.
4. Loose-fitting skirts; no nylon tights or tight blue jeans.
5. Sitz baths 2 or 3 times daily with plain warm water. The vulva should be gently washed with no soap or a mild, nonscented soap (Basis, unscented Dove, Lowila, Oilatum, Castile). The bath should be followed by careful drying (patting, not rubbing). The child should then lie with her legs spread apart for approximately 10 minutes to complete the drying, or use a hairdryer on the cool or low setting.
6. Urination with legs spread apart and labia separated.

Therapy for acute severe edematous vulvitis

1. Sitz baths every 4 hours (with plain water or with a small amount of Aveeno colloidal oatmeal or baking soda added). Soap should not be used, and the vulva should be air dried. Powders should be avoided.
2. Witch hazel pads (Tucks) give soothing relief to most girls (although some complain of discomfort with use) and may be used in place of toilet paper for wiping. After the acute phase of 1 to 2 days, if there is no oozing, the sitz baths can be alternated every 4 hours with painting on a bland solution such as calamine or a mixture of zinc oxide (15%), talc (15%), and glycerine (10%) in water. In this phase, infection may need to be treated with oral antibiotics.
3. In the subacute phase, topical creams can be applied such as hydrocortisone cream 1%, Neosporin Ointment, Sultrin Cream, or A and D ointment.

Occasionally an oral medication to lessen pruritus is indicated such as hydroxyzine hydrochloride (Atarax), 2 mg/kg/day (divided in 4 doses), or diphenhydramine hydrochloride (Benadryl), 5 mg/kg/day (divided in 4 doses).

Therapy for persistent nonspecific vulvovaginitis

1. Broad-spectrum oral antibiotics, such as amoxicillin, amoxicillin-clavulanate (Augmentin), or a cephalosporin for 10 to 14 days; a 1- to 3-month low dose of bedtime cephalexin, amoxicillin-clavulanate, or trimethoprim/sulfamethoxazole may be helpful in the child with many recurrences; or

2. Antibacterial cream locally (Sultrin, AVC Cream) or
3. Irrigation with Betadine 1% solution or
4. Estrogen-containing creams (Premarin Vaginal Cream), applied nightly to the vulva for 2 weeks and then every other night for 2 weeks; a repeat course may be necessary.
5. Hygiene must be stressed.

LICHEN SCLEROSUS

Lichen sclerosus is an uncommon disorder in prepubertal children but should be recognized by the clinician [31–34]. Patients usually complain of itching, irritation, soreness, and dysuria and less commonly of constipation, vaginal discharge, and bleeding. The vulva characteristically has white atrophic, parchment-like skin and evidence of chronic ulceration, inflammation, and subepithelial hemorrhages. The occurrence of bleeding without a history of trauma has caused many patients to be suspected of being victims of sexual abuse. The friction involved with bike riding can produce bleeding. Often, the involvement of the perianal area along with the labia may give the affected area an hourglass configuration. Secondary infection may occur. The condition should be distinguished from vitiligo, which causes loss of pigmentation but not inflammation or atrophy. The occurrence of vulvar lichen sclerosus in monozygotic twin girls suggests a genetic factor [35].

The diagnosis of lichen sclerosus is made clinically and, if necessary, by examining a biopsy specimen (Fig. 3-2, see also Plate 5). Since the etiology is unknown, the best form of therapy is controversial. A graded approach based on symptomatology and clinical appearance seems best. For mild to moderate cases, treatment aims at elimination of local irritants and any vaginitis present and improved hygiene. Harsh soaps should not be overused; the child should be encouraged to wear cotton underpants and loose-fitting pants or skirts to minimize local maceration and irritation. A protective ointment such as A and D Ointment is helpful, and hydroxyzine hydrochloride (Atarax) is given 1 hour before bedtime to lessen the child's nocturnal scratching. The child is encouraged to become an active participant by applying the ointment and avoiding scratching. If this therapy is not adequate, a 1- to 3-month course of a low potency topical steroid cream or ointment such as hydrocortisone 1% or 2.5% or, if necessary, a shorter course of a moderate potency ointment such as fluocinolone acetonide (Synalar 0.025%) can be used, followed by hydrocortisone. Oral antibiotics are prescribed for significant infections.

The next stage of therapy is topical testosterone cream (2% in petrolatum) applied nightly for several months. Although this has been very successful in the treatment of postmenopausal women [36], re-

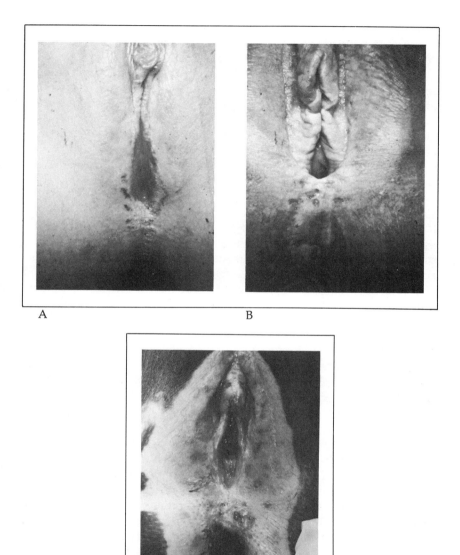

A   B

C

Figure 3-2. Vulvas of three girls with lichen sclerosus.

sults have been more variable in children. Occasionally pubic hair appears, as well as other signs of androgen absorption, so use should be closely monitored in the growing child.

A new therapy that appears very promising in a few children with severe intractable disease treated at our institution is a laser brushing of the vulva under general anesthesia [37]. Long-term data are needed. Although oral potassium para-aminobenzoate has been helpful in a few adults [38], more information is needed on toxicity in adults before undertaking a study in children. In some girls, lichen sclerosus improves with puberty; in many, the symptoms and signs persist [31, 33, 34].

VAGINAL BLEEDING
Vaginal bleeding in the prepubertal child should always be carefully assessed. In the neonate, slight vaginal bleeding is sometimes seen in the first week of life secondary to withdrawal from maternal estrogen. After that, the causes to be considered include vaginitis, lichen sclerosus, condyloma, trauma, a foreign body, a tumor, precocious puberty, blood dyscrasias, hemangiomas, polyps, and urethral prolapse. A good history and physical examination are important in making the differential diagnosis. Acceleration of height and weight or signs of pubertal development before the age of 8 years suggest precocious puberty (see Chap. 5). A history of foreign bodies in the ears or vagina may implicate another foreign body, which may have been placed by the child or by an abuser. Patients with blood dyscrasias typically have other signs of bleeding, such as epistaxis, petechiae, or hematomas.

The physical examination should include a general assessment and a careful gynecologic examination. Trauma and vulvovaginitis are usually evident on inspection. A straddle injury typically causes ecchymoses in the vulva and periclitoral folds. A laceration of the labia minora and periurethral tissue may be seen (see Plate 17). It is very uncommon for a child to have a tear in the hymen without a penetrating injury (e.g., a nail, broom handle, bedpost), and thus in the absence of an appropriate history, sexual abuse should be strongly considered when a hymenal tear is noted (see Plate 16). Good tricks for examining the child who has active bleeding from the vulva are to wipe 2% lidocaine jelly over the cut, place warm water in a syringe to irrigate the tissue gently [39], and/or irrigate using IV tubing and solution. As noted in Figure 3-3, the irrigation allows the blood that may have collected in the vagina from a labial laceration to be washed out and the bleeding source to be identified. If necessary, a meperidine hydrochloride (Demerol) compound can be given intramuscularly for sedation. If an abrasion is oozing, Gelfoam or Surgigel can be applied in the emergency ward. If only a few stitches are necessary

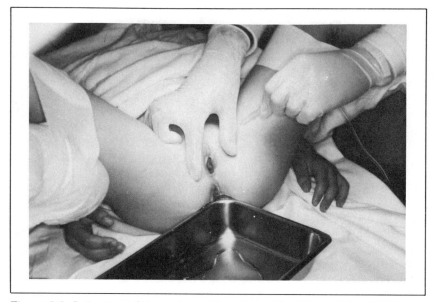

Figure 3-3. Irrigation of the vulva and vagina with saline to identify the source of bleeding.

for repairing a vulvar laceration, some emergency wards have a nitrous oxide protocol for anesthesia if the child is old enough to cooperate. Lidocaine 1 to 2% with epinephrine can then be injected locally with a 25-gauge needle and the repair done with No. 4 chromic running or interrupted sutures. If cooperation is not possible and a hymenal or intravaginal tear or periurethral laceration is noted, an examination and repair should be done under general anesthesia. Straddle injuries may cause deep lacerations in the periurethral tissue; repair requires placement of a Foley catheter and deep sutures. Significant penetrating injuries may have occurred to the upper vagina without obvious symptoms or signs other than a hymenal tear at presentation. Many vulvar injuries heal with little or no residual scarring or other findings.

Most bleeding in the prepubertal girl occurs not because of major trauma but because of vulvovaginitis, scratching due to pinworm infection, or a vaginal foreign body. Vaginitis caused by group A β-streptococci or *Shigella* is especially likely to be accompanied by bleeding. In a child with the recent onset of "drops of blood" seen on the underwear, visualization of the vagina with the patient in the knee-chest position and vaginal cultures are important before anesthesia examination is recommended. If excoriations are noted around the anus and vulva, a Scotch type test should be done to search for pinworms. Intravaginal foreign bodies are usually wads of toilet pa-

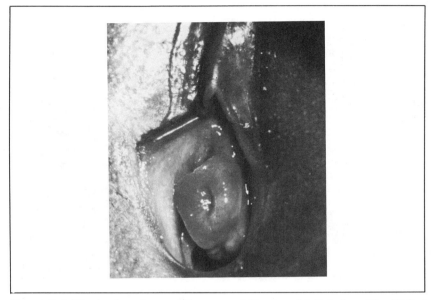

Figure 3-4. Urethral prolapse. (Courtesy of Dr. Arnold Colodny, The Children's Hospital, Boston.)

per but may be pins, tampon cartons, beads, marker tips, crayons, or batteries. A study by Paradise and Willis [28] found that 18 percent of girls under 13 years with vaginal bleeding with or without discharge and 50 percent of those with vaginal bleeding and *no* discharge can be expected to have a foreign body. Most girls with a foreign body do not have a foul-smelling discharge with the bleeding. A tumor is a rare cause of bleeding, but the possibility of this diagnosis makes adequate assessment of the vagina important in the child with unexplained bleeding.

Urethral prolapse usually presents with bleeding, often thought by the parent to be "vaginal bleeding." Examination reveals the characteristic friable red-blue (doughnut-like) annular mass (Fig. 3-4) [40, 41, 42]. The patient may complain of dysuria, bleeding, and pain that has occurred after coughing or straining or following trauma. The peak age of prolapse is 5 to 8 years; the condition appears to occur much more commonly in black girls [43]. The diagnosis is made by the characteristic shape of the lesion and visualization of the vaginal orifice with the patient in the supine or knee-chest position. Prolapse usually resolves with nonsurgical treatment; methods used in (uncontrolled) series of patients include sitz baths, plain or with antiseptic soap (providone-iodine or hexachlorophene) added, application of topical estrogen cream or topical antibiotics, and systemic oral antibiotics. Resolution takes 1–4 weeks. Prolapse with necrotic tissue require surgical intervention.

Cyclic vaginal bleeding without signs of pubertal development is rare; Heller and associates [44, 45] have termed this entity "precocious menarche" (see Chap. 5). Although we have followed several girls with this problem, one of whom has a mother who had the same pattern of bleeding, full examination, under anesthesia if necessary, is essential before regarding vaginal bleeding as an idiopathic or benign disorder.

Bleeding secondary to vulvitis should respond promptly to local measures. Vaginitis due to organisms such as group A β-hemolytic streptococci or *Shigella* requires oral antibiotics.

Removal of foreign bodies may be accomplished in the outpatient setting with the cooperative patient. Soft foreign bodies can often be easily removed by twirling a dry cotton-tipped applicator within the vagina with the patient in the lithotomy or knee-chest position. Gentle irrigation of the vagina with saline or water can usually be accomplished with the child supine using a small urethral catheter attached to a 25-ml syringe. Lubricant or xylocaine jelly can be applied to the introitus to aid in insertion of the small catheter. Metallic items such as safety pins can be removed with bayonet forceps. For the frightened child or the child with a foreign body that is not easily removed, sedation with a meperidine (Demerol) compound or general anesthesia is necessary.

Therapy for a tumor depends on the extent of the lesion and requires referral to a large medical center.

SARCOMA BOTRYOIDES

The malignant tumor that involves the vagina, uterus, bladder, and urethra of very young girls most frequently is sarcoma botryoides, also known as embryonal rhabdomyosarcoma. The symptoms include vaginal discharge, bleeding, abdominal pain or mass, or the passage of grapelike lesions. The peak incidence is in the first 2 years of life, with 90 percent occurring before age 5 years. The growth usually starts on the anterior vaginal wall near the cervix, and as the tumor grows larger, it fills the vagina.

On examination, the tumors appear as a prolapse of grapelike masses through the urethra or vagina. If a vaginal tag is seen on vaginal examination, it should never be assumed to be benign. Growth of the tumor is rapid and prognosis poor unless the diagnosis is made early. A combination of chemotherapy and aggressive surgery along with radiation therapy for some patients can cure more than 90 percent of children with localized pelvic rhabdomyosarcoma [46]. Patients with regional or distant spread do less well.

CLITORAL LESIONS

The clitoral hood may occasionally develop an infection with intense edema and erythema. Antibiotics such as dicloxacillin or a cephalosporin should be given orally and warm soaks applied. Surgical incision and drainage are necessary if the abscess becomes fluctuant.

Hemorrhages may occur around the clitoris in girls with lichen sclerosis, and synechiae may be apparent even after the condition has improved in the vulvar area. An ecchymotic clitoris may also occur secondary to trauma.

Edema of the clitoris may occur with hypoproteinemia in conditions such as the nephrotic syndrome. Recently, a "clitoral tourniquet syndrome" has been described by Press and associates [47]; a hair had become wrapped around the clitoris, which resulted in edema and severe pain. After removal of the hair, the clitoris returned to normal size. The syndrome is similar to strangulation by hair of other parts of the body, such as fingers, toes, or penis. Clitorism, a persistent painful erection of the clitoris, has been reported in one 11-year-old with acute nonlymphocytic leukemia and extremely elevated white count (196,000/mm^3) [48].

CONDYLOMA ACUMINATUM
(HUMAN PAPILLOMAVIRUS)

Condyloma acuminatum ("venereal warts"), caused by human papillomavirus, occurs in infants and children and may have the typical verrucous appearance around the vulva and anus seen in adolescents or may have an atypical appearance resembling a fleshy tumor at the introitus (Fig. 3-5). Human papillomavirus (HPV) can be transmitted to the infant at the time of delivery from an infected mother who may or may not be aware of having the disease. Since the incubation period may be many months, a child with warts in the first 12 to 24 months of life may have been infected at birth. Whether longer intervals of latency to clinical expression occur is unclear. However, beyond this time period, an evaluation for sexual abuse should be undertaken to search for the possible source. The types of warts found in the genital area of girls (types 6 and 11) are not the same as those found on the hands of caregivers (types 1 and 2). It is possible, although as yet unproved, that caregivers can transmit the genital wart virus during shared bathing. Recently we evaluated a 5-year-old with a single wart on her inner thigh that apeared shortly after birth; 5 years later she developed extensive hymenal and vulvar warts [49]. Psychological evaluation revealed that she had been involved in coercive sexual play with a peer. The warts on the inner thigh and the vulva were identical genital types. Thus, the need to pursue a careful history of abuse is essential even if the source seems apparent. Because of the long latency, identifying a perpetrator or determining

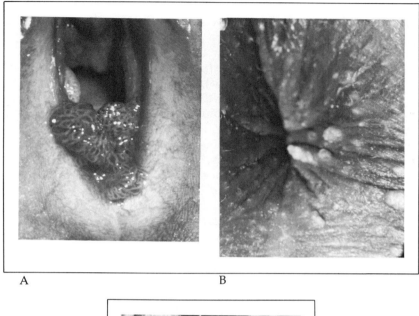

A   B

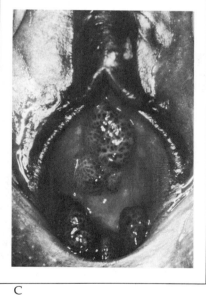

C

Figure 3-5. Condylomata acuminata in three girls. A. Hymenal condyloma. B. Anal condyloma in the sister of A. C. Condyloma presenting in the emergency ward as "vaginal bleeding."

whether the virus was acquired at birth is often not possible, but the child should continue to be followed to try to ensure her safety in her environment.

Thus, evaluation of the child with condyloma acuminatum should include a history for sexual abuse (preferably done by a mental health worker with expertise in the field), careful genital examination, cultures for other sexually transmitted infections (*N. gonorrhoeae, C. trachomatis*), and serology for syphilis.

Treatment of anogenital condyloma is best accomplished with carbon dioxide laser under general anesthesia. As DNA typing becomes more widely available to clinicians, tissue should be obtained for both diagnosis and to help with prognosis. A few lesions can be treated in an outpatient surgery setting; for more extensive lesions, admission to the hospital the night after the procedure is important because children have difficulty voiding and usually need bladder catheterization. Sitz baths and/or a squeeze bottle of warm water can relieve pain. A thin application of silver sulfadiazine (Silvadene) cream is used topically, and oral analgesics are given as needed. The long-term risk of neoplasia, especially of the vulva, is unknown but remains a significant worry. Long-term follow-up is important.

LABIAL ADHESIONS
Agglutination of the labia minora, termed labial adhesions or vulvar adhesions (for the lower half), occurs primarily in young girls between age 3 months and 6 years (Fig. 3-6; see also Plate 4). Adhesions may occasionally occur for the first time after age 6 years, and adhesions present from any age may persist to the time of puberty. It is possible though unproved that hygiene and vulvar irritation can cause a small adhesion to result in near total fusion. Occasionally the vaginal orifice is completely covered, causing poor drainage of vaginal secretions. Parents often become alarmed because the vagina appears "absent." It has been suggested, though far from proved, that fondling and the irritation from sexual abuse may predispose the older girl to labial agglutination [50, 51].

The diagnosis of labial adhesions is made by visual inspection of the vulva. The treatment of labial adhesions remains controversial. Spontaneous separation may occur, particularly with small vulvar adhesions at the posterior forchette and with estrogenization at puberty. If the opening in the agglutination is large enough for good vaginal and urinary drainage, lubrication of the labia with a bland ointment such as A and D Ointment and gentle separation by the mother over several weeks may be helpful. For adhesions that impair vaginal or urinary drainage, the most effective treatment is application of an estrogen-containing cream [52]. We use Premarin Vaginal Cream twice daily for 2 to 3 weeks and then at bedtime for another 2

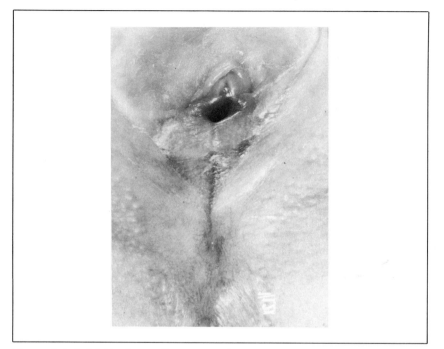

Figure 3-6. Labial/vulvar adhesions with small opening below the clitoris.

weeks. The mother must be shown exactly where the labial adhesion is ("a line") and shown how to rub in the cream with gentle separation. Most failures result from the parent applying the cream over the entire vulva without specific attention to the adhesion. After separation has occurred, the labia should be maintained apart by daily baths, good hygiene, and the application of a bland ointment (such as A and D ointment) at bedtime for 6 to 12 months. Forceful separation is generally contraindicated because it is traumatic for the child and may cause the adhesions to form again.

In occasional patients the extensive, dense labial adhesions fail to respond to the application of estrogen cream (even with proper technique). Separation can be accomplished in the cooperative patient in the office. Approximately 5 minutes after the application of 5% Xylocaine ointment, the physician can slide a Calgiswab gently along the adhesions thinned by the estrogen cream, teasing them apart from anterior to posterior. If this is not easily accomplished or the girl has acute urinary retention, separation in an ambulatory surgical setting is recommended. Rare early adolescents who have had labial adhesions since early childhood do not have the usual spontaneous separation either with their own endogenous estrogen or with topically applied estrogen, seemingly because of the thick bands that

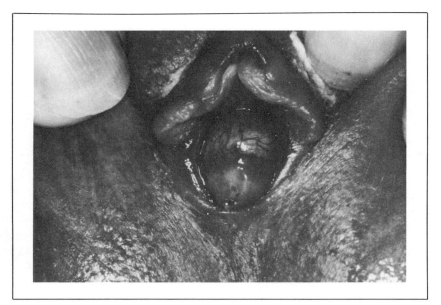

Figure 3-7. Paraurethral cyst in a neonate.

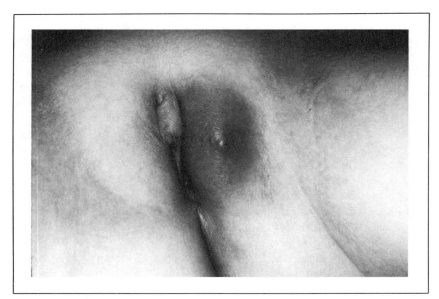

Figure 3-8. Labial abscess.

have formed over time. Our oldest patient with persistent adhesions was 16 years old and required separation under general anesthesia.

MISCELLANEOUS ENTITIES

Other entities that should be recognized by the physician are paraurethral cysts, urethral caruncles, labial abscesses, and congenital failure of midline fusion. Paraurethral cysts (Fig. 3-7) may occur in children, especially in the newborn period. In the newborn, the cysts usually disappear without treatment. Before surgery is undertaken, the possibility of a urologic or gynecologic problem such as urethral diverticulum, ectopic ureterocele, hymenal or vaginal cyst, or obstructed hemivagina should be excluded by examination and ultrasound of the kidneys and bladder preoperatively, and intraoperatively radiopaque dye such as Renografin should be injected into the cyst and imaged to detect an anomaly. Labial abscesses (Fig. 3-8) are treated with antibiotics, sitz baths, and, as indicated, incision and drainage. The failure of midline fusion is congenital and may be confused with trauma or sexual abuse; the child in Plate 6 had excision of the base of the separation at age 4 years and suturing of edges to give a normal vulvar appearance.

REFERENCES
1. Emans SJ, and Goldstein DP. The gynecologic examination of the prepubertal child with vulvovaginitis: Use of the knee-chest position. Pediatrics 1980; 65:758.
2. Paradise JE, Compos JM, Friedman HM, et al. Vulvovaginitis in premenarchal girls: Clinical features and diagnostic evaluation. Pediatrics 1982; 70:193.
3. Altchek A. Pediatric vulvovaginitis. J Reprod Med 1984; 29:359.
4. Capraro VJ. Vulvovaginitis and other local lesions of the vulva. Clin Obstet Gynecol 1974; 1:533.
5. Heller RH, Joseph JH, and David HJ. Vulvovaginitis in the premenarchal child. J Pediatr 1969; 74:370.
6. Ginsburg CM. Group A streptococcal vaginitis in children. Pediatr Infect Dis 1982; 1:36.
7. Figeroa-Colon R, Grunow JE, Torres-Pinedo R, et al. Group A streptococcal proctitis and vulvovaginitis in a prepubertal girl. Pediatr Infect Dis 1984; 3:439.
8. Guss C, and Larsen JG. Group A beta-hemolytic streptococcal proctocolitis. Pediatr Infect Dis 1984; 3:442.
9. Kokx NP, Comstock JA, and Facklam RR. Streptococcal perianal disease in children. Pediatrics 1987; 80:659.
10. Spear RM, Rithbaum RJ, Keating JP, et al. Perianal streptococcal cellulitis. J Pediatr 1985; 107:557.
11. Murphy TV, and Nelson JD. *Shigella* vaginitis: Report of 38 patients and review of the literature. Pediatrics 1979; 63:511.
12. Watkins S, Quan L. Vulvovaginitis caused by *Yersinia* enterocolitica. Pediatr Infect Dis 1984; 3:444.
13. Farrell MK, Billmire ME, Shamroy JA, et al. Prepubertal gonorrhea: A multidisciplinary approach. Pediatrics 1981; 67:151.

14. Folland DS, Burke RE, Hinman AR, et al. Gonorrhea in preadolescent children: An inquiry into source of infection and mode of transmission. Pediatrics 1977; 60:153.
15. Whittington WL, Rice RJ, Biddle JW, et al. Incorrect identification of Neisseria gonorrhoeae from infants and children. Pediatr Infect Dis 1988, 7:3.
16. Alexander ER. Misidentification of sexually transmitted organisms in children: medicolegal implications. Pediatr Infect Dis 1988; 7:1.
17. Ingram DL, White ST, Occhiuti AC, et al. Childhood vaginal infections: association of Chlamydia trachomatis with sexual contact. Pediatr Infect Dis 1986; 5:226.
18. Fuster CD, and Neinstein LS. Vaginal Chlamydia trachomatis prevalence in sexually abused prepubertal girls. Pediatrics 1987; 79:235.
19. Schacter J, Grossman M, Sweet RL, et al. Prospective study of perinatal transmission of Chlamydia trachomatis. JAMA 1986; 255:3374.
20. Bell TA, Stamm WE, Kuo CC, et al. Delayed appearance of Chlamydia trachomatis infection acquired at birth. Pediatr Infect Dis 1987; 6:928.
21. Patamasucon P, Rettig PJ, and Nelson JD. Cefuroxime therapy of gonorrhea and coinfection with Chlamydia trachomatis in children. Pediatrics 1981; 68:534.
22. Bartley DL, Morgan L, and Rimsza ME. Gardnerella vaginalis in prepubertal girls. Am J Dis Child 1987; 141:1014.
23. Hammerschlag MR, Albert S, Rosner I, et al. Microbiology of the vagina in children: Normal and potentially pathogenic organisms. Pediatrics 1978; 68:57.
24. Paradise J. Unpublished data.
25. Fink CW. A perineal rash in Kawasaki disease. Pediatr Infect Dis 1983; 2;140.
26. Rimsza ME, and Chun JJ. Vaginal discharge of "beads" and the new diapers. Pediatrics 1988; 81:332.
27. Tudor RB. Disposable diaper damper. Pediatrics 1988; 81:471.
28. Paradise JE, and Willis ED. Probability of vaginal foreign body in girls with genital complaints. Am J Dis Child 1985; 139:472.
29. Hammerschlag MR, Rettig PJ, and Shields ME. False positive result with the use of Chlamydia antigen detection tests in the evaluation of suspected sexual abuse in children. Pediatr Infect Dis 1988;7:11.
30. Hammerschlag MR. Chlamydia and suspected sexual abuse. Pediatrics 1988; 81:600.
31. Redmond CA, Corvell CA, and Krafchik B. Genital lichen sclerosus in prepubertal girls. Adolesc Pediatr Gynecol 1988; 1:177.
32. Muramatsu T, Kitamura W, and Sakamoto K. Lichen sclerosus et atrophicus in children. J Dermatol 1985; 12:377.
33. Kaufman RH, and Gardner HL. Vulvar dystrophies. Clin Obstet Gynecol 1978; 21:1081.
34. Clark JA, and Muller SA. Lichen sclerosus et atrophicus in children. Arch Dermatol 1967; 95:476.
35. Meyrick Thomas RH, and Kennedy CT. The development of lichen sclerosus et atrophicus in monozygotic twin girls. Br J Dermatol 1986; 114:337.
36. Friedrich EG, and Kalra PS. Serum levels of sex hormones in vulvar lichen sclerosis, and the effect of topical testosterone. N Engl J Med 1984; 310:486.
37. Davis A, and Goldstein DP. Treatment of pediatric lichen sclerosus with the CO_2 laser. Adol Pediatr Gynecol 1989; 2:71.

38. Penneys NS. Treatment of lichen sclerosus with potassium para-aminobenzoate. J Am Acad Dermatol 1984; 10:1039.
39. Davis A. Unpublished observation.
40. Mercer LJ, Mueller CM, and Hajj SN. Medical treatment of urethral prolapse in the premenarchal female. Adolesc Pediatr Gynecol 1988; 1:181.
41. Capraro VJ, Bayonet MP, and Magoss I. Vulvar tumors in children due to prolapse of urethral mucosa. Am J Obstet Gynecol 1970; 108:572.
42. Belman AB, and King LR. The Urethra. In PP Kelalis and LR King (eds.), *Clinical Pediatric Urology*. Philadelphia: Saunders, 1976.
43. Owens SB, and Morse WH. Prolapse of the female urethra in children. J Urol 1968; 100:171.
44. Heller ME, Dewhurst J, and Grant DB. Premature menarche without other evidence of precocious puberty. Arch Dis Child 1979; 54:472.
45. Heller ME, Savage MO, and Dewhurst J. Vaginal bleeding in childhood: A review of 51 patients. Br J Obstet Gynaecol 1970; 85:721.
46. Hendren WH, and Lillehei CS. Pediatric surgery. N Engl J Med 1988; 319:86.
47. Press S, Schachner L, and Paul P. Clitoris tourniquet syndrome. Pediatrics 1980; 66:781.
48. Williams DL, Bell BA, and Ragab AH. Clitorism at presentation of acute nonlymphocytic leukemia. J Pediatr 1985; 107:754.
49. Davis AJ, Emans SJ, Craighill MC, et al. HPV autoinoculation: A case report. Adol Pediatr Gynecol 1989; 2:165.
50. Berkowitz CD, Elvik SL, and Logan MK. Labial fusion in prepubescent girls: A marker for sexual abuse? Am J Obstet Gynecol 1987; 156:16.
51. McCann J, Voris J, and Simon M. Labial adhesions and posterior fourchette injuries in childhood sexual abuse. Am J Dis Child 1988; 142:659.
52. Ariberg A. Topical estrogen therapy for labial adhesions in children. Br J Obstet Gynaecol 1975; 82:424.

4. The Physiology of Puberty

A good understanding of the physiology of puberty and menarche is essential background to the diagnosis of precocious puberty in the child and the management of common menstrual and growth problems of the adolescent. This chapter presents a brief discussion of these issues; more detailed information can be found in the references listed at the end of the chapter.

HORMONAL CHANGES AT PUBERTY
Normal puberty in girls involves the appearance of secondary sex characteristics, the growth spurt, and the achievement of fertility. These changes result from the activation of the hypothalamic pituitary unit and the secretion of sex steroids from the ovary. The hypothalamus is responsible for the synthesis and release of gonadotropin releasing hormone (GnRH), sometimes referred to as luteinizing hormone releasing hormone (LHRH) (Fig. 4-1). GnRH, a decapeptide with a serum half-life of 2 to 4 minutes, is released in pulses into the pituitary portal plexus. GnRH stimulates the synthesis and release of the gonadotropins, follicle-stimulating hormone (FSH) and luteinizing hormone (LH), from the anterior pituitary gland. The secreted FSH and LH are responsible for the stimulation of the ovary and the resultant germ cell maturation and hormone synthesis.

Sex steroids exert a feedback effect upon gonadotropin secretion. The feedback occurs both at the level of the hypothalamus modulating the frequency and amplitude of GnRH release and at the level of the pituitary affecting the amount of LH and FSH in response to GnRH pulses. With negative feedback, small amounts of estrogen from the ovary suppress gonadotropin secretion; with positive feedback, rising levels of estrogen at midcycle trigger increased pulses of LH and FSH, resulting in ovulation. Although both FSH and LH are released in pulses, only the pulses of LH are recognizable by minute-to-minute serum measurements because the half-life of LH is about 30 minutes versus an FSH half-life of 300 minutes.

The hypothalamic-pituitary-ovarian system is remarkably developed at the time of birth. In fact, the hypothalamic portal system is intact by 14 weeks of gestation. The negative feedback system of gonadal steroids on the hypothalamus and pituitary is apparent by midgestation. Gonadotropin and ovarian sex steroid production are important in stimulating germ cell division and follicular development. By 5 to 6 months of gestation, 6 to 7 million oocytes are present, and through the process of atresia, the neonate has approximately 1 to 2 million at birth; by puberty only 0.3 to 0.5 million remain. By 5 days after birth, gonadotropin levels rise sharply to levels consider-

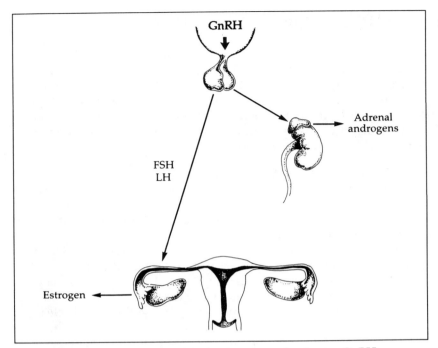

Figure 4-1. Hormones responsible for the onset of puberty. GnRH = gonadotropin releasing hormone; FSH = follicle-stimulating hormone; LH = luteinizing hormone. The stimulus for the rise in adrenal androgens is unclear.

ably higher than those found in the prepubertal child, probably in response to the fall in placental estrogen. A transient rise in plasma estradiol is apparent in female infants, especially during the first 3 months of life. Preantral and antral follicles are seen in the ovary. Thereafter gonadotropin levels gradually fall to childhood levels, although FSH levels may not be maximally suppressed for 1 to 4 years. Females have an elevated FSH/LH ratio compared to males [1, 2].

During the childhood years, there is a down regulation of the hypothalamic pituitary system, with reduction of the amplitude and frequency of GnRH pulses and a decreased pituitary responsiveness to a single dose of GnRH. This inactivity appears to be in response to a central nervous system (CNS) signal, since it occurs even in agonadal patients. For example, levels of FSH and LH in Turner syndrome, which are markedly elevated in the neonatal period, are suppressed between the ages of 4 and 10 years, although the mean levels are higher than the mean levels of normal children of similar ages. In some agonadal children between the ages of 5 and 11 years, basal levels of LH and FSH and responses to GnRH are comparable to those in normal prepubertal children, thus preventing a definitive diagnosis of gonadal failure by hormonal tests alone [3].

In prepubertal girls, GnRH pulses continue to persist at low levels with enhancement during sleep, and the FSH/LH ratio is higher than in earlier or later stages. Prepubertal girls often show very little LH response to a single dose of GnRH but a considerable rise in FSH; however, if GnRH is administered in a physiologic manner over the course of time, the pituitary is capable of response. The ovary increases in size during these years and has evidence of active follicular growth and atresia. The vagina, which is approximately 4 cm in length at birth, grows only 0.5 to 1.0 cm during early childhood but increases in length to 7.0 to 8.5 cm in late childhood. The uterus is about 2.5 cm in length in infancy. The corpus-to-cervix ratio is slightly less than 1:1; it reaches 1:1 at menarche and the adult ratio of 3:1 postmenarcheally.

The earliest change associated with future pubertal maturation is the secretion of adrenal androgens—dehydroepiandrosterone (DHA) and its sulfate (DHAS), as well as androstenedione—between the ages of 6 and 8 years. Termed adrenarche, this process involves the regrowth of the zona reticularis of the adrenal cortex (the zone that is large in the fetal adrenal cortex and regresses after birth) with the increases in the activity of the microsomal enzyme p450c17. The mechanism for this change in adrenal androgen synthesis is unknown. Adrenal androgens continue to rise through ages 13 to 15 years and are primarily responsible for the appearance of pubic and axillary hair in girls (so-called pubarche) [4, 5].

Sometime around or after age 8 years, although no physical changes are present, GnRH secretion is enhanced, first during sleep. There is a resultant increase in pituitary responsiveness with increased secretion of LH and FSH (Fig. 4-2). LH responsiveness to exogenous GnRH testing also increases at this time and allows differentiation between a pubertal and prepubertal pattern. It also appears that the increase in LH bioactivity at puberty exceeds the changes seen in studies that examine the more commonly used radioimmunoassay. Lucky and co-workers [6] found that bioactive LH increased 23.1-fold, while immunoreactive LH increased only 4-fold during puberty, suggesting a role of the pituitary in controlling the maturational process of puberty.

The age-related rise in gonadotropins with an initial sleep enhancement also occurs in patients with Turner syndrome, and menopausal levels of LH and FSH pulses occur at this time. It does not appear that ovarian sex steroids play a critical role in the onset of puberty, since patients with Turner syndrome experience adrenarche (the rise of adrenal adrogens) and an age-related rise in gonadotropins. Pre-

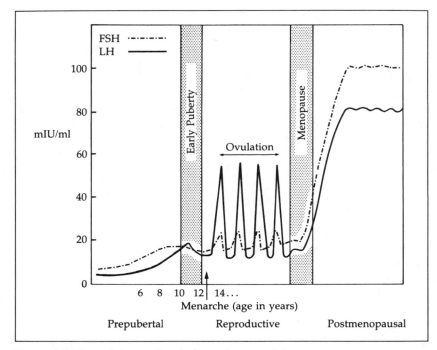

Figure 4-2. Gonadotropin levels from the age of 6 years to menopause. FSH = follicle-stimulating hormone; LH = luteinizing hormone.

pubertal patients with Addison's disease can experience normal gonadarche (the activation of the hypothalamic-pituitary-ovarian axis) but no adrenarche. Patients with the onset of precocious puberty before age 6 typically exhibit gonadarche but not adrenarche. Patients with constitutional delay of puberty frequently have delays of both adrenarche and gonadarche [7]. Sex steroids are important for the development of functional feedback mechanisms [1, 8].

During late prepuberty and early puberty, there is a gradual augmentation of episodic peaks of LH and FSH during sleep. LH stimulates the theca interna cells of the ovary to synthesize precursors, and FSH increases the enzyme aromatase, which is responsible for the conversion of androgen precursors to estrogen. Estrogen peaks 10 to 12 hours after the gonadotropin secretion (Fig. 4-3) [9]. The ovaries are marked by increased follicular growth and on ultrasonography may appear as "enlarged and multicystic" ovaries. As puberty progresses, the ovaries amplify the gonadotropin message and release greater amounts of sex steroids for a given amount of gonadotropins.

The stimulus for this change in CNS activation is unknown given that the system is fully operative in the neonatal period. The "gonadostat theory" with altered sensitivity to sex steroids as a sole

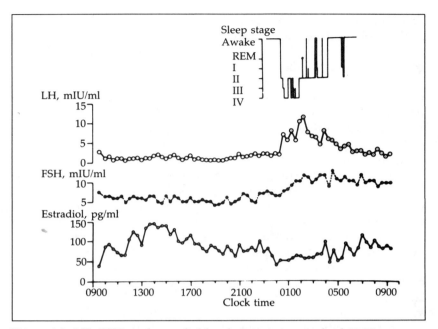

Figure 4-3. LH, FSH, and estradiol levels in a premenarcheal 13 7/12-year-old girl (Tanner stage 3) showing a rise in LH and FSH during sleep and a rise in plasma estradiol during the afternoon. LH = luteinizing hormone; FSH = follicle-stimulating hormone. (From RM Boyar, RH Wu, H Roffwarg, et al. Human puberty: 24-hour estradiol patterns in pubertal girls. J Clin Endocrinol Metab 43:1418, 1976. By permission.)

explanation seems untenable given the evidence of activation in agonadal children. The theory of a metabolic signal or critical percent fat remains speculative because of the many clinical exceptions to the theory and the fact that menarche is a relatively late event in puberty (see Chap. 6). Conflicting studies have suggested a possible role for melatonin or endogenous opiate tone.

Breast budding, estrogenization of the vaginal mucosa, and lengthening of the uterus occur with rising estrogen levels. The physiologic vaginal discharge of puberty or leukorrhea is the desquamation of epithelial cells and mucus from the estrogenized mucosa. The pubertal process is accompanied by a growth spurt, which usually begins gradually around age 9 years and reaches a peak by age 12 years. Both growth hormone and sex steroids appear to contribute to the growth spurt. Growth hormone and somatomedin-C levels increase during puberty as estrogen levels rise [10, 11, 12]. The effect of estrogen on growth hormone and growth is dose related; low doses of estrogen stimulate growth, growth hormone, and somatomedin-C, while at high doses of estrogen, growth hormone, somatomedin-C, and growth are decreased. This observation has led to the use of large pharmacologic doses of estrogen in an attempt to diminish final adult height in girls who are predicted to have excessively tall stature. In contrast, low doses of estrogen replacement in hypogonadal patients result in increased somatomedin-C levels and growth. An increase in weight accompanies the growth spurt in normal girls, and body composition changes through late childhood and adolescence with a particularly apparent increase in percent body fat.

As puberty progresses to adulthood, the levels of FSH and LH reached at night are gradually carried over into the waking hours until the sleep augmentation disappears. Even before menarche, circulating estrogen concentrations in pubertal girls have some cyclicity; eventually these periodic fluctuations are sufficient to result in uterine bleeding. The first 1 to 2 years following menarche are often characterized by anovulatory menses. This period coincides with the rapid growth of the uterus, vagina, tubes, and ovaries. However, with maturation, a mechanism known as the biphasic positive feedback system develops; in this system a rise in plasma estrogen in the latter part of the follicular phase of the menstrual cycle triggers the surge of LH and FSH, which is responsible for ovulation. The change in the sensitivity of the feedback system can be demonstrated by the use of clomiphene citrate, a nonsteroidal, agonist-antagonist estrogen, which when administered to prepubertal and early pubertal girls causes further suppression of gonadotropin levels. However, in late pubertal adolescents and adults, clomiphene causes a rise in gonadotropin levels and ovulation (which makes it useful as a fertility drug).

STAGES OF BREAST AND PUBIC HAIR DEVELOPMENT

In 1969, Marshall and Tanner [13] recorded the rates of progression of pubertal development of 192 English schoolgirls. These stages can be important guidelines in assessing whether an adolescent is developing normally. The Tanner stages for breast development are as follows (Fig. 4-4) [13, 14]:

Stage B1, preadolescent; elevation of the nipple only
Stage B2, breast bud stage; elevation of the breast and nipple as a small mount, enlargement of the areolar diameter
Stage B3, further enlargement of the breast and areola with no separation of the contours
Stage B4, further enlargement with projection of the areola and nipple to form a secondary mound above the level of the breast
Stage B5, mature stage; projection of the nipple only, resulting from recession of the areola to the general contour of the breast

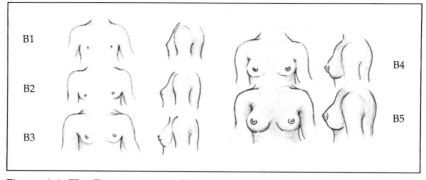

Figure 4-4. The Tanner stages of human breast development. (Adapted from G Ross and R Vande Wiele, The Ovaries. In R Williams [ed.], *Textbook of Endocrinology* [5th ed.]. Philadelphia: Saunders, 1974; and from WA Marshall and JM Tanner, Variations in pattern of pubertal changes in girls. Arch Dis Child 44:291, 1969.)

The pubic hair stages are as follows (Fig. 4-5):

Stage PH1, no pubic hair

Stage PH2, sparse growth of long, straight, only slightly curled hair along the labia

Stage PH3, thicker, coarser, and more curled hair extending sparsely over the junction of the pubis

Stage PH4, hair is adult in type and spreads over the mons pubis but not to the medial surface of the thighs

Stage PH5, hair is spread to the medial surface of the thighs

The mean age of each stage of puberty is shown in Figure 4-6. The ages shown are from British data; American data show development occurring 6 to 9 months earlier.

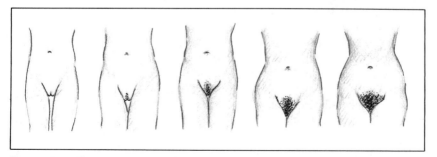

Figure 4-5. The Tanner stages for the development of female pubic hair (Adapted from G Ross and R Vande Wiele, The Ovaries. In R Williams [ed.], *Textbook of Endocrinology* [5th ed.]. Philadelphia: Saunders, 1974; and from WA Marshall and JM Tanner, Variations in pattern of pubertal changes in girls. Arch Dis Child 44:291, 1969.)

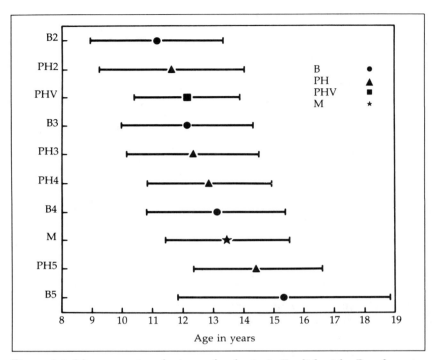

Figure 4-6. Mean age at each stage of puberty in English girls. B = breast; PH = pubic hair; M = menarche; PHV = peak height velocity. The center of each symbol represents the mean; the length of the symbol is equivalent to 2 standard deviations on either side of the mean. (Adapted from WA Marshall and JM Tanner, Variations in pattern of pubertal changes in girls. Arch Dis Child 44:291, 1969.)

The first sign of puberty in 85 to 92 percent of white girls is breast budding. Breast budding usually begins around ages 10½ to 11 years and may initially be unilateral. Some girls pass from B3 directly to B5 and some remain in B4; the best assignment of stages is to observe the changes in the individual patient. In Tanner's series, the mean interval from stage B2 to B5 was 4.2 years. Pubic hair development usually lags by about 6 months and appears at an average age of 11 to 12 years. Pubic hair as the first sign of development may be a normal variant (especially in black girls) but may be a sign in some patients of an excess of androgens that later may cause hirsutism and menstrual irregularity. The mean interval from stages PH2 to PH5 is 2.7 years. Generally, pubic hair will not advance beyond PH2 to PH3 without the presence of gonadal sex steroids. The appearance of breast development usually corresponds to the onset of the growth spurt and precedes pubic hair growth. The timing of these events is variable, but 98.8 percent of girls will have the first signs of sexual development between ages 8 and 13 years. Harlan and associates [15] have reported a high concordance between breast and pubic hair stage (within one ordinal rank) for both black and white girls, with black girls being consistently more advanced in Tanner stages than white girls for each chronologic age.

Breast development before age 8 years would suggest precocious puberty. A girl who has experienced no breast development by age 13 years is two standard deviations from the normal age and has delayed development. She should be evaluated for a pathologic cause of the delay (see Chap. 6). It is also extremely unlikely for a patient to achieve full B5 breast development without pubic hair development, and this would raise the question of an androgen insensitivity (testicular feminization) syndrome or adrenal insufficiency. The development of pubic hair without any evidence of breast development would suggest the presence of androgen alone and would raise the possibility of either estrogen deficiency such as Kallmann's syndrome or a virilized state such as an intersex disorder. The normal changes of LH, FSH, estradiol, testosterone, DHA, DHAS, and androstenedione are shown in Figure 4-7 [16].

GROWTH PATTERNS
The growth spurt is dependent on the onset of puberty. Growth charts, such as those illustrated in Figure 4-8 and Figure 4-9 are helpful to evaluate normal development. Special growth charts for Turner syndrome patients can be obtained from Genentech or its representatives.† The inserts (the increment curves) on the charts in Figure 4-8 represent velocities, that is, the peak is at the maximum rate of linear growth and weight gain. The peak height velocity is attained in the majority of teenagers before the Tanner stages B3 and PH2. The growth chart in Figure 4-9 is data from the National Health Statistics. Because the data in Figure 4-9 is cross-sectional rather than longitudinal data as in Figure 4-8, the pubertal growth spurt is not seen clearly on Figure 4-9. Figure 4-10 shows the growth chart of a patient with precocious puberty; the early acceleration in height and weight gain at the age of 2 to 3 years is followed by premature fusion of the epiphyses and attainment of adult height by the age of 10 years. Figure 4-11 is the growth chart of a patient with delayed development and Crohn's disease; normal linear growth is impaired and the patient is relatively underweight for height. Since the timing of the growth spurt during normal development may be related to weight and body composition, Frisch [18] has developed a method of predicting the age at which the growth spurt begins, based on height and

†Genentech, Inc., 460 Pt Bruno Blvd, San Francisco, CA 94080.

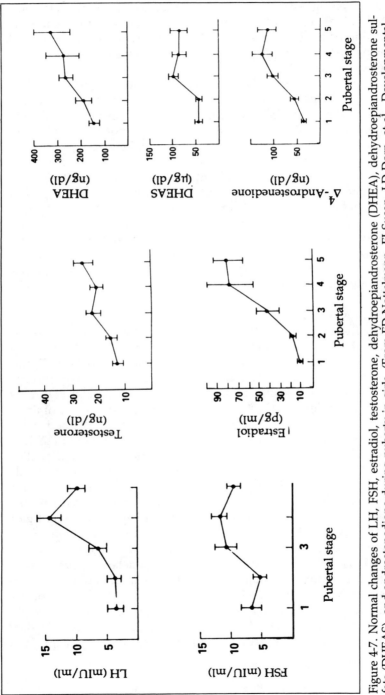

Figure 4-7. Normal changes of LH, FSH, estradiol, testosterone, dehydroepiandrosterone (DHEA), dehydroepiandrosterone sulfate (DHEAS), and androstenedione during puberty in girls. (From ED Nottelmann, EJ Susan, LD Dorn, et al., Developmental processes in early adolescence: Relations among chronologic age, pubertal stage, height, weight, and serum levels of gonadotropins, sex steroids, and adrenal androgens. J Adolesc Health Care 1987;8:246. By permission.)

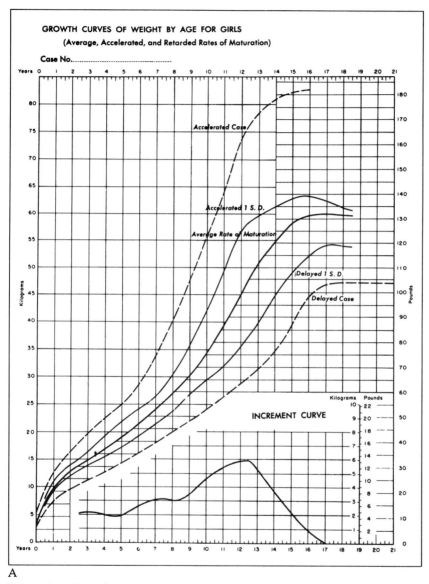

A

Figure 4-8. Growth charts. A. Weight. B. Height. (From N Bayley, Growth curves of height and weight by age for boys and girls, scaled according to physical maturity. J Pediatr 1956;48:187. By permission of the author and the C.V. Mosby Co.)

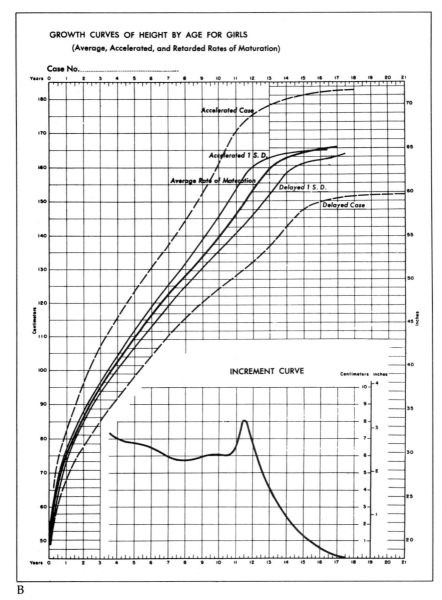

B

Figure 4-8 (Continued)

107

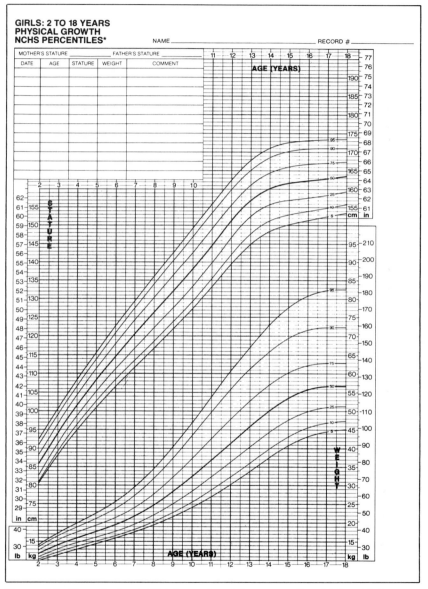

Figure 4-9. Growth chart. Height and weight percentiles. (Adapted from PVV Hamill, et al. Physical growth: National Center for Health Statistics percentiles. Am J Clin Nutr 1979;32:607. Data from the National Center for Health Statistics [NCHS], Hyattsville, MD, by permission of Ross Laboratories.)

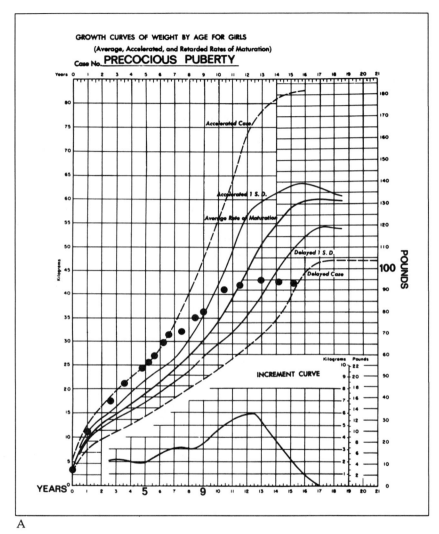

A

Figure 4-10. Growth charts of a patient with idiopathic precocious puberty.
A. Weight. B. Height.

weight at the age of 8 years. The average girl grows 2 to 3 inches over
the 2 years following menarche.

Skeletal proportions are determined by the rate of pubertal development. The upper-lower (U/L) ratio is approximately 1.0 by the age
of 10 years. (L is the distance from the patient's symphysis pubis to
the floor, with the patient standing; U is the height minus L.) At
puberty, the extremities rapidly increase in length, while the vertebral column lengthens more gradually. Initially the U/L ratio may dip

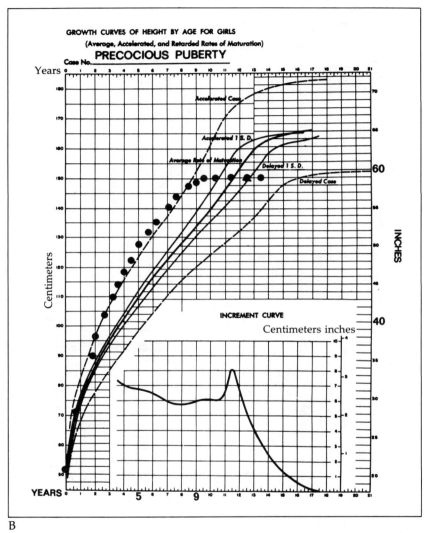

B

Figure 4-10 (Continued)

to 0.9. As the epiphyses of the legs close, the vertebrae continue to
add height, and thus the final adult U/L ratio approximates 1.0. In
patients with hypogonadism, the lower segment becomes relatively
longer because of delayed fusion; thus the U/L ratio may be approximately 0.8. Span (the distance between the fingertips of outstretched
arms) usually reflects the same clinical situation; if the span is more
than 2 inches greater than the height, the patient has eunuchoid
proportions. Athletes with intensive training during the prepubertal
years may have delayed development and menarche, along with de-

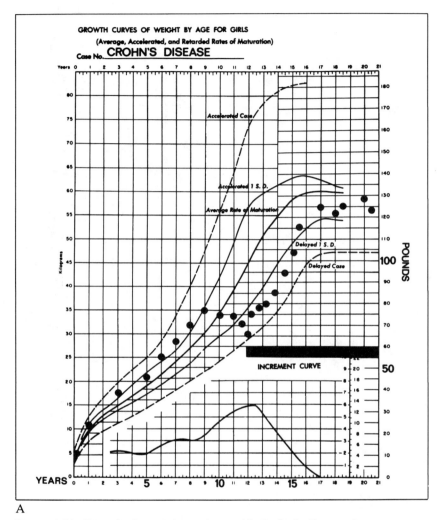

A

Figure 4-11. Growth charts of a patient with Crohn's disease; bar represents treatment with prednisone. A. Weight. B. Height.

layed epiphyseal closure, and therefore may have longer than normal arm span [19, 20].

MENARCHE

The mean age at menarche in Tanner's series in England was 13.46 ± .46 years with a range of 9 to 16 years. In a study by Zacharias and Wurtman [21], the mean age of menarche among student nurses in the United States was 12.65 ± 1.2 years. The National Health Examination Survey [22] estimated the median age at menarche to be 12.77

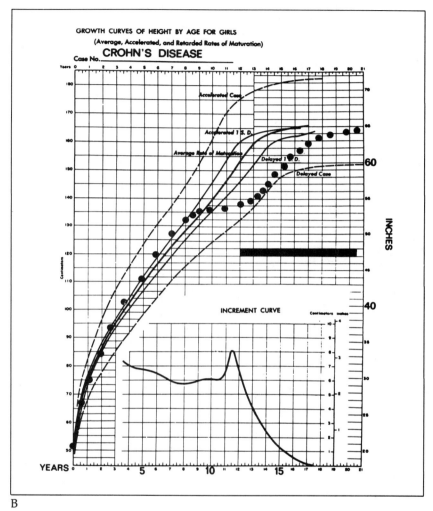

B

Figure 4-11 (Continued)

years (12.8 years for white girls and 12.56 for black girls). Table 4-1 shows that most patients had attained stage 4 breast and pubic hair development at the time of menarche.

In Tanner's series, the mean interval from breast development to menarche was 2.3 ± 0.1 years but the range was 0.5 to 5.75 years. A late onset of pubertal development did not appear to change the intervals in the stages of pubic hair and breast development. Frisch [18] established a nomogram predicting the age of menarche based on height and weight at the ages of 9 to 13 years, using her observation that menarche was associated with the attainment of a critical body

Table 4-1. Percentage of Patients in Stages 1
Through 5 at Time of Menarche

Stage	Breast (% of patients)	Pubic Hair (% of patients)
1	0	1
2	1	4
3	26	19
4	62	63
5	11	14

Source: Adapted from WA Marshall and JM Tanner. Variations in pattern of pubertal changes in girls. Arch Dis Child 1969; 44:291.

weight (an average of 46–47 kg for American and most European girls), with percentage of body fat being the important determinant (see p. 166). According to this theory, a minimum fatness level of about 17 percent of body weight is necessary for the onset of menstrual cycles, and a minimum of 22 percent fat is necessary to maintain regular ovulatory cycles [23]. Early and late maturing girls begin their adolescent growth spurt with a weight of about 30 kg. The apparent decline in the age of menarche from the late 1800s to the mid-1900s has been attributed to improved nutrition and the lack of further decline, in the past two decades, to the attainment of optimal nutrition [24]. Gymnasts, ballet dancers, and long-distance runners with reduced weights and (calculated) body fat compositions often have significant delays in development and menarche, especially if training began in the prepubertal years [19, 25]. Since estrogens are also produced by aromatization of androgen precursors in fat, a low fat composition may contribute less estrogen; estrogen is necessary for hypothalamic pituitary regulation and the onset of vaginal bleeding. The theory remains controversial, however, because GnRH and gonadotropin secretion begins many years before menarche, body fat compositions are often only calculated figures, and weight at the time of menarche can show tremendous variation in individual girls.

In a retrospective series, Zacharias and Wurtman [21, 26] found that the interval between menarche and regular periods was approximately 14 months, and the interval between menarche and painful (presumably ovulatory periods) was approximately 24 months. However, ovulatory cycles can begin in the first year following menarche and may be associated with shortened luteal phases. Data from Finland [27] demonstrated that in the first 2 years after menarche, 55 to 82 percent of cycles were anovulatory (the figure depends on whether only samples drawn fewer than 10 days until the next menstrual bleeding or all samples drawn on day 20 to 23 of the menstrual cycle were considered). By 3 years postmenarche, the percentage of anovulatory cycles decreased to 50 percent and by 5 years to 10 to 20 percent [4, 27]. It appears that the later the age of menarche the longer the interval before 50 percent of cycles are ovulatory. Apter [28] found this interval was 1 year if menarche occurred at an age less than 12 years, 3 years when menarche occurred at 12.0 to 12.9 years, and 4.5 years when menarche was after 13 years of age.

HORMONE LEVELS IN NORMAL OVULATORY CYCLES

The establishment of ovulatory cycles depends on the maturation of a positive feedback mechanism in which rising estrogen levels trigger an LH surge at midcycle. Understanding the hormone changes responsible for ovulation allows the physician to understand the pathophysiology of polycystic ovary syndrome, amenorrhea, and dysfunctional uterine bleeding. Figure 4-12 demonstrates the complex interactions between the changes in the ovary during ovulation and gonadotropins.

The menstrual cycle is divided into a follicular phase, an ovulatory phase, and a luteal phase. In the early follicular phase of the menstrual cycle (shown in Fig. 4-13), pulsatile GnRH released from the hypothalamus stimulates the secretion of FSH and LH from the pituitary. FSH in turn increases the number of granulosa cells in the ovarian follicle, increases the number of receptors for FSH on the granulosa cells, and induces the granulosa cells to acquire an aromatizing enzyme that provides the essential step for the conversion of androgen precursors to estradiol. Estradiol also increases the number of granulosa cells and the number of FSH receptors, which thus leads to further amplification of the effect of FSH. The theca cells, under LH stimulation, secrete androstenedione, testosterone, and estradiol into the bloodstream and also into the follicle as substrate. A dominant follicle emerges by day 5 to 7 of the cycle. The rising estradiol level increases the number of glandular cells and stroma in the endometrium of the uterus. By the midfollicular phase, FSH is beginning to decline in part because of estrogen-mediated negative feedback. Inhibin, which is secreted by granulosa cells and blocks FSH synthesis and release, rises in the late follicular phase of the cycle parallel with estradiol. The highest levels are found during the luteal phase and together with estradiol and progesterone appear to play a role in the regulation of FSH in that phase of the cycle as well. Serum FSH and inhibin levels are inversely related in the mid to late follicular phase and in the luteal phase [28]. Activins also secreted by the granulosa cells stimulate FSH secretion. The dominant follicle has the richest blood supply and the most estrogen production and granulosal aromatase. The increased number of FSH receptors on the dominant follicle allows it to continue to respond even as rising estrogen levels lower FSH. Locally, in the dominant follicle, estradiol levels are

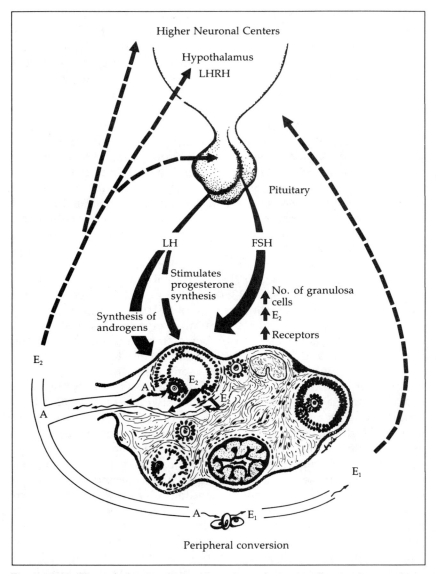

Figure 4-12. Hypothalamic-pituitary-ovarian axis interaction in the regulation of follicular maturation and steroid biosynthesis. LHRH = luteinizing hormone releasing hormone, also termed gonadotropin releasing hormone (GnRH); LH = luteinizing hormone; FSH = follicle-stimulating hormone; E_2 = estradiol; A = androstenedione; E_1 = estrone. The ovary shows the various stages of growth of the follicle and formation and regression of the corpus luteum.

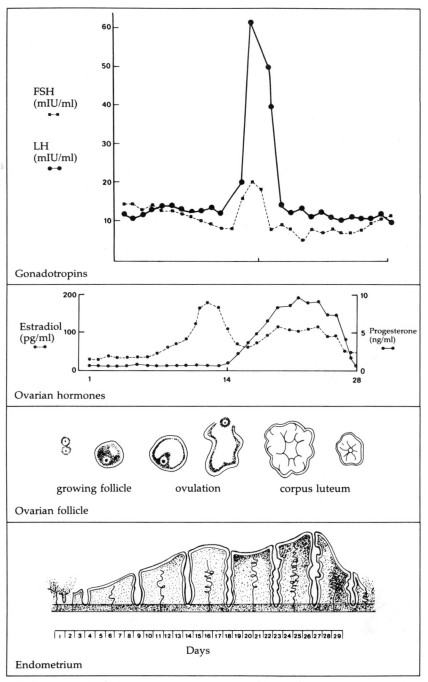

Figure 4-13. Physiology of the normal ovulatory menstrual cycle: gonado-tropin secretion, ovarian hormone production, follicular maturation, and endometrial changes during one cycle. FSH = follicle-stimulating hormone; LH = luteinizing hormone.

greater than androstenedione levels, whereas androstenedione levels are greater than estradiol levels in the atretic follicles.

Crowley's group at the Massachusetts General Hospital [29] has recently characterized the changes in LH that occur during the normal ovulatory menstrual cycle. The LH interpulse interval decreased from a mean of 94 minutes in the early follicular phase to 71 minutes in the late follicular phase, with change in the mean pulse amplitude from 6.5 mIU/ml in the early follicular phase, to 5.1 mIU/ml in the midfollicular phase, and to 7.2 mIU/ml in the late follicular phase. In the luteal phase, the LH pulse interval progressively increased from a mean of 103 minutes in the early luteal phase to 216 minutes in the late luteal phase. The mean pulse amplitude was highest in the early luteal phase (14.9 mIU/ml) and decreased to 12.2 mIU/ml in the midluteal phase and to 7.6 mIU/ml by the late luteal phase. FSH was closely correlated to LH secretion.

In the periovulatory phase of the cycle, the dominant follicle is clearly evident; it has increased receptors for LH and secretes increasing levels of estradiol. The rising estrogen levels produce a further proliferation of the endometrium with thickening of the mucosa and increasing length of the glands. The rising LH levels appear to induce a block in steroid pathways, which initiates secretion of 17-hydroxyprogesterone and progesterone and the gradual luteinization of the granulosa cells. The exact mechanism for the positive feedback effect of rising estrogen and progesterone levels on the midcycle release of multiple pulses of LH is unknown. By midpuberty, the hypothalamic-pituitary unit is capable of this positive feedback response. Following the surge of LH, follicular rupture occurs with expulsion of the oocyte.

The development of the corpus luteum is affected by levels of LH and the rupture of the follicle. As noted, GnRH and thus LH are released in slower pulses. The corpus luteum secretes progesterone and 17-hydroxyprogesterone. Plasma progesterone concentrations are stable over 24-hour studies in the early luteal phase and show no relationship to LH pulses; however, in the mid and late luteal phases, progesterone levels rapidly fluctuate during 24-hour studies from levels as low as 2.3 to peaks of 40.1 ng/ml and correlate with LH pulses [30]. Thus a single progesterone level in the mid to late luteal phase of the cycle may not always predict corpus luteum adequacy.

Under the influence of rising progesterone and estrogen levels, the endometrium enters the secretory phase, which is characterized by coiling of the endometrial glands, increased vascularity of the stroma, and increased glycogen content of the epithelial cells. Maturation of the endometrium is reached within 8 or 9 days after ovulation, and if fertilization does not occur, regression begins. Exact dating of the endometrium is possible because of the changes in morphology. Evidence for ovulation and the occurrence of a luteal phase may be obtained by endometrial biopsy, basal body temperature charts, and measurement of serum progesterone levels. The adequacy of the luteal phase in allowing implantation and successful pregnancy is more difficult to assess.

Without pregnancy and the concomitant rising placental human chorionic gonadotropin (HCG) levels, luteolysis begins and progesterone and estrogen levels begin to decline. Unlike HCG, the luteotropic support of LH cannot extend the life of the corpus luteum beyond 14 days. In contrast to the variable length of the follicular phase, the luteal phase is constant. Thus the life span of the corpus luteum is determined by a preset "clock" with time to allow implantation and retention until trophoblastic HCG intervenes. With the waning of progesterone and estrogen levels, the endometrium undergoes necrotic changes that result in menstrual bleeding. The stage for the new cycle is in fact set in the late luteal phase as plasma FSH begins to rise to initiate follicular development.

A number of studies have recently looked at adolescent cycles as they pass from anovulatory to ovulatory cycles [31–33]. Apter and co-workers [31] reported that in adolescents follicle development was slower and eventual ovulation took place from a smaller follicle than in older women (age 25–35 years). In adults the concentration of FSH decreased from day 4 to day 10 of the cycle, whereas in the adolescent the FSH level increased. The selection of the dominant follicle seemed disturbed, with 7 of 8 adolescent patients studied still having several follicles of 8 to 14 mm on days 12 to 15 of the cycle. In the last 3 days before ovulation, the mean increase in the diameter of the dominant follicle was 2.9 mm in the adolescent group and 5.6 mm in the adult group. Ovulation occurred later in the cycle in adolescents than in adults (mean of 5 days longer). Apter and co-workers had previously shown that a negative correlation was seen between the FSH concentration on days 3 to 4 of the cycle and the length of the follicular phase [33]. In comparison with adolescents, the adults had slightly but significantly higher mean maximal luteal phase progesterone levels.

Apter and co-workers [31] found several patterns in adolescents with anovulatory cycles. One pattern was characterized by low estradiol levels without LH at midcycle and minor or no follicular growth. A second pattern was characterized by developing follicles, slightly higher estradiol, and minor increases in LH at midcycle. A third pattern was identical to an ovulatory pattern with an increase in follicular development, increased estradiol levels, and an LH surge but no evidence of ovulation (no rise in progesterone, no cul-de-sac fluid by ultrasound, menses 3–4 days after the LH surge). Others have found similar patterns in adolescents and adult women involved in strenuous athletic competition. Bonen and associates [34] found that competitive swimmers may have an LH surge at midcycle but no rise in serum progesterone; abnormal FSH secretion in the first half of the cycle may have inadequately prepared the follicle for ovulation. The time from the LH surge to menstruation was 4 or 5 days, similar to the third pattern described by Apter and co-workers. Shangold and associates [35] documented that the luteal phase in a healthy adult runner shortened as she increased her weekly mileage.

In adolescents, the gonadotropin response to a dose of exogenous GnRH appears to change during the follicular phase in the first 2 postmenarcheal years toward that observed in adult women and in the luteal phase from the third to the fifth postmenarcheal year (Fig. 4-14) [35].

Another pattern that appears to occur early in the adolescent years in association with menstrual irregularity is the overproduction of adrenal and ovarian androgens. Venturoli and co-workers [37, 38] found that adolescents with persistent anovulatory menses maintained marked hyperandrogenism, increasingly high LH levels, and enlarged multicystic ovaries. Mean testosterone and androstenedione were higher than in ovulatory cycles and in adult controls. The persistence of this pattern sets the stage for classic polycystic ovary syndrome (see Chap. 7) with rapid pulses of GnRH and LH. In contrast, adolescents with anovulatory cycles and normal LH levels were more similar to ovulatory adolescents. Venturoli and co-workers [37] have suggested that the pulsatile pattern of GnRH and gonadotropin secretion accounts for the endocrine differences in these groups of postmenarcheal adolescents. In addition, they have suggested that in the postmenarcheal period, progesterone, by modulating LH and FSH pulsatility and thus reducing androgen levels and their action on producing atresia of follicles, may be a regulatory factor in enhancing normal cyclicity.

The term *hypothalamic amenorrhea* has been used to apply to the common problem in women in which despite a normal pituitary and ovaries normal cyclic changes do not occur. Recent studies have suggested that abnormalities in pulsatile GnRH are involved and may include a spectrum of changes. The frequency of LH pulses is reduced in most women with hypothalamic amenorrhea [39], suggesting that GnRH pulses are too infrequent to stimulate normal follicular maturation. Santaro and associates [40] have offered a classification of hypogonadotropic hypogonadism based on a comparison of the LH pulse pattern (90-minute intervals) found in the early follicular phase. One pattern was an apulsatile pattern associated with the most profound clinical abnormalities (often primary amenorrhea). A second pattern showed pulses of abnormally low amplitude but a normal number of pulses. A third pattern showed pulses of normal or greater than normal amplitude but low frequency, resembling the normal

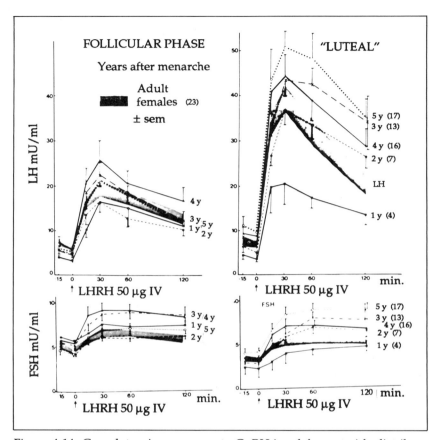

Figure 4-14. Gonadotropin responses to GnRH in adolescent girls distributed according to gynecologic age (years after menarche). Upper panel: LH responses during the follicular and "luteal" phases. Lower panel: FSH responses in the same girls. ■—■ = first postmenarcheal year; ●---● = second postmenarcheal year; X__.__X = third year; ▲—▲ = fourth year; 0 . . . 0 = fifth year. The hatched area represents the mean ± SEM gonadotropin responses in 23 normally cycling adult women. LH and FSH are expressed as milliunits per milliliter MRC international standards 68/40 and 68/39, respectively. The number of subjects is in parentheses. (From T Lemarchand-Beraud, M Zufferey, M Reymond, M Rey, et al., Maturation of the hypothalamic-pituitary-ovarian axis in adolescent girls. J Clin Endocrinol Metab 1982;54:241. By permission.)

luteal phase. A fourth group showed no discernible differences in LH in spite of amenorrhea. This last group may have a difference in night-day secretion or less circulating bioactive gonadotropins. Since patients in the last group have significant spontaneous resumption of normal menses, this pattern may represent a transition. Hyperprolactinemia is also associated with abnormal patterns of pulsatile gonadotropin secretion; bromocryptine therapy caused an increase in LH pulse frequency and a decrease in pulse amplitude in 4 of 5 patients with hyperprolactinemia [41].

CNS opioids appear to play an inhibitory role and catecholamines a stimulatory role on GnRH secretion. Clomiphene appears to be active in promoting fertility by increasing the frequency of LH pulses; the better response to this drug by women with higher estradiol levels can be explained by its ability to increase GnRH pulse frequency in patients with less impairment of GnRH secretion [39]. The ability to deliver pulses of GnRH at physiologic doses of amplitude and frequency has enhanced the ability to induce ovulation and normal female and male sexual maturation in hypogonadal patients [42, 43].

CLINICAL APPLICATIONS
An understanding of the normal cycle is useful in clinical management of patients with menstrual problems. In patients with anovulatory cycles, the endometrium remains in the proliferative stage; menstrual periods may be heavy and irregular. Dramatic relief can often be obtained with medroxyprogesterone (Provera) given 10 to 14 (preferably 12 to 14) days each month to produce a secretory endometrium; 3 to 7 days after the medroxyprogesterone, the patient then has a normal period. In the evaluation of the patient with amenorrhea, a withdrawal flow after intramuscular progesterone or oral medroxyprogesterone implies that the endometrium has been adequately primed with estrogen (see Chap. 6).

Quantitation of serum FSH and LH by radioimmunoassay is readily available, but laboratories vary both in normal values and in units per milliliter (mIU/ml or ng/ml). Because gonadotropins are released in pulses, a single random serum value of LH and FSH may not be helpful to distinguish between low and normal levels of these hormones although future use of sensitive immunofluorometric assays look promising. In Figure 4-12, the variability of values in normal cycles is evident. Levels of 5 to 25 mIU/ml are in the normal range; consistently low values of 2 to 4 mIU/ml may imply hypothalamic or pituitary hypofunction. An FSH level greater than 50 to 60 mIU/ml and an LH level greater than 40 mIU/ml in a prepubertal or poorly estrogenized female imply ovarian failure; such high levels are also found in the postmenopausal woman. Timed urinary collections for assay of FSH and LH may also be helpful to assess patients who have extremely low levels of serum FSH and LH [44]. In addition, an elevated serum LH (in excess of 30 mIU/ml) with a normal FSH in an amenorrheic or oligomenorrheic adolescent may suggest polycystic ovary syndrome (see Chap. 7). Gonadotropin levels and serum androgen levels should be measured in the oligomenorrheic patient who has hirsutism, acne, or signs of virilization. It is always important to know when the levels of FSH and LH were drawn in relation to the menstrual cycle, if any. The last menstrual period should be recorded at the time of the office visit and the patient should be instructed to keep a calendar and call with the date of the next menses. If no menses have occurred by 4 weeks after the visit, the clinician should record this fact to aid in the interpretation of the levels.

Frequent sampling of the serum for LH and FSH levels over a 24-hour period or over a menstrual cycle has been very useful in research settings for investigating normal and abnormal physiology. Clinically, pituitary function can also be studied by the administration of GnRH. A single dose of GnRH is given intravenously or subcutaneously, and serum LH and FSH levels are measured at frequent intervals over a 4-hour period. LH values should increase 150 percent *above* baseline in normal pubertal patients (see Fig. 4-14 for variations with menarcheal age). Girls with isosexual central precocious puberty will respond with a pubertal LH and FSH response, whereas those with premature thelarche or puberty secondary to an ovarian tumor respond with a prepubertal response. Patients with anorexia nervosa and craniopharyngiomas usually have little response to GnRH, whereas those with prolactin-secreting pituitary microadenomas have a normal pubertal response. Patients with Kallmann's syndrome (hypogonadotropic hypogonadism) have heterogeneous responses to GnRH; some may have minimal response to the single dose of GnRH and require longer administration of pulsatile GnRH to cause normal release of LH and FSH. Even patients with anorexia nervosa and amenorrhea can be stimulated to secrete LH and FSH and to ovulate with long-term pulsatile GnRH [45]. As previously mentioned, administration of physiologic pulses of GnRH can be used clinically in the induction of ovulation in infertile women with normal ovarian function and in the stimulation of normal pubertal maturation in men.

The observation [46–48] that pulsatile GnRH results in secretion of LH and FSH but that the continuous infusion of GnRH results in the suppression of LH and FSH has led to new treatment modalities for precocious puberty in children. The use of long-acting GnRH analogues offers the possibility of reversing the pubertal activation of gonadotropins and sex steroids. GnRH analogues are also potentially useful for contraception and for chemical castration therapy for malignancies, endometriosis, polycystic ovary syndrome, and severe premenstrual syndrome.

Measurement of serum estrogen, progesterone, and androgen levels are now possible in many laboratories, although variable quality control and normal levels makes interpretation, especially of androgen levels, problematic at times. In addition, the fact that most of these levels vary during the day and during the menstrual cycle must be kept in mind when drawing conclusions from these levels. For example, girls in the early stages of puberty may have low daytime FSH and LH levels and undetectable or very low estradiol levels in spite of normal maturation. As noted, progesterone is secreted in pulses, and thus a single level cannot assess the adequacy of the luteal phase in infertility patients. The importance of the physical examination should not be underestimated despite the ability to measure many hormone levels. The response of the target organs to these hormones is essential to a correct diagnosis. Pubertal breast development, a pink moist vaginal mucosa, and watery cervical mucus are all signs that suggest functional ovaries and the secretion of estrogen. The physician could infer from the presence of normal axillary and pubic hair functioning adrenal glands and circulating androgens. Hirsutism and clitoromegaly are signs of androgen excess; a patient with these findings will require an evaluation of her hormone status. The assessment of many gynecologic problems depends on a careful physical examination (see Chap. 1) combined with a thorough understanding of normal pubertal development. Primary and secondary amenorrhea, menorrhagia, and virilization can then be evaluated in terms of the hypothalamic-pituitary-ovarian-adrenal axis.

REFERENCES
1. Lee PA. Neuroendocrinology of puberty. Semin Reprod Endocrinol 1988; 6:13–20.
2. Moscicki A-B, and Shafer MA. Normal reproductive development in the adolescent female. J Adolesc Health Care 1986; 7:41S.
3. Conte FA, Grumbach MM, Kaplan SL, et al. Correlation of luteinizing hormone–releasing factor–induced luteinizing hormone and follicle-stimulating hormone release from infancy to 19 years with the changing pattern of gonadotropin secretion in agonadal patients: Relation to the restraint of puberty. J Clin Endocrinol Metab 1980; 50:163.
4. Apter D, Pakarinen A, Hammond GL, et al. Adrenocortical function in puberty. Acta Paediatr Scand 1979; 68:599.
5. Styne DM, and Grumbach MM. Puberty in the male and female: Its physiology and disorders. In SSC Yen and RB Jaffe, Reproductive Endocrinology. Philadelphia: Saunders, 1986.
6. Lucky AW, Rich BH, Rosenfield RL, et al. LH bioactivity increases more than immunoreactivity during puberty. J Pediatr 1980; 97:205.
7. Sklar CA, Kaplan SL, and Grumbach MM. Evidence for dissociation between adrenarche and gonadarche: studies in patients with idiopathic precocious puberty, gonadal dysgenesis, isolated gonadotropin deficiency, and constitutionally delayed growth and adolescence. J Clin Endocrinol Metab 1980; 51:548.
8. Reiter EO. Neuroendocrine control processes. J Adolesc Health Care 1987; 8:479.
9. Boyar RM, Wu RH, Roffwarg H, et al. Human puberty: 24-hour estradiol patterns in pubertal girls. J Clin Endocrinol Metab 1976; 43:1418.
10. Rosenfield RL, and Frulanetto R. Physiologic testosterone in estradiol

induction of puberty increases plasma somatomedin-C. J Pediatr 1985; 107:415.

11. Moll GW, Rosenfield RL, and Fang VS. Administration of low-dose estrogen rapidly and directly stimulates growth hormone production. Am J Dis Child 1986; 140:124.
12. Zachmann M, Prader A, Sobel EH, et al. Pubertal growth in patients with androgen insensitivity: indirect evidence for the importance of estrogens in pubertal growth of girls. J Pediatr 1986; 108:694.
13. Marshall WA, and Tanner JM. Variations in pattern of pubertal changes in girls. Arch Dis Child 1969; 44:291.
14. Ross G, and Vande Wiele R. The ovaries. In R Williams (ed.), *Textbook of Endocrinology* (6th ed.). Philadelphia: Saunders, 1981.
15. Harlan WR, Harlan EA, and Grillo GP. Secondary sex characteristics of girls 12 to 17 years of age: The U.S. Health Examination Survey. J Pediatr 1980; 96:1074.
16. Nottelmann ED, Susan EJ, Dorn LD, et al. Developmental processes in early adolescence: relations among chronologic age, pubertal stage, height, weight, and serum levels of gonadotropins, sex steroids, and adrenal androgens. J Adolesc Health Care 1987; 8:246.
17. Bayley N. Growth curves of height and weight by age for boys and girls, scaled according to physical maturity. J Pediatr 1956; 48:187.
18. Frisch RE. A method of prediction of age and menarche from height and weight at ages nine through thirteen years. Pediatrics 1974; 53:384.
19. Warren MP. The effects of exercise on pubertal progression and reproductive function in girls. J Clin Endocrinol Metab 1980; 51:1150.
20. Frisch RE, Gotz-Welbergen AV, and McArthur JW. Delayed menarche and amenorrhea of college athletes in relation to age of onset of training. JAMA 1981; 246:1559.
21. Zacharias L, and Wurtman R. Age at menarche: Genetic and environmental influences. N Engl J Med 1969; 280:868.
22. MacMahon B. *National Health Examination Survey: Age at Menarche.* DHEW Publication 74-1615, Series 11, No. 133, November 1973.
23. Frisch RE, and McArthur JW. Menstrual cycles: Fatness as a determinant of minimum weight necessary for their maintenance or onset. Science 1974; 185:949.
24. Wyshak G, and Frisch RE. Evidence for a secular trend in age of menarche. N Engl J Med 1982; 306:1033.
25. Frisch RE, Wyshak G, and Vincent L. Delayed menarche and amenorrhea in ballet dancers. N Engl J Med 1980; 303:17.
26. Zacharias L, Wurtman RJ, and Schatzoff M. Sexual maturation in contemporary American girls. Am J Obstet Gynecol 1970; 108:833.
27. Apter D, and Vihko R. Serum pregnenolone, progesterone, 17-hydroxyprogesterone, testosterone, and 5 α-dihydrotestosterone during female puberty. J Clin Endocrinol Metab 1977; 45:1039.
28. Tsonis CG, Messinis IE, Templeton AA, et al. Gonadotropic stimulation of inhibin secretion by the human ovary during the follicular and early luteal phase of the cycle. J Clin Endocrinol Metab 1988; 66:915.
29. Filicori M, Santoro N, Merriam GR, et al. Characterization of the physiological pattern of episodic gonadotropin secretion throughout the human menstrual cycle. J Clin Endocrinol Metab 1986; 62:1136.
30. Filicori M, Butler JP, and Crowley WF. Neuroendocrine regulation of the corpus luteum in the human: Evidence for pulsatile progesterone secretion. J Clin Invest 1984; 73:1638.
31. Apter D, Raisanen I, Ylostalo P, et al. Follicular growth in relation to

serum hormonal patterns in adolescent compared with adult menstrual cycles. Fertil Steril 1987; 47:82.

32. Apter D. Serum steroids and pituitary hormones in female puberty: A partly longitudinal study. Clin Endocrinol 1980; 12:107.

33. Apter D, Viinikka L, and Vihko R. Hormonal pattern of adolescent menstrual cycles. J Clin Endocrinol Metab 1978; 47:944.

34. Bonen A, Belcastro AN, Ling WY, et al. Profiles of selected hormones during menstrual cycles of teenage athletes. J Appl Physiol 1981; 50:545.

35. Shangold M, Freeman R, Thysen B, et al. The relationship between long distance running, plasma progesterone and luteal phase length. Fertil Steril 1979; 31:130.

36. LeMarchand-Berand T, Zafferey M-M, Reymond M, et al. Maturation of the hypothalamic-pituitary-ovarian axis in adolescent girls. J Clin Endocrinol Metab 1982; 54:241.

37. Venturoli S, Porcu E, Fabbri R, et al. Postmenarchal evolution of endocrine pattern and ovarian aspects of adolescents with menstrual irregularities. Fertil Steril 1987; 48:78.

38. Venturoli S, Porcu E, Gammi L, et al. Different gonadotropin pulsatile fashions in anovulatory cycles of young girls indicate different maturational pathways in adolescence. J Clin Endocrinol Metab 1987; 65:785.

39. Marshall JC, and Kelch RP. Gonadotropin-releasing hormone: role of pulsatile secretion in the regulation of reproduction. Seminars in Medicine of the Beth Israel Hospital, Boston. N Engl J Med 1986; 315:1459–1468.

40. Santaro N, Filicori M, and Crowley W Jr. Hypogonadotropin disorders in men and women: Diagnosis and therapy with pulsatile gonadotropin-releasing hormone. Endocr Rev 1986; 7:11.

41. Sauder SE, Frager M, Case GD, et al. Abnormal patterns of pulsatile luteinizing hormone secretion in women with hyperprolactinemia and amenorrhea: Responses to bromocriptine. J Clin Endocrinol Metab 1984; 59:941.

42. Hurley DM, Brian R, Outch K, et al. Induction of ovulation and fertility in amenorrheic women by pulsatile low-dose gonadotropin-releasing hormone. N Engl J Med 1984; 310:1069.

43. Hoffman AR, and Crowley WF Jr. Induction of puberty in men by long-term pulsatile administration of low-dose gonadotropin-releasing hormone. N Engl J Med 1982; 307:1237.

44. Kulin HE, and Santner SJ. Timed urinary gonadotropin measurements in normal infants, children and adults and in patients with disorders of sexual maturation. J Pediatr 1977; 90:760.

45. Nillius SJ, and Wide L. Gonadotropin-releasing hormone treatment for induction of follicular maturation and ovulation in amenorrheic women with anorexia nervosa. Br Med J 1975; 3:405.

46. Knobil E, Plant TM, Wildt L, et al. Control of the rhesus monkey menstrual cycle: Permissive role hypothalamic gonadotropin-releasing hormone. Science 1980; 207:1371.

47. Belchetz PE, Plant TM, Nakai Y, et al. Hypophyseal responses to continuous and intermittent delivery of hypothalamic gonadotropin-releasing hormone. Science 1978; 202:631.

48. Crowley WF Jr, Comite F, Vale W, et al. Therapeutic use of pituitary desensitization with a long-acting LHRH agonist: a potential new treatment for idiopathic precocious puberty. J Clin Endocrinol Metab 1981; 52:370.

5. Precocious Puberty

A thorough understanding of the normal progression of puberty (see Chap. 4) is essential in the evaluation of precocious puberty, premature thelarche, and premature adrenarche. It should be recalled that in normal adolescence, estrogen is responsible for breast development, for maturation of the external genitalia, vagina, and uterus, and initiation of the menses. An increase in adrenal androgens is associated with the appearance of pubic and axillary hair. Excess androgens of either ovarian or adrenal origin may cause acne, hirsutism, voice changes, increased muscle mass, and clitoromegaly. Thus, precocious puberty in females can be divided into two categories: isosexual precocity, in which the patient has normal pubertal development; and heterosexual precocity, in which the patient has evidence of virilization with or without changes characteristic of a normal puberty.

Premature thelarche is defined as the appearance of breast development in the absence of other signs of puberty or growth acceleration. Premature pubarche is the appearance of pubic (or axillary, or both) hair without signs of estrogenization and is usually associated with increased secretion of adrenal androgens (adrenarche). Although usually self-limited, isolated breast budding or pubic hair development may be the first sign of a true precocious puberty. Because most cases of true precocity require fairly sophisticated endocrine studies, referral to an endocrinologist is often necessary. However, the primary care physician can usually initiate the investigation of precocious puberty and can diagnose and follow cases of premature thelarche and adrenarche.

ISOSEXUAL PRECOCIOUS PUBERTY
Over the past century, the age of onset of pubertal development and menarche has steadily declined in the United States, perhaps in part because of improved nutrition. Currently, sexual development in girls before 8 years of age is defined as "precocious." Isosexual precocious puberty can be divided into two categories on the basis of etiology: true isosexual precocity and isosexual pseudoprecocity.

In true isosexual precocity, the stimulus for development arises in the hypothalamus and pituitary gland. In response to rising pituitary gonadotropin levels, the ovarian follicles produce estrogen. The young girl has a growth spurt and develops breasts and may begin menstruation. With the establishment of the cyclic midcycle luteinizing hormone (LH) peak, the child becomes potentially fertile.

In the majority of patients with isosexual precocious puberty, the hypothalamic-pituitary axis is activated prematurely for unknown reasons. In some series, a number of patients with idiopathic precocious puberty have abnormal electroencephalograms (EEGs), suggesting that a neuroendocrine dysfunction may contribute to precocious puberty [1]. Newer methods of imaging the central nervous system (CNS), including computed tomography (CT) and magnetic resonance imaging (MRI), have also identified small CNS abnormalities, such as hypothalamic hamartomas in boys and girls with the onset of sexual precocity before age 3 years [2–4]. In isosexual pseudoprecocity, an ovarian tumor or cyst or rarely an adrenal adenoma may produce estrogen autonomously.

Although the etiology of most cases of precocious puberty in girls is constitutional or idiopathic, the differential diagnosis includes many organic disorders that need to be considered in the evaluation of the girl with early isosexual development [5–10].

TRUE ISOSEXUAL DEVELOPMENT
1. Idiopathic.
2. Cerebral disorders (5–20%): brain tumor (e.g., glioma, hamartoma); neurofibromatosis (optic nerve glioma or hypothalamic glioma); tuberous sclerosis; suprasellar cyst; sarcoid granuloma; hydrocephalus; postinfectious (meningitis, encephalitis, brain abscess); post-traumatic; post–cranial radiation for leukemia or other tumors [11].
3. Congenital adrenal hyperplasia (CAH): Patients with undertreated or late-treated CAH may have early puberty; patients who have been treated for CAH or virilizing tumors may have the onset of precocious puberty following lowering of androgen levels if the skeletal age has reached 11 to 13 years [12].
4. Primary hypothyroidism: Premature breast development usually regresses following thyroid hormone replacement. Absence of a statural growth spurt accompanying breast development may be a clue to hypothyroidism as a cause of premature development.

PSEUDOPRECOCIOUS PUBERTY
1. Ovarian tumors (2–5%): Approximately 60 percent of ovarian tumors that cause sexual precocity are granulosa cell tumors; the remainder are arrhenoblastomas, lipid cell tumors, thecomas, and cysts. Ovarian tumors can secrete estrogens and androgens, thus resulting in both breast and public hair development. Girls with Peutz-Jehgers syndrome have an increased risk of ovarian tumors.
2. Adrenal disorders (rare): Adrenal adenomas may secrete estrogen alone and cause sexual precocity. Adrenal carcinomas that secrete estrogen also produce other hormones that cause heterosexual precocity. Patients with untreated CAH may have virilization as well as some breast development.

3. Gonadotropin-independent sexual precocity occurs in McCune-Albright syndrome. Girls with the McCune-Albright syndrome (polyostotic fibrous dysplasia, café au lait spots) have recurrent ovarian cysts [13, 14]. Ovarian volumes by ultrasonography are often asymmetric and fluctuate in size over time in these girls [15]. Although the mechanism of gonadotropin independence in McCune-Albright syndrome is unknown, the presence of somatic problems as well as endocrine abnormalities implies that the disorder results from a defect in cellular regulation, possibly altered control of intracellular cyclic adenosine monophosphate effects [16]. The fluctuating estrogen levels produced by cysts result in sexual development and anovulatory menses.
4. Gonadotropin-producing tumors (rare): Tumors that secrete both LH-like substances (e.g., human chorionic gonadotropin [HCG]) and estrogen (primary ovarian choriocarcinoma) can cause precocious development. The production of LH alone will cause isosexual precocity in boys but not in girls.
5. Iatrogenic disorders (rare): For example, the use of estrogen-containing creams and medications.

PATIENT ASSESSMENT
The initial assessment of the patient with precocious development should include a careful history and physical examination. It is particularly important to look for a history of birth trauma, encephalitis, personality change, seizures, headaches, visual symptoms, abdominal pain, increased appetite, urinary or bowel changes, or use of medications and creams. The age of onset of precocious development is often not helpful in the differential diagnosis except for cases of hamartomas, which may cause pubertal development at birth or shortly thereafter. Hamartomas may cause precocious puberty directly by secretion of gonadotropin releasing hormone (GnRH) [4], unlike other CNS tumors that cause sexual precocity by destructive effects on regions of the brain that normally suppress gonadotropin secretion.

The age of menarche of sisters, mother, and grandmothers should be recorded; and a family history of neurofibromatosis or tuberous sclerosis should be noted. Vaginal bleeding may be the first sign of precocity in the McCune-Albright syndrome, but this pattern has been noted in idiopathic cases as well. Irregular bleeding occurs in patients with both true precocity and pseudoprecocity. Growth charts should be brought up to date, since the growth spurt often correlates with the onset of development in precocious puberty. The finding of accelerated growth and bone age is important in distinguishing between premature thelarche and true precocity. The photograph and growth charts of an untreated patient with idiopathic precocious puberty are shown in Figure 5-1.

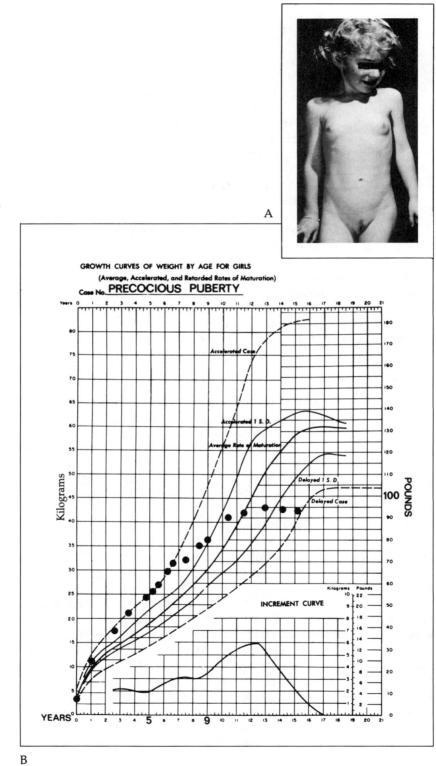

A

GROWTH CURVES OF WEIGHT BY AGE FOR GIRLS
(Average, Accelerated, and Retarded Rates of Maturation)

Case No. PRECOCIOUS PUBERTY

B

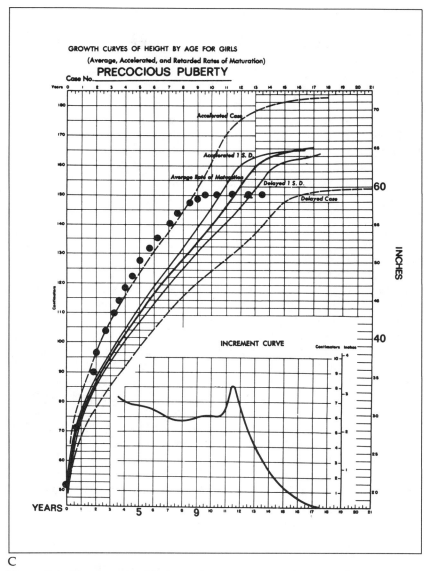

C

Figure 5-1. Photograph of B.S. aged 3⁶/₁₂ years. She was first seen at the clinic because of early development at the age of 3²/₁₂ years. B.S.'s menarche occurred at 5⁶/₁₂ years of age; she attained adult height at 10 years of age. Diagnosis was idiopathic precocious puberty. A. Photograph. B. Weight chart. C. Height chart.

The physical examination should include a careful neurologic assessment, visualization of the optic discs for evidence of papilledema, evaluation of visual fields by confrontation, measurement of the head circumference, and inspection of the skin for café au lait spots. In patients with neurofibromatosis, café au lait spots may be multiple brown macules with smooth edges; whereas in McCune-Albright syndrome, one or more large macules with irregular borders may be found. The thyroid should be palpated and any clinical signs of hypothyroidism (hair and skin changes, low pulse) noted. It is extremely important to note the degree of breast development, pubic and axillary hair growth, and the appearance of the vaginal mucosa. Signs of virilization, clitoromegaly, or voice changes should alert the examiner to the possibility of heterosexual precocity (see p. 137). If the child is approached in a relaxed manner, it is often possible to carry out a thorough bimanual rectal-abdominal examination. Ovarian masses, when present, are usually easily palpated. Ultrasonography of the abdomen is usually done to look for ovarian masses. Girls with true precocity frequently have mildly enlarged ovaries with multiple small follicular cysts similar to the ovaries seen in the adolescent with a normal age of puberty. A single ovarian cyst often occurs in McCune-Albright syndrome.

The laboratory evaluation of the child depends on the initial clinical assessment. If the examination shows clear-cut estrogen effect on the vaginal mucosa and growth charts reveal an acceleration of linear growth, then more extensive testing is needed. If, on the other hand, the clinician suspects premature thelarche, the initial tests would include an x-ray film of the wrist for bone age and a vaginal smear for estrogen effect. Careful growth measurements are recorded, and dimensions and staging of breast development are recorded. If the vagina shows little estrogen effect, and growth rate and bone age are normal, the patient can be followed by her primary care physician at 3-month intervals to observe whether sexual development progresses or acceleration of linear growth occurs. Rarely, a child will have one or several transient episodes of precocious puberty that resolve without therapy.

If the girl has progressive sexual development, advancing bone age, acceleration of growth, or vaginal estrogenization, consultation with a pediatric endocrinologist is important. Tests include serum levels of luteinizing hormone (LH), follicle-stimulating hormone (FSH), estradiol, dehydroepiandrosterone sulfate (DHAS), and thyroid hormones (including TSH), and CT or MRI of the CNS. The vaginal smear for estrogen effect and the ultrasound may be repeated, depending on initial results. Skeletal survey is helpful in patients with suspected McCune-Albright syndrome. In patients with androgen effect, serum androgens and early-morning 17-

hydroxyprogesterone (to look for 21-hydroxylase deficiency) tests are indicated. The GnRH test (see Chap. 4) can help in the differential diagnosis of premature thelarche, gonadotropin-independent precocity, and true precocity.

The bone age will always become significantly greater than the height age in patients with precocious puberty. Although a girl may appear tall at the initial evaluation, she may eventually have a short final height because of premature epiphyseal closure. Approximately 50 percent of patients with precocious puberty have a final height of less than 5 feet. The younger the patient is at the onset of puberty, the shorter she is likely to be. A retarded bone age and short stature suggest the rare diagnosis of hypothyroidism with precocious puberty.

Since LH and FSH secretion is sleep-associated in early puberty, the random daytime serum LH and FSH values may not be helpful in differentiating among premature thelarche, pseudoprecocity, and idiopathic or CNS causes of true precocity. Low daytime levels of gonadotropin are often found in the early stages of true precocity, although Lucky and co-workers [17] have found that bioactive LH is higher in girls with true precocity than in those with premature thelarche. Timed urine collections for FSH and LH levels have been used by Kulin and Santner [18] to help differentiate between premature thelarche and precocious puberty. The finding of a high estradiol level (100–200 pg/ml) and low gonadotropin levels should, however, raise the possibility of an estrogen-secreting tumor or cyst, although this diagnosis should be apparent on ultrasound (see Chap. 13). Likewise, elevated serum levels of LH are suggestive of a gonadotropin-producing tumor or choriocarcinoma; the latter produces HCG, which cross-reacts with LH on the standard assay. An elevated HCG would be detected by a serum or urine pregnancy test. However, unless the tumor also secretes estrogen, elevated LH alone will not produce isosexual precocity. Heterosexual precocity has been reported in a family with isolated elevation of LH [19].

Patients with true precocity exhibit nocturnal pulses of LH and FSH and a pubertal response to the GnRH test, whereas girls with gonadotropin-independent precocity, premature thelarche, or ovarian tumors have a prepubertal response to GnRH. This test is especially useful in following the response of the girl to GnRH analogue therapy to ensure complete suppression of puberty.

The level of DHAS is a marker of adrenal androgen production (Fig. 5-2). Most girls with precocious puberty have age-appropriate DHAS, although a few have premature adrenarche as well. Patients with precocity between 6 and 8 years of age have a mean DHAS similar to normal children with the same bone age [20].

A vaginal smear or urocytogram confirms estrogenization (see

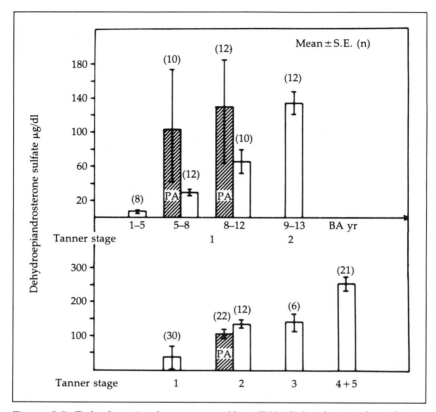

Figure 5-2. Dehydroepiandrosterone sulfate (DHAS) levels in girls with precocious adrenarche (PA) compared to normal girls of various bone ages (BA), and stages of pubic hair development (Tanner 1–4/5). DHAS levels are appropriate for the Tanner stage of pubic hair but are elevated for the bone age. S. E. = standard error; n = number. (From S Korth-Schutz, LS Levine, and MI New, Dehydroepiandrosterone sulfate (DS) levels, a rapid test for abnormal adrenal androgen secretion. J Clin Endocrinol Metab 42:1005, 1976. By permission.)

p. 29) and is useful both in confirming clinical impression and following therapy. A typical smear in a patient with precocious puberty might show 35 percent superficial, 50 percent intermediate, and 15 percent parabasal cells. The findings of estrogen excess (greater than 40% superficial cells) should raise the suspicion of an estrogen-secreting granulosa cell tumor. A high percentage of intermediate cells (95–100%) can be seen in the luteal phase (secretory phase) of the normal ovulatory cycle and with progesterone-secreting thecomas. Clearly, the date of the last menstrual period must be known to evaluate a vaginal smear. Serum estradiol and progesterone levels can aid in the interpretation of vaginal smears. Estradiol levels are elevated in approximately one third of patients with granulosa cell tumors. Serum progesterone and urinary pregnanediol are increased in the luteal phase of isosexual precocity and with ovarian thecomas.

TREATMENT AND FOLLOW-UP
Treatment and follow-up depend on the diagnosis. Ovarian tumors should be surgically removed. Successful treatment of a tumor can be monitored by demonstrating decreasing estrogenization on vaginal smear, cessation of menses, and declining serum or urine estrogen levels. Ovarian cysts that are pure fluid-filled on ultrasound may undergo spontaneous resolution, although some large cysts may require aspiration and, if recurrent, cystectomy (see Chap. 13). Treatment of an ovarian cyst will not result in regression of puberty in girls with true precocity or McCune-Albright syndrome, and thus caution should be exercised not to remove normal follicular cysts accompanying true precocity. The ovarian cysts associated with central precocity should be observed because they will likely regress with suppression of gonadotropins. Hypothalamic tumors and choriocarcinomas are rarely treated successfully by surgery.

Although Depo-Provera and cyproterone acetate have been used in the past to treat precocious puberty, Crowley and co-workers [21] and Comite and associates [22] have pioneered work in Boston and at the National Institutes of Health (NIH) in the use of GnRH agonists to suppress precocious puberty. In girls with central precocity, the advantages of the use of a GnRH agonist are the selective and reversible suppression of LH and FSH, the return of estradiol to the prepubertal range, and the regression (or lack of progression) of breast development and the cessation of menses [7, 10, 21–24]. The pattern of gonadotropin secretion and the response to GnRH is shown before, during, and after GnRH analogue therapy in Figure 5-3. In nine girls treated with GnRH analogue, estradiol fell to less than 20 pg/ml, and maturation index score of the vaginal cytology and the response to GnRH markedly decreased over 18 months (Figure 5-4). Growth velocity and the rate of skeletal maturation decreased. Since bone age advancement is slowed more than height age, predicted adult height increased by this therapy [10, 25] (Figures 5-5, 5-6, and 5-7). Therapy with GnRH analogues is expensive and has required daily injections, since nasal analogues give less complete suppression. Depo forms of GnRH analogues that can be given once a month are promising.

GnRH agonists are also effective in suppressing puberty in girls with precocity secondary to hypothalamic hamartomas and optic nerve gliomas associated with neurofibromatosis [10, 26]. The selective suppression of gonadarche without an effect on adrenarche has allowed important studies on the contribution of adrenal sex steriods and growth hormone in pubertal growth [27]. During treatment with

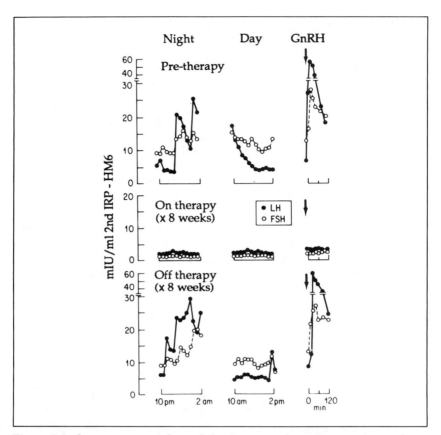

Figure 5-3. Spontaneous night and daytime gonadotropin secretion and response to exogenous GnRH administration in a 2-year-old girl with central precocious puberty before, during, and after discontinuation of GnRH analogue therapy. (From WF Crowley, F Comite, W Vale, et al., Therapeutic use for pituitary desensitization with a long-acting LHRH agonist: A potential new treatment for idiopathic precocious puberty. J Clin Endocrinol Metab 1981;52:370. By permission.)

the analogue, normal age-appropriate progression of adrenarche as determined by measurement of DHAS occurred. Although growth velocity during analogue therapy did not correlate with DHAS levels, there was a relationship between DHAS levels and skeletal maturation. In one study, those with the highest levels of DHAS had the smallest increases in predicted height with analogue therapy [10]. Somatomedin-C levels and nocturnal growth hormone secretion decreased during analogue therapy, suggesting that sex steroids augment growth hormone secretion during puberty.

Important insights have also been gained on behavioral changes associated with gonadarche. Children with sexual precocity do not

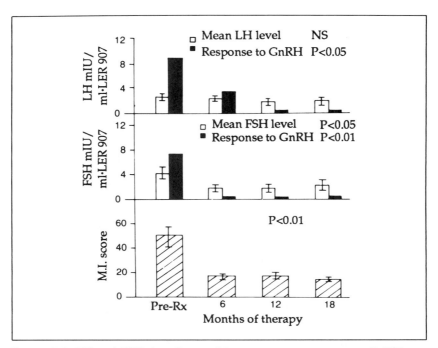

Figure 5-4. LH and FSH, baseline and in response to exogenous GnRH, and maturation index (M.I.) score of vaginal cytology in nine girls with central precocious puberty before and during chronic therapy with GnRH analogue. (From MJ Mansfield, DE Beardsworth, J Loughlin, et al., Long-term treatment of central precocious puberty with a long-acting analogue of luteinizing hormone-releasing hormone. N Engl J Med 1983;309:1286. Reprinted with permission from *The New England Journal of Medicine.*)

automatically manifest intellectual or psychosocial maturity even though parents may have abnormal expectations and fears. The degree of psychological maturity of a young girl is more likely to be related to the life experiences she encounters and transacts, her peer group, parent-child interaction, and sibling relationships. Nevertheless, parents and investigators have noted that girls with sexual precocity often have mood swings, impulsivity, and aggressiveness and return to more age-appropriate behavior with the institution of GnRH agonist therapy [28]. Of utmost importance is the need to tell the young girl that her development is "early," not abnormal and that she will receive medicine to delay her development to a later age. Psychological consultation for the family may be indicated to help them through this major stress.

In girls with McCune-Albright syndrome with gonadotropin-independent puberty and cyclic gonadal steroid production, GnRH agonist therapy does not cause a decrease in estradiol or regression

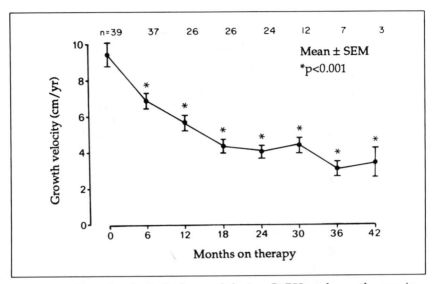

Figure 5-5. Growth velocity before and during GnRH analogue therapy in 32 girls and 7 boys treated between 6 and 42 months. (From PA Boepple, MJ Mansfield, ME Wierman, et al., Use of a potent, long-acting agonist of gonadotropin-releasing hormone in the treatment of precocious puberty. Endocr Rev 1986;7:24. By permission.)

of pubertal changes [29]. Feuillan and colleagues [14] reported success with testolactone, an aromatase inhibitor that blocks the synthesis of estrogens, in 5 girls with McCune-Albright syndrome. Ketoconazole and combination spironolactone and testolactone are experimental treatments being studied in boys with gonadotropin-independent precocity [30, 31].

Follow-up depends on the diagnosis and the treatment undertaken. Girls being treated with GnRH analogue therapy need frequent assessment of compliance with medication, bone age, vaginal cytology for maturation index, growth records, and physical examinations, as incomplete suppression of estrogen by GnRH might actually result in a further decrease in final height. Ultrasound can follow regression of uterine size. The growth chart of a patient treated with analogue is shown in Figure 5-8. The possibility of an initially occult CNS lesion or other diagnosis such as neurofibromatosis needs to be kept in mind during the observation period.

In many patients, particularly those whose puberty begins after age 6 years, whose height prognosis without intervention is good, reassurance and careful follow-up and possibly counseling may be all the intervention that is necessary. Depo-Provera may be used to stop menses when complete suppression of puberty is not required.

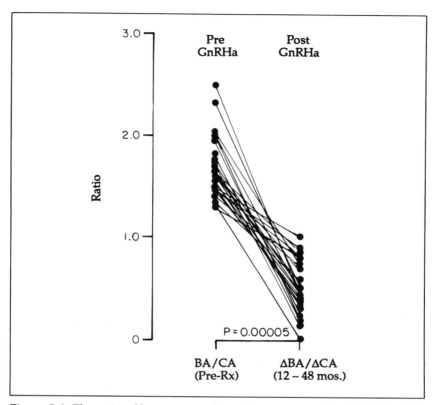

Figure 5-6. The ratio of bone age to chronologic age (*BA/CA*) at the institution of GnRH analogue therapy as compared with the ratio of their change (△*BA*/△*CA*) during GnRH analogue therapy (minimum 12 months) in 26 patients with central precocious puberty. (From PA Boepple, MJ Mansfield, ME Wierman, et al., Use of a potent long-acting agonist of gonadotropin-releasing hormone in the treatment of precocious puberty. Endocr Rev 1986;7:24. By permission.)

HETEROSEXUAL PRECOCIOUS PUBERTY

Heterosexual precocity arises from excess androgen production from an adrenal or ovarian source, which results in acne, hirsutism, and virilization. The differential diagnosis includes (1) congenital adrenocortical hyperplasia (CAH), (2) Cushing's syndrome, (3) adrenal tumors, (4) ovarian tumors such as lipid cell and Sertoli cell tumors, and (5) in one report, familial precocious puberty with isolated elevation of LH [19].

PATIENT ASSESSMENT

The patient should be given a careful physical examination, with emphasis on noting evidence of hirsutism, acne, or clitoral enlarge-

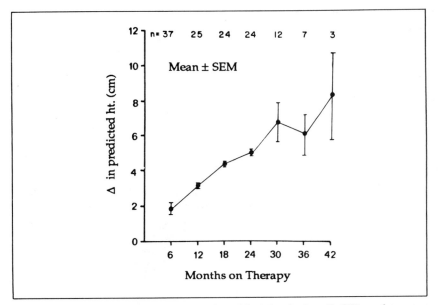

Figure 5-7. The mean change in predicted height during GnRH analogue therapy of central precocious puberty in the patients whose patterns are shown in Figures 5-5 and 5-6. (From PA Boepple, MJ Mansfield, ME Wierman, et al., Use of a potent long-acting agonist of gonadotropin-releasing hormone in the treatment of precocious puberty. Endocr Rev 1986;7:24. By permission.)

ment, and an adequate abdominal and bimanual rectal examination to exclude an ovarian mass. Ovarian tumors are usually palpable.

Laboratory tests include serum levels of LH, FSH, estradiol, de-hydroepiandrosterone (DHA), DHA sulfate (DHAS), 17-hydroxy-progesterone, testosterone, and androstenedione (see Fig. 2-4 for pathways of steroid biosynthesis). A 24-hour urine collection may be assayed for 17-ketosteroids, pregnanetriol, and, if Cushing's syndrome is under consideration, free cortisol level. The baseline 17-hydroxyprogesterone is best drawn between 7 and 8 A.M., since with the diurnal variation of adrenal hormones a normal level may be found in the afternoon in patients with mild deficiencies of 21-hydroxylase. In girls with suspected CAH, a 1-hour adrenocorticotropic hormone (ACTH) test (see Chap. 7) is useful in detecting a block in the adrenal pathways. Quantitation of 17-ketosteroids in a 24-hour urine and serum testosterone level may give a clue to the presence of an adrenal or ovarian source of the excess androgens. Urinary 17-ketosteroids are usually increased with adrenal tumors and CAH, whereas normal urinary 17-ketosteroids and elevated serum testosterone suggest an ovarian tumor. However, some

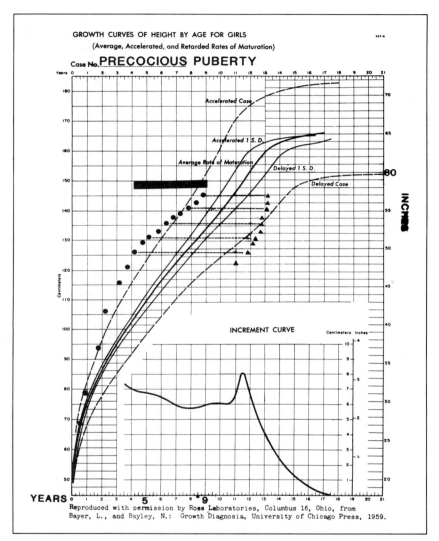

Figure 5-8. Growth chart of a girl with true isosexual precocious puberty. Her onset of breast development occurred at 10 months and her menarche at 1¹⁄₁₂ years. Note the acceleration of growth velocity and bone age. The patient was begun on GnRH analogue (*bar*) at 4²⁄₁₂ years and growth decelerated. Bone age, which is shown with ▲ on the horizontal line to the right of the height measurement, was significantly advanced at the onset of therapy (just under 12 years) but advanced only minimally over the next 4½ years (slightly over 13 years). (Growth chart courtesy of Dr. MJ Mansfield.)

ovarian tumors such as lipid cell tumors, and rare Sertoli-Leydig cell tumors with enzyme activity resembling adrenocortical cells, gonadoblastomas, and adrenocortical rest cells (under increased ACTH stimulation from Cushing's syndrome or CAH) may be accompanied by elevated urinary 17-ketosteroids [32]. Adrenal tumors are usually associated with elevated serum DHA, DHAS, and androstenedione and elevated urinary 17-ketosteroids, not suppressible by dexamethasone. Serum testosterone may be elevated because of direct secretion by the tumor or because of peripheral conversion. Cushing's syndrome should be accompanied by signs of excess cortisol production and poor linear growth. Thus the differential diagnosis is made by careful hormone studies with ACTH testing in cases of suspected CAH, abdominal and bimanual rectoabdominal palpation, ultrasonography, CT or MRI scanning for visualizing adrenals, and laparotomy for tumors.

TREATMENT AND FOLLOW-UP
Ovarian and adrenal tumors should be surgically excised, if possible. Patients with CAH should receive glucocorticoid replacement (e.g., hydrocortisone, 13–25 mg/M^2/day divided into 3 daily doses) and be monitored every 3 months. If the bone age is not too advanced, breast development may regress with treatment of CAH. As noted earlier, some patients may have the onset of true precocity and be candidates for GnRH analogue therapy.

PREMATURE THELARCHE
Premature thelarche is defined as bilateral breast development without any other sign of puberty and is most commonly seen among young girls under 4 years of age. Occasionally, neonatal breast hypertrophy fails to regress within 10 months after birth; this persistent breast development is also characterized as premature thelarche. The typical child with premature thelarche has bilateral breast buds of 2 to 4 cm with little or no change in the nipple or areola. The breast tissue feels granular and may be slightly tender. In some cases, development is quite asymmetric; one side may develop 6 to 12 months before the other. Growth is not accelerated, and the bone age is normal for height age. No other evidence of puberty appears; the labia usually remain prepubertal without obvious evidence of estrogen effect.

A vaginal smear or urocytogram may be atrophic or may show slight evidence of estrogenization. In Collette-Solberg and Grumbach's series [33] of patients with premature thelarche, 8 out of 9 patients showed 5 percent or greater superficial cells on urocytogram, but only 3 showed greater than 10 percent. Silver and Sarni [34] demonstrated a slight estrogen effect on urocytogram in 15 out of 16 girls with premature thelarche as opposed to 7 out of 86 controls. In contrast to patients with isosexual precocity or normal puberty, the patient with premature thelarche still has a high percentage of parabasal cells. For example, a typical smear may show 7 percent superficial, 30 percent intermediate, and 63 percent parabasal and nonnucleated cells [35]. In addition, the evidence of estrogen effect on a vaginal smear or urocytogram is often transient. Similarly, estradiol levels are slightly elevated in some patients [36]. Escobar and associates [37] found that patients who demonstrate premature thelarche have estradiol levels of 7.7 ± 6.6 pg/ml (range <2.5–18.9) compared to 51.6 ± 42.9 pg/ml (range 19–154 pg/ml) in patients who have precocious puberty. Control prepubertal girls have estradiol levels of 1.5 pg/ml (range 0–7.2); however, most assays are not this sensitive. A low estradiol level may be somewhat reassuring, but overlap does occur and estradiol levels may be quite low in early precocious puberty.

In girls with premature thelarche, basal and post-GnRH serum levels of LH and FSH are generally in the prepubertal range, although Ilicki and colleagues [38] have found that basal levels of FSH and the response to GnRH were higher than in prepubertal controls (basal FSH 1.93 versus 0.8 mIU/ml; post-GnRH FSH peak 12.3 versus 7.9 mIU/ml). They have postulated that premature thelarche is due to derangement in maturation of the hypothalamic-pituitary-gonadal axis with higher than normal FSH secretion and increased peripheral sensitivity to the sex hormones. This hypothesis would explain the occurrence of this problem principally in 1- to 4-year-old girls. Premature thelarche is also seen more commonly in very low–birth–weight infants [39]. Thus peripheral sensitivity may play a partial role, but increasing evidence points toward the importance of transient ovarian secretion of estrogen under hypothalamic-pituitary control.

The usual clinical course of regression, or at least lack of progression, of breast development would then correlate with the waning of the estrogen levels as the ovarian follicles become atretic.

PATIENT ASSESSMENT
The assessment of a patient with premature breast development includes a careful review of medications and creams recently used. Occasionally it is discovered that a package of the mother's or sister's oral contraceptive pills has been ingested by the child. Premarin cream applied to the vulva nightly for more than 2 to 3 weeks may result in breast changes.

The physical examination should include notation of the appearance of the vaginal mucosa, size of the breasts, and a rectal-abdominal examination to exclude an ovarian cyst. The uterus should not be enlarged in patients with premature thelarche. Growth charts should be brought up to date and checked to see whether the patient is continuing to grow at her previously established percentile of height and weight. Laboratory tests include vaginal smear or urocytogram for assessment of estrogenization, serum estradiol level, hand and wrist x-ray films for bone age, and possibly ultrasonography of the pelvis.

TREATMENT AND FOLLOW-UP
Treatment consists mainly of reassurance and careful follow-up to confirm that the breast development does not represent the first sign of precocious puberty. A thorough physical examination should be done at each visit. Linear growth and bone age should be followed. Biopsy of the breast tissue is not indicated because removal of the breast bud prevents future normal development. In many cases, breast development does regress with age. Capraro and associates' series [40] of 10 cases, followed for a period of 11 months to 2 years, showed 4 patients with no change in breast size, 2 with decreased breast size, 1 with regression after excision of luteinized follicle cysts, 1 with complete disappearance of breast development, and 2 lost to follow-up. Mothers should be reassured that in most cases pubertal development will occur at the normal adolescent age.

PREMATURE MENARCHE
Premature menarche most likely represents a similar but less common response than premature thelarche to the transient production of estrogen by the ovary. Prepubertal girls may have uterine bleeding lasting 1 to 5 days, once or in cycles for several months, without other evidence of estrogen effect. Blanco-Garcia and co-workers [41] found estradiol levels to be significantly above the normal prepubertal range and a seasonal increase in isolated menses between September and January. Before the clinician can make this diagnosis, other etiologies for vaginal bleeding including infections, trauma, foreign body, and tumors need to be excluded (see p. 82).

PREMATURE ADRENARCHE
Premature adrenarche is defined as the isolated appearance of pubic and, occasionally, axillary hair before the age of 8 years without evidence of estrogenization or virilization. Patients usually also have increased axillary odor. Terminology is sometimes confusing but premature pubarche refers to the clinical manifestations of early pubic (and/or axillary) hair and premature adrenarche to the early maturation of adrenal androgen secretion. In common usage, the terms are often interchanged. Most patients have an increase in urinary 17-ketosteroid production and increased plasma DHA and DHAS, suggesting that hormone biosynthesis in the adrenal gland undergoes

maturation prematurely to a pubertal pattern [42]. Although production of these androgens is suppressible by dexamethasone and therefore dependent on adrenocorticotropic hormone, the mediator for the change at puberty and in premature adrenarche is unknown. Urinary 17-ketosteroid values are elevated for chronologic age, but they correspond with the levels expected for the amount of pubic hair (1–3 mg/24 hours) [42, 43]. DHAS levels are similar to values seen in girls with stage 2 pubic hair (see Fig. 5-2) [44]. Bone age is usually normal or just slightly advanced (appropriate for height). The urocytogram is similar to that seen in normal prepubertal girls: 3 percent superficial, 17 percent intermediate, and 80 percent parabasal and nonnucleated cells [35]. Estradiol levels are prepubertal in these girls [45], as are responses to GnRH testing.

It is not yet known what causes premature adrenarche. The condition appears to be more common in black and Hispanic girls and obese boys and girls [13, 46]. Some medical centers, including ours, have observed that adolescents with androgen excess and polycystic ovary syndrome may have a history of premature adrenarche. Temeck and colleagues [47] have noted that 30 percent of women with hirsutism and late onset 3 β-hydroxysteroid dehydrogenase deficiency had premature adrenarche between 5 and 8 years. More longitudinal studies of girls with premature adrenarche followed into adolescence are needed to answer whether a relationship exists, especially since early intervention with suppression of excess androgens may be helpful in prevention. Importantly, some girls with premature adrenarche do have evidence of a partial deficiency of 21-hydroxylase or 3 β-hydroxysteroid dehydrogenase or are heterozygotes for 21-hydroxylase deficiency [13, 47, 48]. In a referred population with predominance of ethnic groups known to have a high incidence of late onset 21-hydroxylase deficiency (Ashkenazi Jewish, Hispanic, and Italian), Temeck and colleagues [47] found that among girls with premature adrenarche between ages 2 and 7 years, 5 of 19 (26%) had 21-hydroxylase deficiency and 2 of 19 (11%) had 3 β-hydroxysteroid deficiency. At 1 hour after ACTH administration, patients with 21-hydroxylase deficiency showed elevated 17-hydroxyprogesterone and low 17-hydroxypregnenolone to 17-hydroxyprogesterone ratios, and patients with 3 β-hydroxysteroid deficiency had elevated 17-hydroxypregnenolone levels and increased 17-hydroxypregnenolone to 17-hydroxyprogesterone ratios. One patient with 21-hydroxylase deficiency who refused treatment developed hirsutism and polycystic ovaries by the age of 11 years. This study needs to be repeated in ethnic populations with a lower incidence of these disorders, especially among American black children, since premature adrenarche is so common in these girls between ages 5 and 8 years. Thus, the exact percentage of children with these deficiencies, the natural history, and the benefits of intervention need to be defined better, since doing a 1-hour ACTH test in all girls with premature adrenarche would add substantially to the expense of the evaluation. A 1-hour ACTH test is indicated in all girls with elevated baseline (7–8 A.M.) 17-hydroxyprogesterone, significantly advanced bone age, increased linear growth, and any signs of clitoromegaly or virilization. Even in the absence of these indications, white girls, especially those from the ethnic groups with an increased risk of late onset 21-hydroxylase deficiency, should be screened for enzyme deficiencies.

PATIENT ASSESSMENT

The assessment of the patient with premature adrenarche is similar to that for heterosexual precocious puberty. The important findings on physical examination are the presence of pubic hair and axillary odor and the *absence* of breast development, estrogenization of the labia and vagina, and virilization (clitoromegaly).

The laboratory tests include an x-ray film of the wrist for bone age, vaginal smear for estrogenization, and serum DHAS, testosterone, and early-morning (7–8 A.M.) 17-hydroxyprogesterone. A 24-hour urine may be collected for 17-ketosteroids. As noted in the previous section, the criteria for ACTH testing need further refinement. However, many medical centers are performing this test on all patients to detect enzyme deficiencies and better define the potential etiologies for this condition. The differential diagnosis must exclude precocious puberty, CAH, and an adrenal or ovarian tumor. Sometimes the diagnosis of adrenarche is made only in retrospect when further evidence of precocious puberty does not occur. It should be recalled that most patients with precocious puberty have an advanced bone age, growth spurt, and evidence of estrogenization of vaginal smear. Patients with tumors and some patients with CAH have evidence of virilization.

TREATMENT AND FOLLOW-UP

Treatment of premature adrenarche is reassurance and follow-up. The child should be examined every 3 to 6 months initially to confirm the original diagnostic impression; evidence of virilization or early estrogen effect points to a different diagnosis. Growth data should be carefully plotted. It is hoped that treatment of late onset 21-hydroxylase deficiency with corticosteroids will prevent the development of polycystic ovary syndrome in early adolescence. In general, pubertal development at adolescence can be expected to be normal. Whether an increased risk of polycystic ovaries and hirsutism occurs only in those with enzyme deficiencies is not known.

145

REFERENCES
  1. Liu N, Grumbach MM, deNapoli RA, et al. Prevalence of EEG abnor-
     malities in idiopathic precocious puberty and premature pubarche. J Clin
     Endocrinol Metab 1965; 25:1296.
  2. Hochman HI, Judge DM, and Reichlin S. Precocious puberty and hy-
     pothalamic hamartoma. Pediatrics 1981; 67:236.
  3. Cacciari E, Frejaville E, Cicognani A, et al. How many cases of true
     precocious puberty in girls are idiopathic? J Pediatr 1983; 102:357.
  4. Judge DM, Kulin HE, Page R, et al. Hypothalamic hamartoma and
     luteinizing-hormone release in precocious puberty. N Engl J Med 1977;
     296:7.
  5. Sigurjonsdottir TJ, and Hayles AB. Precocious puberty: A report of 96
     cases. Am J Dis Child 1968; 115:309.
  6. Thamdrup E. Precocious sexual development. Dan Med Bull 1961; 8:140.
  7. Lee PA, Page JG, and the Leuprolide Study Group. Effects of leuprolide
     in the treatment of central precocious puberty. J Pediatr 1989; 114:321.
  8. Scully RE, Galdabrini JJ, and McNeely BU (eds.), et al. Case records of the
     Massachusetts General Hospital. N Engl J Med 1979; 300:1322.
  9. Root AW, and Shulman D. Isosexual precocity: current concepts and
     recent advances. Fertil Steril 1986; 45:749.
 10. Boepple PA, Mansfield MJ, Weirman ME, et al. Use of a potent, long
     acting agonist of gonadotropin-releasing hormone in the treatment of
     precocious puberty. Endocr Rev 1986; 7:24.
 11. Leiper AD, Stanhope R, Kiching P, et al. Precocious and premature pu-
     berty associated with treatment of acute lymphoblastic leukaemia. Arch
     Dis Child 1987; 62:1107.
 12. Pescovitz OH, Hench K, Green O, et al. Central precocious puberty
     complicating a virilizing adrenal tumor: Treatment with a long-acting
     LHRH analog. J Pediatr 1985; 106:612.
 13. Wierman ME, Beardsworth DE, Mansfield MJ, et al. Puberty with
     gonadotropins: A unique mechanism of sexual development. N Engl J
     Med 1985; 312:65.
 14. Feuillan PP, Foster CM, Pescovitz OH, et al. Treatment of precocious
     puberty in the McCune-Albright syndrome with the aromatase inhibitor
     testolactone. N Engl J Med 1986; 315:1115.
 15. Foster CM, Feuillan P, Padmanabhan V, et al. Ovarian function in girls
     with McCune-Albright syndrome. Pediatr Res 1986; 20:859.
 16. Lee PA, VanDop C, and Migeon C. McCune-Albright syndrome: Long-
     term follow up. JAMA 1986; 256:2980.
 17. Lucky AW, Rich BH, Rosenfield RL, et al. Bioactive LH: A test to dis-
     criminate true precocious puberty from premature thelarche and ad-
     renarche. J Pediatr 1980; 97:214.
 18. Kulin HE, and Santner SJ. Timed urinary gonadotropin measurements in
     normal infants, children, and adults, and in patients with disorders of
     sexual maturation. J Pediatr 1977; 90:760.
 19. Rosenfield RG, Reitz RE, King AB, et al. Familial precocious puberty
     associated with isolated elevation of luteinizing hormone. N Engl J Med
     1980; 303:859.
 20. Sklar CA, Kaplan SL, and Grumbach MM. Evidence for dissociation be-
     tween adrenarche and gonadarche: Studies in patients with idiopathic
     precocious puberty, gonadal dysgenesis, isolated gonadotropin defi-
     ciency, and constitutionally delayed growth and adolescence. J Clin En-
     docrinol Metab 1980; 51:548.
 21. Crowley WF, Comite F, Vale W, et al. Therapeutic use for pituitary de-

sensitization with a long-acting LHRH agonist: A potential new treatment for idiopathic precocious puberty. J Clin Endocrinol Metab 1981; 52:370.

22. Comite F, Cutler GB, Rivier J, et al. Short-term treatment of idiopathic precocious puberty with a long-acting analogue of luteinizing hormone-releasing hormone. N Engl J Med 1981; 305:1539.
23. Kappy MS, Stuart T, and Perelman A. Efficacy of leuprolide therapy in children with central precocious puberty. Am J Dis Child 1988; 142:1061.
24. Comite F, Cassoria F, Barnes KM, et al. Luteinizing hormone releasing hormone analogue therapy for central precocious puberty. JAMA 1986; 255:2613.
25. Mansfield MJ, Beardsworth DE, Loughlin J, et al. Long-term treatment of central precocious puberty with a long-acting analogue of luteinizing hormone-releasing hormone. N Engl J Med 1983; 309:1286.
26. Laue L, Comite F, Hench K, et al. Precocious puberty associated with neurofibromatosis and optic gliomas. Am J Dis Child 1985; 139:1097.
27. Boepple PA, Mansfield MJ, Link K, et al. Impact of sex steroids and their suppression on skeletal growth and maturation. Am J Physiol 255 (Endocrinol Metab 18) 1988; E559.
28. Sonis WA, Comite F, Glue J, et al. Behavior problems and social competence in girls with true precocious puberty. J Pediat 1985; 106:156.
29. Comite F, Shawker TH, Prescovitz OH, et al. Cyclical ovarian function resistant to treatment with an analogue of leuanizing hormone releasing hormone in McCune-Albright syndrome. N Engl J Med 1984; 311:1032.
30. Laue L, Kenigsberg D, Pescovitz OH, et al. Treatment of familial male precocious puberty with spironolactone and testolactone. N Engl J Med 1989; 320:496.
31. Holland FJ, Fishman L, Bailey JD, et al. Ketoconazole in the management of precocious puberty not responsive to LHRH-analogue therapy. N Engl J Med 1985; 312:1023.
32. Scully RE, Mark EJ, and McNeely BU (eds.). Case records of the Massachusetts General Hospital. N Engl J Med 1982; 306:1348.
33. Collett-Solberg PR, and Grumbach MM. A simplified procedure for evaluating estrogenic effects and the sex chromatin pattern in exfoliated cells in urine. J Pediatr 1965; 66:883.
34. Silver HK, and Sarni D. Premature thelarche. Pediatrics 1964; 34:107.
35. Lencioni LH, and Staffieri JJ. Urocytogram diagnosis of sexual precocity. Acta Cytol (Baltimore) 1969; 13:382.
36. Jenner MR, Kelch RP, Kaplan SI, et al. Hormonal changes in puberty: Plasma estradiol, LH and FSH in prepubertal children, pubertal females, and in precocious puberty, premature thelarche, hypogonadism, and in a child with a feminizing ovarian tumor. J Clin Endocrinol Metab 1972; 34:521.
37. Escobar ME, Rivarola MA, and Bergada C. Plasma concentration of oestradiol-17β in premature thelarche and in different types of sexual precocity. Acta Endocrinol (Copenh) 1976; 81:351.
38. Ilicki A, Lewin RP, Kauli R, et al. Premature thelarche—natural history and sex hormone secretion in 68 girls. Acta Paediatr Scand 1984; 73:756.
39. Nelson KG. Premature thelarche in children born prematurely. J Pediat 1983; 103:756.
40. Capraro VJ, Bayonet-Rivera NP, Aceta T, et al. Premature thelarche. Obstet Gynecol Surv 1971; 26:2.
41. Blanco-Garcia M, Evain-Brion D, Roger M, et al. Isolated menses in prepubertal girls. Pediatrics 1985; 76:43.

42. Rosenfield R. Plasma 17-ketosteroids and 17 β-hydroxysteroids in girls with premature development of sexual hair. J Pediatr 1971; 79:260.
43. Sigurjonsdottir TJ, and Hayles AB. Premature pubarche. Clin Pediatr (Phil) 1968; 7:29.
44. Korth-Schultz S, Levine LS, and New M. Dehydroepiandrosterone sulfate (DS) levels, a rapid test for abnormal adrenal androgen secretion. J Clin Endocrinol Metab 1976; 42:1005.
45. Sklar CA, Grumbach MM, and Kaplan SL. Estradiol values in premature adrenarche. J Pediatr 1978; 94:677.
46. Kaplowitz PB, Cockrell JL, and Young RB. Premature adrenarche. Clin Pediatr 1986; 25:28.
47. Temeck JW, Pang S, Nelson C, et al. Genetic defects of steroidogenesis in premature pubarche. J Clin Endocrinol Metab 1987; 64:609.
48. Granoff AB, Chasalow FI, and Blethen SZ. 17 hydroxyprogesterone responses to adrenocorticotropin in children with premature adrenarche. J Clin Endocrinol Metab 1985; 60:409.

6. Delayed Puberty and Menstrual Irregularities

This chapter presents a simplified approach to patients with delayed sexual development, amenorrhea, and dysfunctional uterine bleeding. Chapters 1 and 4 should be mastered before an evaluation of any of these problems is undertaken. (Embryogenesis is reviewed in Chap. 2.) The goal of a workup of a patient with menstrual irregularities is to rule out a tumor or systemic disease and to make as exact a diagnosis as possible in order to present a discussion and treatment plan to the teenage girl and her parents.

This chapter outlines a program for evaluating the common pubertal and menstrual problems of adolescents: (1) delayed sexual development, (2) delayed menarche with some pubertal development, (3) delayed menarche plus virilization, (4) secondary amenorrhea, (5) oligomenorrhea, and (6) dysfunctional uterine bleeding. The distinction between many of these entities is somewhat artificial because many of the problems that cause pubertal delay can also cause primary amenorrhea or secondary amenorrhea. For example, the patient with 45,X/46,XX (Turner mosaic) or the patient with anorexia nervosa may present to the clinician with no sexual development or primary or secondary amenorrhea. It is thus helpful to the clinician to think about a general approach to define the source of the problem in the hypothalamic-pituitary-ovarian axis and to determine whether a genital anomaly is present.

After the history and physical examination, the differential diagnosis in the hypoestrogenic adolescent can often be divided on the basis of gonadotropin levels (follicle-stimulating hormone [FSH], luteinizing hormone [LH]) into categories of hypergonadotropic hypogonadism (ovarian failure) and hypogonadotropic hypogonadism (hypothalamic or pituitary dysfunction). Other estrogenized patients may have a genital anomaly or polycystic ovary syndrome. This distinction allows the clinician to focus on the etiologies and diagnostic tests that would be useful in formulating a treatment plan. This chapter discusses broad categories of potential problems and then focuses on each of the menstrual complaints that are likely to bring the adolescent to the physician.

A careful history and physical examination are mandatory whenever the patient expresses concern about her physical development. A girl who has not experienced any pubertal development by the age of 13 years is 2 standard deviations beyond the normal age of initiating puberty and deserves a medical evaluation. For the exceptional case in which the girl is known to have a debilitating chronic disease or involvement in a competitive or endurance sport such as ballet or track that may be associated with a delay in development, the diagnostic workup can be postponed until age 14 years. Absence of menarche by age 16 years is usually termed delayed menarche. No menarche by 18 years (some authors use 16 years) is termed primary amenorrhea. Only 3 in 1000 girls will experience menarche after 15½ years. In assessing the individual patient, the physician needs to keep in mind the normal developmental stages of puberty. For example, if the 15-year-old began her sexual development at age 14 years, she can usually be reassured that she can expect her menarche by the age of 16 or 17 years. The patient should be observed for a reassuring steady progression of growth and development. A halt in maturation signifies the need to do a thorough endocrine evaluation. Likewise, the girl who started her development at age 12 and has not had her menarche by age 16 years deserves an evaluation for the cause, including a careful pelvic examination to exclude a genital anomaly before serum hormone levels are obtained.

The definition of secondary amenorrhea, and thus guidelines for timing of the evaluation, are problematic in the adolescent, since pregnancy is such a frequent etiology for this complaint. Denial of intercourse is common among teenagers. Young adolescents may not understand their anatomy well enough to answer questions accurately or may have become pregnant by rape or incest. Thus a pregnancy test should be done whenever an adolescent expresses concern about a menstrual period being late, even if only by 2 or 3 weeks. A call or visit from a teenager concerned about a late period should prompt the physician to explore with the teenager a history of unprotected intercourse. Adolescents who are not sexually active are less likely to contact their physicians about mildly irregular or late menses. Nevertheless, a pregnancy test should be obtained promptly in adolescents with late menses, even if sexual activity is denied. Hormone tests and further evaluation of amenorrhea is usually reserved for adolescents who have had 3 to 6 months of amenorrhea without an obvious cause (such as dieting) and those with persistent oligomenorrhea, estrogen deficiency, or androgen excess (hirsutism, acne). Several illustrative case histories are included at the end of each section.

The pertinent past history depends in part on the presenting complaint and may include the following:

1. Neonatal history: maternal ingestion of hormones such as androgens or progestins that can cause clitoromegaly, maternal history of miscarriages, birth weight, congenital anomalies, lymphedema (Turner syndrome), neonatal problems suggestive of hypopituitarism such as hypoglycemia.

2. Family history: heights of all family members; age of menarche and fertility of sisters, mother, grandmothers, and aunts (familial disorders include delayed menarche, testicular feminization, congenital adrenal hyperplasia, and chromatin-positive gonadal dysgenesis); history of ovarian tumors (e.g., gonadoblastomas in intersex disorders); history of endocrine (autoimmune) disorders such as thyroiditis and Addison's disease.
3. Previous surgery, irradiation, or chemotherapy.
4. Review of systems with special emphasis on a history of chronic disease, abdominal pain, diarrhea, headaches, neurologic symptoms, ability to smell, weight changes, eating disorders, sexual activity, medications, substance abuse, emotional stresses, competitive athletics, and hirsutism.
5. Age of initiation of pubertal development, if any, and rate of development.
6. Growth data plotted on charts, such as those illustrated in Chapter 4.

The physical examination should involve a general assessment including height and weight (plotted on growth charts), blood pressure, palpation of the thyroid, and Tanner staging of breast development and pubic hair. The breasts should be compressed gently to examine for the presence of galactorrhea, since patients frequently do not report this sign. A search should also be made for congenital anomalies, especially midline facial defects that may be associated with hypothalamic-pituitary dysfunction and somatic stigmata of Turner syndrome. Renal and vertebral anomalies may be associated with Müllerian malformations. A neurologic examination is important in patients with delayed or interrupted puberty and should include an assessment of the ability to smell, fundoscopic examination, and visual field tests (by confrontation).

In the initial examination of the adolescent with no pubertal development, the gynecologic examination usually involves inspection of the external genitalia looking for clitoromegaly, estrogen effect, and a normal hymen. Since the cause of the problem is likely an ovarian or hypothalamic-pituitary problem, visualizing the cervix is much less crucial in girls with no pubertal maturation than in the evaluation of the teenager with delayed menarche. However, in the nonobese prepubertal teenager, a simple rectoabdominal examination will often allow palpation of the cervix and the uterus. In addition, the knee-chest position (see p. 13) can be used in the unestrogenized adolescent (just as in the prepubertal child) to view the vagina and the cervix. For the adolescent with pubertal development and delayed menarche, it is crucial to exclude a genital anomaly. Techniques for examining the adolescent girl are in Chap. 1. The girl with secondary amenorrhea, oligomenorrhea, and dysfunctional uterine bleeding needs a gynecologic assessment, which usually involves a speculum examination or at minimum a bimanual rectoabdominal examination.

The degree of estrogenization noted at the time of the initial examination can often help the clinician decide the extent of the workup indicated. The finding of a reddened, thin vaginal mucosa is consistent with estrogen deficiency and is more worrisome than the finding of an estrogenized, pink, moist vaginal mucosa. Obtaining a vaginal smear at the time of the examination can confirm the clinical assessment of estrogenization (see p. 29). A progesterone challenge with oral medroxyprogesterone (10 mg twice a day for 5 days or once a day for 10 days, in the patient with no possibility of pregnancy) can be used to assess whether the endometrium is primed with estrogen. This test is not indicated in the patient with delayed development or in the patient who clearly appears estrogen deficient on clinical examination since withdrawal bleeding will not occur. Ultrasonography should not be a routine part of the evaluation but can be extremely useful to confirm uterine agenesis, Müllerian anomalies, and adnexal masses in an adolescent with questionable findings on bimanual examination or evidence of an anomaly. The physician should be cautious in the interpretation of the pelvic ultrasound in the adolescent with no puberty (no estrogenization) because the uterus may not be well visualized and thus assumed to be absent. If questions are raised at the time of the initial evaluation, the ultrasound can be repeated after a course of estrogen therapy.

In adolescents, assessment of the pattern of growth can yield valuable information to make a diagnosis. Failure of statural growth for several years may occur with Crohn's disease or an acquired endocrine disorder or may indicate that the adolescent has reached a bone age of 15 years and her epiphyses have fused. In conditions caused by poor nutrition such as eating disorders and inflammatory bowel disease, weight is typically affected more than height. The patient is thus underweight for her height. In contrast, patients with acquired hypothyroidism, cortisol excess, and Turner syndrome are typically overweight for height. Bone age can be helpful in assessing patients with delayed development. For example, hypothyroidism tends to delay bone age more than height age (height age is the age at which the patient's height would be on the fiftieth percentile on a growth chart). With constitutional delay, both bone age and height age are similarly delayed. Menarche is more closely linked to bone age than to chronologic age.

Initial screening tests include a complete blood count (CBC) with sedimentation rate and serum FSH and LH levels. Although an elevated sedimentation rate may be a clue to the diagnosis of a chronic disease such as Crohn's disease, a normal erythrocyte sedimentation rate does not exclude this diagnosis. High LH and FSH levels imply ovarian failure and should be repeated before a definitive statement is made to the patient and family. Low to normal levels of FSH and LH imply a central nervous system (CNS) etiology—for example, a CNS tumor, hypopituitarism, or hypothalamic dysfunction, which may be primary or secondary to a chronic disease, stress, or an eating disorder. It is important to remember that although constitutional delayed puberty is common in boys, it is less common as an etiology in girls. A definitive diagnosis is likely in the girl with delayed or interrupted puberty. The spectrum of disorders that were seen in a study of 252 patients evaluated between 1960 and 1980 in the Reproductive Unit of the Medical College of Georgia is shown in Table 6-1 [1]. It should be remembered, however, that this series was based on a referral population, and a different balance of diagnoses is likely to be seen by the primary care physician.

HYPERGONADOTROPIC HYPOGONADISM
(HIGH FSH AND LH LEVELS)
Adolescents with elevated gonadotropins may have an abnormal karyotype (such as Turner syndrome or XY gonadal dysgenesis) or a normal karyotype (such as autoimmune oophoritis, XX premature menopause, or ovarian failure associated with radiation or chemotherapy). These patients typically present with delayed development but may present with primary or secondary amenorrhea after undergoing some or even complete pubertal maturation. In the adolescent population, most patients with ovarian failure have gonadal dysgenesis; in contrast, a higher percentage of patients in the adult population have autoimmune ovarian failure as a cause of premature menopause. It is important to remember that some patients with premature menopause may have fluctuating levels of gonadotropins and estradiol for months to years and may recover menstrual function spontaneously with the rare possibility of fertility. Although Alper and co-workers [2] reported that 6 of 80 (7.5%) women conceived after the diagnosis of premature ovarian failure, patients presenting with elevated gonadotropins during adolescence are less likely to have a reversal of the hypogonadism. In addition patients with autoimmune ovarian failure may develop adrenal insufficiency, and thus long-term follow-up is indicated.

Initial evaluation of the adolescent with elevated gonadotropins (in the absence of a history of radiation therapy or chemotherapy) includes a karyotype. In patients with 46,XX ovarian failure, further studies include assessment for autoimmune ovarian failure (see p. 160) and serum levels of progesterone, 11-deoxycorticosterone,

Table 6-1. Etiologic Breakdown of 252 Patients Presenting with Pubertal Abnormalities

	Group total	No.	%
Hypergonadotropic hypogonadism:			
CIOF	69		27
CCOF	40		16
46,XX		34	14
46,XY		6	2
Total	109		43
Hypogonadotropic hypogonadism:			
Reversible	48		19
Physiologic delay		35	14
Weight loss/anorexia nervosa		6	2
Primary hypothyroidism		3	1
Congenital adrenal hyperplasia		3	1
Cushing's syndrome		1	0.5
Irreversible	29		12
Congenital deficiency syndromes			
Isolated GnRF deficiency		13	5
Forms of hypopituitarism		6	2
Congenital CNS defects		2	1

155

	n	%
Acquired anatomic lesions		
Prolactin-secreting adenoma	3	1
Unclassified pituitary adenoma	2	1
Craniopharyngioma	1	0.5
Unclassified malignant pituitary tumor	1	0.5
Postsurgical hypopituitarism (craniopharyngioma)	1	0.5
Total	77	31
Eugonadism:		
Anatomic	46	18
Rokitansky syndrome	37	15
Transverse vaginal septum	7	3
Imperforate hymen	2	1
Inappropriate positive feedback	17	7
Androgen insensitivity syndrome	3	1
Total	66	26

CIOF = chromosomally incompetent ovarian failure; CCOF = chromosomally competent ovarian failure; GnRF = gonadotropin releasing factor; CNS = central nervous system.

Source: RH Reindollar, JR Byrd, and PG McDonough, Delayed sexual development: A study of 252 patients. *Am J Obstet Gynecol* 140:371, 1981. With permission.

and corticosterone (in the hypertensive patient with delayed puberty) to look for 17α-hydroxylase deficiency. Laparoscopy or laparotomy with gonadal biopsy is rarely indicated.

Gonadal Dysgenesis

Slightly over one half of patients with gonadal dysgenesis have a 45,X karyotype (Turner syndrome). The classic stigmata of Turner syndrome include short stature (final height less than 58 inches); widely spaced nipples; webbed neck; low hairline; short fourth or fifth, or both, metacarpals; cubitus valgus; ptosis; low-set ears; narrow, high-arched palate; lymphedema; and multiple pigmented nevi. Associated problems include cardiac anomalies (especially coarctation of the aorta), renal anomalies, hearing impairment, otitis media and mastoiditis (in about one-third), and an increased incidence of hypertension, achlorhydria, diabetes mellitus, and Hashimoto's thyroiditis [3–5]. A young adolescent with Turner syndrome has prepubertal female genitalia, bilateral streak gonads, and a normal uterus and vagina capable of responding to exogenous hormones; she may have sparse or absent pubic and axillary hair in spite of levels of dehydroepiandrosterone sulfate (DHAS), which correspond to pubic hair stages 2 to 3. A growth chart of a Turner syndrome patient is shown in Figure 6-1. The older adolescent (15 or 16 years old) with undiagnosed or untreated Turner syndrome usually has pubic and axillary hair but no breast development or estrogenization of the vaginal mucosa (no ovarian function). Although a few 45,X patients will produce estrogen during adolescence and young adulthood, estrogenization should at least raise the possibility of a theca lutein cyst or germ cell tumor.

The other 40 to 50 percent of patients with gonadal dysgenesis have a mosaic karyotype (e.g., 46,XX/45,X) or a structural abnormality of the second X chromosome. Such patients may show none or all of the classic stigmata of Turner syndrome. Patients with Turner mosaic may have (1) sexual infantilism, (2) some sexual development and primary amenorrhea, (3) secondary amenorrhea and short stature, or (4) regular menses and normal stature. Girls with mosaic blood karyotypes, especially involving only the loss of the short arm of the X chromosome, are more likely to have pubertal maturation. Gonadal failure is indicated by elevated gonadotropin levels.

Rarely, there have been pregnancies reported among patients with 45,X and mosaic blood karyotypes, even among some with elevated gonadotropin levels (which indicates poor ovarian function). The outcome of the reported pregnancies has been poor with an increased risk of abortion, stillbirth, and chromosomally abnormal babies [6, 7]; however, these studies have been disputed.

The follow-up of the patient diagnosed with Turner syndrome

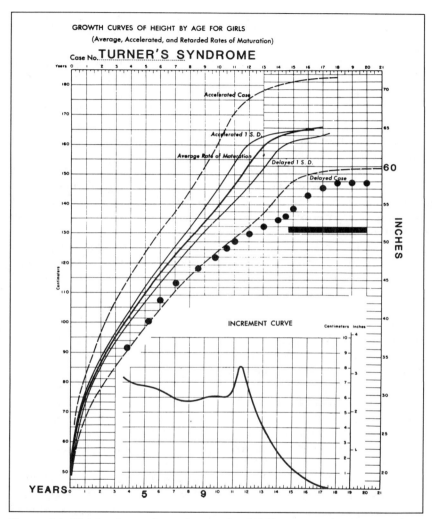

Figure 6-1. Height chart of a patient with 45,X Turner syndrome treated with estrogen (indicated by bar) to induce secondary sexual characteristics.

should include ultrasound examination of the kidneys, cardiac assessment, monitoring for hypertension, glucose intolerance, and thyroid dysfunction (those with isochromosome of the long arm of X are especially at risk of Hashimoto's thyroiditis) [3, 5, 8, 9]. After finding evidence of increased aortic root diameters in Turner patients, Allen and colleagues [3] have suggested that these patients should be monitored with periodic cardiac evaluations and echocardiography to follow aortic root diameter as well as detect bicuspid aortic valve, coarctation of the aorta, and hypertension. Patients who are untreated or who have persistently high gonadotropin levels, or both, may show enlarged pituitary fossae, which suggests hyperplasia of the pituitary gland [10].

Patients with a 45,X karyotype should remain under surveillance for the possibility of a gonadal tumor and the presence of an undetected Y line. If a pelvic examination is difficult, annual x-ray films to detect calcification or ultrasonography of the pelvis (to detect gonadal tumors) can be done. Hormonal therapy is discussed on p. 179. Special growth charts with percentiles for Turner syndrome can be obtained from Genentech.*

The term *pure gonadal dysgenesis* includes patients with normal or tall stature and the gonadal abnormality of Turner syndrome. Breast development is absent or poor; gonadotropin levels are high. Proportions are usually eunuchoid; karyotype is usually 46,XX or 46,XY. The lack of a testis in XY patients results from the lack of testicular determining factor on the Y chromosome (see Chap. 2); the streak gonads do not produce androgens or Müllerian inhibiting substance. The patients appear as normal prepubertal females including a normal Müllerian system. Because of the presence of the Y, these patients are at increased risk of gonadal tumors and thus require removal of the gonads. Patients with XX ovarian failure may have a family history of premature menopause. Krauss and colleagues [11] have reported a family with a deletion on the long arm X chromosome in the area responsible for follicular maintenance.

OVARIAN FAILURE SECONDARY TO RADIATION OR CHEMOTHERAPY

A past history of a malignancy treated with radiation to the pelvis or abdomen and/or chemotherapy suggests a diagnosis of ovarian failure. Data [12] from The Children's Hospital, Boston, on long-term survivors of childhood malignancy have demonstrated ovarian failure in 68 percent of patients who had both ovaries within the abdominal radiotherapy fields, in 14 percent whose ovaries were at the edge of the treatment field, and in none of the patients with one or both ovaries outside of an abdominal treatment field. A dose of 800 rads or more to the pelvis is associated with ovarian failure, with lower doses capable of producing some damage. The likelihood of ovarian failure is both dose and age related; the higher the dose and the older the patient, the greater the possibility of ovarian damage [13–15]. Thus children and adolescents have a better outcome than women in their thirties. In addition to ovarian failure, an adolescent who received pelvic radiation therapy before puberty often has a very small cervix and uterus despite estrogen therapy. Oophoropexy to move the

*Genentech, Inc., 460 Pt Bruno Blvd., San Francisco CA 94080.

ovaries laterally or medially from the treatment field and shielding the ovaries with lead blocks can lower the radiation dose but have only been partially successful in preserving fertility. Transplanting the ovaries outside the pelvis and the use of drugs such as oral contraceptives [16] and gonadotropin releasing hormone (GnRH) analogues to suppress function during treatment may offer future promise to preserve function in some patients.

Chemotherapeutic agents that have been associated with premature ovarian failure in adults include cyclophosphamide, chlorambucil, busulfan, L-PAM, MOPP (mechlorethamine, vincristine, procarbazine, and prednisone), and MVPP (nitrogen mustard, vinblastine, procarbazine, and prednisolone) [2, 13, 17, 18]. Children and adolescents appear more resistant to the deleterious effects of these agents, although long-term effects have not been fully assessed. In a review of 30 studies that evaluated patients who had received chemotherapy for renal disease (cyclophosphamide), Hodgkin's disease, or acute lymphocytic leukemia, Rivkees and Crawford [18] concluded that chemotherapy-induced damage was more likely to occur in sexually mature than prepubertal girls and with higher doses of alkylating agents. They found gonadal dysfunction at follow-up in none of the girls given cyclophosphamide during prepuberty and midpuberty versus 58 percent of those who were sexually mature. For Hodgkin's disease, 7 percent of those treated in midpuberty and 71 percent of the sexually mature had gonadal dysfunction. For leukemia, the percentages were 10 percent for those treated before puberty, 36 percent for midpuberty, and 22 percent for those sexually mature. Even in girls who appear to go through a normal or early puberty, prior treatment of acute lymphocytic leukemia can result in elevated FSH levels and decreased plasma inhibin levels, despite normal plasma estradiol levels [19]. The total dose is also important in relation to the age of the patient. For cyclophosphamide, a dose of 5.2 gm is associated with amenorrhea in women over 40 years, whereas a dose of 20.4 gm is needed for the same effect in women 20 to 29 years of age [20].

Adolescents may experience amenorrhea and elevated gonadotropins while receiving these drugs and subsequently return to normal menstrual function and normal hormone levels months to several years after completing the course. Although chemotherapy is not a common cause of ovarian failure in adolescents, some patients do experience permanent ovarian failure, which may become apparent later after therapy.

The combination of chemotherapy and radiation therapy, especially in Hodgkin's disease, often significantly impairs ovarian function. Patients less than 30 years of age have the best chance for recovery of function [21]. Further controlled trials of GnRH analogue are needed to assess protection, if any, of ovarian function. Fortunately for women who do have normal ovarian function, there is no evidence of any effect of the therapy on conception rates, fetal anomalies, or spontaneous abortion [13, 14].

Autoimmune Oophoritis

The possibility of autoimmune oophoritis needs to be considered in any patient with normal karyotype and ovarian failure, because she may subsequently develop other endocrinopathies. In studies of adults with premature ovarian failure evaluated in medical centers, 20 to 50 percent have been reported to have evidence of autoimmune disease [1, 22–25]. Alper and Garner [22] found that 18 percent of women with premature ovarian failure had a family history of autoimmune diseases, all of whom proved to have autoimmune disease themselves. Associated diseases have included thyroid disorders, Addison's disease, hypoparathyroidism, myasthenia gravis, pernicious anemia, and vitiligo. Antibodies against theca interna and corpus luteum cells and FSH receptors have been described. Using an assay to examine for the presence of ovarian antibodies (an indirect fluorescent antibody assay using human ovarian tissue), Damewood and associates [24] found that localization of staining occurred in the primary oocytes and in the granulosa cells of large secondary follicles. Patients may not have positive anti-ovarian antibody tests because the right antigens may not be included in the assay or the pathogenesis of the ovarian failure may involve cell-mediated immunity. According to Scully [26], the primordial follicles are normal but the theca cell layer around the developing follicle is infiltrated with lymphocytes and plasma cells, and subsequently inflammatory cells infiltrate the granulosa cell layer of the graafian follicle. Many of these young women have antibodies to thyroglobulin and to other endocrine organs.

Patients with autoimmune oophoritis may have a variable course with spontaneous remissions and the resumption of normal ovarian function [2, 27]. Amenorrhea and infertility persist in most patients. Whether corticosteroids or combined estrogen-progestin therapy leads to any better prognosis is unclear, since controlled studies have not been performed. Rabinowe and colleagues [28] have reported a 32-year-old woman with antiovarian antibodies and "immune associated" (Ia) T lymphocytes who responded with a rise in estradiol levels and menses when given oral corticosteroids. Estrogen therapy has been postulated to shift the FSH to a more bioactive FSH. The best approach for defining prognosis in these patients is controversial. Transvaginal ultrasound can give good definition of ovarian structure. Others advocate ovarian biopsy obtained at laparotomy. For most, in vitro fertilization with donor oocytes offers the best possibility for a pregnancy.

At the initial assessment of the patient with suspected autoimmune ovarian failure, baseline thyroid function tests, calcium, phosphorus, and hemoglobin should be obtained and, if available, serum sent for antibodies to thyroid, adrenal, ovary, and parietal cells. Because of the risk of adrenal insufficiency, an adrenocorticotropic hormone (ACTH) test with measurement of cortisol levels at 0 and 30 or 60 minutes has been suggested as an appropriate screening test, with repeated measurements done annually to determine adrenal reserve.

RESISTANT OVARY SYNDROME
In resistant ovary syndrome, a rare condition, the ovaries appear normal at laparoscopy. Biopsy specimens reveal numerous primordial follicles [29]. The ovaries may lack a receptor for gonadotropin function. During an infertility evaluation, a trial of exogenous human gonadotropin may be indicated to exclude the remote possibility that the patient has an abnormally structured FSH and LH.

17 α-HYDROXYLASE DEFICIENCY
The extremely rare disorder 17 α-hydroxylase deficiency is not truly gonadal failure but rather an enzyme deficiency that results in adrenal insufficiency, hypertension, and lack of gonadal sex steroids, including androgens and estrogens. XX patients have a female phenotype but no secondary sexual characteristics or sexual hair. XY patients may have a female phenotype, vaginal agenesis, and lack of Müllerian structures but, unlike patients with androgen insensitivity (testicular feminization), do not have pubertal breast development.

OTHER CAUSES OF OVARIAN FAILURE
Ovarian failure also occurs in patients with galactosemia (even those treated from infancy [30]), myotonia dystrophica, trisomy 21, sarcoidosis, and ataxia telangiectasia. Ovarian destruction has followed mumps oophoritis, rarely gonococcal salpingitis, ovarian infiltrative processes (tuberculosis and mucopolysaccharidosis), and ovarian hemorrhage.

HYPOGONADOTROPIC HYPOGONADISM
(LOW TO NORMAL FSH AND LH LEVELS)
Hypogonadotropic hypogonadism is the general term used for the diagnosis of patients with a delay in sexual development or menses associated with low to normal levels of gonadotropins. This may include patients with a central etiology for the disorder such as chronic disease or undernutrition, a hypothalamic etiology such as

Kallmann's syndrome or a tumor, or a pituitary cause such as a microadenoma or infiltrative disease. A normal physiologic delay in puberty or menarche is a diagnosis of exclusion and requires a careful medical evaluation before watchful waiting or hormonal therapy.

One of the most common causes of delayed puberty is poor nutrition. Poor intake, malabsorption, and increased caloric requirements commonly occur in such chronic diseases as cystic fibrosis, sickle cell disease, renal disease, celiac disease, and Crohn's disease [31–34]. The diagnosis is frequently evident before puberty but especially in the case of Crohn's disease may have a subtle presentation with growth failure alone in the teenage years. On careful history, most, but not all, patients with Crohn's disease will have a history of intermittent crampy abdominal pain, diarrhea, or constipation. The sedimentation rate is usually, but not invariably, elevated, and mild anemia and hypoalbuminemia may be present as clues. When the diagnosis is in doubt, gastrointestinal workup is often indicated before assuming that low caloric intake is responsible for the problem. Renal problems associated with impaired growth include renal tubular acidosis, glomerular diseases treated with corticosteroids, and end-stage renal failure.

Self-imposed caloric restriction and intermittent dieting are common among adolescent girls, most of whom view themselves as overweight. Society's preoccupation with a thin physique may lead parents and children to restrict the diet inappropriately and cause weight loss or growth failure. Although anorexia nervosa is typically associated with secondary and to a lesser extent primary amenorrhea, "fear of obesity" can cause significant growth failure even in prepubertal children [35]. Because of the rarity of this presentation, however, it behooves the clinician to exclude a hypothalamic tumor, a malabsorptive state, and chronic disease in the prepubertal child with apparent eating disorder (see p. 165 for discussion of anorexia nervosa). Children may also have inadequate access to food because of family psychosocial problems, alcoholism, drug abuse, lack of financial resources, or homelessness.

Girls who are involved in competitive endurance sports such as track, ballet, and gymnastics frequently have a delay in pubertal development and irregular menses [36, 37]. It is likely that this delay results from self-imposed caloric restriction coupled with high energy output and stress and probably the tendency of these sports to attract late maturers (see p. 168).

Delayed puberty may also be caused by endocrinopathies, including hypothyroidism, diabetes mellitus, and Cushing's syndrome. Acquired hypothyroidism may have a subtle onset that may be missed except for the slowing of statural growth. In contrast to the patients with malabsorptive problems, patients with hypothyroidism are typically overweight for height, but not massively obese. Patients who have received total nodal radiation therapy for Hodgkin's disease may develop hypothyroidism. Girls with poorly controlled diabetes mellitus may have short stature and delay in puberty as well as irregular menstruation [38]. The use of pharmacologic doses of corticosteroids to treat many medical diseases frequently causes an iatrogenic Cushing's picture. Substance abuse and psychological problems such as severe depression may also be associated with an interruption of the pubertal process.

Hypothalamic dysfunction may be caused by a congenital defect such as Kallmann's syndrome in which there is a lack of pulsatile release of GnRH, sometimes associated with midline craniofacial defects or anosmia. Distinguishing this entity from delayed puberty may be difficult if the patient with delayed puberty has not begun to show a normal postpubertal response to GnRH. Patients with delayed puberty or menarche frequently have a history of other members of the family experiencing a significant delay. This history alone, however, should not prevent a workup in girls with delayed development, since other conditions can be present. Central lesions that need to be excluded include tumors, hydrocephalus, brain abscesses, and infiltrative lesions such as tuberculosis, sarcoidosis, histiocytosis X, and CNS leukemia. Follow-up is critical to make sure that normal puberty occurs, since one of these conditions may become apparent later.

Craniopharyngiomas typically present between ages 6 and 14 years and cause headaches, poor growth, delayed development, and diabetes insipidus. Children who have received cranial radiation for leukemia therapy frequently have abnormalities of growth hormone secretion and may have interference with pulsatile GnRH secretion as well [39, 40]. Iron deposition from hemochromatosis and iron overload associated with transfusion therapy in thalassemia major can result in pubertal delay. Iron deposition in the thalassemic patient may also cause hypothyroidism, diabetes, cardiac failure, and pituitary dysfunction. Whether chelation therapy will result in an improved outcome for growth and development is still being evaluated [41, 42]. Hypogonadotropic hypogonadism is also associated with the Laurence-Moon-Biedl and Prader-Willi syndromes. Medications and illicit drugs such as cocaine can cause hyperprolactinemia (see Table 6-2).

Pituitary causes of interrupted development and irregular menses include hypopituitarism, either congenital or acquired, and tumors. Acquired hypopituitarism can result from head trauma [43], postpartum shock and necrosis, and rarely from an autoimmune process [44]. The most common pituitary tumor in adolescence is a prolactinoma that typically causes primary or secondary amenorrhea, rather than complete absence of pubertal development (see p. 171). Galactorrhea is uncommon in patients with primary amenorrhea in spite of the elevated serum prolactin levels and is found in only one half to two thirds of adolescents with secondary amenorrhea and prolactinomas. Although prolactinomas are a frequent cause of amenorrhea in adult women presenting to teaching centers for infertility evaluations, these tumors are an important but rare cause of menstrual irregularity in the adolescent. Nonetheless, obtaining a serum prolactin level offers a simple test for this problem and is indicated in patients with low or normal FSH and LH levels and interrupted puberty or menses. An entity known as "empty sella" can occur in children as well as adults and may be associated with hypothalamic-pituitary dysfunction (although the incidence of this abnormality in the general population is unknown). Shulman and co-workers [45] have suggested that primary empty sella with a normal-sized sella may be associated with pituitary hypoplasia, an unrecognized pituitary insult, dysfunction of the hypothalamus or higher centers resulting in diminished pituitary growth, or herniation of cerebrospinal fluid through an incompetent sellar diaphragm.

Thus the evaluation of the adolescent found to have low to normal FSH and LH levels needs to focus on excluding a systemic disease, poor nutrition, CNS disorder, or endocrinopathy. This may include careful assessment of the growth charts, neurologic examination, CBC, sedimentation rate, thyroid function tests (including thyroid-stimulating hormone [TSH]), prolactin, skull x ray with cone-down view of the sella, and bone age. Caloric counts of food diaries and gastrointestinal evaluation are indicated in those with poor nutrition. Evidence for other chronic diseases such as cystic fibrosis, renal failure, diabetes, or liver disease should be assessed. A skull x ray is useful only if calcification is present (e.g., from a craniopharyngioma) or the sella enlarged or eroded. If a hypothalamic or pituitary tumor is under consideration or if the etiology of the delayed puberty clearly stems from the CNS without obvious explanation (e.g., thin ballet dancer), then evaluation should include computed tomography (CT) scan or magnetic resonance imaging (MRI).

Neuroendocrine studies with GnRH testing can be useful for the patient in the early stages of delayed puberty; a normal pubertal response to GnRH suggests constitutional delay, whereas failure to respond frequently occurs in patients with Kallmann's syndrome. Repeated pulsatile GnRH is usually needed to stimulate FSH and LH secretion in the patient with Kallmann's syndrome. Other studies of overnight secretion of pituitary hormones and tests of cortisol and growth hormone secretion are important in the evaluation of patients with evidence of panhypopituitarism and some tumor patients. Patients with a history of CNS radiation for leukemia should have growth monitored carefully and neuroendocrine testing done if linear growth is abnormal. Formal visual field testing is helpful in patients with hypothalamic and pituitary tumors.

EATING DISORDERS

As previously mentioned, many adolescents pursue thinness to the extreme of causing delayed development, delayed menarche, and secondary amenorrhea. Even simple weight loss in the adolescent may result in a delayed period or several months of amenorrhea. Adolescents with bulemia and normal weight for height may have regular menses but may also have secondary amenorrhea or irregular menses. Two peaks of presentation of anorexia occur, at age 13 years and at 18 years, the first associated with pubertal maturation and body image concerns and the second the age of separation and choices about jobs and college. The older girl has a less favorable prognosis for recovery. The typical girl is from a middle or upper socioeconomic family and is an overachiever, often in both academics and sports. In spite of achievements, she feels inadequate and senses a pervasive lack of control in her life. Patients with other medical problems such as Turner syndrome or diabetes mellitus may develop an eating disorder. Although in the past a 25 percent loss of body weight was part of the criteria for the diagnosis of anorexia nervosa, *The Diagnostic and Statistical Manual of Mental Disorders IIIR (DSM-IIIR)* now accepts a loss of 15 percent of expected body weight. Treating patients early in the course of the illness even before these guidelines are met may yield a better prognosis. The girls are often preoccupied with thoughts of food; some may restrict intake to several hundred calories per day, while others may binge and then purge by self-induced vomiting or laxative abuse. Since these girls are frequently secretive about their eating patterns, it is useful for the physician to develop some techniques for eliciting an accurate history. Rather than asking, "Do you vomit?", the physician can say, "Do you have difficulty keeping your weight where you want it to be? Have you ever had to use vomiting or medicines to control it?" These questions allow the physician to begin the dialogue with the teenager on appropriate health care.

A number of medical problems have been associated with anorexia and bulemia. Dehydration and electrolyte imbalance may be a problem for these patients. Vital signs are usually depressed, with low temperature, blood pressure, and pulse rate. Other signs include dry, yellow (secondary to carotenemia) skin, lanugo, bruises, edema (during refeeding), murmurs, abdominal bloating, constipation, and cold intolerance. The differential diagnosis includes inflammatory bowel disease, celiac disease, Addison's disease, hyperthyroidism, malignancy, diabetes mellitus, depression, and CNS tumors.

Laboratory studies are tailored to the presentation and the likelihood of other medical illness. Initial screening tests usually include a CBC, sedimentation rate, blood urea nitrogen (BUN), creatinine, electrolytes, and urinalysis. In patients with amenorrhea, a pelvic assessment (which may include external genital examination and rectoabdominal palpation) is usually all that is indicated at diagnosis. A pregnancy test should be done if there is any suspicion of sexual activity or if the vagina appears estrogenized in a girl with secondary amenorrhea. Serum tests for FSH, LH, and prolactin are helpful in establishing the diagnosis of hypothalamic amenorrhea in the patient with an eating disorder and persistent amenorrhea. In girls with anorexia nervosa, serum levels of FSH and LH are low; the 24-hour secretory pattern of LH pulses may be immature [46]. The estradiol level (if measured) is usually less than 20 pg/ml, and the vaginal smear for estrogen effect is immature. Progesterone challenge is not indicated in patients with no evidence of normal estrogenization. It should be noted, however, that a girl with Turner syndrome and severe anorexia nervosa may have suppression of gonadotropin levels. CT or MRI scanning are indicated in patients with neurologic symptoms, headaches, and atypical presentations (especially prepubertal girls). Other tests may include thyroid function tests, malabsorption studies, and electrocardiogram.

Treatment includes medical monitoring including frequent weight checks, nutritional rehabilitation with slow weight gain, and psychotherapy for the patient and family. The patient needs to be educated about the consequences of her medical choices including from the gynecologic point of view the concern that long-term estrogen deficiency is associated with lower bone mass and may place her at risk of osteoporosis and fractures [47, 48]. Hospitalization is often necessary in the treatment of these girls, and a number of different therapeutic programs have been advocated.

Frisch and McArthur [49, 50] have proposed a chart for examining the relationships of height and weight on menstrual function. Although individual patients clearly show variation in the recovery of menstrual function at a particular weight and the tenth percentile of the weight/height chart may not hold for different ages during adolescence, the guidelines are useful in counselling patients to develop target weights. For example, using Figure 6-2, an adolescent who is 5 feet 5 inches would be expected to weigh a minimum of 44 kg (97 pounds) at the time of menarche, but if she later lost weight and developed secondary amenorrhea, she would need to achieve a weight of 49 kg (108 pounds) to regain her menses. Another method of determining a normal weight is to determine height age and then find the corresponding weight for that height age on the National Growth Charts. Another rule of thumb for the older adolescent is to

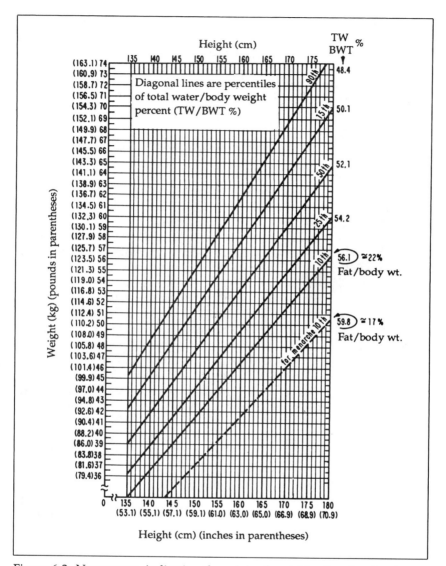

Figure 6-2. Nomogram, indicating the minimal weight a female of a given height should weigh to be likely to have normal menses. The lowest diagonal line is the tenth percentile of total water/body fat for menarche. The second lowest diagonal line is the tenth percentile for 18-year-old adolescents; this diagonal often corresponds to the weight needed for restoration of menses in an adolescent with weight loss and secondary amenorrhea. (From RE Frisch and JW McArthur, Menstrual cycles: Fatness as determinant of minimum weight for height necessary for their maintenance or onset. *Science* 1974, 185:949. By permission of the American Association for the Advancement of Science and Dr. Rose Frisch. Figure provided by Dr. Rose Frisch, Center for Population Studies, Cambridge, Mass.)

take the height in inches and double the number to give an approximation of the tenth percentile weight in pounds. Patients benefit from being given a range (goal plus 10 pounds) of weights, not a single number. Patients who regain a normal weight for height but persist with amenorrhea frequently continue to have abnormal eating patterns and preoccupation with food.

ATHLETIC AMENORRHEA

In the past decade, as more young women have participated in sports, the issue of athletic amenorrhea has received increasing attention. The incidence of amenorrhea in a variety of sports is unclear in large part because of the varying definitions used for secondary amenorrhea. However, it is clear that competitive athletes involved in sports associated with low weight for height, low percentage body fat, high energy drain, low caloric intake, and stress are likely to experience menstrual irregularity [51–58]. Endeavors such as gymnastics, ballet, and running are particularly likely to be associated with menstrual problems. However, other adolescent athletes such as swimmers may have menstrual dysfunction. In contrast, adolescents involved in normal after-school sports programs do not appear to be at increased risk of disruption of menstrual cycles [59], although the possibility of more subtle changes in GnRH pulsations or anovulation have not been examined in this population. Ellison and Lager [60] have found lowered salivary progesterone levels in recreational runners (average 12.5 miles/week). It is clear that many competitive athletes with seemingly regular menses in fact have anovulatory cycles or short luteal phases.

The age of thelarche and menarche is often delayed in thin athletes, especially ballet dancers and runners [37, 61, 62]. Malina [63] has proposed that some of this delay may be attributed to the preselection of girls with the thin body type and familial late development who excel in athletic endeavors, but some of the delay likely also results from the commitment to the sport. Frisch and co-workers [64] found that athletes who began their training premenarcheally experienced a delay in menarche and a higher incidence of amenorrhea than did athletes who began their training postmenarcheally. Each year of training before menarche delayed menarche by 5 months.

The intensity of the exercise and the age of the athlete also appear to be contributing factors. In most studies, the greater number of miles per week run is associated with a higher incidence of amenorrhea. For example, in a survey of college runners, Feicht and associates [65] found that the incidence of amenorrhea was 20 percent for women running 20 miles per week and 43 percent for those running 60 to 80 miles per week. A lower incidence of amenorrhea (19%) was found in the runners participating in the marathon trial of the

1984 Olympics [66]. Young runners and nulliparous runners are more likely to experience irregular cycles [67].

Diet may be suboptimal in many adolescent athletes, especially those participating in sports in which thinness is perceived as an advantage. In an attempt to separate weight loss from strenuous exercise, Bullen and colleagues [55] carried out a prospective study of menstrual cycles, assigning one group to weight maintenance and the other to weight loss. They found that exercise, especially if accompanied by weight loss, could reversibly disturb menstrual function. Those in the weight loss group experienced more delayed menses, and a higher percentage of patients had loss of the LH surge. It is important to note that some of the changes were detected only by the serial hormonal measurements.

Diets low in calories and red meat and high in carotene have been associated with amenorrhea [68–71]. Deuster and co-workers [70] found that 3-day diet records of amenorrheic runners had lower fat and zinc intake and higher vitamin A intake (probably in the form of beta carotene) and crude fiber intake. Pirke and associates [71] reported that weight loss using a vegetarian diet was more likely to induce menstrual dysfunction than a nonvegetarian diet. It is important to remember that girls with anorexia nervosa may have joined the track team and be exercising compulsively (often beyond the expectation of the coach) to lose additional weight. Eating disorders, including food restriction, binging, and purging, are prevalent especially among dancers.

Stress associated with the athletic endeavor also may increase the incidence of amenorrhea. Gadpaille and colleagues [72] have found an association between athletic amenorrhea, eating disorders, and a family history of major affective disorders. Whether this will be confirmed by others awaits further studies.

The mechanism of exercise-related menstrual changes is unclear [73–78]. Higher levels of estrogen during exercise caused by diminished clearance may inhibit gonadotropin release. Prolactin levels increase acutely with exercise but return to normal within 30 minutes of exercise, and 24-hour prolactin levels are not increased [74–76]. ACTH and β-endorphin also increase with exercise, and the endorphins may alter the pattern of GnRH release [77]. Naloxone, an opiate antagonist, can increase the amplitude of LH pulsations in some runners. Chin and associates [78] have proposed that periodic elevations of catecholamines during exercise may interfere with GnRH release. A normal LH response to GnRH in most runners also suggests that the defect is at the level of the hypothalamus. As noted in Chapter 4, a variety of patterns of GnRH and gonadotropin patterns can be seen in these young women.

Since athletes may suffer from other medical conditions, the evaluation of the athlete should follow the same pattern as that used to assess other adolescents. Pregnancy should always be excluded in the adolescent who is late for her menses. Clearly athletes can also have premature ovarian failure, polycystic ovary syndrome, thyroid disorders, and hyperprolactinemia causing amenorrhea.

Although previously it was assumed that athletic activity and menstrual dysfunction were a normal problem without sequelae, recent studies have focused on the possibility of lowered bone mass associated with estrogen deficiency. Using CT of the vertebral trabecular bone, Cann's group [79] found osteopenia in young adult women with exercise-related amenorrhea. Marcus and co-workers [80] found that while eumenorrheic runners had better bone density than sedentary eumenorrheic women, amenorrheic runners had decreased bone density by CT. Using dual photon densitometry, Drinkwater and colleagues [81] also found lower vertebral bone density in amenorrheic young adult runners than in cycling runners. Densitometry of the radius has yielded conflicting results, and bone loss is often not reflected well at this site.

In a survey of ballet dancers, Warren and associates [62] found that the incidence of stress fractures rose with increasing age of menarche and that the incidence of secondary amenorrhea was twice as high among dancers with stress fractures as those without. The intervals of amenorrhea were often marked by profound hypoestrogenism. Ballet dancers with delayed menarche also were more likely to have scoliosis. Ballet dancers frequently have the onset or return of menses following weight gain or a decrease in the amount of exercise (e.g., summer vacation, sidelined because of an injury).

Reassuringly, the lowered bone density appears to be at least partially reversible in girls who begin to menstruate normally. Runners who regained their menses after a mean of 40 months of amenorrhea experienced an increase in bone density in the 14-month follow-up [82]. With the improvement in technology to measure spine and hip bone density, athletes at risk of osteoporosis because of estrogen deficiency may benefit from early diagnosis and monitoring during treatment (decrease in exercise, gain in weight, and estrogen replacement). Wyshak and colleagues [83] have questioned the risk of bone fractures to former college athletes by surveying older women and observing no difference in risk between former college athletes and nonathletes. However, it is likely that athletes of today are quite different from those of the past, and the pursuit of thinness is a significant factor in the 1970s and 1980s. Noteworthy was a lower rate of cancers of the reproductive system and breast cancer in former athletes.

Adolescent athletes with amenorrhea deserve a medical evaluation and discussion of therapeutic options (see p. 176).

HYPERPROLACTINEMIA

The advent of sensitive hormone assays for prolactin in the early 1970s allowed the detection of and new therapies for prolactin-secreting pituitary tumors. Much new information has become available on the spectrum of disease, the natural history of prolactinomas, and outcome of surgically treated patients [84–94]. Nevertheless, controversy still exists on the best management of many patients. In addition, it is very important for the clinician to remember that stalk compression can cause hyperprolactinemia, and thus mild elevations of prolactin levels in association with a CNS tumor do not necessarily imply the presence of a prolactinoma. For example, patients with craniopharyngiomas, somatotropic tumors causing acromegaly, cysts (suprasellar arachnoid cysts and Rathke's cleft cyst), and nonfunctioning tumors may have elevated prolactin values (typically <200 ng/ml). In general the level of prolactin correlates with the size of the prolactinoma, and thus a large tumor occurring with a low serum prolactin level should raise the consideration of a tumor other than a prolactinoma.

The normal serum prolactin level of women ranges from 1 to 20 ng/ml with a mean of 8.9 ng/ml (although laboratories vary in reported values) [89]. Prolactin is secreted episodically, it has a half-life of around 20 minutes, and peak secretion occurs during sleep. Patients with pituitary tumors often have abolition of the sleep-related rhythm and have elevated prolactin values night and day.

Unlike most pituitary hormones, prolactin is regulated primarily by inhibition from the hypothalamus through secretion of a prolactin inhibiting factor (PIF). PIF is either dopamine or a dopamine-like agent, since dopamine and dopaminergic drugs, such as bromocriptine, lower serum prolactin levels. Drugs such as phenothiazines and other tranquilizers that block dopamine receptors and agents such as reserpine and alpha methyldopa that cause dopamine depletion in tuberoinfundibular neurons raise prolactin levels.

The relative importance of other inhibiting factors such as GnRH-associated peptide (GAP) and prolactin releasers such as estrogens, thyrotropin releasing hormone (TRH), and serotonin is not fully elucidated. Estrogens stimulate prolactin release and result in an increase in the size and number of lactotropes. Prolactin secretion is increased during pregnancy, with prolactin levels peaking at term (100–300 ng/ml). Prolactin levels rise with each episode of nursing in the initial postpartum period, but by 4 to 6 months prolactin levels are normal and the prolactin response to suckling no longer occurs. Although some patients taking or discontinuing oral contraceptives develop galactorrhea, studies have not shown an association between oral contraceptives and the development of prolactinomas. Hypothyroidism (with elevated TRH and TSH levels) is often associated with

Table 6-2. Differential Diagnosis of
Hyperprolactinemia and/or Galactorrhea

Postpartum and postabortion

Pituitary tumor

Hypothalamic diseases and tumors: craniopharyngioma, sarcoidosis, histiocytosis X, encephalitis, Chiari-Frommel, pituitary stalk section or compression

Hypothyroidism

Drug-induced: phenothiazines, reserpine, prostaglandins, methyldopa,
amitriptylene, cimetidine, benzodiazepines, haloperidol, cocaine, metoclopramide

Chronic renal failure

Local factors: chest wall surgery, trauma, nipple stimulation, herpes zoster,
atopic dermatitis, thoracic burns

Tumors: bronchogenic or renal carcinoma

Other: stress, sleep-induced, hypoglycemia

Idiopathic

---

elevated prolactin levels, possibly related to the decreased dopamine
levels in hypothyroidism. The observation that TRH can cause release
of prolactin has been used to study patients with elevated prolactin
levels.

Prolactin secretion is also affected by breast stimulation in some
nonpregnant women and can increase following ingestion of a large
meal, during major stress (such as general anesthesia for surgery),
orgasm, hypoglycemia, and marathon running [95, 96]. Thus optimally, the serum prolactin level should not be drawn after a large
meal, strenuous exercise, or breast examination.

Hyperprolactinemia can occur because of a number of conditions
including physiologic stimuli (pregnancy, exercise, stress), drugs, hypothyroidism, renal failure (decreased clearance of prolactin), hyperplasia of lactotropes (functional hyperprolactinemia), or a pituitary
tumor (see Table 6-2). The presenting complaint in the adolescent
may be galactorrhea, interrupted pubertal development, or primary
or secondary amenorrhea. The absence of galactorrhea is not unusual
in the adolescent, especially in the girl with hyperprolactinemia and
primary amenorrhea. Amenorrheic patients with low to normal FSH
and LH, including those who withdraw to progestin or who have
polycystic ovary syndrome, should have a serum prolactin measured.
Galactorrhea with normal menses and normal serum prolactin virtually excludes a tumor, although galactorrhea is unusual in this setting
without a prior pregnancy [98].

The evaluation of the adolescent with hyperprolactinemia should
include a gynecologic history of pregnancies and abortions, medica-

tions and illicit drugs, menstrual history, hirsutism or acne, symptoms of thyroid dysfunction, visual changes, and headaches. The physical examination should include a careful neurologic assessment, including fundoscopic examination and visual field test by confrontation, palpation of the thyroid, notation of vital signs, a careful breast examination, and evaluation of androgen excess and estrogenization by vaginal examination.

Pregnancy, hypothyroidism, renal and hepatic disease, polycystic ovary syndrome, and ingestion of drugs (including cocaine) should be ruled out in the patient with hyperprolactinemia. In most of these conditions, prolactin values are elevated to only 30 to 100 ng/ml. Repeat serum prolactin values should be measured with optimal conditions of no exercise, meals, or breast stimulation. Thyroid function tests should include a TSH level. Anteroposterior and lateral cone-down views of the sella are useful only in detecting calcification or lesions large enough to cause erosion or enlargement of the sella. Detection of small lesions requires CT or MRI scanning. Tomograms of the sella should be restricted to specific preoperative needs.

A prolactin in excess of 100 ng/ml is suggestive of a prolactin-secreting tumor; Turksoy and co-workers [97] found that 17 out of 18 patients with proven microadenomas had prolactin level greater than 160 ng/ml. However, a tumor can be seen with only a minimal elevation of prolactin, especially in the case of nonfunctioning tumors that cause stalk compression. Prolactinomas are classified as microadenomas (< 10 mm) and macroadenomas (> 10 mm). Even the newest radiologic scanners can miss small lesions. In fact, it is likely that patients classified as having "functional hyperprolactinemia" represent a spectrum of findings from mild hyperplasia of lactotropes to small pituitary microadenomas.

Even stimulation tests and suppression tests are not reliable in excluding a small tumor. Hyperprolactinemia of many etiologies will respond to bromocriptine therapy. The TRH test may be of some help, since patients with functional hyperprolactinemia usually respond with a doubling of serum prolactin level, whereas 78 to 95 percent of those with pituitary tumors will have a blunted or no response because either the TRH receptors are absent or the prolactin-secreting cells are already secreting maximally. Response to GnRH is usually normal in patients with both functional hyperprolactinemia and microadenomas. Formal pituitary function testing is thus usually reserved for evaluation of preoperative status and macroadenomas and is not necessary in patients with prolactin-secreting microadenomas.

Estrogen status should be assessed in these young women by serum estradiol level, vaginal smear, and progestin challenge. Klibanski and associates [99] have found reduced bone density in young women with hyperprolactinemia and serum estradiol levels of less than 20 pg/ml. Bone density improved with the institution of effective therapy [100].

Once the diagnosis of a prolactin-secreting pituitary tumor is made, the clinician needs to consider the size, the estrogen status, and the desire for fertility. Some authors have suggested observing patients with small microadenomas and functional hyperprolactinemia, since studies of the natural history of these lesions have suggested that many lesions will stay the same size or regress with lowering of serum prolactin and reestablishment of menses over time [93]. However, since most adolescents with microadenomas are estrogen deficient, treatment with bromocriptine to restore menses and estrogen levels seems indicated. The years of adolescence are especially important in establishing peak bone mass.

Transphenoidal surgery of microadenomas is 90 percent successful in the immediate postoperative period [101, 102], but long-term follow-up has found that 40 to 50 percent of patients recur with hyperprolactinemia (even though a lesion may not be demonstrable on CT scan) [91, 103]. A normal prolactin value 6 months after surgery indicates that a cure is likely. The rationale for surgery has been that medical therapy with bromocriptine would likely have to be continued indefinitely; however, more recent data from published studies and our own experience would suggest that after 2 years of bromocriptine therapy, some patients have normal prolactin levels and menses following discontinuation of the medication [90, 94].

The best form of treatment for macroadenomas is still controversial. Medical therapy with bromocriptine is advocated by many, especially since the cure rate with surgery is less than 40 percent. Bromocriptine can reduce prolactin levels substantially and cause shrinkage of the tumor over weeks to months (see Case 9) [104, 105]. Cytoplasmic volume of cells is decreased. In most patients, bromocriptine will have to be continued indefinitely, which is very expensive. Abrupt cessation of medication can result in increased tumor size. However, more experience and long-term follow-up are needed in the gradual withdrawal of bromocriptine after 2 to 3 years of therapy to see if medication needs to be continued in all patients. Tumor enlargement may occur in some patients despite bromocriptine therapy because of the presence of a nonfunctioning or non-prolactin-secreting tumor [106] or the occurrence of intrapituitary hemorrhage or tumor necrosis. Since prolactin levels may fall with bromocriptine therapy in spite of continued tumor enlargement, successful management must be monitored by prolactin levels, CT or MRI, and clinical assessment. Combined therapy with surgery and radiation has also been advocated for large tumors but may lead to hypopituitarism. Controlled clinical studies are needed to answer many of these questions to allow physicians to give the best possible therapies for macroadenomas.

Adolescents treated with bromocriptine for microadenomas usually have resumption of menses and restoration of fertility. Patients thus need to be counselled to use effective barrier contraception if they become sexually active. In young women desiring fertility, bromocriptine has been used effectively to lessen prolactin levels. Discontinuation of bromocriptine therapy is recommended as soon as a pregnancy is diagnosed, although the incidence of congenital malformation in infants exposed to bromocriptine appears to be no higher than in a normal population. The long-term risk to the fetus is unknown. A major worry in these patients is that with high placental estrogens the tumor would rapidly enlarge during pregnancy and cause symptoms of visual field defects, headaches, and diabetes insipidus. Tumor-related complications appear to occur in about 15 percent of bromocriptine-induced pregnancies but are uncommon in patients with microadenomas (<5%) [107, 108]. Careful follow-up is thus important with monitoring of clinical status (headaches and visual symptoms), serum prolactin level, and possibly monthly visual field tests. A prolactin level of greater than 500 ng/ml, headaches, visual field changes, and/or diabetes insipidus suggest tumor enlargement. Complications of tumor enlargement are usually reversible with the reinstitution of bromocriptine therapy for the remainder of the pregnancy. Prolactin levels fall after delivery, and there appears to be no contraindication to breast-feeding.

The best approach to the patient with a macroadenoma who desires a pregnancy has not been established, and more information is needed on the benefits of surgery and/or radiation versus the use of bromocriptine therapy before and, if necessary, throughout pregnancy. The risk of symptomatic tumor enlargement with macroadenomas is 15 to 35 percent for tumors previously treated with bromocriptine, as compared to 4 to 7 percent for those previously treated with surgery and/or radiation therapy. In these high-risk patients, careful monitoring throughout pregnancy of clinical status and monthly formal visual field testing is essential. Imaging is indicated for patients with symptomatic enlargement of the tumor and in all patients postpartum. Bromocriptine is reinstituted in symptomatic patients; some require surgery during pregnancy.

The decision to institute bromocriptine therapy is thus based on indications for treating estrogen deficiency, the desire for fertility, or the desire for cessation of lactation. Bromocriptine is usually prescribed in slowly increasing dosages, starting with one half of a 2.5-mg tablet at bedtime, followed a week later by one tablet at bedtime, followed in one week by one 2.5-mg tablet twice a day. A dosage of 5.0 to 7.5 mg per day is usually adequate in most patients with mild to moderate hyperprolactinemia, although some patients do require a higher dose. Patients must be warned to be careful rising from bed in the morning because of the possibility of postural hypotension; some patients notice nausea, headache, dizziness, nasal congestion, and fatigue with bromocriptine therapy. In patients unable to tolerate oral bromocriptine because of nausea, Vermesh and co-workers [109] have reported that vaginal administration of this drug can result in detectable plasma bromocriptine levels and reduction of prolactin. Teguride, a new dopamine agonist drug, appears to have fewer side effects than bromocriptine and potent prolactin-inhibiting effects, with 1 mg of teguride having similar effect to 2.5 mg of bromocriptine [110]. Other dopamine agonists appear to have similar efficacy and require additional testing.

Long-term follow-up of patients is essential whatever treatment option is chosen—observation, bromocriptine, or surgery/radiation. Clinical status including estrogenization, menstrual pattern, and neurologic and visual symptoms should be assessed. Prolactin levels should be followed. Formal visual field testing should be performed periodically depending on the size of the lesion. Imaging with CT or MRI is important regardless of whether the prolactin has diminished with bromocriptine therapy. Radiation to the eyes should be minimized, and thus MRI is especially useful for long-term follow-up in patients with macroadenomas who require more surveillance.

EUGONADISM
The term *eugonadism* has been used to include patients with normal estrogenization but failure of a normal menstrual pattern. Patients with genital anomalies such as obstructed outflow and uterine agenesis would be in this category (see p. 194). In addition, patients with polycystic ovary syndrome typically have normal to elevated levels of estrogens but oligomenorrhea and often evidence of androgen excess (see p. 246; Chap. 7). Patients with many of the central problems, systemic illnesses, stress, and weight loss may also fit midway between the categories of eugonadism and hypogonadotropic hypogonadism because estrogen levels fall into the range seen in the follicular phase of the cycle but normal cyclicity does not occur.

TREATMENT GUIDELINES
Treatment is aimed at the etiology of the problem, especially in patients with CNS tumors, Crohn's disease, or anorexia nervosa. For example, nutritional rehabilitation and corticosteroids or surgery may cause the teenager with Crohn's disease to begin spontaneous pubertal maturation. Adequate weight gain and psychotherapy may result in progression of puberty and menses in the girl with anorexia nervosa. The girl with end-stage renal failure often experiences menarche following a successful renal transplant; in fact, ovulatory cycles may result in an unwanted pregnancy for the adolescent who has not previously used birth control.

For many patients with irreversible estrogen deficiency or significant constitutional delay, estrogen replacement therapy is needed to bring about normal secondary sexual characteristics at an age commensurate with the peer group. Although few adolescents experience vasomotor symptoms such as those seen in the postmenopausal woman or following oophorectomy, estrogen replacement reverses vaginal atrophy, decreases the risk of osteoporosis and fractures, and likely lessens the risk of cardiovascular disease because of beneficial changes in lipoproteins [111–115].

Since many girls with gonadal dysgenesis, premature ovarian failure, or Kallmann's syndrome do not come to medical attention until 13 to 16 years of age, therapy is undertaken at that time. The goals of therapy are to induce normal breast development and menses, increase growth velocity, and promote normal bone mass. In adolescents and young adults, the risk of low bone density appears to be especially related to the lack of spontaneous development, low weight, and radiation therapy [116]. Thus patients should be identified for replacement therapy as early as possible. Patients with known chemotherapy and especially radiation therapy should have bone age and ovarian status evaluated at a chronological age of 10 to 12 years and should be considered for replacement therapy when the diagnosis of ovarian failure is established.

The optimal age for treating patients with a delay in sexual development because of athletics or anorexia nervosa is unknown. In general, it seems preferable for patients to "earn" their estrogenization, pubertal development, and menses by making the necessary changes in life-style, especially improving nutrition. Coaches, parents, and athletes should be counselled about optimal diet, to establish normal growth and development. However, with the increasing evidence of the potential for osteoporosis the health care provider should inform the patient about these concerns and offer estrogen replacement at least by the mid-teens (e.g., 3 years postmenarche or age 16 years). In girls with a normal age of pubertal development and estrogenization followed later by amenorrhea and estrogen deficiency, instituting medical treatment and counselling to try to bring about a change in life-style for at least a year before offering estrogen replacement appears to be a reasonable approach. Some patients will reduce their exercise; others may find their regimen important for optimal performance or they may be in a compulsive pattern associated with an eating disorder. Weight, height, body fat percentage (if possible), and diet should be monitored. Previously, patients were often allowed to remain estrogen deficient for years or even a decade or more, increasing the risk of osteoporosis. Although some anorexic and athletic patients will refuse medical intervention, the potential problems of estrogen deficiency should be discussed with the patient and her family. Calcium replacement alone has not been shown to be efficacious in the postmenopausal woman and thus should be considered an adjunct to the total health care of the young woman. An intake of 1200 to 1500 mg of calcium is recommended by diet (see Appendix 3 for handout) or supplemental calcium.

Single photon densitometry of the radius can be used to provide a baseline measurement and to impress the patient of the need to take the potential medical complication of bone loss seriously. However, this technique may not demonstrate the actual degree of osteopenia. Newer techniques including dual photon absorptiometry (DPA) may well yield further information on the risks of estrogen deficiency in the young and most importantly the optimal dose of replacement to achieve normal bone mass.

The dosages of estrogen for inducing secondary sexual characteristics and menses have been apparent for a number of years, but the optimal preparation and dosage for long-term replacement are still a subject of controversy. Conjugated estrogens (Premarin), 0.3 mg, or 5 to 10 μg of ethinyl estradiol,* given daily for 12 to 18 months, is satisfactory to induce breast development. Oral contraceptives are not recommended for initial therapy because the progestin may impair breast development. The estrogen dose is then raised to 0.625 mg (and then stepwise to 0.9 and 1.25 mg) of conjugated estrogens or 20 μg (to 35 μg) of ethinyl estradiol, given in cycles of 25 to 27 days/ month along with a progestin. Elevated gonadotropin levels usually only partially suppress, even with what appears to be adequate doses. The progestin can be used for 5 days a month for the first 3 months and thereafter increased to 10 and subsequently 13 to 14 days (e.g., given on days 13–25 each month). The most commonly used progestin is medroxyprogesterone (Provera), 10 mg; doses as low as 5 mg may be sufficient to protect the endometrium from endometrial hyperplasia, although studies in adolescents are needed. Endometrial cancer has been reported in patients with gonadal dysgenesis, especially those treated with unopposed estrogens, and thus adequate progestin is important in addition to the estrogen [117, 118]. Used sequentially in the postmenopausal woman, the progestins norethindrone and norgestrel may be more likely to lower high-density lipoprotein (HDL) cholesterol [119] unless used in small doses. Endometrial biopsy is indicated in young women taking estrogen replacement therapy who develop irregular bleeding without obvious etiology (missed pills, pelvic infection). Padwick and colleagues [120] have suggested that in postmenopausal women treated with daily estrogens, the optimal dose of progestin can be determined by observing the bleeding pattern. The progestin was given for the first 12 days of each month; women who had bleeding on or before day 10 after the addition of progestin had predominantly proliferative endometrium,

*The lowest dose of ethinyl estradiol commercially available is 20 μg.

whereas those with bleeding on day 11 or later had a wholly or predominantly secretory endometrium.

Previous studies in postmenopausal women have demonstrated that doses of 0.625 mg of conjugated estrogens, 0.3 mg of conjugated estrogens plus calcium, and 20 to 25 μg of ethinyl estradiol can be used to maintain bone density [112, 113, 121–124]. These doses, however, may not be applicable to the adolescent patient who needs to increase bone mass, not just maintain bone density. Our studies of adolescents with estrogen deficiency states treated with conjugated estrogens, 0.625 mg for 21 days of the month, have shown that a regimen started at a mean age of 16 years can prevent further bone loss but cannot bring bone mass up to the levels of age-matched controls [116]. In addition, exercise and calcium intake in adolescents are often inadequate and need to be encouraged as part of a total therapeutic approach. More studies are needed in determining an optimal dose for long-term treatment of adolescents and young adults. Doses more likely to be effective are conjugated estrogens (Premarin)—1.25 mg, transdermal β-estradiol patches (Estraderm)—0.1 mg, ethinyl estradiol—30 to 35 μg, micronized estradiol (Estrace)—2 mg, all given in cycles (along with 13–14 days of progestin), but none of these has been subjected to long-term studies. Many adolescents tolerate the estradiol patches well and find changing them twice a week preferable to daily oral medication (oral progestin is still necessary). However, other adolescents complain of the patch falling off, have allergic reactions to the adhesive, or do not like the idea of having a potentially visible acknowledgement of a medical problem. Counselling needs to take these issues into account in the choice of therapy. Adolescents prefer to have menses, and thus continuous estrogen and progestin used in the postmenopausal woman are not indicated in this age group. After normal breast development and menses have occurred, oral contraceptives with 30 to 35 μg of ethinyl estradiol may be another option for the adolescent, although side effects may be greater than with sequential estrogen and progestin. Since use of replacement estrogen is long-term, patients should be carefully instructed in the potential side effects and monitored with measurement of blood pressure, Papanicolaou smears, and serum lipids.

The estrogen replacement therapy of Turner syndrome patients is especially difficult. Patients with Turner syndrome have short stature, and therapy with growth hormone appears promising in altering adult final height. Thus delaying epiphyseal closure by postponing the use of estrogen would seem indicated. On the other hand, patients with Turner syndrome show evidence of demineralization from an early age, and adolescents with Turner syndrome have low bone density for age. In contrast, patients with normal estrogenization and Turner syndrome have normal bone density [116]. Thus two competing aims present a dilemma for the physician designing optimal therapy for these girls.

In the past, androgens including oxandrolone were given by some centers during late childhood and early adolescence to try to promote growth [125–128]. Although these hormones did result in a significant increase in growth velocity during the first year of treatment, final adult height did not appear to be improved [128]. The observation that low-dose estrogen promoted bone growth led to several trials of using ethinyl estradiol at 100 ng/kg/day starting in late childhood [129–131]. Short-term results appeared beneficial, with a significant growth acceleration in most Turner patients treated for 6 to 12 months, but our center and others have found that bone age also increased and final height did not appear to be increased. The low-dose estrogen therapy did, however, result in increased somatomedin-C levels and psychological gains with the height spurt. Although the institution of estrogen therapy in mid-adolescence might be expected to cause shorter stature than institution in late adolescence because of closure of epiphyses, in fact we could not find any difference in final height between those treated at a mean age of 14.3 years and those treated at a mean age of 17.2 years [132]. Some, but not all studies, have found that stature of the Turner patients is related to mean mid-parental height [128, 132].

The newest mode of therapy for Turner patients has been the use of synthetic growth hormone [133–135]. Long-term controls are lacking, but Rosenfield and associates [133] have demonstrated encouraging results with the use of growth hormone (alone and combined with oxandrolone) in promoting growth. In the first year of therapy of Turner patients, the mean growth rate for controls was 3.8 cm/year, for human growth hormone (met-hGH) 6.6 cm/year, oxandrolone 7.9 cm/year, and for combination therapy with human growth hormone and oxandrolone 9.8 cm/year. The control and oxandrolone alone groups were discontinued after the first year, and thus final height data must now use historical controls. Height velocity did decrease after the first year, but the growth rate was still increased over the control year with combination therapy (7.4 cm in the second year, 6.1 cm in the third year) and in the second year with met-hGH (5.4 cm in the second year, 4.4 cm in the third year). Growth rates with injections of growth hormone (6 times a week) or with growth hormone plus oxandrolone (3 times a week) appear to be comparable. Because of the potential for advancement of bone age with androgens, growth hormone alone (6 times/week) should be used in young children when growth rate declines. Oxandrolone is no longer available and whether other androgens (e.g., fluoxymesterone) should be given or whether growth hormone alone is indicated for late childhood and early adolescence is unclear. Recommendations on optimal management are likely to evolve over the next few years. Some centers are combining estrogen and growth hormone therapy. Treatment with growth hormone is expensive and may have long-term side effects not presently known. Thus patients and parents need to be informed about the benefits and risks of treatment.

Treatment of adolescents with oligomenorrhea and anovulatory cycles aims at giving normal menstrual flow and protection of the endometrium from hyperplasia. Progestins such as medroxyprogesterone, 10 mg, can be prescribed for 13 to 14 days each month (or every 2 months in patients with scant withdrawal flow). Patients with chronic anovulatory states such as polycystic ovary syndrome have increased risk of endometrial carcinoma and should receive long-term progestin therapy (13–14 days per month) or oral contraceptives (see Chap. 7).

Even though fertility considerations are beyond the scope of this book, it is useful to be able to provide some information to the teenager with estrogen deficiency states. Most patients with irreversible ovarian failure such as Turner syndrome who desire to have children will choose adoption; however, advances in technology have now shown that oocyte donation and in vitro fertilization are possible in women with ovarian failure [136–138]. Patients with autoimmune oophoritis and resistant ovary syndrome have been reported to have rare pregnancies spontaneously (because of the waxing and waning nature of the disorder) and with estrogen therapy, corticosteroids (autoimmune disease), and gonadotropin therapy. Patients with GnRH deficiency can be induced to ovulate with GnRH pulsatile therapy and with gonadotropins. Although GnRH can also be used to induce pubertal development, oral estrogens are clearly easier and less expensive for this purpose. In addition, an 18-year-old female with Kallmann's syndrome who had been treated long-term with GnRH was reported to develop urticaria associated with anti-GnRH–antibodies [139]. Patients with hypothalamic dysfunction and infertility need to have the issue of weight, exercise, and stress addressed and then, depending on the etiology, need to be treated with clomiphene citrate, gonadotropins, or GnRH. Ovulation can usually be induced in patients with hyperprolactinemia by the use of bromocriptine (see p. 175).

The most important part of the therapy undertaken by the physician is the ability to listen to questions and respond in a straightforward fashion. The adolescent needs to know that her parents do not have secrets about her medical condition. Drawings that underscore how normal she is and potential technology available in the future are extremely meaningful. The positive aspects of her condition and her ability to function as a normal woman should be emphasized. Patients may cope better with the issue of infertility if they receive information in response to their own questions. The girl with ovarian failure can be counselled about the many other young patients with infertility; she may know a couple who has spent years in infertility treatments. The fact that she can make plans that are right for her from the beginning of her marriage can be helpful in her thinking about the future. Acceptance of estrogen therapy is generally the easier part of the counselling, given the widespread lay information on osteoporosis.

Groups are available in many metropolitan centers for counselling patients (e.g., Turner groups). Young adolescents frequently resist going to meetings, but parents, older adolescents, and young adults often find the support helpful. Teenagers also often discover meeting another patient with the same condition one-on-one beneficial. For example, before surgery for reconstruction for vaginal agenesis, a girl may find it useful to meet an older patient who has already been through the experience. Many girls are relieved to discuss their diagnosis openly, since before the initial medical visit they have often feared worse problems, including cancer, which has impaired development or menses. Grief and mourning over the lack of function is normal, and frequent visits can help the patient come to terms with the problem. Denial of the diagnosis between visits is common, and the same questions may arise each time. The physician frequently needs to do much of the talking during these appointments with statements such as "I have other girls in my practice with this problem, and I find they worry about . . . ." Sometimes, a young patient will request to be excused from physical education class so that her lack of development will not be the subject of peer discussion; this request should be honored. The empathic physician or nurse can greatly aid the patient in acceptance of the medical diagnosis and the treatment plan.

DELAYED SEXUAL DEVELOPMENT
The absence of breast budding by the age of 13 years is 2 standard deviations beyond normal and requires an evaluation. If the teenager is a thin competitive athlete, then hormonal testing can be delayed until 14 years. The stigmata of Turner syndrome, especially short stature, or a falloff in height and weight gain, suggestive of malnutrition or a systemic disease, may prompt an earlier diagnosis. A patient history and physical examination along with evaluation of growth records are essential. The chief complaint may be "no development," and yet evidence of breast budding and a growth spurt may indicate that development has indeed occurred and that observation is indicated. Pubic hair may imply that the patient is about to begin her thelarche as well, but remember that the patients with ovarian failure will develop some pubic hair because of the rise of adrenal androgens. As noted on p. 151, the physical examination includes a general assessment as well as external genital examination. Estrogen effect on the vaginal mucosa can be assessed visually and with the help of a

vaginal smear. Visualizing the cervix is much less important in the girl with no development than in the girl with primary amenorrhea. However, examination of the patient in the knee-chest position or rectoabdominal palpation is reassuring that the uterus is present.

Initial studies in the evaluation of delayed development include a wrist x ray for bone age, CBC with sedimentation rate, thyroid function tests (including TSH), FSH, and LH. In the absence of short stature suggesting gonadal dysgenesis, a serum prolactin is often drawn as part of the initial work-up. The differential diagnosis is made by separating patients' conditions into hypergonadotropic hypogonadism and hypogonadotropic hypogonadism (Fig. 6-3). Patients with elevated gonadotropins have ovarian failure and need to have a karyotype; patients with a normal XX karyotype should be

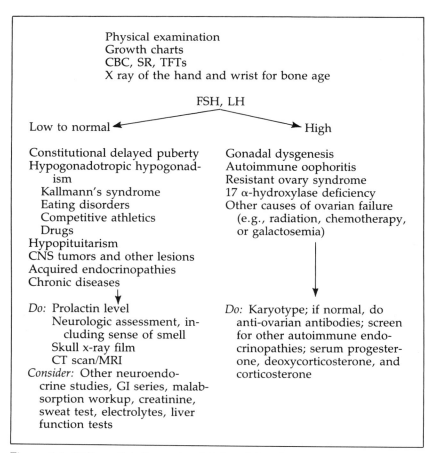

Figure 6-3. Differential diagnosis of delayed development.

assessed for autoimmune disease. Adolescents with low or normal gonadotropin levels require evaluation for a systemic disease or a CNS disorder. Studies may include prolactin level, somatomedin-C, skull x ray, CT or MRI scan, GnRH testing, and other neuroendocrine tests (e.g., growth hormone stimulation tests, cortisol response). Visual field testing is indicated in the presence of a CNS lesion. Other tests for systemic disease depending on clinical suspicion may include a malabsorption workup, sweat chloride, BUN, creatinine, electrolytes, calcium, phosphorus, urinary osmolality, and electrolytes. Patients thought to have a constitutional delay of puberty should be kept under surveillance for the possibility of an initially undetected CNS tumor or systemic disease.

In patients with ovarian failure, therapy as outlined on p. 176 should be undertaken as soon as the diagnosis is made in early adolescence. In patients with a constitutional delay, reassurance may be all that is necessary; however, many girls by 14 to 15 years of age will elect to take exogenous hormones to promote normal breast development. Therapy can be stopped after attainment of secondary sexual characteristics to reassess whether the patient has a normal delay or hypothalamic dysfunction. If no spontaneous development continues, then estrogen can be reinstituted for courses of 3 to 6 months with periodic discontinuation of therapy. Many patients have the onset of pubic hair after instituting estrogen replacement therapy; however, girls with previous CNS tumors and those with panhypopituitarism often have adrenal insufficiency and thus have absent or only scanty pubic and axillary hair.

Case 1. S. T. came to the clinic at the age of 15 years with "no development." She had always been the shortest member of her class. The review of systems was unremarkable. Physical examination (Fig. 6-4) revealed a short teenager with many of the stigmata of Turner syndrome (low hairline, webbed neck, ptosis, "fishmouth," increased carrying angle, and short fourth metacarpals). Her height was 54 inches and her weight, 105 pounds; blood pressure was 125/80; and pulse rate was 78/min. Breast development was stage 1; no pubic or axillary hair was present.

Pertinent laboratory tests showed FSH level of 143 mIU/ml, LH of 135 mIU/ml, a chromatin-negative buccal smear, and karyotype of 45,X. The patient was started on conjugated estrogens; then after 1 year, regular menstrual periods were established with the addition of medroxyprogesterone therapy. At the age of 20 years, her therapy changed to oral contraceptives.

Case 2. C. O. was referred to our unit at the age of 15^{10}/$_{12}$ because of delayed development. She was the 7 pound, 6 ounce product of a normal pregnancy and delivery. Her developmental milestones were normal; however, she was always the shortest member of her class (she was an "A" student in the tenth grade). The review of systems was negative. The family history revealed that one of her father's sisters had her menarche at the age of 20 years. On physical examination (Fig. 6-5), C. O. was a short, pleasant teenager with a height of 55¾ inches and a weight of 86 pounds; blood pressure was 105/70;

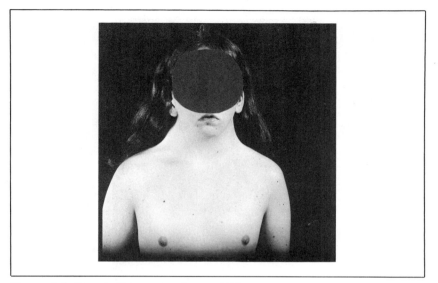

Figure 6-4. Case 1, Turner syndrome (XO).

pulse rate was 66/min. Fundi were normal. Breast development was stage 1, although the areolae were slightly puffy with a diameter of 2.4 cm. There was no pubic or axillary hair. As an outpatient, C. O. had a normal CBC, blood urea nitrogen, thyroid function tests, and urinalysis; FSH level was 7.7 mIU/ml and LH 6.3 mIU/ml. She was admitted for an extensive neuroendocrine evaluation, which included skull x-ray films, CT scan, metyrapone test, growth hormone levels, and GnRH test, all of which were normal.

Because no organic lesion was found, the patient was started on conjugated estrogens (Premarin), 0.3 mg daily, and within a short period of time she began to have breast development. Pubic hair appeared gradually. One year later the estrogen dosage was increased to 0.625 mg given in cycles with 10 mg of medroxyprogesterone (Provera). The hormone therapy was discontinued after 18 months, and C. O. continued to have normal cyclic menses. One year later, she had an unplanned pregnancy, which she decided to terminate. She admitted that she never thought *she* could get pregnant. Her cycles have remained normal, and she is currently using contraception.

Case 3. L. C. presented to the clinic at age 16⁶/₁₂ years because of no sexual development. She recalled being short since age 8 or 9 years. She had had several moves with her family at that time, and two of her grandparents had died when she was between age 8 and 12 years. She had otherwise always been in good health and specifically denied headaches, frequent infections, eating disorders, and gastrointestinal symptoms. Her family members had not experienced any delays in pubertal development. Her father was 65 inches tall; her mother was 62 inches tall and had had menarche at age 13 years.

Physical examination revealed a healthy, intelligent, short girl with normal blood pressure and pulse rate. Weight was 105 pounds and height 58¼ inches. Breast development was Tanner stage 1, and pubic hair was stage 2. No axillary hair was present. The external genitalia were normal but unes-

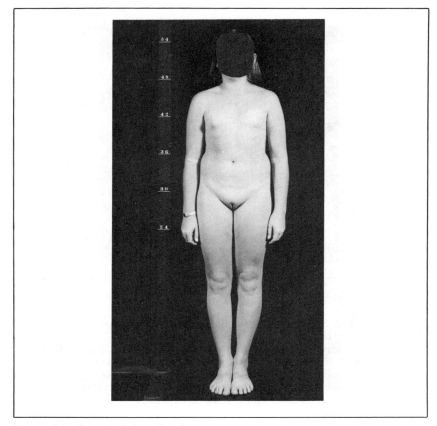

Figure 6-5. Case 2, delayed puberty.

trogenized, and a small uterus was palpable on rectoabdominal examination. Neurologic examination including a sense of smell was normal. Growth charts (Fig. 6-6) showed the patient to be slightly overweight for height; bone age was 10%12 years, with a height age of 11%12 years. LH was 2.2 mIU/ml, FSH less than 2 mIU/ml, estradiol less than 20 pg/ml, DHAS 109 μg/dl, and prolactin 2.2 ng/ml. Thyroid function tests, creatinine, urinalysis, CBC, and sedimentation rate were normal. As noted in Figure 6-3, with the finding of low levels of gonadotropins, further tests of CNS were undertaken. Skull x rays and CT scan were normal. An overnight study of gonadotropin levels showed no detectable pulsations of LH or FSH (all values < 2.0 mIU/ml), and GnRH testing showed a prepubertal pattern of LH and FSH. Cortisol and growth hormone responses were normal overnight and with insulin testing.

A diagnosis of hypogonadotropic hypogonadism was made, and the patient was started on estrogen therapy, initially 0.3 mg of conjugated estrogens, which was subsequently increased to 0.625 mg and then 1.25 mg. With 2 years of therapy, she has developed pubertal breasts with areola 2.5 cm and glandular tissue 6 × 6 cm, and pubic hair is now stage 3. Bone age was 13 years at a chronological age of 18 years, and a significant growth spurt can be seen in Figure 6-6. Whether this case represents GnRH a permanent hy-

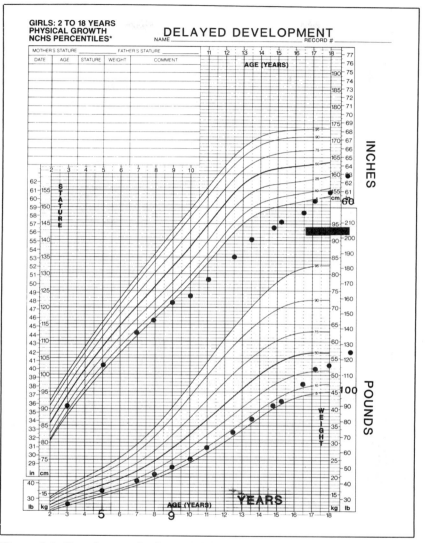

Figure 6-6. Case 3, growth chart of delayed development.

pogonadotropic state or less likely a significant constitutional delay will become more apparent after therapy is discontinued.

Case 4. M. C. was referred to the Adolescent Clinic by the Renal Clinic at age 15⁶/₁₂ because of delayed development. She had been diagnosed with immune complex nephritis at age 8 years and had begun dialysis for end-stage renal disease at age 11 years, at the same time she recalled the onset of pubic hair. She had a successful renal transplant at age 13 years. At the time of her clinic visit she had a normal serum creatinine and was taking prednisone, 15

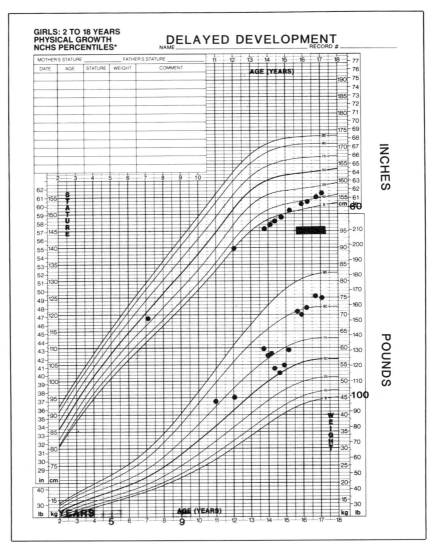

Figure 6-7. Case 4, growth chart of patient with delayed development, renal transplant, and XY gonadal dysgenesis.

mg every other day, and azathioprine, 100 mg daily. She was concerned because she had never had the onset of breast development or menses.

Physical examination revealed a short, overweight, pleasant teenager. Height was 59½ inches, weight 131 pounds (Fig. 6-7). Blood pressure and pulse were normal. Breast development was Tanner stage 1, and pubic hair scant stage 2 to 3; no axillary hair was present. The abdominal examination revealed several large scars with a kidney palpable in the right lower quadrant. Pelvic examination revealed a prepubertal unestrogenized introitus; examination in the knee-chest position showed a normal vagina and cervix. Rectoabdominal examination showed a small cervix palpable. Although the initial thought was that M. C.'s delay in puberty was likely to be caused by her chronic illness, the fact that she had started her pubic hair development at age 11 years and not progressed to a normal puberty in spite of the establishment of normal renal function following the transplant suggested other diagnoses. Bone age was 10⁶/₁₂ years. Thyroid function tests were normal, but surprisingly gonadotropin levels were elevated, with LH 216 mIU/ml and FSH 297 mIU/ml. Because of gonadal failure, a karyotype was done and revealed 46,XY. With the diagnosis of XY gonadal dysgenesis, M. C. had surgery to remove the intra-abdominal gonads. Pathology revealed bilateral gonadoblastomas with early invasive dysgerminoma. The 18-month follow-up has not revealed any recurrent tumor. M.C. has also been treated with estrogen replacement therapy, with the development of small breasts and menses. Bone age after 1 year of estrogen therapy was 12⁶/₁₂ years. Weight remains a significant problem for M. C.

DELAYED MENARCHE WITH SOME PUBERTAL DEVELOPMENT

The adolescent evaluated for a delay in the onset of menarche needs assessment not only for many of the disorders covered in the previous sections but also for the possibility of a genital anomaly, such as uterine agenesis. The lack of menses by age 15 to 16 years requires thoughtful consideration of the differential diagnosis (Figs. 6-8 and 6-9). The timing and tempo of the patient's previous pubertal growth and development are important. Bone age is more closely related to the onset of menses than is chronologic age. Although most girls have the onset of menses within 2 to 2½ years of the onset of breast development, the range is considerable and an individual girl may not have the onset of menarche for 4 years. An interruption in the pattern of normal puberty should alert the physician to the possibility of a hypothalamic-pituitary-ovarian disorder, and thus evidence of estrogenization is essential in determining the extent of evaluation. A girl with delayed menarche who has a late onset of normal puberty and a family history of delayed development is less worrisome than the adolescent who began her development at age 11 years and still has no menses at age 16 years.

A careful physical examination gives an excellent indication of endogenous hormone levels. The presence of normal breast development and an estrogenized vagina implies that the patient is making estrogen. A vaginal smear can be obtained to confirm the degree of estrogen effect. The genital examination is crucial in the patient with delayed menarche. Although most patients with imperforate hymen should be detected in the newborn nursery or early childhood, some patients are not diagnosed until adolescence. A bulging bluish-tinged hymen may be noted in the adolescent with an imperforate hymen and blood filled vagina (hematocolpos). The patient with vaginal and uterine agenesis has normal-appearing external genitalia and thus is not usually detected until a pelvic examination is done for primary amenorrhea.

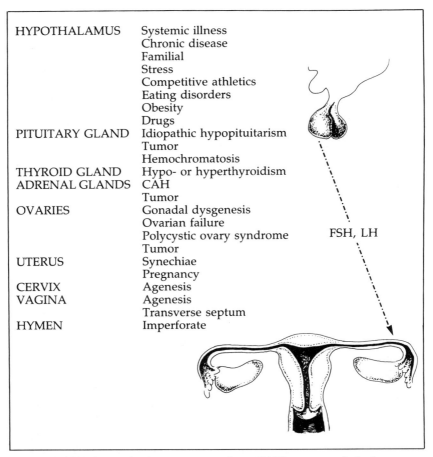

HYPOTHALAMUS	Systemic illness
	Chronic disease
	Familial
	Stress
	Competitive athletics
	Eating disorders
	Obesity
	Drugs
PITUITARY GLAND	Idiopathic hypopituitarism
	Tumor
	Hemochromatosis
THYROID GLAND	Hypo- or hyperthyroidism
ADRENAL GLANDS	CAH
	Tumor
OVARIES	Gonadal dysgenesis
	Ovarian failure
	Polycystic ovary syndrome
	Tumor
UTERUS	Synechiae
	Pregnancy
CERVIX	Agenesis
VAGINA	Agenesis
	Transverse septum
HYMEN	Imperforate

FSH, LH

Figure 6-8. Etiology of primary amenorrhea. CAH = congenital adreno-cortical hyperplasia.

To determine the presence of a normal vagina and uterus, the physician needs to adapt the examination to the individual patient. A gentle one-finger examination of the vagina will establish vaginal patency and allow palpation of the cervix and uterus by bimanual vaginal-abdominal examination. Visualization of the cervix and assessment of estrogenization of the cervical mucus and vaginal walls are usually possible with a small Huffman speculum. Occasionally the hymenal opening is too tight to admit a finger or speculum comfortably; then the vagina should be probed gently with a saline-moistened cotton-tipped applicator or urethral catheter to make sure it is the normal length. In a patient with vaginal agenesis, a cotton-

Figure 6-9. Workup of delayed menarche in females with some pubertal development.

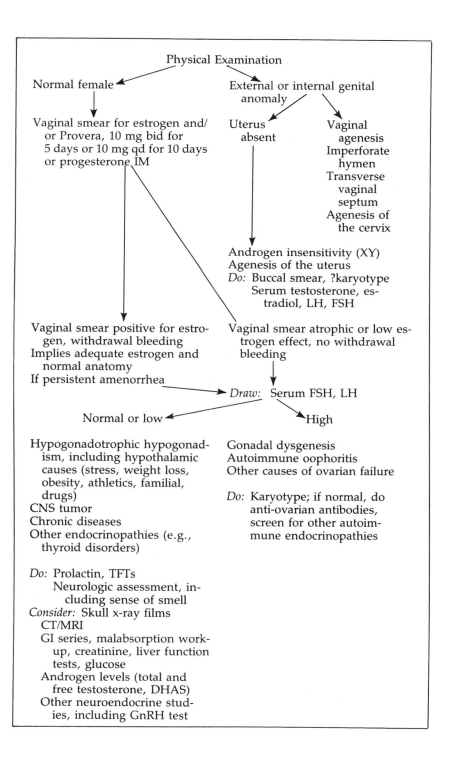

tipped applicator can usually be inserted only 1 to 2 cm. The uterus and adnexa can be palpated by rectoabdominal palpation with the patient in the lithotomy position. Ultrasonography can be used for confirmation of findings. During the physical examination and history, it is important to look for signs of androgen excess, including evidence of progressive hirsutism, clitoromegaly, and severe acne. Very rarely, pregnancy will occur without menarche.

If the genital examination is normal, assessment of estrogen effect by vaginal smear and progesterone withdrawal allows the clinician to think about diagnoses associated with eugonadism such as polycystic ovary syndrome and those associated with estrogen deficiency such as ovarian failure and hypothalamic disorders. After pregnancy is excluded, a course of progesterone can be given to verify that the uterus is present and that the endometrium has been sufficiently stimulated with estrogen to cause withdrawal flow. Although a withdrawal flow to progesterone is generally reassuring, patients with prolactinomas and those in the early years of premature menopause may have a normal response. A serum level for estradiol, although taken at only one point in time, can be helpful in confirming the clinical impression of the degree of estrogenization. In general, unless the clinician can find factors such undernutrition or profound stress accounting for the lack of cycles, simple screening tests including CBC, sedimentation rate, FSH, LH, prolactin, thyroid function tests, and urinalysis should be done to establish a diagnosis. A wrist x ray for bone age is useful in those who have not completed skeletal maturation.

The levels of gonadotropins are useful, as noted in the previous section, in determining the type of investigation. Low to normal levels imply that an evaluation needs to focus on the hypothalamic pituitary axis; elevated gnadotropins imply ovarian failure. Further tests are similar to those indicated in the previous sections and in Figures 6-3 and 6-9.

In the apparently estrogenized patient with failure to have withdrawal bleeding from progesterone and normal gonadotropin levels, the presence of a normal endometrium can be established by giving estrogen and progestin for two to three cycles. However, a diagnosis of uterine synechiae (Asherman's syndrome) is sufficiently rare in the absence of a history of infection or abortion that this part of the evaluation can be delayed until other diagnoses are considered.

EVALUATION OF PATIENTS WITH WITHDRAWAL BLEEDING
AFTER PROGESTERONE

Delayed menarche (with adequate estrogen and normal anatomy)
In most cases, the normal teenager with delayed menarche is healthy and will eventually begin spontaneous periods. Factors such as

weight (either too little or too much), stress, athletics, and depression appear to act at the hypothalamic level to prevent the onset of normal cycles (see p. 161). Adolescents who are not engaged in competitive athletics but who are underweight and then gain 5 to 10 pounds may have the spontaneous onset of menses. An adequate work-up consists of a careful physical examination, vaginal smear for estrogenization, progesterone test for withdrawal bleeding, hemoglobin level, and urinalysis. Thyroid disease and diabetes mellitus should be excluded as possible diagnoses by physical examination or laboratory tests (serum glucose, thyroid function tests, including TSH).

If by the age of 16 years an adolescent has not begun spontaneous menses, it is prudent to check a serum FSH, LH and prolactin. Menstrual cycles can be induced by the administration of medroxy-progesterone (Provera), 10 mg orally for 12 to 14 days (at least every 6 to 8 weeks). This medication will produce a secretory endometrium and withdrawal menses in the presence of normal estrogenization and the presence of a uterus. Progestin therapy can also prevent endometrial hyperplasia, which can occur in the presence of unopposed estrogen stimulation. Although the presence of withdrawal flow to progesterone is generally reassuring about the continuing presence of normal circulating levels of estrogen and a normal hypothalamic-pituitary axis, persistence of amenorrhea, any signs of headache, visual symptoms, galactorrhea, or an interruption in the tempo of the pubertal process necessitates further tests (Fig. 6-9). Based on these tests, the clinician should pursue a diagnosis. The presence of an increased LH/FSH ratio or evidence of androgen excess should raise the possibility of polycystic ovary syndrome. Low to normal levels of FSH and LH and normal prolactin level are suggestive of hypothalamic dysfunction; a lateral skull film with cone-down view of the sella can exclude calcification and an enlarged sella.

A quandary for the physician may be whether to obtain a cranial CT or MRI scan in the patient with a normal sella film and normal serum gonadotropin and prolactin values. Unfortunately, there are no absolute guidelines because most pituitary tumors associated with pubertal development followed by primary or secondary amenorrhea in this age group secrete prolactin and thus will be detected by this assay. Given the likelihood that most adolescents have hypothalamic amenorrhea due to stress, athletics, or weight changes, and nonfunctioning tumors are rare, a CT or MRI scan is generally reserved for the evaluation of the patient with interrupted puberty, abnormal sella seen on x ray of the skull, and/or neurologic signs or symptoms. A CT or MRI may also be indicated in the evaluation of the older adolescent and young adult woman who has no obvious etiology for persistent amenorrhea.

EVALUATION OF PATIENTS WITH NO WITHDRAWAL BLEEDING AFTER PROGESTERONE

Low to normal follicle-stimulating and luteinizing hormone levels

In contrast to the patients with sexual infantilism discussed on p. 183, low levels of gonadotropins may induce some ovarian function with low levels of estrogen, scanty breast development, and slight maturation of the vaginal mucosa and labia. In some cases, gonadotropin and estrogen levels appear to be normal at the onset of puberty and then diminish because of depression, stress, or weight loss. It is important with all these patients to exclude the possibility of an organic lesion (e.g., CNS tumor) or a systemic disease.

If possible, therapy should be directed at the underlying cause of hypogonadotropism. For example, weight loss due to depression should be treated with psychiatric and dietary counselling. Athletic training schedules may need to be modified to allow the patient to go through the normal pubertal process. Achieving better glucose control in the young diabetic or decreased disease activity in Crohn's disease will often bring about menarche.

Estrogen deficiency in the adolescent is important because the clinician must try to make a definitive diagnosis and must continue to consider the possibility of an underlying problem not initially evident. In addition, the psychological problems associated with incomplete sexual development and the potential consequences of long-term estrogen deficiency, including osteoporosis, necessitate that the clinician and patient consider estrogen replacement therapy. By age 15 to 16 years, failure to complete sexual development and estrogen deficiency should be treated with estrogen replacement as outlined on p. 178. If skeletal age is mature and no further growth can be anticipated, increasing the dose of estrogen can be accomplished more rapidly. Therapy should be discontinued intermittently (e.g., once a year for 2–3 months) to determine if the hypothalamic-pituitary axis has commenced more normal functioning. Estrogen-progestin therapy can also be given in alternate months to see if normal menses begin. Clearly patients with GnRH deficiency require long-term replacement therapy until fertility treatment is initiated, whereas those with delayed maturation will begin spontaneous menses.

High follicle-stimulating and luteinizing hormone levels

Conditions in which there are high FSH and LH levels and usually no withdrawal bleeding after progesterone are gonadal dysgenesis and other forms of ovarian failure (see p. 153).

EXTERNAL OR INTERNAL GENITAL ANOMALIES

Imperforate hymen and transverse vaginal septum

The diagnosis of imperforate hymen should be made early in a child's life, but occasionally a patient reaches menarcheal age before the diagnosis is made. The patient may have a history of cyclic abdominal pain, often for several years, or may be asymptomatic. A bluish, bulging hymen and vagina distended with blood are found on genital inspection and rectoabdominal palpation. The repair of imperforate hymen can be accomplished in infancy, childhood, or adolescence when the diagnosis is made. One method utilizes a bovie (with the plastic shield cut back and placed back on so that three-fourths of the tip is shielded) to excise the hymen close to the hymenal ring. Shielding the tip prevents inadvertent injury to the surrounding tissues. The surgeon then performs a small perineoplasty, utilizing a vertical incision, which is then closed horizontally. Marcaine, 0.5%, is injected into the repair area at the conclusion of the procedure for postoperative analgesia. In treating adolescents, puncture of a hematocolpos without definitive surgical repair should be avoided, since the viscous menstrual products will not drain and the small perforations will allow ascension of bacteria and infection.

The rare complete transverse vaginal septum may be low or high in the vagina, but the external genital examination appears normal. The vagina appears short and a mass is palpable above the examining finger and on rectoabdominal palpation. Obstruction with a high transverse septum results in hematometra and endometriosis [140]. Almost 50 percent of vaginal septi occur in the upper vagina, followed by 40 percent in the middle vagina, and 14 percent in the lower vagina. It should be noted that most transverse vaginal septi have a central small perforation but still may present with hematocolpos in the adolescent, mucocolpos in the child, and pyohematocolpos (because of ascending infection). MRI may be helpful to define the thickness of the septum preoperatively. Surgical approaches depend on the septal thickness and the need for vaginoplasy. Incision of small septi may be acceptable. End-to-end anastomosis is applicable for thicker septi. A Z-plasty technique will probably prevent scar formation perpendicular to the vaginal axis. To prevent injuries to the urethra or rectum, a urinary catheter and a finger in the rectum can guide surgery. If necessary, a probe can be passed transfundally to tent up the septum.

Agenesis of the vagina/cervix/uterus
Vaginal agenesis is usually accompanied by uterine agenesis, although infrequently a patient will have a normal, but obstructed uterus or rudimentary uterus with functional endometrium. Another rare variant is the presence of a uterus but agenesis of the cervix; such patients present with pain and a distended uterus, a condition that has not to date been particularly amenable to surgical attempts at reconstruction [141–143]. Ultrasonography and MRI can aid in defining anatomy preoperatively.

Patients with Müllerian anomalies often have associated skeletal (congenital scoliosis, Klippel-Feil syndrome, and limb bud defects), renal, and cardiac anomalies and, rarely, malposition of the ovary [144]. Müllerian aplasia has also been associated with maternal deficiency of galactose-1-phosphate uridyl transferase [145]. Patients with Mayer-Rokitansky-Kuster-Hauser syndrome are XX and have normal ovaries and hormonal patterns but have absent or rudimentary uterus and fallopian tubes, and have absence of the upper two thirds of the vagina. Müllerian aplasia is estimated to occur in about 1 in 4000 births. The presence of normal breast and pubic hair development, normal female serum testosterone and pubertal estradiol levels, and chromatin-positive buccal smear makes this syndrome the likely diagnosis. Ultrasonography, which should be done to assess renal status, can confirm normal ovaries and lack of a uterus. Remnants of uterine structures are occasionally (8%) present and sometimes cause pain and require surgical excision. Although chromosomes studies may not be necessary for all of these girls, the finding of an elevated testosterone level, abnormal buccal smear, lack of breast development, absent pubic hair, or virilization mandates further studies for an intersex state.

Patients with obstruction require immediate surgery to establish normal flow, whereas those with vaginal and uterine agenesis can elect the timing of the intervention. Diagnostic laparoscopy is useful in cases of abdominal pain when functioning remnants are suspected; its routine use for diagnosis is not advised. The timing for the creation of a vagina preferred by most patients is the mid to late teens; surgery is usually done in the summer so that the patient has adequate time for recovery without having to miss school or answer embarrassing questions from her peers.

The nonsurgical approach for creation of a vagina involves the use of graduated Lucite dilators (Frank method). The smallest dilator is pressed firmly (until she feels mild discomfort, not pain) against the vaginal dimple backward and inward in the lithotomy position three times daily for at least half an hour the first week. During the second week the patient is instructed to insert the tube downward and inward in the line of the normal vaginal axis. A bicycle stool has also been used to facilitate vaginal dilatation (Ingram modification). The method is simple and nonoperative and works best when a vaginal dimple is already present.

If dilators are unsuccessful or if the patient prefers surgery after a thorough discussion of the advantages and disadvantages, surgical creation of a vagina can be accomplished by two techniques. The McIndoe-Read procedure utilizes a split-thickness skin graft (0.018–0.022 inches) taken from the buttocks (to make sure that the graft is aesthetic, the patient can tan in her bikini in advance so that the graft can be taken from the white, untanned skin). The skin graft is placed over a stent, dermal side out (Counsellor technique) (Fig. 6-10). With

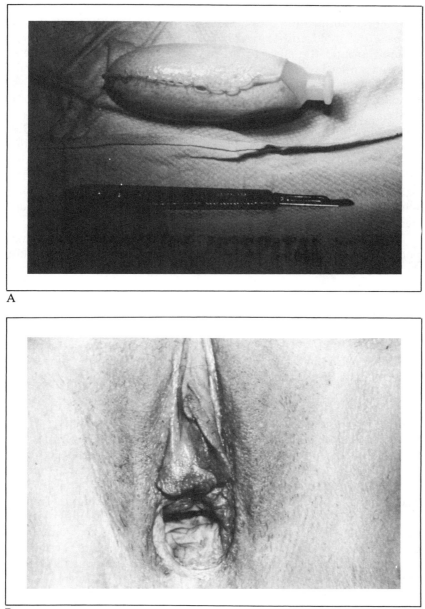

A

B

Figure 6-10. Creation of a vagina in a girl with vaginal and uterine agenesis. A. Split-thickness skin graft using Padgett's dermatome on a Counsellor stent. B. Postoperative vagina.

the patient in the lithotomy position, a transverse incision is made at the vaginal dimple and a cavity dissected with good hemostasis and asepsis; the mold and skin graft are inserted and the labia minora secured around the stent to prevent expulsion. The Foley catheter inserted earlier is removed and suprapubic bladder drainage accomplished. After 7 to 10 days of bed rest and a low residue diet, the stent is removed and the graft revised. Frank dilators are begun to prevent contraction of the graft. The patient is seen for frequent follow-up to check the graft. Once the graft has taken, the patient is instructed to wear the dilator at night for 6 months (unless she has regular intercourse). Since the failure to comply with follow-up treatment can lead to vaginal stenosis, surgery should not be contemplated until the patient understands the procedure and her involvement. Talking with another patient who has already had successful surgery is very helpful for many adolescents.

The Williams vulvovaginoplasty involves the creation of a vaginal pouch by making a U-shaped incision and using full-thickness skin flaps from the labia majora to create a "kangaroo-like" pouch, horizontal to the perineum. A dilator is used daily for 3 to 4 weeks but is not necessary after that. The axis of the vagina is different for coitus, but difficulties can be overcome. This operation does not enter the pelvic structures, and thus the risk of fistula formation is low. It is particularly useful in patients with a previously failed vaginoplasty and those who have had radical pelvic surgery or irradiation. Some gynecologists find this operation the treatment of choice for vaginal agenesis.

Androgen insensitivity

The patient with androgen insensitivity (testicular feminization), a form of male pseudohermaphroditism, has good breast development and absent or very sparse pubic and axillary hair. The vagina is short, and the uterus and cervix are absent. The chromosome pattern is XY. The gonads, which may be intra-abdominal or in the inguinal rings, are testes; thus the serum testosterone level is in the range of the normal male. Because of insensitivity to androgens and enhanced estrogen production, the patient develops a female habitus and external genitalia. The lack of pubic and axillary hair is the result of end-organ failure to respond to adrenal and testicular androgens.

Because the testes in such patients have a high rate of malignant degeneration, they should be prophylactically removed after the patient has attained full height and breast development. There are rare children who have had malignant degeneration of XY gonads during childhood; therefore, it is suggested that patients in whom the diagnosis is made before puberty be monitored for pelvic pathology. X-ray films and ultrasonography of the pelvis can be used to supplement rectoabdominal examination. Breast development is usually better in patients who have their gonads in place during adolescent development than those who have had gonadectomy in childhood. After surgery, the patient should receive estrogen replacement.

Before surgery is undertaken, the patient needs to understand her anatomy. The physician should stress the patient's femininity and her ability to have normal sexual relations; she must, however, ultimately accept the fact that she cannot have menses or bear children. Relating the patient's condition to "genes" or "chromosomes" is more helpful than telling her that she is a "male" or "XY." If the question "Am I XY?" arises in the course of discussion, the physician needs to answer the question honestly and at the same time reemphasize that the patient's phenotype is female. The necessary laparotomy should be explained as removal of "gonads" rather than testes; gonads can be viewed as organs that did not develop into either testes or ovaries because of the "chromosome problem." The tumor risk can be openly discussed.

Partial androgen insensitivity has also been reported [146]; the patient had an XY karyotype, labial fusion, a blind vas deferens, and testes located in the labioscrotal folds. At puberty, the patient developed breasts and pubic and axillary hair. Because of the absence of the uterus, the patient sought medical care for amenorrhea.

Case 5. E. B. came to the clinic at the age of 16 years with a history of "no periods." Breast and pubic hair development had started at the age of 11 or 12 years. She had noted a slight whitish vaginal discharge for several years. On physical examination, E. B. was a healthy, attractive teenage girl with a height of 64 inches and a weight of 125 pounds. Breast development was stage 5, and pubic hair stage 4. Pelvic examination revealed a well-estrogenized vagina and a normal cervix and uterus. A vaginal smear showed 20 percent superficial and 80 percent intermediate cells. Following an intramuscular injection of 100 mg of progesterone-in-oil, she had a 4-day period. She began spontaneous menses 2 months later and has continued normal menstrual cycles.

Case 6. P. M. visited the clinic at the age of 18 years. Her complaint was "no periods." Breast development occurred when she was 13 years old, but pubic and axillary hair had not appeared. She had recently gained 70 pounds, seemingly because of the anxiety over her lack of periods. On physical examination, P. M. was an attractive, overweight young woman with a height of 64 inches and a weight of 187 pounds. Blood pressure was 140/80; pulse rate was 80/min. Breasts were stage 5 and pendulous. No axillary or pubic hair was present. Pelvic examination revealed a short vagina with no cervix or uterus. Laboratory tests showed a chromatin-negative buccal smear with fluorescent Y bodies in 60 percent of the cells. Karyotype was XY. Serum testosterone was 281 ng/100 ml (the level for a normal female <75 ng/100 ml). A diagnosis of androgen insensitivity was made. After surgery to remove the intraabdominal testes, P. M. was started on conjugated estrogens. She required extensive counselling concerning the issue of her femininity and her inability to bear children. She subsequently lost 35 pounds by dieting.

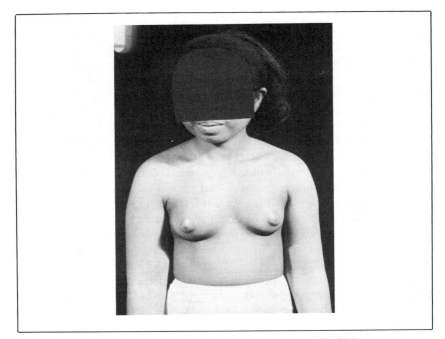

Figure 6-11. Case 7, gonadal dysgenesis, karyotype 46,X,i(Xq).

Case 7. R. L. sought medical attention at the age of 18 years because of "no periods." She recalled that her breast and pubic hair development had started at the age of 12 years. She had always been the shortest member of her class, and she had worn bilateral hearing aids since age 11. On physical examination (Fig. 6-11), R. L. was a short, overweight female with a height of 51 inches and a weight of 105 pounds. She had hypertelorism, ptosis, a low hairline, an increased carrying angle, and short fourth metacarpals. Breast development was stage 5; pubic hair was stage 4. Pelvic examination revealed a poorly estrogenized vagina with a small cervix and uterus. Vaginal smear showed no evidence of estrogenization. Laboratory tests revealed a serum FSH of 258 mIU/ml and LH of 173 mIU/ml (indicative of ovarian failure). Karyotype was 46,X,i(Xq). The patient was given cyclic doses of conjugated estrogens (Premarin) and medroxyprogesterone (Provera) and had normal withdrawal flow each month. She was subsequently changed to cyclic oral contraceptives.

Case 8. C. J. was seen at the clinic at 16 years of age because of lack of periods. Pubic and axillary hair had been present for 4 years. She had never had any significant breast development. She had been slightly overweight until the age of 15 years when she went on a crash diet and lost 25 pounds. On physical examination, C. J. was 64¼ inches tall and weighed 110 pounds (Fig. 6-12). Breasts were stage 1 with areola of 1.5 cm. Pubic hair was stage 3. Vagina was poorly estrogenized and the uterus was small. Neurologic assessment, including sense of smell, was normal. Laboratory tests included the following: FSH, 9.5 and 2.6 mIU/ml; LH, 2.0 and less than 2.0 mIU/ml;

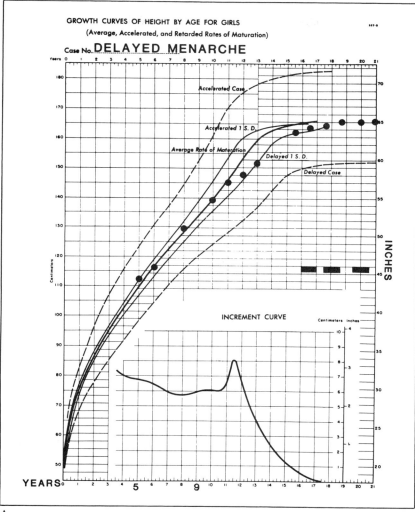

A

Figure 6-12. Case 8, delayed menarche. Growth charts: A. Height.
B. Weight. Bar indicates treatment with estrogen-progestin therapy.

prolactin, 3.6 ng/ml. Skull x-ray films were normal, and bone age was 14 years.

Although the weight loss at the age of 15 years may have further suppressed the hypothalamic-pituitary axis, the history of long-standing lack of estrogenization indicated the need to evaluate the patient further. GnRH testing revealed a normal LH rise with a minimal rise of FSH. Cranial CT scan was normal. The patient was given estrogen-progestin therapy, and she developed normal breasts and menstrual periods. She discontinued medication

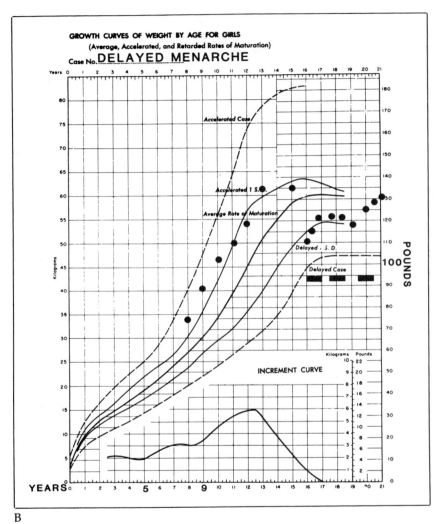

B

Figure 6-12 (Continued)

for 3 to 6 months each year, but initially she did not menstruate during that time and her breast development regressed. She had difficulty with substance abuse and bulimia during her twenties but she maintained a normal weight of 125 pounds. Finally at age 27 years, she began spontaneous menses and had an unplanned pregnancy 1 year later, which she carried to term.

Case 9. N. K. was referred to the Adolescent Unit at age 17 for primary amenorrhea. She was an "A" student in her senior year of high school at a boarding school and was involved in athletics. Her breast and pubic hair development started at age 10 years but subsequently stopped at age 12 years. She never had the onset of menses. She had had significant headaches for 4 years, which seemed to increase during the school year. Physical examination revealed a pleasant, bright young woman with a height of 64 inches and weight of 111 pounds. Blood pressure and pulse were normal. Breasts were Tanner stage 3 with small areolae, 1.7 cm on the right and 2.0 cm on the left, and glandular tissue 4 × 4 cm on the right and 5 × 6 cm on the left. No galactorrhea was present. Pubic hair was stage 3 to 4; the vaginal introitus was poorly estrogenized. The vagina was normal in length, and rectoabdominal examination revealed a cervix. Neurologic examination including fundi, visual fields by confrontation, and sense of smell was normal. The growth chart (Fig. 6-13) revealed no increase in height since age 12⁶/₁₂ years.

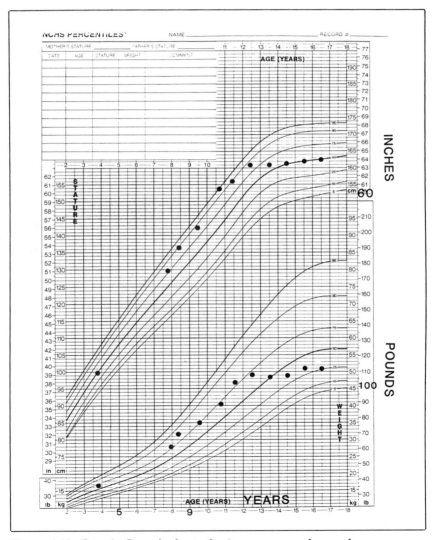

Figure 6-13. Case 9. Growth chart of primary amenorrhea and a prolactinoma.

The history and examination suggested normal initiation of puberty followed by arrest and regression of estrogenization. Laboratory tests showed a bone age of 14 years, normal CBC and thyroid function tests, low gonadotropin levels (LH 5.2 mIU/ml and FSH < 2.0 mIU/ml), and undetectable estradiol, with markedly elevated prolactin of 13,000 ng/ml (normal < 25 ng/ml). Skull x ray showed an enlarged sella turcica, and cranial CT demonstrated a large pituitary and suprasellar mass (Fig. 6-14A). Formal visual field testing was normal. Neuroendocrine studies revealed prepubertal LH and FSH response to GnRH, growth hormone deficiency, flat prolactin response to TRH, and normal cortisol levels.

After neurosurgical consultation, N. K. was started on bromocriptine therapy. The dosage was gradually increased on a weekly basis; the prolactin levels fell progressively, and the tumor showed significant reduction in size

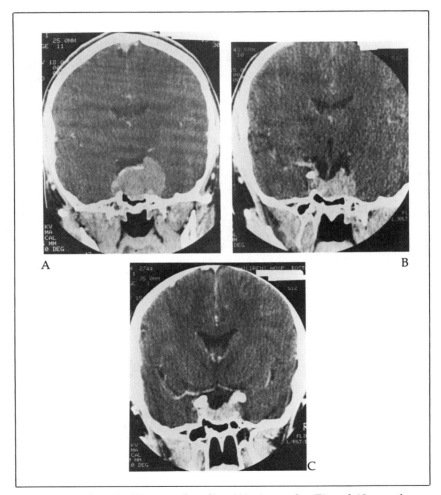

Figure 6-14. Case 9. CT scans: baseline (A); 6 months (B) and 12 months (C) after initiating bromocriptine therapy.

(Fig. 6-14B and C). Headaches disappeared. After 2 years of therapy, she is currently receiving 5 mg of bromocriptine in the morning and 11.25 mg in the evening, with prolactin levels between 48 and 75 ng/ml. Although she initially had difficulty tolerating the bromocriptine because of postural symptoms accompanying exercise, she is currently asymptomatic. LH and FSH levels have increased, and estradiol levels have ranged between 53 and 283 pg/ml. Breast development and vaginal estrogenization have progessed, and N. K. had normal withdrawal flow to medroxyprogesterone given 1 year after starting the bromocriptine (during her first year of college). Her first spontaneous menses occurred 2 months later, and over the following 6 months she had one withdrawal flow to medroxyprogesterone and two spontaneous menses 1 month apart. The long-term prognosis is unclear, and it is likely that other modalities of therapy may be undertaken before fertility can be considered.

DELAYED MENARCHE WITH VIRILIZATION/HIRSUTISM
Progressive hirsutism or virilization, or both, in association with delayed menarche is uncommon. Patients with amenorrhea and hirsutism usually have polycystic ovary syndrome or late onset congenital adrenocortical hyperplasia. An abrupt onset of the hirsutism may signal a tumor. Patients with true virilization are rarer and may have polycystic ovary syndrome, late onset congenital adrenal hyperplasia, an ovarian or adrenal tumor, mixed gonadal dysgenesis, an incomplete form of androgen insensitivity, gonadal dysgenesis (with virilization), or true hermaphroditism.

The diagnosis and treatment of many of these disorders is discussed in Chapter 7. A physical examination is critical to establish the presence of breast development and a normal female genital tract. Laboratory tests to evaluate the hirsute adolescent with primary amenorrhea include serum levels of testosterone (total and free), dehydroepiandrosterone (DHA) and its sulfate (DHAS), androstenedione, 17-hydroxyprogesterone (early morning), FSH, LH, and prolactin. A one-hour ACTH test can be used to detect adrenal enzyme deficiencies. Depending on these tests and the concern about tumors and intersex states, other studies may include 24-hour urine for 17-ketosteroids, buccal smear, karyotype, ultrasonography, CT/MRI of the adrenals (and sometimes pelvis), and laparoscopy or laparotomy.

Congenital Adrenocortical Hyperplasia
In the past, the diagnosis of congenital adrenocortical hyperplasia (CAH) usually implied the virilized female newborn with or without a salt-losing tendency. Some patients, however, may have a mild block of their adrenal steroid synthesis (11 β-hydroxylase, 21-hydroxylase, or 3 β-hydroxysteroid dehydrogenase deficiency) and therefore may not manifest clitoromegaly or hirsutism until puberty. Patients may present to the clinician with delayed menarche, oligomenorrhea, or hirsutism. Those with 11 β-hydroxylase deficiency may have associ-

ated hypertension. The pathways of steroid biosynthesis are shown in Figure 7-5.

Many patients who have classical CAH, even though they have been observed and treated since infancy, may visit their physician because of menstrual irregularities, including delayed menarche. Klingensmith and associates [147] found that all adolescents with CAH who had urinary 17-ketosteroid excretion in excess of 6.2 mg/24 hours had some menstrual irregularities—secondary amenorrhea, oligomenorrhea, or persistent anovulatory cycles. Many of the older adolescents with CAH were not taking medication regularly; many of the younger adolescents had not had their dosage of medication changed to keep up with their accelerated growth. During the adolescent years, dosages need to be regulated by monitoring height and weight and measuring levels of urinary 17-ketosteroids, serum 17-hydroxyprogesterone and testosterone (Δ^4-androstenedione and DHAS), and plasma renin. In adolescents who have achieved full growth, continuous adrenal suppression and improved menstrual regularity can often be achieved by switching to twice a day prednisone or once a day dexamethasone. Fertility is possible for the majority of non-salt-losing CAH patients, although some have persistent anovulatory cycles and develop enlarged polycystic-like ovaries. Money and Schwartz [148] have noted a delay in the dating age and first romance, difficulty in establishing friendships, and inhibition of erotic arousal and expression in patients with early onset CAH.

The diagnosis of so-called late onset CAH may be difficult because the initial hormone profile may resemble that seen in patients with polycystic ovary syndrome (PCO). A rapid ACTH test is helpful in differentiating PCO from 21-hydroxylase deficiency. An intravenous injection of 0.25 mg of cosyntropin (Cortrosyn) is given. The 17-hydroxyprogesterone is measured at 0 and 60 minutes with a rise of greater than 6 ng/100 ml/min seen in patients with late onset 21-hydroxylase deficiency CAH (see p. 259 for ACTH testing).

CAH and late onset CAH with 21-hydroxylase deficiency are both autosomal recessive disorders. In addition, patients with so-called cryptic 21-hydroxylase deficiency have been identified; these patients have biochemical evidence of 21-hydroxylase deficiency but without clinical evidence of excess virilism, amenorrhea, or infertility [149] (see Chap. 7).

OVARIAN AND ADRENAL TUMORS

A patient may have virilization from either an ovarian or adrenal tumor, both before and after the onset of puberty or menarche. A serum testosterone value greater than 150 to 200 ng/100 ml, androstenedione greater than 500 ng/100 ml, DHAS greater than 700 µg/100 ml *or* urinary 17-ketosteroid excretion greater than 25 mg/24 hours should make the clinician suspicious of a tumor. Adrenal tumors will typically not show suppression of elevated 17-ketosteroids with dexamethasone administration; rare adrenal tumors secrete testosterone with normal levels of DHA and 17-ketosteroids [150]. Rarely, testosterone levels in a patient with a testosterone-secreting adenoma will be LH responsive and suppressible with birth control pills; however, the baseline levels of testosterone are typically greater than 150 to 200 ng/100 ml. Since the source of the excess androgen may be difficult to identify initially, a careful physical examination (including palpation of the ovaries), ultrasonography, CT or MRI imaging, and rarely selective catheterization of the adrenal and ovarian veins are necessary for localization. Surgical treatment is indicated.

POLYCYSTIC OVARY SYNDROME
A discussion of the polycystic ovary syndrome can be found on page 212 and Chap. 7. In rare cases, the syndrome is responsible for delayed menarche and moderate virilization or progressive hirsutism, or both.

MIXED GONADAL DYSGENESIS
At puberty, patients with mixed gonadal dysgenesis (MGD) show virilization (without evidence of estrogen effect) because the functioning intra-abdominal testis produces testosterone. The reported chromosome patterns of patients with MGD have included 46,XY; 45,X/46,XY; 45,X/46,XX/46,XY; and 45,X (some likely missed a second line). Essential is mosaicism with a 45,X stem and a stem with a Y (fragment) [147]. The gonadal constitution in Federman's series in *Abnormal Sexual Development* [147] consisted of the following:

	Patients
Testis plus streak gonad	24
Unilateral testis only	9
Streak gonad plus tumor	7
Testis plus tumor	1
Unilateral tumor only	1
Total	42

A uterus could be palpated in all patients, although it may be asymmetric because of the presence of a testis. Because of dysgenetic intra-abdominal testis has a high incidence of malignant transformation, it should be removed. Fertility is impossible. Patients can be given cyclic estrogen-progestin therapy to produce menses.

INCOMPLETE FORMS OF ANDROGEN INSENSITIVITY
Patients with incomplete androgen insensitivity have a 46,XY chromosomal pattern, agenesis of the uterus, hirsutism, clitoral enlargement, and absence of breast development. Unlike classic testicular

feminization (see p. 198 and Chap. 2, p. 61), which has enhanced estrogen production, the estrogen levels in these patients are low, and therefore breast development is absent at puberty. Treatment consists of surgical removal of the testes and replacement treatment with estrogens [151, 152, 153].

GONADAL DYSGENESIS (45,X) WITH VIRILIZATION
Rarely, patients with gonadal dysgenesis may show virilization at puberty. The streak gonads may contain Leydig-like cells that presumably secrete androgens. The possibility of a tumor should be excluded. The presence of a Y fragment may be detected by DNA probes.

TRUE HERMAPHRODITISM
A true hermaphrodite is a person with ovarian and testicular tissue. The majority of true hermaphrodites are 46,XX, although there are some persons with mosaic patterns, including 46,XX/XY (which may be an overlap with MGD) and 46,XX/47,XXY. Some appear to be almost normal females who develop mild to moderate virilization at puberty, depending on the balance of ovarian and testicular function. Gonadotropin concentrations may be normal or high. The majority of patients with this rare diagnosis are first noted as newborns with ambiguous genitalia (see Chap. 2).

SECONDARY AMENORRHEA
PATIENT EVALUATION
Many of the causes of delayed menarche are also responsible for secondary amenorrhea; however, the two most common causes of missed periods in the adolescent are pregnancy and stress. A period that is 2 to 3 weeks overdue should be investigated to rule out pregnancy (see p. 35 for a review of pregnancy tests). The physician should never assume that the girl is not pregnant simply because she denies a history of sexual intercourse. Many older teenagers are still fearful of admitting a past history of intercourse; a youngster aged 11 or 12 may not understand her own anatomy well enough to answer the questions accurately.

Stress and changes in environment are responsible for most cases of missed periods in adolescents. Young women are especially likely to have irregular periods with fevers, emotional upset, weight changes, or changes in environment such as summer camp, boarding school, or college. Furthermore, the involvement of increasing numbers of young adolescents in competitive athletics has been accompanied by increasing reports of menstrual irregularities (see p. 167 for discussion of athletic amenorrhea). In spite of the association of competitive athletics with menstrual irregularities, each patient should be considered individually since amenorrhea may be due to pregnancy or can be a sign of a significant medical problem.

For example, the patient with classic anorexia nervosa may come to the physician because of secondary amenorrhea; an increased level of activity, which may include jogging and other exercises, may initially mask the diagnosis. Frequently, the magnitude of the weight loss is evident only after a careful history and after weight charts from the pediatrician's office or school are obtained. Both parents and patient may initially deny any change in weight or presence of emotional problems (see p. 165 for discussion of eating disorders). Similarly, a patient with depression may rapidly gain weight and become amenorrheic. The adolescent may inaccurately view the weight gain as secondary to the loss of periods and retention of blood. The patient with anorexia or depression requires counselling for emotional problems as well as reassurance about the probable return of her cycles.

Patients who have chronic diseases frequently benefit from an explanation of the cause of their menstrual irregularity. Failure to use contraceptives and an unwanted pregnancy may result if they do not understand that they are potentially fertile.

Teenagers may have irregular periods or amenorrhea for 3 to 6 months in the first 2 to 3 years after menarche. Which patients should be evaluated? Generally, the abrupt cessation of menses for 4 months after regular cycles have begun or persistent oligomenorrhea should be taken as an indication for an evaluation. Clearly, many patients will not visit the physician until 2, 3, or 8 months after amenorrhea occurs. Since the workup is simple (it includes a physical examination, pregnancy test, progesterone test, and simple laboratory studies), there is no need for the patient to wait an arbitrary length of time.

The history in the patient with secondary amenorrhea should focus on issues of stress, recent changes in the environment, weight change, and involvement in competitive athletics. Review of systems should include questions about headaches, visual changes, galactorrhea, hirsutism, acne, chronic disease, and any medications or illicit drug use. Amenorrhea following delivery may be due to pregnancy, or rarely Sheehan's postpartum pituitary necrosis, or Asherman's syndrome. Recent sexual activity and contraceptive use should also be assessed. The general physical examination should include a fundoscopic examination and a check of visual fields by confrontation. The thyroid gland should be palpated, and the blood pressure and pulse rate noted. The areolae should be gently compressed to determine if galactorrhea, usually not noted by the patient, is present. The physician should also search for evidence of androgen excess, including progressive hirsutism, clitoromegaly, or severe acne, and note any ovarian enlargement (although this may prove difficult

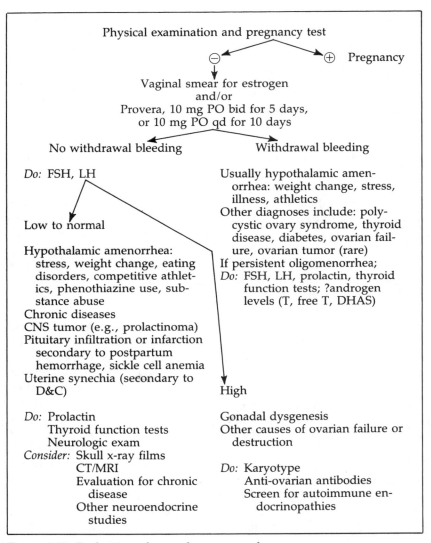

Figure 6-15. Evaluation of secondary amenorrhea.

in the obese or poorly relaxed adolescent patient). The evaluation of the patient with androgen excess is considered in Chap. 7.

Assessment of the estrogen status by vaginal smear, examination of cervical mucus, estradiol level, or the progesterone challenge test allows the physician to divide patients into two large categories (Fig. 6-15). If a sexually active patient is late with her period, progesterone challenge should never be used as a provocative test for pregnancy. A pregnancy test and physical examination are more appropriate. In the sexually active adolescent, it may be best to do two highly sensitive pregnancy tests, 2 weeks apart, with the girl using abstinence or condoms/foam, before doing a progestin challenge (progesterone-in-oil, 50 to 100 mg intramuscularly, may be preferable). If pregnancy is not a consideration, oral medroxyprogesterone (10 mg 2 times a day for 5 days or once daily for 10 days) is usually selected for progesterone challenge. Generally, progesterone will not induce menses in a patient who has hypopituitarism due to a tumor; profound hypothalamic suppression from anorexia nervosa, or massive weight gain; or ovarian failure because the endometrium is not primed with estrogen. These patients deserve an evaluation with laboratory tests to determine the cause of the estrogen deficiency. Unless the patient has a history suggestive of Asherman's syndrome (uterine scarring and synechiae usually secondary to a dilatation and curettage, following postpartum or postabortal endometritis), most adolescents are not prescribed a combined estrogen-progestin challenge as part of the initial evaluation until laboratory studies have been obtained. The patient with Asherman's syndrome will be estrogenized on vaginal examination and vaginal smear but will not have withdrawal bleeding to either progestin alone or combined estrogen-protestin therapy. Because of the rarity of this diagnosis in adolescents, before undertaking an extensive evaluation of the uterus of the adolescent who fails to withdraw from estrogen-progestin and does not have a history suggestive of Asherman's syndrome, a higher dose of estrogen should be administered for several months and compliance ensured with a pill count. In addition, it should be remembered that adolescents using low-dose birth control pills (which may have been provided confidentially by another clinic) may have scanty or absent withdrawal flow.

Most patients who do have withdrawal bleeding to progesterone are normal; however, disorders such as the polycystic ovary syndrome, ovarian tumors, Cushing's disease, thyroid disease, and diabetes should be excluded by physical examination, history, or the appropriate laboratory tests. Even in patients with a positive progesterone challenge test, prolonged amenorrhea (> 6 months) or persistent oligomenorrhea without an explanation should be evaluated by measurement of serum FSH, LH, and prolactin levels and thyroid function tests (T4, TT3, TSH). An elevated LH (> 30 mIU/ml) and normal FSH may suggest the diagnosis of polycystic ovary syndrome and the need to measure androgen levels (free and total testosterone, DHAS) even in the absence of obvious androgen excess. Patients with ovarian failure or premature menopause may continue to have sporadic menses in spite of elevated FSH and LH. In addition, although patients with prolactin-secreting microadenomas usually eventually become estrogen deficient, patients with small tumors may continue to have irregular periods and withdrawal flow to progesterone. It should be remembered that many patients with prolactinomas do not have galactorrhea. Clearly, any patient with galactorrhea should have a neuroendocrine evaluation as outlined on p. 171.

The management of teenage pregnancy and the diagnosis of ectopic pregnancy are discussed in Chapter 16.

WITHDRAWAL FLOW AFTER PROGESTERONE CHALLENGE

Hypothalamic amenorrhea

In most patients who have abundant, watery cervical mucus, a positive vaginal smear for estrogen, or a normal response to progesterone, periods will return spontaneously without treatment. Medroxyprogesterone (Provera), 10 mg orally for 12 to 14 days (13–14 days for prolonged therapy), is usually given every 6 to 8 weeks to prevent endometrial hyperplasia owing to prolonged estrogen stimulation and to reassure the physician that the patient is continuing to make estrogen. Underweight adolescents should be encouraged to gain weight. Athletes should receive an explanation of the hypothalamic cause of their amenorrhea and be reassured about their normal reproductive anatomy. Birth control pills should not be used to induce menstrual periods artificially unless the patient is sexually active and needs birth control or has a prolonged hypoestrogenic state (and needs estrogen replacement).

Polycystic ovary syndrome

Polycystic ovary syndrome is a common cause of secondary amenorrhea in both adolescents and older women. Formerly, this diagnosis was usually made in infertile patients in their mid- to late twenties, but increasing awareness of this syndrome has resulted in earlier diagnosis. The classic Stein-Leventhal syndrome described in 1935 [154] was characterized by polycystic ovaries, oligomenorrhea, and infertility; return of normal menstrual function followed wedge resection of the ovaries. However, it is now clear that there is a spectrum of disorders, sometimes called polycystic ovary syndrome (PCO) or androgenizing ovary syndrome. These disorders demonstrate disturbed hypothalamic-pituitary-ovarian feedback. LH levels are usually elevated (often > 30 mIU/ml); LH pulsations have increased amplitude and a tonic, rather than a cyclic, secretion. The LH appears to stimulate excessive androstenedione secretion from the theca cells of the ovary. FSH levels are generally slightly suppressed. The insufficient FSH results in a deficiency of the aromatase needed for the conversion of the androstenedione to estradiol in the ovarian follicle. The end result is anovulation and the production of excess androgens (see Chap. 7).

Adolescents who have oligomenorrhea and persistently elevated serum LH and low to normal FSH levels probably represent one end of a spectrum of disturbed feedback. In some patients, the elevated

LH with anovulation is a stress-induced phenomenon; in others, it appears to be a precursor to polycystic ovary syndrome. Although serum androgen levels may be normal at the initial evaluation, later in adolescence some of these patients do appear to develop enlarged tender cystic ovaries or elevated testosterone levels, or both (see Chap. 7). It should also be remembered that normal perimenarcheal adolescents may have enlarged multicystic ovaries on ultrasound. Other patients in the spectrum of PCO have elevated serum LH and androgen levels that are often accompanied by mild to moderate hirsutism. During adolescence, many of these patients appear to have normal-sized ovaries both by palpation and ultrasonography (thus the term *androgenizing ovary syndrome*); it is not known whether the ovaries in some of these adolescents enlarge over the course of time to become classic polycystic ovaries. Some adolescents, however, have not only elevated LH and testosterone, but also enlarged polycystic ovaries. The far end of the PCO spectrum is represented by the adolescent who has severe hirsutism—and often virilization—that is associated with the proliferation of hyperplastic theca cells in the ovarian stroma (ovarian hyperthecosis), often associated with acanthosis nigricans and insulin resistance.

Not only is PCO a confusing group of disorders, but polycystic ovaries can occur as a phenomenon that results from the androgen excess seen with congenital adrenal hyperplasia, Cushing's disease, and hyperprolactinemia. In the last, the elevated prolactin is usually associated with a selective increase in dehydroepiandrosterone sulfate (DHAS) and low or normal LH and FSH levels [155].

The diagnosis of PCO is usually made by excluding other diagnoses by finding an abnormal endocrine profile: elevated LH, normal FSH (or a ratio of LH/FSH > 2.5:1), and elevated total testosterone or free testosterone (or both). Serum DHAS and urinary 17-ketosteroid excretion may be mildly elevated in hirsute patients. The current hypothesis for the pathogenesis of PCO, the differential diagnosis, and treatment are included in Chapter 7. Patients with normal-sized ovaries and no evidence of progressive hirsutism should be given cyclic medroxyprogesterone, 10 mg a day for 13 to 14 days each month, or oral contraceptives to prevent endometrial hyperplasia. Careful long-term follow-up is indicated in all patients with anovulatory cycles and PCO because of the later increased incidence of endometrial carcinoma.

No Withdrawal Flow after
Progesterone Challenge
Low to normal follicle-stimulating and luteinizing hormone levels
The conditions that occur in the presence of low to normal FSH and LH levels are CNS tumor, chronic disease, pituitary infarction,

uterine synechia, and hypothalamic amenorrhea (see p. 161). The profound suppression of hypothalamic function found in patients with anorexia nervosa and depression is responsible for evidence of poor estrogenization; intramuscular progesterone or medroxyprogesterone will not induce a menstrual period in most of these patients. In patients with profound weight loss, periods may not recommence for months, sometimes years, after normal weight is reestablished. Frisch and McArthur [49] have shown that the mean weight necessary to reestablish menses is greater than the original mean weight at menarche. For example, the patient with a final height of 63 inches may weigh 91 pounds at menarche; if she loses weight and develops secondary amenorrhea, her periods may not resume until she achieves a weight of 102 pounds. Guidelines for instituting estrogen therapy in these girls is on p. 179.

As noted in Figure 6-15, it is important to exclude the possibility that a prolactinoma is the cause of secondary amenorrhea. The diagnosis, assessment, and management of patients with prolactinomas are discussed on p. 171; however, it should be remembered that many patients with prolactin-secreting microadenomas do not have galactorrhea.

The finding of an enlarged sella turcica on routine skull x-ray films should be further investigated with cranial CT scan or MRI. Occasionally, the enlargement represents the so-called empty sella syndrome (see p. 164).

High follicle-stimulating and luteinizing hormone levels
High FSH and LH levels indicate ovarian failure, which may be secondary to gonadal dysgenesis, radiation therapy, chemotherapy, autoimmune oophoritis, and other conditions (see p. 153). For example, ovarian fibrosis and failure have been associated with cyclophosphamide therapy. Patients with a history of prepubertal irradiation to the pelvis may develop secondary sexual characteristics and menses and then later in adolescence have secondary amenorrhea and ovarian failure. Patients with Addison's disease should be observed for the later development of autoimmune ovarian failure. In rare cases, ovarian destruction has followed a severe gonococcal infection.

Some patients may have fluctuating levels of FSH and LH along with intervals of normal cyclic menses before they become permanently amenorrheic.

Case 10. A. N., aged 15, came to the clinic because of fatigue. Further questioning revealed that her last menstrual period was 2 months previously. Her menarche was at the age of 12 years, and she had had regular cycles until the missed period. Although she initially denied the possibility of pregnancy, the

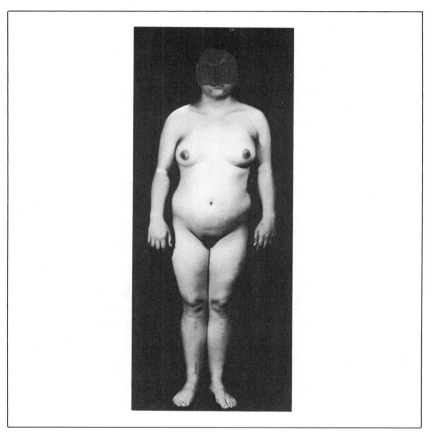

Figure 6-16. Case 11, gonadal dysgenesis, 45,X/46,XX karyotype.

pregnancy test was positive and her uterus was 8-weeks' size. After an abortion, she decided to take oral contraceptive pills.

Case 11. B. D., aged 17, was noted to have a history of amenorrhea for 6 months. Breast and pubic hair development began at the age of 12 years. Menarche occurred at the age of 14 years, but she had only two to three periods each year. She denied sexual activity. On physical examination (Fig. 6-16), B. D. was a short young woman with several stigmata of Turner syndrome (webbed neck, ptosis, low hairline, and short fourth metacarpals). Her height was 57¾ inches, and her weight was 100 pounds. Breasts and pubic hair were stage 5. Pelvic examination revealed a poorly estrogenized vagina with a small cervix and uterus; the vaginal smear showed no estrogenization. The patient had no response to an injection of 100 mg of intramuscular progesterone-in-oil. FSH concentration was 197 mIU/ml and LH 150 mIU/ml; karyotype was 45,X/46,XX. She was placed on cyclic estrogen and progestin and had withdrawal flow each month.

Case 12. B. T., a 17-year-old student at a local boarding school, had amenorrhea for 3 years. She had had menarche at the age of 12 years, followed by regular menses for 2 years until she became amenorrheic. The amenorrhea had been attributed to the stress of boarding school.

Physical examination revealed a healthy young woman with a height of 63 inches, weight of 119 pounds. Vaginal examination showed poor estrogenization. Laboratory tests showed elevated gonadotropin levels: FSH, 63.9 and greater than 100 mIU/ml; LH, 60.8 and 94.5 mIU/ml. Karyotype was 46,XX; antiovarian antibodies were negative; thyroid tests were normal.

This case of premature ovarian failure underscores the importance of examining the amenorrheic adolescent and establishing a diagnosis.

Case 13. K. M. was brought to the Adolescent Clinic at age $12^{6}/_{12}$ years for amenorrhea. She had started her breast and pubic hair development at age $10^{6}/_{12}$ years and had her menarche at age $11^{9}/_{12}$ years. She had subsequently had two monthly cycles and then amenorrhea for 9 months. She recalled having been short for some time. She had been treated with iron for anemia. She denied constipation, fatigue, hot-cold intolerance, or school problems. Her mother was 60 inches and her father $67\frac{1}{2}$ inches; her 17-year-old brother was 69 inches. On physical examination, K. M. had a height of $55\frac{1}{2}$ inches, weight 84 pounds. Blood pressure was 112/70, and pulse was 66/min. Breast and pubic hair development were both Tanner 4. The introitus was well estrogenized, and rectal examination showed a normal-sized uterus. Although the history of irregular menses was not particularly unusual in an early adolescent, the growth chart (Fig. 6-17) was a clue to the diagnosis. The patient had had little increase in height between ages $8\frac{1}{2}$ and $10\frac{1}{2}$ years but then had experienced the growth spurt of pubertal development. Additionally she had been treated for anemia. Bone age was 11 years (delayed for a postmenarcheal adolescent), and indeed thyroid function test showed hypothyroidism with a T4 of 1.8 μg/100 ml, thyroid-binding globulin index (TBGI) of 0.75, total T3 of 54 ng/100 ml, and TSH of 990 μU/ml. Gonadotropin levels were normal (LH, 3.6 mIU/ml; FSH, 9.0 mIU/ml). She was started on levothyroxine (Synthroid) and experienced some behavioral problems at school as she converted from a placid child to a rebellious adolescent. Menses resumed after 2 months of thyroid replacement, and she is currently on a dose of 0.125 mg daily. School performance and adolescent adjustment gradually improved over the following years.

Case 14. Identical twins M. R. and S. R. presented at age 20 years with amenorrhea of 2 years' duration. Both had experienced menarche between the ages of 13 and 14 years and had had regular monthly menses until age 18 years when they both increased their level of athletic training in preparation for college athletics. M. R. lost 20 pounds, and S. R. lost 15 pounds. Both had subsequently maintained stable weights between 112 and 120 pounds for the past 2 years with heights of 66 inches. Both continued to be active in competitive sports throughout the year. Physical examination of both patients revealed Tanner stage 5 breast and pubic hair development with markedly diminished estrogenization on vaginal examination. The remainder of the pelvic examinations and general assessments were normal. Laboratory values for the two girls were remarkably similar: LH was 4.6 mIU/ml for S. R., 4.7 mIU/ml for M. R.; FSH, 10.6 mIU/ml for S. R., 11.3 mIU/ml for M. R.; prolactin, 3.1 ng/ml for S. R. and 3.7 mIU/ml for M. R.; estradiol, 27 pg/ml for S. R. and 28 pg/ml for M. R. Vaginal smears were slightly different, with S. R., who had lost less weight, having a better maturation index: 15 percent superficial:85 percent intermediate for S. R. versus 16 percent superficial:53

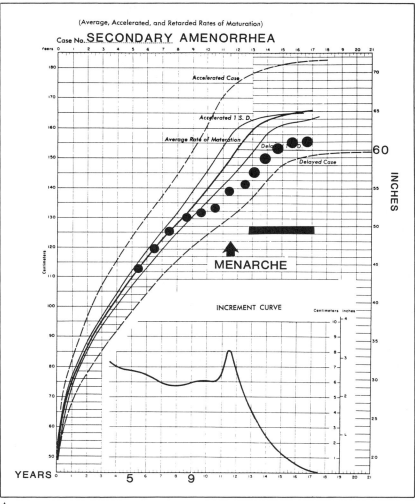

A

Figure 6-17. Case 13. Growth charts: A. Height. B. Weight. The bar and the larger dots represent therapy with thyroid replacement.

percent intermediate:31 percent parabasal for M. R. The options of weight gain, decreased activity level, improved calcium intake, and estrogen replacement were discussed with the two young women. They both elected to increase dietary calcium and to use transdermal estradiol patches (Estraderm) and medroxyprogesterone (13 days/month) for 9 months. Withdrawal flow was normal; however, they discontinued the medication because of concerns about bloating. Six months later they began to decrease athletic activity in preparation for graduation from college. Estradiol levels were 47 pg/ml for M. R. and 49 pg/ml for S. R. It is hoped that estrogenization will continue to improve and spontaneous menses will return after graduation.

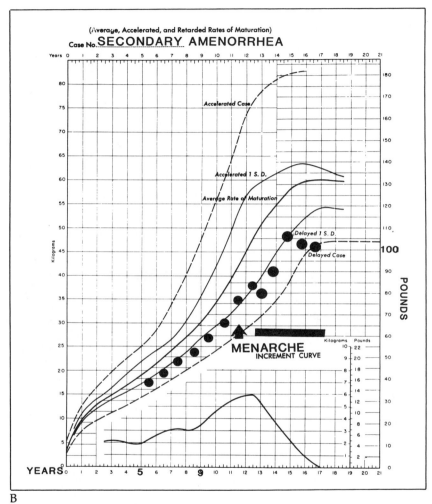

B
Figure 6-17 (Continued)

SECONDARY AMENORRHEA WITH HIRSUTISM
OR VIRILIZATION

The differential diagnosis of secondary amenorrhea with hirsutism or
virilization, or both, includes polycystic ovary syndrome, congenital
(or late onset) adrenocortical hyperplasia, Cushing's syndrome, and
ovarian and adrenal tumors. The entities are discussed in the section
Delayed Menarche with Hirsutism in this chapter and especially in
Chapter 7. In addition to a careful physical examination, the evaluation includes laboratory tests such as serum levels of testosterone
(total and free), DHA, DHAS, androstenedione, 17-hydroxyproges-
terone (early morning), FSH, LH and prolactin. Measurement of

urinary 17-ketosteroids, ACTH stimulation testing, and dexamethasone suppression testing may be included. Ultrasonography, CT, MRI, and/or laparoscopy may be indicated in some of these patients.

OLIGOMENORRHEA

Teenagers with periods every 2 to 3 months often consult the physician. Many teenage girls feel different from their friends who are having regular monthly cycles. These menses may or may not be ovulatory. Premenstrual symptoms, dysmenorrhea, and a shift in the basal body temperature curve (see p. 42) that is confirmed by a rise in serum progesterone suggest ovulation. Scanty, irregular periods without cramps are most likely anovulatory and may characterize the early teenage years.

Adolescents who have evidence of androgen excess at any age, those who have persistent oligomenorrhea 3 to 4 years after menarche, and those with 4 to 6 months of amenorrhea deserve the same consideration as patients with secondary amenorrhea. Recall that girls with earlier menarche have the onset of ovulatory menses sooner than those with menarche after age 13 (see p. 113). The causes of oligomenorrhea are essentially the same as those shown in Figure 6-8. Fluctuating weight with rapid gain, followed by crash dieting, may disturb hypothalamic-pituitary function in the adolescent and result in irregular periods. Ballet dancers and competitive athletes, such as runners and gymnasts, may have oligomenorrhea, especially those who started training in the prepubertal years. In addition, it should be remembered that the sexually active patient who has a history of irregular periods but who is not using contraception may have an unplanned pregnancy despite any number of negative pregnancy tests in the past.

The importance of evaluating cases of persistent oligomenorrhea was noted in a review at The Children's Hospital. The charts of all adolescents who had a workup for oligomenorrhea not associated with weight loss and who had been evaluated over a 2-year period were reviewed [156]. The 42 adolescents ranged in age from 15 to 20 years, with an average age of 17.3 years. All patients were at least 2 years postmenarche, with an average of 4.4 years. None were athletes. Twenty had a history of vaginal bleeding every 2 to 3 months; 15 bled every 4 to 6 months, and 7 reported bleeding every 7 to 12 months. A careful physical examination was done, which included noting the stage of hirsutism (see Chap. 7). Nineteen (group I) patients were found to have evidence of androgen excess (hirsutism, clitoromegaly, and/or severe acne) with PCO or adrenal androgen excess, and 23 patients (group II) had no evidence of androgen excess. In the group without androgen excess, 4 patients had persistently elevated LH levels that ranged from 34.5 to 41.0 mIU/ml, with normal FSH, DHAS, and total and free testosterone levels. Two of these patients had enlarged ovaries by palpation, suggesting a diagnosis of PCO. One of the patients with normal ovaries by palpation has subsequently become hirsute with an elevated free testosterone level. The majority of group II patients (15 out of 23) had low to normal levels of LH and FSH, suggesting hypothalamic suppression. None of these patients were overweight, and many of them seemed to be under academic stress. Six of the 15 have subsequently returned to normal monthly menses. Although 3 group II patients were diagnosed as having ovarian failure, this is an uncommon diagnosis and may reflect the fact that our hospital is a referral center. The demonstration of a prolactinoma in one young adolescent with oligomenorrhea and withdrawal flow to progesterone challenge confirms the need to measure the level of prolactin in patients with persistent symptomatology.

Lest the physician feel that expensive laboratory tests should be done on all adolescents with irregular periods, it should be pointed out that the patients in our series were not adolescents with occasional irregular menses. The mean age was over 17 years, and many had noted increasing hair growth. At most, these adolescents had one cycle every 2 to 3 months, and most had significantly fewer periods. Only 9 out of the 42 girls had ever had monthly menses. The most striking finding was the high incidence of abnormal hormone profiles among obese adolescents with mild to moderate hirsutism. (The treatment of androgen excess is discussed in detail in Chap. 7.) Patients with hypothalamic suppression and a normal physical examination deserve reassurance and a careful explanation of menstrual cycles. The statement, "You're normal, don't worry," is not sufficient. Such patients should not be treated with oral contraceptives to produce "normal cycles." Medroxyprogesterone acetate (Provera), 10 mg a day for 13 to 14 days each month, can be used to prevent endometrial hyperplasia; it is also especially useful to treat patients with a history of hypermenorrhea associated with irregular periods. The importance of establishing an exact diagnosis in patients with oligomenorrhea is particularly important in contraceptive counselling. If the young woman has a history of irregular menses associated with hypothalamic suppression (which has been adequately evaluated), she may prefer a barrier method of contraception. The worry associated with amenorrhea and the need for frequent pregnancy tests is a drawback. If she uses the Pill, her menses are likely to return to the pre-Pill status after she discontinues its use (see Chap. 15). The adolescent who has the abnormal hormone profile and hirsutism of polycystic ovary syndrome benefit from the suppression of ovarian function that oral contraceptive pills induce.

In older adolescents who have menses every 2 months with premenstrual symptoms and dysmenorrhea, the likelihood of ovulation is high, and no therapy is necessary. Basal body temperature charts can be useful in demonstrating ovulation, although they are not always accurate. Ovulatory cycles are indicated by a shift in basal body temperature chart 2 weeks before the next menses and a rise in serum progesterone level. An endometrial biopsy can provide confirmatory evidence of a secretory endometrium. All of these tests are generally reserved for the investigation of infertile patients.

DYSFUNCTIONAL UTERINE BLEEDING: POLYMENORRHEA, HYPERMENORRHEA

One of the most common problems reported to the practitioner seeing adolescents is irregular, profuse menstruation. Rarely, a teenager with her first period might even show a decrease of 10 to 20 percentage points in her hematocrit. More often, a teenager who has had several years of regular cycles begins to have periods every 2 weeks or prolonged bleeding for 14 to 20 days after 2 to 3 months of amenorrhea. A young adolescent is prone to anovulatory periods with incomplete shedding of a proliferative endometrium; the older adolescent may develop anovulatory cycles with stress or illness. A study of FSH/LH patterns in perimenarcheal girls with dyfunctional bleeding suggests the prevalence of a maturation defect [157]. The higher than normal levels of FSH in relation to LH may result in rapid follicular maturation and increased synthesis of estrogen, and absence of the midcycle surge of LH. Although dyfunctional uterine bleeding (DUB) may appear to be a defect in positive feedback and the establishment of ovulatory cycles, in fact most adolescents are anovulatory in the first years following menarche and yet do not present with this problem. Thus the group of adolescents with DUB appear to have delayed maturation of normal negative feedback cyclicity; rising levels of estrogen do not cause a fall in FSH and subsequent suppression of estrogen secretion, and thus the endometrium becomes excessively thickened. In contrast, normal adolescents have an intact negative feedback mechanism that allows for orderly growth of the endometrium and withdrawal flow before the endometrium is excessively thickened. In addition, the occasional ovulatory cycle stabilizes endometrial growth and allows an intermittent more complete shedding. Adolescents with conditions that cause sustained anovulation may also be likely to present with DUB; such problems include eating disorders, weight changes, athletic competition, chronic illnesses, stress, drug abuse, endocrine disorders, and most importantly polycystic ovary syndrome.

In deciding whether the pattern of the adolescent is normal or abnormal, the clinician needs to be cognizant of normal variation. The adult menstrual cycle is 21 to 45 days, and an adult tends to have the same interval on a month-to-month basis. Although adolescents have a similar range of normal cycles, a given adolescent has more variability within this range than does the adult woman. Normal duration of flow is 3 to 7 days, with a flow of greater than 8 to 10 days excessive. Normal blood loss is 30 to 40 ml per menstrual period, which usually translates into 10 to 15 soaked tampons or pads per cycle. However, estimation of blood loss by self-report of the adolescent (and adult women) is unfortunately inaccurate with the exception of very scanty flow [158]. Even using the number of tampons or pads changed in a day cannot give the clinician an assessment of the likelihood of significant DUB, defined as a blood loss of greater than 80 ml per menstrual period, an amount that would result in iron deficiency anemia. Thus the hematocrit should be measured in the girl with the report of possible DUB to determine the extent of blood loss; if the story of bleeding is very impressive in spite of a normal or near normal hematocrit, a reticulocyte count is very useful in assessing the amount of blood loss.

The list of diagnoses to be considered in approaching the problem of DUB is long but necessitates the careful consideration and examination of each patient. Importantly, disorders of pregnancy and the possibility of pelvic infection must be appraised early in the evaluation. The differential diagnosis is included in Table 6-3. A highly sensitive pregnancy test should be performed in the initial evaluation; ectopic pregnancy should be a consideration, especially in the adolescent with a previous history of pelvic inflammatory disease or sexually transmitted diseases (see Chap. 10). Adolescents with pelvic inflammatory disease and endometritis caused by *Neisseria gonorrhoeae* or *Chlamydia trachomatis* frequently present with heavy or irregular bleeding. The possibility of these infections also needs to be considered in the adolescent taking oral contraceptives who develops new breakthrough bleeding. Thus a crucial part of the evaluation in an adolescent who might ever have been sexually active (history notwithstanding) is a culture for *N. gonorrhoeae* and *C. trachomatis*. A sedimentation rate should be done if infection is a likely possibility.

Patients with blood dyscrasias usually have other signs of bleeding such as petechiae, ecchymoses, or epistaxis; however, the teenager with von Willebrand's disease may not have a prior history of injuries and thus may be diagnosed because of profuse menstruation starting with her menarche. Likewise the teenager with chronic thrombocytopenic purpura or the cardiac patient on warfarin may have heavy menstrual bleeding.

Irregular, heavy menstruation may accompany endocrine disorders that are also associated with secondary amenorrhea and anovulation. Adrenal problems such as late onset 21-hydroxylase deficiency, Cushing's disease, and Addison's disease cause anovulation; Addi-

Table 6-3. Differential Diagnosis of Vaginal Bleeding in the Adolescent Girl

Dysfunctional uterine bleeding

Disorders of pregnancy: threatened, incomplete, or missed abortion; molar pregnancy; ectopic pregnancy

Pelvic inflammatory disease: salpingitis, endometritis

Blood dyscrasias: thrombocytopenia (e.g., idiopathic thrombocytopenic purpura, leukemia, aplastic anemia, hypersplenism), clotting disorders, von Willebrand's disease and other disorders of platelet function, iron deficiency

Endocrine disorders: hypo- or hyperthyroidism, adrenal disease, diabetes mellitus, hyperprolactinemia, polycystic ovary syndrome, ovarian failure

Vaginal abnormalities: carcinoma, adenosis (secondary to maternal diethylstilbestrol)

Cervical problems: cervicitis, polyp, hemangioma, carcinoma

Uterine problems: congenital anomalies, submucous myoma, polyp, carcinoma, use of intrauterine contraceptive device, breakthrough bleeding associated with the use of oral contraceptives, ovulation bleeding

Ovarian cysts and tumors

Endometriosis

Systemic diseases

Trauma

Foreign body (e.g., retained tampon)

Medications: anticoagulants, platelet inhibitors, androgens

son's disease is also often associated with ovarian failure. Patients with hyperprolactinemia usually have amenorrhea but early may have DUB from anovulation or a shortened luteal phase. Similarly, patients with ovarian failure from Turner syndrome or chemotherapy/radiation therapy may have DUB before amenorrhea. The anovulation of PCO is present early in adolescence; 20 to 30 percent of PCO patients experience DUB. This diagnosis needs to be considered in adolescents with persistent DUB and those presenting initially with evidence of androgen excess (hirsutism, acne) because these girls are at increased risk of endometrial hyperplasia and the early development of endometrial carcinoma (rarely, even in the teenage years). Thus therapy with progestins or oral contraceptives needs to be continued long-term in these girls.

Uterine abnormalities presenting with irregular bleeding include submucous myomas, congenital anomalies, IUD use, and breakthrough bleeding on oral contraceptives. With congential anomalies, the tip-off is sometimes the presence of regular red menstrual bleeding followed by brown or prune-colored spotting intermenstrually; the bloody fluid may have a foul odor if infected by anaerobes. The normal uterus empties in a cyclic pattern, and the obstructed uterus or vagina empties through a fistula slowly over the month (see p.

290). The possibility of breakthrough bleeding in the adolescent taking oral contraceptives needs to be kept in mind, since the adolescent may have obtained the pills confidentially from a clinic and yet be brought to another physician by her mother for irregular menses. Unless the girl is seen alone and asked specifically about the use of pills, the history may not become apparent. An occasional patient may have slight vaginal bleeding for 1 or 2 days at midcycle because of a fall in estrogen levels at ovulation. A carefully kept menstrual calendar helps make the diagnosis. The bleeding may be more apparent to the adolescent who is exercising vigorously that day because of more rapid emptying of the vagina of the menstrual blood.

Carcinoma of the vagina is a rare problem among teenagers. However, since the in utero exposure to diethylstilbestrol has been implicated in the later development of vaginal and cervical adenocarcinoma in female offspring, it certainly behooves the physician to examine patients with a positive maternal history (see Chap. 12). Cervical problems may also cause bleeding, especially with trauma or postcoitally. Cervicitis from sexually transmitted infections such as Trichomonas and C. trachomatis can be associated with bleeding. Young women with cystic fibrosis often have a large cervical ectropion with chronic inflammation; the cervix may be friable and bleed easily with coitus or insertion of a speculum. Hemangiomas rarely occur on the cervix and cause bleeding especially with trauma or coitus. Given the epidemic of sexually transmitted disease and the exposure of adolescents to human papillomavirus, the possibility of cervical cancer must be kept in mind.

Endometriosis has been associated with irregular menses from anovulation and also with the occurrence of brown spotting in the premenstrual phase of the cycle. Ovarian abnormalities include tumors and cysts that may cause hypermenorrhea.

Systemic diseases may interfere with normal cyclicity because of an impact on ovulation, an interference with normal coagulation, or a local endometrial infection such as tuberculosis (a common etiology in third world countries but exceedingly rare in the United States). Patients on renal dialysis frequently have either amenorrhea or excessive menstrual flow; the menorrhagia may increase the transfusion requirement of the patient and thus frequently requires ongoing management with progestins or oral contraceptives.

Trauma may occur because of acute falls, waterskiing injuries, foreign objects introduced for masturbation, or sexual assault. The most frequent foreign body is a retained tampon, sometimes left in the vagina for weeks to months. The young adolescent may have tried a tampon and not realized the need for removal or may have put two tampons in the vagina and forgotten to remove one. The bleeding of a retained tampon is usually accompanied by a foul-smelling discharge.

Contraceptive sponges may fragment and be retained as a foreign body within the vagina, necessitating removal by the clinician.

Medications such as anticoagulants and platelet inhibitors can be associated with excessive bleeding. Adolescent athletes taking anabolic steroids may develop masculinization and anovulatory cycles with irregular bleeding or amenorrhea.

Categorizing bleeding as cyclic or acyclic may help the clinician focus on the appropriate diagnosis. For example, an adolescent with normal cyclic intervals but very heavy bleeding at the time of each cycle may have a blood dyscrasia or a uterine problem (submucous myoma or IUD). An adolescent with normal cycles but superimposed abnormal bleeding at any time throughout the cycle may have a foreign body within the vagina, uterine polyp, vaginal malignancy, congenital malformation of the uterus with obstruction, infection, cervical abnormality, or endometriosis. Adolescents with no cyclicity apparent or cycles of less than 21 days or more than 40 to 45 days usually have anovulatory dysfunctional uterine bleeding with lack of normal negative feedback. However, the other disorders associated with anovulation need to be considered, including psychosocial problems, eating disorders, athletic competition, PCO, ovarian failure, ovarian tumors, and endocrinopathies.

PATIENT ASSESSMENT
The history is crucial in determining the likely diagnoses as well as the urgency for immediate treatment because of profound anemia or postural symptoms. Questions should focus on date of menarche, menstrual pattern, duration, quantity and color of the flow, and the presence of dysmenorrhea. The dates of the last menstrual period and the previous menstrual period should be recorded. A menstrual calendar is invaluable. The use of tampons, contraceptive sponges, or other foreign objects should be elicited. The patient should be asked whether she is sexually active (realizing that the history must be taken confidentially and the answers may not always be honest), whether the bleeding was postcoital, and if she is using oral contraceptives or an IUD. The patient should also be queried about previous sexually transmitted diseases and recent exposure to a new partner or a partner with urethritis or other "infection." A general review of systems including recent stresses, weight changes, eating disorders, athletic competition, chronic diseases, bleeding disorders, medications, illicit drugs, syncope, visual changes, headaches, gastrointestinal symptoms, and a family history of PCO and bleeding disorders is essential.

The physical examination should include a general assessment with attention to the height, weight, body type and fat distribution (Cushing's syndrome, Turner syndrome), blood pressure (standing and sitting), evidence of androgen excess (acne, hirsutism, clitoromegaly), thyroid palpation, breast examination to detect galactorrhea, other signs of bleeding such as petechiae or bruises, and a pelvic examination. In most virginal adolescents and all sexually active adolescents, a one-finger digital examination can be done initially to check for foreign bodies within the vagina and to palpate the cervix. A speculum appropriate for the size of the hymenal opening can then be chosen, usually a Huffman in the virginal patient and a Pederson for the sexually active adolescent. Generally, a virginal patient can cooperate fully if the need for the examination is carefully explained and the examiner elicits her help. Sometimes the application of a small amount of lubricating jelly or xylocaine jelly to the introitus can aid in the insertion. In some girls who have never used tampons, the opening is too small to allow a speculum examination. In these cases, a rectoabdominal examination suffices; if the patient then does not respond to simple hormonal treatment, ultrasonography of the pelvis and/or anesthesia examination can be done. Clearly many adolescents in the early months postmenarche may have several closely spaced menses and then revert to a normal pattern and can be simply observed without a full pelvic examination. However, even a virginal girl with continuous spotting, cyclic bleeding with superimposed bleeding throughout the cycle, bleeding sufficient to cause anemia, or persistent DUB deserves a careful gynecologic assessment.

During the speculum examination, cultures should be obtained for *N. gonorrhoeae* and *C. trachomatis* in any patient who gives a history of being sexually active and any patient whom the clinician suspects may have had intercourse. In the absence of bleeding at the time of the examination, wet preps can also be done to look for other sexually transmitted diseases and a Papanicolaou smear can be obtained. A bimanual examination should be done to assess uterine tenderness and enlargement and adnexal pain and masses. A soft mass along the anterior-lateral vaginal wall is most likely an obstructed unilateral genital tract.

Laboratory tests should include a urine human chorionic gonadotropin (HCG) using a sensitive test with monoclonal antibody technology (such as the ICON) and a CBC with differential and estimate of platelets by smear. Reticulocyte count is helpful in girls who give an impressive history of bleeding and yet have a normal or only slightly depressed hemoglobin to assess the amount of bleeding. A sedimentation rate is useful if pelvic infection is a consideration. Coagulation studies (prothrombin time, partial thromboplastin time, bleeding time) and platelet count are indicated in patients with heavy cyclic bleeding from menarche and those with a significant drop in hemoglobin or a hemoglobin less than 10 gm at presentation. Blood is sent for type and cross-match in girls with acute hemorrhage or low hemoglobin for whom transfusion may be necessary.

Other tests depend on the physical examination and the length of the history of dysfunctional uterine bleeding. Blood tests, if indicated, should be drawn before hormone therapy and include blood sugar, thyroid function tests (including TSH), LH, FSH, prolactin, and, especially in those with hirsutism or acne, androgens (total and free testosterone, DHAS). Progesterone level in the presumed luteal phase of the cycle, and basal body temperature charts can aid in the evaluation of ovulatory versus anovulatory menses. Ultrasonography can be helpful when a pelvic mass is felt, a uterine anomaly is suspected, or bimanual examination cannot be accomplished in a young adolescent with significant bleeding. If a uterine anomaly, submucous myoma, or endometrial polyp is suspected, hysterosalpingogram (usually under general anesthesia) and hysteroscopy are diagnostic aids.

TREATMENT
The goals of the assessment are to determine which adolescent needs medical treatment and which adolescent can be observed with the hope that further maturation of the hypothalamic-pituitary-ovarian axis will result in normal cycles. The objective of hormonal treatment is to give estrogens to heal over the bleeding sites by causing further proliferation and to give progestins to induce endometrial stability. The aim should be to stop bleeding, prevent a recurrence, and provide long-term follow-up to the patient. Although opinion clearly varies on the best mode of therapy [157, 159, 160], the following classification and treatment schedules have been helpful in our clinics.

Mild dysfunctional bleeding
1. Menses are longer than normal or cycle is shortened for 2 or more months. Flow is slightly to moderately increased.
2. Hemoglobin level is normal.
3. Observation and reassurance is usually adequate. The patient should be encouraged to keep a menstrual calendar so that the need for intervention in the future can be assessed. Iron supplements will prevent anemia (especially if dietary intake is borderline). Antiprostaglandin medications, such as mefenamic acid (Ponstel), 500 mg 3 times a day during menstruation, have been reported to reduce blood loss in patients with menorrhagia [161].

Moderate dysfunctional bleeding
1. Menses are moderately prolonged or cycle remains shortened with frequent menses (every 1–3 weeks). Flow is moderate to heavy.

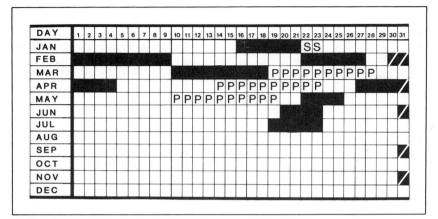

Figure 6-18. A 14-year-old girl comes to the clinic on March 19 with a history of frequent periods (every 17–22 days). She is not bleeding at the time of her visit. Her examination and laboratory studies are normal. She is treated with medroxyprogesterone (Provera), 10 mg daily for 10 days and then for 10 days from the 14th to the 23rd day of the two subsequent cycles. Her menses return to normal in June and July. (*S* = spotting; *P* = Provera; *solid bars* = bleeding. On the normal menstrual calendar, the months without 30 or 31 days have *slashed bars*.)

2. Hemoglobin level often shows a mild anemia.
3. Treatment consists of the use of birth control pills or medroxyprogesterone (Provera). Hormones should not be prescribed if the patient is pregnant. Birth control pills are more effective at stopping dysfunctional bleeding that is in progress. However, if the patient is not bleeding at the time of the visit, the patient or parent dislikes the use of birth control pills, or there is a medical contraindication to the use of estrogen (see Chap. 15), medroxyprogesterone can be tried as initial therapy. Medroxyprogesterone, 10 mg once or twice a day for 10 to 14 days, is started on the 14th day of the menstrual cycle (day 1 is the first day of the last period) or at the time of the visit. After the patient has withdrawal flow, she starts medroxyprogesterone on day 14 again (Fig. 6-18). The pattern is continued for 3 to 6 months. A system that uses the calendar month (i.e., medroxyprogesterone, 10 mg once or twice a day the first 10 to 14 days of each month) is simpler for many patients to remember; however, day 14 to 25 of the cycle should be used if the calendar month method fails. If the girl starts bleeding even before she gets to day 14 of her cycle, then starting the medroxyprogesterone on day 10 or day 12 of the cycle for 2 months or switching to an oral contraceptive will give better cycle control. Norethindrone acetate (Norlutate), 10 mg daily for 10 to 14 days, can be given instead of medroxyprogesterone. For adolescents

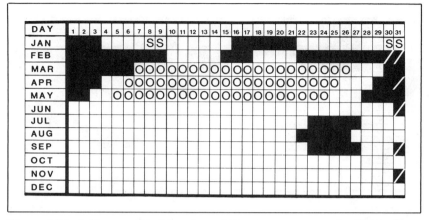

Figure 6-19. A 14-year-old girl arrives at the emergency ward with profuse vaginal bleeding that followed markedly irregular cycles for the previous 3 months. Her pelvic examination and clotting studies are normal; hematocrit is 28 percent. She is placed on Ovral every 4 hours; bleeding ceases the following day. She is continued on Ovral for the remainder of the cycle and then given cyclic Lo/Ovral or Ovral for two additional months. (S = spotting; O = Ovral; *solid bars* = bleeding. On the normal menstrual calendar, the months without 30 or 31 days have *slashed bars*.)

who require *ongoing* therapy for persistent dysfunctional uterine bleeding (especially associated with PCO), *13 to 14 days* of progestin should be prescribed each month to prevent endometrial hyperplasia.

For patients with heavy or prolonged dysfunctional bleeding, the initial use of an oral contraceptive, such as Ovral, Lo/Ovral, or Norinyl (Ortho-Novum) 1/50 or 1/35 for 21 days, is preferable (Fig. 6-19). Ovral is particularly useful in the treatment of heavy dysfunctional bleeding because of the content of a strong progestin coupled with 50 μg of ethinyl estradiol. The patient can usually be told to take one twice a day for 3 or 4 days until the bleeding stops and then one a day to finish a 21-day cycle. Lo/Ovral can be used similarly in the young adolescent but sometimes may need to be increased initially to 3 or 4 times a day to stop menstrual flow and then reduced to once a day. Norinyl (Ortho-Novum) 1/35 (or 1/50) has also been used successfully in some patients, given once or twice a day for 21 days. The clinician needs to keep in contact with the patient, since hormonal therapy can cause nausea and noncompliance and adequate doses must be prescribed to prevent further bleeding.

The urgency of gaining cycle control is related to the amount of bleeding and the hematocrit; thus in some adolescents with heavy bleeding and anemia, starting with Ovral 4 times a day may be neces-

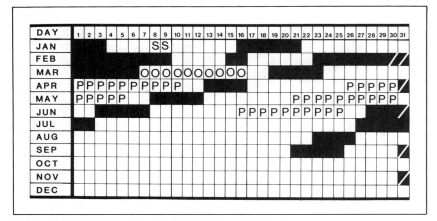

DAY	1	2	3	4	5	6	7	8	9	10	11	12	13	14	15	16	17	18	19	20	21	22	23	24	25	26	27	28	29	30	31
JAN								S	S																						
FEB																															
MAR								O	O	O	O	O	O	O	O	O	O	O													
APR	P	P	P	P	P	P	P	P	P																		P	P	P	P	P
MAY	P	P	P	P	P																	P	P	P	P	P	P	P	P	P	P
JUN																	P	P	P	P	P	P	P	P	P						
JUL																															
AUG																															
SEP																															
OCT																															
NOV																															
DEC																															

Figure 6-20. The same case as illustrated in Figure 6-19; however, the patient experiences moderate nausea and vomiting on Ortho-Novum therapy. The bleeding stops on Ortho-Novum 1/50 daily, and the course is shortened to 10 days. Medroxyprogesterone (Provera), 10 mg daily, is given for 3 months from day 14 to 23 of each cycle. (S = spotting; O = Ortho-Novum; P = Provera.)

sary to stop bleeding within 24 to 36 hours. A useful regimen is Ovral 4 times a day for 4 days, 3 times a day for 3 days, and twice a day for 2 weeks. With these doses of estrogen, antiemetics such as chlorpromazine, 5 to 10 mg, may need to be prescribed and taken by the patient 2 hours before each dose of Ovral to prevent nausea.

Occasionally patients experience excessive nausea in spite of antiemetics; in these cases, the 21-day course of hormone can be shortened to 10 days and medroxyprogesterone started on a cyclic basis (Fig. 6-20). An alternative regimen with norethindrone acetate (Norlutate), similar to that for Ovral, can also be used: 5 mg 4 times a day for 4 days, 3 times a day for 3 days, and then twice a day for 2 weeks. Failure to control bleeding with any of the above regimens should make the clinician consider a diagnosis other than dysfunctional bleeding (Fig. 6-21).

A normal withdrawal flow will follow 2 to 4 days after the last hormone tablet. The patient should then be given cyclic medroxyprogesterone for 3 to 6 months. If the history of dysfunctional bleeding has been long, the patient may require treatment with cyclic oral contraceptives for 2 to 3 months before switching to medroxyprogesterone. A lower dose contraceptive such as Lo/Ovral or Triphasil can usually be prescribed after the initial month of Ovral. The patient should receive careful instructions on 21-day versus 28-day pills, otherwise confusion may result and placebos used on hormone days or a 7-day withdrawal time not observed. Oral contraceptives should be continued if birth control is needed. A course of oral iron plus folic acid (1 mg daily) should be prescribed to correct anemia.

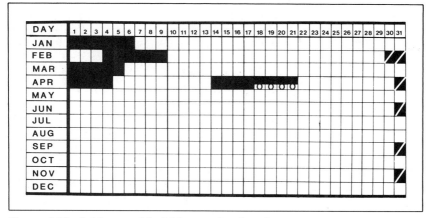

Figure 6-21. A 14-year-old girl is examined in the emergency ward on April 18; she has had profuse vaginal bleeding for 4 days. She has had 1 year of normal cycles. Her last normal menstrual period was 2 weeks previously. She is virginal, and examination is difficult because of poor relaxation. Hematocrit is 33 percent. She is placed on 2 tablets of Ortho-Novum 1/50 every 4 hours for 2 days and then twice a day. She continues to bleed and is seen in the clinic on April 21. Ultrasonography of her pelvis reveals a mass in the right pelvis and an absent right kidney. Anesthesia examination and laparoscopy demonstrate an obstructed right uterine horn and duplicated vagina that is obstructed on the right. (O = Ortho-Novum; *solid bars* = bleeding. On the normal menstrual calendar, the months without 30 or 31 days have *slashed bars*.)

Severe dysfunctional bleeding

1. Prolonged bleeding with disruption of normal menstrual cycles; very heavy flow.
2. Hemoglobin level reduced, often to less than 9 gm. Clinical signs of blood loss may be present.
3. Treatment: The patient should be admitted if initial hemoglobin is less than 7 gm, if orthostatic signs are present or bleeding is heavy and hemoglobin is less than 10 gm. Transfusion should be considered if there are clinical signs of acute blood loss or the hemoglobin level is extremely low. Clotting studies should be done. If the hemoglobin is 9 to 10 gm and the patient and family are reliable and can maintain close telephone contact, the patient can be treated at home and followed daily until bleeding ceases. For most patients, hospitalization is necessary.

An effective treatment is Ovral every 4 hours until bleeding slows or stops (usually 4–8 tablets), then every 6 hours for 24 hours, every 8 hours for 48 hours, and then twice a day to complete a 21-day course of hormones. Alternatively, the Ovral regimen can start with every 4 hours until bleeding is controlled and then can be tapered to one tablet 4 times a day for 4 days, 3 times a day for 3 days, and twice a day for 2 weeks; this schedule may be especially easy for emergency ward personnel to administer. Norinyl (Ortho-Novum) 1/50 has been used in similar doses. In acute severe hemorrhage, some physicians use conjugated estrogens (Premarin), 25 mg intravenously every 4 hours for 2 to 3 doses, whereas others use only oral medications because of concern about possible thromboembolism. Intravenous estrogen appears to increase clotting at the level of the capillary and thus is effective very rapidly. If intravenous estrogen is used, oral hormones such as Ovral need to be started at the same time to stabilize the endometrium. Antiemetics are usually needed with any of the high-dose estrogen therapies. Transfusion needs are individualized on the basis of hemoglobin, blood loss, postural symptoms, and rapidity of gaining control of the bleeding.

If there is a contraindication to the use of estrogen, a trial of progestin such as norethindrone acetate (Norlutate), 5 to 10 mg, or medroxyprogesterone, 10 mg, can be given every 4 hours and then tapered to the regimen of 4 times a day for 4 days, 3 times a day for 3 days, and then twice a day for 2 weeks. Norlutate appears to be more effective than medroxyprogesterone.

Occasionally only very high doses of progestin (medroxyprogesterone, 40 to 80 mg/day, or DepoProvera, 100 mg intramuscularly daily for up to a week and then weekly to monthly) are effective to cause endometrial atrophy; breakthrough bleeding can be avoided by using a several-day course of estrogen (conjugated estrogens, 2.5 mg for 5 to 7 days or an occasional transdermal estradiol patch). Patients may become cushingoid with these high doses and injections are contraindicated in patients with bleeding disorders. More evaluation of the potential use of long-acting GnRH analogues is needed, although both the route of administration and the initial agonist phase are current disadvantages.

If the regimen of hormone tablets every 4 hours fails to control bleeding within 24 to 36 hours, the possibility of pelvic pathology should be excluded by anesthesia examination and dilatation and curettage. Dilatation and curettage may be needed earlier to treat the group of patients who cannot be given estrogen. Although this procedure can be both diagnostic and curative, the overwhelming majority of adolescents can be managed successfully with hormonal therapy. In addition, the adolescent with a long history of anovulation still needs follow-up therapy to prevent a recurrence of heavy bleeding.

A normal withdrawal flow follows 2 to 4 days after the last hormone tablet. In patients with significant anemia the placebo (off pill) interval may be shortened to 4 to 5 days. The patient should then be cycled for 3 to 4 months with one tablet daily of Ovral (28 day) or, if tolerated without breakthrough bleeding, a pill with 30–35 μg of ethinyl estradiol (Lo/Ovral, Norinyl [Ortho-Novum] 1/35). Iron and folic acid therapy should be instituted along with hormone therapy as soon as the situation has stabilized (1–2 days).

FOLLOW-UP

Patients with low platelets, leukemia, or aplastic anemia may require long-term management. Suppression of menses by continuous use of Lo/Ovral (21d) for several months is helpful in treating menorrhagia; longer use may result in breakthrough bleeding. Medroxyprogesterone (Provera) 10 mg (tapered to 5 mg) daily has been used to create amenorrhea for months and even years [162]. As platelet levels improve, patients should be changed to cyclic therapy with a low-dose progestin-dominant pill. Patients who have weight loss and other symptoms from radiation or chemotherapy may become amenorrheic and not require further hormonal therapy.

Patients with von Willebrand's disease frequently do well on a low-dose cyclic oral contraceptive pill such as Lo/Ovral (28 day) or Triphasil/Trilevlen to reduce menstrual flow. Since DDAVP may also be helpful in some of these girls, provocative testing by a hematologist is useful in planning therapy.

Patients with a long history of anovulatory cycles and dysfunctional uterine bleeding have an increased risk of later infertility and endometrial carcinoma. This risk is especially a problem for patients with polycystic ovary syndrome [163]. Thus regular withdrawal with progestins (such as medroxyprogesterone 13-14 days/month) or oral contraceptives are needed on a long-term basis in these high-risk girls. Careful follow-up is essential.

Case 15. A. J. was a 17-year-old young woman who presented to the Adolescent Clinic for evaluation of heavy bleeding and pain. Her menarche occurred at age 13, and she had always had regular menses lasting 4 to 6 days with mild dysmenorrhea. Her last menstrual period had begun 7 days before and instead of decreasing by the sixth day, the flow had increased and was accompanied by moderately severe cramps. She denied ever having been sexually active.

Physical examination revealed an afebrile, cooperative patient. Abdominal examination showed bilateral lower abdominal tenderness; pelvic examination showed a 1- to 2-fingerbreadth introitus with moderate vaginal bleeding and cervical motion and adnexal tenderness. Cultures were taken from the endocervix for *C. trachomatis* and *N. gonorrhoeae*. Urine ICON for HCG was negative. Since the clinical impression was pelvic inflammatory disease in spite of a negative history of sexual activity, a CBC and sedimentation rate were drawn and the patient was treated with intramuscular ceftriaxone and oral doxycycline. She returned in 2 days and was markedly improved. Laboratory tests showed a hematocrit of 36 percent, white blood count (WBC) of 13,600, and a sedimentation rate of 26 mm/hour. Endocervical cultures were positive for both *N. gonorrhoeae* and *C. trachomatis*. The patient finally admitted to having been sexually active, and her boyfriend was also treated. The patient was started on oral contraceptives for birth control. Her follow-up cultures were negative, but her Papanicolaou smear and subsequent biopsies showed dysplasia and changes consistent with infection with human papillomavirus. Despite an initial history from a patient who denies sexual activity, the clinician seeing adolescents needs to keep the possibility of pelvic inflammatory disease in mind in the evaluation of adolescents with pelvic or abdominal pain or irregular bleeding.

Case 16. N. T. is a 19-year-old who presented to the clinic with a complaint of irregular menses and abdominal pain. Her menarche was at age 13 years, and she had a long history of irregular menses occurring every 3 to 8 weeks. She had previously been treated with oral contraceptives for dysfunctional bleeding and had discontinued her pills 2 months prior to the appointment. Her last menstrual period had started 5 days before the visit, and she had experienced increasing bleeding and cramps. Her prior menstrual period had been 6 weeks ago. Physical examination was remarkable for bilateral lower abdominal tenderness and rebound. Pelvic examination revealed moderate bleeding and cervical motion and adnexal tenderness. Cultures were taken from the endocervix for *N. gonorrhoeae* and *C. trachomatis*. The initial diagnosis was pelvic inflammatory disease, and the patient was admitted to the hospital and started on antibiotics. Urine ICON was positive, and quantitative HCG was 340 mIU/ml. Hematocrit was 35 percent, WBC 9000, and sedimentation rate 36 mm/hour. The repeat HCG was unchanged, and the *Chlamydia* culture was positive. Laparoscopy revealed pelvic inflammatory disease and an ectopic pregnancy. These two diagnoses are important considerations for the physician seeing adolescents with vaginal bleeding.

Case 17. P. H. was a 13-year-old asthmatic who was brought to the emergency ward for a 1-week history of vomiting and headache and a 1-day history of bizarre behavior and hallucinations. She had been on theophylline for many years, and initial impression was that she might have taken a drug overdose. Her menarche had occurred at age 11 years, and she had had regular menses until 16 days before the visit when she began to bleed heavily with clots. Physical examination revealed a pale, disoriented girl with heavy bleeding on vaginal examination. The introitus appeared virginal, and bimanual examination showed a normal uterus and adnexa. Hematocrit was 8.5 percent, WBC 6000, and platelets 14,000. She was transfused with 6 units of blood, given 25 mg of Premarin intravenously, and started on Ovral therapy every 4 hours. After bleeding slowed, she was tapered to 1 tablet of Ovral every 6 hours for 2 days, every 8 hours for 2 days, and then maintained on twice daily tablets for 2½ months until her platelet count was sufficient to allow menstrual flow. Bone marrow evaluation showed aplastic anemia. Because she lacked a matched donor for a bone marrow transplant, she was treated with antithymocyte globulin with a 1-year remission. She has been maintained on cyclic birth control pills without excessive bleeding, since she is now sexually active.

REFERENCES
1. Reindollar RH, Byrd JR, and McDonough PG. Delayed sexual development: A study of 252 patients. Am J Obstet Gynecol 1981; 140:371.
2. Alper MM, Garner MB, and Seibel MM. Premature ovarian failure: Current concepts. J Reprod Med 1986; 31:699.
3. Allen DB, Hendricks SA, and Levy JM. Aortic dilation in Turner's syndrome. J Pediatr 1986; 109:302.

4. Engel E, and Forbes A. Cytogenetic and clinical findings in 48 patients with congenitally defective or absent ovaries. Medicine (Baltimore) 1965; 44:135.
5. Lippe B. Geffner ME, Dietrich RB, et al. Renal malformations in patients with Turner syndrome: Imaging in 141 patients. Pediatrics 1988; 82:852.
6. Groll M, and Cooper M. Menstrual function in Turner's syndrome. Obstet Gynecol 1976; 47:225.
7. Reyes FI, Koh KS, and Faiman C. Fertility in women with gonadal dysgenesis. Am J Obstet Gynecol 1976; 126:668.
8. Gruneiro de Papendieck L, Lorcansky S, Coco R, et al. High incidence of thyroid disturbances in 49 children with Turner syndrome. J Pediatr 1987; 111:258.
9. Miller MJ, Geffner ME, Lippe BM, et al. Echocardiography reveals a high incidence of bicuspid aortic valve in Turner syndrome. J Pediatr 1983; 102:47.
10. Samaan NA, Stepanas AV, Danziger J, et al. Reactive pituitary abnormalities in patients with Klinefelter's and Turner's syndrome. Arch Intern Med 1979; 139:198.
11. Krauss CM, Turksoy RN, Atkins L, et al. Familial premature ovarian failure due to an interstitial deletion of the long arm of the X-chromosome. N Engl J Med 1987; 317:125.
12. Stillman RJ, Schinfeld JS, Schiff I, et al. Ovarian failure in long-term survivors of childhood malignancy. Am J Obstet Gynecol 1981; 139:62.
13. Damewood MD, and Grochow LB. Prospects for fertility after chemotherapy or radiation for neoplastic disease. Fertil Steril 1986; 45:443.
14. Bookman MA, Longo DL, and Young RC. Late complications of curative treatment in Hodgkin's disease. JAMA 1988; 260:680.
15. Hammond CB, and Maxson WS. *Current Concepts. Physiology of the Menopause: Premature Menopause.* Kalamazoo, Mich.: Upjohn, 1983.
16. Chapman RM, and Sutcliffe SB. Protection of ovarian function by oral contraceptives in women receiving chemotherapy for Hodgkin's disease. Blood 1981; 58:849.
17. Watson AR, Taylor J, Rance CP, et al. Gonadal function in women treated with cyclophosphamide for childhood nephrotic syndrome: a long-term follow-up study. Fertil Steril 1986; 46:331.
18. Rivkees SA, and Crawford JD. The relationship of gonadal activity and chemotherapy-induced gonadal damage. JAMA 1988; 259:2123.
19. Quigley C, Cowell C, Jimenez M, et al. Normal or early development of puberty despite gonadal damage in children treated for acute lymphoblastic leukemia. N Engl J Med 1989; 321:143.
20. Shalet SM. Effects of cancer chemotherapy on gonadal function of patients. Cancer Treat Rev 1980; 7:141.
21. Horning SJ, Hoppe RT, Kaplan HS, et al. Female reproductive potential after treatment for Hodgkin's disease. N Engl J Med 1981; 304:1377.
22. Alper MM, and Garner PR. Premature ovarian failure: Its relationship to autoimmune disease. Obstet Gynecol 1985; 66:27.
23. Aiman J, and Smentek C. Premature ovarian failure. Obstet Gynecol 1985; 66:9.
24. Damewood MD, Zacur HA, Hoffman GJ, et al. Circulating antiovarian antibodies in premature ovarian failure. Obstet Gynecol 1986; 68:850.
25. Ahonen P, Miettinen A, and Perheentupa J. Adrenal and steroidal cell antibodies in patients with autoimmune polyglandular disease type I and risk of adrenocortical and ovarian failure. J Clin Endocrinol Metab 1987; 64:494.

26. Scully RE (ed.). Case records of the Massachusetts General Hospital: Case 46-1987. N Engl J Med 1987; 317:1270.
27. Rebar RW, Erickson GF, and Yen SSC. Idiopathic premature ovarian failure: clinical and endocrine characteristics. Fertil Steril 1982; 37:35.
28. Rabinowe SL, Berg MJ, Welch WR, et al. Lymphocyte dysfunction in autoimmune oophoritis: resumption of menses with corticosteroids. Am J Med 1986; 81:347.
29. Scully RE (ed.). Case records of the Massachusetts General Hospital: Case 46-1986. N Engl J Med 1986; 315:1336.
30. Kaufman FR, Kogut MD, Donnell GN, et al. Hypergonadotrophic hypogonadism in female patients with galactosemia. N Engl J Med 1981; 304:994.
31. Finan AC, Elmer MA, Sasnow SR, et al. Nutritional factors and growth in children with sickle cell disease. Am J Dis Child 1988; 142:237.
32. Platt OS, Rosenstock W, and Espeland MA. Influence of sickle hemoglobinopathies on growth and development. N Engl J Med 1984; 311:7.
33. Rosenbach Y, Dinari G, Zahavi I, et al. Short stature as the major manifestation of celiac disease in older children. Clin Pediatr 1986; 25:13.
34. Weizman Z, Hamilton JR, Kopelman HR, et al. Treatment failure in celiac disease due to coexistent exocrine pancreatic insufficiency. Pediatrics, 1987; 80:924.
35. Pugliese MT, Lifshitz F, Grad G, et al. Fear of obesity: A cause of short stature and delayed puberty. N Engl J Med 1983; 309:513.
36. Frisch RE, Gotz-Welbergen AV, McArthur JW, et al. Delayed menarche and amenorrhea of college athletes in relation to age of onset of training. JAMA 1981; 246:1559.
37. Warren MP. The effects of exercise on pubertal progression and reproductive function in girls. J Clin Endocrinol Metab 1980; 51:1150.
38. Djursing H. Hypothalamic-pituitary-gonadal function in insulin treated diabetic women with and without amenorrhea. Dan Med Bull 1987; 34:139.
39. Cicognani A, Cacciari E, Vecchi V, et al. Differential effects of 18- and 24-gy cranial irradiation on growth rate and growth hormone release in children with prolonged survival after acute lymphocytic leukemia. Am J Dis Child 1988; 142:1199.
40. Costin G. Effect of low-dose cranial radiation on growth hormone secretory dynamics and hypothalamic-pituitary function. Am J Dis Child 1988; 142:847.
41. Maurer HS, Lloyd-Still JD, Ingrisano C, et al. A prospective evaluation of iron chelation therapy in children with severe β-thalassemia. Am J Dis Child 1988; 142:287.
42. Borgna-Pignatti C, DeStefano P, Zonta L, et al. Growth and sexual maturation in thalassemia major. J Pediatr 1985; 106:150.
43. Miller WL, Kaplan SL, and Grumbach MM. Child abuse as a cause of past-traumatic hypopituitarism. N Engl J Med 1980; 302:724.
44. Barkan AL, Kelch RP, and Marshall JC. Isolated gonadotrope failure in the polyglandular autoimmune syndrome. N Engl J Med 1985; 312:1535.
45. Shulman DI, Martinez CR, Bercu BB, et al. Hypothalamic-pituitary dysfunction in primary empty sella syndrome in childhood. J Pediatr 1986; 108:540.
46. Boyar RM, Katz J, Finkelstein JW, et al. Anorexia nervosa: Immaturity of the 24-hour luteinizing hormone secretory pattern. N Engl J Med 1974; 291:861.
47. Ayers JWT, Gidwani GP, Schmidt IMV, et al. Osteopenia in hypoestrogenic young women with anorexia nervosa. Fertil Steril 1984; 41:224.

48. Rigotti NA, Nussbaum SR, Herzog DB, et al. Osteoporosis in women with anorexia nervosa. N Engl J Med 1984; 311:1601.
49. Frisch RE, and McArthur JW. Menstrual cycles: Fatness as a determinant of minimum weight for height necessary for their maintenance or onset. Science 1974; 185:949.
50. Frisch RE. Fatness and fertility. Sci Am, March 1988; 88.
51. Abraham SF, Beumont PJV, Fraser IS, et al. Body weight, exercise and menstrual status among ballet dancers in training. Br J Obstet Gynecol 1982; 89:507.
52. Baker ER. Menstrual dysfunction and hormonal status in athletic women: A review. Fertil Steril 1981; 36:691.
53. Baker ER, Mathur RS, Kirk RF, et al. Female runners and secondary amenorrhea: Correlation with age, parity, mileage, and plasma hormonal and sex-hormone-binding globulin concentrations. Fertil Steril 1981; 36:183.
54. Bonen A, Belcastro AN, Ling WY, et al. Profiles of selected hormones during menstrual cycles of teenage athletes. J Appl Physiol 1981; 50: 545.
55. Bullen BA, Skrinar GS, Beitins IZ, et al. Induction of menstrual disorders by strenuous exercise in untrained women. N Engl J Med 1985; 312:1349.
56. Schwartz B, Cumming DC, Riordan E, et al. Exercise-associated amenorrhea: A distinct entity? Am J Obstet Gynecol 1981; 141:662.
57. Shangold MM. Causes, evaluation and management of athletic oligo/ amenorrhea. Med Clin North Am 1985; 69:83.
58. Sanborn CF, Martin BJ, Wagner WW. Is athletic amenorrhea specific to runners? Am J Obstet Gynecol 1982; 143:859.
59. Wilson C, Emans SJ, Mansfield J, et al. The relationship of calculated percent body fat, sports participation, age, and place of residence on menstrual patterns in healthy adolescent girls at an independent New England high school. J Adolesc Health Care 1984; 5:248.
60. Ellison PT, and Lager C. Moderate recreational running is associated with lowered salivary progesterone profiles in women. Am J Obstet Gynecol 1986; 154:1000.
61. Frisch RE, Wyshak G, and Vincent L. Delayed menarche and amenorrhea in ballet dancers. N Engl J Med 1980; 303:17.
62. Warren MP, Brooks-Gunn J, Hamilton LH, et al. Scoliosis and fractures in young ballet dancers: Relation to delayed menarche and secondary amenorrhea. N Engl J Med 1986; 314:1348.
63. Malina RM. Menarche in athletes: a synthesis and hypothesis. Ann Hum Biol 1983; 10:1.
64. Frisch RE, Gotz-Welbergen AV, McArthur JW, et al. Delayed menarche and amenorrhea of college athletes in relation to age of onset of training. JAMA 1981; 246:1559.
65. Feicht CB, Johnson TS, Martin BJ, et al. Secondary amenorrhoea in athletes. (letter to the editor). Lancet 1978; 2:1145.
66. Glass AR, Deuster PA, Kyle SB, et al. Amenorrhea in olympic marathon runners. Fertil Steril 1987; 48:740.
67. Dale E, Gerlabh DH, and Wilhite AL. Menstrual dysfunction in distance runners. Obstet Gynecol 1979; 54:47.
68. Brooks SM, Sanborn CF, Albrecht BH, et al. Diet in athletic amenorrhea (letter to the editor). Lancet 1984; 1:559.
69. Kemmann E, Pasquale SA, and Skaf R. Amenorrhea associated with carotenemia. JAMA 1983; 249:926.
70. Deuster PA, Kyle SB, Moser PB, et al. Nutritional intakes and status of

highly trained amenorrheic and eumenorrheic women runners. Fertil Steril 1986; 46:636.

71. Pirke KM, Schweiger U, Laessle R, et al. Dieting influences the menstrual cycle: vegetarian versus nonvegetarian diet. Fertil Steril 1986; 46:1083.

72. Gadpaille WJ, Sanborn CF, and Wagner WW. Athletic amenorrhea, major affective disorders, and eating disorders. Am J Psychiatry 1987; 144:939.

73. Baker E, and Demers L. Menstrual status in female athletes: Correlation with reproductive hormones and bone density. Obstet Gynecol 1988; 72:683.

74. Chang FE, Richards SR, Kim MH, et al. Twenty four-hour prolactin profiles and prolactin responses to dopamine in long distance running women. J Clin Endocrinol Metab 1984; 59:631.

75. Hale RW, Kosasa T, Krieger J, et al. A marathon: The immediate effect on female runners' luteinizing hormone, follicle-stimulating hormone, prolactin, testosterone, and cortisol levels. Am J Obstet Gynecol 1983; 146:550.

76. Shangold MM, Gatz ML, and Thysen B. Acute effects of exercise on plasma concentration of prolactin and testosterone in recreational women runners. Fertil Steril 1981; 35:699.

77. Russell JB, Mitchell D, Musey PI, et al. The relationship of exercise to anovulatory cycles in female athletes: Hormonal and physical characteristics. Obstet Gynecol 1984; 63:452.

78. Chin WN, Chang FE, Doods WG, et al. Acute effects of exercise on plasma catecholamines in sedentary and athletic women with normal and abnormal menses. Am J Obstet Gynecol 1987; 157:938.

79. Cann CE, Martin MC, Genant HK, et al. Decreased spinal mineral content in amenorrheic women. JAMA 1984; 251:626.

80. Marcus R, Cann C, Madvig P, et al. Menstrual function and bone mass in elite women distance runners: Endocrine and metabolic features. Ann Intern Med 1985; 102:158.

81. Drinkwater BL, Nilson K, Chesnut CH, et al. Bone mineral content of amenorrheic and eumenorrheic athletes. N Engl J Med 1984; 311:277.

82. Drinkwater BL, Nilson K, Ott S, et al. Bone mineral density after resumption of menses in amenorrheic athletes. JAMA 1986; 256:380.

83. Wyshak G, Frisch RE, Albright TE, et al. Bone fractures among former college athletes compared with nonathletes in the menopausal and postmenopausal years. Obstet Gynecol 1987; 69:121.

84. Chang RJ, Keye WR, and Young JR. Detection, evaluation, and treatment of pituitary microadenomas in patients with galactorrhea and amenorrhea. Am J Obstet Gynecol 1977; 128:356.

85. Cowden EA, Thomson JA, Doyle D, et al. Tests of prolactin secretion in diagnosis of prolactinomas. Lancet 1979; 1:1156.

86. Forsbach G, Soria J, Canales E, et al. Gonadotropic responsiveness to clomiphene, LH, estradiol, and bromocriptine in galactorrheic women. Obstet Gynecol 1977; 50:139.

87. Reichlin S. The prolactinoma problem. N Engl J Med 1979; 300:313.

88. Weibe RH, Hammond CB, and Handwerger S. Prolactin-secreting pituitary microadenoma: Detection and evaluation. Fertil Steril 1978; 29:282.

89. Kleinberg DL, Noel GL, and Frantz AG. Galactorrhea: A study of 235 cases, including 48 with pituitary tumors. N Engl J Med 1977; 296:589.

90. Blackwell RE, and Younger JB. Long-term medical therapy and follow-up of pediatric-adolescent patients with prolactin-secreting macroadenomas. Fertil Steril 1986; 45:713.

91. Schlechte JA, Sherman BM, Chapler FK, et al. Long-term follow-up of women with surgically treated prolactin-secreting pituitary tumors. J Clin Endocrinol Metab 1986; 62:1296.
92. Pereira MC, Sobrinho LG, Afonso AM, et al. Is idiopathic hyperprolactinemia a transitional stage toward prolactinoma? Obstet Gynecol 1987; 70:305.
93. Sisam DA, Sheehan JP, and Sheeler LR. The natural history of untreated microprolactinomas. Fertil Steril 1987; 48:67.
94. Rasmussen C, Bergh T, and Wide L. Prolactin secretion and menstrual function after long-term bromocriptine treatment. Fertil Steril 1987; 48:550.
95. Dessypris A, Karonen SL, and Adlercreutz H. Marathon run effects on plasma prolactin and growth hormone. Acta Endocrinol [Suppl] (Copenh.) 1979; 255:187.
96. Noel GL, Suh HK, Stone JG, et al. Human prolactin and growth hormone release during surgery and other conditions of stress. J Clin Endocrinol Metab 1972; 35:840.
97. Turksoy RN, Farber M, and Mitchell GW. Diagnostic and therapeutic modalities in women with galactorrhea. Obstet Gynecol 1980; 56:323.
98. Dawajan V, Kletsky O, and March CM. The significance of galactorrhea in patients with normal menses, oligomenorrhea, and secondary amenorrhea. Am J Obstet Gynecol 1978; 130:894.
99. Klibanski A, Neer RM, Beitins IZ, et al. Decreased bone density in hyperprolactinemic women. N Engl J Med 1980; 303:1511.
100. Klibanski A, and Greenspan SL. Increase in bone mass after treatment of hyperprolactinemia amenorrhea. N Engl J Med 1986; 315:542.
101. Post KD, Biller BJ, and Adelman LS. Selective transphenoidal adenomectomy in women with galactorrhea-amenorrhea. JAMA 1979; 242:158.
102. Keye WR, Chang RT, Monroe SE, et al. Prolactin-secreting pituitary adenomas in women: II. Menstrual function, pituitary reserves, and prolactin production following microsurgical removal. Am J Obstet Gynecol 1979; 134:360.
103. Serri O, Rasio E, Beauregard H, et al. Recurrence of hyperprolactinemia after selective transphenoidal adenomectomy in women with prolactinoma. N Engl J Med 1983; 309:280.
104. Thorner MO, Martin WH, Rogol AD, et al. Rapid regression of pituitary prolactinomas during bromocriptine treatment. J Clin Endocrinol Metab 1980; 51:438.
105. McGregor A, Scanlon MF, Hall K, et al. Reduction in size of a pituitary tumor by bromocriptine therapy. N Engl J Med 1979; 300:291.
106. Horvath E, Kovacs K, Smyth HS, et al. A novel type of pituitary adenoma: Morphological features and clinical correlations. J Clin Endocrinol Metab 1988; 66:1111.
107. Shewchuk AB, Adamson GD, Lessard P, et al. The effect of pregnancy on suspected pituitary adenomas after conservative management of ovulation defects associated with galactorrhea. Am J Obstet Gynecol 1980; 136:659.
108. Griffith RW, Turkalj I, and Braun P. Outcome of pregnancy in mothers given bromocriptine. Br J Clin Pharmacol 1978; 5:227.
109. Vermesh M, Fossum GT, and Kletzky OA. Vaginal bromocriptine: pharmacology and effect on serum prolactin in normal women. Obstet Gynecol 1988; 72:693.
110. Ciccarelli E, Touzel R, Besser M, et al. Terguride—a new dopamine agonist drug: A comparison of its neuroendocrine and side effect profile with bromocriptine. Fertil Steril 1988; 49:589.

111. Weiss NS, Ure CL, Ballard JH, et al. Decreased risk of fractures of the hip and lower forearm and postmenopausal use of estrogen. N Engl J Med 1980; 303:1195.
112. Lindsay R. Estrogen therapy in the prevention and management of osteoporosis. Am J Obstet Gynecol 1987; 156:1347.
113. Ettinger B, Genant HK, and Cann CE. Long-term estrogen replacement therapy prevents bone loss and fractures. Ann Intern Med 1985; 102:319.
114. Richelson LS, Wahner HW, and Melton LJ III. Relative contributions of aging and estrogen deficiency to postmenopausal bone loss. N Engl J Med 1984; 311:1273.
115. Johansen BW, Kaij L, Kullander S, et al. On some late effects of bilateral oophorectomy in the age range 15–30 years. Acta Obstet Gynecol Scand 1975; 54:449–561.
116. Emans SJ, Grace E, Woods ER, et al. Estrogen deficiency in adolescents and young adults: The impact on bone density and the effects of estrogen replacement therapy (in press).
117. Benjamin I, and Block RE. Endometrial response to estrogen and progesterone therapy in patients with gonadal dysgenesis. Obstet Gynecol 1977; 50:136.
118. Van Campenhout J, Choquette P, and Vauclair R. Endometrial pattern in patients with primary hypoestrogenic amenorrhea receiving estrogen replacement therapy. Obstet Gynecol 1980; 56:349.
119. Hirvonen E, Malkonen M, and Manninen V. Effects of different progestogens on lipoproteins during postmenopausal replacement therapy. N Engl J Med 1981; 340:560.
120. Padwick ML, Pryse-Davies J, and Whitehead MI. A simple method for determining the optimal dosage of progestin in postmenopausal women receiving estrogens. N Engl J Med 1986; 315:930.
121. Riggs BL, Wahner HW, Dunn WL, et al. Differential changes in bone mineral density of the appendicular and axial skeleton with aging: relationship to spinal osteoporosis. J Clin Invest 1981; 67:328.
122. Horsman A, Jones M, Francis R, et al. The effect of estrogen dose on postmenopausal bone loss. N Engl J Med 1983; 309:1405.
123. Quigley ME, Martin PL, Burnier AM, et al. Estrogen therapy arrests bone loss in elderly women. Am J Obstet Gynecol 1987; 156:1516.
124. Lindsay R, Hart DM, and Clark DM. The minimum effective dose of estrogen for prevention of postmenopausal bone loss. Obstet Gynecol 1984; 63:759.
125. Rosenbloom AL, and Frias JL. Oxandrolone for growth promotion in Turner's syndrome. Am J Dis Child 1973; 125:385.
126. Urban MD, Lee PA, Dorst JP, et al. Oxandrolone therapy in patients with Turner's syndrome. J Pediatr 1979; 94:823.
127. Moore DC, Tattoni DS, Ruvalcaba RH, et al. Studies of anabolic steroids. J Pediatr 1977; 90:462.
128. Sybert VP. Adult height in Turner syndrome with and without androgen therapy. J Pediatr 1984; 104:365.
129. Ross JL, Cassorla FG, Skerda MC, et al. A preliminary study of the effect of estrogen dose on growth in Turner's syndrome. N Engl J Med 1983; 309:1104.
130. Ross JL, Long LM, Skerda M, et al. Effect of low doses of estradiol on 6-month growth rates and predicted height in patients with Turner syndrome. J Pediatr 1986; 109:950.
131. Martinez A, Heinrich JJ, Domene H, et al. Growth in Turner's syndrome: Long-term treatment with low dose ethinyl estradiol. J Clin Endocrinol Metab 1987; 65:253.

132. Demetriou E, Emans SJ, and Crigler JF, Jr. Final height in estrogen-treated patients with Turner syndrome. Obstet Gynecol 1984; 64:459.
133. Rosenfeld RG, Hintz RL, Johanson AJ, et al. Three year results of a randomized prospective trial of methionyl human growth hormone and oxandrolone in Turner syndrome. J Pediatr 1988; 113:393.
134. Raiti S, Moore WV, Van Vliet G, et al. Growth-stimulating effects human growth hormone therapy in patients with Turner syndrome. J Pediatr 1986; 109:944.
135. Ross JL, Long LM, Skerda M, et al. Growth response relationship between growth hormone dose and short term growth in patients with Turner's syndrome. J Clin Endocrinol Metab 1986; 63:1028.
136. Navot D, Laufer N, Kopolovic J, et al. Artificially induced endometrial cycles and establishment of pregnancies in the absence of ovaries. N Engl J Med 1986; 314:806.
137. Seibel MM. A new era in reproductive technology: In vitro fertilization, gamete intrafallopian transfer, and donated gametes and embryos. N Engl J Med 1988; 316:828.
138. Asch RH, Balmaceda JP, Ord T, et al. Oocyte donation and gamete intrafallopian transfer in premature ovarian failure. Fertil Steril 1988; 49:263.
139. Claman P, Elkind-Hirsch K, Oskowitz SP, et al. Urticaria associated with antigonadotropin-releasing hormone antibody in a female Kallman's syndrome patient being treated with long-term pulsatile gonadotropin-releasing hormone. Obstet Gynecol 1987; 69:503.
140. Rock JA, Zacur HA, Dlugi AM, et al. Pregnancy success following surgical correction of imperforate hymen and complete transverse vaginal septum. Obstet Gynecol 1982; 59:448.
141. Farber M, and Marchant DJ. Congenital absence of the uterine cervix. Am J Obstet Gynecol 1975; 121:414.
142. Dillon WP, Mudalier N, and Wingate M. Congenital atresia of the cervix. Obstet Gynecol 1979; 54:126.
143. Markham SM, Parmley TH, Murphy AA, et al. Cervical agenesis combined with vaginal agenesis diagnosed by magnetic resonance imaging. Fertil Steril 1987; 48:143.
144. Rock JA, Parmley T, Murphy AA, et al. Malposition of the ovary associated with uterine anomalies. Fertil Steril 1986; 45:561.
145. Cramer DW, Ravnikar VA, Craighill M, et al. Müllerian aplasia associated with maternal deficiency of galactose-1-phosphate uridyl transferase. Fertil Steril 1987; 47:930.
146. Federman D. Abnormal Sexual Development. Philadelphia: Saunders, 1968.
147. Klingensmith GJ, Garcia SC, Jones HW, et al. Effects of glucocorticoid treatment in congenital adrenal hyperplasia in girls. J Pediatr 1976; 90:996.
148. Money J, and Schwartz M. Dating, Romantic and Nonromantic Friendships, and Sexuality in 17 Early Treated Adrenogenital Females, Age 16–25. In PA Lee, LP Plotnick, AA Kowarski, et al. (eds.), Congenital Adrenal Hyperplasia. Baltimore: University Press, 1977.
149. Levine LS, Dupont B, Lorenzen F, et al. Cryptic 21-hydroxylase deficiency in families of patients with classical congenital adrenal hyperplasia. J Clin Endocrinol Metab 1980; 51:1316.
150. Kamilaris TC, DeBold CR, Manolas KJ, et al. Testosterone-secreting adrenal adenoma in a peripubertal girl. JAMA 1987; 258:2558.
151. Wilson JD, Harrod MJ, Goldstein JL, et al. Familial incomplete male pseudohermaphroditism, type 1. N Engl J Med 1974; 290:1097.

152. Griffin JE, and Wilson JD. The syndromes of androgen resistance. N Engl J Med 1980; 302:198.
153. Amrhein J, Klingensmith GJ, Walsh PC, et al. Partial androgen insensitivity: Reinfenstein syndrome revisited. N Engl J Med 1977; 297:350.
154. Stein IF, and Leventhal ML. Amenorrhea associated with bilateral polycystic ovaries. Am J Obstet Gynecol 1935; 29:181.
155. Lobo RA, Kletzky OA, Kaptein EM, et al. Prolactin modulation of DHEAS secretion. Am J Obstet Gynecol 1980; 138:632.
156. Emans SJ, Grace E, and Goldstein DP. Oligomenorrhea in adolescent girls. J Pediatr 1980; 97:815.
157. Ansel S, and Jones G. Etiology and treatment of dysfunctional uterine bleeding. Obstet Gynecol 1974; 44:1.
158. Fraser IS, McCarron G, and Markham R. A preliminary study of factors influencing perception of menstrual blood loss volume. Am J Obstet Gynecol 1984; 149:788.
159. Cloessens EA, and Cowell CA. Acute adolescent menorrhagia. Am J Obstet Gynecol 1981; 139:277.
160. Altchek A. Dysfunctional uterine bleeding in adolescence. Clin Obstet Gynecol 1977; 20:633.
161. Fraser IS, Pearse C, Shearman RP, et al. Efficacy of mefenamic acid in patients with a complaint of menorrhagia. Obstet Gynecol 1981; 58:543.
162. Muram D. Unpublished data.
163. Southam AL, and Richart RM. The prognosis for adolescents with menstrual abnormalities. Am J Obstet Gynecol 1966; 94:637.

7. Hirsutism

Signs of androgen excess, especially hirsutism and acne, can be a troubling problem for the adolescent girl. Although the degree of hirsutism may be related to familial or racial factors that determine the capacity of the hair follicle to respond to androgen levels, in most cases excess androgen production from the ovaries and/or adrenal glands is responsible for the clinical problem of hirsutism. Oligomenorrhea or anovulatory dysfunctional uterine bleeding accompanying the signs of androgen excess should especially alert the clinician to the possibility of polycystic ovary syndrome (PCO). Whatever the cause of the hirsutism, the patient will benefit from a careful explanation of the diagnosis and suggestions about therapy.

DEFINING HIRSUTISM

Two types of hair are found on the human body: terminal hair (> 0.5 cm in length, coarse, and usually pigmented) and vellus or lanugo (downy, fine, light-colored hair). An increase in the distribution and quantity of terminal hair may bring the patient to the physician with the complaint of hirsutism. Hirsutism may also be noted by the physician during a routine physical examination or during an evaluation of irregular menses. Excessive downy hair is usually referred to as *hypertrichosis* and occurs, for example, in adolescents with anorexia nervosa.

The clinician may encounter difficulty in establishing whether the amount of hair is excessive, since the spectrum of "normal" is at best ill-defined. McKnight [1] studied 400 young women in Wales in an attempt to establish the prevalence of terminal hair. Her study found that the great majority of women had terminal hair on the lower arm and leg (84%), and most also had terminal hair on the upper arm and leg (70%). Twenty-six percent had terminal hair on the face, usually on the upper lip. In 10 percent of the women, the facial hair was noticeable, and in 4 percent, it was characterized as a "true disfigurement." Seventeen percent had hair on the chest or breast, usually periareolar; 35 percent had hair on the abdomen, usually along the linea alba up to the umbilicus; 16 percent had hair in the lumbosacral area; and 3 percent had hair on the upper back. Nine percent had considerable hair in most or all of these areas and were therefore considered "hirsute." Hirsutism is race and age dependent with increasing hirsutism with age, especially in the postmenopausal woman. Clearly the appreciation of the problem is often subjective and related to a comparison of the degree of hirsutism to that noted in other female family members. For this reason, scoring systems that

Table 7-1. Causes of Hirsutism in Adolescents

Familial
Drugs (phenytoin, danazol, diazoxide, minoxidil, glucocorticoid excess, androgens)
Pregnancy
Hypothyroidism
Central nervous system injury
Hyperprolactinemia
Stress
Anorexia nervosa, malnutrition
Adrenal disorders
    Congenital adrenal hyperplasia (21-hydroxylase, 11 β-hydroxylase, 3 β-hydroxysteroid dehydrogenase deficiencies)
    Cushing's disease
    Tumors
Ovarian disorders
    Polycystic ovary syndrome (PCO)
    Hyperthecosis
    Tumors
    Enzyme deficiency (e.g., 17-ketosteroid reductase deficiency)
Peripheral tissue
    ? Excessive activity of 5 α-reductase and/or 17-ketosteroid reductase
Male pseudohermaphroditism, mixed gonadal dysgenesis
Idiopathic hirsutism

are reproducible for different patients and visits and can be useful for comparing diagnostic categories and outcomes are helpful in practice and research settings [2, 3].

ETIOLOGY OF HIRSUTISM
The differential diagnosis of hirsutism is listed in Table 7-1. Many patients with mild hirsutism and regular menses have a familial or racial predisposition. Drugs such as phenytoin, corticosteroids, danazol, diazoxide, minoxidil, and androgens cause hirsutism. Anabolic steroids used by athletes may also cause virilization. Pregnancy, hypothyroidism, anorexia nervosa, malnutrition, and chronic central nervous system disorders (e.g., mental and motor retardation) can be accompanied by excess hair growth.

Most cases of significant hirsutism are the result of overproduction of androgens from an ovarian and/or adrenal source [4–12]. In the past, using only measurements of urinary 17-ketosteroids, clinicians erroneously believed that the majority of cases of hirsutism were idiopathic. Recent studies have shown that most women with hirsutism have increased testosterone production rates. Increased levels of free testosterone are detectable in 80 to 85 percent of hirsute women.

Hyperandrogenism is not demonstrable by usual laboratory tests in approximately 15 percent of women. In these cases, hirsutism may be due to an androgen other than testosterone and androstenedione, an elevated level not detected because of the normal fluctuation of secretion, or the presence of more numerous hair follicles. In addition, enhanced sensitivity to androgens may be present at the peripheral level (increased 5 α-reductase activity in the skin, increased utilization of androgens reflected by increased androstanediol glucuronide, and/ or possibly an abnormality of testosterone release from the binding globulin). Testosterone induces the production of enzymes in the hair follicle, and thus once a terminal hair begins to grow, less androgen is required to stimulate its continued growth. This factor probably accounts, in part, for the fact that a less than optimal response is frequently achieved by hormone suppression therapy, which by biochemical parameters (lowering of free testosterone) should be successful.

Occasionally, stress may precipitate excess luteinizing hormone (LH) secretion and increased production of androgens from the theca cells; the abnormal hormone production reverses when the acute stress is over. With their immature hypothalamic-pituitary-ovarian axis, adolescents may be particularly prone to this type of disorder. Adolescents with oligomenorrhea in the first few years after menarche may have mild elevations of androgens and a PCO-like picture. With time, some of these girls appear to manifest the typical PCO and others appear to progress to normal ovulatory cycles [13].

Hyperprolactinemia may be accompanied by increased secretion of adrenal androgens (especially dehydroepiandrosterone sulfate [DHAS]) and may also be associated with PCO. The rare diagnosis of male pseudohermaphroditism or mixed gonadal dysgenesis (with a Y line or Y fragment) may present with virilization at puberty [14, 15, 16]. Any signs of rapid progression of hirsutism or the presence of virilization (clitoromegaly, temporal hair recession, deepening of the voice, changes in muscle pattern) should prompt an immediate assessment of hormone status to exclude the possibility of a tumor or male gonad.

OVARIAN AND ADRENAL CAUSES OF HIRSUTISM
Overproduction of androgens from the ovary and/or adrenal glands is responsible for hirsutism in most adolescents; indeed ovarian androgens account for most of the clinical symptoms seen in PCO. The rate of testosterone production in adult women correlates most closely with the degree of hirsutism-virilization. Mildly increased facial hair; increased facial hair and menstrual disturbances; facial hair, menstrual disturbances, and clitoromegaly; and increased muscle mass along with all of these represent a spectrum of hirsutism that

corresponds to stepwise levels of increased testosterone production [17, 18]. Serum *total* testosterone levels frequently do not correlate with the severity of the patient's hirsutism or testosterone production rate; rather free or unbound testosterone levels correlate better with clinical signs and testosterone production rate. All but a small fraction of serum testosterone is bound, mainly to sex hormone binding globulin (SHBG), also termed testosterone-estradiol binding globulin (TEBG). Although normal adult women have twice the SHBG concentration of normal men, hirsute women with elevated androgen levels have SHBG levels lower than normal women. Thus, in patients with PCO, the mild elevation of serum total testosterone plus the increase in the percent of testosterone that is not bound to SHBG results in a significant rise in the concentration of free (active) testosterone.

The source of androgens must be understood to assess the results of laboratory tests. The major adrenal androgens are dehydroepiandrosterone (DHA) and its sulfate (DHAS) and androstenedione with a small amount of testosterone secreted. The ovaries secrete primarily testosterone and androstenedione. In normal women, approximately 80 to 90 percent of DHA is secreted by the adrenal glands and 10 to 20 percent by the ovaries. Greater than 90 percent of DHAS is secreted by the adrenal glands. The diurnal variation of DHA is similar to that of cortisol, with peak levels in the early morning. DHAS has a long half-life with less fluctuation in levels, and thus measurement of DHAS is more easily interpreted by the clinician evaluating hirsute patients. Androstenedione is secreted equally by the adrenal glands and the ovaries in normal women. Urinary 17-ketosteroids include DHA, DHAS, and androstenedione.

The source of testosterone is more variable; 0 to 30 percent comes from the adrenal, 5 to 20 percent from the ovaries, and 50 to 70 percent of serum levels is produced by peripheral conversion of precursors (such as DHA and androstenedione). In hirsute women with PCO, the ovaries are responsible for a much greater percentage of the testosterone production. Most adolescents with significant or progressive hirsutism, especially if accompanied by irregular menses, have elevation of one or more serum androgen levels.

Polycystic ovary syndrome (PCO) is the cause of hirsutism in most adolescent patients. The term *polycystic ovary syndrome* is not a single, well-defined entity but rather a spectrum of clinical disorders associated with increased androgen production from the ovaries and/or adrenal glands, often with abnormal gonadotropin secretion and insulin resistance [11, 12, 19–23]. Clinical presentations may vary and include hirsutism, obesity, oligomenorrhea, anovulation, and infertility. Many adolescent patients do not fit the original description of Stein-Leventhal syndrome. Ovarian morphology in PCO is also variable and ranges from normal-appearing ovaries to enlarged ovaries with a thickened capsule, multiple small peripheral cysts and increased stroma, or hyperthecosis (islands of luteinized theca cells deep within the ovarian stroma). In fact, almost all patients with ovarian hyperandrogenism have major contributions from both stromal and thecal sources [11]. The spectrum of ovarian pathology in ovarian androgen excess is mirrored in ultrasound findings. Ovaries may appear normal on ultrasound, although more commonly the ovaries appear enlarged with multiple tiny cysts. These "polycystic" ovaries may also occur normally in perimenarcheal adolescents who are anovulatory, furthering the difficulty of using ultrasound technique to help make the diagnosis of PCO. In addition, PCO-like ovaries can occur secondary to androgen excess from untreated or undiagnosed congenital adrenocortical hyperplasia (CAH) and adrenal adenomas or carcinomas or secondary to any condition that causes chronic anovulation (including Cushing's disease, hypothyroidism, and hyperprolactinemia).

Patients with PCO usually have a normal age of menarche, although occasionally PCO may cause delayed menarche with hirsutism or virilization (see p. 205). Although most adolescents with PCO are overweight for height, a normal weight does not exclude the diagnosis. The majority of patients have irregular menses from the time of menarche and often have hirsutism and/or acne beginning either before or around the time of menarche. As noted in Chapter 5, recent interest has focused on the possible relationship between premature adrenarche and the later development of PCO, especially in regard to mild defects in cortisol synthesis. The abnormal gonadotropin secretory patterns associated with PCO are apparent very early in adolescence, suggesting a central defect [24]. Only rarely have specific abnormalities in ovarian steroidogenesis (e.g., 17-ketosteroid reductase deficiency) been reported [25]. PCO has a familial incidence, but the inheritance patterns have not been defined.

A major feature of PCO is chronic anovulation. The pituitary gland has heightened sensitivity to gonadotropin releasing hormone (GnRH) and exaggerated pulsatile release of LH. The LH levels are often tonically elevated to above 30 mIU/ml or have an elevated LH/FSH ratio of greater than 2:1 or 2.5:1 (some groups use 3:1). The high LH levels stimulate the ovary to secrete increased amounts of androgen from the stromal tissue; the androgens are converted peripherally to estrone and estradiol. Estrogens, which are secreted tonically rather than cyclically, are hypothesized to augment pituitary sensitivity to GnRH [26, 27] (Figs. 7-1 and 7-2). Investigators in Crowley's group at the Massachusetts General Hospital [28] have suggested a role of circulating estradiol levels in increasing the frequency of GnRH release and thus LH pulse frequency, and Dunaif [29] has shown that androgens do not appear to alter gonadotropin release

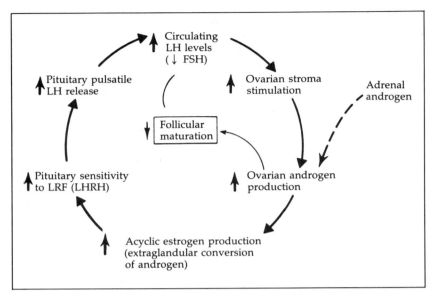

Figure 7-1. Yen's proposed mechanism for persistent anovulation in poly-cystic ovary syndrome. LH = luteinizing hormone; FSH = follicle-stimulating hormone; LHRH = luteinizing hormone releasing hormone (also termed GnRH). (From SSC Yen, Chronic Anovulation. In SSC Yen and RB Jaffe [eds.], *Reproductive Endocrinology*. Philadelphia: Saunders, 1978. By permission.)

directly. Under chronic LH stimulation, the polycystic ovaries secrete excess androstenedione and testosterone [11, 12, 30]. The action of testosterone is further augmented because androgens decrease SHBG and thereby increase the level of free testosterone. In contrast, estrogen increases SHBG. Thus sex steroids tend to amplify their own effects. In hirsute women, the low SHBG level facilitates the rapid uptake of free androgens and their peripheral conversion to estrogen. Peripheral conversion of androgens to estrogens takes place in adipose tissue, which is increased in many PCO patients, thus increasing estrogen production. With low levels of SHBG, PCO patients have free estradiol levels that are higher than in normal women in the midfollicular phase of the cycle [28, 31]. The constant, acyclic levels of estradiol cause abnormal feedback to the pituitary and hypothalamus, and unopposed stimulation of the endometrium by estradiol and estrone places the PCO patient at higher risk for developing uterine cancer [32].

In contrast to elevated LH levels seen in many patients with PCO, FSH levels are low to normal. As noted by Rebar and others [26, 28], the low levels may result from several factors: (1) the inhibitory feedback of estrogen on FSH, (2) the relative insensitivity of FSH secretion

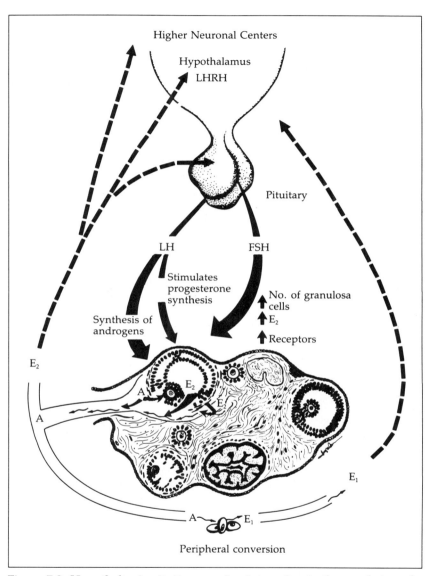

Figure 7-2. Hypothalamic-pituitary-ovarian interaction in the regulation of follicular maturation and steroid biosynthesis. LHRH = luteinizing hormone releasing hormone (also termed GnRH); LH = luteinizing hormone; FSH = follicle-stimulating hormone; E_2 = estradiol; A = androstenedione; E_1 = estrone. The ovary shows the various stages of growth of the follicle and formation and regression of the corpus luteum.

to GnRH, and (3) the production of inhibin from the PCO ovaries that could inhibit the release of FSH. Estradiol may cause decreased dopamine secretion at the hypothalamic level that leads to increased GnRH pulses, which in turn may selectively increase LH secretion and LH bioactivity and decrease FSH secretion. In the ovary a relative aromatase defect secondary to FSH deficiency and high intraovarian androgen levels impair follicular maturation and cyclic production of estradiol and induce follicular atresia.

A number of metabolic abnormalities have also been noted in PCO. Obesity is common in adolescents with PCO. An abnormal pattern of serum lipids occurs in some patients [33, 34, 35]. In comparison to controls, PCO women may have higher levels of triglycerides and very-low-density lipoprotein cholesterol and lower levels of high-density lipoprotein cholesterol, in part secondary to the obesity but also likely related to the androgen excess [35]. Hyperinsulinemia is evident in many patients both in the fasting and glucose-stimulated state [11, 36]. The presence of acanthosis nigricans (velvety, verrucous, hyperpigmented skin often over the nape of the neck, in the axillae, beneath the breasts, and in other body folds) has been associated with more severe insulin resistance and hyperthecosis. Burghen and colleagues [21] found a positive correlation between fasting insulin levels and circulating testosterone and androstenedione levels, an association confirmed by others. A specific syndrome of hyperandrogenism (HA), insulin resistance (IR), and acanthosis nigricans (AN) has been termed HAIR-AN. Insulin resistance and glucose patterns vary from high insulin levels and diabetic glucose tolerance curves to mild elevation of insulin levels with normal glucose levels both fasting and after a carbohydrate challenge. Three categories have been defined: type A, a genetic disorder often associated with obesity, with insulin resistance caused by a decreased number of insulin receptors or a decreased function of the receptor; type B, often associated with autoimmune disorders, with insulin resistance due to circulating antibodies; and type C, often associated with obesity, with insulin resistance due to "postreceptor" defects [11]. Ovarian stromal hyperthecosis is common in patients with the HAIR-AN syndrome. Barbieri [11] has suggested that if women with significant ovarian androgen excess (serum testosterone > 100 ng/100 ml) are studied, approximately 50 percent will have insulin resistance and compensatory hyperinsulinemia. Several groups have reported that approximately 5 percent of hyperandrogenic women have acanthosis nigricans [11, 37].

The cause of PCO is unknown, but several hypotheses have been proposed. Yen [10] has suggested that an exaggerated adrenarche (with excess adrenal androgen production) could result in increased peripheral conversion of androgens to estrogens. The noncyclic production of estrogen would then lead to inappropriate gonadotropin secretion with tonic, elevated LH and, subsequently, inappropriate ovarian androgen secretion. Emotional stress at puberty could perhaps cause increased adrenocorticotropic hormone (ACTH) production or adrenal sensitivity, or both. Since the percent conversion of androstenedione to estrone is related to body weight, obesity at the time of puberty and during adolescence might be an additive factor [38, 39]. Although PCO-like syndromes associated with CAH and adrenal tumors are reversible with the removal of the androgen excess, true PCO appears to persist and recur despite interruption of the cycle with suppression of ovulation, use of long-acting gonadotropin analogues, or pregnancy. In addition, the pattern of abnormal diurnal secretion of LH appears to be present early in adolescence [24]. Thus a hypothesis suggesting that a primary central abnormality in the regulation of gonadotropin secretion exists is attractive. Indeed, the fact that many women with PCO have elevated circulating levels of prolactin and endorphin suggests that disorders of hypothalamic-pituitary function are not limited to gonadotropin secretion [11, 40–43]. Lobo and colleagues [44] have suggested that psychological stress and neurotransmitter levels may be linked to some of the abnormal gonadotropin patterns.

Recently, Barbieri and associates [11] have postulated that hyperinsulinemia and insulin resistance are not just associated with androgen excess but may play a role in causing the abnormalities seen in PCO. They have proposed that both insulin and LH regulate ovarian stromal and thecal androgen production. In support of the theory are in vitro studies that have shown that insulin and insulin-like growth factors (IGF-I) can stimulate androgen accumulation in incubations of ovarian stroma obtained from hyperandrogenic women [45]. In addition, lowering androgen levels to the normal range in women with PCO using long-acting GnRH analogues, cyproterone acetate, or bilateral oophorectomy does not improve the insulin resistance [46]. Dunaif and colleagues [47] have shown that insulin infusion in PCO patients but not normal women causes an increase in androstenedione. Another study [48] has demonstrated that an acute glucose load can produce a large rise in insulin and increases in circulating androgens (androstenedione, testosterone, and dihydrotestosterone) in women with the HA-IR syndrome (hyperandrogenism, insulin resistance), but not in control women or hyperandrogenic non-insulin-resistant women. Since a diet high in simple carbohydrates may stimulate more endogenous insulin production than diets rich in fibers and complex carbohydrates, Barbieri and associates [11] have postulated that diet intervention as well as weight loss and exercise might be helpful in reducing the degree of hyperandrogenism. They have proposed two basic subgroupings of ovarian hyperandrogenism. Patients in one subgroup, HA-IR, have hyperandrogenism, marked insulin resistance, chronic hyperinsulinemia, normal or slightly elevated LH, and normal prolactin, often associated with ovarian stromal hyperthecosis. Patients in the second subgroup, HA-nonIR, have hyperandrogenism, minimal insulin resistance, markedly elevated LH, and often slightly elevated prolactin.

Although only rarely is a true enzymatic deficiency in the ovaries demonstrable, Barnes and colleagues [49] have recently suggested that women with PCO have both pituitary and ovarian responses to the gonadotropin-releasing-hormone agonist nafarelin similar to that seen in normal men. They have hypothesized that regulation of cytochrome P-450c17 (17-hydroxylase and C-17, 20-lyase) is abnormal and that this enzyme is overstimulated because of excessive levels of LH or because of an intrinsic defect within the thecal-interstitial cells. Thus the ovaries may play more of a role than suggested by theories that explain the pathogenesis solely on the basis of a central etiology.

The role of the adrenal glands in the pathogenesis of PCO is controversial. Direct catheterization of ovarian and adrenal veins has provided conflicting data. Not only is bilateral sampling of the ovaries difficult to achieve, but pulsatile secretion and enhanced output of steroids from the ovary with the dominant follicle limit interpretation [5, 50, 51]. Although many patients with PCO have mildly elevated DHAS levels and evidence of hyperresponsive adrenal glands on ACTH testing and adrenal scintiscans [6, 52], most adolescents with androgen excess do not have adrenal enzyme deficiencies. Lucky and colleagues [53] have hypothesized that some patients have an exaggerated adrenarche.

Depending on the population studied (ethnic origin and referral versus primary care practice), late onset 21-hydroxylase deficiency, also termed nonclassical CAH, is found in 1 to 10 percent of adult women with hirsutism [54–61]. The gene for this disorder is common, and the deficiency is particularly prevalent among Ashkenazi Jews (1 in 30). Our study of adolescents in a referral center found that 2 of 22 adolescent girls and young women with hirsutism had this deficiency by ACTH testing [59]. In a study of 100 consecutive women presenting with classic features of PCO, Benjamin and colleagues [61] reported that 4 percent of women had homozygous CAH and 15 percent had heterozygous CAH.

New and colleagues have been in the forefront of unraveling much of the family pedigrees and genetics of patients with nonclassical CAH. Nonclassical CAH is an autosomal recessive disorder with a gene located on chromosome 6, in proximity to the HLA locus. The association of this disorder with HLA-B14;DR1 has been a useful marker in distinguishing nonclassical from classical CAH, which is associated with HLA-Bw47;DR7 [62, 63]. Patients with nonclassical CAH have a spectrum of clinical presentations; some have severe hirsutism and menstrual irregularity, others are asymptomatic. Asymptomatic patients with nonclassical CAH and abnormal hormone levels are termed "cryptic." Speiser and New [62] have also identified a group of patients termed compound heterozygotes with one severe (classical) and one mild (nonclassical) 21-hydroxylase allele; these patients have a higher 17-hydroxyprogesterone response to ACTH than homozygous nonclassical patients but were no more likely to have signs of androgen excess.

ACTH testing with measurement of 17-hydroxyprogesterone levels at baseline and 60 minutes later has been the cornerstone of diagnosis of CAH [58, 59, 64], although overlap between heterozygotes and normals and heterozygotes and homozygotes for nonclassical CAH does occur. The use of early morning levels (7–9 A.M.) of serum or salivary 17-hydroxyprogesterone appears to be a useful screening test for this disorder [65, 66]. We have found that early morning levels of 17-hydroxyprogesterone drawn in the follicular phase of the cycle can be helpful for screening; a level greater than 100 ng/100 ml or clinical suspicion should be followed by a one hour ACTH test (standards are on p. 259 and in Fig. 7-6). Fiet and associates [67] have also recently suggested that both baseline and stimulated plasma 21-deoxycortisol levels may be even better markers for CAH.

Controversy still surrounds the prevalence of 3 β-hydroxysteroid dehydrogenase deficiency causing hirsutism in a general population. These patients typically have elevation primarily of DHAS, not testosterone. In a referral population in New York, Pang and co-workers [58] found that 17 of 116 hirsute women had evidence of a partial 3 β-hydroxysteroid dehydrogenase block on ACTH testing (see p. 259). The number who have a primary block versus a block secondary to the abnormal androgen milieu is unknown. Deficiencies of 11 β-hydroxylase and 17-ketosteroid reductase are quite rare [25, 67]. Neither 11-hydroxylase nor 3 β-hydroxysteroid dehydrogenase deficiency is HLA-linked [69]; the structural gene for cytochrome P-450c11 enzyme (for 11-hydroxylation, 18-hydroxylation, and 18-oxidation) is located on chromosome 8. Lee and colleagues [70] have recently reported a familial hypersecretion of adrenal androgens transmitted as a dominant non-HLA-linked trait; the affected family members had premature adrenarche, hirsutism, and amenorrhea. More needs to be learned about such disorders. In addition, a subset of patients with PCO have hyperprolactinemia and elevated DHAS.

Other diagnoses to be considered in the patient with hirsutism are Cushing's disease and the rare ovarian or adrenal tumor. Cushing's disease, albeit rare, should be excluded in the hypertensive obese adolescent with irregular menses and hirsutism. Tests include 24-

hour urinary free cortisol excretion and an overnight dexamethasone test with measurement of cortisol level. Tumors should be considered in patients with virilization, rapid onset of hirsutism, or markedly elevated baseline androgen levels [71, 72, 73]. Adrenal carcinomas are usually palpable at the time of diagnosis; these lesions typically secrete DHA and androstenedione, which are converted to testosterone in the periphery. Some do secrete testosterone directly. Since some lesions lack the ability to convert DHA to DHAS, both these hormones need to be measured in the patient suspected of having a tumor. Adrenal adenomas can be quite small at presentation in spite of high levels of androgens. Ovarian tumors may cause hirsutism (see Chap. 13) and with the exception of luteomas are usually palpable on bimanual examination or detectable by ultrasound. Occasional small ovarian tumors are also suppressible by estrogen-progestin therapy.

PATIENT EVALUATION
The initial history should focus on (1) recent changes in the amount of hair, (2) location of new hair, (3) relation of hair development to the onset of puberty and menses, (4) acne, (5) drug intake (especially anabolic steroids in athletes), (6) stress, (7) change in weight, voice pitch, and scalp hair distribution, (8) onset of skin changes suggestive of acanthosis nigricans, (9) family history of hirsutism, PCO, adrenal enzyme deficiencies, diabetes, hyperinsulinism, or infertility, and (10) ethnic background. Increased terminal hair over the face (especially the chin), sternum, upper abdomen, or back is usually a sign of significant hirsutism. Hirsutism associated with menstrual irregularity deserves careful attention. A history of virilization or an abrupt onset of hirsutism should raise the suspicion of a tumor.

The physical examination should include looking for signs of thyroid disorders, galactorrhea, acne, acanthosis nigricans, stigmata of Cushing's disease, and abdominal and pelvic masses. Acanthosis nigricans is usually associated with hyperinsulinemia and PCO/hyperthecosis but can occur secondary to an ovarian neoplasm. The distribution and quantity of the hair should be noted. Hirsutism should be scored in order to assess the degree of the problem and to provide baseline data for follow-up. Bardin and Lipsett [2] have suggested a criteria of 1 + for each portion of the face involved (upper lip, chin, sideburns) and a 4 + for the entire beard area. A more time-consuming but preferable method is the use of the Ferriman and Gallwey scoring system (Fig. 7-3). Based on a study of 430 women aged 15 to 74 years, a score above 7 was found in 4.3 percent of women and above 10 in 1.2 percent. The appearance of the patient can be circled on a flow sheet in the chart and the total score recorded. The presence of any signs of virilization—temporal hair recession, deepening of the voice, clitoral enlargement (Fig. 7-4), or changes in body fat or muscle distribution—should prompt an assessment to exclude a tumor, adrenal enzyme deficiency, or intersex disorder.

The width of the clitoral glans should be measured; a normal width is considered to be less than 5 mm. If the patient has hirsutism, signs of virilization and/or irregular menses, a vaginal or rectal bimanual examination should be done to assess ovarian size.

LABORATORY STUDIES

The aim of laboratory tests is to try to define an etiology for the patient's hirsutism. PCO should be thought of as a diagnosis of exclusion. Levels of serum androgens need to be sent to a qualified laboratory, and standards for normals must have been developed and reported. Since levels vary throughout the day, morning sampling is preferred. Because of the expense of hormone tests, some endocrinologists prefer to draw two or three samples (either 20 minutes apart or on subsequent days at 8:00 A.M.), pool equal aliquots of serum from each of the samples, and then obtain a single determination. Others do a single sample initially, and if androgens are all normal on the random sample in a hirsute patient, the levels are repeated or several aliquots pooled. In patients with mild hirsutism, apparent skin sensitivity to androgens and the level of serum free testosterone seem to contribute equally; thus about half of patients with mild hirsutism may have normal free testosterone levels [74]. Even women with moderate to severe hirsutism, normal ovarian function, and normal menses can have seemingly normal serum androgen levels.

Although recommendations vary depending on the clinical presentation, the initial laboratory evaluation of a case of significant or progressive hirsutism should include serum levels of testosterone, free testosterone, DHAS, LH, FSH, and prolactin. Although some centers only measure total testosterone levels in hirsute adult women with the aim of using the test primarily to exclude a tumor, we have found that measuring free testosterone is helpful because adolescents may have only mild hirsutism and irregular menses at initial presentation of PCO. The presence of an abnormal level is useful in establishing a likely diagnosis and outlining therapy and follow-up. Thyroid function tests are also frequently measured. If virilization is present or a tumor is under consideration, serum levels of DHA and androstenedione are added, and sometimes a 24-hour urine test for 17-ketosteroids is collected. Some centers have also found androstanediol glucuronide to be helpful, since an increased level reflects utilization of androgens by target tissue [75, 76]. Androstanediol glucuronide, although not an androgen itself, is a metabolite of the pathway of testosterone to dihydrotestosterone which is an important step in androgen expression. Levels of this metabolite also ap-

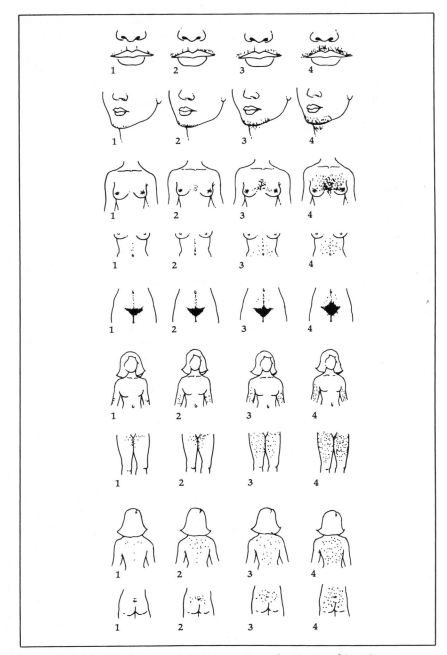

Figure 7-3. The Ferriman and Gallwey system for scoring hirsutism.
A score of 8 or more indicates hirsutism. (From R Hatch, RL Rosenfield,
MH Kim, et al., Hirsutism: Implications, etiology, and management.

(Grade 0 at all sites indicates absence of terminal hair.)

Site	Grade	Definition
1. Upper Lip	1	A few hairs at outer margin.
	2	A small moustache at outer margin.
	3	A moustache extending halfway from outer margin.
	4	A moustache extending to mid-line.
2. Chin	1	A few scattered hairs.
	2	Scattered hairs with small concentrations.
	3 & 4	Complete cover, light and heavy.
3. Chest	1	Circumareolar hairs.
	2	With mid-line hair in addition.
	3	Fusion of these areas, with three-quarter cover.
	4	Complete cover.
4. Upper back	1	A few scattered hairs.
	2	Rather more, still scattered.
	3 & 4	Complete cover, light and heavy.
5. Lower back	1	A sacral tuft of hair.
	2	With some lateral extension.
	3	Three-quarter cover.
	4	Complete cover.
6. Upper abdomen	1	A few mid-line hairs.
	2	Rather more, still mid-line.
	3 & 4	Half and full cover.
7. Lower abdomen	1	A few mid-line hairs.
	2	A mid-line streak of hair.
	3	A mid-line band of hair.
	4	An inverted V-shaped growth.
8. Arm	1	Sparse growth affecting not more than a quarter of the limb surface.
	2	More than this; cover still incomplete.
	3 & 4	Complete cover, light and heavy.
9. Forearm	1, 2, 3, 4	Complete cover of dorsal surface; 2 grades of light and 2 of heavy growth.
10. Thigh	1, 2, 3, 4	As for arm.
11. Leg	1, 2, 3, 4	As for arm.

Figure 7-3 (Continued). Am J Obstet Gynecol 140:815, 1981. (The chart is adapted from D Ferriman and JD Gallwey, Clinical assessment of body hair growth in women. J Clin Endocrinol Metab 21:1440, 1961. By permission.)

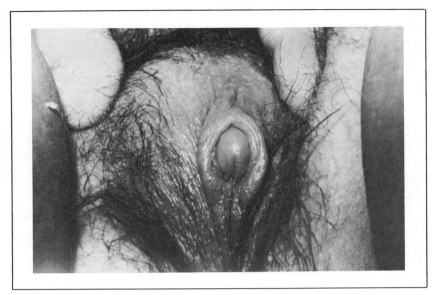

Figure 7-4. Clitoral enlargement in a patient with late onset 21-hydroxylase deficiency congenital adrenal hyperplasia.

pear to correlate with clinical response to spironolactone therapy of patients with idiopathic hirsutism [76]. If stigmata of Cushing's disease are present, a 24-hour urine should be collected for urinary free cortisol, and an 8 A.M. cortisol level after a bedtime (11 P.M.) dose of 1 mg of dexamethasone should be measured. If the serum level of cortisol is not well suppressed (< 5 μg/100 ml), or urinary free cortisol is abnormal, formal dexamethasone suppression testing is done. A pituitary adenoma should be excluded in hyperandrogenic adolescents with hyperprolactinemia.

A testosterone level above 150 to 200 ng/100 ml (depending on the laboratory normal values), DHAS above 700 μg/100 ml, androstenedione above 500 ng/100 ml, or urinary 17-ketosteroids above 25 mg/24 hours should raise the suspicion of a tumor or intersex disorder. Because of the need for extensive tests to exclude a tumor, it is critical that a markedly elevated testosterone be verified in a specialized endocrine laboratory; commercial laboratories may use less specific assays that include cross-reacting substances and thus falsely elevate the total testosterone value. Another guideline is the presence of 3 daily samples that reach a value 2.5 times greater than the upper limit of normal for that laboratory; however, testosterone levels between 100 and 200 ng/100 ml may occasionally be associated with tumors [77]. A karyotype is reserved for adolescents with significant virilization (especially associated with vaginal/uterine agenesis), a serum testosterone in the male range, or elevated FSH and is helpful in detecting mixed gonadal dysgenesis or male pseudohermaphroditism.

The need to do ACTH testing on all patients with hirsutism is controversial. Since testing is expensive, our current approach is to suggest that ACTH testing for 21-hydroxylase deficiency be done on girls with clitoromegaly, elevated DHAS, history of premature adrenarche, family history of CAH, ethnic history of a high prevalence of CAH, and most importantly a high baseline level of 17-hydroxyprogesterone. Girls with "typical PCO" can have 17-hydroxyprogesterone measured between 7 and 8 A.M. in the follicular phase of the menstrual cycle. If the level is above 100 ng/100 ml, ACTH testing should be done. Alternatively, all patients with significant hirsutism can be given a modified ACTH test with measurement of 17-hydroxyprogesterone at baseline and 60 minutes after 0.25 mg of ACTH. The rise seen with late onset CAH is typically greater than 6.5 ng/100 ml/min with levels above 1000 ng/100 ml (usually > 2000 ng/100 ml) at 60 minutes. Pang and colleagues [58] reported that women with nonclassical CAH had 60-minute stimulated levels of 17-hydroxyprogesterone of 5404 ± 3234 ng/100 ml (normal 334 ± 194 ng/100 ml) with markedly abnormal ratio of 17-hydroxypregnenolone to 17-hydroxyprogesterone of 0.4 ± 0.2 (normal 3.4 ± 1.5). Heterozygotes for nonclassical CAH may have a rise in 17-hydroxyprogesterone intermediate between the normal range and the homozygous response.

Deficiency of 3 β-hydroxysteroid dehydrogenase has been found to be an important cause of hirsutism by some groups [58, 78, 79]. These patients usually present with elevated DHAS and not with a marked increase in testosterone. Detection of 3 β-hydroxysteroid dehydrogenase deficiency requires the measurement of multiple hormone levels at baseline and 60 minutes later and the results of the ratios compared to the standards developed by Pang and colleagues [58]; stimulated 17-hydroxypregnenolone rose to 2276 ± 669 ng/100 ml (normal 985 ± 327 ng/100 ml) and DHA to 2787 ± 386 ng/100 ml (normal 1050 ± 384 ng/100 ml) with increased stimulated ratios of 17-hydroxypregnenolone to 17-hydroxyprogesterone (11 ± 2.0) and DHA to androstenedione (7.5 ± 2.3; normal 4.6 ± 1.5) (Figs. 7-5 and 7-6).

In our clinic, we do a dexamethasone suppression test for 5 days following the ACTH test in girls in whom corticosteroids are being considered as treatment for CAH or more rarely PCO with significant adrenal androgen excess. Testosterone, free testosterone, DHA, DHAS, androstenedione, and cortisol are measured at baseline and on the morning of the fifth day of dexamethasone (0.5 mg 4 times a

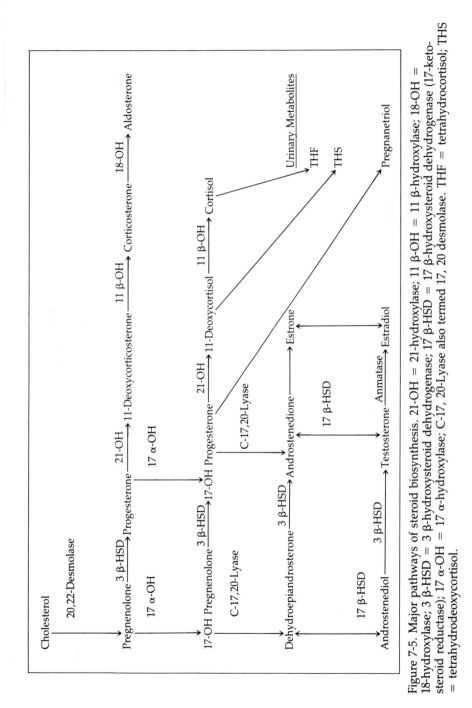

Figure 7-5. Major pathways of steroid biosynthesis. 21-OH = 21-hydroxylase; 11 β-OH = 11 β-hydroxylase; 18-OH = 18-hydroxylase; 3 β-HSD = 3 β-hydroxysteroid dehydrogenase; 17 β-HSD = 17 β-hydroxysteroid dehydrogenase (17-keto-steroid reductase); 17 α-OH = 17 α-hydroxylase; C-17, 20-Lyase also termed 17, 20 desmolase. THF = tetrahydrocortisol; THS = tetrahydrodeoxycortisol.

day). Other centers have used 7- or 14-day tests. In patients with PCO, DHA and DHAS typically suppress to less than 80 percent and 50 percent, respectively, with a dexamethasone test, but unless the level of free testosterone also falls into the normal range, clinical improvement on the lower doses of dexamethasone prescribed for maintenance (0.1–0.5 mg/day) is unlikely [80].

With evolving information on the metabolic abnormalities associated with PCO, clinicians are likely to become more involved in testing lipid levels, carbohydrate tolerance with an oral glucose tolerance test, and insulin levels.

Ultrasonography can be helpful in assessment of the ovaries of obese and poorly relaxed adolescents. However, many adolescents with PCO have normal-sized ovaries, and normal anovulatory adolescents may have multifollicular ovaries. Thus ultrasonography can be used as an adjunct but not as the sole criteria for making the diagnosis of PCO. Vaginal ultrasound appears promising to define ovarian morphology in more detail in these patients. The adrenal glands can also be visualized by ultrasonography, but computed tomography (CT) or magnetic resonance imaging (MRI) should be ordered if an adrenal tumor is suspected. Laparoscopy is not useful in making the diagnosis of PCO in adolescents and is generally reserved for infertility evaluations. In rare cases, exploratory laparotomy with bivalving of the ovaries may be necessary if the evaluation strongly indicates the presence of a small ovarian tumor, not palpable on pelvic examination or visible on ultrasound. Fortunately, MRI is showing promise in this type of evaluation.

The diagnosis of PCO is made by exclusion of other clinical entities and the finding of elevated free testosterone in the setting of anovulatory cycles and androgen excess (hirsutism, acne). The total testosterone level is also often elevated. Typically, but not always, the LH levels are above 30 mIU/ml and/or the ratio of LH/FSH is above 2.5 (LH and FSH should be assayed against the same reference standard). It should be remembered that an increased LH/FSH ratio may occur secondary to androgen excess per se, such as with ovarian tumors, CAH, and hyperthecosis. Intermittent sampling may also miss the abnormal gonadotropin ratio. An increased LH/FSH ratio in the absence of elevated free testosterone does not make a diagnosis of PCO, although the patient may later develop the more evident clinical and laboratory picture. In some clinical research centers, further confirmatory studies of PCO are done, such as looking for an exaggerated LH response with normal FSH response to GnRH and increased androstenedione , and/or testosterone response to human chorionic gonadotropin (HCG) stimulation. Suppression-stimulation testing, however, cannot be used to exclude a neoplasm definitively in the patient with markedly elevated testosterone.

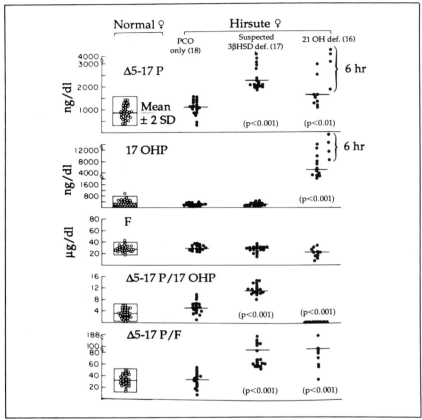

A

Figure 7-6. A. Serum hormone responses to ACTH stimulation 60 minutes after 0.25 mg intravenously in normal women and women with hirsutism (PCO, suspected 3 β-hydroxysteroid dehydrogenase, and 21-hydroxylase deficiency).

TREATMENT

Treatment of hirsutism aims at the cause, if possible. The sooner a diagnosis is made, the more amenable the hirsutism usually is to treatment. Patients with late onset CAH should receive glucocorticoid therapy, usually with low-dose dexamethasone or prednisone. Overtreatment should be avoided to prevent side effects. Patients with ovarian or adrenal tumors are usually managed surgically. Treatment of hyperprolactinemia and/or prolactinomas with bromocriptine may lower the DHAS level.

The majority of patients who have progressive hirsutism and menstrual irregularities will be found to have PCO. The potential aims of therapy should be discussed with each patient and a therapeutic decision made. The aims may include any or all of the four potential

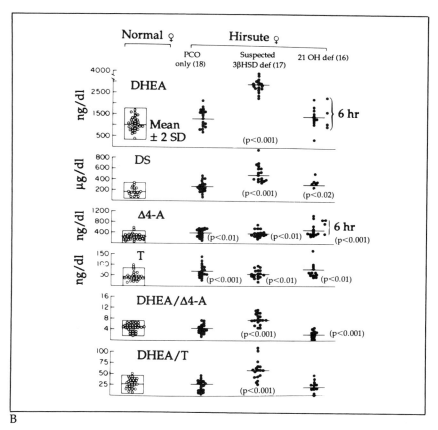

Figure 7-6 B. Serum androgen levels 60 minutes after ACTH stimulation in normal women and women with hirsutism. 3 β-HSD def = 3 β-hydroxyster oid dehydrogenase deficiency, 21 OH def = 21-hydroxylase deficiency; △5-17P = 17-hydroxypregnenolone, 17 OHP = 17-hydroxyprogesterone, F = cortisol; DHEA = dehydroepiandrosterone, DS = dehydroepiandrosterone sulfate; △4-A = androstenedione; T = testosterone. (From [58].)

problems: (1) protecting the endometrium from continuous stimulation with estrogen and the increased likelihood of endometrial cancer, (2) managing the irregular menses, (3) improving the hirsutism or at least preventing further new hair growth, and (4) aiding the infertility patient. In the non–sexually active adolescent without significant or progressive hirsutism, the first two problems can be easily managed by the use of progestin withdrawal (13–14 days of 10 mg medroxyprogesterone every 4–6 weeks). For the adolescent with significant hirsutism, with enlarged ovaries, or in need of contraception, oral contraceptives are generally well tolerated. The oral contraceptive suppresses the hypothalamic-pituitary-ovarian axis, lowering ovarian secretion of steroids. In addition, the estrogen increases

SHBG and thereby decreases free testosterone. Although studies have been carried out using numerous different oral contraceptive pill formulations [30, 81], we have preferred to use low-dose pills with an estrogenic dominance such as Brevicon/Modicon or Demulen 1/35. Other norethindrone-containing pills such as Norinyl 1+35/Ortho-Novum 1/35, Tri-Norinyl, or Ortho-Novum 7/7/7 can also be used provided that acne does not worsen during therapy. In general, the more androgenic progestin norgestrel should be avoided in these girls. New formulations using combinations of ethinyl estradiol–desogestrel appear promising [82, 83]. Occasionally suppression of androgens and LH requires a 50-μg oral contraceptive pill (Demulen 1/50 or Norinyl 1+50/Ortho-Novum 1/50) [84], but we try to lower the dosage to a 35-μg pill once lowering of free testosterone is achieved. In adolescents who will be taking the pills for many years, we usually measure the free and total testosterone at the end of the hormone tablets of the first package or preferably in the second or third week of hormones of the second cycle to make sure that adequate suppression has occurred. It is important to exclude the rare tumor in adolescents with a pretreatment serum testosterone greater than 150 to 200 ng/100 ml (done in a reliable laboratory) even if suppression occurs because tumors can be suppressed by oral contraceptives, norethindrone, and GnRH analogues [84].

Hirsutism improves in 50 to 70 percent of hirsute women treated with birth control suppression [80, 85]. The adolescent girl needs to understand that the goal is to prevent the growth of new hairs while she uses cosmetic measures such as electrolysis to treat preexisting hair follicles. Oral contraceptives also lower elevated DHAS levels in many patients being treated for PCO and additionally provide regular menses and protection of the endometrium from unopposed estrogen stimulation [80, 86].

Although studies in adult women have suggested both short-term and long-term benefit in the remission of high androgen levels and the establishment of normal menses after dexamethasone therapy, our experience in treating adolescents with PCO and hirsutism with corticosteroids has been different [4, 23, 85, 87, 88]. Many patients with PCO do have elevated adrenal androgen levels (without an adrenal enzyme deficiency) and will experience lowering of serum androgen levels during a dexamethasone test, but few adolescents have clinical improvement in hirsutism or regularity of menses with long-term corticosteroid suppression. In our studies and those of others, the best predictor of success seems to be a lowering of free testosterone level to the normal range with *both* a 5-day dexamethasone test (0.5 mg 4 times a day) and a maintenance dose of once daily dexamethasone [80, 89]. If dexamethasone is selected, the maintenance dose should be started slowly in 0.1 mg increments (dose is 0.1–0.5

mg, with the usual dose 0.25 mg per day). Adrenal androgens suppress at lower doses than cortisol [90] but still may not remain in the normal range once the high-dose dexamethasone is discontinued [80]. In our experience with hirsute adolescents, daily doses of 0.5 mg of dexamethasone may result in overtreatment, weight gain, and striae. We now prefer to use the shorter-acting prednisone (e.g., 5 mg once daily, or occasionally 2.5 mg twice daily) in the occasional adolescent with PCO who would appear to benefit from adrenal suppression. Others have prescribed cortisone acetate (12.5 mg in the morning, 25 mg at night for 1 month, and then 25 mg at night). The morning cortisol level should remain above 2 μg/100 ml. The results of a study of 14 girls with adrenal androgen excess (Fig. 7-7) show the difficulty of suppressing free testosterone in hirsute girls with dexamethasone therapy, especially in contrast to the results achieved with oral contraceptive therapy. In addition, girls treated with corticosteroids need to wear MediAlert bracelets and be cautioned about the consequences of adrenal suppression. Whether other schedules of dexamethasone or other glucocorticoids might yield better results has not been determined.

Spironolactone has been used in a number of studies in adult women but in relatively few adolescents for the treatment of hirsutism. Spironolactone is an aldosterone antagonist with antiandrogenic effects; this drug blocks the ability of cells to produce testosterone and displace androgens from their binding sites, thus lessening hair growth and sebum production. This drug is particularly useful with idiopathic hirsutism. The drug has been administered in several regimens, usually at 100 to 200 mg/day in two divided doses [91, 92]. The cyclic administration on days 4 to 22 of the cycle appears to reduce the occurrence of irregular menses. The dosage of 100 mg/day (given as 50 mg twice daily) is less likely to be associated with metrorrhagia than the higher 200 mg/day [93]. Side effects (which include polyuria, polydipsia, headache, increased body weight, and increased appetite) are usually transient and disappear without any intervention. Possible long-term problems have not been fully defined. Adolescents cannot use this drug if they are at *risk* of pregnancy because the drug can prevent normal masculinization of the male fetus. Thus, for the most part, we have used this drug in addition to oral contraceptives in the adolescent with severe hirsutism.

Cyproterone acetate along with low-dose estrogen replacement has been used in Europe and has yielded excellent results. Cimetidine has also been studied [94] but appears not to be very efficacious clinically. Cimetidine blocks the action of androgens at the hair follicle by inhibiting the binding of dihydrotestosterone to androgen receptors. GnRH analogues may also be promising in diminishing ovarian steroidogenesis, but estrogen-progestin would need to be adminis-

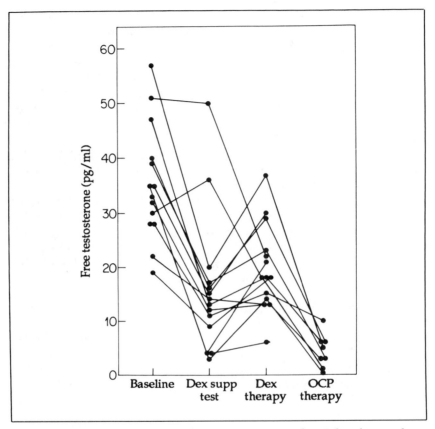

Figure 7-7. Free testosterone levels before therapy, after 4 day dexamethasone suppression test, and during long-term dexamethasone therapy in
14 hirsute adolescent patients (without 21-hydroxylase deficiency) and in
8 patients receiving oral contraceptive therapy. In this study, the normal
range of free testosterone was 3.3 to 15 pg/ml. Dex = dexamethasone;
OCP = oral contraceptive pill. (From SJ Emans, E Grace, ER Woods, et al.,
Treatment with dexamethasone of androgen excess in adolescent patients.
J Pediatr 112:821, 1988. By permission.)

tered to replace estrogen [95–98]. Ketoconazole is also being studied,
but potential toxicity may limit its use. Bromocriptine has been prescribed in both hyperprolactinemic PCO and normoprolactinemic
PCO [99, 100, 101], but the efficacy in treating androgen excess is
questionable. Topical anti-androgens are under investigation and
may hold promise for the treatment of this frustrating disorder.

Weight loss is an important adjunct to hormonal intervention because fat cells appear to be responsible for some of the peripheral

conversion of the prehormone androstenedione [39, 102, 103, 104]. Obesity per se is associated with increases in testosterone and DHAS in adults as well as adolescent girls. In addition, hyperinsulinism, which may drive the elevated androgen levels, may improve with weight loss. Barbieri and associates' [11] intriguing hypothesis that diets that are high in fiber and complex carbohydrates may lower insulin output and improve androgen levels needs to be tested.

The patient also needs help in achieving good cosmetic results in the short and long run. Bleaching of the fine hair, especially on the face, can be accomplished with 6% hydrogen peroxide or commercial preparations of facial bleaches (e.g., Jolen). The addition of 10 drops of ammonia per 30 ml of peroxide just before use will activate the peroxide and increase bleaching. Depilatories, shaving, and wax epilation remove hair temporarily. Electrolysis, if done by an experienced person, permanently destroys the hair bulb and, in most cases, avoids pitlike scars and regrowth of incompletely destroyed hairs [105]. Patients should have their own individual electrolysis needle; many carry their own needle to each treatment.

Ovulation induction in infertile PCO patients is beyond the scope of this book but may involve adrenal suppression, clomiphene citrate, menotropins (Pergonal) and HCG, low-dose FSH, pulsatile GnRH, and GnRH analogues followed by Pergonal [106]. Although frequently used in the past, wedge resection of the ovaries is not a first-line therapy and should not be used for the treatment of androgen excess in adolescents because of the risk of subsequent pelvic adhesions.

REFERENCES

1. McKnight E. The prevalence of "hirsutism" in young women. Lancet 1964; 1:410.
2. Bardin CW, and Lipsett MB. Testosterone and androstenedione blood production rates in normal women and women with idiopathic hirsutism or PCO. J Clin Invest 1967; 46:891.
3. Ferriman D, and Gallwey JD. Clinical assessment of body hair growth in women. J Clin Endocrinol Metab 1961; 21:1440.
4. Abraham G, Chakmakjian ZH, Buster JE, et al. Ovarian and adrenal contributions to peripheral androgens in hirsute women. Obstet Gynecol 1975; 46:169.
5. Farber M, Millan B, Turksoy RN, et al. Diagnostic evaluation of hirsutism in women by selective bilateral adrenal and ovarian venous catheterization. Fertil Steril 1978; 30:283.
6. Givens J, Andersen R, Ragland J, et al. Adrenal function in hirsutism: I. Diurnal change and response of plasma androstenedione, testosterone, 17-hydroxyprogesterone, cortisol, LH and FSH to dexamethasone and ½ unit ACTH. J Clin Endocrinol Metab 1975; 40:988.
7. Maroulis GB. Evaluation of hirsutism and hyperandrogenemia. Fertil Steril 1981; 36:273.

8. Hatch R, Rosenfield RL, Kim MH, et al. Hirsutism: Implications, etiology and management. Am J Gynecol 1981; 140:815.
9. Rosenfield RL, Ehrlich EN, and Cleary RE. Adrenal and ovarian contributions to the elevated free plasma and androgen levels in hirsute women. J Clin Endocrinol Metab 1972; 34:92.
10. Yen SSC. The polycystic ovary syndrome. Clin Endocrinol 1980; 12:177.
11. Barbieri RL, Smith S, and Ryan KJ. The role of hyperinsulinemia in the pathogenesis of ovarian hyperandrogenism. Fertil Steril 1988; 50:197.
12. McKenna TJ. Pathogenesis and treatment of polycystic ovary syndrome. N Engl J Med 1988; 318:558.
13. Siegberg R, Nilsson CG, Stenman UH, et al. Endocrinologic features of oligomenorrheic adolescent girls. Fertil Steril 1986; 46:852.
14. Rosen GF, Vermesh M, d'Ablaing G, et al. The endocrinologic evaluation of a 45,X true hermaphrodite. Am J Obstet Gynecol 1987; 157:1272.
15. Rosen GF, Kaplan B, and Lobo RA. Menstrual function and hirsutism in patients with gonadal dysgenesis. Obstet Gynecol 1988; 71:677.
16. Caufriez A. Male pseudohermaphroditism due to 17-ketoreductase deficiency: Report of a case without gynecomastia and without vaginal pouch. Am J Obstet Gynecol 1986; 154:148.
17. Rosenfield RL. Relationship of androgens to female hirsutism and infertility. J Reprod Med 1973; 11:87.
18. Rosenfield RL. Studies of the relation of plasma androgen levels to androgen action in women. J Steroid Biochem 1975; 6:695.
19. Coney P. Polycystic ovarian disease: current concepts of pathophysiology and therapy. Fertil Steril 1984; 42:667.
20. Lobo RA, and Goebelsmann U. Effect of androgen excess on inappropriate gonadotropin secretion as found in the polycystic ovary syndrome. Am J Obstet Gynecol 1982; 142:394.
21. Burghen GA, Givens JR, and Kitabchi AE. Correlation of hyperandrogenism with hyperinsulinism in polycystic ovary disease. J Clin Endocrinol Metab 1980; 50:113.
22. Shoupe D, Kumar DO, and Lobo RA. Insulin resistance in polycystic ovary syndrome. Am J Obstet Gynecol 1983; 147:588.
23. Loughlin T, Cunningham S, Moore A, et al. Adrenal abnormalities in polycystic ovary syndrome. J Clin Endocrinol Metab 1986; 62:142.
24. Zumoff B, Freeman R, Coupey S, et al. A chronobiologic abnormality in luteinizing hormone secretion in teenage girls with the polycystic-ovary syndrome. N Engl J Med 1983; 309:1206.
25. Pang S, Softness B, Sweeney WJ, et al. Hirsutism, polycystic ovarian disease, and ovarian 17-ketosteroid reductase deficiency. N Engl J Med 1987; 316:1295.
26. Rebar R, Judd HL, and Yen SSC, et al. Characterization of the inappropriate gonadotropin secretion in polycystic ovary syndrome. J Clin Invest 1976; 57:1320.
27. DeVane G, Czekala N, Judd H, et al. Circulating gonadotropins, estrogens, and androgens in polycystic ovarian disease. Am J Obstet Gynecol 1975; 121:496.
28. Waldstreicher J, Santoro NF, Hall JE, et al. Hyperfunction of the hypothalamic-pituitary axis in women with polycystic ovarian disease: Indirect evidence for partial gonadotrophic desensitization. J Clin Endocrinol Metab 1988; 66:165.
29. Dunaif A. Do androgens directly regulate gonadotropin secretion in the polycystic ovary syndrome? J Clin Endocrinol Metab 1986; 63:215.
30. Givens JR, Andersen RN, and Wiser WL. The effectiveness of two oral

contraceptives in suppressing plasma androstenedione, testosterone, LH, and FSH, and in stimulating plasma testosterone-binding capacity in hirsute women. Am J Obstet Gynecol 1976; 124:333.

31. Lobo RA, Granger L, Goebelsmann U, et al. J Clin Endocrinol Metab 1981; 52:156.

32. Farhi DC, Nosanchuk J, and Silverberg SG. Endometrial adenocarcinoma in women under 25 years of age. Obstet Gynecol 1986; 68:741.

33. Mattsson L, Cullberg G, Hamgerber L, et al. Lipid metabolism in women with polycystic ovary syndrome: possible implications for an increased risk of coronary heart disease. Fertil Steril 1984; 42:579.

34. Wild RA, and Bartholomew MJ. The influence of body weight on lipoprotein lipids in patients with polycystic ovary syndrome. Am J Obstet Gynecol 1988; 159:423.

35. Wild RA, Painter PC, Coulson PB, et al. Lipoprotein lipid concentrations and cardiovascular risk in women with polycystic ovary syndrome. J Clin Endocrinol Metab 1985; 61:946.

36. Moller DE, and Flier JS. Detection of an alteration in the insulin-receptor gene in a patient with insulin resistance, acanthosis nigricans, and the polycystic ovary syndrome (type A insulin resistance). N Engl J Med 1988; 319:1526.

37. Flier JS, Eastman RC, Minaker KL, et al. Acanthosis nigricans in obese women with hyperandrogenism. Diabetes 1985; 34:101.

38. Siiteri PK, and MacDonald PC. Role of extraglandular estrogen in human endocrinology. In RO Greep and E Astood (eds.) Handbook of Physiology: Endocrinology. Washington, DC: American Physiological Society, 1973, 2(part 1):615.

39. Reid RL, and Van Vugt DA. Weight-related changes in reproductive function. Fertil Steril 1987; 48:905.

40. Shoupe D, and Lobo RA. Evidence for altered catecholamine metabolism in polycystic ovary syndrome. Am J Obstet Gynecol 1984; 150:566.

41. Aleen FA, and McIntosh T. Elevated plasma levels of endorphin in a group of women with polycystic ovary disease. Fertil Steril 1984; 42:686.

42. Luciano AA, Chapler FK, and Sherman BM. Hyperprolactinemia in polycystic ovary syndrome. Fertil Steril 1984; 41:719.

43. Barnes RB, Mileikowski GN, Cha KY, et al. Effects of dopamine and metoclopramide in polycystic ovary syndrome. J Clin Endocrinol Metab 1986; 63:506.

44. Lobo RA, Granger LR, Paul WL, et al. Psychological stress and increases in urinary norepinephrine metabolites, platelets, serotonin, and adrenal androgens in women with polycystic ovary syndrome. Am J Obstet Gynecol 1983; 145:496.

45. Barbieri RL, Makris A, Randall RW, et al. Insulin stimulates androgen accumulation in incubations of ovarian stroma obtained from women with hyperandrogenism. J Clin Endocrinol Metab 1986; 62:905.

46. Geffner ME, Kaplan SA, Bersch N, et al. Persistence of insulin resistance in polycystic ovarian disease after inhibition of ovarian steroid secretion. Fertil Steril 1986; 45:327.

47. Dunaif A, Graf M, Laumas V, et al. Insulin infusion increases androgen and estrogen production in polycystic ovary syndrome, but not in normal women. (Abst 878) Presented in 69th Meeting of Endocrine Society, Indianapolis, June 10–12, 1987.

48. Smith S, Ravnikar VA, and Barbieri RL. Androgen and insulin response to an oral glucose challenge in hyperandrogenic women. Fertil Steril 1987; 48:72.

49. Barnes RB, Rosenfield RL, Burstein S, et al. Pituitary-ovary responses to Nafarelin testing in the polycystic ovary syndrome. N Engl J Med 1989; 320:559.
50. Kirschner MA, and Jacobs JB. Combined ovarian and adrenal vein catheterization to determine the site(s) of androgen overproduction in hirsute women. J Clin Endocrinol Metab 1971; 33:199.
51. Wentz AC, White RL, Migeon CJ, et al. Differential ovarian and adrenal vein catheterization. Am J Obstet Gynecol 1976; 125:1000.
52. Gross MD, Wortsman J, Shapiro B, et al. Scintigraphic evidence of adrenal cortical dysfunction in polycystic ovary syndrome. J Clin Endocrinol Metab 1986; 62:197.
53. Lucky AN, Rosenfield RL, McGuire J, et al. Adrenal androgen hyperresponsiveness to adrenocorticotropin in women with acne and/or hirsutism: adrenal enzyme defects and exaggerated adrenarche. J Clin Endocrinol Metab 1986; 62:840.
54. Blankenstein J, Faiman C, Reyes F, et al. Adult onset familial adrenal hyperplasia due to incomplete 21-hydroxylase deficiency. Am J Med 1980; 68:441.
55. Lobo RA, and Goeblesmann U. Adult manifestation of congenital adrenal hyperplasia due to incomplete 21-hydroxylase deficiency mimicking polycystic ovary disease. Am J Obstet Gynecol 1980; 138:720.
56. Migeon CJ, Rosewaks Z, Lee P, et al. The attenuated form of 21-hydroxylase deficiency as an allelic form of 21-hydroxylase deficiency. J Clin Endocrinol Metab 1980; 51:647.
57. Kohn B, Levine LS, Pollack MS, et al. Late-onset steroid 21-hydroxylase deficiency: A variant of classical congenital adrenal hyperplasia. J Clin Endocrinol Metab 1982; 55:817.
58. Pang S, Lerner A, Stoner E, et al. Late-onset adrenal steroid 3β-hydroxysteroid dehydrogenase deficiency. I. A cause of hirsutism in pubertal and postpubertal women. J Clin Endocrinol Metab 1985; 60:428.
59. Emans SJ, Grace E, Fleischnick E, et al. Detection of late-onset 21-hydroxylase deficiency congenital adrenal hyperplasia in adolescents. Pediatr 1983; 72:690.
60. Chrousos GP, Loriaux DL, Mann DL, et al. Late-onset 21-hydroxylase deficiency mimicking idiopathic hirsutism or polycystic ovarian disease. Ann Intern Med 1982; 96:143.
61. Benjamin F, Deutsch S, Saperstein H, et al. Prevalence of and markers for the attenuated form of congenital adrenal hyperplasia and hyperprolactinemia masquerading as polycystic ovarian disease. Fertil Steril 1986; 46:215.
62. Speiser PW, and New MI. Genotype and hormonal phenotype in nonclassical 21-hydroxylase deficiency. J Clin Endocrinol Metab 1987; 64:86.
63. Speiser PW, New MI, and White PC. Molecular genetic analysis of nonclassic steroid 21-hydroxylase deficiency associated with HLA-B14, DR1. N Engl J Med 1988; 319:19.
64. New MI, Franzieska L, Lerner AJ, et al. Genotyping steroid 21-hydroxylase deficiency: Hormonal reference data. J Clin Endocrinol Metab 1983; 57:320.
65. Zerah M, Pang S, and New MI. Morning salivary 17-hydroxyprogesterone is useful screening test for nonclassical 21-hydroxylase deficiency. J Clin Endocrinol Metab 1987; 65:227.
66. Dewailly D, Vantyghem-Haudiquet MC, Sainsard C, et al. Clinical and biological phenotypes in late-onset 21-hydroxylase deficiency. J Clin Endocrinol Metab 1986; 63:418.

67. Fiet J, Gueux B, Gourmelen M, et al. Comparison of basal and adrenocorticotropin-stimulated plasma 21-deoxycortisol and 17-hydroxy-progesterone values as biological markers of late-onset adrenal hyperplasia. J Clin Endocrinol Metab 1988; 66:659.
68. Cathelineau G, Brerault JL, Fiet J, et al. Adrenocortical 11 α-hydroxylation defect in adult women with postmenarchial onset of symptoms. J Clin Endocrinol Metab 1980; 51:345.
69. Globerman H, Rosler Ä, Theodor R, et al. An inherited defect in aldosterone biosynthesis caused by a mutation in or near the gene for steroid 11-hydroxylase. N Engl J Med 1988; 319:1193.
70. Lee PA, Migeon CJ, Bias WB, et al. Familial hypersecretion of adrenal androgens transmitted as a dominant, non-HLA linked trait. Obstet Gynecology 1987; 69:259.
71. Kamilaris TC, DeBold R, Manolas KJ, et al. Testosterone-secreting adrenal adenoma in a peripubertal girl. JAMA 1987; 258:2558.
72. Lee PDK, Winter RJ, and Green OC. Virilizing adrenocortical tumors in childhood: Eight cases and a review of the literature. Pediatrics 1985; 76:437.
73. Chetkowski RJ, Judd HL, Jagger PI, et al. Autonomous cortisol secretion by a lipoid cell tumor of the ovary. JAMA 1985; 254:2628.
74. Reingold SB, and Rosenfield RL. The relationship of mild hirsutism or acne in women to androgens. Arch Dermatol 1987; 123:209.
75. Paulson RJ, Serafini PC, Catalino JA, et al. Measurements of 3 α, 17 β-androstanediol glucuronide in serum and urine and the correlation with skin 5 α-reductase activity. Fertil Steril 1986; 46:222.
76. Kirschner MA, Samojlik E, and Szmal E. Clinical usefulness of plasma androstanediol glucuronide measurements in women with idiopathic hirsutism. J Clin Endocrinol Metab 1987; 65:597.
77. Meldrum DR, and Abraham GE. Peripheral and ovarian venous concentrations of various steroid hormones in virilizing ovarian tumors. Obstet Gynecol 1979; 53:36.
78. Bongiovanni AM. Acquired adrenal hyperplasia: With special reference to 3 β-hydroxysteroid dehydrogenase. Fertil Steril 1981; 35:599.
79. Lobo RA, and Goebelsmann U. Evidence for reduced 3 β-ol-hydroxysteroid dehydrogenase activity in some hirsute women thought to have polycystic ovary syndrome. J Clin Endocrinol Metab 1981; 53:394.
80. Emans SJ, Grace E, Woods ER, et al. Treatment with dexamethasone of androgen excess in adolescent patients. J Pediatr 1988; 112:821.
81. Talbert LM, and Sloan C. The effect of a low-dose oral contraceptive on serum testosterone levels in polycystic ovary disease. Obstet Gynecol 1979; 53:694.
82. Nappi C, Farace MJ, Leone F, et al. Effect of a combination of ethinyl estradiol and desogestrel in adolescent with oligomenorrhea and ovarian hyperandrogenism. Eur J Obstet Gynecol Reprod Biol 1987; 25:209.
83. Jung-Hoffmann C, and Kuhl H. Divergent effects of two low-dose oral contraceptives on sex hormone-binding globulin and free testosterone. Am J Obstet Gynecol 1987; 156:199.
84. Scully RE (ed.). Case Records of the Massachusetts General Hospital. Case 22-1988. N Engl J Med 1988; 318:1449.
85. Ettinger B, Goldfield EB, Burrill KC, et al. Plasma testosterone stimulation-suppression dynamics in hirsute women. Am J Med 1973; 54:195.
86. Wiebe RH, and Morris CV. Effect of an oral contraceptive on adrenal and ovarian androgenic steroids. Obstet Gynecol 1984; 63:12.

87. Abraham G, Maroulis G, Boyers S, et al. Dexamethasone suppression test in the management of hyperandrogenized patients. Obstet Gynecol 1981; 57:158.
88. Abraham GE, Maroulis GB, Buster JE, et al. Effect of dexamethasone on serum cortisol and androgen levels in hirsute patients. Obstet Gynecol 1976; 47:395.
89. Moll GW, and Rosenfield RL. Plasma free testosterone in the diagnosis of adolescent polycystic ovary syndrome. J Pediatr 1983; 102:461.
90. Rittmaster R, Loriaux DL, and Cutler GB. Sensitivity of cortisol and adrenal androgens to dexamethasone suppression in hirsute women. J Clin Endocrinol Metab 1985; 61:462.
91. Shapiro G, and Evron S. A novel use of spironolactone: Treatment of hirsutism. J Clin Endocrinol Metab 1980; 51:429.
92. Cumming DC, Yang JC, Rebar RW, et al. Treatment of hirsutism with spironolactone. JAMA 1982; 247:1295.
93. Helfer EL, Miller JL, and Rose LI. Side-effects of spironolactone therapy in the hirsute woman. J Clin Endocrinol Metab 1988; 66:208.
94. Vigersky RA, Mehlman I, Glass AR, et al. Treatment of hirsutism. J Clin Endocrinol Metab 1980; 51:429.
95. Steingold K, DeZiegler D, Cedars M, et al. Clinical and hormonal effects of chronic gonadotropin-releasing hormone agonist treatment in polycystic ovarian disease. J Clin Endocrinol Metab 1987; 65:773.
96. Couznet B, LeStrat N, Brailly S, et al. Comparative effects of cyproterone acetate or a long-acting gonadotropin-releasing hormone agonist in polycystic ovarian disease. J Clin Endocrinol Metab 1986; 63:1031.
97. Steingold KA, Judd HL, Nieberg RK, et al. Treatment of severe androgen excess due to ovarian hyperthecosis with a long-acting gonadotropin-releasing hormone agonist. Am J Obstet Gynecol 1986; 154:1241.
98. Andreyko JL, Monroe SE, and Jaffe RB. Treatment of hirsutism with a gonadotropin-releasing hormone agonist (Nafarelin). J Clin Endocrinol Metab 1986; 63:854.
99. El Tabbakh GH, Loutfi IA, Azab I, et al. Bromocriptine in polycystic ovarian disease: A controlled clinical trial. Obstet Gynecol 1988; 71:301.
100. Steingold KA, Lobo RA, Judd HL, et al. The effect of bromocriptine on gonadotropin and steroid secretion in polycystic ovarian disease. J Clin Endocrinol Metab 1986; 62:1048.
101. Seibel MM, Oskowitz S, and Kamrava M. Bromocriptine response in normoprolactinemic patients with polycystic ovary disease: a preliminary report. Obstet Gynecol 1984; 64:213.
102. Glass AR, Dahms WT, and Abraham GE. Secondary amenorrhea in obesity: Etiologic role of weight related androgen excess. Fertil Steril 1978; 30:243.
103. Harlass FE, Playmate SR, and Fariss BL. Weight loss is associated with correction of gonadotropin and sex steroid abnormalities in the obese anovulatory female. Fertil Steril 1984; 42:649.
104. Hosseinian AH, Kim MH, and Rosenfield C. Obesity and oligomenorrhea are associated with hyperandrogenism independent of hirsutism. J Clin Endocrinol Metab 1976; 42:765.
105. Arndt K. Manual of Dermatologic Therapeutics (4th ed.). Boston: Little, Brown, 1989.
106. Kamrava MM, Seibel MM, Berger MJ, et al. Reversal of persistent anovulation in polycystic ovarian disease by administration of chronic low-dose follicle-stimulating hormone. Fertil Steril 1982; 37:520.

8. Pelvic Pain, Dysmenorrhea, and the Premenstrual Syndrome

Pelvic pain is a frequent complaint of adolescent and adult women and can be characterized as acute or chronic. Pelvic pain can arise from diseases or conditions affecting the reproductive tract, the gastrointestinal tract, the kidneys and bladder, and the musculoskeletal system. In addition, life stresses and psychosocial problems may serve to exaggerate the intensity of the symptoms and the response of the patient to the pain. This chapter discusses the approach to the girl with acute and chronic pelvic pain, the diagnosis and treatment of dysmenorrhea, and a brief overview of the premenstrual syndrome.

ACUTE PELVIC PAIN

The adolescent girl presenting with acute pelvic pain necessitates aggressive diagnosis and management because of the possibility of a life-threatening condition such as a ruptured ectopic pregnancy. Some of the common causes of acute pain to be considered in the differential diagnosis are shown in Table 8-1. Gynecologic causes include infection; rupture of an ovarian cyst, endometrioma, or ectopic pregnancy; and torsion of a cyst, tumor, or normal ovary or tube. Genital tract obstruction and dysmenorrhea may cause the patient to present with acute symptoms, although these entities are more commonly associated with chronic pelvic pain. Symptoms associated with infection usually occur over several days, whereas pain with torsion or rupture usually begins abruptly and the patient can tell precisely when the symptoms began. Vomiting may occur with onset of pain. However, intermittent or partial torsion may produce crampy pain for several days to a week or more before an acute episode of complete torsion with infarction of the ovary. Pelvic inflammatory disease (PID) discussed on p. 358, and ectopic pregnancy, discussed on p. 528, are extremely important to consider in the differential diagnosis. Dysmenorrhea with increasing pelvic pain as the menses end should make the clinician think of PID. Many physicians still have difficulty accepting the notion that a young adolescent may be sexually active and therefore the physician may omit performing a pelvic examination.

In deciding whether the pain is gynecologic in origin, the physician must consider gastrointestinal causes such as appendicitis, intestinal obstruction or perforation, volvulus, inflammatory bowel disease, infections (e.g., *Giardia, Shigella, Salmonella*), lactose intolerance, irritable bowel syndrome, and constipation. Urinary tract infections and calculi may present with acute pain. Orthopedic causes of pain are

Table 8-1. Differential Diagnosis of Acute Pelvic Pain in Adolescent Girls

Gynecologic causes
  Infection—pelvic inflammatory disease, postabortion endometritis
  Rupture of a follicular cyst, corpus luteum cyst, endometrioma, tumor,
    or ectopic pregnancy; mittelschmerz
  Torsion of an ovarian cyst, ovarian tumor, normal ovary, or fallopian
    tube
  Ectopic pregnancy (without rupture)
  Threatened/spontaneous abortion
  Endometriosis
  Genital tract obstruction
  Dysmenorrhea
Gastrointestinal causes
  Appendicitis
  Gastroenteritis
  Mesenteric adenitis
  Intestinal obstruction or perforation
  Volvulus
  Meckel's diverticulum
  Inflammatory bowel disease
  Porphyria
  Trauma
  Bowel spasm
  Constipation
Urinary tract causes
  Infection
  Calculi
Orthopedic causes
  Slipped capital-femoral epiphysis
  Bone and joint infections in the sacrum, ilium, and hip
  Vertebral osteomyelitis
  Psoas and iliacus abscess
Psychosomatic

frequently forgotten and can be missed initially if the evaluation does not involve a complete history as well as an examination of the range of motion of the hips and spine and tests of the sacroiliac joints (pelvic compression and figure-of-four test in which the sacroiliac joint is stressed with one hand on the ilium and the other on the opposite flexed knee [Patrick or Fabere test]).

The evaluation of the patient with acute pelvic pain should include a history of the location and radiation of the pain, factors that relieve and exacerbate the pain (e.g., walking, exercise, eating, urination, bowel movement), the date of the last menstrual period, contraceptive and sexual history, associated symptoms (e.g., fever, chills, diarrhea, vomiting, dysuria), and previous pelvic pain and/or surgery. Prepubertal girls (and adolescents less commonly) may have torsion of a normal adnexa (ovary and/or tube) and several weeks to years later experience a torsion of the other adnexa with subsequent sterility. Psychosocial history should be elicited to assess if stress, substance use, or sexual abuse might be contributing factors.

A complete physical examination should be undertaken with special attention to palpation of the abdomen, looking for evidence of masses, tenderness, organomegaly, or peritoneal irritation. Depending on the age of the patient and the size of the hymenal opening, a bimanual vaginal-abdominal, rectoabdominal, or rectovaginal-abdominal examination, always in the lithotomy position, should be done to assess the size of the uterus, the possibility of cervical motion tenderness, and any ovarian or adnexal tenderness. A speculum examination to assess the vagina and cervix should be done in all sexually active girls and in virginal girls if the examination can be accomplished without trauma. Tests for *Chlamydia trachomatis* and *Neisseria gonorrhoeae* should be obtained in all girls who might have ever been sexually active. Lubricant should not be used for the digital vaginal or speculum examination unless cervical specimens have already been obtained.

Laboratory tests depend on the initial assessment and usually include a complete blood count with differential and erythrocyte sedimentation rate, a urinalysis and urine culture, cervical cultures, a sensitive pregnancy test, and a stool specimen for occult blood. A high white count usually indicates infection, inflammation, or ischemia such as secondary to adnexal torsion or bowel obstruction. In acute hemorrhage, the hematocrit may not reflect the extent of blood loss.

In adolescents in whom a mass is palpated or an adequate pelvic examination is not possible, ultrasonography can be used as an aid in the diagnosis of pelvic pathology. Ultrasound may not be necessary to evaluate a 5-cm cyst, and physical examination can be used to follow the finding clinically; however, adequate examination or repeat examinations in young adolescents may be difficult. It is important to remember that adolescents normally have 1- to 2-cm follicles, which though often termed "cysts" on ultrasound reports are incidental findings. Endometriosis and pelvic inflammatory disease cannot be excluded by a normal ultrasound (see p. 38).

A patient experiencing intermittent edema and enlargement of an ovary associated with episodes of acute pelvic pain may be experiencing intermittent torsion of a normal adnexa. The ultrasound of ovarian torsion may reveal an echogenic mass, and cul-de-sac fluid is usually present with hemorrhagic, necrotic ovarian tissue. Ovarian torsion is more common on the right and may mimic acute appendicitis, with right lower quadrant pain, vomiting, rebound, tender-

Table 8-2. Principal Laparoscopic Diagnoses in 121
Adolescent Females 11 to 17 Years Old with Acute
Pelvic Pain (The Children's Hospital, Boston, 1980–1986)

Diagnosis	No. of Patients
Ovarian cyst	47 (39%)
Acute pelvic inflammatory disease	21 (17%)
Adnexal torsion	9 (8%)
Endometriosis	6 (5%)
Ectopic pregnancy	4 (3%)
Appendicitis	13 (11%)
No pathology	21 (17%)

ness, and leukocytosis. Girls in the 7- to 10-year-old range are especially prone to this problem. Whether pexing of the contralateral ovary can be helpful in preventing a second episode needs evaluation.

Gastrointestinal and skeletal x rays, bone scans, and other radiologic studies should be ordered as clinically indicated by the history and abdominal and musculoskeletal examinations.

Depending on clinical and laboratory assessment, patients will fall into one of several categories [1]. Some conditions such as acute hemoperitoneum, ruptured tubo-ovarian abscess, appendicitis, and some other gastrointestinal surgical emergencies require definitive surgery. Some conditions such as gastroenteritis, urinary tract infection, and pelvic inflammatory disease require medical management; others require further investigation (e.g., urinary calculi). Not infrequently, the diagnosis remains in doubt, and laparoscopy may be invaluable for a definitive assessment. Often, in cases of ruptured ovarian cysts or hemorrhagic corpus luteum, free blood and clots can be aspirated and hemostasis ensured by fulguration of the bleeders through the laparoscope.

The principal findings in 121 adolescents (11–17 years old) who were laparoscoped by the Gynecology Service of The Children's Hospital, Boston, for acute pelvic pain between 1980 and 1986 are shown in Table 8-2 [1]. The most common diagnosis was a complication of an ovarian cyst. Interestingly, the causes of acute pelvic pain did not appear to be age related (Table 8-3).

MITTELSCHMERZ
Mittelschmerz is the term applied to so-called ovulatory pain. The patient typically complains of dull, aching pain at midcycle in one lower quadrant, lasting from a few minutes to 6 to 8 hours. In rare instances, the pain is described as severe and crampy and persisting for 2 to 3 days. The etiology of this pain in unknown, but the spillage

Table 8-3. Age-related Prevalence of Principal Laparoscopic
Findings in 121 Adolescent Females 11 to 17 Years Old
with Acute Pelvic Pain (The Children's Hospital, Boston, 1980–1986)

	No. of Patients		
Diagnosis	Age 11–13	Age 14–15	Age 16–17
Ovarian cyst	12 (50%)	16 (35%)	19 (37%)
Acute pelvic inflammatory disease	4 (17%)	7 (16%)	10 (19%)
Adnexal torsion	0 (0%)	7 (16%)	2 (4%)
Endometriosis	0 (0%)	2 (4%)	4 (7%)
Ectopic pregnancy	0 (0%)	3 (7%)	1 (2%)
Appendicitis	3 (13%)	4 (9%)	6 (12%)
No pathology	5 (20%)	6 (13%)	10 (19%)
Total	24 (20%)	45 (37%)	52 (43%)

of fluid as the follicle cyst ruptures and expels the oocyte may irritate the peritoneum. Ultrasonography studies have detected small quantities of fluid in 40 percent of cycles at mid–menstrual cycle in normal women [2].

In most cases, the diagnosis of mittelschmerz is evident from the recurrent nature of the mild discomfort. Documentation of the midcycle occurrence of the pain by menstrual charts is helpful. If the patient is being examined for the first episode or for an exceptionally severe episode, other diagnoses must be excluded, including appendicitis, torsion or rupture of an ovarian cyst, and ectopic pregnancy.

Therapy for mittelschmerz should aim foremost at a careful explanation to the teenager of the benign nature of the pain. A heating pad and analgesics such as prostaglandin inhibitors (ibuprofen, naproxen sodium) and rarely oral contraceptives may be prescribed.

CHRONIC PELVIC PAIN
The diagnosis of chronic pelvic pain is similar to that for acute pelvic pain except that the tempo of the investigation is slowed and an accurate assessment of psychosocial issues and the impact of the pain on the life of the teenager is essential. Chronic pain can be a significant source of frustration for the patient and her parents, and the seeking of multiple opinions from the medical community is not unusual. Many of these teenagers will have missed many days of school and will be far behind in their schoolwork. If, for example, bowel spasm resulted in the initial symptoms of pain, reluctance to return to school may intensify the pain, causing further absences. Although short-term tutoring may be essential, the physician should work with the adolescent and her family to encourage the adolescent

to return to normal social interaction and to school. Granting a request for long-term home tutoring is rarely in the best interests of the adolescent. On the other hand, a definitive diagnosis is extremely important because of frequent concern on the part of parents or patient that cancer or some other life-threatening condition is present. The complaints of the adolescent should be assessed thoroughly so that she feels that her symptoms are taken seriously by the physician. A recommendation "to see a counselor" may be interpreted by the adolescent as "the pain is in your head." In addition, important diagnoses such as pelvic inflammatory disease or endometriosis may be missed unless a complete assessment is undertaken in the patient with persistent pelvic pain. The physician needs to reassure the patient that efforts will be made to sort out her problem and that she will not be abandoned even if no diagnosis can be established.

The evaluation of the girl with chronic pelvic pain requires a similar history and physical examination to that described in the section Acute Pelvic Pain. The common problems included in the differential diagnosis are shown in Table 8-4. The history and assessment should take into account gynecologic, gastrointestinal, urologic, musculoskeletal, and psychosomatic etiologies. A complete physical examination including abdominal palpation, musculoskeletal assessment, and pelvic examination should be performed. It is helpful to ask the patient during the examination to point with one finger to the location of the pain and then to ask her what factors (e.g., exercise, sexual activity, food, urination, bowel movement) relieve or exacerbate the pain. For example, girls with endometriosis may have a constellation of symptoms including cyclic severe dysmenorrhea, rectal pressure and other bowel problems, and dyspareunia. Increased symptoms with activity may occur with adhesions and with many of the musculoskeletal problems. Since constipation and other GI disorders (irritable bowel syndrome, lactose intolerance) are such common causes of pelvic discomfort in adolescents, a careful bowel history, dietary history (including gum chewing and carbonated beverages), and rectal examination are important. A trial of stool softeners, high fiber diet, and increased fluid intake are often essential before proceeding to other diagnoses.

The musculoskeletal examination should assess the range of motion of the hips and spine, check for a normal straight-leg raising test and the absence of symptoms with pelvic compression, and look for bone tenderness. Neoplasms of the pelvis and lower spine may be missed on plain x-ray films and may require a bone scan for detection. Stress fractures of the pubic ramus and ischium can occur in runners and may present with hip or groin pain, exacerbated by activity, and bone tenderness.

As noted in a previous section, the pelvic examination should be

Table 8-4. Differential Diagnosis of Chronic Pelvic Pain in Adolescent Girls

Gynecologic causes
  Dysmenorrhea
  Mittelschmerz
  Endometriosis
  Chronic pelvic inflammatory disease
  Ovarian cyst
  Genital tract malformation and obstruction
  Pelvic congestion
  Pelvic serositis
  Multicystic enlarged ovaries
  Postoperative adhesions
Gastrointestinal causes
  Constipation
  Bowel spasm
  Fecalith of the appendix
  Infections
  Inflammatory bowel disease
  Dietary intolerance (e.g., lactose intolerance)
Urinary tract causes
  Infection
  Hydronephrosis and obstructing lesions
Orthopedic causes
  Herniated intervertebral disc
  Chronic slipped capital-femoral epiphysis
  Osteitis pubis
  Neoplasms of the pelvis and lower spine
  Stress fractures of the pelvis
  Spondylolysis
Psychosomatic

performed in the lithotomy position to assess adequately all the reproductive structures. A speculum examination (usually possible with a Huffman speculum, even in virginal girls) is important to identify genital tract obstruction and anomalies and to obtain tests for *C. trachomatis* and *N. gonorrhoeae* and Pap smear (if patient was ever or is possibly sexually active or is over 18 years). The bimanual palpation (rectoabdominal or rectovaginal-abdominal) should attempt to localize tender areas, and the posterior cul-de-sac should be assessed for pain and nodularity suggestive of endometriosis.

The laboratory evaluation usually includes a complete blood count with differential and sedimentation rate, urinalysis and urine culture, and cervical cultures. Pelvic ultrasonography can be used to assess a mass or a suspected genital tract malformation and to screen patients in whom a satisfactory pelvic examination is not possible. It is advisable to ask the radiologist to screen the kidneys by ultrasound to look for unilateral renal agenesis in patients with a possible genital tract anomaly. In our clinic, we have evaluated a small number of girls in the earliest stages of pubertal development with persistent pelvic discomfort and large tender multifollicular ovaries (Fig. 8-1); the patients have been treated symptomatically with analgesics and low doses of nonsteroidal anti-inflammatory agents, and the symptoms have resolved with further pubertal development. Operative treatment should be avoided unless torsion or tumor is suspected. In many girls, multicystic ovaries are asymptomatic and noted on ultrasound done for other reasons. Gastrointestinal series, urologic studies, bone scans, and specialist consultation should be done as needed and not routinely in all girls with chronic pelvic pain.

For adolescents with significant, undiagnosed *pelvic* pain (not vague abdominal pain), laparoscopy has become an invaluable aid to diagnosis [1, 3, 4]. Laparoscopy allows the physician to make or confirm a specific diagnosis, to take biopsies, to lyse adhesions, and to perform some laparoscopic procedures. If endometriosis is a consideration based on the symptoms and outpatient examination and if laser laparoscopy is available, the gynecologist should discuss the possibility of laser surgery during the laparoscopy or laparotomy with the patient and her family before the procedure to avoid a second anesthetic. Negative findings at laparoscopy can be equally valuable in reassuring the patient and her family and to help her accept the concept of having a functional problem that often responds to medical and psychological therapy.

The indications for laparoscopy in the evaluation of the adolescent girl with chronic pelvic pain are dysmenorrhea unresponsive to prostaglandin inhibitors and/or ovulation suppression with oral contraceptive pills over a 3- to 6-month interval; confirmation or exclusion of clinically suspected endometriosis, chronic pelvic inflammatory disease, ovarian cysts, pelvic adhesions, or appendiceal fecalith; and evaluation of undiagnosed pain after an appropriate evaluation and treatment with a stool softener. The results of laparoscopy in the diagnosis of chronic pelvic pain at The Children's Hospital between July 1974 and December 1983 are shown in Table 8-5. It should be noted that patients with suspected pelvic inflammatory disease on the basis of history and elevated sedimentation rate were not included in this series, since the laparoscopy in these patients was performed to confirm the diagnosis and evaluate the severity rather than to establish the diagnosis of chronic pelvic pain. Other series of laparoscopic findings in adolescents have found a higher proportion of patients having pelvic inflammatory disease; this may reflect both the population studied (inner city versus suburban), the inclusion-exclusion criteria, the ability to recognize very early endometriosis, and the distribution of the age of the girls. For example, in a study of 100 women between the ages of 15 and 19 years, Strickland and co-workers [3] found that 46 had a normal pelvis, 29 had evidence of

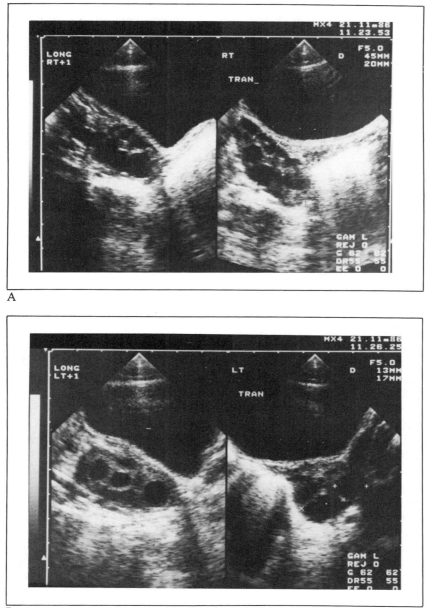

A

B

Figure 8-1. Longitudinal and transverse ultrasounds of enlarged multicystic ovaries in an 11-year-old girl with chronic pelvic pain. A. Right ovary. B. Left ovary. Such ovaries are often found without symptoms in early pubertal girls.

Table 8-5. Postoperative Diagnosis in 282 Adolescent Females
with Chronic Pelvic Pain (The Children's Hospital, Boston, 1974–1983)

Diagnosis	No. of Patients
Endometriosis	126 (45%)
Postoperative adhesions	37 (13%)
Serositis	15 (5%)
Ovarian cyst	14 (5%)
Uterine malformation	15 (5%)
Others*	4 (2%)
No pathology	71 (25%)

*Ileitis, infarcted hydatid of Morgagni, pelvic congestion.

pelvic inflammatory disease, 12 had endometriosis, and 13 had other pelvic pathology (including paratubal cysts, multicystic ovaries, and adhesions).

At The Children's Hospital, laparoscopy is performed under general endotracheal anesthesia, usually in the ambulatory surgery unit. A 7-mm Wolf or Stortz laparoscope is used with a second trocar site established in the suprapubic area and a uterine mobilizer attached to the cervix to allow mobilization of the uterus.

As noted in Table 8-5, three quarters of the girls laparoscoped at The Children's Hospital for chronic pelvic pain had intrapelvic pathology, with endometriosis diagnosed most frequently (see following section). The age-related incidence of findings is shown in Table 8-6. As one would expect, the finding of endometriosis increases with age. The next most common finding was postoperative adhesions, which were usually associated with a history of appendectomy or ovarian cystectomy. In most of these girls, the pain was acyclic, often aggravated by physical activity or coitus, and relieved by rest. Preoperative pelvic examination frequently revealed some adnexal thickening and cul-de-sac or adnexal tenderness and nodularity.

The most puzzling finding was the presence of serositis characterized by hyperemia and granuloma-like lesions of the pelvic peritoneum and uterine serosa. Biopsies of these lesions showed mesothelial hyperplasia with hemosiderin deposits. It is unclear whether these findings represent early endometriosis, a reaction to hemoperitoneum from leaking corpus luteum or retrograde menstruation, a viral infection, or a nonspecific finding. Treatment was variable with predominantly the use of ovulation suppression with oral contraceptives or antiprostaglandins; because of the small number of

Table 8-6. Age-Related Incidence of Laparoscopic Findings in 129
Adolescent Females with Chronic Pelvic Pain (The Children's Hospital,
Boston, 1980–1983)

Diagnosis	No. of Patients				
	Age 11–13	Age 14–15	Age 16–17	Age 18–19	Age 20–21
Endometriosis	2 (12%)	9 (28%)	21 (40%)	17 (45%)	7 (54%)
Postoperative adhesions	1 (6%)	4 (13%)	7 (13%)	5 (13%)	2 (15%)
Serositis	5 (29%)	4 (13%)	0 (0%)	2 (5%)	0 (0%)
Ovarian cyst	2 (12%)	2 (6%)	3 (5%)	2 (5%)	0 (8%)
Uterine malformation	1 (6%)	0 (0%)	1 (2%)	0 (0%)	1 (0%)
Others	0 (0%)	1 (3%)	2 (4%)	1 (3%)	0 (0%)
No pathology	6 (35%)	12 (37%)	19 (36%)	11 (29%)	3 (23%)

patients, the natural history is unknown except that a few have subsequently developed endometriosis.

Other findings included pelvic inflammatory disease with adhesions (see p. 358), ovarian cysts (see p. 425), genital tract malformations with obstruction (see p. 290), and cases of ileitis, infarcted hydatid of Morgagni, and pelvic congestion. The pain in the patients with chronic pelvic inflammatory disease was generally acyclic and not related to physical activity; pelvic examination revealed tender or nontender adnexal thickening in most of these girls.

No apparent gynecologic cause of the chronic pain was found in one quarter of the patients. Most of the girls with negative findings (74%) were improved at follow-up. Whether the knowledge of normal anatomy contributed to the positive outcome is unknown, although several patients with a past history of pelvic inflammatory disease were considerably reassured. Other centers have reported finding a larger percentage of normal laparoscopic examinations. The much higher number of patients with early endometriosis in The Children's Hospital series may reflect the difficulty identifying very early endometriosis, thus underscoring the need for biopsy of hyperemic petechial lesions.

The data collected at our institutions and others emphasize the need to take the symptoms of chronic pelvic pain seriously. A careful history, pelvic examination, appropriate laboratory tests, and laparoscopy as indicated, should be done in the pursuit of a diagnosis and treatment. The results of treatment of the first 140 patients in our earlier series are shown in Table 8-7.

Table 8-7. Results of Initial Treatment
in 140 Adolescent Females with Chronic Pelvic Pain

Condition	No. Patients	Improved	Recurrence
Endometriosis alone	66	47 (71%)	19 (29%)
Postoperative adhesions	18	16 (89%)	2 (11%)
Uterine anomalies			
With endometriosis	8	8 (100%)	0 (0%)
Without endometriosis	4	4 (100%)	0 (0%)
Pelvic inflammatory disease	10	5 (50%)	5 (50%)
Hemoperitoneum	6	5 (83%)	1 (17%)
Functional ovarian cysts	5	4 (80%)	1 (20%)
Serositis	4	3 (75%)	1 (25%)
No pathologic condition seen	19	14 (74%)	5 (26%)
Total	140	106 (76%)	34 (24%)

Goldstein DP, deCholnoky C, Emans SJ, et al. Laparoscopy in the diagnosis and management of pelvic pain in adolescents. J Reprod Med 1980; 24:254.

ENDOMETRIOSIS

As noted in Tables 8-5 and 8-6, endometriosis is the most common pelvic pathology in adolescents with chronic pelvic pain who do not have a history of pelvic inflammatory disease. The history usually reveals cyclic and acyclic pelvic pain, with the most severe symptoms just before and during the menses. In our clinic, 64 percent of adolescents with endometriosis had cyclic pain and 36 percent acyclic pain [5]. Some patients also experience an increase in symptoms at midcycle. The pain tends to increase in severity over time and may occur throughout the month. Although oral contraceptives and antiprostaglandin medications may give some initial relief, the pain is usually not totally relieved and begins to increase in intensity with subsequent cycles. Other symptoms include dyspareunia, painful defecation (sometimes with bloody stools during menstruation), premenstrual staining (often brown or prune colored) and irregular bleeding, suprapubic pain, dysuria, hematuria, and infertility. In our clinic, 28 percent of adolescents with endometriosis had abnormal bleeding, 25 percent dyspareunia, and 21 percent gastrointestinal symptoms [5]. Most adolescents with diagnosed endometriosis present with symptoms of pain, although adult women may be asymptomatic and be detected because of evaluation for infertility. The cause of the pain seems to be related to prostaglandin release and may be incapacitating in patients with both mild and extensive disease. Swelling and bleeding within the implants in response to cyclic hormone production may cause discomfort.

Pelvic examination in the adult woman with endometriosis classi-
cally reveals tender nodules in the posterior vaginal fornix and along
the uterosacral ligaments. The ovary may be involved with an endometrioma or dense periovarian adhesions, and the uterus may be
fixed and retrodisplaced. In contrast, adolescents with endometriosis
often have only mild to moderate tenderness (without nodularity or
masses) on examination. Among our patients diagnosed with endometriosis, 20 to 30 percent have a normal pelvic examination at initial
assessment. In adolescents, an abnormal examination is most easily
elicited in the late luteal phase of the cycle. Importantly, the pelvic
examination most frequently reveals tenderness rather than nodules
or masses.

Patients may have a mother or sister with endometriosis. Simpson
and associates [6] reported a 6.9 percent rate of endometriosis in
first-degree relatives of women with the disease compared to only 1
percent of control relatives. Although previously thought of as a diagnosis only in women from 30 to 50 years of age, endometriosis clearly
occurs in the adolescent, especially the older adolescent. As noted in
Table 8-6, endometriosis among patients complaining of chronic
pelvic pain increases with age, from 12 percent in the 11- to 13-year-
old group to 54 percent in the 20- to 21-year-old group. The origin of
endometriosis is disputed and includes retrograde menstruation,
congenital rests of endometrial tissue, and spread of endometrial cells
hematogeneously and through the lymphatic system (sometimes to
distant sites including lungs, skin, thigh, extremities and bowel).
Factors such as shorter cycle lengths, longer duration of flow, and
possibly heavier flow in women with endometriosis compared to
control women lend credence to the hypothesis that retrograde menstruation is primarily responsible for endometriosis [7]. In addition,
endometriosis is particularly common at the site of entry from the
tubes into the peritoneal cavity (the fallopian tube ostia) and the
adjacent structures (ovary and uterosacral ligament at the base of
the broad ligament) and in fixed structures [8]. Jenkins and co-
workers [9] have noted that endometriosis of the anterior compartment (anterior cul-de-sac, anterior broad ligament, and anterior
uterine serosa) was more common in patients with anterior uteri
(41%) than in patients with posterior uteri (12%), again supporting
the hypothesis of retrograde menstruation and the position of the
uterus in determining the location of endometriosis. Since endometrial tissue is dependent on hormones for growth, the ovary is an
optimal site and is, in fact, the most common single site of endometriosis [9]. Given that retrograde menstruation commonly occurs as
noted at the time of laparoscopy in menstruating women and in the
peritoneal dialysates of menstruating women with renal failure, the
extent of the reflux may be different or immunologic responses may

be variable in women developing endometriosis from those free of the disease. Women with endometriosis are more likely to have a history of severe cramps; whether the greater uterine contractility predisposes these patients to endometriosis or whether the cramps are secondary to the early development of endometriosis is unanswered. Former intrauterine device (IUD) use is also a risk factor for endometriosis, possibly because of retrograde menstruation from increased flow [10]. The role of endogenous estrogens is also under study. Smokers who began their habit before age 17 years and smoked a pack or more a day have a lower risk of endometriosis, possibly because of lower estrogen levels [7]. Regular strenuous exercise may also lower the risk of endometriosis.

The diagnosis of endometriosis must be established by laparoscopy and biopsy. Treatment with potent drugs should not be undertaken without a firm diagnosis. Endometriosis is staged using the criteria of the American Fertility Society, which is based on a point system (Fig. 8-2) [11]. Most adolescents have stage I implants; however, adolescents with obstructing genital tract malformations often have severe endometriosis classified as stage III or IV, even in early adolescence. Implants have also been categorized on the basis of morphologic appearance: red, petechial implants; reddish brown, intermediate implants; and dark brown, "powder burn" implants. Because petechial implants produce the most prostaglandins, they may be especially prone to cause symptoms. The implants seen in adolescents may not be typical of the lesions seen in adult women, and thus biopsies can help to confirm the diagnosis. Adolescents may have pearly granular punctations (so-called white implants) of the pelvic peritoneum or small hemorrhagic or petechial spots. The earliest sign is hemosiderin staining of the peritoneal surfaces in dependent areas of the pelvis [8]. Scarring around the endometrial implants occurs later and can result in adhesions. In the ovary, large endometrial cysts can develop, so-called endometriomas or "chocolate cysts," probably at the site of the postovulatory corpus luteum [8].

The importance of finding endometriosis early lies not only in the relief of symptoms but also, hopefully, in the preservation of reproductive potential. The optimal therapy for adolescents and adult women with endometriosis is still debated. The patient needs to understand the pros and cons of each surgical and medical option and that recurrence of endometriosis is common. Adolescents need to know that studies in adult women have not shown increased infertility in patients with minimal or mild endometriosis.

The basis of medical therapy for pain is to take advantage of the reliance of endometrial tissue on steroid hormones for growth and function. One strategy is to create an acyclic, low-estrogen environ-

THE AMERICAN FERTILITY SOCIETY
REVISED CLASSIFICATION OF ENDOMETRIOSIS

Patient's Name _____ Date _____

Stage I (Minimal) - 1-5
Stage II (Mild) - 6-15
Stage III (Moderate) - 16-40
Stage IV (Severe) - >40
Total_____

Laparoscopy_____ Laparotomy_____ Photography_____
Recommended Treatment_____
_____
Prognosis_____

PERITONEUM	ENDOMETRIOSIS		<1cm	1-3cm	>3cm
	Superficial		1	2	4
	Deep		2	4	6
OVARY	R	Superficial	1	2	4
		Deep	4	16	20
	L	Superficial	1	2	4
		Deep	4	16	20

	POSTERIOR CULDESAC OBLITERATION	Partial	Complete
		4	40

	ADHESIONS		<1/3 Enclosure	1/3-2/3 Enclosure	>2/3 Enclosure
OVARY	R	Filmy	1	2	4
		Dense	4	8	16
	L	Filmy	1	2	4
		Dense	4	8	16
TUBE	R	Filmy	1	2	4
		Dense	4*	8*	16
	L	Filmy	1	2	4
		Dense	4*	8*	16

*If the fimbriated end of the fallopian tube is completely enclosed, change the point assignment to 16.

Additional Endometriosis: _____   Associated Pathology: _____
_____   _____
_____   _____
_____   _____

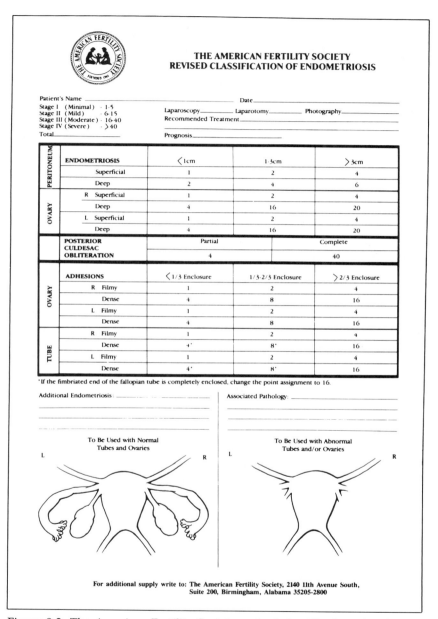

To Be Used with Normal Tubes and Ovaries

To Be Used with Abnormal Tubes and/or Ovaries

L   R   L   R

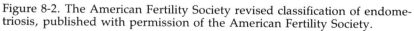

For additional supply write to: The American Fertility Society, 2140 11th Avenue South, Suite 200, Birmingham, Alabama 35205-2800

Figure 8-2. The American Fertility Society revised classification of endometriosis, published with permission of the American Fertility Society.

ment to prevent bleeding in the implants and to prevent additional seeding of the pelvis during retrograde menstruation [12]. In recent studies this goal has been pursued by the use of gonadotropin releasing hormone (GnRH) agonists, similar to the use in precocious puberty, to produce a low-estrogen state. The side effects include menopausal symptoms such as hot flashes, vaginal dryness, and decreased libido [13, 14]. The most worrisome possibility of GnRH analogue therapy is decreased bone density, which may be reversible on cessation of therapy. Daily medroxyprogesterone may lessen the menopausal symptoms; research is needed to find potential therapies for maintaining bone density with a hypoestrogenic environment. Thus, the place of GnRH agonists in the 1990s is as yet unknown.

Another strategy is to produce a high androgen state with androgens or synthetic progestins (with androgenic properties) to produce atrophy of endometriotic implants. This strategy also results in an acyclic low-estrogen state by interrupting ovarian follicular development [12, 14]. This goal can be accomplished by the use of danazol. Although danazol appears to be a very effective drug, many adolescents complain of the side effects including weight gain, edema, irregular menses, acne, oily skin, hirsutism, and a deep voice change. Other problems with this medication include decreased high-density lipoprotein (HDL) cholesterol, a mild increase in insulin resistance, alteration in liver proteins, and androgenic effects on the developing fetus (if the adolescent becomes pregnant while taking the drug). The drug should therefore be avoided in patients with hepatic dysfunction, severe hypertension, congestive heart failure, and borderline renal function. Danazol offers effective contraception at doses of 400 to 800 mg/day [12]; sexually active patients treated with less than 400 mg/day require additional methods of contraception. A 6-month course is commonly prescribed, but courses should be individualized. A 3-month course has been used preoperatively in patients with advanced endometriosis scheduled for surgery. The recurrence rate of symptoms and physical findings in patients treated with danazol is approximately 5 to 20 percent per year [12]. A prospective randomized study in adult women has failed to show that danazol was superior to placebo in improving pregnancy rates in women with minimal endometriosis [15], in agreement with a previous study [16]. A comparative trial of a GnRH agonist, nafarelin, administered by nasal spray, and oral danazol (800 mg/day) showed similar reduction in the extent of disease as assessed by laparoscopy, symptoms, and pregnancy rate [13]. Another 19-nortestosterone derivative, gestrinone, a progesterone agonist-antagonist and androgen agonist, appears to be effective in the treatment of endometriosis in European and U.S. studies, with side effects similar to those of danazol.

Daily oral progestins such as medroxyprogesterone acetate and intramuscular medroxyprogesterone acetate (Depo Provera) for 6 to 9 months can also be used [5, 17]. The principal complaint in adolescents is weight gain and irregular menses. "Pseudopregnancy" with continuous oral contraceptives for 9 to 12 months may exacerbate symptoms initially because of the swelling of implants secondary to the estrogen in the oral contraceptives but may with continued use give some patients relief of symptoms. A progestin-dominant pill such as Lo/Ovral can be initiated; the pill may be doubled or tripled or estrogen added if breakthrough bleeding occurs. Ortho-Novum 1/35 (Norinyl 1 + 35) and Loestrin 1/20 or 1.5/30 may be used similarly; triphasics are not suitable because of the change in progestin dose. The principal problems with the pseudopregnancy are headaches, fluid retention, nausea, weight gain, emotional lability, and hypertension.

In our clinic, most patients have fulguration of implants using laser (or electrocautery) and lysis of adhesions at the time of laparoscopy and are then placed on pseudopregnancy or danazol for 9 to 12 months or started immediately on cyclic oral contraceptives. If pseudopregnancy is prescribed, the patient is switched to cyclic oral contraceptives at the end of the course. Cyclic oral contraceptives are prescribed indefinitely with the hope that scantier menses will lessen the chance of recurrence. Danazol has also been used successfuly in some adolescents in our clinic. Therapy clearly needs to be individualized because adolescents are very conscious of side effects and will become noncompliant. Frequent appointments, support, and careful listening and response to concerns and questions are an important part of the medical care. It is important for the clinician to keep in mind other diagnoses in addition to the endometriosis such as irritable bowel syndrome, lactose intolerance, or psychological issues in the adolescent with persistent pain. Large endometriomas need to be excised followed by ovarian reconstruction. In persistent cases, conservative laparotomy with fulguration of implants, lysis of adhesions, presacral neurectomy and uterine suspension is performed.

Future developments in the treatment of endometriosis may be able to take advantage of the protein growth factors that regulate the epithelial and stromal elements of the endometrium. Modulation of the immune system, which may possibly play a critical role in pain, scarring, and infertility, may offer another method of treating endometriosis. Some adult women with stage II, III, and IV endometriosis have elevated levels of serum CA-125, and this marker may provide a potential means for following treatment (the sensitivity of the test is too low for detection of early endometriosis) [12, 18, 19]. Studies have not been done in adolescents (usually with stage I endometriosis).

UTERINE AND VAGINAL MALFORMATIONS WITH OBSTRUCTION

Uterine and vaginal malformation may come to the attention of the clinician because of acute or chronic pelvic pain, abnormal vaginal bleeding, or foul-smelling vaginal discharge (often worsened at the time of menses). Between 1970 and 1986, 27 patients presented to The Children's Hospital with obstructing malformations [20, 21]. The anatomy of the first 16 patients is shown in Figure 8-3, and a patient presenting with an obstructed hemivagina is shown in Figure 8-4. Patients 1, 2, 3, and 4 had obstruction at the level of the uterus. Patients 5 through 11 had vaginal obstruction; patient 11 had a pinhole opening in a transverse vaginal septum that did not allow menstrual drainage. Patients 12 through 16 had combined uterine and vaginal obstruction. Patients 14 through 16 had complex malformations with a normal-appearing cervix on speculum examination and an occult fistula-like cervix that could not be visualized or sounded without an anesthesia examination. Each of these girls had a unilateral vaginal pouch with a small fistula draining the pouch. Patient 16 also had an obstructed right uterine horn.

Of the total 27 patients, 20 were postmenarcheal with a mean menarchal age of 12.3 years. The mean age of the onset of symptoms was 13.6 years, and the average age of diagnosis was 14.4 years. Pelvic pain was present in 63 percent of patients, abnormal bleeding (frequently thought to be dysfunctional bleeding) was present in 26 percent, purulent discharge in 15 percent, urinary tract symptoms in 15 percent, and the inability to use tampons in 4 percent. Two patients were detected early because of known unilateral renal agenesis. On examination, 63 percent of the patients had a pelvic mass detected, and 4 patients had absence of the vaginal canal [21].

Other anomalies were common in these girls. Renal anomalies were frequent, with ipsilateral renal agenesis most common. Of the patients with an obstructed uterus, 33 percent had a double collecting system. Of the patients with vaginal obstruction, 67 percent had unilateral renal agenesis. Of the patients with combined uterine and vaginal obstruction, 83 percent had unilateral renal agenesis. Other extragenital malformations included orthopedic (11%) with congenital scoliosis and limb bud deformity, congenital heart disease, imperforate anus, and other urologic abnormalities. Fourteen of the 27 (52%) had endometriosis, and an additional 2 patients had extensive adhesions. Associated anomalies have been noted in other series [22, 23, 24].

Treatment depends on the lesion. Ultrasonography, laparoscopy, careful examination under anesthesia, and intraoperative hysterosalpingograms are useful in defining anatomy in these patients so that appropriate reconstruction can be carried out. Type I uterine obstructive abnormalities should be repaired by either metroplasty or removal of the blind horn, depending on the size of the horn and its condition. Since patients with a unicornuate uterus have an increased risk of premature labor, metroplasty may improve reproductive outcome, although no controlled studies of excision of the blind horn versus metroplasty have been done. Excision of the rudimentary blind horn will prevent endometriosis by eliminating reflux. Patients 5 through 8 had fenestration of the blind pouch using a wide incision to allow adequate drainage; because of distorted anatomy, a second procedure is often necessary. A hemihysterectomy and unilateral salpingo-oophorectomy were necessary in one of these girls because of extensive endometriosis and adhesions. Patients with a didelphic uterus usually have adequate reproductive outcomes and thus metroplasty is not necessary. Patient 9 was treated by excision of the transverse vaginal septum. Patient 10 was treated by creation of a neovagina and anastomosis to the cervix, and patient 11 with excision of the transverse vaginal septum. Patients with combined uterine and vaginal obstruction are difficult to diagnose and treat. Patients 12 and 13 were treated with hysterectomy. Although Farber [25] has reported success in a rare patient with cervical agenesis, infection and potential mortality from sepsis are significant risks because of recurring obstruction [20, 26]. Patients 14, 15, and 16 were treated with fenestration of the blind pouch and metroplasty, which is important to prevent future obstruction through the fistulous cervix.

Although rare, these entities are challenging and frequently missed in the early adolescent years because the complaints of pelvic pain, irregular bleeding, or vaginal discharge may be attributed to functional disturbances [20, 21, 27, 28]. The new classification of uterine anomalies by the American Fertility Society should allow for studies of the reproductive outcome of each type of anomaly and better information on prognosis for physicians and patients [28].

DYSMENORRHEA

Dysmenorrhea is probably the most common gynecologic complaint of adolescents. Analyzing data from the National Health Examination Survey for 12- to 17-year-old girls, Klein and Litt [29] found that 59.7 percent of 2,699 adolescents reported dysmenorrhea, and of those with dysmenorrhea, 14 percent frequently missed school because of cramps. In a survey of private school girls (mean age 15.5 ± 1.1 years) done by our clinic, dysmenorrhea was reported as mild by 32 percent, moderate by 15 percent, and severe by 6 percent [30]. Most dysmenorrhea in adolescents is primary (or functional), but as noted in the section Chronic Pelvic Pain, dysmenorrhea can be secondary to endometriosis, obstructing Müllerian anomalies, and other pelvic pathology.

In typical histories, the 14- or 15-year-old teenager, 1 to 3 years after

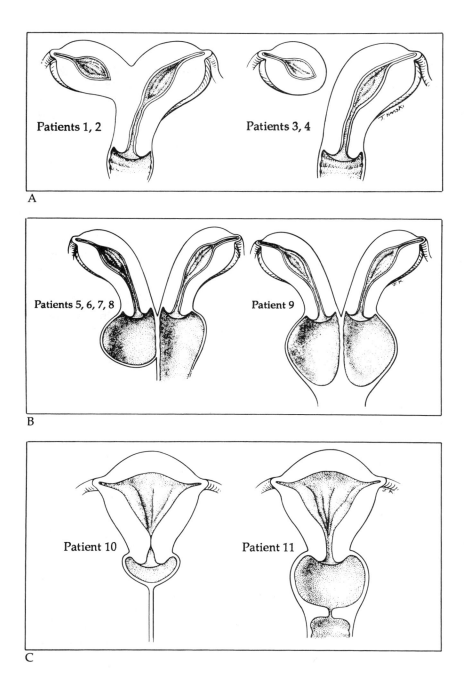

A

B

C

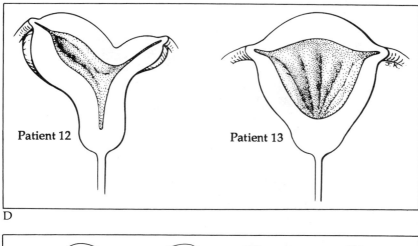

D

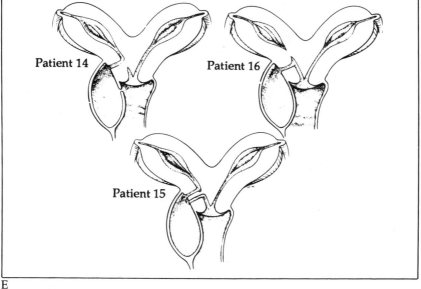

E

Figure 8-3. Obstructing malformations of the uterus and vagina. A. Type I: Uterine obstruction. B and C. Type II Vaginal obstruction B. with duplication, C. without duplication. D and E. Type III: Combined uterine and vaginal obstruction D. Cervix absent, E. Cervix present. (From O Pinsonneault and DP Goldstein, Obstructing malformations of the uterus and vagina. Fertil Steril. 44:241, 1985. Reproduced with permission of the publisher, The American Fertility Society.)

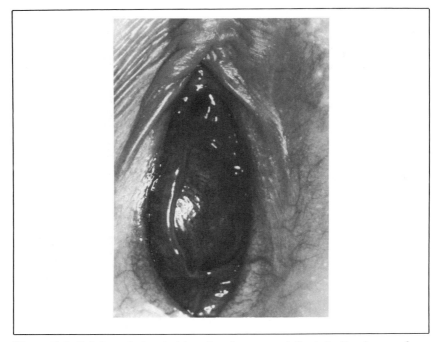

Figure 8-4. Bulging obstructed hemivagina seen at the introitus in an adolescent with pelvic pain.

menarche, begins to develop crampy lower abdominal pain with each menstrual period. Usually the pains start within 1 to 4 hours of the onset of the menses and last for 24 to 28 hours. In some cases, the pain may start 1 to 2 days before the menses and continue for 2 to 4 days into the menses. Nausea or vomiting (or both), diarrhea, lower backache, thigh pain, headache, fatigue, nervousness, dizziness, or rarely syncope may accompany the cramps. Although dysmenorrhea is usually associated with the onset of ovulatory menses, some adolescents may experience cramps from the first few cycles (which are often anovulatory) or with episodes of anovulatory dysfunctional bleeding associated with heavy menses and clots.

ETIOLOGY

Until recently, the etiology of primary dysmenorrhea was poorly understood. Pickles [31] was the first to suggest that dysmenorrhea might be related to a "menstrual stimulant" found in human menstrual fluid that induced smooth muscle contractions. In later studies, he found that the substance was a mixture of prostaglandins $F_{2\alpha}$ ($PGF_{2\alpha}$) and E_2 (PGE_2) [32, 33]. Menstrual fluid prostaglandin levels were several-fold higher in ovulatory compared to anovulatory cycles. Eglinton and associates [34] found that the endometrial content of $PGF_{2\alpha}$ and the ratio of $PGF_{2\alpha}$ to PGE_2 are higher during the secretory than during the follicular phase of the menstrual cycle. In 5 women with anovulatory cycles, endometrial $PGF_{2\alpha}$ content during the late part of the menstrual cycle was only 20 percent of that found in ovulatory patients [35]. Uterine jet washings, endometrial sampling, and collection of menstrual fluid have generally confirmed higher endometrial prostaglandin levels in women with primary dysmenorrhea than in those without symptoms [33, 36–39].

In the uterus, phospholipids from the dead cell membranes are converted to arachidonic acid, which can be metabolized by at least two enzymes: lipoxygenase, which begins the production of leukotrienes, and cyclo-oxygenase, which leads to cyclic endoperoxides (PGG_2 and PGH_2). The cyclic endoperoxides are then converted by specific enzymes to prostacyclin, thromboxanes, and the prostaglandins PGD_2, PGE_2, and $PGF_{2\alpha}$. Prostaglandin $PGF_{2\alpha}$ mediates pain sensation and stimulates smooth muscle contraction, whereas PGE_2 potentiates platelet disaggregation and vasodilatation [40]. Exogenously administered PGE_2 and $PGF_{2\alpha}$ can produce uterine contractions as well as systemic symptoms such as vomiting, diarrhea, and dizziness. Although plasma levels of prostaglandins are normal in dysmenorrheic women, increased sensitivity or generalized overproduction of prostaglandins may occur.

The prostaglandin hypothesis has been further strengthened by the observation that drugs that inhibit prostaglandin synthesis could relieve dysmenorrhea and the associated symptoms [40–50]. A number of clinical studies have found that nonsteroidal anti-inflammatory drugs (NSAIDs) are effective in the relief of pain. NSAID agents are divided into two classes: carboxylic acids and enolic acids. Enolic acid agents include phenylbutazone and piroxicam and act by inhibition of the isomerase/reductase step in the production of PGE_2 and $PGF_{2\alpha}$. Phenylbutazone is not prescribed in dysmenorrhea because of side effects, and piroxicam requires further studies to delineate its role in the therapy of this problem. The carboxylates, most frequently used in the treatment of dysmenorrhea, can be divided into four categories: salicylic acids/esters (aspirin, diflunisal), acetic acids (indomethacin, sulindac, tolmetin), propionic acids (ibuprofen, naproxen, fenoprofen, ketoprofen, flurbiprofen), and fenamates (mefenamic acid, meclofenamate, tolfenamic acid, flufenamic acid) [40]. The salicylic acids and esters appear to inhibit cyclo-oxygenase; but aspirin has little potency compared to some of the other NSAIDs in reducing prostaglandin synthesis and may increase menstrual flow [51]. Thus aspirin is used less often than previously in the treatment of dysmenorrhea. Indomethacin is the best known drug of the acetic acid group for treating dysmenorrhea, but side effects have prevented its use for most, if not all, patients. Thus the clinician selects chiefly from the two last groups, propionic acids and fenamates, for clinical treatment.

Ibuprofen and naproxen have been most widely studied for the relief of pain in dysmenorrhea. For examples, Chan and associates [42–44] correlated the relief of dysmenorrhea by ibuprofen with the reduction in menstrual prostaglandin release as measured by a method that can detect menstrual prostaglandin activity in tampon specimens. Total menstrual prostaglandin release per cycle fell from a control level of 59.8 ± 7.2 to 16.8 ± 2.3 (μg $PGF_{2\alpha}$ equivalents) with the use of ibuprofen [42]. Numerous clinical studies have found these agents to be effective in both adult and adolescent women, with pain relief in 67 to 86 percent of patients. The sodium salt of naproxen (Anaprox) has a more rapid absorption than naproxen and can give very rapid relief of symptoms. The newly released prostaglandin inhibitor flurbiprofen (ANSAID), at doses of 50 mg every 6 hours or 100 mg every 12 hours, also appears to be very effective in the relief of dysmenorrhea [52, 53].

The fenamates are potent inhibitors of prostaglandin synthesis and in addition can antagonize the action of already formed prostaglandins [49, 50]. This increased activity may give this class of drug a theoretic advantage in treatment, although comparative controlled drug trials are not available for reaching a conclusion. A trial of mefenamic acid (Ponstel) is useful when propionic acids are ineffective in the individual patient. Recent clinical studies of meclofenamate (Meclomen) have shown effectiveness [54, 55]; this drug also inhibits the activity of 5-lipoxygenase, but the clinical importance of the inhibition of leukotrienes is unknown.

Oral contraceptives lessen dysmenorrhea, probably in part related to their anti-ovulatory actions as well as their ability to produce endometrial hypoplasia, less menstrual flow, and subsequently less prostaglandins [42].

With the advent of the research on prostaglandins as the cause of dysmenorrhea, the potential influence of psychological issues on dysmenorrhea has received little attention. However, in a study of adolescents treated for dysmenorrhea with naproxen sodium therapy (Anaprox), DuRant and colleagues [56] made the interesting observation that girls with increased life crisis events experienced greater symptom severity in the first month of therapy than other girls. It is possible that prostaglandins may increase in response to physical and psychological stress or that the patient may be more keenly aware of pain when distressed by other problems in her life. As therapy was continued, life stress ceased to have a significant influence on severity of dysmenorrhea symptoms. Those with persistent symptoms, however, did have lower self-concept at follow-up, perhaps because of their initial high expectation of receiving relief.

PATIENT ASSESSMENT

In assessing the adolescent with dysmenorrhea, the physician needs to know the patient's menstrual history, timing of the cramps, and premenstrual symptoms, as well as her response to the cramps. Key questions would be as follows: Is she missing school? If so, how many days? Does she miss other activities? A party? Does she have nausea and vomiting, diarrhea, or dizziness? What medications has she used before? What is the nature of the mother-daughter interaction? Did the mother or sister have cramps? Is there a family history of endometriosis? Girls with disability from cramps out of proportion to the apparent severity may have school phobia, a prior episode of sexual abuse, or significant psychosocial problems. The questions about previous medications are particularly crucial because with the availability of ibuprofen over-the-counter, many adolescents have tried this medication in subtherapeutic doses and have subsequently discarded the usefulness of ibuprofen.

For the virginal girl of 13 or 14 years who has mild cramps the first day of her menses, a normal physical examination, including inspection of the genitalia to exclude an abnormality of the hymen, is reassuring. It is not necessary to do a speculum examination. Treatment includes a careful explanation to the patient of the nature of the problem and a chance for her to ask questions regarding her anatomy. Mild analgesics, such as aspirin, acetaminophen, and especially over-the-counter ibuprofen (Advil, Nuprin, Midol 200 in doses of one to two 200-mg tablets) usually give symptomatic relief.

Adolescent girls with moderate or severe dysmenorrhea should have a careful pelvic examination. In the majority of adolescents who are carefully prepared, a vaginal examination is atraumatic. In some patients, a rectoabdominal examination in the lithotomy position is all that is possible, but even this will exclude adnexal tenderness and masses. The uterosacral ligaments should be palpated carefully for tenderness or the presence of nodules, which would suggest endometriosis. Ultrasonography is useful in defining suspected uterine and vaginal anomalies with obstruction but will not detect abnormalities such as adhesions or endometriosis.

TREATMENT

If the examination is normal, treatment should be directed at symptomatic relief. The most common approach is to prescribe one of the NSAID compounds: naproxen sodium (Anaprox), 550 mg given immediately and then 275 mg every 6 hours; naproxen sodium double-strength (Anaprox DS), 500 mg twice a day; naproxen (Naprosyn), 250 to 375 mg 2 to 3 times a day; ibuprofen, 400 mg every 4 to 6 hours to 800 mg 3 times a day (with a loading dose of 800–1200 mg); or mefenamic acid (Ponstel), 500 mg given immediately and then 250 mg every 6 hours. As noted previously, flurbiprofen (50 mg every 6 hours or 100 mg 2 to 3 times daily) and meclofenamate (100 mg initially, followed by 50 to 100 mg every 6 hours) are also promising but more expensive than ibuprofen.

For most patients, effective relief can be obtained by starting the antiprostaglandin medicine at the onset of the menses and continuing for the first 1 to 2 days of the cycle (or for the usual duration of cramps). The patient should be told to start as soon as she knows her menses are coming—"the first sign of cramps or bleeding." A loading dose is important in patients with symptoms that are severe and occur rapidly. In this situation, a rapidly absorbed drug such as Anaprox would be preferable. Generally, giving the medicine at the onset of the menses prevents the inadvertent administration of the drug to a pregnant woman. However, a non–sexually active patient with severe cramps accompanied by early vomiting (and thus the inability to take medication) may often benefit from starting the drug 1 or 2 days before the onset of her menses. A patient may respond to a higher dose or to another NSAID. Since life stresses may lessen the pain relief in the first cycle, the determination of effectiveness in an individual patient should be based on the response in more than one cycle. Usually medication is prescribed for two to three cycles before changing. In addition, a patient may have taken inadequate doses of a medicine previously, particularly ibuprofen, to obtain relief.

The NSAID compounds should be avoided in preoperative patients and patients with known or suspected ulcer disease, gastrointestinal bleeding, clotting disorders (because of effects on platelet aggregation), renal disease, allergies to aspirin or NSAIDs, or aspirin-induced asthma. All the NSAIDs should be taken with food, even though some patients prefer liquids on the first day of the cycle. The side effects of these drugs appear minimal in short-term use, but the possibility of allergy and gastrointestinal irritation and bleeding should be explained to the patient. Some patients complain of fluid retention or fatigue with the use of these agents.

In some patients, NSAID drugs are contraindicated or produce undesirable side effects. In these girls, acetaminophen can be prescribed, often combined with 15 to 30 mg of codeine. Usually only a few pills are needed each month. However, adolescents may complain of dizziness and nausea with codeine-containing medications.

The adolescent should be seen initially every 3 or 4 months to evaluate the effectiveness of the medication. Such visits also facilitate the doctor-patient rapport that is essential in the treatment of this problem. Although a few adolescents will use cramps as an excuse to stay out of school or to gain sympathy from their parents, patients should not be made to feel emotionally unstable because they complain of cramps. Some girls can continue to exercise during their menses; others find the discomfort may be too great on the first day. It is likely that girls who are involved in competitive sports and who have fewer ovulatory menses have less dysmenorrhea.

If the patient fails to respond to antiprostaglandin drugs and continues to have severe pain or vomiting or at initial evaluation needs birth control, a course of oral contraceptives (e.g., Norinyl 1+35, Ortho-Novum 1/35, Triphasil/TriLevelen, Tri-Norinyl, Ortho-Novum 7/7/7) should be tried. A pelvic examination is necessary before this medication is prescribed. Cramps are usually substantially, if not completely, relieved with the anovulatory cycles and scantier flow. If severe cramps persist despite three to four cycles of ovulation suppression therapy or the examination reveals tenderness or nodularity, laparoscopy is indicated to exclude endometriosis or other organic causes.

If dysmenorrhea is relieved by oral contraceptive pills, medication is usually prescribed for 3 to 6 months and then discontinued (frequently during the summer when school attendance will not be disrupted). Often the patient will continue to have relief from cramps for several additional (commonly anovulatory) cycles before the more severe dysmenorrhea recurs. When the cramps recur, a trial of other antiprostaglandin drugs should again be attempted before reinstituting oral contraceptives. The sexually active adolescent with severe dysmenorrhea usually prefers to continue long-term on oral contraceptives. The return of increasingly severe dysmenorrhea in spite of continued use of oral contraceptives raises the possibility of organic disease such as endometriosis and calls for a reevaluation and consideration of laparoscopy for diagnosis.

PREMENSTRUAL SYMPTOMS
Premenstrual symptoms are commonly reported by adolescents and adult women and include bloating, weight gain, breast soreness, hunger, thirst, fatigue, acne, constipation, hot flashes and chills, difficulty concentrating, and mood change (irritability or depression) in the luteal phase of the cycle [57–59]. Girls with migraine headaches may suffer an increase in headaches premenstrually and with menses; similarly, girls with epilepsy may note an increase in seizure severity and/or frequency premenstrually or with the onset of menses. Retarded girls may have behavior outbursts that are difficult for their caretakers, and psychotic patients may exhibit more uncontrollable actions. Although most adolescents are aware of some pre-

menstrual symptoms, active listening, reassurance, and a few suggestions about diet and exercise are usually sufficient. Adolescents who experience severe symptoms often are under stress and have other psychosocial issues that need to be addressed, not just with medical evaluation of the premenstrual symptoms, but also with psychological counselling. About 20 to 40 percent of adult women of reproductive age have sufficiently bothersome symptoms to cause a temporary deterioration in interpersonal relationships or job effectiveness; less than 5 percent of adult women have severe symptoms [57, 60].

The cause of premenstrual syndrome (PMS) has been variously attributed to estrogen and progesterone because of the occurrence of these symptoms in the luteal phase of the cycle and the disappearance when ovulation is inhibited with the use of GnRH agonists [61]. Although several forms of progesterone have been prescribed for treatment, double-blind studies have not demonstrated efficacy for this approach [62]. In fact, a recent study has suggested that higher adverse premenstrual scores occurred in menstrual cycles with high luteal phase plasma progesterone and estradiol concentrations [63]. Other studies have not detected a difference in hormone levels between women with a mood disorder of premenstrual syndrome and those without symptoms [64].

Reid and Yen [65] have proposed a hypothesis that endogenous opiates may trigger the symptoms. In an assessment of the pattern of symptoms, Reid [66] has attributed the changes in the 2 weeks before menses—breast swelling and tenderness, lower abdominal bloating, and constipation—to the production of endogenous central, and perhaps peripheral, opiates. Since weight may not increase in spite of bloating, changes that the patient notes may occur because of local fluid shifts and bowel wall edema. The release of the opiates may also increase appetite and result in unusual food cravings as well as fatigue, depression, and emotional lability. Later in the cycle the shift toward anxiety and irritability, vague abdominal cramps with loose bowel movements or diarrhea, headaches, chills, and sweats may result from withdrawal of endogenous opiates as hormone levels fall. In sensitive women, cyclic exposure to and subsequent withdrawal from the central effects of the neuropeptides may result in a cascade of neuroendocrine changes that cause clinical symptomatology. Support for this hypothesis has come from animal experiments, the observation of the effects of opiates on nonaddicts and the consequences of withdrawal in addicts, and the improvement in symptoms with the administration of opiate antagonists [67].

In the next decade, therapeutic approaches to premenstrual syndrome may be improved by increased understanding of the pathophysiology and the interaction of biologic and psychological factors. Biologic factors that cause premenstrual syndrome may be influenced by personal psychological and social factors [59]. Alteration of the ovulatory menstrual cycle can alleviate symptoms. GnRH agonists can prevent the cyclic progesterone and estrogen production; however, this approach may be more useful as a probe in defining the etiology of the problem than as a long-term treatment because of the potential for osteoporosis in estrogen-deficient patients. Preventing ovulation but allowing some estrogen secretion might protect the bones from osteoporosis but would potentially place the endometrium at risk of unopposed estrogen and carcinoma. Danazol may inhibit ovulation but is likely to have undesirable side effects in adolescents. Although oral contraceptives have given variable results in adult women with premenstrual syndrome, many adolescents, especially those with premenstrual exacerbation of seizures or headaches, show striking improvement on pills with 30 to 35 μg of estrogen and a medium dose of progestin. Administration of an oral opiate antagonist such as naltrexone [67] appears to be a promising experimental approach. Preliminary clinical studies are underway; however, until side effects are better known, these drugs will be most useful in elucidating the pathogenesis of this disorder. Much more needs to be learned before drugs have a major role in the treatment of premenstrual syndrome in adolescents.

For most adolescents, premenstrual symptoms are mild and the recognition that they are a real entity can be reassuring. For those troubled by their symptoms, the cyclic occurrence should be established by recording symptoms on a special calendar for two to three cycles (many are in use by PMS clinics) [59]. Otherwise mood alterations and depression occurring throughout the cycle may be attributed to "premenstrual syndrome" and adequate psychological intervention not undertaken. A calendar is also useful in deciding which symptoms are most troubling to the patient. Although no controlled studies have demonstrated benefit in diet or exercise, most centers start with this approach because the life-style changes are healthy and undoubtedly give the adolescent a sense of control over her life. Patients are instructed to avoid salty foods, alcohol, caffeine, chocolate, and concentrated sweets and to eat four to six smaller meals per day during the premenstrual period. A written sheet with foods to avoid (e.g., cola, coffee, hot dogs, canned foods, chips) and to add to the diet (e.g., unsalted popcorn, raw vegetables and fruits, skim milk, complex carbohydrates, high-fiber foods, low-fat meats) is helpful to the young woman. A program of aerobic exercise should be strongly encouraged, and areas of stress should be identified. Stress reduction programs such as biofeedback or self-hypnosis may be helpful. Many patients experience an increased sense of well-being and control with a program of improved nutrition, exercise, and stress management.

Drug therapy may be considered in adolescents with significant symptoms that have not responded to nonpharmacologic management. The physician or nurse-clinician should realize that most drug trials are hampered by the definition of premenstrual syndrome, the sample size, and the strong placebo effect. In addition, adolescents are often at risk of unprotected intercourse and pregnancy, and many of the medications should not be prescribed to potentially pregnant teenagers. In addition, although many patients complain of weight gain, actual daily measurements may reveal no change; rather fluid shifts and bowel wall edema may result in the symptomatology. For true edema and weight gain from fluid retention, a mild diuretic such as chlorothiazide, 250 to 500 mg once or twice daily during the last week of the cycle (plus supplemental potassium by diet), or spironolactone can be given. Although diuretics are often prescribed, they are frequently ineffective.

Mefenamic acid (Ponstel, 250 mg every 8 hours starting on day 16 of the cycle, increased to 500 mg on day 19 of the cycle) has been shown in one small study of 15 women with premenstrual syndrome to improve fatigue, headache, and general aches and pains; this medication may be especially useful in those patients with severe dysmenorrhea as well [68]. Other nonsteroidal anti-inflammatory drugs (NSAIDs) used in treating dysmenorrhea (see p. 297) may be similarly useful, but none of these should be prescribed to the adolescent at risk of pregnancy. Oral contraceptives may be effective in adolescent girls and are especially useful if birth control is also needed.

A variety of other drugs have been used in adult women, but none of the studies has focused on adolescents. For example, low-dose danazol (200–400 mg/day) has appeared beneficial in a small study [69]; however, reliable contraception is needed at doses of less than 400 mg/day. Alprazolam (0.25 mg 3 times daily from day 20 until the second day of menstruation and then tapered by one tablet per day) relieved premenstrual symptoms in a double-blind study of women with premenstrual syndrome [70], but concern about patients' becoming dependent on this drug and having withdrawal symptoms has made us reluctant to use this type of drug in adolescents. Bromocriptine has been used in adult women to alleviate breast soreness, but this symptom is rarely a major complaint of adolescents. In adolescents with breast soreness, we prefer to suggest reducing caffeine consumption and prescribe a small dose of NSAIDs. The plethora of drugs shown to be effective in small studies suggests that more data are clearly needed to document efficacy before exposing adolescents to the potential risks of these medications. In addition, adolescents need to be questioned whether they are taking over-the-counter medications. Vitamin B_6 has been popular with some self-help groups. Studies of the efficacy have been conflicting, and a recent placebo-controlled study of 150 mg of vitamin B_6 found that while some premenstrual symptoms such as dizziness and behavioral symptoms were improved, most patients still experienced significant symptomatology [71]. In view of concern about the toxic potential of this vitamin even in low doses to cause sensory neuropathy, patients need to be cautioned about this indication.

Premenstrual exacerbation may occur in some rare medical conditions such as hepatic porphyria [72]. In addition, recent case reports have indicated that rare patients develop sensitivity to progesterone and may have hives or even life-threatening allergic reaction during the luteal phase (reversed by GnRH agonists or oophorectomy) [73, 74].

REFERENCES
1. Goldstein DP. Acute and chronic pelvic pain. Pediatr Clin North Am 1989; 365:573.
2. Hann LE, Hall DA, Black EB, et al. Mittleschmerz: Sonograph Demonstration. JAMA 1979; 241:2731.
3. Strickland DM, Hauth JC, and Strickland KM. Laparoscopy for chronic pelvic pain in adolescent women. Adolesc Pediatr Gynecol 1988; 1:31.
4. Goldstein DP, deCholnoky C, Emans SJ, et al. Laparoscopy in the diagnosis and management of pelvic pain in adolescents. J Reprod Med 1980; 24:251.
5. Goldstein DP, deCholnoky C, and Emans SJ. Adolescent endometriosis. J Adol Health Care 1980; 1:37.
6. Simpson JL, Elias S, Malinak LR, et al. Heritable aspects of endometriosis: I. Genetic studies. Am J Obstet Gynecol 1980; 137:327.
7. Cramer DW, Wilson L, Stillman RJ, et al. The relationship of endometriosis to menstrual characteristics, smoking, and exercise. JAMA 1985; 255:1904.
8. Haney AF. Endometriosis. Pathogenesis and Pathophysiology. In EA Wilson (ed.), Endometriosis. New York: Liss, 1987:23.
9. Jenkins S, Olive DL, and Haney AF. Endometriosis: Pathogenetic implications of the anatomic distribution. Obstet Gynecol 1986; 67:335.
10. Kirshon B, and Poindexter AN. Contraception: A risk factor for endometriosis. Obstet Gynecol 1988; 71:829.
11. American Fertility Society. American Fertility Society Classification of Endometriosis. Fertil Steril 1985; 43:351.
12. Barbieri RL (ed.), and Hornstein MD. Medical Therapy for Endometriosis. In EA Wilson, Endometriosis. New York: Liss, 1987:111.
13. Henzl MR, Corson SL, Moghissi K, et al. Administration of nasal nafarelin as compared with oral danazol for endometriosis. N Engl J Med 1988; 318:485.
14. Barbieri RL. New therapy for endometriosis. N Engl J Med 1988; 318:512.
15. Bayer SR, Seibel MM, Saffan DS, et al. Efficacy of danazol treatment for minimal endometriosis in infertile women. J Reprod Med 1988; 33:179.

16. Hull ME, Moghissi KS, Magyar DF, et al. Comparison of different treatment modalities of endometriosis in infertile women. Fertil Steril 1987; 47:40.
17. Luciano AA, Turksoy RN, and Carleo J. Evaluation of oral medroxyprogesterone acetate in the treatment of endometriosis. Obstet Gynecol 1988; 72:323.
18. Barbieri RL. CA-125 in patients with endometriosis. Fertil Steril 1986; 45:767.
19. Patton PE, Field CS, Harms RW, et al. CA-125 levels in endometriosis. Fertil Steril 1986; 45:770.
20. Pinsonneault O, and Goldstein DP. Obstructing malformations of the uterus and vagina. Fertil Steril 1985; 44:241.
21. Davis A, Pinsonneault O, and Goldstein DP. Congenital obstructive Müllerian malformations in 28 patients (in press).
22. Tran ATB, Arensman RM, and Falterman KW. Diagnosis and management of hydrohematometrocolpos syndrome. Am J Dis Child 1987; 141: 632.
23. Biedel CW, Pagon RA, and Zapata JO. Müllerian anomalies and renal agenesis: autosomal dominant urogenital dysplasia. J Pediatr 1984; 104: 861.
24. Horejsi J. Incomplete reduplication of internal genitalia and unilateral renal aplasia syndrome. Adolesc Pediatr Gynecol 1988; 1:42.
25. Farber M. Congenital atresia of the uterine cervix. Sem Reprod Endocrinol 1986; 4:33.
26. Niver DH, Barrette G, and Jewelewicz R. Congenital atresia of the uterine cervix and vagina: three cases. Fertil Steril 1980; 33:25.
27. Rock JA, and Jones HW. The clinical management of the double uterus. Fertil Steril 1977; 28:798.
28. Freeman MF. Uterine anomalies. Sem Reprod Endocrinol 1986; 4:39.
29. Klein JR, and Litt IF. Epidemiology of adolescent dysmenorrhea. Pediatrics 1981; 68:661.
30. Wilson C, Emans SJ, Mansfield J, et al. The relationship of calculated percent body fat, sports participation, age, and place of residence on menstrual patterns in healthy adolescent girls at an independent New England high school. J Adolesc Health Care 1984; 5:248.
31. Pickles VR. A plain muscle stimulant in the menstruum. Nature 1957; 180:1198.
32. Pickles VR, and Cletheroe HJ. Further studies of the menstrual stimulant. Lancet 1960; 2:959.
33. Pickles VR, Hall WJ, Best FA, et al. Prostaglandins in endometrium and menstrual fluid from normal and dysmenorrheic subjects. Br J Obstet Gynaecol 1965; 72:185.
34. Eglinton G, Raphael RA, Smith GN, et al. Isolation and identification of two smooth muscle stimulants from menstrual fluid. Nature 1963; 200:960.
35. Pickles VR. Prostaglandins in human endometrium. Int J Fertil 1967; 12: 335.
36. Downie J, Poyser NL, and Wunderlich M. Levels of prostaglandins in human endometrium during the normal menstrual cycle. J Physiol 1974; 236:465.
37. Demers L, Halbert DR, Jones PE, et al. Prostaglandin levels in endometrial jet wash specimens during normal cycles. Prostaglandins 1975; 10: 1057.
38. Halbert IR, Demers L, Fontana J, et al. Prostaglandin levels and endome-

trial jet wash specimens in patients with dysmenorrhea before and after indomethacin therapy. Prostaglandins 1975; 10:1047.

39. Ylikorkala O, and Dawood MY. New concepts in dysmenorrhea. Am J Obstet Gynecol 1978; 130:833.

40. Smith RP. Primary dysmenorrhea and the adolescent patient. Adolesc Pediatr Gynecol 1988; 1:23.

41. Alvin PE, and Litt IF. Current status of the etiology and management of dysmenorrhea in adolescence. Pediatrics 1982; 70:516.

42. Chan WY, Dawood MY, and Fuchs F. Prostaglandins in primary dysmenorrhea. Comparison of prophylactic and nonprophylactic treatment with ibuprofen and use of oral contraceptives. Am J Med 1981; 70:535.

43. Chan WY, and Hill JC. Determination of menstrual prostaglandin levels in non-dysmenorrheic and dysmenorrheic subjects. Prostaglandins 1978; 15:365.

44. Chan WY, Dawood MY, and Fuchs F. Relief of dysmenorrhea with the prostaglandin synthetase inhibitor ibuprofen: effect on prostaglandin levels in menstrual fluid. Am J Obstet Gynecol 1979; 135:102.

45. Henzl MR, Buttram V, Segre EJ, et al. The treatment of dysmenorrhea with naproxen sodium. Obstet Gynecol 1977; 127:818.

46. Pulkkinen MO, and Csapo AI. Effect of ibuprofen on menstrual blood prostaglandin levels in dysmenorrheic women. Prostaglandins 1979; 18:137.

47. Larkin RM, Van Arden DE, and Poulson AM. Dysmenorrhea: treatment with an anti-prostaglandin. Obstet Gynecol 1979; 54:456.

48. Corson SL, and Bolognese SL. Ibuprofen therapy for dysmenorrhea. J Reprod Med 1978; 20:246.

49. Budoff PW. Use of mefenamic acid in the treatment of primary dysmenorrhea. JAMA 1979; 241:2713.

50. Anderson AB, Fraser IS, Haynes PJ, et al. Trial of prostaglandin-synthetase inhibitors in primary dysmenorrhea. Lancet 1978; 1:345.

51. Klein JR, Litt IF, Rosenberg A, et al. The effect of aspirin on dysmenorrhea in adolescents. J Pediatr 1981; 98:987.

52. Kristna UR, Naik S, Mandlekar A, et al. Flurbiprofen in the treatment of primary dysmenorrhea. Br J Clin Pharmacol 1980; 9:605.

53. DeLia JE, Emery MD, Taylor RH, et al. Flurbiprofen in dysmenorrhea. Clin Pharmacol Ther 1982; 32:76.

54. Smith RP, and Powell JR. Simultaneous objective and subjective evaluation of meclofenamate sodium in the treatment of primary dysmenorrhea. Am J Obstet Gynecol 1987; 157:611.

55. Smith RP. The dynamics of nonsteroidal anti-inflammatory therapy for primary dysmenorrhea. Obstet Gynecol 1987; 70:785.

56. DuRant RH, Jay MS, Shoffitt T, et al. Factors influencing adolescents' responses to regimens of Naproxen for dysmenorrhea. Am J Dis Child 1985; 139:489.

57. Committee on Gynecologic Practice. Premenstrual Syndrome. ACOG Committee Opinion, No. 66, January 1989.

58. Fisher M, Trieller K, and Napolitano B. Premenstrual symptoms in adolescents. J Adolesc Health Care 1989; 10:369.

59. Keye W Jr (ed.), *The Premenstrual Syndrome.* Philadelphia: Saunders, 1988.

60. Johnson SR, McChesney C, Bean JA. Epidemiology of premenstrual symptoms in a nonclinical sample: 1. Prevalence, natural history and help-seeking behavior. J Reprod Med 1988; 33:340.

61. Muse KN, Cetel NS, Futterman LA, et al. The premenstrual syndrome: effects of "medical ovariectomy." N Engl J Med 1984; 311:1345.

62. Maddocks S, Hahn P, Moller F, et al. A double-blind placebo-controlled trial of progesterone vaginal suppositories in the treatment of premenstrual syndrome. Am J Obstet Gynecol 1986; 154:573.
63. Hammerback S, Damber JE, and Backstrom T. Relationship between symptom severity and hormone changes in women with premenstrual syndrome. J Clin Endocrinol Metab 1989; 68:125.
64. Rubinow DR, et al. Changes in plasma hormones across the menstrual cycle in patients with menstrually related mood disorder and in control subjects. Am J Obstet Gynecol 1988; 158:5.
65. Reid RL, and Yen SSC. Premenstrual syndrome. Am J Obstet Gynecol 1981; 139:85.
66. Reid RL. Endogenous opiate peptides and premenstrual syndrome. Semin Reprod Endocrinol 1987; 5:191.
67. Chuong CJ, Coulam CB, Bergstralh, et al. Clinical trial of naltrexone in premenstrual syndrome. Obstet Gynecol 1988; 72:332.
68. Mira M, NcNeil D, Fraser IS, et al. Mefenamic acid in the treatment of premenstrual syndrome. Obstet Gynecol 1986; 68:395.
69. Sarno AP, Miller EJ Jr, and Lundblad EG. Premenstrual syndrome: beneficial effects of periodic, low-dose danazol. Obstet Gynecol 1987; 70:33.
70. Smith S, Rinehart JS, Ruddock VE, et al. Treatment of premenstrual syndrome with alprazolam: Results of a double-blind, placebo-controlled, randomized crossover clinical trial. Obstet Gynecol 1987; 70:37.
71. Kendall KE, and Schnurr PP. The effects of vitamin B_6 supplementation on premenstrual symptoms. Obstet Gynecol 1987; 70:145.
72. Bargetzi MJ, Meyer UA, and Birkhaeuser MH. Premenstrual exacerbations in hepatic porphyria: prevention by intermittent administration of an LH-RH agonist in combination with a gestagen. JAMA 1989; 261:864.
73. Slater JE. Recurrent anaphylaxis in menstruating women: Treatment with a luteinizing hormone-releasing hormone agonist: A preliminary report. Obstet Gynecol 1987; 70:542.
74. Meggs WJ, Pescovitz OH, Metcalfe D, et al. Progesterone sensitivity as a cause of recurrent anaphylaxis. N Engl J Med 1984; 311:1236.

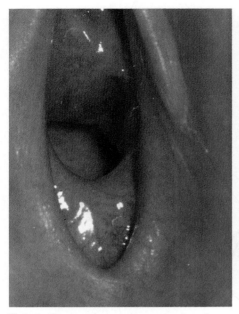

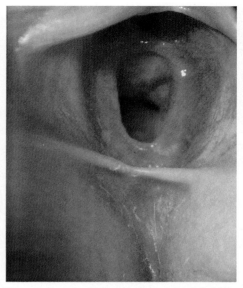

Plate 2. Annular hymen in a prepubertal child.

Plate 1. Crescent hymen in a prepubertal child.

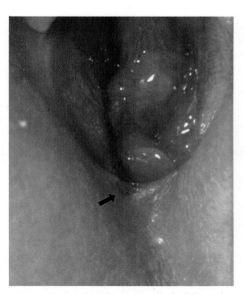

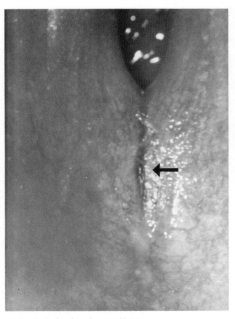

Plate 3. Redundant hymen with friability of the posterior forchette (*arrow*) with separation of the labia to visualize the hymen.

Plate 4. Labial/vulvar adhesion.

Plate 1 from SJ Emans. Vulvovaginitis in the child and adolescent. *Pediatr in Rev* 1986;8:12. By permission.

Plates 8, 10, and 13 are from SJ Emans, et al. Genital findings in sexually abused, symptomatic and asymptomatic girls. *Pediatrics* 1987;79:778. By permission.

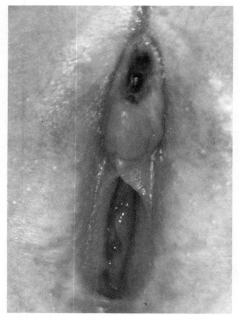

Plate 5. Lichen sclerosis with white epithelium, ecchymoses, and fissures.

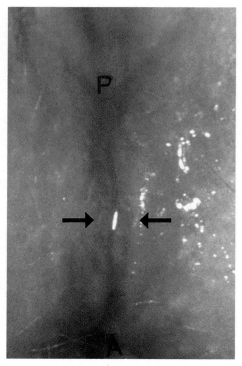

Plate 6. Failure of midline fusion (*arrows*) between the posterior forchette (*P*) and the anus (*A*).

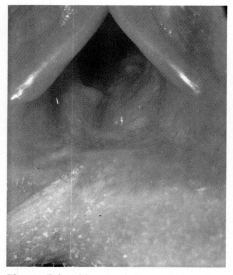

Plate 7. Dilated hymenal ring and laceration of the hymen at 6 o'clock in a 9-month-old sexually and physically abused infant.

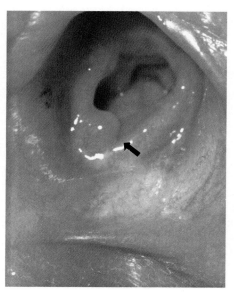

Plate 8. Incomplete tear of the hymen at 6 o'clock (*arrow*) with adjacent "bump" in a 3-year-old child with a history of sexual abuse and insertion of a magic marker 4 days before the examination.

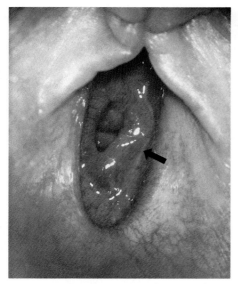

Plate 9. Edema of the hymen from 1 o'clock to 6 o'clock (*arrow*) in a 3½-year-old with a stick inserted within the vagina 2 weeks previously, causing vaginal bleeding.

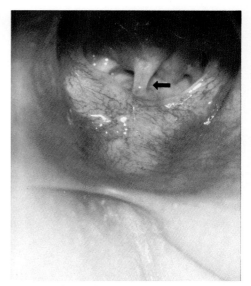

Plate 10. Threadlike adhesion (*arrow*) between the anterior and posterior vaginal walls in a child with a previous history of sexual abuse and insertion of objects within the vagina.

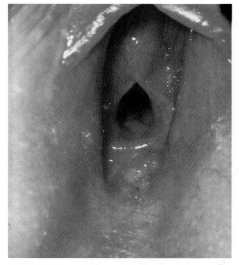

Plate 11. Rounding and scarring of the lower hymenal border with an adhesion from the hymen to the vagina in a 5-year-old girl with chronic sexual abuse.

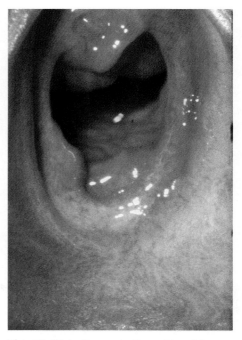

Plate 12. Distortion and attenuation of the lower hymenal border with an adhesion between the hymen and vagina in a sexually abused 4-year-old girl (her 2½-year-old sister was the index case with *N. gonorrhoeae* vaginitis).

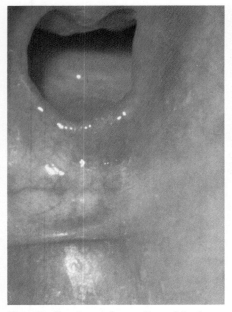

Plate 13. Scarring and rounding of the lower half of the hymen with an adhesion between the hymen and vagina at 5 o'clock in a 9-year-old girl with a 2-year history of chronic sexual abuse.

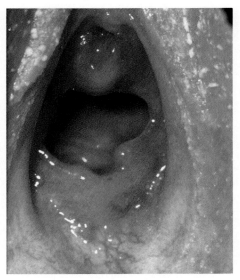

Plate 14. Rounded and distorted lower hymenal border with an indentation at 6 o'clock with two adjacent "bumps" in an 11-year-old girl with a long history of sexual abuse.

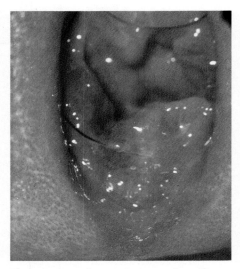

Plate 15. Acute hymenal tears and small hemorrhages at 4 and 8 o'clock in a 12-year-old rape victim, examined 3 days after the assault.

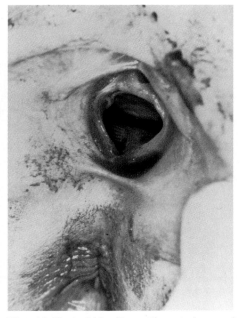

Plate 16. Vaginal bleeding with acute hymenal laceration at 6 o'clock. This finding should prompt an evaluation for sexual abuse.

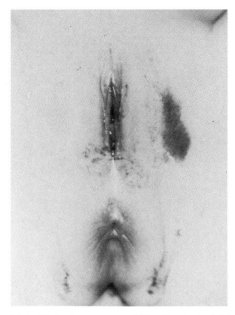

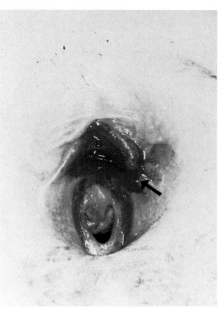

Plate 17. Ecchymoses and bleeding in a child following a straddle injury. **A.** Perineum.

B. Close-up of the vulva with laceration by the labia minora and periurethral tissues (*arrow*). (Note the normal hymen.)

9. Vulvovaginal Complaints in the Adolescent

In the adolescent, vaginitis represents a common gynecologic problem despite the fact that the adolescent has developed a more resistant, estrogenized vaginal epithelium, pubic hair, and labial fat pads. The striking difference between prepubertal and adolescent vaginitis is the shift in etiology. Vulvovaginitis in the prepubertal child is often nonspecific and results from poor perineal hygiene, whereas vaginitis in the adolescent usually has a specific etiology, often related to sexual contact. A complaint of vaginal discharge may also be the presenting symptom of the adolescent with cervicitis secondary to *Neisseria gonorrhoeae*, *Chlamydia trachomatis*, or herpes simplex. In addition to these true infections, physiologic leukorrhea, a normal desquamation of epithelial cells secondary to estrogen effect, is probably the most common cause of discharge in the pubescent girl.

This chapter includes a description of the various causes of vaginitis as well as of vulvar disease, toxic shock, and the urethral syndrome. Infections with *N. gonorrhoeae* and *C. trachomatis* are covered in Chapter 10 and human papillomavirus (HPV) in Chapter 11.

VAGINAL DISCHARGE
The evaluation of vaginal discharge in the adolescent should include a history of symptoms (pruritus, odor, quantity), other illnesses (e.g., diabetes), recent medications (e.g., broad-spectrum antibiotics, birth control pills), and in utero exposure to diethylstilbestrol (DES). A history of broad-spectrum antibiotics or poorly controlled diabetes mellitus is frequently a clue to the diagnosis of *Candida* vaginitis. The patient should be questioned about recent sexual relations, since treatment failure in an adolescent girl often occurs because of reexposure to an untreated contact. It should be remembered that several infections may coexist; a patient may be adequately treated for one infection and still have a second or third infection. For example, an adolescent may have *C. trachomatis* cervicitis, *Trichomonas* vaginitis, and vulvar condylomata. In addition, the use of oral broad-spectrum antibiotics for the treatment of the vaginitis may be followed by a second infection with *Candida*. Commonly in the evaluation of sexually transmitted vaginitis, the clinician needs to address the issue of birth control as well. Although close family contact has been blamed for the spread of some infections, the clinician should assume that most, if not all, cases of *Trichomonas*, condyloma, and genital herpes in adolescents are sexually acquired either through consenting sexual relationships or sexual abuse.

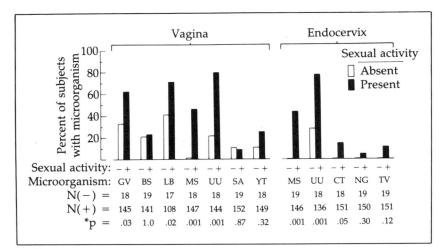

Figure 9-1. Microbiologic isolations from vagina and endocervix in adolescent girls by presence or absence of sexual activity. BS = group B streptococcus, CT = *Chlamydia trachomatis*; GV = *Gardnerella vaginalis*; LB = lactobacillus; MS = *Mycoplasma* species; NG = *Neisseria gonorrhoeae*; SA = *Staphylococcus aureus*; TV = *Trichomonas vaginalis*; UU = *Ureaplasma urealyticum*; YT = yeast. *Chi square statistic except for CT, NG, and TV Fischer exact test. (From MA Shafer, RL Sweet, MJ Ohm-Smith, Microbiology of the lower genital tract in postmenarcheal adolescent girls: Differences by sexual activity, contraception, and presence of nonspecific vaginitis. J Pediatr 1985; 107:974. By permission.)

The microbiologic flora of the adolescent vagina and cervix divided by those who give a history of being sexually active and those who deny sexual activity has been recently reported by Shafer and co-workers [1] and is extremely helpful to clinicians (Fig. 9-1).

An adolescent may have symptoms for weeks or months before seeking medical help because of anxiety about a pelvic examination or because of guilt or trauma from a previous episode of rape, intercourse, touching, or sexual abuse. Therefore, it is important to explain carefully to the adolescent both the details of the pelvic examination and the possible causes of discharge.

Assessment of the adolescent usually includes a speculum examination to obtain specimens of the vaginal discharge for wet preparations, pH, and in sexually active patients endocervical cultures for *N. gonorrhoeae* and *C. trachomatis* (described in Chap. 1). A speculum examination may be omitted in the virginal adolescent 12 to 13 years old with a history of a whitish mucoid discharge, since samples for wet preparations obtained with a saline-moistened, cotton-tipped applicator or Calgiswab gently inserted through the hymenal ring are sufficient to confirm the diagnosis of leukorrhea. In the older adolescent with persistent discharge (even if the history makes leukorrhea likely) and in all sexually active adolescents, a speculum examination should be done to assess the appearance of the cervix, since patients with cervicitis may complain of vaginal discharge.

Inspection of the vulva is often helpful in the differential diagnosis of vaginitis. A small magnifying glass can be of immense help. A red, edematous vulva with satellite red papules is characteristic of acute *Candida* vulvovaginitis. Fissures and excoriations are seen with subacute or chronic *Candida* infections. Small vesicles or ulcers are typical of herpetic vulvitis. Symptomatic gonococcal cervicitis and pelvic inflammatory disease may be accompanied by a greenish-yellow discharge oozing from the vaginal introitus and the urethra.

Insertion of a speculum appropriate to the size of the hymenal ring should be preceded by a gentle one-finger digital examination of the vagina. A Huffman speculum can be used for most virginal adolescents. The slightly larger Pederson speculum allows better visualization of the cervix in the virginal adolescent who has a wider hymenal opening and in the sexually active adolescent.

The appearance of the vaginal secretions often gives a clue to the diagnosis. A thick, curdy discharge is typical of *Candida;* a yellow, bubbly, frothy discharge is typical of *Trichomonas vaginalis.* In patients with *Trichomonas* infections and those with cervicitis, the cervix may be friable and may bleed during the collection of the samples. A cervical ectropion is present in many adolescents; however, very large ectropions may be responsible for persistent vaginal discharge in older adolescents, even in the absence of infection. The presence of a mucopurulent discharge from the endocervix and ectropion characterizes cervicitis and is typical of infections with *N. gonorrhoeae, C. trachomatis,* and herpes. Other infectious agents, not as yet well defined, may cause persistent mucopus from a cervical ectropion in spite of eradication of *N. gonorrhoeae* and *C. trachomatis.* If a large ectropion is associated with any abnormality of the shape of the cervix or the presence of glandular cells extending into the anterior vaginal wall (adenosis), in utero exposure to DES should be strongly suspected in girls born before 1974 (see Chap. 12).

Microscopic examination of the wet preparations usually provides the diagnosis (see Chap. 1). On the saline preparation slide, trichomonads are seen as dancing flagellated organisms. Sheets of epithelial cells are characteristic of leukorrhea. So-called clue cells (epithelial cells coated with large numbers of refractile bacteria that obscure the cell borders) are seen in bacterial vaginosis. The potassium hydroxide (KOH) preparation is used to demonstrate the pseudohyphae of *Candida* (Fig. 9-2).

Large numbers of white cells may be seen in the presence of *Trichomonas,* to a lesser extent with *Candida* vaginitis, and with cervicitis. The presence of white cells in the absence of a diagnosis sug-

310

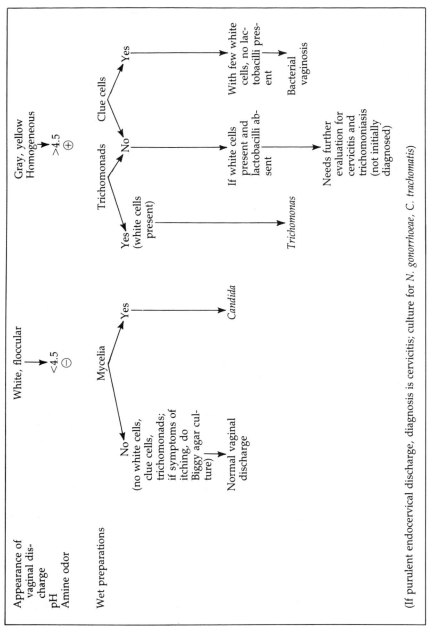

Figure 9-2. Differential diagnosis of vaginitis.

gests that further tests and a follow-up visit in 2 weeks may be necessary. For example, the wet preparation may miss the diagnosis of *Trichomonas* because of a sensitivity of only 50 to 75 percent depending on the number of organisms and the microscopist. As cultures and direct immunofluorescent and enzyme immunoassay methods become more available, the clinician will find diagnosis in such patients more rewarding.

The presence of an amine odor when a drop of discharge is mixed with 10% KOH is a positive "whiff" test and occurs most commonly with bacterial vaginosis but may sometimes occur with *Trichomonas* as well. The pH of the vaginal secretions is helpful in the differential diagnosis. A normal pH of less than 4.5 is found in patients with normal leukorrhea and *Candida* vaginitis, whereas the pH is elevated above 4.5 in patients with *Trichomonas* vaginitis and bacterial vaginosis. Gram stain of the vaginal discharge can be used to look for lactobacillus organisms, typical of normal discharge, and to detect alterations in the flora seen in bacterial vaginosis in which gram-variable coccobacilli and curved gram-negative rods are observed.

Gram stain of the endocervical mucopus should be examined for increased numbers of polymorphonuclear leukocytes (PMNs). In sexually transmitted disease (STD) clinics, greater than 10 PMNs/oil immersion field (1000×) has been associated with *C. trachomatis* cervical infection. However, this finding is less helpful in detection of this important infection in asymptomatic adolescents (see Chap. 10). Likewise, the finding of a positive yellow swab test (a yellow color noted on the white cotton-tipped applicator inserted into the endocervical canal and twirled) is associated with *C. trachomatis* cervicitis in STD clinics. Increased white cells and the presence of gram-negative intracellular diplococci are often found on the Gram stain of patients with endocervical *N. gonorrhoeae*. Specific cultures (or other tests such as direct immunofluorescent smears, immunoassays, or DNA probes) should be done to detect *N. gonorrhoeae* and *C. trachomatis* in sexually active adolescents. If the discharge is itchy or cheesy and yet no pseudohyphae are seen on KOH preparation, a culture for *Candida* on Biggy agar (Scott) is helpful.

The Papanicolaou (Pap) smear may also give helpful clues to the diagnosis. Herpes simplex is associated with intranuclear inclusions and multinucleate giant cells and HPV with koilocytosis, squamous atypia, and cervical intraepithelial neoplasia. *Chlamydia* has been associated with inflammation, cytoplasmic inclusions, and transformed lymphocytes or increased histiocytes. *Trichomonas* may be seen on Pap smear, but false-positive smears are not infrequent and should be confirmed with wet preparation or culture in the asymptomatic patient. The Pap smear has been noted to have a sensitivity of 17 to 58 percent for the detection of *C. trachomatis*, 3 to 49 percent for *Candida*,

25 percent for bacterial vaginosis, 33 to 79 percent for *Trichomonas*, and 25 to 66 percent for herpes simplex [2]. The positive predictive value differs depending on the prevalence of the infection in the population and the specificity. In addition, the time involved in obtaining the report makes it unlikely that the Pap smear will be a major method of diagnosis of most infections.

Although not generally available for routine diagnosis of cervical and vaginal infections, the colposcope may also be helpful in making the diagnosis. In a study of STD patients, Paavonen and colleagues [3] found that endocervical mucopus was associated with *N. gonorrhoeae*, *C. trachomatis*, and herpes simplex; ulcers/necrotic areas and increased surface vascularity with herpes simplex; strawberry cervix (uniformly arranged red spots or stippling of a few millimeters in size, located on the squamous epithelium covering the ectocervix) with *Trichomonas*; hypertrophic cervicitis with *C. trachomatis*; and immature metaplasia with *C. trachomatis* and cytomegalovirus.

Therapy is aimed at the specific etiology. Patients should avoid chemical douches, since a recent report [4] found that commercial douche preparations used with a disposable bottle were associated with an increased risk of pelvic inflammatory disease. In contrast, the use of water with or without vinegar for douching was not associated with pelvic inflammatory disease. Although this observation needs to be studied further in other centers, douching has not been shown to be of benefit in the treatment of specific infections. When one sexually transmitted infection is detected, the clinician should test the patient for other STDs, including considering a blood test for syphilis. Counselling about prevention and the use of condoms is essential.

In most situations, therapy should include the following:

1. Warm baths once or twice a day (baking soda may be added if the vulva is irritated). Only bland soaps should be used.
2. Careful drying after the bath and application of a small amount of baby powder (no talc) to the vulva.
3. Frequent changes of white cotton underpants or panty shields to absorb the discharge.
4. Good perineal hygiene (including wiping from front to back after bowel movements).
5. Avoidance of bubble bath.

LEUKORRHEA

Agent: A normal estrogen effect.

Symptoms: A whitish mucoid discharge that usually starts before menarche and may continue for several years. With the establishment of more regular cycles, the adolescent may notice a cyclic variation in vaginal secretions: copious watery secretions at midcycle and then a stickier, scantier discharge in the second half of the cycle associated with rising progesterone levels.

Diagnosis: The wet preparation reveals epithelial cells without evidence of inflammation.

Treatment: Most health classes that discuss puberty and menarche do not include an explanation of the change in vaginal secretions. The physician can reassure the patient by explaining vaginal physiology and can suggest measures to help if she is bothered by the discharge—baths, cotton underpants, and as needed, some form of panty shield (e.g., Light Days, Carefree shields) that she can change frequently. If an older adolescent is troubled by excessive discharge, especially during jogging or athletics, evaluation of the cervix and vagina may be indicated. Use of a conventional tampon (not a superabsorbent tampon) during athletics for a few hours at midcycle can help the adolescent cope with the heavy discharge. It is extremely important that the adolescent not be overtreated with vaginal creams and given the impression that the leukorrhea represents an infection. It is also important to discourage daily use of tampons because of the possibility of vaginal ulcers.

TRICHOMONAL VAGINITIS

Agent: Trichomonas vaginalis; a small, flagellated parasite.

Symptoms: Frothy, malodorous yellow discharge that may cause itching, dysuria, postcoital bleeding, or dyspareunia or any combination of these symptoms. May be asymptomatic and found on culture, Pap smear, or wet preparation [5].

Source: Usually sexually acquired. Males are usually asymptomatic but may reinfect the female after she is treated. Since *Trichomonas* may survive for several hours in urine and wet towels, the possibility of transmission by sharing washcloths has been suggested. It is unlikely that this is a frequent occurrence given the association of this infection with other sexually transmitted diseases. The incubation time has been estimated to be between 4 and 20 days with an average of 7 days.

Diagnosis: The vulva may be erythematous or excoriated with visible discharge evident on inspection. The classic yellow-green discharge is seen in 20 to 35 percent of patients; more usually the discharge is gray. A frothy discharge is seen in about 10 percent of women and may also occur with bacterial vaginosis. Grossly visible punctate hemorrhages and swollen papillae (strawberry cervix) are seen in only about 2 percent of patients; however, in an STD population, colposcopy of the cervix found that 15 percent of patients with *Trichomonas* had a strawberry cervix. By colposcopy this special finding had a 45 percent sensitivity and a 99 percent specificity for *Trichomonas* [3].

The positive wet preparation may show flagellated organisms dancing under the coverslip along with an increase in the number of white cells on low and high dry power of the microscope [5–13]. The vaginal wet mount is far from a perfect tool and detects 64 percent of infections in asymptomatically infected women, 75 percent of those presenting with clinical vaginitis, and 80 percent of those with characteristic symptoms. Philip and co-workers [14] found wet mount was positive only in patients whose cultures had more than 10^5 CFU/ml. Use of Feinberg-Whittington or Diamond's culture has a sensitivity of 86 to 97 percent. Pap smears have a detection rate of only 50 to 56 percent, and false-positives are not infrequent. In a study by Krieger and associates [7], monoclonal antibody staining detected 86 percent of positive specimens including 92 percent of those with positive wet mounts and 77 percent of those missed on wet mount. Enzyme-linked immunoassay methods are also under study.

Treatment: Metronidazole, 2.0 gm orally all in one dose, is effective in 86 to 95 percent of patients [15, 16]. It is important that the sexual partner be treated with the same dose at the same time (although single dose may be less effective in men than women). Side effects of metronidazole include nausea, vomiting, headache, metallic aftertaste, and rare blood dyscrasias. The patient should be instructed to avoid alcohol and intercourse until both partners are treated. If the physician does not wish to treat the partner or the partner does not wish to be treated, the partner can be referred to his own physician (although trichomonads are difficult to document in the male), or the male partner can wear a condom or avoid intercourse for 2 weeks with the hope that the organisms will be eradicated by the host.

If the organisms persist in the vagina after two courses of single-dose metronidazole and reinfection is not the cause, a longer course of metronidazole can be tried—500 mg orally twice daily for 7 days. Recurrent infection necessitates retreating the partner and making sure the relationship is monogamous; otherwise, the patient should understand the futility of repeated treatment.

Rarely a patient will have *Trichomonas* infection that has relative resistance to metronidazole and is refractory to treatment [17, 18]. The patient can be treated with 2 gm/day of metronidazole orally for 3 to 5 days (possibly, plus with vaginal insertion of a 500-mg tablet daily). Lossick and colleagues [18] reported the need for an average oral dose of 2.6 gm/day of metronidazole for a mean period of 9 days to cure refractory *Trichomonas*. Neurologic side effects are common if more than 3 gm is taken orally in a day. A complete blood count (CBC) should be done prior to prolonged therapy.

Although a 10-year follow-up study [19] showed no association between the use of metronidazole and cancer, the duration of follow-up was short; thus the shortest course and lowest dose that result in cure are preferred.

Pregnancy: Metronidazole should be avoided during pregnancy and breast-feeding. Although no birth defects have been associated with the drug, it is contraindicated in the first trimester. If a symptomatic patient in the second or third trimester has been unresponsive to a regimen of clotrimazole (Gyne-Lotrimin, Mycelex) 1% cream or 100-mg vaginal tablets at bedtime for 7 nights or other local measures, a single 2-gm dose of metronidazole may be prescribed.

CANDIDA VAGINITIS

Agent: Candida albicans accounts for 60 to 80 percent of vaginal fungal infections; other *Candida* species including *Torulopsis glabrata* (20%) and *Candida tropicalis* (6–23%) also cause similar symptoms [20, 21]. *C. tropicalis* may be more difficult to eradicate with current therapies.

Symptoms: Thick, cheesy, pruritic discharge. The vulva may be red and edematous. Itching may occur at midcycle and after menses and for some patients seems to remit at midcycle. Patients may complain of dyspareunia with an increase in symptoms after intercourse. Many patients have external dysuria and irritation.

Source: Predisposing factors to *Candida* vaginitis include diabetes mellitus, pregnancy, antibiotic use (e.g., tetracycline for acne), corticosteroids, obesity, and tight-fitting undergarments. The frequency of positive cultures rises from 2.2 to 16 percent by the end of pregnancy. The increase in clinical infections appears to be associated with the rise in pH seen in late pregnancy as well as premenstrually [22]. Infections are more common in the summer. Whether small numbers of *Candida* are part of normal flora is debated, but it appears that eradication of *Candida* by culture is important in patients with frequent recurrences.

Although *Candida* is not seen more commonly in STD clinics than in other settings, suggesting that sexual transmission is not a major mode of spread, recent research has focused on the role of sexual transmission in patients with recurrent *Candida* vulvovaginitis [23, 24]. Sexual partners of women with recurrent *Candida* vaginitis are more likely to have positive oral and ejaculate cultures than controls. Women with recurrent infections are more likely than controls to have positive oral cultures as well. Thus studies are needed to determine if treatment of the male partner with oral clotrimazole troches or oral ketoconazole would be useful in treating women with recurrent vaginitis. Thus, in the history, the physician should ask about symptoms and medical problems in the male partner,

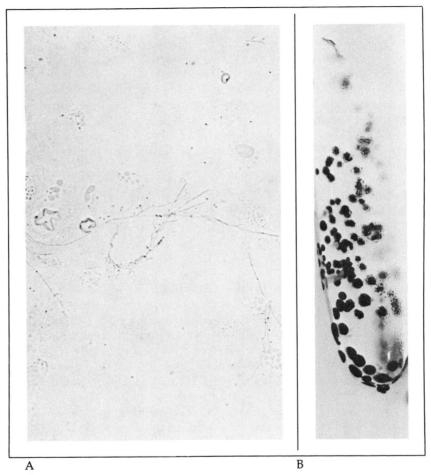

A   B

Figure 9-3. *Candida* vaginitis. A. Potassium hydroxide preparation showing pseudohyphae (From Syntex slide collection, Palo Alton, CA. With permission.) B. Biggy agar culture with multiple brown colonies.

since men with diabetes mellitus and conditions requiring long-term antibiotics may be predisposed to *Candida* genital infections. *Diagnosis:* The vulva is usually red and may be edematous, with small satellite red papules or fissures at the posterior forchette. The KOH preparation shows filamentous forms in 80 to 90 percent of symptomatic patients (Fig. 9-3A). In patients with suggestive signs or symptoms and especially patients previously labelled as having "recurrent *Candida* infections," culture of the vagina is extremely useful. The easiest office culture is Biggy agar, which can be read for the presence of brown colonies after 3 to 7 days of incubation

(Fig. 9-3B). Sabouraud agar can also be used. Most patients with symptomatic infections will have a large number of colonies; however, even a few colonies may be significant in the woman with frequent infections who has recently finished a treatment course. In difficult diagnostic cases, the patient may be shown how to inoculate a culture at home with a cotton-tipped applicator at the time of increased symptomatology.

Treatment: The imidazoles are the mainstay of treatment of *Candida* vaginitis. Courses of therapy range from a single dose to 3 to 7 days of therapy with creams or suppositories. (Pregnant patients should have 7-day courses.) The suppositories are less messy but may not treat vulvar infection as well. In addition, the symptomatic male partner can use the cream as well. Some packaging contains both suppositories and cream (e.g., Monistat Dualpack). Efficacy, as judged by symptomatic improvement and negative cultures after any of the available treatment courses with imidazoles, is approximately 85 to 90 percent at the end of therapy and 75 percent 3 weeks later. Nystatin is probably less efficacious because it requires the patient to be compliant with 2 weeks of therapy; however, it is useful in women who develop allergic symptoms with the use of the imidazoles and in women in the first trimester of pregnancy (although there is no evidence of adverse effects to date, imidazoles should be avoided in the first trimester). Allergic symptoms to the imidazoles are often manifested by increased burning and itching after several days of therapy. Nystatin is also cheaper for the patient than the imidazoles.

Treatment doses are as follows [25–31]:

Clotrimazole, 100-mg vaginal suppository for 7 nights
Clotrimazole, two 100-mg vaginal suppositories for 3 nights
Clotrimazole 1% cream, 1 applicatorful for 7 nights
Miconazole, 200-mg vaginal suppository for 3 nights
Miconazole, 100-mg vaginal suppository for 7 nights
Miconazole 2% cream, 1 applicatorful for 7 nights
Butaconazole 2% cream, 1 applicatorful for 3 nights
Terconazole 0.4% cream, 1 applicatorful for 7 nights
Terconazole, 80-mg vaginal suppository for 3 nights
Nystatin, 100,000-unit vaginal suppository for 14 nights
Clotrimazole, 500-mg vaginal suppository for 1 night

The base of the terconazole suppository may interact with latex products, including diaphragms, and thus the patient should be informed of this possibility.

Recurrent infections can be very difficult to treat. The most important issue is to make sure that the diagnosis is in fact *Candida*. Patients may have inflammation of the minor vestibular glands, HPV infection, or allergies to soaps, spermicides, or rarely semen. Once the diagnosis of *Candida* is confirmed, the clinician should check for predisposing factors such as diabetes. Looser fitting clothing and the use of nondeodorized panty shields can be recommended. Any douching equipment should be cultured or discarded. The potential for a gastrointestinal reservoir in the patient or partner should be considered. In addition, the patient may not have purchased the medication because of cost or may not have finished the previously prescribed dosage.

Many patients who have experienced frequent recurrences of *Candida* vulvovaginitis in the past can be maintained symptom free with *one* of the following treatments: by using vaginal clotrimazole (100 mg) 6 days a month *or* vaginal clotrimazole (500 mg) once a month *or* an antifungal vaginal cream for 2 to 3 days before and after each menses *or* a vaginal cream "always on Sunday" *or* a vaginal cream for 1 to 3 days at the first sign of itching.

The use of oral ketoconazole has been studied in adult women with *Candida* infections. This drug is efficacious in treating *Candida* vulvovaginitis and in preventing recurrences while the patient is taking the drug. Sobel [32] reported in a prospective controlled study of women with recurrent vulvovaginal candidiasis that symptomatic recurrences over a 6-month interval occurred in 71 percent of women treated with placebo compared with 29 percent treated with 400 mg of ketoconazole for 5 days at the onset of each menses for six cycles and 4.8 percent of women given 100 mg of ketoconazole daily for 6 months. At the end of 12 months of follow-up, the number of asymptomatic women was 24 percent for the placebo group versus 43 and 52 percent for the two dosages of ketoconazole. Thus relapse is common, and the risks of using a drug with a small chance of hepatotoxicity need to be addressed. It is unlikely that many adolescents would be candidates for this form of therapy.

Whether the elimination of gastrointestinal carriage (rectal and oral) is efficacious in long-term prevention of recurrences is disputed. The evidence from studies with oral ketoconazole suggests that many patients will have recurrences despite prolonged therapy. Treatment with oral nystatin had not been of demonstrated benefit. Clotrimazole troches may be useful for treating oral carriage in male partners of patients and the patients themselves, but further studies are needed. A short course of 3 days of oral ketoconazole given to male partners did not result in different cure rates or recurrence rates in women with *Candida* vaginitis [24].

BACTERIAL VAGINOSIS

Agent: Bacterial vaginosis, formerly termed "nonspecific vaginitis," results from the complex alteration of microbial flora of the vagina. Although *Gardnerella vaginalis* is found in most patients with this diagnosis, this organism is found in many asymptomatic patients including virginal young women. Thus this syndrome seems to result from an increased concentration of *G. vaginalis,* anaerobic organisms (especially *Bacteroides* and *Mobiluncus* species) and *Mycoplasma hominis* with an absence of normal hydrogen peroxide producing lactobacilli [33–40]. The overgrowth results in an elevated vaginal pH and production of amines (putrescine and cadaverine), which cause the typical malodor that patients experience. Gasliquid chromatographic studies show an increase in acetate, proprionate, isobutyrate, butyrate, and isovalerate with an increase in succinate-lactate ratio of 0.4. Bacterial vaginosis occurs in 4 to 15 percent of college students, 10 to 25 percent of pregnant women, and 33 to 37 percent of women attending an STD clinic. The presence of bacterial vaginosis has been associated with postpartum endometritis, premature labor and premature rupture of membranes, irregular menstrual bleeding, and salpingitis [41]. The relationship of this condition to nongonococcal, nonchlamydial pelvic inflammatory disease needs further clarification, since the organisms cultured are similar.

Symptoms: Malodorous discharge; associated symptoms may be abdominal pain and irregular or prolonged menses.

Source: Usually seen in sexually active patients. Risk factors include presence of an intrauterine device, prior STD, smoking, low socioeconomic status, nonwhite race, and uncircumcised partner.

Diagnosis: The pelvic examination reveals a homogeneous, malodorous, yellow, white, or gray discharge adherent to the vaginal walls, in contrast to the normal clumped or floccular discharge. Three of four criteria should be met to make the clinical diagnosis: (1) homogeneous discharge; (2) pH above 4.5 (in one study $\geq$ 4.7 [34]); (3) positive "whiff" test (mixing 1 drop of the discharge with 1 drop of 10% KOH to see if an amine odor is liberated); (4) the presence of clue cells (making up at least 20% of the cells) (Fig. 9-4). Gram stain of the vaginal discharge is also very useful. A positive determination is made if 4 or fewer lactobacilli are seen per oil immersion field and *Gardnerella* morphologic types plus one or more other bacterial morphologic types (gram-positive cocci, small gram-negative rods, curved gram-variable rods, or fusiforms) are detected. In a highprevalence population at an STD clinic, Eschenbach and colleagues [34] found that the Gram stain had a 97 percent sensitivity, 79 percent specificity, and 69 percent positive predictive value for bac-

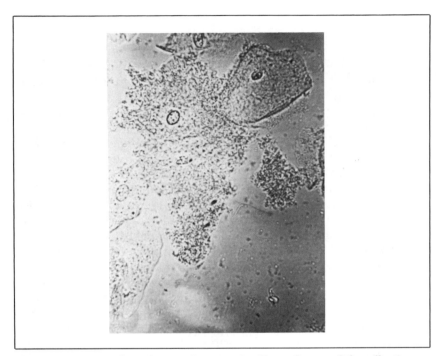

Figure 9-4. Clue cells in bacterial vaginosis. (From Syntex slide collection, with permission.)

terial vaginosis. Homogeneous discharge was found in 69 percent, pH 4.7 or greater in 97 percent, positive whiff test in 43 percent, and clue cells (≥20% of epithelial cells) in 78 percent of patients with bacterial vaginosis. The whiff test was the least sensitive test, and the pH was the least specific test since 47 percent of patients without bacterial vaginosis had elevated pH. The finding of a pH 4.4 or less and a predominance of lactobacilli on wet mount or Gram stain is useful in excluding the diagnosis of bacterial vaginosis. Cultures for *G. vaginalis* are not helpful and should not alone be diagnostic of this condition.

Treatment: Treatment is usually given only to symptomatic women; however, as research elucidates the possible link between this alteration in flora and pelvic inflammatory disease and pregnancy risks, it is possible that treatment will be recommended for asymptomatic women as well.

The standard therapy for nonpregnant patients is metronidazole, 500 mg twice a day for 7 days, which results in cure rates of 85 percent [42, 43]. Alternative treatments include clindamycin, 300 mg twice a day for 7 days [44]; amoxicillin (500 mg) plus clavulanic acid (Augmentin) 3 times a day for 7 days, and possibly 2% clindamycin cream (not yet available) daily for 7 days. Single-dose metronidazole (2 gm) is less effective (67–90%), especially if follow-up is done at 3 weeks instead of just 1 week after the completion of therapy [43, 45, 46, 47]. Treatment with two doses of metronidazole (2 gm) given 2 days apart on day 1 and day 3 appears promising [47]. Other less effective regimens are ampicillin, 500 mg 4 times a day, or amoxicillin, 500 mg 3 times a day, for 7 or 14 days. Although the sexual partner is often colonized with the same flora, treatment of the partner with metronidazole has not diminished recurrences in the woman; thus condoms should be recommended for several weeks with the hope of altering flora. Studies using other drugs and protocols for partners of women with frequent recurrences are needed.

Patients with multiple symptomatic recurrences can be tried with therapy of 7 to 14 days of Augmentin plus, when available, intravaginal clindamycin 2% cream. Other regimens include oral cephalexin, 500 mg 4 times a day for 7 days; oral cephradine, 500 mg 4 times a day for 5 to 7 days; or metronidazole, 1 gm twice a day for 7 days. Women with recurrences appear to fail to recolonize the vagina with *Lactobacillus* species. Treatment of the male partner may be considered in these circumstances.

Asymptomatic patients are generally not treated, although this recommendation may change. Patients with Pap smear abnormalities and those who are preoperative should be treated. The patient should be told of the possibility of developing characteristic symptoms. A positive culture for *G. vaginalis* does not make the diagnosis of bacterial vaginosis, which must be established by multiple criteria.

Vaginitis Secondary to a Foreign Body
Agent: In adolescents, usually a retained tampon.
Symptoms: Foul-smelling, often bloody discharge.
Diagnosis: Examination.
Treatment: Removal of the foreign body and irrigation of the vagina with warm water.

Gonorrhea
Agent: Neisseria gonorrhoeae.
Symptoms: Often asymptomatic. In symptomatic patients, gonorrhea may cause a purulent vaginal discharge from cervicitis, urethritis, pelvic inflammatory disease, proctitis, pharyngitis, and arthritis (see Chap. 10).
Source; Sexual contact.
Diagnosis: Culture on Thayer-Martin-Jembec (Scott) or Transgrow

media. Gram stain of the discharge may reveal gram-negative, intracellular diplococci (suggestive but not conclusive evidence of infection in women).
Treatment: See Chapter 10.

CHLAMYDIAL INFECTION
Agent: Chlamydia trachomatis (D,E,F,G,H,I,J,K).
Symptoms: The serotypes D–K of *C. trachomatis* have been associated with nongonococcal urethritis in men, and mucopurulent cervicitis, salpingitis, perihepatitis, and the urethral syndrome in women.
Source: Sexually transmitted.
Diagnosis: Culture on McCoy cells; direct immunofluorescent smear (MicroTrak), enzyme immunoassays, and under development, DNA probes.
Treatment: See Chapter 10.

NONSPECIFIC VULVITIS
Agent: A nonspecific vulvar irritation may be caused by hot weather, nylon underpants, obesity, or poor hygiene or from sitting on sand.
Symptoms: Pruritus, pain, dysuria.
Diagnosis: By history, and exclusion of a specific vaginitis, allergy, or papillomatosis (HPV) of the vulva (see Chap. 11).
Treatment: Hydrocortisone cream 1% applied 3 times daily to the vulva; white cotton underpants; avoidance of precipitating factors.

GENITAL HERPES
Agent: Usually herpes simplex type 2 (HSV-2), but 5 to 15 percent of first episodes are type 1 (HSV-1). Herpes infections can be divided into primary first episodes in which the patient has no antibody to HSV-1 or HSV-2, nonprimary first episodes in which the patient does have antibody to one type (usually a type 2 infection with antibodies to type 1), and recurrences. Primary first episodes are responsible for approximately 60 percent of first episodes and nonprimary infections for the other 40 percent of first episodes. Three percent of nonprimary first episodes and 2 percent of recurrences are HSV-1 [48].
    When Lafferty and associates [49] examined patients with simultaneous oral and genital HSV infections, results showed that oral labial recurrences occurred in 5 of 12 with HSV-1 and 1 of 27 with HSV-2, whereas genital recurrences occurred in 2 of 27 with HSV-1 and 24 of 27 with HSV-2. Mean monthly recurrences were 0.33/month for genital HSV-2, 0.12/month for oral HSV-1, 0.02/month for genital HSV-1, and 0.001/month for oral HSV-2. Over the course of a year after the first episode, 14 percent of patients with

HSV-1 and 60 percent of those with HSV-2 will have a recurrence. The recurrence rate may decrease after the first year [49–52].

Asymptomatic genital shedding of HSV occurs in 1.6 to 8.0 percent of women seen in STD clinics and 0.25 to 1.5 percent of women seen in private gynecology practices. Although symptomatic patients are most infectious, asymptomatic patients may spread HSV to sexual partners [53]. Seroepidemiologic studies in adults have suggested that the prevalence of HSV-2 is greater than previously thought (<1% in under 15 year olds to 20% in the group 30 to 40 years old).

Patients may have vulvar, cervical, urethral, or rectal infections. HSV may occur in 5 percent of women with dysuria and frequency. Rarely, HSV has been associated with endometritis and salpingitis. The estimated number of physician-patient consultations for genital herpes has increased 15-fold from 1966 to 1984 [54].

Symptoms: In primary infections, vesicles appear on the labia, vagina, or cervix (or all three); they rupture in 1 to 3 days and produce small painful ulcers. The patient experiences local burning and irritation, dysuria, and inguinal adenopathy. Systemic symptoms are often present, including headache, fever, myalgia, and malaise. Patients may also have neurologic symptoms such as aseptic meningitis, sacral anesthesia, urinary retention, and constipation that may last for 4 to 8 weeks. Anorectal symptoms from primary involvement may cause discharge, pain, and tenesmus. Large numbers of virus are shed from the lesions and, usually, from the cervix. Positive cultures persist for 8 to 10 days and sometimes for as long as 2 weeks. Symptoms improve in 10 days to 3 weeks (Fig. 9-5).

The symptoms associated with recurrences are less marked and shorter in duration (3–5 days) than those of primary infections. The number of lesions is also less, and lesions are generally external rather than vaginal or cervical. The mean healing time was 8.0 ± 2.8 days in a study by Guinan and co-workers [55] of college students. Many patients experience a prodrome of neuralgia in the buttocks, groin, or legs and itching or burning 24 hours before the herpetic lesions recur. Virus is shed in lesser amounts for 4 to 5 days and is usually markedly diminished by the sixth to seventh day.

Nonprimary first-episode infections with HSV have a time course for symptoms and viral shedding that is intermediate between primary herpes and recurrent herpes (Fig. 9-6).

Extragenital sites may occur on the buttocks, groin, thighs, pharynx, fingers, and conjunctiva.

Source: Sexually acquired. The incubation period is 2 to 10 days.

Diagnosis: Inspection and cultures. A tender, painful vesicle, pustule, or yellowish ulcer should make the clinician think of HSV. A scrap-

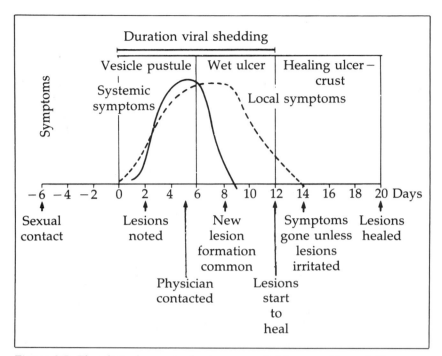

Figure 9-5. The clinical course of primary genital herpes. (From L Corey, HG Adams, ZA Brown, et al., Genital herpes simplex virus infections: Clinical manifestation, course, and complications. Ann Intern Med 1983; 98:958. With permission.)

ing from the base of a lesion, which is stained with Wright's stain (a Tzanck preparation), may reveal multinucleate giant cells and inclusions. This test is inexpensive and highly specific, but only about 30 to 50 percent sensitive for detection of HSV. The Pap smear may show characteristic changes of intranuclear inclusions and multinucleated cells but is only 40 to 50 percent sensitive. Colposcopy of the cervix may reveal ulcers and necrotic areas and increased surface vascularity. Paavonen and colleagues [3] found that cervical ulcers or necrotic areas were 68 percent sensitive and 98.5 percent specific for the diagnosis of cervical HSV.

The best diagnostic technique is viral culture. HSV grows rapidly, and within several days a definitive diagnosis of HSV-1 or HSV-2 can usually be made (laboratories generally hold the culture for 2 weeks before reporting a negative). The rate of positivity of the culture depends on the timing and the type of infection. For example, HSV can be cultured from 94 percent of vesicles, 70 percent of ulcers (82% first episode, 42% recurrent), and 27 percent of crusted lesions. Culture of the cervix will yield HSV in 80 to 88

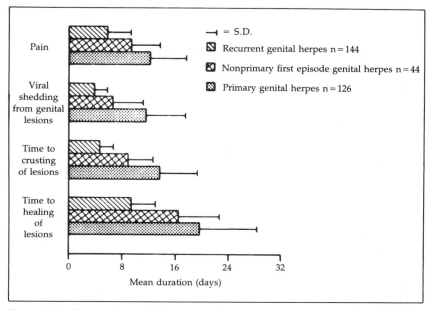

Figure 9-6. Comparison of the mean duration of symptoms and signs in female patients with first episode, nonprimary first episode, and recurrent genital herpes. SD = standard deviation. (From L Corey, HG Adams, ZA Brown, et al., Genital herpes simplex virus infections: Clinical manifestation, course, and complications. Ann Intern Med 1983; 98:958. With permission.)

percent of primary first episodes, 65 percent of nonprimary first episodes, and 12 percent of recurrent episodes. To culture a genital lesion, the vesicle should be unroofed and a sterile swab rubbed vigorously over the base. An ulcer can be similarly swabbed. The swab should then be placed immediately into viral transport media and processed as soon as possible.

Immunofluorescent techniques using fluorescein-labelled anti-HSV are 50 to 60 percent sensitive, depending in part on the site of sampling (vulvar lesions are more likely to be positive than cervical swabs). Another technique is use of ELISA (enzyme-linked immunosorbent assay) for direct examination of patient specimens; however, the technique is only 34 to 70 percent sensitive. In an obstetric population, 56 of 3,237 women had false-positive tests, which could have resulted in unnecessary cesarean sections [56]. It is likely that DNA probes will be useful in more rapid detection techniques in the future.

Documenting a conversion from no antibodies to a positive titer in a previously uninfected patient (no HSV-1 or HSV-2) can be useful in some clinical situations where cultures are negative and primary infection is suspected. The absence of antibody on two occasions 2 to 3 weeks apart can help eliminate the diagnosis. A rise of IgM antibody followed by IgG antibody is most convincing. A fourfold rise in titer is more difficult to interpret because it may indicate a new infection with a different type or a significant recurrence. In addition, the antibody tests done by many commercial laboratories have cross-reactivity between HSV-1 and HSV-2. Assays vary in sensitivity and thus interpretation can be problematic. Titers with type specific assays are useful in research settings and for retrospective diagnosis.

The differential diagnosis of genital ulcers is considered on p. 328.

Treatment: Current antiviral therapy with acyclovir can shorten the duration of symptoms and viral shedding, prevent the formation of new lesions, and reduce systemic symptoms, but it is not curative and initial therapy does not prevent later recurrences [57–59]. Oral acyclovir, 200 mg 5 times a day for 10 days, is helpful in patients with symptomatic primary genital herpes. Adjunctive measures include sitz baths in tepid water or Burow's solution, dry heat (low or cool setting on a hair dryer), and/or lidocaine (Xylocaine) jelly 2% applied to the genital area. Patients may need to void in the shower or into a sitz bath if the lesions cause urinary retention. Analgesics may be necessary, but narcotics have the potential to worsen urinary retention. Occasionally patients with severe genital lesions and systemic symptoms require hospitalization and treatment with oral or intravenous acyclovir, urinary catheterization, and bed rest. Side effects of intravenous acyclovir include phlebitis and transient reversible elevation of serum creatinine. Care must be taken to ensure adequate hydration. Nausea, vomiting, diarrhea, and headache may occur with intravenous or oral acyclovir. Topical acyclovir can cause burning symptoms with application and, except in the rare patient who cannot tolerate the oral acyclovir, offers no advantages; simultaneous usage does not improve efficacy. *Candida* vaginitis often accompanies or follows genital HSV.

Recurrences can usually be treated symptomatically with local measures. However, if recurrences are severe, acyclovir, 200 mg 5 times a day, can be taken for 5 days or 800 mg twice a day for 5 days at the first sign of prodromal symptoms. Frequent recurrences can be suppressed with acyclovir, 200 mg 2 to 5 times a day or 400 mg twice a day (individualized dose) for 6 months; however, such a course does not change the natural history of HSV, and recurrences begin anew after the treatment period is ended [59, 60]. Toxicity does not appear to be a problem even with treatment up to 3 years. Acyclovir-resistant strains are not commonly recovered from healthy patients treated for 4 months [61], but resistant strains are emerging among immunosuppressed and HIV-positive patients treated with long-term acyclovir. Acyclovir should not be used for recurrent herpes in pregnancy.

Although there is an increased incidence of cervical dysplasia and carcinoma in situ in patients with antibodies to HSV-2, this virus most likely is a cofactor in the pathogenesis of human papillomavirus (HPV)–induced dysplasia. In addition, the presence of HSV-2 is likely a marker for other STD exposure. Thus these patients require counselling about the necessity of Pap smear screening and contraceptive counselling.

Cultures of pregnant women with a previous history of HSV have not been found to be cost-effective in preventing neonatal HSV. Women at high risk of transmitting infection to their newborns are those with a primary infection during the third trimester [62] and those with active genital lesions at the time of vaginal delivery. Unfortunately, many mothers who deliver babies with severe HSV are asymptomatic [63–66]. The development of sensitive, rapid diagnostic tests that can be done at the time of labor may make future decision-making easier for delivery vaginally or by cesarean section. Current guidelines have been outlined by the American College of Obstetrics and Gynecology (ACOG) and the Infectious Disease Society for Obstetrics and Gynecology [67].

Patients with genital lesions from HSV should not have intercourse until the lesions heal. Although condoms prevent the transmission of virus, the location of lesions makes protection with barrier methods difficult. Patients should be educated about the risk of recurrence, the possibility of transmission (especially with the onset of prodromal symptoms), and the avoidance of self-inoculation to mouth and fingers. Cultures and tests should be done for other sexually transmitted diseases.

Vaccine trials are in progress, but there is no evidence yet that viral antibody titers can prevent infection. Certainly high titers do not prevent recurrences in already established infections. The safety of a live virus vaccine is unknown in view of the ability of HSV to transform cells, and thus new technology may make possible the development of a killed vaccine [50].

PEDICULOSIS PUBIS (CRABS)
Agent: Phthirius pubis (crab lice).
Symptom: Pruritus.
Source: Close physical contact; infested blankets and clothing.
Diagnosis: On inspection, small, moving adult lice or minute, firmly attached flakes (1–2 mm) are visible on the pubic hair. Under the low-power microscope, the flakes are nits.
Treatment: 1% Lindane (Kwell) shampoo should be lathered into the

pubic hair and left on for 5 minutes. The newer 1% permethrin creme rinse (NIX) is used for 10 minutes and appears to be equally efficacious [68]. After rinsing, the hair should be cleaned with a fine-tooth comb. Repeat treatment with 1% Lindane in 1 week will lessen recurrences. Clothing and blankets should be laundered or dry cleaned, or set aside for 2 weeks. Alternatively, pyrethrins (RID, A-200 Pyrinate) may be used.

PINWORMS
Agent: *Enterobius vermicularis* (pinworm).
Symptoms: Pruritus, mostly around the anus.
Source: Oral-anal spread; more common in young children.
Diagnosis: A piece of Scotch tape or a commerical pinworm tape is blotted around the anus as soon as the patient awakens in the morning. The tape is affixed to a glass slide and is examined for the presence of typical ova. Rarely, an adult pinworm may be seen in the vagina.
Treatment: Mebendazole (Vermox), 100 mg orally once.

MISCELLANEOUS CAUSES OF VAGINAL DISCHARGE
Some of the other causes of vaginitis include allergic vulvovaginitis (from soaps, chemical douches, contraceptive creams, vaginal antibiotic creams, and, occasionally, sperm), psychosomatic vulvovaginitis, and chronic discharge from an intrauterine device (IUD) string. Rectovaginal fistulas (seen mostly in Crohn's disease) and Müllerian anomalies with obstruction can also cause chronic vaginal discharge.

VULVAR ULCERS AND NEVI
The diagnosis of vulvar ulcers is sometimes difficult. The most common causes of ulcers in adolescents are genital herpes, chancroid, and syphilis. Syphilis is characterized by a nonpainful hard ulcer and a positive rapid plasma reagin (RPR) test by the seventh day of the ulcer (see p. 371). Genital herpes is characterized by painful, usually multiple, shallow ulcers that are positive on Tzanck preparation and culture (see p. 322). Rarely, Epstein-Barr virus infection (mononucleosis) can be associated with painful genital ulcers [69].

In the last 5 years, chancroid has reemerged as a potential etiology of genital ulcers. In 1986, 4,318 cases were reported, the largest number since 1952. The cases have principally occurred in men who frequented prostitutes or in those who have travelled to areas within the U.S. that have recently experienced outbreaks (Orange County, California; Palm Beach, Florida; Pennsylvania; and Boston) or endemic areas outside the United States (Dominican Republic and Haiti) [70, 71]. The disease typically presents as multiple purulent ulcers, often with ragged edges, and tender unilateral or bilateral inguinal adenopathy. Diagnosis is made by excluding the diagnosis of genital herpes or syphilis. Culture of *Haemophilus ducreyi* is the only sure means of diagnosis, but special media and conditions are necessary. Detection from the direct smears of the base of the genital lesion is the method commonly used by clinicians. The specimen is obtained from the ulcer base, which may involve peeling off the crust or wiping away excess pus (but not extensive cleaning). The cotton swab is used to touch first the base and then the edges of the ulcer. The swab is then rolled onto a slide in a circle about the size of a dime, and the slide is allowed to air dry and is Gram stained. The use of indirect immunofluorescence of ulcer smears using a monoclonal antibody directed against *H. ducreyi* and a dot-immunobinding serologic test offer promise but require more studies to determine sensitivity and specificity. Thus patients with ulcers without a history of blisters who do not have herpes or syphilis and have significant painful inguinal adenopathy should be suspected of having chancroid and treated with either erythromycin base, 500 mg orally 4 times a day for 7 days; or ceftriaxone, 250 mg intramuscularly [70–72]. Alternatives are trimethoprim-sulfamethoxazole, (160/800 mg) 1 double-strength tablet twice a day for 7 days (less reliable because of emerging resistance); amoxicillin (500 mg) with clavulanic acid (125 mg) 3 times a day for 7 days (not evaluated in the United States); or ciprofloxacin, 500 mg twice a day for 3 days (only in nonpregnant patients >16 years old). A clinical response should be evident within several days; patients should be seen in 7 days to make sure that ulcer healing is occurring and that adenopathy is less painful. Nodes may progress to fluctuation inspite of adequate medical therapy and require needle aspiration [72]. If a response to therapy has not occurred by day 7, the diagnosis may be different (e.g., herpes), the patient may be noncompliant with medication, the organisms may be resistant to the antibiotic chosen, or the patient may be infected with HIV. Sexual contacts (within the 10 days preceding the onset of symptoms) should be examined and treated. Serologic testing for syphilis should be considered within 3 months after therapy. Genital ulcers are of particular worry in the 1990s because of the association of genital ulcers with acquiring HIV infection.

Lymphogranuloma venereum (LGV) is caused by three serotypes (L-1, L-2, and L-3) of *C. trachomatis;* it is rare and more common in men than women. The ulcer in LGV is usually transient, and the patient is usually seen by the clinician for the late sequelae (enlarged inguinal nodes and rectal strictures). An LGV titer is used to make the diagnosis. Treatment is doxycycline 100 mg twice a day for 21 days.

The diagnosis of carcinoma, pemphigus, or granuloma inguinale generally requires the taking of a biopsy specimen. Granuloma inguinale, a rare disease, causes painful ulcerations with red granulation tissue or keloidlike depigmented scars, elephantoid enlargement of the external genitalia, and fistulas.

Ulcers can also occur with chronic fistulas or Crohn's disease; local application of zinc oxide paste may help alleviate symptoms. A course of oral metronidazole (Flagyl) has proved beneficial in some patients with chronic fistulas.

The mouth should always be examined in patients with vulvar ulcers. Behçet's disease is a multisystem disorder characterized by recurrent oral and genital ulcers, often associated with uveitis (70–80%) and, less commonly, arthritis, phlebitis, and rashes. The disease occurs more often in men than women. Although the disease usually does not appear until the third decade of life, rare cases in young children and adolescents have been reported [73, 74]. Therapy is unsatisfactory and includes high-estrogen oral contraceptives, corticosteroids, colchicine and immunosuppressive agents (e.g., azathioprine, chlorambucil).

Although most darkly pigmented lesions seen on the vulva of adolescent girls represent lentigo (a benign "frecklelike" increase in the concentration of melanocytes in the basal layer of the epithelium) or a compound, junctional, or intradermal nevus, the rare occurrence of melanoma or other form of carcinoma makes it essential to perform an excisional biopsy to establish a benign diagnosis.

An atlas of vulvar pathology can be very helpful to the clinician who sees adolescents with gynecologic problems.

TOXIC SHOCK SYNDROME

Toxic shock syndrome (TSS) received much publicity in the early 1980s as a disease that was occurring in young women primarily in association with one brand of tampon (Rely). Since that time, there has been recognition of milder cases than the original Centers for Disease Control (CDC) definition as well as newer information on toxin production and risk factors [75].

Although the original description of toxic shock by Todd and associates [76] suggested a disease of boys and girls, it is now apparent that toxic shock is predominantly (70–80%) a disease of young menstruating women who use tampons. Almost all cases in men and nonmenstruating women have been associated with a focal infection (infected wound, abscess, augmentation mammoplasty, and pneumonia [especially associated with influenza]). The disease in menstruating young women is associated with elaboration of an exotoxin, toxic-shock syndrome toxin (TSST-1) by *Staphylococcus aureus*. *S. aureus* has been cultured from the vagina of 98 percent of women with TSS versus 7 percent of controls. TSS has a peak occurrence on the fourth day of the menses and has been associated with continuous tampon use.

TSS continues to be reported, although the originally blamed tampon (Rely) was removed from the market in 1980. The incidence of TSS after 1980 has been reported to be 2 to 4/100,000 woman-years [77]. In a study looking at time intervals based on the change in tampon types, Pettiti and Reingold [78] reported the incidence of TSS per 100,000 women to be 0.4 from 1972 to 1977 (absorbency low), 1.5 from 1977 to 1979 (superabsorbent tampons, not Rely), 2.4 from 1979 to 1980 (Rely and other superabsorbent tampons), 2.2 from 1980 to 1985 (Rely off the market), 0.8 from April 1985 to December 1985 (polyacrylate rayon removed from tampons, absorbency low). In a study of TSS from 1983 to 1984, Berkley and co-workers [77] found that users of all tampons had a 32.8-fold increase in risk compared to nonusers. Regardless of the chemical composition, increasing absorbency increased the odds ratio for TSS. Although Mills and colleagues [79] found that in vitro the fiber polyacrylate rayon bound magnesium ions and increased the production of TSST-1 by *S. aureus*, the epidemiologic study by Berkley and co-workers [77] did not find an elevated odds ratio for cases of TSS when absorbency was controlled. Polyacrylate-containing tampons were removed from the market in 1985. Given the current information and the tremendous variability of absorbency with the current terminology of regular, super, and super-plus, mandatory labelling with standardized absorbency might allow the consumer to diminish her risk of TSS [80]. Factors that appear to promote the occurrence of TSS are the neutral pH of the vagina during menstruation and the introduction of oxygen into the vagina with the insertion of tampons. Cases of TSS do, however, occur during menses in women not using tampons, and there has been a gradual increase in the percentage of cases of TSS not related to menstruation.

Contraceptive sponge use and to a lesser extent diaphragm use have been associated with rare cases of TSS. The relative risk of nonmenstrual TSS associated with the sponge has been estimated to be increased 7.8 to 40-fold over the risks of nonusers [81]. Although in vitro data suggest that *S. aureus* and TSST-1 production are inhibited by the sponge [82], clinicians should base their counselling on the rare possibility of TSS (the risk of death estimated at 0.1–0.6/100,000 woman-years [83]) and discuss the symptoms with each patient using this method of contraception.

The toxin TSST-1 has been isolated in 90 to 100 percent of menstrual cases of TSS, whereas this toxin has been reported in only 50 to 62 percent of nonmenstrual cases, suggesting that other toxins are involved in the pathogenesis of nonmenstrual TSS. Most individuals develop antibody to TSST-1 by age 20 years. TSS occurs predominantly in the population that lacks antibody, because of either a genetic factor or lack of exposure. Young patients, especially adolescents, would be expected to be at increased risk for TSS. Almost half of the 30 patients studied by Bergdoll and associates [84] had no antibody to this toxin during convalescence. This toxin appears to block B-lymphocytes from making antibody. Women who have not made antibody to TSST-1 at follow-up are at high risk of recurrence with future menses and tampon usage.

Milder cases of TSS have also been described [85]; physicians and patients need to be aware of more minor symptomatology occurring with tampon (or sponge) use in order to intervene effectively. The criteria set up by the Center for Disease Control to study the epidemiology of TSS is for the more severe manifestation of the syndrome. These criteria are as follows:

1. Fever (temperature ≥ 38.9°C)
2. Rash (diffuse macular erythroderma that looks like sunburn)
3. Desquamation 1 to 2 weeks after the onset of the illness, particularly of palms and soles
4. Hypotension (systolic blood pressure ≤ 90 mm Hg for adults, or below the fifth percentile by age for children less than 16 years, or orthostatic decrease ≥ 15 mm Hg in diastolic blood pressure, or orthostatic syncope)
5. Involvement of three or more of the following organ systems:
   a. Gastrointestinal (vomiting or diarrhea)
   b. Muscular (severe myalgia or creatinine phosphokinase level > two times the upper limits of normal)
   c. Mucous membranes (vaginal, oropharyngeal, or conjunctival hyperemia)
   d. Renal (blood urea nitrogen or creatinine > two times the upper limit of normal or > 5 white cells/high power field in the absence of urinary tract infection)
   e. Hepatic (total bilirubin, AST (SGOT), ALT (SGPT) > two times the upper limit of normal)
   f. Hematologic (platelet count < 100,000/mm^3)
   g. Central nervous system (disorientation or alterations in consciousness when fever and hypotension are absent)
6. Negative results on the following tests, if obtained:
   a. Blood, throat, or cerebrospinal fluid cultures
   b. Serologic tests for Rocky Mountain spotted fever, leptospirosis, or measles

Adolescents with any of these symptoms or with vomiting, diarrhea, and rash during menstruation should be instructed to remove the tampon (or sponge) and go to the emergency room. Patients with TSS should be managed in the same way as those suffering from other forms of shock, including most importantly the administration of fluid. Laboratory tests include hematology and chemistry profiles, along with coagulation parameters. Hypocalcemia and hypomagnesemia and elevated CPK are common findings. A vaginal examination should be done along with removal of the tampon (if still in place). Gram stain of the vaginal pool should be done. Cultures of blood, rectum, vagina, oropharynx, anterior nares, and urine should be obtained. Penicillinase-resistant antistaphylococcal antibiotics should be administered for 2 weeks (iv, po). Although evidence is lacking, many clinicians favor irrigating the vagina with saline, Betadine solution, or vancomycin or gentamicin solution. In patients with deep abscesses in which eradication of toxin-producing staphylococci is unlikely to occur rapidly or particularly severe cases of TSS, immunoglobulin therapy (which has high levels of antibody to TSST-1) and possibly steroids may improve outcome. Further studies are needed.

Because there is an approximately 30 percent risk of recurrence, patients should be warned to avoid tampons for at least 6 months. The presence of high levels of antibody to TSST-1 at follow-up in a patient with no antibody at presentation is reassuring. Serial cultures of the vagina may be difficult to interpret, since other strains of S. aureus may be present. Testing for TSST-1–producing strains requires a specialized laboratory. Sources of antibody testing to TSST-1 at baseline and follow-up can be done in some academic centers; the CDC or Dr. Jeffrey Parsonnet (Dartmouth Medical School, Hanover, NH) may be contacted by clinicians for further information. Tampon use can be resumed with seroconversion.

The use of all tampons in the United States fell initially in response to the publicity about TSS in the early 1980s. A significant number of young women desire to continue tampon use. There is insufficient knowledge to give absolute guidelines to patients, but we suggest (1) avoiding superabsorbent tampons (this should be easier with mandatory labelling), (2) using tampons intermittently by using pads at night, (3) changing tampons every 4 to 6 hours, and especially (4) removing tampons and calling a physician if vomiting, diarrhea, rash, or fever occurs. The recommendation about frequency of changing tampons has not been subjected to critical study.

DYSURIA IN ADOLESCENT GIRLS

Dysuria is a common symptom in adolescent girls and is discussed in this section because vaginitis and vulvar lesions may produce symptoms usually associated with a urinary tract infection (UTI). The clinician needs to do a careful gynecologic assessment of adolescents who complain of dysuria. Studies [86–88] in adult women have revealed that only one half of the women with dysuria had bacteriuria with more than 10^5 organisms/ml. Vaginitis, vulvitis, infection with genital

Table 9-1. Etiology of Dysuria in Adolescent Girls

Diagnosis	No. of Patients
Vaginitis from	
Candida	10 (19%)
Trichomonas	8 (15%)
Candida and *Trichomonas*	2 (4%)
Bacterial vaginosis	2 (4%)
Bacterial UTI	9 (17%)
Bacterial UTI and vaginitis	9 (17%)
Other diagnoses	
Genital herpes	2 (4%)
N. gonorrhoeae	1 (2%)
C. trachomatis	1 (2%)
N. gonorrhoeae and *C. trachomatis*	1 (2%)
Skene's gland abscess	1 (2%)
Nonspecific vulvitis	2 (4%)
Traumatic urethritis	1 (2%)
Urethral syndrome of unclear etiology	4 (8%)

From E Demetriou, SJ Emans, and RP Masland, Dysuria in adolescent girls. Pediatrics 1982; 80:299.

herpes, *N. gonorrhoeae, C. trachomatis,* and bacteriuria with fewer than 10^5 organisms/ml are responsible for most of the remaining group. The results of a study of 53 adolescent girls (mean age 17.5 years, 77% sexually experienced) who came to our clinic because of dysuria are shown in Table 9-1 [89]. Pyuria on urinalysis was seen most frequently with UTI and *Trichomonas* vaginitis; however, patients with gonococcal and mixed gonococcal-chlamydial infection (one case of each) also had pyuria, as has been documented previously. If the study were repeated today, the percentage with *C. trachomatis* cervicitis and urethritis would be substantially higher. None of the patients who had acute urethral syndrome with unclear cause had pyuria. Stamm and associates [88, 90] have suggested that women who do not have bacteriuria of greater than 10^4 organisms/ml, gonorrhea, or vaginitis, but who have pyuria, have either low counts of bacteriuria (coliforms or *Staphylococcus saprophyticus*) or infection with *C. trachomatis*. In contrast, of the undiagnosed group without pyuria, few women had demonstrable infection. This observation led to a follow-up study [91] in which women with dysuria and frequency, in whom the usual causes were excluded, were given antibiotic treatment. Women with pyuria improved on doxycycline, 100 mg orally twice daily for 10 days, whereas those without pyuria did as well on placebo treatment. Pyuria was defined in this study as being 8 or more leukocytes/mm^3 of urine. This method was more accurate than methods generally available to clinicians because a hemocytometer chamber was used to count leukocytes.

When we assess an adolescent with dysuria, we take a history that asks specifically about onset of symptoms, sexual activity (recent and past), symptoms of urethritis in the boyfriend, previous UTIs, and internal dysuria (pain felt inside the body) versus external dysuria (pain felt as urine passes over the inflamed labia). If the patient reports a clear-cut external dysuria and discharge, it is highly likely that the patient's symptoms are due to vaginitis or a vulvar cause. Although adult women who have internal dysuria and frequency usually have a UTI, many of the adolescent girls in our clinic have vaginitis either alone or in combination with a UTI. In contrast to older women, adolescents are less able to differentiate internal versus external dysuria. Pain only at the end of urination suggests a UTI.

The laboratory evaluation of the adolescent with dysuria should include urinalysis, urine culture (if UTI is suspected), wet preparations of the vaginal secretions, and (in sexually active patients) endocervical culture for gonorrhea and a test for *C. trachomatis*. Incubating dipslides such as Uricults* in the office is inexpensive. Inspection of the genitalia should be done to exclude urethral or vulvar pathology. Speculum examination should be done for sexually active patients. In virginal patients, samples for wet preparations can be obtained with a saline-moistened, cotton-tipped applicator gently inserted through the hymenal ring. A culture for *Candida* should be done in patients with itching or vulvar erythema in whom the KOH preparation does not reveal *Candida*.

The diagnosis is generally UTI or a specific gynecologic infection [89, 92]. In patients who have undiagnosed dysuria and persistent pyuria on urinalysis, cultures or rapid tests for *Chlamydia* should be obtained from the endocervix and urethra. The patient should ask her partner again about symptoms of urethritis so that urethritis from *C. trachomatis* can be treated in him at the same time. The patient with pyuria should then be treated with a course of antibiotics effective against low-count UTIs and *Chlamydia*.

Adolescents with uncomplicated cystitis may be treated with single-dose antibiotics or a 10-day course. The most well-studied single doses are amoxicillin (3 gm) or trimethoprim-sulfamethazole (320 mg/1600 mg—4 tablets), the cure rates with the latter being slightly higher than the former [93, 94]. In a comparative trial of single dose versus 10 days of trimethoprim-sulfamethoxazole, Fihn and coworkers [95] found that a 10-day course yielded higher rates of cure at 2 weeks from the start of therapy, but at 6 weeks the difference was

*Orion Diagnostica, Helsinki, Finland.

not significant. The group suggested that an intermediate duration of treatment such as 3 days might be efficacious. The 10-day course increases the cost and the possibility of allergic symptoms, diarrhea, and *Candida* vaginitis. The oral quinolones hold promise for effective single-dose therapy of gonorrhea and UTI; a longer course is necessary to eradicate *Chlamydia*. Quinolones should not be used in pregnant women or children. For example, in nonpregnant adult patients, ciprofloxacin, 250 mg twice a day for 10 days, appears to be equally efficacious to trimethoprim-sulfamethoxazole for 10 days with fewer adverse side effects. Although Carlson and Mulley [94] and others have found that single-dose antibiotics are the most cost-effective strategy in treating young women with dysuria and advocate doing cultures and further laboratory evaluation only on those with persistent symptoms, the adolescent may be less precise in giving symptomatology, less likely to return for follow-up diagnosis, and more likely to have *Chlamydia* infection, which is not adequately treated with single-dose medication. Thus we recommend that a diagnosis be made in adolescents at the same time as treatment is initiated.

Ultrasonography of the kidneys should be performed in adolescents with complicated UTIs, pyelonephritis, inadequate response to antibiotics, and recurrent cystitis. The lack of response to a single dose of antibiotics can indicate a patient at higher risk of upper tract infection, and thus is another indicator of the need to evaluate the kidneys. In contrast to recommendations in children in which ultrasonography of the kidneys and voiding cystourethrogram (VCUG) should be performed with the *first* UTI, VCUG is generally ordered in adolescents who have an abnormal ultrasound or clinical pyelonephritis.

Patients often have recurrent UTIs in relation to coitus and especially diaphragm use. Other diaphragms or other methods of contraception may need to be considered (see Chap. 15). Coitus-related UTI can be treated with frequent voiding (every 2 hours during the day), voiding after intercourse, and suppressive antibiotics. Antibiotic regimens include trimethoprim-sulfamethoxazole, 80/160 mg, one-half tablet daily or one-half tablet 3 times per week, postcoital antibiotics [96, 97], or single-dose therapy with each infection [98, 99]. The use of prophylactic antibiotics is considered cost-effective when women experience more than two infections per year. Self-administration of antibiotics at the time of the UTI appears to be most useful in women who are accurate at self-diagnosis and have only one to two infections per year. Patients can be taught how to perform Uricult tests at home for diagnosis and to follow up symptoms. One drawback to self-therapy is the failure to reduce the proportion of patients with enterobacterial colonization of the urethra and vagina [99].

Currently, the patients without pyuria or a diagnosis fall into the small category of urethral syndrome of unclear etiology. Antibiotics do not benefit these patients. Studies in the future are likely to shed light on the diagnosis and treatment of this group.

REFERENCES
1. Shafer MA, Sweet RL, Ohm-Smith MS, et al. Microbiology of the lower genital tract in postmenarchal adolescent girls: Differences by sexual activity, contraception, and presence of nonspecific vaginitis. J Pediatr 1985; 107:974.
2. Roongpisuthipong A, Grimes DA, and Hadgu A. Is the Papanicolaou smear useful for diagnosing sexually transmitted diseases? Obstet Gynecol 1987; 69:820.
3. Paavonen J, Stevens CD, Wohler-Hanssen P, et al. Colposcopic manifestations of cervical and vaginal infections. Obstet Gynecol Survey 1988; 43:373.
4. Wolner-Hanssen P, Eschenbach D, Paavonen J, et al. Vaginal douching is an independent risk factor for pelvic inflammatory disease (Abstract #26). Infectious Disease Society for Obstetrics-Gynecology, Aug. 1988.
5. Wolner-Hanssen P, Krieger JN, Stevens CE, et al. Clinical manifestations of vaginal trichomoniasis. JAMA L989; 261:571.
6. Lossick JG. The diagnosis of vaginal trichomonias. JAMA 1988; 259:1230.
7. Krieger JN, Tam MR, Stevens CE, et al. Diagnosis of trichomoniasis: Comparison of conventional wet-mount examination with cytologic studies, cultures, and monoclonal antibody staining of direct specimens. JAMA 1988; 259:1223.
8. Fouts AC, and Kraus SJ. *Trichomonas vaginalis:* reevaluation of its clinical presentation and laboratory diagnosis. J Inf Dis 1980; 141:137:143.
9. Rein MF, and Muller M. *Trichomonas vaginalis* and trichomoniasis. In KK Holmes, P Mardh, Sparling PF, et al (eds.), *Sexually Transmitted Diseases* (2nd ed.). New York: McGraw-Hill Inc. 1990.
10. Jirovec O, and Petru M. *Trichomonas vaginalis* and trichomoniasis. Adv Parasitology 1968; 6:117.
11. Spence MR, Hollander DH, Smith J, et al. The clinical and laboratory diagnosis of *Trichomonas vaginalis* infection. Sex Transm Dis 1980; 7:168.
12. Mason PR, Super H, and Fripp PJ. Comparison of four techniques for the routine diagnosis of *Trichomonas vaginalis* infection. J Clin Pathol 1976; 29:154.
13. McLellan R, Spence MR, Brockman M, et al. The clinical diagnosis of trichomoniasis. Obstet Gynecol 1982; 60:30–34.
14. Philip A, Carter-Scott P, Rogers C. An agar culture technique to quantitative *Trichomonas vaginalis* in women. J Infect Dis 1987; 55:304.
15. Hager WD, Brown ST, Kraus SJ, et al. Metronidazole for vaginal trichomoniasis: Seven day vs. single dose regimen. JAMA 1980; 244:1219.
16. Dykers J. Single dose metronidazole for *Trichomonas:* Patient and consort. N Engl J Med 1975; 293:23.
17. Muller M, Miengasser J, and Miller W. Three metronidazole-resistant strains of *Trichomonas vaginalis* from the U.S. Am J Obstet Gynecol 1980; 138:808.
18. Lossick JG, Muller M, and Garrell TE. In vitro drug susceptibility and doses of metronidazole required for cure in cases of refractory vaginal trichomoniasis. J Infect Dis 1986; 153:948.
19. Beard CM, Niller KL, O'Fallon WM, et al. Lack of evidence for cancer due to use of metronidazole. N Engl J Med 1979; 301:519.

20. Horowitz BJ, Edelstein SW and Lippman L. *Candida tropicalis* vulvovaginitis. Obstet Gynecol 1985; 66:229.
21. Robertson WH. Mycology of vulvovaginitis. Am J Obstet Gynecol 1988; 158:989.
22. Galask RP. Vaginal colonization by bacteria and yeast. Am J Obstet Gynecol 1988; 158:993.
23. Horowitz BJ, Edelstein SW, and Lippman L. Sexual transmission of candida. Obstet Gynecol 1987; 69:883.
24. Bisschop MP, Merkus JM, Scheygrand H, et al. Cotreatment of the male partner in vaginal candidiasis: a double blind randomized control study. Br J Obstet Gynecol 1986; 93:79.
25. Leonderslot EW, Goormans E, Wiesenhaan PE, et al. Efficacy and tolerability of single-dose versus six-day treatment of candidal vulvovaginitis with vaginal tablets of clotrimazole. Am J Obstet Gynecol 1985; 152:953.
26. Bradbeer CS, Mayhew SR, and Barlow D. Butoconazole and miconazole in treating vaginal candidiasis. Genitourin Med 1985; 61:270.
27. Fleury F, and Hodgson C. Single-dose treatment of vulvovaginal candidiasis with a new 500 mg clotrimazole vaginal tablet. Adv Ther 1984; 1:349.
28. Droegemueller W, Adamson DG, Brown D, et al. Three-day treatment with butoconazole nitrate for vulvovaginal candidiasis. Obstet Gynecol 1984; 64:530.
29. Masterton G, Napier IR, Henderson JN, et al. Three-day clotrimazole treatment in candidal vulvovaginitis. Br J Vener Dis 1977; 53:126.
30. Adamson GD. Three-day treatment of vulvovaginal candidiasis. Am J Obstet Gynecol 1988; 158:1002.
31. Horowitz BJ. Antifungal therapy in the management of chronic candidiasis. Am J Obstet Gynecol 1988; 158:996.
32. Sobel JD. Recurrent vulvovaginal candidiasis: A prospective study of the efficacy of maintenance ketoconazole therapy. N Engl J Med 1986; 315:1455.
33. Speigel CA, Amsel R, Eschenbach D, et al. Anaerobic bacteria in nonspecific vaginitis. N Engl J Med 1980; 303:601.
34. Eschenbach DA, Hillier S, Critchlow C, et al. Diagnosis and clinical manifestations of bacterial vaginosis. Am J Obstet Gynecol 1988; 158:819.
35. Larsson PB, and Bergman BB. Is there a causal connection between motile curved rods, *Mobiluncus* species, and bleeding complications? Am J Obstet Gynecol 1986; 154:107.
36. Speigel CA, Amsel R, and Holmes KK. Diagnosis of bacterial vaginosis by direct gram stain of vaginal fluid. J Clin Microb 1983; 18:170.
37. Bump RC, Zuspan FP, Buesching WJ, et al. The prevalence, six-month persistence, and predictive values of laboratory indicators of bacterial vaginosis (nonspecific vaginitis) in asymptomatic women. Am J Obstet Gynecol 1984; 150:917.
38. Amsel R, Totten PA, Spiegel CA, et al. Nonspecific vaginitis: Diagnostic criteria and microbial and epidemiologic associations. Am J Med 1983; 74:14.
39. McCormack WM, Hayes CH, and Rosner B. Vaginal colonization with *Cornyebacterium vaginale*. J Infect Dis 1979; 136:740.
40. Hillier SL. In vitro inhibition of vaginal microorganisms by lactobacilli (Abstract #24). Infectious Disease Society for Obstetrics-Gynecology, August 1988.
41. Gravett MG, Nelson HP, DeRouen T, et al. Independent associations of

bacterial vaginosis and *Chlamydia trachomatis* infection with adverse pregnancy outcome. JAMA 1986; 256:1899.

42. Pheifer T, Forsyth P, Durfee M, et al. Non-specific vaginitis: Role of *Haemophilus vaginalis* and treatment with metronidazole. N Engl J Med 1978; 298:1429.
43. Swedberg J, Steiner JF, Deiss F et al. Comparison of single-dose vs. one-week course of metronidazole for symptomatic bacterial vaginosis. JAMA 1985; 254:1046.
44. Greaves WL, Chungafung J, Morris B, et al. Clindamycin versus metronidazole in the treatment of bacterial vaginosis. Obstet Gynecol 1988; 72:799.
45. Purdon A, Hanna JH, Morse PL, et al. An evaluation of single-dose metronidazole treatment for *Gardnerella vaginalis* vaginitis. Obstet Gynecol 1984; 64:271.
46. Minkowski WL, Baker CJ, Alleyne D, et al. Single oral dose metronidazole therapy for *Gardnerella vaginalis* vaginitis in adolescent females. J Adolesc Health Care 1983; 4:113.
47. Jerve F, Berdal TB, Bohman P, et al. Metronidazole in the treatment of non-specific vaginitis (NSV). Br J Vener Dis 1984; 60:171.
48. Reeves WC, Corey L, Adams HG, et al. Risk of recurrence after first episodes of genital herpes. N Engl J Med 1981; 305:315.
49. Lafferty WE, Coombs RW, Benedetti J, et al. Recurrences after oral and genital herpes simplex virus infection: Influence of site of infection and viral type. N Engl J Med 1987; 316:1444.
50. Reeves WC, Corey L, and Adams HG. Risk of recurrence after first episodes of genital herpes. N Engl J Med 1981; 305:315.
51. Corey L, Adams HG, Brown ZA, et al. Genital herpes simplex virus infections: Clinical manifestations, course and complications. Ann Intern Med 1983; 98:958.
52. Corey L, and Holmes KK. Genital herpes simplex virus infections: Current concepts in diagnosis, therapy, and prevention. Ann Intern Med 1983; 98:973.
53. Rooney JF, Felser JM, Ostrove JM, et al. Acquisition of genital herpes from an asymptomatic sexual partner. N Engl J Med 1986; 314:1561.
54. Becker TM, Blount JH, and Guinan ME. Genital herpes infections in private practice in the United States, 1966 to 1981. JAMA 1985; 253:1601.
55. Guinan ME, MacCalman J, and Kern ER. The course of untreated recurrent genital herpes simplex infection in 27 women. N Engl J Med 1981; 304:759.
56. Warford AL, Levy RA, Rekrut KA, et al. Herpes simplex virus testing of an obstetric population with an antigen enzyme-linked immunosorbent assay. Am J Obstet Gynecol 1986; 154:21.
57. Bryson YJ, Dillon M, Lovett M, et al. Treatment of first episodes of genital herpes simplex virus infection with oral acyclovir. N Engl J Med 1983; 308:916.
58. Reichman RC, Badger GJ, Mertz GJ, et al. Treatment of recurrent genital herpes simplex infections with oral acyclovir. JAMA 1984; 251:2103.
59. Straus SE, Takiff HE, Seidlin M, et al. Suppression of frequently recurring genital herpes: A placebo-controlled double-blind trial of oral acyclovir. N Engl J Med 1984; 310:1545.
60. Douglas JM, Critchlow C, Benedetti J, et al. A double-blind study of oral acyclovir for suppression of recurrences of genital herpes simplex virus infection. N Engl J Med 1984; 310:1551.

61. Lehrman SN, Douglas JM, Corey L, et al. Recurrent genital herpes and suppressive oral acyclovir therapy: Relation between clinical outcome and in-vitro drug sensitivity. Ann Intern Med 1986; 104:786.
62. Brown ZA, Vontver LA, Benedetti J, et al. Effects on infants of a first episode of genital herpes during pregnancy. N Engl J Med 1987; 317:1246.
63. Prober CG, Hensleigh PA, Boucher FD, et al. Use of routine viral cultures at delivery to identify neonates exposed to herpes simplex virus. N Engl J Med 1988; 318:887.
64. Arvin AM, Hensleigh PA, Prober C, et al. Failure of antepartum maternal cultures to predict the infant's risk of exposure to herpes simplex virus at delivery. N Engl J Med 1986; 315:798.
65. Prober CG, Sullender WM, Yasukawa LL, et al. Low risk of herpes simplex virus infections in neonates exposed to the virus at the time of vaginal delivery to mothers with recurrent genital herpes simplex virus infections. N Engl J Med 1987; 316:240.
66. Growdon WA, Apodaca L, Cragun J, et al. Neonatal herpes simplex virus infection occurring in second twin of an asymptomatic mother: Failure of a modern protocol. JAMA 1987; 257:508.
67. Gibbs RS, Amstey MS, Sweet RL, et al. Management of genital herpes infection in pregnancy. Obstet Gynecol 1988; 71:779.
68. Kalter DC, Sperber J, Rosen T, et al. Treatment of pediculosis pubis. Arch Dermatol 1987; 123:1315.
69. Portnoy J, Ahronheim GA, Ghibu F, et al. Recovery of Epstein-Barr virus from genital ulcers. N Engl J Med 1984; 311:966.
70. Schmid GP, Sanders L, Jr, Blount JH, et al. Chancroid in the United States: Reestablishment of an old disease. JAMA 1987; 258:3265–3268.
71. CDC. Chancroid—Massachusetts. MMWR 1985; 34:711.
72. Schmid GP. The treatment of chancroid. JAMA 1986; 255:1757.
73. Silber TJ, and Olsen J. Recurrent genital ulcer in an adolescent as a manifestation of Behçet's disease. J Adolesc Health Care 1988; 9:231.
74. Ammann AJ, Johnson A, Fyfe G, et al. Behçet syndrome. J Pediatr 1985; 107:41.
75. Wager GP. Toxic shock syndrome: A review. Am J Obstet Gynecol 1983; 146:93.
76. Todd J, Fishaut M, Kapral F, et al. Toxic shock syndrome associated with phage group-1 staphylococci. Lancet 1978; 2:1116.
77. Berkley SF, Hightower AW, Broome CV, et al. The relationship of tampon characteristics to menstrual toxic shock syndrome. JAMA 1987; 258:917.
78. Pettitti DB, and Reingold A. Tampon characteristics and menstrual toxic shock syndrome. JAMA 1988; 259:686.
79. Mills JT, Parsonnet J, Tsai Y, et al. Control of production of toxic-shock-syndrome toxin-1 (TSST-1) by magnesium IM. J Infect Dis 1985; 151:1158.
80. CDC. Dangerous delays in tampon absorbency warnings. JAMA 1987; 258:949.
81. Faich G, Pearson K, Fleming D, et al. Toxic shock syndrome and the vaginal contraceptive sponge. JAMA 1986; 255:216.
82. Remington KM, Buller RS, and Kelly, JR. Effect of the Today contraceptive sponge on growth and toxic shock syndrome toxin-1 production by *Staphylococcus aureus*. Obstet Gynecol 1987; 69(4):563.
83. Reingold AL. Toxic shock syndrome and the contraceptive sponge. JAMA 1986; 255:242.
84. Bergdoll MS, Reiser RF, Crass BA, et al. A new staphylococcal entero-

toxin F, associated with toxic-shock-syndrome *Staphylococcus aureus* isolates. Lancet 1981; 1:1017.
85. Bass JW, Harden LB, and Peixotto JH. Probable toxic shock syndrome without shock and multisystem involvement. Pediatrics 1982; 70:279.
86. Brooks D, and Maudar A. Pathogenesis of the acute urethral syndrome in women and its diagnosis in general practice. Lancet 1972; 2:893.
87. Komaroff AL, Pass TM, McCue JD, et al. Management strategies for urinary and vaginal infections. Arch Intern Med 1978; 138:1069.
88. Stamm WE, Wagner KF, Amsel R, et al. Causes of the acute urethral syndrome in women. N Engl J Med 1980; 303:409.
89. Demetriou E, Emans SJ, and Masland RP. Dysuria in adolescent girls. Pediatrics 1982; 80:299.
90. Stamm WE, Counts GW, Running KR, et al. Diagnosis of coliform infection in acutely dysuric women. N Engl J Med 1982; 307:463.
91. Stamm WE, Running K, McKevitt M, et al. Treatment of acute urethral syndrome. N Engl J Med 1981; 304:956.
92. Komaroff AL. Acute dysuria in women. N Engl J Med 1984; 310:368.
93. Morgan PP. Randomized clinical trials need to be more clinical. JAMA 1985; 253:1782.
94. Carlson KJ, and Mulley AG. Management of acute dysuria: A decision-analysis model of alternative strategies. Ann Intern Med 1985; 102:244.
95. Fihn SD, et al. Trimethoprim-sulfamethoxazole for acute dysuria in women: a single-dose or ten-day course: A double-blind, randomized trial. JAMA 1988; 260:627.
96. Plau A, Sachs T, and Englestein D, Recurrent urinary tract infection in premenopausal women. Prophylaxis based on an understanding of the pathogenesis. J Urol 1983; 129;1152.
97. Vosti KL. Recurrent urinary tract infection prevention by prophylactic antibiotics after sexual intercourse. JAMA 1975; 1231:934.
98. Stamm WE. Prevention of urinary tract infections. Amer J Med 1984; 76:148.
99. Wong ES, McKevitt M, Running K, et al. Management of recurrent urinary tract infections with patient-administered single-dose therapy. Ann Intern Med 1985; 102:302.

SUGGESTED FURTHER READING

Corey L. First episode, recurrent, and asymptomatic herpes simplex infections. J Am Acad Dermatol 1988; 18:169.
CDC. 1989 Sexually Transmitted Diseases Treatment Guidelines. MMWR 1989; 38(S-8):1.
Johnson RE, Nahmias AJ, Magdar LS, et al. A seroepidemiologic survey of the prevalence of herpes simplex virus type 2 infection in the United States. N Engl J Med 1989; 321:7.
Crumpacker CS. Molecular target of antiviral therapy (Seminars in Medicine). N Engl J Med 1989; 321:163.
Mertz GJ, Jones CC, Mills J, et al. Long-term acyclovir suppression of frequently recurring genital herpes simplex virus infection: A multicenter double-blind trial. JAMA 1988; 260:201.
Holmes KK, Mardh P, Sparling PF, et al. (eds.). *Sexually Transmitted Diseases* (2nd ed.). New York: McGraw-Hill, 1990.
Kaufman RH, Friedrich EG, Gardner HL. *Benign Diseases of the Vulva and Vagina.* Chicago: Yearbook, 1989.

10. Gonorrhea, *Chlamydia trachomatis*, Pelvic Inflammatory Disease, and Syphilis

School lectures, popular magazines, and scientific journals currently point to the epidemic of reported cases of sexually transmitted diseases (STDs), including *Neisseria gonorrhoeae*, *Chlamydia trachomatis*, herpes (see p. 332), and human papillomavirus (see p. 385) and to the increased prevalence of syphilis. The increase is probably the result of many factors, including earlier sexual relations among teenagers, decreased use of the condom, increased health facilities for teenagers allowing better treatment and reporting, and the recognition of asymptomatic infections in males and females. Adolescents infected with *N. gonorrhoeae* and *C. trachomatis* are at particular risk of upper genital tract infections including pelvic inflammatory disease (PID) and the sequelae of infertility, ectopic pregnancy and chronic pain. Although most infections occur in young women between 15 and 24 years of age, very young teenagers who are sexually active have an especially high risk of acquiring these pathogens. More widespread screening to detect asymptomatic infections of *N. gonorrhoeae* and *C. trachomatis* and better recognition of the symptoms of upper tract infections are needed to improve health care for teenage women.

GONOCOCCAL INFECTIONS
Gonococcal infections may be symptomatic or asymptomatic. Screening endocervical cultures indicates that the asymptomatic rate of gonorrhea ranges from 0.2 to 13 percent in adult women, depending on the clinical setting. Adolescents seen in private practices in the suburbs have a significantly lower rate than adolescents seen in large outpatient hospital clinics serving an inner city population. In homes for juvenile delinquents, the asymptomatic rate of gonorrhea among teenage girls was found to be 10 to 12 percent [1, 2]. Hein and associates [3] found a rate of 7 percent among girls admitted to a New York detention center. Saltz and associates [4] reported isolating *N. gonorrhoeae* from 3 percent of 100 adolescents in a clinic that serves low- and middle-income urban families. Among a sample of 500 New England college students, *N. gonorrhoeae* was recovered from only 2 out of 500, or 0.4 percent (88% of the 486 who answered the questionnaire were sexually experienced) [5]. Thus the risk of being infected varies with the population studied and the number of sexual partners. Screening sexually active teenagers in low-risk groups once a year or less and high-risk groups at least every 6 months appears to

be a prudent policy. A young woman who has recently changed sexual partners or has symptoms should also be cultured.

Although it has been estimated that 75 to 90 percent of all gonococcal infections in women, and 10 to 40 percent of infections in men, are asymptomatic, many of these patients on careful questioning do, in fact, have symptoms. Culturing the endocervix is the best screening test for detecting infection in adolescent girls. Routinely culturing the rectum and pharynx is not cost-effective in adolescent populations; in addition, treatment regimens generally take into account the need to eradicate *N. gonorrhoeae* at all sites [6].

Isolating *N. gonorrhoeae*, a fastidious gram-negative diplococcus, requires special techniques. Culture swabs should always be plated directly onto the appropriate medium. Thayer-Martin plates must be transported immediately to the laboratory and incubated under increased carbon dioxide tension. Two alternatives, Transgrow and modified Thayer-Martin-Jembec, offer selective media that have the advantage of being transport media. Transgrow bottles should be held upright when the swab is streaked over the agar; isolation of the gonococcus is improved if the medium is incubated at 37°C for 12 to 18 hours before mailing. The Jembec media with the carbon dioxide generating tablet inserted into the well is easier to use, more sensitive, and therefore generally preferable in clinical practice. It is critical that *N. gonorrhoeae* be properly identified, since cultures of vaginal discharge in prepubertal girls may yield other *Neisseria* such as *N. cinerea* that may initially be diagnosed as *N. gonorrhoeae*. In prepubertal children with presumptive *N. gonorrhoeae*, confirmatory testing should be done.

The Gram stain is considered positive if gram-negative intracellular diplococci are seen within polymorphonuclear leukocytes. Although the specificity of this finding is 95 percent for the diagnosis of *N. gonorrhoeae*, the sensitivity is variable, close to 100 percent in men with symptomatic urethritis but less than 60 percent for cervical and rectal infections [7]. Enzyme immunoassays such as Gonozyme and the new rapid Testpack are more sensitive than Gram stain but less sensitive than culture in the diagnosis of cervical gonorrhea. DNA probes for gonorrhea such as the GenProbe PACE system (direct chemiluminescent DNA probe test) are under investigation, with preliminary sensitivities of 90 to 93 percent [8, 9]. However, a major drawback for enzyme immunoassays and DNA probes is the inability to test the organisms for antibiotic resistance, an increasing problem in the past decade.

GONOCOCCAL CERVICITIS AND URETHRITIS

The presenting complaints of patients with gonococcal cervicitis include vaginal discharge, dysuria, urinary frequency, and dys-

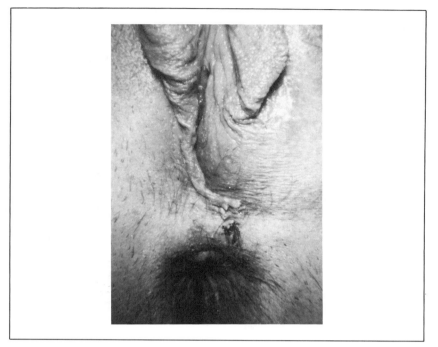

Figure 10-1. Bartholin's gland abscess.

pareunia. On examination, the cervix may be tender to palpation; Gram stain of the purulent discharge may be positive, but the diagnosis of gonorrhea in women must be confirmed by culture. However, treatment can be instituted on the basis of symptoms and a positive smear.

Gonococcal urethral and cervical infections often coexist in the woman. The urethral infection may be asymptomatic, or the patient may present with urinary frequency, internal dysuria, suprapubic pain, and purulent discharge from the urethra or Skene's glands. Urinalysis may show pyuria, and Gram stain of the purulent discharge may be positive for gram-negative intracellular diplococci. The urethral discharge should be cultured for *N. gonorrhoeae*. As noted in Chapter 9, the differential diagnosis of dysuria include (low count) urinary tract infections, chlamydial urethritis, and vulvovaginal infections.

Labial pain and swelling may be present if the young woman has a Bartholin's gland infection (which may be associated with infections caused by *N. gonorrhoeae*, *Chlamydia*, or other organisms) (Fig. 10-1). Depending on assessment, the abscess is usually treated with incision and drainage using a Word catheter, cultures are taken, and the patient is given a course of antibiotics. Marsupialization is necessary for recurrent infections.

TREATMENT OF ASYMPTOMATIC INFECTIONS, CONTACTS, URETHRITIS, AND CERVICITIS

Treatment of *N. gonorrhoeae* must take into account the sites infected, the prevalence of antibiotic resistance in the community, the high rate of coexisting *C. trachomatis* infections in adolescents, allergies, pregnancy, and the likelihood of compliance. Antibiotic resistance can be plasmid-mediated, chromosomally mediated, or both. The most important variations currently identified in the United States are plasmid-mediated penicillin resistance (penicillinase-producing *N. gonorrhoeae* [PPNG]), chromosomally mediated resistance to penicillin (CMRNG), which can also include resistance to tetracycline, and plasmid-mediated high-level tetracycline resistance (TRNG) [2, 10–13]. In 1985, more than 8800 cases of PPNG were reported; in 1986, 16,608 cases of PPNG [13]; and in 1987, more than 25,000 cases. Since rates of resistance are quite variable throughout the United States, each locale needs to make sure that isolates are tested at minimum for beta lactamase production and if possible for resistance. For example, in Dade County, Florida, 22 percent of the isolates were PPNG in 1986.

Nonepidemic areas are defined as having less than 1 percent of gonorrhea isolates in a 2-month period caused by PPNG. Endemic areas are defined as locales with 1 to 3 percent of gonorrhea caused by PPNG. All isolates from treatment failures, from children, and from complicated infections (PID, disseminated gonococcal infections, ophthalmia) should be tested for antimicrobial resistance. The Centers for Disease Control (CDC) has outlined an aggressive management program to prevent the further spread of resistant organisms. Hyperendemic areas are defined as those with greater than 3 percent of all gonorrhea isolates being PPNG. Vigorous contact tracing and control measures are indicated. Ceftriaxone intramuscularly is the drug of choice for the treatment of gonorrhea. Spectinomycin is an alternative, although it does not eradicate pharyngeal gonorrhea. Spectinomycin and the quinolones are not effective against incubating syphilis. Spectinomycin-resistant strains have been reported in the Far East [11].

Because of the 15 to 40 percent prevalence of coexisting *C. trachomatis* infections in heterosexual patients with gonorrhea, the single-dose therapy should be followed with a course of doxycycline, tetracycline, or erythromycin [12–14].

The recommendation of the 1989 Sexually Transmitted Diseases Treatment Guidelines [12] for gonorrhea is

Ceftriaxone, 250 mg intramuscularly once
plus
Doxycycline, 100 mg orally 2 times a day for 7 days

The ceftriaxone can be mixed with 1% lidocaine (without epinephrine) to reduce patient discomfort with the injection. A history of allergy to penicillin and cephalosporins should be taken before initiating treatment. Fortunately, the crossreactivity between third-generation cephalosporins and penicillin is rare, and a history of the type of penicillin allergy should be carefully documented. Ceftriaxone should be withheld only in the rare patient with a history of immediate and/or anaphylactic reaction to penicillin. In these cases spectinomycin, 2.0 gm intramuscularly, should be used, followed by doxycycline.

Other alternatives with less data for the treatment of gonorrhea include ofloxacin, ciprofloxacin, 500 mg orally once; norfloxacin, 800 mg orally once; cefuroxime axetil, 1 gm orally once with probenecid, 1 gm; cefotaxime, 1 gm intramuscularly once; and ceftizoxime, 500 mg intramuscularly once [14–17]. All of these regimens are followed by doxycycline, 100 mg orally 2 times a day for 7 days. The quinolones (ofloxacin, ciprofloxacin, norfloxacin) are not prescribed to patients pregnant or under 17 years old. A penicillin such as amoxicillin, 3 gm orally with 1 gm probenecid, followed by doxycycline may be used for treatment if the infection is known to have been acquired from a source proven *not* to have penicillin-resistant gonorrhea. Oral ampicillin or amoxicillin may cause nausea and vomiting; the dose should always be taken in the office to ensure compliance. Oral medications may be preferred for rape victims who have already been traumatized at the time of the emergency ward visit; technically the risk of acquiring penicillin-resistant NG, the possibility of pregnancy, and the age of the patient must be considered.

Tetracycline, 500 mg orally 4 times a day for 7 days, can be substituted for doxycycline, although compliance is likely to be lower since this drug has to be taken 4 times a day between meals and the cost of generic doxycycline is not substantially higher than tetracycline. For patients who cannot take doxycycline (e.g., pregnant patients), erythromycin base or stearate, 500 mg orally 4 times a day for 7 days, or erythromycin ethylsuccinate, 800 mg orally 4 times a day for 7 days, can be substituted. Some patients cannot tolerate the 500-mg dose of erythromycin without nausea and vomiting; in these cases the erythromycin base can be given 250 mg orally 4 times a day for 14 days.

Newer antimicrobial agents and combinations are likely to be introduced in the 1990s. Aztreonam (1.0 gm intramuscularly) and the quinolones need more clinical studies. Rosoxacin appears effective against both PPNG and non-PPNG infections but central nervous system side effects are common and resistance has emerged in some parts of the world. In addition to efficacy against gonorrhea, ofloxacin, 300 mg twice a day for 7 days, appears effective against *C. trachomatis* [17]. Although trimethoprim-sulfamethoxazole, 9 tablets (720 mg/3600 mg) daily, for 5 days is effective in treating both *N. gonorrhoeae* infections (including pharyngeal infections) and *C. trachomatis*, a high number of patients experience adverse neurologic side effects including dizziness, light-headedness, tremor, and impaired speech and cognition [18]. Amoxicillin 3 gm plus clavulanic acid orally appears promising in the treatment of men with urethritis caused by both PPNG and non-PPNG.

Patients are instructed to abstain from sexual relations for 7 days. Since treatment failure is rare with ceftriaxone/doxycycline, a test of cure done 1 to 2 months after treatment allows an opportunity for rescreening. Test of cure should be done 4 to 7 days after completion of alternative treatment. Adolescent girls are more likely to return than adolescent boys. Most positive cultures on follow-up are the result of reinfection. True treatment failures should be given ceftriaxone or spectinomycin and sensitivity testing performed on the isolate.

A serologic test for syphilis should be sent at the time of therapy. If the initial test is negative, a follow-up blood test 1 month later is necessary only if the patient was treated with spectinomycin or the quinolones. The pros and cons of HIV testing should be presented.

Every patient should be interviewed to find contacts for the period of the duration of symptoms plus 30 days (90 days is preferable for PPNG isolates). Regardless of symptoms, all contacts should be cultured and treated at the same visit.

Gonococcal Pharyngitis
The incidence of symptomatic and asymptomatic pharyngitis among teenagers reflects the population studied. Gonococcal pharyngitis is related to the practice of fellatio. It may be asymptomatic, or it may occur as patchy erythema (viruslike throat) or less commonly with a red, edematous uvula with vesiculopustular lesions on the soft palate and tonsillar pillars (strep-like) [13, 19, 20]. This infection spontaneously clears in 10 to 12 weeks; however, patients are at risk for disseminated disease during this time. Diagnosis is by culture on selective media. Treatment should be ceftriaxone, 250 mg intramuscularly once. Nonpregnant patients (over 16 years old) who cannot tolerate ceftriaxone can be treated with ciprofloxacin, 500 mg orally as a single dose; a repeat culture should be done 4 to 7 days later. Single-dose ampicillin is not effective against pharyngeal gonorrhea, and thus if

the gonorrhea is known to be penicillin-sensitive, a longer course of ampicillin, 3.5 gm orally initially (with 1 gm probenecid), followed by 500 mg orally 4 times a day for the next 2 days is another option. Although trimethoprim-sulfamethoxazole, 9 tablets a day for 5 days, has also been shown to be effective, neurologic side effects can be significant.

Gonococcal Proctitis
Gonococcal infection of the rectum may occur asymptomatically, or the patient may have an anal discharge of blood and pus (acute proctitis) or a low-grade proctitis with pain on defecation. In suspected cases, a cotton-tipped applicator should be inserted into the rectum to obtain a sample of the pus for culture; the specimen should be obtained by direct visualization if possible [21]. Proctitis can be more difficult to treat than urethritis, but the treatment courses for women are the same as noted for cervicitis.

Gonococcal Arthritis
The diagnosis of gonococcal arthritis depends largely on clinical suspicion because the source of the gonococcus in adolescent girls is usually an asymptomatic or low-grade cervicitis or pharyngeal infection [22, 23]. Two forms of gonococcal arthritis have been described by Holmes and others [24, 25], although many patients do not fit this classic description. In young women, the early form begins at the onset or just following a menstrual period and is characterized by migratory polyarthralgias, tenosynovitis, fever, chills, and skin lesions (pinpoint erythematous papules that may progress to purpuric vesiculopustular lesions) (Fig. 10-2). There are usually less than 20 skin lesions, chiefly in a peripheral distribution. Gram stain and culture from these lesions are positive in about 10 percent of patients [23], but direct fluorescent antibody staining of biopsies detects *N. gonorrhoeae* in more than half of these patients. Blood cultures may be positive if taken within 2 days of the onset of symptoms. Joint fluid, usually scanty, is negative for the gonococcus.

The late form of gonococcal arthritis is characterized by a monoarticular effusion, most often involving the knee, followed by elbows, ankles, wrists, small joints of the hands and feet, and shoulders. A positive synovial fluid culture occurs in 20 to 50 percent of cases. Synovial fluid containing less than 20,000 leukocytes/mm^3 are usually negative, whereas fluids containing more than 80,000/mm^3 are usually positive. Blood cultures are negative and systemic symptoms are usually absent.

Hospitalization is indicated for unreliable patients and patients with purulent joint effusions or uncertain diagnosis. Treatment includes *one* of the following: ceftriaxone, 1 gm intramuscularly or intra-

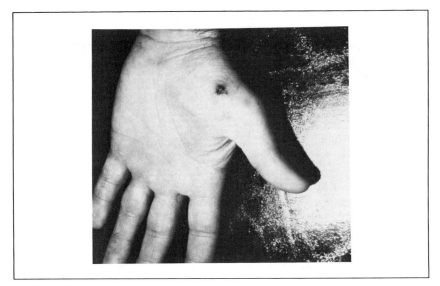

Figure 10-2. Skin lesion of gonococcemia.

venously, every 24 hours; or ceftizoxime, 1 gm intravenously, every 8 hours; or cefotaxime, 1 gm intravenously, every 8 hours. Patients who are allergic to β-lactam drugs should be treated with spectinomycin, 2 gm intramuscularly every 12 hours. If the *N. gonorrhoeae* is proven to be penicillin-sensitive, parenteral therapy can be changed to ampicillin, 1 gm intravenously every 6 hours. Patients should also be tested for *C. trachomatis* genital infection. If reliable testing is not available, the patient should be treated empirically for *Chlamydia*. Patients who are reliable and have uncomplicated disease may be discharged 24 to 48 hours after all symptoms resolve to complete a total of 7 days of antibiotic therapy with oral cefuroxime axetil, 500 mg 2 times a day, or amoxicillin, 500 mg with clavulanic acid 3 times a day, or, if not pregnant and over 16 years old, ciprofloxacin, 500 mg 2 times a day [12].

Immobilization of the joint is helpful. Although open drainage of joints other than the hip is not indicated, repeated aspiration may be necessary [12, 26].

REITER'S SYNDROME

Reiter's syndrome is characterized by the triad of arthritis, urethritis, and ocular abnormalities, frequently following a disease such as *N. gonorrhoeae* or *C. trachomatis* urethritis or enteric infections such as with *Shigella*, *Salmonella*, or *Yersinia*. The joints affected are primarily knees, ankles, feet, and wrists in an oligo- or monoarticular pattern; sacroiliitis and spondyloarthropathies can also occur. Ocular problems include iritis and conjunctivitis. Dermatologic findings include keratoblennorrhagica, mucocutaneous lesions, and oral ulcers. Treatment should aim at the detection and antimicrobial therapy of the genital infection and the use of nonsteroidal anti-inflammatory agents for the reactive arthritis. The eyes should be carefully followed by an ophthalmologist and treated with topical and systemic agents as indicated [27, 28].

GONOCOCCAL EYE INFECTIONS
Although gonococcal ophthalmia in the newborn is well-known to pediatricians, adolescent girls and boys can develop purulent discharge from gonococcal conjunctivitis. Periorbital edema and pain, gaze restriction, keratitis, and preauricular adenopathy can occur. Ceftriaxone, 1 gm intramuscularly, should be administered, and evaluation and follow-up by an ophthalmologist are essential. The possibility of concurrent chlamydial eye infection or genital infections with *N. gonorrhoeae* or other STDs should be evaluated.

MISCELLANEOUS INFECTIONS
Gonococcal endocarditis and meningitis have been reported. Meningitis should be treated with ceftriaxone 1 to 2 gm intravenously every 12 hours for 10 to 14 days; endocarditis with a similar dose for 4 weeks. The possibility of a complement deficiency should be investigated.

GONOCOCCAL VULVOVAGINITIS IN THE PREPUBERTAL CHILD
Gonococcal infection in the prepubertal child is usually manifested as a purulent vulvovaginitis rather than a cervicitis. The infection may also be asymptomatic or be evident as a thin mucoid discharge. Thus, a Gram stain and culture are important in the evaluation of vaginal discharge in a prepubertal girl. Although the Gram stain is helpful, *Neisseria meningitides* rarely causes vaginitis; therefore, it is essential that the diagnosis be proved by cultures with confirmatory testing.

Once a diagnosis is made, the child should be interviewed by an experienced social worker, psychologist, or pediatrician to try to elicit a history of sexual abuse or misuse. Play therapy and repeated interviews may be necessary to establish the history, since in most cases of sexual abuse, the abuser is known to the child and is often a family member. All family members and caretakers of the child should be cultured. The source of infection is frequently found to be an older male relative or stepparent. Mothers and sisters are frequently infected. Although it is possible that *N. gonorrhoeae* can be transmitted by sexual play between siblings and peers, the clinician should strongly suspect sexual abuse in all cases of prepubertal gonorrhea

[29, 30]. Since sexual abuse often involves vulvar coitus or oral sex rather than penetration, a physical examination in many abused girls shows a normal hymen (see Chap. 17). Although contacts may be easier to culture and follow-up may be significantly improved if the child is hospitalized [30], we use an outpatient approach for most cases. Cases of suspected child sexual abuse must be reported to the mandated state agency.

Prior to treatment, rectal and pharyngeal cultures for *N. gonorrhoeae* should be obtained from the child with vaginal gonorrhea as well as vaginal culture for *C. trachomatis* and a serology for syphilis. For children over 100 pounds ($\geq$ 45 kg), adult schedules for treating cervicitis and urethritis are used. For children under 100 pounds ($<$ 45 kg), the recommended regimen is ceftriaxone, 125 mg intramuscularly once. Children allergic to cephalosporins are treated with spectinomycin, 40 mg/kg intramuscularly once. Patients under 45 kg with bacteremia or arthritis are treated with ceftriaxone, 50 mg/kg (maximum 1 gm) once daily for 7 days [12]. Coinfection with *C. trachomatis* should be treated with erythromycin, 50 mg/kg/day in 4 divided doses, or in children older than 8 years, with doxycycline, 100 mg 2 times a day for 7 days.

Follow-up cultures of the throat, rectum, and vagina should be taken 7 to 14 days after treatment. Reinfection is likely if the source is not identified and treated. Persistent vaginal discharge in a girl who has been adequately treated and had negative cultures for gonorrhea may result from a coinfection with *C. trachomatis* that was not adequately treated with single-dose therapy. The family may have been noncompliant with the 7-day course of doxycycline or erythromycin. All patients should be evaluated for coinfection with syphilis.

Only a few cases of salpingitis secondary to *N. gonorrhoeae* have been reported in prepubertal girls, and thus no data exist on the best form of treatment. Antibiotics with similar spectrum as used in adolescent and adult PID are appropriate.

CHLAMYDIA TRACHOMATIS
The past decade has recognized the importance of the epidemic of *C. trachomatis* infections among sexually active patients, especially adolescents. The serotypes D-K have been associated with nongonococcal urethritis and epididymitis in men and mucopurulent cervicitis, salpingitis, urethritis (pyuria-dysuria syndrome, see p. 333), postabortal and postpartum endometritis, perihepatitis, and infertility in women. Cervical infection with *C. trachomatis* has been associated with premature rupture of membranes, preterm labor, and low birth weight [31]. Both men and women may have conjunctivitis, Reiter's syndrome, and rectal infections. Infants born to mothers with chlamydial genital infections may have conjunctivitis and pneumonia.

Washington and colleagues [32] have estimated that the projected annual cost of chlamydial infections by 1990 may exceed $2.18 billion.

C. *trachomatis* is a common infection, occurring in 5 to 15 percent of asymptomatic sexually active patients, 20 to 30 percent of patients seen in STD clinics, 40 to 50 percent of symptomatic patients, and 15 to 50 percent of patients with *N. gonorrhoeae*. Adolescent girls are at high risk of acquiring a cervical infection with *C. trachomatis* because of the increased number of partners, the presence of columnar cells on the cervical ectropion exposed to the vaginal environment, the lack of barrier contraception, and the use of oral contraceptives. It is estimated that sexually active women less than 20 years old have chlamydial infection rates two- to three-fold higher than adult women. Prevalence figures vary depending on the population studied, with rates from 4.9 percent in a college population in the mid 1970s to 27 percent in inner city pregnant teens [33–43]. Most clinics can expect that 8 to 15 percent of sexually active adolescents screened will have *C. trachomatis* endocervical infections (Table 10-1).

Risk factors for acquiring *C. trachomatis* are young age (<20 years), new partner within 2 months, no contraception or a nonbarrier method, black race, number of partners, cervical ectopy, friability or mucopus, and pregnancy. In a study of 1059 women attending family planning clinics with a 9.3 percent prevalence of *C. trachomatis* infection, Handsfield and co-workers [44] found that the presence of two or more of the following risk factors identified 90 percent of infections: age less than 25 years, intercourse with a new partner within 2 months, examination showing purulent or mucopurulent cervical exudate, bleeding induced by swabbing the endocervical mucosa, and use of no contraception or a nonbarrier method.

In STD clinics, the presence of mucopurulent cervical discharge, a positive yellow swab test (a white cotton-tipped applicator is twirled in the endocervical canal and the color compared to a white background), and the presence of white cells on a Gram stain of the endocervical discharge have all been associated with *C. trachomatis* infection. Brunham and associates [45] in a study of 100 women in an STD clinic found that of those with *C. trachomatis* isolated, 89 percent had 10 or more polymorphonuclear leukocytes per oil immersion field; in contrast, only 17 percent of those without *C. trachomatis* had 10 or more white cells. However, examining this test in an adolescent clinic, Moscicki [46] found the positive predictive value of finding more than 5 white cells per oil immersions field (1000×) to be only 36 percent for all adolescents studied. The positive predictive value was 53 percent in a black population with a prevalence of *C. trachomatis* of 30 and 13 percent in a white population with a prevalence of infection of 7 percent.

Given the difficulty in identifying risk factors for individual sexu-

Table 10-1. Prevalence of C. trachomatis in the Cervix

Reference	n	Age/Symptoms/Race	% Chlamydia	% GC
Shafer et al. [33]	363	13–20 yr 50% black 32% white 11% Hispanic Symptoms in 24%	14	7
Bump et al. [34]	68	14–17 yr 72.5% black 27.5% white Asymptomatic	19	6
Chacko [35]	70	13–18 yr Pregnant—black, urban, low SES	27	
	190	13–18 yr Nonpregnant	23	
Fraser et al. [36]	125	14–20 yr	8	12
Bell et al. [37]	100	Adolescents in a juvenile detention center 52% black—urban clinic	20	18
Fisher et al. [38]	150	14–21 yr Suburban clinic	14.5	
McCormack et al. [39]	439	College students (1974–75)	4.9	0.4
Ismail et al. [40]	201	13–19 yr Pregnant, low SES	21.3	
Khurana et al. [41]	49	15–19 yr Pregnant, low SES	18.4	
Harrison et al. [42]	162	53% undergrad college health center 86% white 10% Hispanic	8	1.2
Skjeldestad et al. [43]	599	Pregnant women in Norway <20 yr 20–24 yr >24 yr	5.8 25.8 8.9 2.3	

GC = N. gonorrhoeae; SES = Socioeconomic status.

ally active teenagers, the best policy is to screen adolescents once or twice a year, after a change in sexual partners, and with any suggestive symptoms. In the presence of a positive endocervical culture, Jones and co-workers [47] found that 40 percent have positive cultures from the endometrium and evidence of silent upper tract infection. More adolescents with endocervical infection with *C. trachomatis* go on to develop salpingitis than do adult women, and thus clinicians need to make sure that adolescents are receiving needed medical care and counselling about this infection and other STDs.

A number of detection methods for diagnosing *C. trachomatis* are now available, and improved methods using DNA probes are likely to be in clinical use soon. In prepubertal children, in whom the diagnosis of sexual abuse must be considered in the presence of *C. trachomatis* vaginal infection, culture is essential because of the possibility of false-positive indirect tests. In adolescents, culture using McCoy cells and subsequent identification using fluorescent antibody stain 2 to 3 days later is considered the "gold" standard against which other methods are judged; however, in some locations, cultures are impractical because of transport of specimens or too expensive because of lack of interested laboratories. Culture will not detect nonviable organisms that may be found in upper genital tract infections. Care must be taken when cultures are obtained to make sure that a Dacron swab is used and that the endocervix is scraped to obtain cells, since *C. trachomatis* is an intracellular organism. Although the specificity is 100 percent, it is estimated that the sensitivity of the culture is only 80 to 90 percent. The use of a special cytobrush may improve detection of the organism.

Nonculture methods appear to have a greater potential for infection control. Commonly used methods of detection include the direct smear using the SYVA MicroTrak system and enzyme immunoassays (Chlamydiazyme, CellTech). An office-based test (Testpack CHLAMYDIA) has also become available and appears to have a sensitivity of 76 percent and a specificity of 99.5 percent in five high-risk populations [48]. The MicroTrak kit includes urethral and cervical swabs and a cytobrush. In nonpregnant girls, the cytobrush can markedly improve the collection of endocervical cells and the number of positive smears. After applying a fluorescein-conjugated monoclonal antibody, the microscopist looks for the presence of yellow-green elementary bodies. The value of this test depends on the prevalence of *C. trachomatis* in the population studied, whether single- or double-pass cultures are used as the standard, and whether 1, 5, or 10 elementary bodies are considered a positive test. For example, the sensitivity of this test has ranged from a low of 61 percent in a study by Shafer and colleagues [33] of females in an adolescent clinic with a prevalence of 14 percent, to a sensitivity of 80 percent in

The Children's Hospital (Boston) clinics with a prevalence of 15 percent, to a sensitivity of 93 percent in an STD clinic with a prevalence of 23 percent [49]. The positive predictive value of this test ranges from 80% in populations with a 10% prevalence of infection to a predictive value of 95% in populations with a prevalence of 30%.

Chlamydiazyme is an enzyme-linked immunoabsorbent assay (ELISA) and requires a spectrophotometer. This test also has had a range of sensitivities and specificities depending on the study; Amortegui and Meyer [50] found a sensitivity of 82 percent in a population with a prevalence of 8.8 percent, compared to a study by Baselski and co-workers [51] that found a sensitivity of 96 percent in a pregnant group with a prevalence of 21.1 percent. Positive predictive values have ranged from 32 to 87 percent depending on the population studied [52]. Lebar and associates [53] reported a 97 percent sensitivity in a population with a 16 percent incidence of infection using another immunoassay (Boots CellTech IDEA III). Both of these nonculture methods have the problem of false-positive and false-negative results. Better detection techniques including DNA hybridization tests will likely be available to the clinician in the near future. Sensitivities are reported for DNA tests to be 87 to 92 percent with specificities of 95 to 99 percent [53–55]. Thus, symptomatic patients with mucopurulent cervical infection and their partners should be treated even if these detection methods are negative, given the limitations of methodology. However, young women with cervical ectopy may have persistent or recurrent mucopus in spite of the eradication of *N. gonorrhoeae* and *C. trachomatis*, and thus additional research is needed to elucidate other infectious agents responsible for this condition.

In choosing a test for office practice, clinicians need to look at the comparison of the test with culture, the expense, the timing to obtain results, the sensitivity, and predictive value in the population of patients for whom they will be providing care. Cultures are of greatest value in screening populations with a low risk of chlamydial infection. Trachtenburg and colleagues [56] have estimated that with a prevalence of more than 2 percent, screening would pay for itself. Analyzing costs of various strategies, Phillips and co-workers [57] found that using a rapid test to detect *C. trachomatis* would reduce overall health costs if the prevalence was 7 percent or greater and that routine cultures would be cost-effective with a prevalence over 14 percent. Doing urethral cultures in addition to endocervical screening detects additional patients who are infected with *C. trachomatis* but adds to cost.

In Papanicolaou (Pap) smears from women seen in STD clinics, increased numbers of histiocytes and polymorphonuclear leukocytes and the presence of transformed leukocytes have been associated with *C. trachomatis* infection with sensitivities of 17 to 95 percent, specificities of 61 to 100 percent, and positive predictive values of 40 to 100 percent [58, 59]. Since it is likely that an adolescent would already have been screened for *C. trachomatis*, reports of the Pap smear are difficult to use in selective screening but certainly should encourage follow-up evaluation if findings suggestive of Chlamydia are noted. Colposcopic evaluation has suggested an association between *C. trachomatis* infection and endocervical mucopus, hypertrophic cervicitis, and immature metaplasia [60].

Serologies for IgG and IgM to *C. trachomatis* are primarily a research tool. A conversion from lack of antibody to the presence of a titer 3 weeks after PID, the presence of IgM, and a fourfold rise in antibody titer have been used to confirm the role of *C. trachomatis* retrospectively in clinical cases of salpingitis. Antibodies to *C. trachomatis* are more common in women with PID, tubal infertility, and ectopic pregnancy than in control women without these disorders. In children, infections with so-called TWAR agents may give cross-reacting rises in antibody titers to *C. trachomatis*.

In addition to genital tract infections, *C. trachomatis* has been recognized increasingly as an etiologic agent in perihepatitis or Fitz-Hugh–Curtis syndrome. Salpingitis may or may not be present. The patient typically presents with right upper quadrant pain, often pleuritic, and laboratory evaluation reveals an increased sedimentation rate and a positive endocervical culture for *C. trachomatis*. Ultrasonography may be necessary to exclude biliary tract disease in patients with this type of pain. Liver function tests are usually normal in chlamydial perihepatitis, in contrast to abnormal liver function tests that may accompany gonococcal perihepatitis.

Although *C. trachomatis* has been cultured from the pharynx in 3.7 percent of men and 3.2 percent of women in an STD clinic [62], a positive culture was not associated with symptoms. This organism is rarely cultured from patients with symptomatic pharyngitis and thus does not appear to be an important etiologic agent for this disease. Similarly, *C. trachomatis* has been cultured from the rectum of 5.2 percent of women attending an STD clinic. A positive rectal culture in women tends to correlate with concurrent genital infection, not rectal symptoms [62], although mild proctitis has been associated with non-lymphogranuloma venereum immunotypes in homosexual men [63].

Treatment of *C. trachomatis* cervical and urethral infections in women is *one* of the following [52, 64]:

1. Doxycycline, 100 mg orally 2 times a day for 7 days
2. Tetracycline, 500 mg 4 times a day for 7 days
3. Erythromycin base or stearate, 500 mg 4 times a day for 7 days
4. Erythromycin ethylsuccinate, 800 mg 4 times a day for 7 days

To improve compliance, the twice a day dosing with doxycycline is the first choice for therapy. Pregnant patients should be treated with erythromycin; for those who cannot tolerate the high doses, a lower dose of 250 mg of erythromycin base or 400 mg of erythromycin ethylsuccinate can be given 4 times daily for 14 days. Erythromycin estolate, associated with hepatotoxicity, should not be used in pregnant women. Ofloxacin has been approved for treatment in older, non-pregnant teens. Amoxicillin, 500 mg 3 times daily for 7 days, was effective in treating pregnant women [65]. Sulfamethazole, 500 mg four times a day for 10 days, is probably also effective. Trimethoprim-sulfamethazole (160 mg/800 mg), twice a day for 10 days; has a failure rate of 8 to 10 percent. Clindamycin is effective against *Chlamydia* in vitro and results in clinical and bacteriologic cure in patients given clindamycin and tobramycin for PID.

Patients should be examined for other STDs, and partners should receive adequate diagnosis and treatment at the same visit. It is important to remember that *C. trachomatis* can remain asymptomatic in the cervix for months and probably years [66], and thus pinpointing the source can be problematic in many adolescents. Although the CDC does not recommend test of cure cultures if laboratory resources are scarce, in adolescents the high risk of reexposure to an untreated partner, the possibility of noncompliance, and the morbidity associated with the infection in young women should make clinicians place a high priority on follow-up cultures and continued screening. Since the cultures may not become positive for 3 to 6 weeks, delaying a test of cure to this time interval would be appropriate. As with all STDs, patients should be thoroughly counselled about the need to have monogamous relationships and the use of barrier contraception or abstinence. It is crucial that partners be treated.

Better screening tools for men are needed, since current screening is directed only at women. In our unit, the use of the leukocyte esterase dipstick on the man's first-catch urine (first 12 ml) has allowed us to do selective screening. The finding of a 1 + or 2 + leukocyte esterase dipstick on a 7-L Chemstrip is highly associated with the presence of urethral infection with *C. trachomatis* or *N. gonorrhoeae* [67].

PELVIC INFLAMMATORY DISEASE

ETIOLOGY

The term *pelvic inflammatory disease* (PID) refers to infection in the upper genital tract that involves the fallopian tubes. PID may occur as a sexually acquired acute salpingitis, a postpartum or postabortal infection, or the chronic sequelae to a previous acute or silent salpingitis. This section concentrates on acute salpingitis.

It has been estimated that 1 million women in the United States are treated for acute salpingitis each year, with 16 to 20 percent of cases occurring in adolescents. Adolescents represent an especially high-risk group because they often have multiple sexual partners and have high prevalence of infections with *N. gonorrhoeae* and *C. trachomatis*. Women with multiple partners have a 4.6-fold increased risk of PID. The use of nonbarrier methods of contraception makes adolescents more likely to acquire endocervical infections, and the immaturity of their immune systems appears to increase their susceptibility to ascending infection. It has been estimated that adolescents with a gonococcal or chlamydial endocervical infection have a 30 percent chance of developing PID, as opposed to a 10 percent risk in the older woman. The intrauterine device (IUD) has been associated with an increased risk of PID and is rarely a good choice for contraception in the adolescent [68–71].

The use of the oral contraceptive pill appears to lessen the risk of gonococcal PID, perhaps because of changes in cervical mucus, lighter menstrual flow, diminished uterine contractions, less retrograde menstruation, and less canal dilatation. Since most studies have been limited to hospitalized cases of PID, which represent only 25 percent of all cases, it is unclear whether the protection of the pill can be generalized to other forms of PID [72]. Since the use of oral contraceptives has been associated with chlamydial cervical infection in adolescent girls (probably in part because of the pill's effect on persistence of the cervical ectopy as well as possible altered attachment of organisms to endocervical cells in the presence of estrogen), studies are needed on this high-risk population. One study from Sweden [73] in adult women has suggested that chlamydial PID rates are lower in oral contraceptive users. It has been estimated that the risk of PID in a sexually active 15-year-old is 1 in 8, as contrasted to the risk in women 24 years and older of 1 in 80. Since a history of previous PID is a risk factor for PID and the sequelae of infertility, ectopic pregnancy, and pelvic pain are related to the number of episodes, it is clear that adolescents deserve prompt attention to complaints that may suggest a diagnosis of PID.

Although in the past PID has been divided into gonococcal and nongonococcal PID on the basis of the presence or absence of *N. gonorrhoeae* in the endocervical culture, the more appropriate designations are gonococcal, chlamydial, and nongonococcal nonchlamydial PID. A positive cervical culture for gonorrhea is found in 20 to 80 percent of patients with PID, with estimates around 25 to 40 percent. Holmes and colleagues [71] found gonorrhea in 49 percent of initial episodes of PID versus 34 percent with recurrent attacks. It is uncommon to isolate gonococci after three or more episodes of PID. In patients with positive gonococcal cultures from the endocervix, the fallopian tube culture is most likely to be positive during the first 2 days of symptoms. Eschenbach and associates [74] found *N. gonor-rhoeae* in the peritoneal exudate from 8 out of 21 patients with, and in none of the 33 patients without, cervical gonococcal infections; and Sweet and co-workers [75] isolated *N. gonorrhoeae* from the cul-de-sac in 32 percent of 26 patients and from the fallopian tube in 19 percent.

Chlamydial infection is found in 20 to 45 percent of patients with PID. In patients with acute PID, Mardh and his collaborators [76] isolated *C. trachomatis* from 19 of 53 cervical cultures and from 6 of 20 specimens of the fallopian tube. Although initial studies in the United States did not suggest that *Chlamydia* was a significant cause of upper genital tract disease, more recent studies have confirmed a similar proportion of PID with a chlamydial etiology in the United States and Scandinavia. Of great concern in the evaluation of adolescents is a recent study that found that 40 percent of patients with asymptomatic endocervical chlamydial infection also have evidence of endometrial infection [47]. The course of chlamydial PID can be subacute and indolent, and adolescents frequently delay seeking medical attention. The sedimentation rate associated with chlamydial PID is often quite elevated and the tubal damage significant at the time of presentation.

Nongonococcal nonchlamydial PID involves a number of organisms including coliforms, *Gardnerella vaginalis*, *Hemophilus influenzae* group B streptococci, *Bacteroides* species (e.g., *Bacteroides fragilis* and *bivius*), peptostreptococcus, peptococcus, and *Mycoplasma hominis* [71–78]. The role of *M. hominis* is still debated [79, 80]. *M. hominis* is frequently cultured from the cervix of both women with PID and those without PID; however it does appear to be responsible for infection in a small number of patients. The flora seen in nongonococcal nonchlamydial PID is strikingly similar to that occurring in bacterial vaginosis, and thus what has been thought of in the past as a benign condition appears to be a risk factor for PID. Although it has been suggested that the gonococcus paves the way for other invaders from the lower genital tract, in fact anaerobic organisms are frequently found within the first 24 hours of symptoms. Gonococcal and chlamydial PID must also be considered to have a polymicrobial etiology, and thus antimicrobial therapy must be directed against all the potential organisms.

Both gonococcal and chlamydial PID are temporally related to menses. Sweet and co-workers [81] found that 81 percent of women with PID occurring within 7 days of the onset of menses had an infection with either gonorrhea or chlamydia. In contrast, of the PID occurring greater than 14 days after the onset of menses, 66 percent were nongonococcal nonchlamydial infections. Overall 55 percent of gonococcal PID and 57 percent of chlamydial PID occurred in the first 7 days of the cycle. The increased risk of ascending infection during the menses may occur because of loss of the cervical mucus plug;

shedding of the endometrium, which may have offered protection from infection; the presence of menstrual blood, which is an excellent culture medium; and the reflux of blood into the fallopian tubes. It appears that once the gonococci reach the tubal epithelium, they penetrate the cells and cause cell destruction with production of a purulent exudate. The infection then reaches the fimbriated ends of the tubes and causes pelvic peritonitis. If the tubes are blocked, a pyosalpinx may develop; if the ovaries are involved, a tubo-ovarian abscess may occur. About one-fourth of hospitalized PID patients have palpable adnexal swelling, and 7 to 16 percent develop an abscess. It is likely that chlamydial infection spreads in a similar fashion to gonococcal infection by direct canalicular spread along the endometrial surface to the tubes. Other postulated modes of spread for bacteria include transport via attachment to sperm or *Trichomonas,* transfer with retrograde menstruation, or perhaps lymphatic spread (which may occur with mycoplasma). The use of commercial douches may also be associated with an increased risk of salpingitis (see p. 312).

DIAGNOSIS
The classic picture of acute salpingitis includes lower abdominal pain, vaginal discharge, and fever and chills, usually following the onset of a menses in a sexually active young woman. Symptoms may be less specific and include menstrual irregularities, dyspareunia, vomiting, diarrhea, constipation, dysuria, and urinary frequency. Patients with chlamydial PID are less likely to be febrile and more likely to have long-standing milder symptoms and breakthrough bleeding on oral contraceptives than those with gonococcal or anaerobic PID. The markedly elevated sedimentation rate often contrasts with the mild symptoms of chlamydial PID. Golden and colleagues [77] found that adolescent patients with chlamydia-associated PID in contrast to girls with gonococcus-associated PID had a longer duration of symptoms (6.2 versus 3.1 days), lower temperature (37.8°C versus 38.5°C), and lower white count (11,055 versus 14,648 μl). Such associations have not been found in all studies. Symptoms are often unreliable to distinguish PID patients from a group of women with a visually normal pelvis; signs found to be different include longer duration of pain (7–14 days) and irregular bleeding [82].

The diagnosis of PID is made by finding signs of genital infection, lower abdominal pain, and pelvic tenderness. The abdominal pain and adnexal tenderness are typically bilateral, although Falk [83] reported an 8 percent incidence of unilateral salpingitis confirmed by laparoscopy. Pain on cervical motion is usually present but may also occur with other pelvic pathology. Rebound tenderness may not be present early in the disease if peritonitis is not present. Liver tenderness caused by perihepatitis (Fitz-Hugh–Curtis) may occur in both gonococcal and chlamydial infections [61, 84, 85]. The patient may complain of pleuritic right upper quadrant pain with radiation to the right shoulder and back. It is always wise to ask if the patient's sexual partner has any symptoms of urethritis or has recently been treated for a STD.

The laboratory tests should include a complete blood count (CBC), sedimentation rate, serologic test for syphilis, Gram stain of the endocervical discharge, cultures or other tests for *N. gonorrhoeae* and *C. trachomatis*, and a sensitive pregnancy test (such as the urine ICON). The CBC may show a normal or elevated white blood cell count. The sedimentation rate is greater than 15 mm/hour in 75 to 80 percent of patients. In a study by Wolner-Hanssen and associates [82] comparing women subjected to laparoscopy because of signs and symptoms of acute salpingitis, 75 percent of those with PID compared to 31 percent of those with visually normal pelvis had an elevated sedimentation rate. Some clinicians also find that an elevated C-reactive protein is helpful in making the diagnosis. The Gram stain of a purulent cervical discharge may reveal gram-negative intracellular diplococci in about half of patients with gonococcal PID. The finding of 10 or more white cells on a cervical Gram stain ($1000 \times$) may also be a clue to chlamydial disease. The absence of any white cells in the cervical secretions and vaginal discharge suggests a different diagnosis from PID. A pregnancy test should always be obtained and the possibility of an ectopic pregnancy considered in the adolescent with acute abdominal pain; it is important to remember that an adolescent may have more than one diagnosis, such as chlamydial PID and ectopic pregnancy (see Case 16, p. 234). Ultrasonography (especially newer techniques using vaginal probes) can be extremely useful in ruling out other diagnoses and defining masses in the adnexa. Mean adnexal volume appears to be larger in adolescents with PID versus controls, even in those PID patients without tubo-ovarian abscesses [86]. Golden and colleagues [77] reported that 19 percent of adolescents with PID in their hospital had tubo-ovarian abscesses by ultrasound (not laparoscopy), and in 12 of 17 the abscesses were identified by ultrasound before being diagnosed by their examiners. Tubo-ovarian abscesses can be followed in the hospital with ultrasound.

The diagnosis of PID is sometimes difficult to make. Laparoscopic studies of patients with a presumptive diagnosis of acute salpingitis have concluded that the clinical diagnosis is confirmed by visual inspection in only 60 to 70 percent of cases [87–90]. An additional 5 percent of patients with negative examinations by laparoscopy do have gonococci present in the cervical culture. Jacobson [87, 88] found that 12 percent of patients with "clinical PID" had in fact a different diagnosis—acute appendicitis, ectopic pregnancy, ruptured corpus luteum, ovarian abscess, or endometriosis. In a significant number of

Table 10-2. Clinical Criteria for the Diagnosis of Acute PID

All three of the following must be present:
1. History of lower abdominal pain and the presence of abdominal tenderness, with or without rebound tenderness
2. Tenderness with motion of the cervix and uterus
3. Adnexal tenderness

Plus one or more of the following:
1. Temperature ≥38°C
2. White blood cell count ≥10,500/mm³
3. Elevated sedimentation rate >15 mm/hr
4. Evidence of *N. gonorrhoeae* and/or *C. trachomatis* in the endocervix: Gram stain from the endocervix positive for gram-negative intracellular diplococci *or* a monoclonal directed smear positive for *Chlamydia* (or similar rapid tests) *or* >5 white blood cells per oil immersion field on Gram stain of endocervical discharge.
5. Pelvic abscess or inflammatory complex on bimanual examination or by sonography
6. Purulent material (white blood cells present) from peritoneal cavity by culdocentesis or laparoscopy

Adapted from AE Washington, et al. [68], WD Hager, et al. [91] and RC Sweet. Pelvic inflammatory disease and infertility in women. Infect Dis Clin North Am 1987; 1:199.

patients, no pelvic pathology was found. Westrom [89] has found that the diagnosis of PID was much more likely if it not only were based on finding signs of genital infection, lower abdominal pain, and pelvic tenderness, but also included one or more of the following: (1) sedimentation rate greater than 15 mm/hour, (2) a rectal temperature greater than 38°C, or (3) palpable adnexal masses. If all these criteria were present, the diagnosis of PID was confirmed in 96 percent of patients. A clinical diagnosis plus a positive culture or rapid diagnostic test for *N. gonorrhoeae* or *C. trachomatis* allows correct diagnosis in 90 percent of patients. Clearly, a clinician cannot expect all the criteria to be present to initiate therapy; otherwise many adolescents would be undertreated and thus likely to develop sequelae. Criteria for the diagnosis of PID were published in 1983 by Hager and associates [91] and subsequently modified (Table 10-2).

Laparoscopy has proved invaluable in clarifying the etiologic agents and the clinical accuracy of diagnosis in PID. Laparoscopy is indicated if the diagnosis is in doubt, especially in patients recurrently labeled with PID but never meeting satisfactory criteria. It should also be used in research settings, especially when clinical trials of antibiotics are undertaken. Care should be taken in making sure that cultures taken at laparoscopy are processed so that fastidious organisms will not be missed. Fluorescein-conjugated antibody staining of endometrial and tubal specimens may be more sensitive than culture techniques for *C. trachomatis* [92].

INPATIENT THERAPY FOR ACUTE PELVIC INFLAMMATORY
DISEASE

Although antibiotics result in the resolution of symptoms in most patients, the long-term results of treatment are still far from satisfactory. Given the frequency of noncompliance with medical therapy during adolescence and the risk of future reproductive problems, adolescents should be considered a high priority for inpatient therapy for PID. Indeed some centers admit all adolescents routinely for parenteral therapy. In addition, all patients who have questionable diagnosis, suspected pelvic abscess, upper quadrant pain, peritoneal signs, temperature greater than 38°C, or vomiting, are prepubertal or pregnant, are possibly noncompliant to outpatient treatment (including medication and follow-up appointments), or fail to respond to outpatient treatment within 48 hours deserve inpatient therapy.

Effectiveness of therapy is improved with prompt institution of antibiotic therapy. Viberg [93] found that none of the patients treated within 2 days of the onset of symptoms were involuntarily infertile, and all had patent fallopian tubes. In contrast, if treatment was instituted after the sixth day, only 70 percent had tubal patency.

In selecting antibiotics for inpatient and outpatient treatment of PID, the clinician needs to take into account the polymicrobial etiology of the disease, regardless of whether *N. gonorrhoeae* or *C. trachomatis* is cultured. It is especially important to make sure that the antibiotics are known to be effective against *Chlamydia*, since clinical improvement may occur in spite of persistence of positive endometrial cultures for *Chlamydia*. For example, in a study of women treated with parenteral second- and third-generation cephalosporins, 94 percent showed prompt clinical improvement and yet *C. trachomatis* was recovered from 87 percent of the post-treatment endometrial aspirates [94]. In contrast, patients treated with clindamycin plus tobramycin had negative post-treatment cultures for *Chlamydia*. In patients with severe disease or abscess formation, antibiotics effective against anaerobes must be included. The risk of abscess formation and infertility in nongonococcal PID is higher than in gonococcal PID. Antimicrobial regimens that include clindamycin are especially effective in the medical treatment of tubo-ovarian abscesses.

A number of drug regimens have been used in the past and ongoing trials of new combinations are in progress [95]. The CDC Guidelines have recommended *one* of two regimens:

1. Cefoxitin, 2 gm intravenously every 6 hours, or cefotetan, 2 gm intravenously every 12 hours, *plus* doxycycline, 100 mg orally or intravenously every 12 hours

   The doxycycline can be given orally if gastrointestinal function is normal. The above regimen is continued for at least 48 hours after the patient improves clinically. After discharge from the hospital, the patient is continued on doxycycline 100 mg orally twice daily for a total of 10 to 14 days. (Other cephalosporins such as ceftizoxime, cefotaxime, and ceftriaxone, which give adequate coverage of gonococci, facultative gram-negative aerobes, and anaerobes, may be utilized [12].)

2. Clindamycin, 900 mg intravenously every 8 hours (or 600 mg intravenously every 6 hours) *plus* gentamicin, 2.0 mg/kg loading dose intramuscularly or intravenously followed by a maintenance dose of 1.5 mg/kg every 8 hours (in patients with normal renal function).

The regimen is continued for at least 48 hours after the patient improves clinically. After discharge from the hospital the patient is continued on doxycycline, 100 mg orally twice daily for a total of 10 to 14 days. Clindamycin, 450 mg orally 4 times a day can be used as an alternative to complete 10 to 14 days of therapy. Doxycycline remains the regimen of choice for out-patient therapy for chlamydial PID. (Tobramycin can be substituted for gentamicin in the above regimen [96].)

Despite concerns about whether the second regimen would cover gonococci and *Chlamydia,* patients treated with these drugs do experience comparable clinical and bacteriologic cure rates of PID. Although there is synergism between these two drugs, the magnitude does not appear to be sufficient to explain the beneficial clinical effect against gonococci [97]. The first regimen may not give as good coverage as the second in the treatment of pelvic abscesses. A study by Sweet and co-workers [98] found that cefotetan plus doxycycline was equally effective to cefoxitin plus doxycycline; however, four failures had sonographically diagnosed tubo-ovarian abscesses that responded to clindamycin plus gentamicin. Dodson and associates [99] have reported a cure rate of 97.7 percent in PID patients (64% gonococcal PID; 51 percent had ultrasound findings compatible with pelvic abscess) with a combination of aztreonam, a monocyclic β-lactam antibiotic, and clindamycin. Parenteral ciprofloxacin appears to be promising as a single agent with a comparable *clinical* cure rate, but more evidence is needed on *microbiologic* cure of the endometrium and fallopian tubes [100, 101]. Resistance to quinolones may become a problem.

Most patients with PID respond well clinically to broad-spectrum antibiotics. However, patients with tubo-ovarian abscesses can be difficult to manage. Such abscesses occur mostly in the third and fourth decades of life but can occur in adolescents as well. Ultrasonography, and in some cases computed tomography (CT) and magnetic resonance imaging (MRI) (for patients in whom sonography does not provide adequate information), can be used along with clini-

366

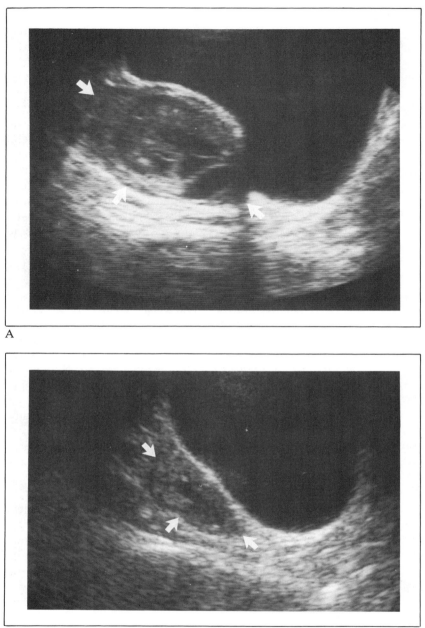

A

B

Figure 10-3. Pelvic ultrasounds of an adolescent referred to The Children's Hospital, Boston, after 1 month of pelvic pain, negative pregnancy test, elevated sedimentation rate, a positive cervical culture for *C. trachomatis*, and noncompliance with outpatient antibiotics. A. Longitudinal sonogram of the right adnexa showing a complex mass behind the bladder (*arrows*).

cal assessment to make the diagnosis and document improvement. Since appreciation of abscesses is often difficult in the patient with a tender pelvis, ultrasonography should be used frequently as an aid to the clinician (Fig. 10-3). Anaerobic organisms, in particular *Bacteroides fragilis*, are strongly associated with abscess formation. A study of 232 abscesses by Landers and Sweet [102] found that 68 percent of patients treated with a regimen that included clindamycin responded to medical management, measured by improved symptoms, decreased fever and tenderness, lowered white blood cell count, and shrinkage of adnexal masses. They have recommended the combination of tobramycin and clindamycin for the treatment of these patients because the spectrum covered includes most organisms cultured from abscesses and clindamycin has excellent penetration into abscess cavities. Other antibiotics with good activity against the anaerobes and good penetration of abscesses include cefoxitin and metronidazole. Although a trial of metronidazole plus tobramycin gave equivalent results in the treatment of a variety of pelvic infections as did clindamycin and tobramycin, metronidazole in combination with an aminoglycoside does not provide adequate coverage against aerobic streptococci, *N. gonorrhoeae,* or microaerophilous streptococci [102]. Some centers prefer to use triple antibiotics in patients with tubo-ovarian abscesses, such as gentamicin and ampicillin *plus* either metronidazole or clindamycin.

Laparoscopy is utilized early at admission in centers obtaining bacteriologic cultures from the fallopian tubes and those verifying the diagnosis for inclusion in studies of PID. Laparoscopy is also useful in patients in whom the diagnosis is in doubt at admission or in patients who fail to respond to medical therapy. Surgery is also indicated in patients with ruptured abscesses. In a study published in 1985, Landers and Sweet [102] found that 60 to 70 percent of patients responded promptly to medical management and 30 to 40 percent failed to respond within 48 to 72 hours as defined by persistent fever, increasing size of the abscess, persistent leukocytosis, increasing sedimentation rate, or suspicion of rupture. It should be noted that

Figure 10-3 (Continued). A right ovary could not be identified separate from this structure. These findings can be seen with a number of disorders including tubo-ovarian abscess, hemorrhagic ovarian cyst, ectopic pregnancy, or inflammation of nongynecologic origin, such as appendicitis. The patient was treated with cefoxitin and doxycycline for 10 days as an inpatient and then took an additional 14-day course of oral metronidazole and doxycycline as an outpatient. B. Resolution of the tubo-ovarian abscess 4 weeks after therapy. The right ovary is now well visualized and is normal, except for the presence of a small amount of residual fluid within it (*arrows*). (Readings of scans courtesy of Jane Share, M.D.)

the sedimentation rate may lag several days behind clinical improvement and may even rise initially. Bilateral abscesses and those greater than 8 cm in diameter are less likely to respond to medical management alone. With the advent of better anaerobic drug combinations in the last 5 years, it is likely that fewer patients will fail to respond to medical management. Surgical intervention may include percutaneous drainage guided by CT or real-time ultrasound (the majority that have been drained have been unilocular abscesses), transabdominal laparotomy with drainage or extirpation of the abscess, with or without unilateral adnexectomy or total abdominal hysterectomy and bilateral salpingo-oophorectomy. Although long-term data are not available on fertility outcome and are critically needed to evaluate new approaches, some centers have advocated a more aggressive early surgical approach to large tubo-ovarian abscesses with aspiration of the abscess, gentle washing of the abscess cavity, instillation of antibiotics, and closed drainage to gravity. Other centers (including ours) have taken a more conservative surgical approach and feel that preservation of fertility is more likely if the patient is treated medically with appropriate antibiotics with performance of surgery later, if necessary, when the infection has been thoroughly treated. Fertility after treatment of tubo-ovarian abscesses may be 20 to 50 percent with conservative medical and surgical approaches.

After inpatient parenteral therapy, oral antibiotics, as previously indicated, are continued to complete a 10- to 14-day course. Patients with severe disease including tubo-ovarian abscesses are usually treated for a longer course with oral clindamycin or a two-drug regimen such as oral doxycycline plus metronidazole. More data are needed on the use of outpatient regimens of ciprofloxacin (for >16 years) and amoxicillin-clavulanate (Augmentin).

With discharge from the hospital, the patient should be seen weekly, and sexual contacts should be identified and treated with regimens effective against both *C. trachomatis* and *N. gonorrhoeae* to prevent reinfection. The patient should be recultured 2 to 4 weeks after the completion of therapy. Patients should abstain from sexual relations for 3 to 4 weeks. STD counselling is essential to minimize the chance of reinfection and to protect against other infections such as human papillomavirus (HPV) and human immunodeficiency virus (HIV).

OUTPATIENT THERAPY OF ACUTE PELVIC INFLAMMATORY DISEASE

Although most adolescents with PID should be treated as inpatients, the reliable patient with *mild* signs and symptoms, a temperature less than 38°C, and no vomiting can be given single-dose ceftriaxone, 250 mg intramuscularly (or cefoxitin, 2 gm intramuscularly plus probenecid, 1 gm orally, or equivalent cephalosporin), followed by doxycycline, 100 mg orally twice daily for 10 to 14 days. Our clinic and others have found an initial dose of 500 mg ceftriaxone particularly effective in ambulatory patients. For patients who do not tolerate doxycycline, the CDC lists erythromycin, 500 mg 4 times a day for 10 to 14 days as an alternative, but states that only limited clinical data are available. Inpatient therapy is probably preferable in these circumstances until better oral alternatives are studied.

It is essential that the clinician feel comfortable that the patient has the resources to purchase the antibiotics and will return in 48 to 72 hours to assess whether the treatment is effective. A lack of response, vomiting of the antibiotics, or noncompliance should prompt hospitalization. The patient is advised to abstain from intercourse for 3 to 4 weeks and her sexual partner(s) should be seen for appropriate cultures and treatment.

In a study of 24 women with probable PID (based on clinical criteria and endometrial biopsy), Wolner-Hanssen and colleagues [103] found that a single dose of 2 gm of cefoxitin and 1 gm of probenecid orally followed by doxycycline, 100 mg twice daily for 14 days, resulted in a clinical cure or improvement in 92 percent of the patients; two microbiologic failures had been reexposed. A combined oral treatment of Augmentin, 625 mg 3 times daily, plus doxycycline, 100 mg twice daily, resulted in 3 of 47 rapidly becoming worse and being hospitalized, 9 (20%) discontinuing medication because of gastrointestinal side effects, and the remaining cured or improved. The authors felt that the regimen could not be recommended as a first-line therapy [104]. Ciprofloxacin with activity against *N. gonorrhoeae, C. trachomatis,* and aerobic bacteria appears promising in the oral treatment of non-pregnant adults (>16 years) with PID. In a study of three antibiotic regimens [105], ciprofloxacin failed to eradicate anaerobic bacteria (especially *Bacteroides bivius* and *Peptococcus asaccharolyticus*) from the endometrial cavity as effectively as cefoxitin/doxycycline or clindamycin/gentamicin in spite of initial clinical cures. In another study [17], oral ciprofloxacin, 750 mg twice a day, resulted in clinical cure in 85 percent of 20 women with salpingitis. Optimal dosage and combinations with other antibiotics need further investigation.

CONSEQUENCES OF ACUTE PELVIC INFLAMMATORY DISEASE

Infertility, ectopic pregnancies, and chronic abdominal pain are the principal sequelae of acute PID. Thus, the aim of the clinician must be to treat adequately and promptly and to prevent recurrences. Women with a first episode of PID have a two- to threefold increased risk of a second episode of PID compared to women who have never had PID. During the treatment of the infection, it should be explained to the patient how the disease is sexually transmitted and how to prevent recurrences. The importance of monogamous relationships, use of the condom, and treatment of both partners should be stressed. A single episode of gonococcal salpingitis appropriately treated carries a low risk of later infertility, and patients can generally be reassured of this. However, recurrences markedly increase the risk of tubal occlusion.

Tubal occlusion may be more common in nongonococcal infections, although newer data have questioned this. Unfortunately, if the issue of possible infertility is overemphasized to the young adolescent, she may discontinue effective contraception and take risks to prove her own fertility. In a study of laparoscopically proved PID, tubal occlusion was verified after one infection in 12.8 percent of patients, after two infections in 35.5 percent, and after three or more infections in 75 percent [106]. Other studies have suggested an infertility risk of 10 to 12 percent with the first infection, 23 to 25 percent with the second, and 50 percent with the third [107, 108]. In general, the more severe the PID, the higher the risk of future infertility.

In addition to infertility, previous salpingitis is a major cause of ectopic pregnancy. Studies have found a 6- to 10-fold increase in ectopic pregnancy in PID patients [68, 109]. Adolescents who have had PID should be counselled about this risk, and ectopic pregnancy should always be considered in the differential diagnosis of the adolescent with acute abdominal pain (see Chap. 16). The clinician should maintain a high index of suspicion in following the pregnancy of an adolescent with a history of PID.

PID may also result in chronic pain. Westrom [89] found that 63 percent of patients with chronic PID were infertile. Physical examination may reveal adnexal tenderness or masses. The sedimentation rate may be normal or elevated. Laparoscopy is necessary to establish the diagnosis and to evaluate the extent of the disease. Adolescents with endometriosis can be incorrectly diagnosed as having PID, and they may receive multiple courses of antibiotics before the correct diagnosis is made by laparoscopy.

Therapy must be individualized. Treatment may include an extended course of oral antibiotics such as doxycycline, clindamycin, trimethoprim-sulfamethazole, Augmentin, or possibly ciprofloxacin; nonsteroidal anti-inflammatory drugs for pain; oral contraceptives to suppress cyclic ovarian function; and conservative surgery with lysis of adhesions and, if the uterus is retroverted, suspension of the uterus. The patient should be cultured and treated with appropriate antimicrobial agents for subsequent episodes of PID and the sexual partner also examined and treated.

SYPHILIS

After a steady decline in primary and secondary syphilis and congenital syphilis in the early 1980s, a dramatic increase in disease occurred in 1987. Reported cases increased 23 percent in the first 3 months of 1987 as compared to the first 3 months of 1986 [110]. The areas reporting the large increases were California, Florida, and New York City, with the disease showing a striking increase among blacks and Hispanics. In 1986, more cases of congenital syphilis were reported to the CDC than for any of the previous 15 years (almost 1/10,000 live-born infants) [111, 112]. Adolescents with syphilis frequently do not present to the clinician at the time of the primary chancre but rather may be seen with rash or lymphadenopathy or detected by screening [113].

Sexually active adolescents should be screened for syphilis when they present with any suspicious oral or genital lesions, unexplained skin rash, other STDs (such as gonorrhea, chlamydial infection, PID, HPV, HIV), or pregnancy. There are no guidelines for routine screening of asymptomatic adolescents, but high-risk behaviors such as multiple partners, nonuse of barrier methods, prostitution, drug abuse, juvenile delinquency, and previous STDs suggest the need for annual screening in these individuals. For example, in a detention center in New York City serving juveniles 9 to 18 years of age, the prevalence rate for syphilis was 0.6 percent for boys and 2.5 percent for girls [114]. The presence of genital ulcers is likely to increase the risk of acquiring HIV infection.

The nontreponemal test (VDRL, RPR) can be accurately quantitated in serum; only the VDRL is used for cerebrospinal (CSF) determinations. A rising titer is indicative of recently acquired infection, a reinfection, or a relapse. A decline in titer is generally indicative of adequate treatment of the early stage of syphilis. Patients with primary syphilis will show a nonreactive RPR within 1 year; patients with secondary syphilis will become nonreactive within 2 years; those in the macular and maculopapular stage of the rash at diagnosis and treatment return to seronegativity more rapidly than patients with papular and/or pustular rashes [115]. Patients who are reinfected with syphilis also take longer to revert to a nonreactive RPR test. Patients who have early latent syphilis for less than 1 year generally revert to a negative test within 4 years, whereas only 20 to 45 percent of late latent patients become nonreactive within 5 years. Many in the latter group remain sero-fast [116, 117, 118]. Brown and co-workers [119] have analyzed data from the Early Syphilis Study and generated curves describing the VDRL decline with time. The curves describe an approximately fourfold decline in titer at 3 months and an eightfold decline in 6 months in patients with primary and secondary syphilis. Retreatment rates for the less effective regimens of erythromycin and spectinomycin exceeded 10 percent. The same laboratory and the same test (either VDRL or RPR) should be used to follow a patient after therapy.

The RPR is now an extremely sensitive test; it is positive by the seventh day of the chancre, at the time many patients actually seek medical help. For this reason, dark-field examination of suspected lesions is not used as frequently in Massachusetts for diagnosing syphilis. However, dark-field examination is still a useful test, since different states use different nontreponemal tests that have varying sensitivities, some of which may not become positive for 2 to 3 weeks after the chancre has appeared. Other methods for direct examination of a lesion include direct fluorescent antibody test for *Treponema pallidum* (DFA-TP), silver stains, and H and E stains. The clinician seeing adolescents should gather information from the state-run STD clinics periodically to keep abreast of current information. In less than 2 percent of patients with secondary syphilis, the RPR test may appear to give a false-negative result because of a prozone reaction. Most commercial laboratories do not do titers unless the undiluted specimen is positive. Thus, if syphilis is suspected and the reagin test appears nonreactive or weakly reactive, a second serum specimen should be sent with instructions to dilute the serum.

False-positive reagin tests occur in 1 out of 3000 to 5000 healthy patients. Infections such as mononucleosis, hepatitis, malaria, and vaccinia, immunizations, and collagen diseases may result in false-positive RPR tests. The specific or treponemal tests are useful to make the diagnosis in situations in which false-positive reactions might occur and in the diagnosis of late syphilis. The most commonly used treponemal test is the fluorescent treponemal antibody absorption test (FTA-ABS). False-positive results are infrequent but have been reported in patients with elevated globulins. The FTA-ABS is not recommended for routine screening of low-risk populations because the test remains positive usually for life whether the syphilis has been treated or not. Other treponemal tests include fluorescent treponemal antibody absorption double staining (FTA-ABS DS), microhemagglutination assay for antibody to *T. pallidum* (MHA-TP), hemagglutination treponemal test for syphilis (HATTS), and Bio-Enzebead Test (ELISA). Special tests, which include DNA and Reiter absorptions for the FTA test, eliminate most of the false-positive results and can be performed by the STD Laboratory Program of the CDC on request (which may sometimes be indicated in the diagnosis and treatment of the pregnant woman [112]).

The diagnosis during pregnancy is particularly urgent to prevent congenital syphilis. The CDC has recommended that if a patient has a reactive nontreponemal test (e.g., VDRL) and a nonreactive treponemal test (e.g., MHA-TP) and no clinical or epidemiologic evidence of syphilis, no treatment is necessary but both tests should be repeated in 4 weeks. In caring for seropositive women, efforts should always be made to document previous titers and forms of treatment. Patients should be retreated if there is clinical (dark-field positive lesions) or serologic evidence (a sustained ≥2 weeks fourfold increase in quantitative nontreponemal test) or a history of recent sexual exposure to an infectious person [112]. In general, high-risk seropositive women should be considered infected and treated unless the clinician is certain about recent therapy.

STAGES OF SYPHILIS
The stages of syphilis are as follows:

1. Primary syphilis. Ten to ninety days (average 3 weeks) after oral or genital exposure to an infected partner, the young woman may develop a hard, painless chancre on her vulva, vagina, cervix, anal area, or mouth, accompanied by nontender lymphadenopathy. The lesions are often asymptomatic and may be missed. The serologic test for syphilis becomes positive 4 to 6 weeks after exposure; thus, a negative test at the time a lesion is first noted does not rule out the diagnosis. The RPR test is usually positive if the chancre has been present for 7 days. If the initial VDRL or RPR is negative with a suspicious lesion, repeat tests are indicated at 1 week, 1 month, and 3 months to exclude syphilis. If possible, a dark-field examination of the clear fluid expressed from the chancre or a DFA-TP of the lesion should be done by an experienced physician. The dark-field examination can be repeated for 3 consecutive days, and the serologic test repeated. Even without therapy, the lesion(s) will heal spontaneously in 2 to 4 weeks, leaving a small scar.

2. Secondary syphilis. If the chancre is untreated, the patient may experience, 6 weeks to several months later, the symptoms of secondary syphilis, including a generalized rash (often present on the palms and soles), fever, malaise, alopecia, weight loss, lymphadenopathy, condylomata lata, or mucous membrane lesions. The rash generally progresses from macular to maculopapular, to papular, and lastly, to pustular lesions [120]. The serum RPR test at this time is positive.

3. Latent syphilis. By definition, this is the state of syphilis in which the patient has no symptoms and the spirochete is "hidden." However, the patient may be infectious and may later develop symptoms of tertiary syphilis. This stage is divided by history and serology into early latent (<1 year) and late latent of more than 1 year's duration.

4. Late syphilis. Except for gummas, which are probably a hypersensitivity phenomenon, the late manifestations of syphilis (neurologic and cardiovascular problems) are the result of a vasculitis. Late

syphilis usually occurs in patients beyond the adolescent age group, although very rarely neurosyphilis or cardiovascular lesions can develop in adolescents as a sequela of untreated congenital syphilis.

TREATMENT
Primary or secondary syphilis or contact history
Benzathine penicillin G, 2.4 million units intramuscularly at a single session is the treatment of choice. (Massachusetts uses benzathine penicillin, 2.4 million units once weekly for 2 weeks, a total dose of 4.8 million units.)

Penicillin-allergic patients should be treated with doxycycline, 100 mg orally twice a day for 2 weeks or tetracycline, 500 mg orally 4 times a day for 2 weeks. Compliance with this regimen is extremely important, as is serologic follow-up. Patients who cannot tolerate doxycycline or tetracycline should have their penicillin allergy confirmed; choices are erythromycin, 500 mg orally 4 times a day for 2 weeks with close serologic follow-up, or penicillin desensitization so that benzathine penicillin can be used. Preliminary data suggest that ceftriaxone, 250 mg intramuscularly for 10 days is effective, but close follow-up of serologies is mandatory [12].

Patients should be re-examined and serologic tests checked at 3 and 6 months. If nontreponemal antibody titers have not declined fourfold at 3 months with primary and secondary syphilis and by 6 months in early latent syphilis, or if signs or symptoms persist and reinfection is ruled out, the patients should have an examination of the CSF and be retreated appropriately.

Latent syphilis
Early latent syphilis of less than 1 year's duration can be treated with a single dose of penicillin (in Massachusetts a total of 4.8 million units), as for primary syphilis.

Syphilis of more than 1 year's duration, except neurosyphilis, should be treated with 2.4 million units of benzathine penicillin G, intramuscularly once a week for 3 consecutive weeks. Ideally all patients with syphilis of more than 1 year's duration should have a CSF examination [12]. The CDC has indicated that a CSF examination is indicated in patients with neurologic and psychiatric signs and symptoms suggestive of neurosyphilis, treatment failure, serum nontreponemal antibody titer 1:32 or more, other evidence of active syphilis (aortitis, gumma, iritis), nonpenicillin therapy planned, or positive HIV antibody test. If neurosyphilis is found, then patients should be treated with the regimen below.

The efficacy of alternative drugs to penicillin in the treatment of syphilis of greater than 1 year's duration is less well established. Penicillin-allergic (nonpregnant) patients may be treated with doxycycline, 100 mg orally twice a day for 4 weeks or tetracycline, 500 mg orally 4 times a day for 4 weeks. In patients who cannot tolerate tetracycline, penicillin allergy should be confirmed by history and testing, and penicillin desensitization should be considered [12].

Neurosyphilis
A dose of aqueous penicillin G, 12 to 24 million units is administered as 2 to 4 million units every 4 hours intravenously for 10 to 14 days. If outpatient compliance can be ensured, an alternative treatment is procaine penicillin, 2.4 million units intramuscularly daily plus pro-benecid, 500 mg orally 4 times a day, both for 10 to 14 days. Many then give benzathine penicillin G, 2.4 million units intramuscularly weekly for 3 doses [12]. The CDC recommends that if pleocytosis was initially present in the CSF, CSF examination should be repeated every 6 months until the cell count is normal. If no decrease occurs by 6 months or if the cell count is not normal by 2 years, retreatment should be strongly considered [12].

Syphilis and HIV infection
Because of concern about the development of neurosyphilis in pa-tients with impaired immune responses secondary to HIV infection, more data are needed on the optimal therapy in these patients. Longer courses of treatment, and perhaps long-term suppressive therapy, may be necessary. Current recommendations call for the usual treatment schedule for early syphilis with careful quantitative nontreponemal tests done at 1, 2, and 3 months and then at 3 month intervals thereafter until a satisfactory serologic response occurs. If the titer does not decrease appropriately, the patient should be reevaluated and the CSF examined. Although some recommend a CSF examination for all stages of syphilis in HIV-infected patients, such an examination should precede treatment of patients with latent syphilis of more than 1 year's duration or unknown duration. If this is not possible, the patient should be treated with doses for neurosyphilis. Consultation with an infectious disease expert, state laboratory, or the CDC is recommended.

Syphilis in pregnancy
Pregnant patients should be screened in the first trimester and at term for syphilis; high-risk patients should also be screened early in the third trimester. Pregnant patients with syphilis should be treated as soon as the diagnosis is made to prevent fetal death and congenital syphilis. Patients who are not allergic to penicillin should be treated with the same dosage schedules recommended for nonpregnant pa-tients. Penicillin should be given to pregnant women even if they have a history of penicillin allergy if their skin tests to minor and

major determinants are negative or their skin tests are positive and they have been desensitized. Ziaya and colleagues [121] have described an intravenous method of penicillin desensitization, and oral penicillin V has been advocated as well. Both methods of desensitization should be used only in consultation with an expert and in a facility with emergency procedures available [12]. Tetracycline is not recommended during pregnancy because of adverse effects on the fetus, and erythromycin is not optimal because of the possibility of inadequate treatment of the mother and fetus. Following treatment, pregnant women should have monthly quantitative nontreponemal serologic tests for the remainder of the pregnancy. Women should be retreated if they show a fourfold rise in titer or do not show a fourfold decrease in titer in 3 months.

Congenital syphilis

With the increase in syphilis in adolescent and adult women, more cases of congenital syphilis are being diagnosed. The CDC has recommended that infants should be evaluated if they are born to seropositive (nontreponemal test confirmed by a treponemal test) mothers who [12]:

1. Have untreated syphilis
2. Were treated for syphilis less than 1 month before delivery
3. Were treated for syphilis during pregnancy with a nonpenicillin regimen
4. Did not have the expected decrease in nontreponemal antibody titers after treatment for syphilis
5. Did not have a well-documented history of treatment, or
6. Were treated but had insufficient follow-up

Evaluation of the neonate should include careful physical examination with special attention to skin lesions, mucocutaneous lesions, hepatosplenomegaly, jaundice, microcephaly, anemia, edema, lymphadenopathy, rhinitis, CNS involvement, and intrauterine growth retardation; roentgenograms of the long bones; and serum for nontreponemal and treponemal tests and total IgM [122, 123]. If possible, FTA-ABS on the purified 19S-IgM fraction should be done [12]. Microscopic examination of the placenta and any skin lesions can also be helpful. A CSF analysis should be done for VDRL, cells, and protein. Regardless of CSF results, all infants with a diagnosis of confirmed or compatible syphilis are treated with a regimen effective against neurosyphilis.

Infants should be treated if their mothers have untreated syphilis or evidence of relapse or reinfection. Other criteria are (1) any evidence of active disease, (2) a reactive CSF-VDRL, (3) an abnormal CSF finding regardless of CSF serology, (4) quantitative nontreponemal serologic titers that are fourfold (or more) higher than their mother's, or (5) positive FTA-ABS-19S-IgM antibody.

Treatment is aqueous penicillin G, 50,000 units/kg intravenously every 8 to 12 hours (100,000 to 150,000 units/kg daily) for 10 to 14 days or procaine penicillin G, 50,000 units/kg intramuscularly daily for 10 to 14 days.

Asymptomatic infants whose mothers were *adequately* treated during pregnancy and in whom follow-up can be ensured do not need to be treated. However, many of these infants are lost to follow-up [123], and thus some CDC consultants recommend treating these infants with benzathine penicillin, 50,000 units/kg intramuscularly in a single dose before discharge [112].

Follow-up should be done at 1, 2, 3, 6, and 12 months with serologic tests performed until they become nonreactive. Patients with persistent, stable, low titers, patients with increasing titers, and patients with a reactive CSF-VDRL at 6 months are candidates for retreatment. Uninfected infants who are seropositive at birth should have nontreponemal antibody titers that are decreasing at 3 months and have disappeared at 6 months [12].

FOLLOW-UP

Adolescent patients should have careful tracing of contacts performed by the state health department. Contacts should be evaluated clinically and with serologic tests. Patients exposed within the preceding 90 days may have negative tests in spite of infection and should be presumptively treated. Patients exposed more than 90 days previously can await the results of serologic tests if follow-up is certain.

Serologic tests should be carefully followed in the patient diagnosed with syphilis. State and CDC health care providers can be extremely helpful in the interpretation of titers. Compliance with testing is especially important in individuals treated with nonpenicillin regimens. Counseling about risk reduction is crucial in adolescents who have had syphilis since the same risk factors associated with the acquisition of syphilis place the patient at risk of acquiring HIV.

REFERENCES
1. Ris HW, and Dodge RW. Gonorrhea in adolescent girls in a closed population. Am J Dis Child 1972; 123:185.
2. Litt IF, Edberg SC, Finberg L, et al. Gonorrhea in children and adolescents. J Pediatr 1974; 85:595.
3. Hein K, Marks A, and Cohen M. Asymptomatic gonorrhea: Prevalence in a population of urban adolescents. J Pediatr 1977; 90:634.
4. Saltz GR, Linnemann CC, Brookman RR, et al. *Chlamydia trachomatis* cervical infections in female adolescents. J Pediatr 1981; 98:981.

5. McCormack WM, Eveard JR, Laughlin CF, et al. Sexually transmitted conditions among women college students. Am J Obstet Gynecol 1981; 139:130.
6. Keith L, Mass W, Berger G, et al. Gonorrhea detection in a family planning clinic: A cost-benefit analysis of 2000 triplicate cultures. Am J Obstet Gynecol 1975; 121:399.
7. Hook EW, and Holmes KK. Gonococcal infections. Ann Intern Med 1985; 102:229.
8. Granato PA, and Roefaro FM. Evaluation of a prototype DNA probe test for noncultural diagnosis of gonorrhea. J Clin Microbiol 1989; 27(4): 632.
9. Gegg CV, Kranig BD, Gonzalez C, et al. Direct identification in urogenital specimens using the PACE DNA probe test: Confirmation by discrepant analysis (Abstract #1181). Presented at 28th Interscience Conference of Antimicrobial Agents and Chemotherapy, Oct. 1988.
10. Handsfield HH, Sandstrom EG, Knapp JS, et al. Epidemiology of penicillinase-producing *Neisseria gonorrhoeae* infections: Analysis by auxotyping and serogrouping. N Engl J Med 1982; 306:950.
11. Boslego JW, Tramont EC, Takafuji ET, et al. Effect of spectinomycin use on the prevalence of spectinomycin-resistant and of penicillinase-producing *Neisseria gonorrhoeae*. N Engl J Med 1987; 317:272.
12. CDC 1989 STD Treatment Guidelines. MMWR 1989; 38(S-8):1.
13. Penicillinase-producing *Neisseria gonorrhoeae*—United States, 1986. MMWR 1987, 36:107.
14. Rice RJ, and Thompson SE. Treatment of uncomplicated infections due to *Neisseria gonorrhoeae*. JAMA 1986; 255:1739.
15. Gottlieb A, and Mills J. Cefuroxime axetil for treatment of uncomplicated gonorrhea. Antimicrob Agents Chemother 1986; 30:333.
16. Crider SR, Colby SD, Miller LR, et al. Treatment of penicillin-resistant *Neisseria gonorrhoeae* with oral norfloxacin. N Engl J Med 1984; 311:137.
17. Hoyme UB, Buehler K, and Schindler AE. Preliminary results of treatment of uncomplicated salpingitis with ciprofloxacin. (Abstract) Inf Dis Soc Obstet Gynecol, August 1988.
18. Stamm WE, Guinan ME, Johnson C, et al. Effect of treatment regimens for *Neisseria gonorrhoeae* on simultaneous infection with *Chlamydia trachomatis*. N Engl J Med 1984; 310:545.
19. Wiesner PJ, Tronca E, Bonin P, et al. Clinical spectrum of pharyngeal gonococcal infection. N Engl J Med 1973; 288:181.
20. DiCaprio JM, Reynolds J, Frank G, et al. Ampicillin therapy for pharyngeal gonorrhea. JAMA 1978; 239:1631.
21. Felman YV, and Nikitas JA. Anorectal gonococcal infection. NY State J Med 1980; 80:1631.
22. Cramolino GM, and Litt IF. The pharynx as the only positive culture site in an adolescent with disseminated gonorrhea. J Pediatr 1982; 100:644.
23. Al-Suleiman SA, Grimes EM, and Jonas HS. Disseminated gonococcal infections. Obstet Gynecol 1983; 61:48.
24. Holmes KK, Counts GW, Beaty HW, et al. Disseminated gonococcal infection. Ann Intern Med 1971; 74:979.
25. Keiser H, Rubin FL, Wolinsky E, et al. Clinical forms of gonococcal arthritis. N Engl J Med 1968; 279:234.
26. Blankenship RM, Holmes RK, Sanford JP, et al. Treatment of disseminated gonococcal infection. N Engl J Med 1974; 290:267.
27. Keat A. Reiter's syndrome and reactive arthritis in perspective. N Engl J Med 1983; 309:1606.

28. Jay MS, Seymore C, Jay WM, et al. Reiter's syndrome in an adolescent female with systemic sequelae. J Adol Health Care 1987; 8:280.
29. Folland DS, Burke RE, Hinman AR, et al. Gonorrhea in preadolescent children: An inquiry into source of infection and mode of transmission. Pediatrics 1977; 60:153.
30. Farrell MK, Billmire ME, Shamroy JA, et al. Prepubertal gonorrhea: A multidisciplinary approach. Pediatrics 1981; 67:151.
31. Gravett MG, Nelson HP, and DeRouen T, et al. Independent association of bacterial vaginosis and *Chlamydia trachomatis* with adverse pregnancy outcome. JAMA 1986; 256:1899.
32. Washington AE, Johnson RE, and Sanders LL. *Chlamydia trachomatis* infections in the United States. JAMA 1987; 257:2072.
33. Shafer MA, Vaughan E, Lipkin ES, et al. Evaluation of fluorescein-conjugated monoclonal antibody test to detect *Chlamydia trachomatis* endocervical infection in adolescent girls. Pediatrics 1986; 108:779.
34. Bump RC, Sachs LA, Buesching WJ, et al. Sexually transmissible infectious agents in sexually active and virginal asymptomatic adolescent girls. Pediatrics 1986; 77:488.
35. Chacko MR. *Chlamydia trachomatis* infection in sexually active adolescents: Prevalence and risk factors. Pediatrics 1984; 73:836.
36. Fraser GJ, Rettig PJ, and Kaplan DW. Prevalence of cervical *Chlamydia trachomatis* and *Neisseria gonorrhoeae* in female adolescents. Pediatrics 1983; 71:333.
37. Bell TA, Farrow JA, Stamm WE, et al. Sexually transmitted diseases in females in a juvenile detention center. Sex Transm Dis 1985; 12:140.
38. Fisher M, Swenson PO, Risucci D, et al. *Chlamydia trachomatis* in suburban adolescents. J Pediatr 1987; 111:617.
39. McCormack WM, Alpert S, McComb DE, et al. Fifteen-month follow-up study of women infected with *Chlamydia trachomatis*. N Engl J Med 1979; 300:123.
40. Ismail MA, Chandler AE, Beem MO, et al. Chlamydial colonization of the cervix in pregnant adolescent. J Reprod Med 1985; 30:549.
41. Khurana CM, Deddish PA, and delMundo F. Prevalence of C. *trachomatis* in the pregnant cervix. Obstet Gynecol 1985; 66:241.
42. Harrison HR, Costin M, and Meder JB. Cervical *Chlamydia trachomatis* infection in university women: Relationship to history, contraception, ectopy and cervicitis. Am J Obstet Gynecol 1985; 153:244.
43. Skjeldestad FE, and Dalen A. The prevalence of C. *trachomatis* in the cervix of puerperal women, and its consequences for the outcome of pregnancy. Scand J Prim Health Care 1986; 4:209.
44. Handsfield HH, Hasman LL, Roberts PL, et al. Criteria for selective screening for *Chlamydia trachomatis* infection in women attending family planning clinics. JAMA 1986; 255:1730.
45. Brunham RC, Paavonen J, Stevens CE, et al. Mucopurulent cervicitis—the ignored counterpart in women of urethritis in men. N Engl J Med 1984; 311:1.
46. Moscicki B, Shafer MA, Millstein SG, et al. The use and limitations of endocervical gram stain and mucopurulent cervicitis as predictors for *Chlamydia trachomatis* in female adolescents. Am J Obstet Gynecol 1987; 157:65.
47. Jones RB, Mammel JB, Shepard MK, et al. Recovery of *Chlamydia trachomatis* from the endometrium of women at risk for chlamydial infection. Am J Obstet Gynecol 1986; 155:35.
48. Coleman P, Varitek V, Grier T, et al. TESTPACK CHLAMYDIA: A new

rapid assay for the direct antigen detection of *Chlamydia trachomatis* (Abstract #1184). Presented at 28th Interscience Conference on Antimicrobial Agents and Chemotherapy, 1988.

49. Tam MR, Stamm WE, Handsfield HH, et al. Culture-independent diagnosis of *C. trachomatis* using monoclonal antibodies. N Engl J Med 1984; 310:1146.

50. Amortegui AJ, and Meyer MP. Enzyme immunoassay for detection of *C. trachomatis* from the cervix. Obstet Gynecol 1985; 65:523.

51. Baselski VS, McNeeley SG, Ryan G, et al. A comparison of non culture-dependent methods for detection of *C. trachomatis* infections in pregnant women. Obstet Gynecol 1987; 70:47.

52. CDC. *Chlamydia trachomatis* infections: Policy guidelines for prevention and control. MMWR 1985; 34:3S.

53. Lebar W, Herschman B, Pierzchala J, et al. Comparison of DNA probe, monoclonal enzyme immunoassay and cell culture for the detection of *Chlamydia trachomatis* (Abstract #1185). Presented at 28th Interscience Conference on Antimicrobial Agents and Chemotherapy, 1988.

54. Pao CC, Lin SS, Yang TE, et al. Deoxyribonucleic acid hybridization analysis for the detection of urogenital *Chlamydia trachomatis* infections in women. Am J Obstet Gynecol 1987; 156:195.

55. Putbrese SC, Meier FA, Johnson BA, et al. Comparison of an isotopic DNA probe and ELISA for detecting *Chlamydia trachomatis* directly in urogenital clinical specimens (Abstract #1186). Presented at 28th Interscience Conference on Antimicrobial Agents and Chemotherapy, 1988.

56. Trachtenberg AI, Washington E, and Halldorson S. A cost-based decision analysis for *Chlamydia* screening in California family planning clinics. Obstet Gynecol 1988; 81:101.

57. Phillips RS, Aronson MD, Taylor WC, et al. Should tests for *Chlamydia trachomatis* cervical infection be done during routine gynecologic visits? Ann Intern Med 1987; 107:188.

58. Kiviat NB, Paavonen J, Brockway J, et al. Cytologic manifestations of cervical and vaginal infections: 1. Epithelial and inflammatory cellular changes. JAMA 1985; 253:989.

59. Roongpisuthipong A, Grimes DA, and Hadgu A. Is the Papanicolaou smear useful for diagnosing sexually transmitted diseases. Obstet Gynecol 1987; 69:820.

60. Paavonen J, Stevens CE, Wolner-Hanssen P, et al. Colposcopic manifestation of cervical and vaginal infections. Obstet Gynecol 1988; 47:373.

61. Katzman DK, Friedman IM, McDonald CA, et al. *Chlamydia trachomatis* Fitz-Hugh–Curtis syndrome without salpingitis in female adolescent. Am J Dis Child 1988; 142:996.

62. Jones RB, Rabinovitch RA, and Katz BP. *C. trachomatis* in the pharynx and rectum of heterosexual patients at risk for genital infections. Ann Intern Med 1985; 102:757.

63. Quinn TC, Goodell SE, Mkrtichian E, et al. *Chlamydia trachomatis* proctitis. N Engl J Med 1981; 305:195.

64. Sanders LL, Harrison HR, and Washington AE. Treatment of sexually transmitted chlamydial infections. JAMA 1986; 255:1750.

65. Crombleholme W, Schachter J, Sweet R, et al. Amoxicillin vs. erythromycin for treatment of *Chlamydia trachomatis* (CT) in pregnancy (Abstract #591). Presented at 28th Interscience Conference on Antimicrobial Agents and Chemotherapy, 1988.

66. McCormack WM, Alpert S, McComb DE, et al. Fifteen-month follow-up

study of women infected with *Chlamydia trachomatis*. N Engl J Med 1979; 300:123.
67. Sadof MD, Woods ER, and Emans SJ. Dipstick leukocyte esterase activity in first-catch urine specimens: A useful screening test for detecting sexually transmitted disease in the adolescent male. JAMA 1987; 258:1932.
68. Washington AE, Sweet RL, and Shafer MB. Pelvic inflammatory disease and its sequelae in adolescents. J Adol Health Care 1985; 6:298.
69. Mascola L, Cates W, Reynolds GH, et al. Gonorrhea and salpingitis among American teenagers, 1980–1981. MMWR 1983; 32:25SS.
70. Brunham RC, Binns B, Guijon F, et al. Etiology and outcome of acute pelvic inflammatory disease. J Infect Dis 1988; 158:510.
71. Holmes KK, Eschenbach DA, and Knapp JS. Salpingitis, an overview of etiology. Am J Obstet Gynecol 1980; 138:893.
72. Washington AE, Gove S, Schachter J, et al. Oral contraceptives, *Chlamydia trachomatis* infection, and pelvic inflammatory disease. JAMA 1985; 253:2246.
73. Wolner-Hanssen P, Svensson L, Mardh PA, et al. Laparoscopic findings and contraceptive use in women with signs and symptoms suggestive of acute salpingitis. Obstet Gynecol 1985; 66:233.
74. Eschenbach D, Buchanan TM, Pollack HM, et al. Polymicrobial etiology of acute pelvic inflammatory disease. N Engl J Med 1975; 293:166.
75. Sweet RL, Mills J, Hadley KW, et al. Use of laparoscopy to determine the microbiologic etiology of acute salpingitis. Am J Obstet Gynecol 1979; 134:68.
76. Mardh PA, Ripa T, Svensson L, et al. *Chlamydia trachomatis* infection in patients with acute salpingitis. N Engl J Med 1977; 296:1377.
77. Golden N, Neuhoff S, and Cohen H. Pelvic inflammatory disease in adolescents. J Pediatr 1989; 114:138.
78. Paavonen J. *Chlamydia trachomatis* in acute salpingitis. Am J Obstet Gynecol 1980; 138:957.
79. Cassell GH, and Cole BC. Mycoplasmas as agents of human disease. N Engl J Med 1981; 304:80.
80. Taylor-Robinson D, and McCormack WM. The genital mycoplasmas. N Engl J Med 1980; 302:1003.
81. Sweet RL, Blankfort-Doyle M. Robbie MO, et al. The occurrence of chlamydial and gonococcal salpingitis during the menstrual cycle. JAMA 1986; 255:2062.
82. Wolner-Hanssen P, Mardh PA, Svensson L, et al. Laparoscopy in women with chlamydial infection and pelvic pain: A comparison of patients with and without salpingitis. Obstet Gynecol 1983; 61:299.
83. Falk V. Treatment of acute non-tuberculous salpingitis with antibiotics alone and in combination with glucocorticoids. Acta Obstet Gynecol Scand 1965; 44(Suppl 16):65.
84. Kornfeld SJ, and Worthington MG. Culture-proved Fitz-Hugh–Curtis syndrome. Am J Obstet Gynecol 1981; 139:106.
85. Litt IF, and Cohen MI. Perihepatitis associated with salpingitis in adolescents. JAMA 1978; 240:1253.
86. Golden N, Cohen H, Gennari G, et al. The use of pelvic ultrasonography in the evaluation of adolescents with pelvic inflammatory disease. Am J Dis Child 1987; 141:1234.
87. Jacobson L. Laparoscopy in the diagnosis of acute salpingitis. Acta Obstet Gynecol Scand 1964; 43:160.

88. Jacobson L, and Westrom L. Objectivized diagnosis of acute pelvic inflammatory disease. Am J Obstet Gynecol 1969; 105:1088.
89. Westrom L. Incidence, prevalence and trends of acute PID and its consequences in industrialized countries. Am J Obstet Gynecol 1980; 138:1006.
90. Jacobson L. Differential diagnosis of acute PID. Am J Obstet Gynecol 1980; 138:1006.
91. Hager WD, Eschenbach DA, Spence MR, et al. Criteria for diagnosis and grading of salpingitis. Obstet Gynecol 1983; 61:113.
92. Kiviat NB, Wolner-Hanssen P, Peterson M, et al. Localization of *Chlamydia trachomatis* infection by direct immunofluorescence and culture in pelvic inflammatory disease. Am J Obstet Gynecol 1986; 154:865.
93. Viberg L. Acute inflammatory conditions of the uterine adnexa. Acta Obstet Gynecol Scand 1964; 43:5.
94. Sweet RL, Schachter J, and Robbie MO. Failure of β-lactam antibiotics to eradicate *Chlamydia trachomatis* in the endometrium despite apparent clinical cure of acute salpingitis. JAMA 1983; 250:2641.
95. Brunham RC. Therapy for acute pelvic inflammatory disease: A critique of recent treatment trials. Am J Obstet Gynecol 1984; 148:235.
96. Wasserheit JN, Bell TA, Kiviat NB, et al. Microbial causes of proven pelvic inflammatory disease and efficacy of clindamycin and tobramycin. Ann Intern Med 1986; 104:187.
97. Berkeley AS, Freeman KS, Senterfit LB, et al. An evaluation of synergistic activity between clindamycin and gentamicin in inhibiting the in vitro growth of *Neisseria gonorrhoeae* (Abstract #21). Inf Dis Soc Obstet Gynecol, Aug. 1988.
98. Sweet RL, Schachter J, Landers DV, et al. Treatment of hospitalized patients with acute pelvic inflammatory disease: Comparison of cefotetan plus doxycycline and cefoxitin plus doxycycline. Am J Obstet Gynecol 1988; 158:737.
99. Dodson MG, Faro S, and Gentry LO. Treatment of acute pelvic inflammatory disease with Aztreonam, a new monocyclic β-lactam antibiotic and clindamycin. Obstet Gynecol 1986; 67:657.
100. Apuzzio J, Stankiewicz R, Jain S, et al. Evaluation of ciprofloxacin with clindamycin-gentamicin in the treatment of pelvic infection in the female (Abstract #1168). Presented at 28th Interscience Conference on Antimicrobial Agents and Chemotherapy, 1988.
101. Thadepalli H, Mathai D, and Savage E. Ciprofloxacin therapy for pelvic inflammatory disease (PID) in hospitalized patients (Abstract #1169). Presented at 28th Interscience Conference on Antimicrobial Agents and Chemotherapy, 1988.
102. Landers DV, and Sweet RL. Current trends in the diagnosis and treatment of tuboovarian abscess. Am J Obstet Gynecol 1985; 151:1098.
103. Wolner-Hanssen P, Paavonen J, Kiviat N, et al. Outpatient treatment of pelvic inflammatory disease with cefoxitin and doxycycline. Obstet Gynecol 1988; 81:595.
104. Wolner-Hanssen P, Paavonen J, Kiviat N, et al. Ambulatory treatment of suspected pelvic inflammatory disease with Augmentin, with or without doxycycline. Am J Obstet Gynecol 1988; 158:577.
105. Ohm-Smith M, Crombleholme WR, and Sweet RL. In vitro activity of ciprofloxacin against anaerobic bacteria recovered from patients with acute PID (Abstract #28). Presented at Interscience Conference on Antimicrobial Agents and Chemotherapy, 1988.

106. Westrom L. Effect of acute pelvic inflammatory disease on fertility. Am J Obstet Gynecol 1975; 121:707.
107. Svenson L, Mardh PA, and Westrom L. Infertility after acute salpingitis with special reference to *Chlamydia trachomatis*. Fertil Steril 1983; 40:322.
108. Westrom L. Influence of sexually transmitted diseases on sterility and ectopic pregnancy. Acta Eur Fertil 1985; 16:21.
109. Curran JW. Economic consequences of PID in the United States. Am J Obstet Gynecol 1980; 138:848.
110. CDC. Increases in primary and secondary syphilis—United States. MMWR 1987; 36:393.
111. CDC. Syphilis and congenital syphilis—United States, 1985–1988. MMWR 1988; 37:486.
112. CDC. Guidelines for the prevention and control of congenital syphilis. MMWR 1988; 37:S1.
113. Silber TJ, and Niland NF. The clinical spectrum of syphilis in adolescence. J Adolesc Health Care 1984; 5:112.
114. Alexander-Rodriguez T, and Vermund SH. Gonorrhea and syphilis in incarcerated urban adolescents: Prevalence and physical signs. Pediatrics 1987; 80:561.
115. Fiumara NJ. Treatment of primary and secondary syphilis. JAMA 1980; 243:2500.
116. Fiumara NJ. Treatment of early latent syphilis of less than a year's duration. Sex Transm Dis 1978; 5:85.
117. Fiumara NJ. Serologic responses to treatment of 128 patients with late latent syphilis. Sex Transm Dis 1979; 6:243.
118. Felman YM, and Nikitas JA. Syphilis serology today. Arch Dermatol 1980; 116:84.
119. Brown ST, Zaidi A, Larsen SA, et al. Serological response to syphilis treatment: A new analysis of old data. JAMA 1985; 253:1296.
120. Fiumara NJ. The surgical diagnosis: Ruling out VD. Part 2. Syphilis. Infect Surg 1984; 359.
121. Ziaya PR, Hankins GD, Gilstrap LC, et al. Intravenous penicillin desensitization and treatment during pregnancy. JAMA 1986; 256:2561.
122. Mascola L, Pelosi R, Blount JH, et al. Congenital syphilis revisited. Am J Dis Child 1985; 139:157.
123. Srinivasan G, Ramamurthy RS, Bharathi A, et al. Congenital syphilis: A diagnostic and therapeutic dilemma. Pediatr Infect Dis 1983; 2:436.

SUGGESTED READING
Hammerschlag MR. Chlamydial infections. J Pediatr 1989; 114:727.
Holmes KK, Mardh P, Sparling PF, et al. (eds.). *Sexually Transmitted Diseases* (2nd ed.). New York: McGraw-Hill, 1990.
Stamm WE. Diagnosis of *Chlamydia trachomatis* genitourinary infections. Ann Intern Med 1988; 108:710.

11. Human Papillomavirus (HPV) and Human Immunodeficiency Virus (HIV)

Two sexually transmitted viruses have special significance for physicians caring for patients in the 1990s: human papillomavirus (HPV) and human immunodeficiency virus (HIV). HPV has become the most prevalent sexually transmitted viral infection, and its association with genital neoplasia poses special risks for the sexually active adolescent population. Although adolescent cases of acquired immunodeficiency syndrome (AIDS) represent only a small fraction of total cases of AIDS in the United States, the long latency period and the potential for spread of sexually transmitted diseases including HIV among adolescents make prevention and management of this infection a task for physicians providing medical care for adolescents. These two viruses may also occur in the same patient: the presence of genital warts appears to be a risk factor for the acquisition of HIV infection, and the presence of HIV infection and the accompanying immunosuppression can result in the occurrence of severe HPV genital infections.

HUMAN PAPILLOMAVIRUS

HPV is a DNA virus with more than 50 subtypes recognized since the recombinant DNA technology with hybridization techniques have been applied to the study of this virus. Some HPV types are specific for common warts and for deep plantar and palmar warts; others have a specific predilection for anogenital tissues. Infections with the genital types may be apparent clinically with or without the aid of magnification or may be subclinical and become apparent only at the time of the evaluation of an abnormal Papanicolaou (Pap) smear or with the biopsy of clinically normal appearing tissues [1, 2]. With an incubation period of 1 to 8 months, the manifestations of clinical disease may appear to "spread" because of the appearance of new lesions [3]. The infection should be thought of as a multicentric infection with the capacity of the virus to have clinical lesions seen on the vulva, vagina, urethra, cervix, and anus [4, 5]. A single viral subtype may be involved, or multiple subtypes may be present [6].

The common genital subtypes are 6, 11, 16, 18, 31, 33, 35, and 39. Types 6 and 11 are most often associated with exophytic "cauliflower" genital warts often appearing around the posterior fourchette and labia minora (Figs. 11-1, 11-2). "Flat condyloma" are generally types 16 or 18. Epidemiologic studies have found high prevalences of HPV infection in sexually active patients. Risk factors for acquisition

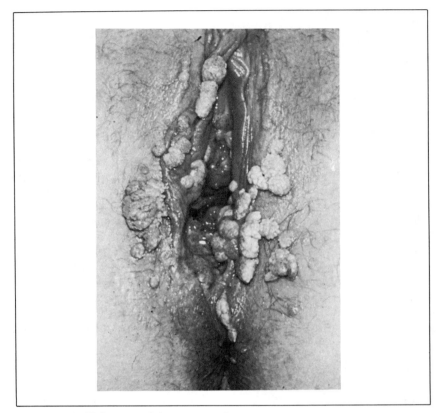

Figure 11-1. Vulvar condyloma accuminata.

of this virus include multiple sexual partners, lack of condom use, previous sexually transmitted diseases, and sexual relations with an infected partner. In an inner city adolescent clinic, cervicovaginal washings for HPV DNA were positive in 32 percent of patients [7]. Moscicki and co-workers [8] found that in a sexually active adolescent population that included suburban middle class and upper middle class adolescents, 19 percent had detectable HPV DNA using a Vira-Pap probe; 16 of the 171 had detectable HPV 16/18. Factors related to the detection of HPV in this study were multiple partners (the most important factor), oral contraceptive use, a history of *Chlamydia trachomatis*, and substance abuse. The prevalence of HPV in an inner city obstetrics clinic was 11.1 percent in the first trimester [9]. In a city hospital colposcopy clinic, 59.7 percent of patients had HPV DNA detected [10]. The worrisome issue in the striking prevalence of this infection is not just the expense and patient discomfort in treating the warty lesions, but more importantly the association of HPV, especially the subtypes 16 and 18, with the occurrence of genital dysplasia

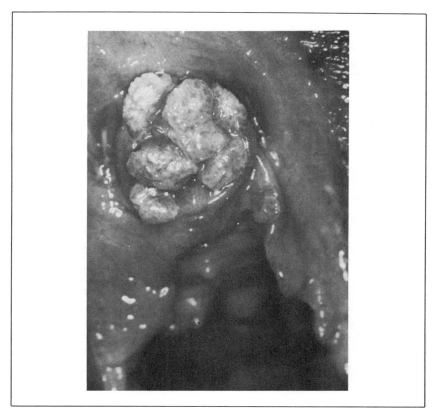

Figure 11-2. Urethral condyloma. (Courtesy of Dr. Ann Davis.)

and cancers [11–15]. During adolescence, high-risk sexual behaviors increase the probability that the patient will be exposed to HPV, and in addition young age may increase the acquisition of HPV because of the active zone of transformation and squamous metaplasia on the cervix. The high prevalence of HPV 16 and 18 in the adolescent age group is particularly worrisome. Abnormal Pap smears, cervical dysplasia, and invasive cancer are seen more commonly in young women than previously. Vulvar cancer can occur in adolescents with condylomas present since childhood [16, 17]. Given the prevalence of the infection, HPV may be thought of as a necessary but not sufficient factor in oncogenesis [18]. Other cofactors may be cigarette smoking [19, 20], immunosuppression [21, 22], other vaginal infections including allergic responses to *Candida* [23] and genital herpes simplex, and widespread transition zones in the vagina such as occurs with in utero exposure to diethylstilbestrol (DES) [24].

The most common clinical manifestation of HPV disease is the appearance of warty condyloma on the vulva or anus 4 to 6 weeks after an exposure to HPV. However, because of the long latency, the lesions may recur months to years after sexual contact due to the presence of virus in the previously clinically normal-appearing tissues. Perianal warts occur commonly in homosexual males and in females engaging in anal intercourse but also often occur in girls denying anal intercourse, suggesting contiguous spread.

Another common clinical manifestation of HPV in adolescents is an abnormal Pap smear. The Pap smear may reveal koilocytes (squamous cells with dense, sometimes granular, "raisinoid" nuclei and a perinuclear halo, also termed balloon cells), dyskeratosis, and/or evidence of cervical intraepithelial neoplasia. As noted in the section on Pap smears in Chapter 1, narrative summaries of Pap cytologic findings are preferred, and careful consultation between the physician and the cytology laboratory is important to ensure that the terminology used (including koilocytosis, koilocytotic atypia) is being interpreted similarly by both the clinician and the cytologist and pathologist. Although Pap smears are not without their problems of sensitivity and specificity, they remain a useful screening technique for cervical dysplasia and cancer [18, 25, 26, 27]. HPV infection and cervical intraepithelial neoplasia (CIN) represent a continuum, *not* a stepwise change. Twenty to thirty percent of Pap smears with atypia or koilocytosis have CIN on cervical biopsy [28, 29]. HPV DNA is present in cervical cells from 90 percent of patients with CIN versus 10 percent of controls. Although rates of both koilocytes and HPV antigen decrease in both severe CIN and invasive cancer, HPV DNA can still be recovered from cellular DNA. HPV types 16 and 18 are present in 70 percent of CIN and cancer with small percentages for types 10, 11, 31, 33, and 35; type 6 is rarely present in cervical cancer. Reid and colleagues [3] found that only 1 of 80 cervical biopsy specimens that were positive for type 6 or 11 had a diagnosis of CIN greater than grade 2. In contrast, 42 of 48 (90%) of cervical biopsies that had CIN grade 3 or invasive cancer were positive for types 16, 18, or 31. However, 10 percent of condyloma and CIN grade 1 were associated with types 16, 18, or 31. Only 31 percent of patients with types 6 or 11 presented with abnormal Pap smears in contrast to 93 percent of those with types 16, 18, or 31. Invasive vulvar cancers can be associated with types 6, 11, and 16 [3, 30].

The rate of progression from HPV cervical disease to dysplasia is variably reported, with higher degrees of dysplasia more likely to progress [31–34]. Nash and colleagues [31] found that about one-third of patients with histologically confirmed HPV cervical infection progressed to CIN within 1 year. Another study found that 14 percent progressed to dysplasia or carcinoma in situ within 2 years [33]. Nasiell and co-workers [32] calculated that the yearly risk for a woman with mild dysplasia to develop severe dysplasia/carcinoma in situ was 560 times greater than for a woman without dysplasia. Lesions with aneuploidy are much more likely to progress to invasive disease than those with polyploid lesions. Twenty-six percent of patients with mild cervical atypia in whom dysplasia could not be excluded and 50 percent of those with warty atypia progressed to CIN or frank cancer [33]. These percentages may be lower than occurs with natural progression because the biopsy in itself may be helpful in stimulating the immune system against HPV. Spontaneous regression with HPV 16 lesions is low. Colposcopy alone without the use of biopsy cannot be used to predict the outcome of HPV lesions [35].

Among patients with vulvar HPV disease, many have coexisting cervical disease. Although numbers vary in studies, Spitzer and associates [4] reported that 78 percent of patients with overt vulvar condylomas had HPV cervical disease by colposcopy and biopsy. Others have found approximately one third to have cervical disease in the presence of vulvar disease. Although colposcopy clinics are often overbooked, optimally adolescents with vulvar condyloma and certainly any changes of HPV on Pap smear (atypia, koilocytosis, and CIN) should be evaluated by an experienced colposcopist. Patients with genital warts should be evaluated with more frequent Pap smears than the annual examination recommended for sexually active teens. For example, we typically obtain Pap smears every 3 months during active disease and then, after resolution of the warts, every 3 to 6 months for 2 to 3 years.

In addition to gross warts and abnormal Pap smears, HPV may also be detected by the application of 3 to 5% acetic acid to the vulva, vagina, and cervix, a procedure that is important in identification of other foci and previously undetected disease in adolescents at high risk for sexually transmitted diseases. The procedure causes slight burning or a "cold" sensation and is time-consuming but is extremely useful in identifying subclinical HPV. The aceto-white lesions may be seen with the naked eye but are particularly visible with the use of magnification of the colposcope. Lesions on the vulva are often referred to as microcondylomata of the labia and should not be confused with the normal, usually symmetric, vestibular papillae that generally do not stain aceto-white. These HPV lesions should be recognized by the clinician as reservoirs of HPV infection, and they also may cause vestibular pruritus, burning, and dyspareunia [36].

Biopsies of the lesions for pathology and DNA probes are useful in detecting the presence of CIN and vulvar and vaginal intraepithelial neoplasia. Techniques for detection of HPV include filter hybridization and in situ hybridization. Commercially available probes have been used to screen for cervical infections with HPV and may ultimately help to elucidate the natural history of various HPV types. These technologies can be used on cervical/genital smears, cervicovaginal lavage [37], or biopsies. It is unknown at present whether all sexually active patients should undergo some type of routine screening or whether patients found to harbor HPV types 16 or 18 should receive extra surveillance and routine colposcopy. Newer procedures (e.g., the polymerase chain reaction) may become available clinically to help answer more questions. A combination of HPV detection methods and Pap smears may be a useful technique in high-risk patients.

Treatment of these lesions has evolved over the past few decades and particularly the past 5 years with more changes expected in the next decade. Since HPV infection is often multicentric and normal-appearing skin is often infected with latent HPV, treatment should be directed at clinical disease and CIN, vulvar intraepithelial neoplasia (VIN), and vaginal intraepithelial neoplasia (VAIN), *not* with the hope of eradication of *all* virus from anogenital tissues. Treatment must also take into account the presence of an infected sexual partner. Barrasso and co-workers [38] found that 64.4 percent of male sexual partners of women with cervical flat condylomata or CIN had evidence of HPV infection; in 42.5 percent the lesions were detected only after the application of acetic acid. Similar percentages of infected men have been found in other studies [39, 40]. Many men are not aware of the existence of lesions and may have penile intraepithelial neoplasia at the time of evaluation [41]. Proper referral of the male partners to a physician experienced in HPV detection (acetic acid soak, magnification) is crucial to treating the young woman. Colposcopy is useful in the detection of condyloma in men as well as women [42]. Although condom use is efficacious in preventing some HPV spread, the contact of vulva and scrotum may further spread the infection.

Most office therapies are aimed at treatment of exophytic warts of the external genitalia. The goal is local destruction with the hope that the patient's own host responses will augment the effect. Any treatment must be compared against the possibility of spontaneous resolution; exophytic warts usually regress over 3 to 5 years. Destructive therapies include podophyllin, trichloroacetic acid (TCA), liquid nitrogen, cryotherapy, and laser. Although a long used medication, application of 25% podophyllin in tincture of benzoin has problems with use; this compound needs to be washed off after 4 to 6 hours (1–4 hours with first application), must be applied frequently, is contraindicated in pregnancy, is not a pure compound, and is contraindicated in well-vascularized perianal and vaginal tissues because of absorption and the possibility of toxic reactions. These problems have led many physicians to use another chemical compound, TCA, in strengths of 25 to 85 percent. TCA must be used carefully to prevent burns to the patient; the most effective strength, 85%, needs to be applied just to the lesion; immediately afterward aloe vera gel or normal saline can be used to ease the burning sensation. Unlike podophyllin, TCA does not need to be washed off. The TCA is reapplied weekly. If the lesions fail to respond or progress between treatments, laser or cryocautery can be discussed with the patient.

The advantage of treatment with the carbon dioxide laser is that cure rates appear good and vulvar, vaginal, cervical, and perianal disease can be treated concurrently [34]. The disadvantages are that general anesthesia is generally required, costs are high, and postoperative pain can be significant. After laser therapy, the patient needs to be instructed in using sitz baths (with 5 tablespoons of epsom salts per 5 gallons of water) and voiding into the water if dysuria causes urinary retention, drying the vulva with a hair dryer, rinsing with povidone-iodine (Betadine, 1 ounce added to 2 ounces of warm water) using a squirt bottle after a bowel movement or urination, application of silver sulfadiazine (Silvadene) cream in a thin layer every 4 to 12 hours for 10 to 30 days, narcotics/analgesics for pain, avoidance of sex for at least 1 month and thereafter with a condom, and use of a stool softener [43]. Problems include postoperative pain, bleeding, and scarring (vulvar coaptations, vaginal strictures, and cervical os stenosis). It is important to remember that the laser cannot effectively eliminate all multicentric subclinical HPV infection of the lower genital tract [44], even when inducing substantial morbidity. Although controversial, incorporating surrounding tissue into the field may reduce the chance of recurrence for vulvar epithelial neoplasia and vulvar and/or anal/perianal condyloma [43, 45]. More studies are needed to improve results. Physicians using laser technology for treatment of HPV infections need to avoid contact with the laser vapor, which contains intact HPV DNA [46].

5-Fluorouracil (5-FU) cream, although not approved by the Food and Drug Administration for the therapy of HPV, has been used in a number of medical centers and can be useful for the treatment of vaginal and urethral condyloma [47]. Protocols that are modeled on those of Krebs [47, 48, 49] have proved useful in the care of some patients at The Children's Hospital in Boston [2]. 5-FU is often used as prophylaxis following laser therapy, especially for immunosuppressed patients who have a high risk of relapse. For prophylaxis, the patient applies 4 to 5 ml (applicator size of 5 or 10 ml must be determined by pharmacy availability) of 5% 5-FU *deeply* into the vagina once every 2 weeks just prior to bedtime, inserting a tampon after the application to prevent seepage of the medication onto the vulva. A small amount of petroleum jelly can be placed at the introitus, although the efficacy of treating coexisting vulvar disease may be lessened. The tampon should be removed the next morning and the patient should bathe. A very thin film of 5-FU is applied over the vulva at night once every 2 weeks, taking care to apply it in the areas previously involved with HPV. The first application of 5-FU is started as soon as sufficient healing has occurred following laser therapy, not later than 4 weeks. At a follow-up of 9 to 22 months after complete ablation of clinical HPV, 13 percent of patients treated with prophylactic 5-FU and 38 percent of those without additional treatment had recurrent lesions [48].

For treatment of vaginal condyloma, a dose of 3 ml of 5-FU can also be used on a weekly basis for 10 weeks; care must be taken as noted to prevent seepage at the introitus by inserting a tampon, and hands must be washed. Krebs [47] reported that 85 percent of women treated with 10 weekly applications of 5% 5-FU (approximately 1.5 gm/vaginal treatment) had no evidence of disease at 3-month follow-up. Alternatively, 2 ml of 5-FU can be applied every third night, just before retiring, for 2 weeks [2]. 5-FU is also recommended for urethral condyloma and can be applied every third night, and the patient is then instructed to void 4 hours later and bathe. However, the clinician needs to be aware of the potential for *serious* side effects. This medication is contraindicated in pregnancy, and adolescents must be using a reliable form of contraception consistently and understand the risks of noncompliance. Counselling should be documented in the medical record. In addition, the adolescent must be able to follow directions, since erosive vulvitis will occur if 5-FU is improperly used; hands must be washed after applications. Bone marrow suppression and gastrointestinal side effects have not been a problem because of the small amount of the total dose absorbed; this amount may increase when applied to eroded epithelium.

The newest form of therapy is interferon and is usually reserved for resistant HPV disease [50]. Multiple injections of interferon alfa-2b are needed. Although initial rates of cure reported were very encouraging, other studies have not yielded as good results. Friedman-Kien and colleagues [51] found that therapy eliminated warts in 62 percent of patients treated with intralesional interferon alfa twice weekly for up to 8 weeks versus only 21 percent treated with placebo. Side effects included fevers, flu-like symptoms, myalgias, and malaise and usually disappeared by the end of the third week of therapy. Other studies are examining lower doses to try to minimize side effects [52]. Studies using intramuscular interferon have also shown promise in treating recalcitrant disease [53]. Safety has not been established in those below 18 years. Effective contraception must be used, since it is currently unknown whether this drug is harmful to the fetus or a woman's reproductive capacity [54]. No studies have been done on male fertility. Most patients with HPV disease unresponsive to TCA prefer a one-time treatment with laser to multiple injections of interferon over a period of weeks to months, but older adolescents might prefer this outpatient treatment for cost or convenience reasons.

The treatment of cervical HPV infections depends on the results of colposcopy and cervical biopsy [2, 55]. Adolescents tolerate cervical biopsies better if they are given a dose of a nonsteroidal anti-inflammatory drug prior to the procedure. If the biopsy confirms HPV without dysplasia, options include observation or treatment with TCA, cryotherapy, or laser. Observation may be difficult to rationalize in an adolescent population in which follow-up may be unreliable and infected partners may not be treated. Cryotherapy is the most common form of treatment and has a failure rate of approximately 12 percent with one treatment. TCA treatment of the cervix may have a cure rate of 82 percent at 3 months, but more long-term studies are needed [56]. If the biopsy shows dysplasia, appropriate therapy includes cryotherapy, laser, and cone biopsy. Careful follow-up at 3 months after treatment is important; Falcone and Ferenczy [57] have recommended combined cytologic testing and colposcopy, and, if appropriate, histologic examination, at 3 months followed by cytologic follow-up (Pap smears) at subsequent visits [57].

Immunocompromised patients are particularly difficult to treat. The risk of vulvar and anal carcinoma in renal transplant patients is significantly higher than in normal patients; the risk of CIN has been estimated to be 16-fold higher than in the general population [21]. Treatment often involves laser therapy followed by long-term pro-phylaxis with 5-FU.

The increase in vulvar and cervical disease noted by physicians caring for adolescents has been mirrored by an increase in anogenital HPV infections seen in prepubertal children. Although many of the infants seen with condyloma in the first 12 to 24 months of life have acquired HPV from the mother at the time of vaginal delivery [58], the most common mode of transmission after this time is sexual abuse (see Chaps. 3 and 17). Infections in immunocompromised girls, especially those with HIV infection, may be severe [59]. Laryngeal papillomatosis can also occur in children secondary to transmission of HPV, usually type 11, at birth; this troubling infection often presents with hoarseness in the first 5 years of life (also later) and may require multiple interventions. Virus can be detected in tissues even when patients are in clinical remission [60]. Most children with juvenile laryngeal papillomas are born to mothers with a history of genital HPV infection [61]. However, the exact risk of laryngeal disease in a child born to a mother with HPV is unknown but may be between 1:200 and 1:1500 [62], and thus more studies are needed before delivery techniques are altered in an attempt to prevent this infection in the offspring. Interferon therapy may not be as useful as was hoped. Rare squamous cell carcinoma of the lung and head and neck cancers have been reported to be associated with genital types of HPV [63, 64].

Prevention of HPV infection is key, and many of the techniques discussed in the section on sex education and HIV are applicable to the prevention of HPV. Condoms and other newly released barrier methods (vaginal condoms) are the only methods known to decrease HPV infections. Sexual partners should always be evaluated to prevent further spread. Because immunocompromised patients are at special risk from this virus, patients require adequate counselling prior to becoming sexually active. They need to know about the importance of using condoms and avoiding infected partners.

Many questions remain to be answered in the care of patients with HPV infection [65]. Should all sexually active adolescents be screened not only with Pap smears but also for HPV infection? Should the management be different for the asymptomatic patient with type 16 HPV? How should latent infections be managed? Can host immunity be altered to affect better management and perhaps "cure" rates? Much research is needed to answer these and other questions in the future.

HUMAN IMMUNODEFICIENCY VIRUS
Like the epidemic of HPV infections, the emergence of HIV infections in the adolescent age group will have profound consequences for the delivery of health care in the United States. Information is updated almost weekly with new studies, books, and review articles [66–82]. Because of the rapid changes in understanding the pathophysiology, diagnosis, and treatment of HIV infection and guidelines for prevention, care, and infection control, this section will focus on an overview of epidemiology and the potential consequences for adolescent girls.

As of July 1989, over 100,000 cases of AIDS in the United States and its territories had been reported to the Centers for Disease Control (CDC). The percentages by race and gender of cases (1981–1988) are shown in Tables 11-1 and 11-2. Although homosexual/bisexual behavior remains a major risk factor for AIDS, a history of intravenous drug use has become an increasingly important risk factor for acquiring HIV infection. The percentage of adolescent/adult males with a history of intravenous drug abuse as the only risk factor rose from 14 percent in 1987 to 20 percent in 1988. Women frequently have a personal history of drug use or are the heterosexual partner of a person at risk for HIV infection. Blacks and Hispanics from coastal communities such as New York City, New Jersey, and Florida are disproportionately represented among adolescent/adult women with AIDS and among infants born with HIV infection. Reports of AIDS cases in

Table 11-1. Percent Distribution of AIDS Cases, by Transmission Category and Year of Report, United States, 1981–1988

Category	AIDS Cases (%)				
	Before 1985	1985	1986	1987	1988
Adult Male (≥13 years)					
Homosexual/bisexual only	69	72	71	70	63
IV-drug user	15	15	15	14	20
Homosexual and IV-drug user	10	8	8	8	7
Hemophiliac	1	1	1	1	1
Heterosexual					
Heterosexual contact	<1	<1	1	1	1
Born in Pattern II country*	3	1	1	1	1
Transfusion	1	1	2	2	2
Undetermined	2	2	2	3	4†
Total	100	100	100	100	100
Adult Female (≥13 years)					
IV-drug user	58	53	49	49	53
Coagulation disorder	<1	1	<1	<1	<1
Heterosexual					
Heterosexual contact	16	21	28	27	26
Born in Pattern II country*	8	6	6	4	3
Transfusion	8	11	10	13	10
Undetermined	10	9	6	6	8†
Total	100	100	100	100	100
Pediatric (<13 years)					
Coagulation disorder	4	6	6	7	7
Transfusion	11	14	13	14	11
Mother with/at risk for AIDS/HIV infection					
IV-drug user	45	47	44	41	40
Sex with person at risk	11	17	24	21	21
Born in Pattern II country*	22	14	6	7	7
Other	0	2	5	8	9
Undetermined	6	0	2	3	6†
Total	100	100	100	100	100

*Pattern II countries are WHO-designated countries with predominantly heterosexual transmission of HIV.
†Of patients initially reported with an undetermined transmission category, 75% are reclassified into known risk categories following investigation. Increases in the proportion of cases with undetermined risk in more recent reporting periods reflect a higher proportion of patients who have not been investigated.
From U.S. Department of Health and Human Services, CDC. AIDS and human immunodeficiency virus infection in the United States: 1988 update. MMWR 1989; 38(S-4):17.

Table 11.2. Racial/Ethnic Distribution of the U.S. Population Compared with AIDS Cases, 1981–1988*

Category	Racial/Ethnic Group (%)				
	White	Black	Hispanic	Asian/Pacific Islander	American Indian/ Alaskan Native
U.S. population	80	12	6	2	1
All AIDS cases	59	27	13	1	<1
Adult AIDS cases					
Male	62	24	13	1	<1
Female	29	54	16	1	<1
Pediatric cases	25	55	20	<1	<1

*Excluding U.S. territories.
Source: U.S. Department of Health and Human Services, CDC. AIDS and human immunodeficiency virus infection in the United States: 1988 update. MMWR 1989; 38(S-4):18.

women from 1981 to 1986 found that over 70 percent were black or Hispanic and over 80 percent were of childbearing age [83].

Epidemiologic surveys have found varying percentages of populations infected with HIV. For example, blood donors (a highly self-selected population) had a prevalence of 0.018 percent for 15 million Red Cross donors [69]. In contrast, the infection rate for civilian applicants for military service was 0.14 percent for 1,798,600 applicants screened between October 1985 and September 1988 (0.15% in men and 0.07% in women). Among the first 84,089 residential Job Corps entrants tested, 0.41 percent were positive. Populations from high-risk urban settings have much higher prevalences. The prevalence of positive tests for applicants for military service from the Bronx was 16/1000 [68]. At an inner city clinic for sexually transmitted diseases in Baltimore, 5.2 percent of patients were seropositive for HIV. HIV-positivity was higher among men (6.3%) than women (3.0%) and among blacks (5.0%) than whites (1.2%) [84]. In men, HIV seropositivity was associated with a history of syphilis and in women with a history of genital warts. In a Baltimore emergency ward, 4 percent of adult patients had unrecognized HIV infection [85].

A study in Massachusetts using newborns' blood samples as an indicator of maternal serologic status found that 2.1/1000 women were positive for HIV infection, with the rate of seropositivity especially high in inner city hospitals (8/1000) [86]. In New York City (1987–88) the prevalence was 1.25 percent among newborns, with a seropositivity of 2.2 percent in zip code areas with high rates of drug abuse [87]. Seroprevalence of HIV among intravenous drug users in drug treatment programs in the United States has ranged from 0 to 65 percent with highest rates in the Northeast (10–65%) and Puerto Rico

(45–59%) [88]. Higher rates occur in black and Hispanic drug users than in white drug users [89]. In a study in San Francisco, intravenous cocaine significantly increased the risk of HIV infection with a seroprevalence of 35 percent in daily cocaine users [90]. Sixty to ninety percent of hemophiliac males, many of whom are adolescents, are infected with HIV.

Adolescents currently account for only 1 percent of the cases of AIDS, with many of these adolescents living in New York City. However, this small percentage likely represents only the tip of the iceberg of HIV infections. With the long latency of HIV infection before a presentation with clinical AIDS, many girls who are infected with HIV during adolescence will not present with clinical symptoms until their twenties and thus will not be counted as "adolescent AIDS." Dr. Karen Hein [66] has spearheaded efforts to highlight the alarming statistics and issues that make the adolescent population at high risk of acquiring HIV infection [68]. The prevalence of HIV infections clearly poses a particular risk to young women who may pass HIV unknowingly to their infants. In a study of AIDS in New York City adolescents, the male to female ratio was 2.9:1, in contrast to the overall ratio in U.S. adults of 15:1. Females in New York City acquire HIV infection from intravenous drug abuse and from heterosexual contacts, often with older males with risk factors for HIV infection (50–60% of intravenous drug users in New York City are HIV-positive [91]). Indeed, 45 percent of female AIDS cases in New York City (aged 13–21 years) reported heterosexual contact as their primary risk behavior. Ten percent of mothers of babies born with AIDS in New York City are under 21 years of age. In the United States, AIDS accounts for 3 percent of all deaths among women 25 to 34 years old [69].

Adolescents need to receive special attention in research and treatment because they have different needs from adults and have the potential to be "the next wave" of the HIV epidemic [68]. The number of reported AIDS cases in adolescents is doubling each year. Adolescents are at particular risk of acquiring HIV infection because of their high prevalence of other sexually transmitted diseases. The frequency of other sexually transmitted disease is worrisome not only because of what it indicates about behavior and risk patterns in adolescence but also because infections such as genital ulcers, warts, and syphilis may increase the risk of acquiring HIV [92, 93]. Adolescents may have many serial monogamous relationships and believe themselves therefore to be at low risk of sexually transmitted disease in spite of having multiple partners over a year; other teens may have multiple partners. The term "sexual adventurer" has been applied by Sorenson [94] to adolescents with a total of 17 partners by age 19 years and who in the month before interview had an average of 3.2 partners. Forty-one percent of sexually experienced adolescent males and 13 percent of sexually experienced females fit this definition and are thus at high risk of acquiring sexually transmitted infections [66].

Young adolescents, often in the stage of concrete thinking, have difficulty thinking through the consequences of actions and the potential long-term effects. Peer pressure to use drugs or have sex may override distant risks [66]. The high pregnancy rate among adolescents, discussed in Chapter 16, has similar parallel to the problems with sexually transmitted diseases. Denial is common among adolescents. Contraception is often episodic, and the most widely used prescription method, oral contraceptives, offers no protection against sexually transmitted infections. Hein [66] has pointed out that for adolescents, "the idea of being an asymptomatic carrier of a deadly disease is a particularly hard one to accept for themselves or others."

Other factors such as immunologic immaturity or a large cervical ectropion may render an adolescent particularly susceptible to acquiring HIV infection. More research is clearly needed to elucidate issues of special significance to adolescents. Of particular worry is that in Central Africa where spread is largely heterosexual, females in the age group of 15 to 19 years old have the highest percentage of HIV positivity, in part reflecting the social pattern of older men having sexual relationships with adolescent females [66].

The major epidemic of drug abuse in the 1980s, especially the use of cocaine and crack, has been important in fueling the HIV epidemic because HIV-infected drug users are frequently young adult minority men who are also sexually active, often with multiple and younger partners. Drug abuse in the female may serve to increase acquisition of HIV from at-risk behaviors facilitated by impairment of judgment under the influence of drugs, involvement with needle-sharing peer groups, and encouragement of the selling of sex to obtain money or drugs. Thus adolescent girls who use only non-intravenous drugs often have increased risk of HIV from their life-style. Although surveys of high school seniors have suggested a decline in drug use and cocaine, school dropout rates in urban centers can be 40 percent, and these youngsters are frequently at-risk teens not reached by such surveys. Prostitutes, runaways, and adolescents in detention centers are at particular risk of HIV infection. The average age of first intercourse in girls in detention centers is 12 years versus 16 years for other adolescents [66, 68].

Poor adolescents frequently have little access to health care or prenatal services and may not enter the health care system at a stage in their pregnancy when they can benefit from HIV testing and counselling. Many adolescents do not personally know someone with AIDS and therefore continue to feel invulnerable [66, 95]. Blinded serosurveys can increase awareness of the infection within the community.

The number of adolescents with bisexual or homosexual behaviors is unknown but represents another group of adolescents at risk of HIV. Ethical and legal issues regarding HIV testing need further discussion and resolution [96, 97].

The clinician often feels bewildered by the magnitude of the problem. Only recently have surveys of adolescents begun to shed some information on sexual practices and beliefs. Adolescents frequently have misinformation and tend to overestimate the risks of HIV infection from casual contact or blood donation. Adolescents engaging in high-risk behaviors are least likely to be in school where they can be reached by curricula and are less likely to be engaging in risk reduction. In a survey of eighth and tenth grade students in randomly selected classrooms in a national probability sample of 217 schools in 20 states, 94 percent believed that sexual intercourse with someone with HIV increases the likelihood of becoming infected, 91 percent believed sharing needles increases the likelihood, 86 percent believed that the use of condoms decreases the likelihood, but 47 percent believed that "donating blood increased the likelihood" [98]. A survey of students in the ninth to twelfth grades found a considerable range of knowledge about ways that AIDS is *not* transmitted; only 29 to 47 percent knew AIDS could not be acquired from mosquito and other insect bites, 42 to 65 percent knew AIDS could not come from use of public toilets, and 50 to 75 percent knew a blood test could not transmit AIDS. A range of 84 to 98 percent knew that AIDS *was* transmitted by sharing needles used to inject drugs, and 88 to 98 percent knew it was transmitted through sexual intercourse [99].

The lack of information has led many school systems to adopt new curricula, some excellent, others a lecture or two. The push for AIDS education as the only effective tool has brought more sex education into school systems that had previously avoided discussion of sensitive topics. Many of these schools are ill-prepared to offer a curriculum to meet the needs of today's youth and focus only on AIDS education rather than a more broad range of topics such as other sexually transmitted diseases, contraception, pregnancy options, and sexual decision-making [100, 101]. Frequently these courses are delayed until high school even though many adolescents are already engaging in high-risk behavior in the middle school. Although it is clear that adolescents and adults can acquire knowledge from the media and courses [102], the greater issue for prevention of the spread of HIV is the effect of these courses on behavior change. Behavior change and risk reduction can occur with education in white homosexual men and to some extent among drug users, but recidivism is common unless behavior is consistently reinforced [103, 104, 105]. The evidence for behavior change in adolescents is less clear with current interventions. An increase in condom use following an educational intervention may not occur. In a survey of well-educated adolescent girls in a private practice, knowledge was not sufficient to alter behavior [106]. Although most adolescents said that they would alter behavior in the future with another partner, they were unwilling to change current behavior. Those with a prior sexually transmitted disease were not more likely to use condoms in the future than those who had never experienced such disease. Of those who did alter behavior, peer influence was most effective in promoting change.

Strategies for reaching adolescents must continue to be developed [66, 68, 107, 108]. The CDC has recommended age-appropriate curricula from kindergarten to twelfth grade taught by qualified teachers [109]. Other useful strategies for reaching adolescents and promoting change are the development of effective audiovisual materials such as "Sex, Drugs, and AIDS," with a national clearinghouse to make these available to schools and community groups, telephone hot lines*, media advertising of condoms and barrier contraceptives, development of adolescent resource groups, and networks of agencies serving youth to develop and disseminate educational materials especially for high-risk youth not served by schools. A clear prevention message needs to come from schools, television, magazines, films, clergy, parents, health care providers, and government agencies and should reflect differences in ethnic, religious, and community values [110]. The group targeted should be active participants in formulating the program. AIDS education needs to be a component of all programs rather than set apart. Since in the adolescent age group, drug use and high-risk sexual behaviors are often interrelated, interventions need to be targeted to the individual's specific risks [111]. Surveys of adolescent attitudes, knowledge, and behavior are important to design these programs. Involvement of families in the education process can facilitate communication.

Peer-based education along with school and community courses should be actively evaluated to examine knowledge acquisition and behavior change. Small discussion groups and role playing to help adolescents acquire the skills to deal with the pressure for drugs and sex are needed. "Just Say No" is a simplistic response to a complicated issue. Films need to be followed by thoughtful discussions of the implications. A new book by Dr. Hein is now available for teens at low cost and others are being published (see Appendix 5). Fear is not as successful at changing behavior as social skills training. Negotiation of sexual relationships is especially important for girls. Education needs to promote a sense of responsibility and empowerment to help adolescents make wise choices.

---

*CDC AIDS Hotline 1-800-342-AIDS, Spanish 1-800-344-SIDA, hearing impaired 1-800-AIDS-TTY.

Methadone programs are needed for adult as well as adolescent drug users, and needle exchange programs deserve further assessment. Outreach programs should be created to provide contraceptives to at-risk women of reproductive age. Not only do condoms need to be distributed widely to make them available and acceptable, but advertising must be targeted to particular ethnic/cultural groups. Many girls have difficulty purchasing condoms despite their fear of AIDS [112]. More funding is needed in many areas of HIV education and prevention, including further evaluation of the in vitro activity of nonoxynol 9 against HIV and the potential use of antiviral systemic agents (e.g., AZT) in the prevention of HIV following a high-risk rape [113, 114].

Community physicians may be called upon to address a community or school group [108, 109, 115]. A single lecture by a health professional is unlikely to change behavior, but it can increase knowledge and lead to further discussion. The physician should plan to cover such topics as a history of the epidemic, the asymptomatic nature of HIV infection, the definition of AIDS, answers to "How can I get it?" and "How can I not get it?", and the risks of sexual behavior and intravenous drug use. Physicians need to become involved in the policy of community and state organizations and in professional organizations.

In their office settings, physicians need to offer sensitive conselling that allows patients to assess their risks [66, 68, 108, 116]. The physician should criticize behaviors, not the teen herself, and help her to make responsible choices by examining options. Adolescents who are not sexually active, have never used intravenous drugs, and have not received blood transfusions between 1977 and 1985 can be counselled and their fears discussed. Typical questions from these adolescents are "What is AIDS? Is the disease common? Can you get it from drinking from a cup or swimming in a pool? Can I tell if someone is infected? How do babies get AIDS? Can it be transmitted by kissing?" The need to avoid risk behaviors including shared ear-piercing equipment and parenteral steroids for body-building and the lack of worry about household or school contacts (e.g., sharing water fountains, mosquito bites) needs emphasis. Patients undergoing elective surgery should be encouraged to use autologous donation if blood will be needed to minimize even the low risk of blood units infected with HIV or HTLV-1 [117, 118]. These adolescents need support for remaining abstinent and information about ways to cope with peer pressure and express affection, romance, and love without putting themselves at risk. The physician should be a good listener and acknowledge to the adolescent girl that living with the fear of AIDS (the "worried well" [68]) has increased the stresses of growing up in the 1990s.

For the sexually active teen who is not in a high-risk group, the physician needs to stress the importance of the patient discussing risk factors with her partner. She needs to understand her inability to "tell" who is infected. The benefits of long-term, mutually monogamous relationships and the use of condoms need to be stressed. The clinician can help the adolescent reassess sexual decision-making. Adolescents often engage in anal intercourse because of the decreased pregnancy risk, failing to realize that anal receptive intercourse is particularly risky for the acquisition of HIV infection. During the counselling session, the epidemic of *Chlamydia* and HPV should be discussed, since the high prevalence of these infections can serve as a reminder to the potential for HIV within the adolescent population. Most adolescents are aware of a friend who has had *Chlamydia* or genital warts. The physician needs to exchange ideas with the patient and help the adolescent to understand that she does have the ability to make wise choices. Helping the adolescent see that drug and alcohol use may interfere with wise sexual decision-making is an important task for the health care provider.

High-risk adolescents deserve special attention, for they tend to be least knowledgeable about HIV infections. These teens need counselling about the benefits and problems of testing, how to gain knowledge of the HIV status of the partner, the use of condoms, pregnancy continuation versus termination, and concrete services if infected [66]. Adolescent males with hemophilia and HIV infection may feel particularly isolated from heterosexual relationships and have difficulty communicating with their partner about their HIV status and using condoms [119]. The clinician may encounter difficulty advising which individual pregnant adolescent from a high prevalence community to have HIV testing done because risk factors may not be evident from the history. The patient may deny her own drug abuse or may not be knowledgeable about her partner's risk factors. In a survey of cord blood samples in New York City in which 2 percent were seropositive, only 7 of 12 seropositive women had risk factors as defined by the CDC [120]. Women at particular risk are those with partners known to be HIV-positive, intravenous drug users or their partners, prostitutes, women whose male partners have had a homosexual experience, hemophiliacs and partners of hemophiliacs, women or women whose partners have immigrated from Africa or Haiti after 1975 [121]. The CDC and the American College of Obstetrics and Gynecology have developed guidelines for the care of pregnant patients with HIV infection [122]. Clearly testing before pregnancy in these high-risk young women would be preferable, although knowledge of HIV status was only one determinant in decision-making about pregnancy termination in a high-risk group of women from the Bronx [123]. Better techniques for detection of HIV infection in newborns are under study [124].

The issue of testing continues to evoke heated debate and is likely to evolve further. In 1988, a Working Group of the conference entitled "AIDS in Adolescents; Exploring the Challenge" [97], cosponsored by many groups including the Society for Adolescent Medicine, National Institute on Drug Abuse, the Bureau of Maternal and Child Health and Resources Development, the National Institute of Mental Health, and the National Institute on Child Health and Human Development, suggested that voluntary testing for HIV infection be *offered* to any adolescent:

who has signs of symptoms consistent with AIDS or AIDS related complex
who is pregnant and (1) is known to be at risk of HIV infection or (2) is at
    unknown risk but is living in a geographic area of high prevalence
who voluntarily requests testing after the benefits and problems have been
    explained.

Further they suggested that an offer of voluntary testing should be *considered* for adolescents:

who engage in high risk behaviors, especially in geographic areas of high
    seroprevalence
who received multiple transfusions or clotting factors between 1978 and
    1985.

The decisions should be made on a case-by-case basis with consent of the adolescent and expected benefits for that patient. The working group suggests that informed consent should include at minimum:

a comprehensive, age-appropriate, culturally relevant explanation of risks
    and benefits (this discussion may take many visits before a decision is
    made)
information on what data will be disclosed in the medical record
identification of who will have access to that information
identification of a significant adult for support.

Even though adolescents receive the best medical care in a single comprehensive setting, the Working Group recognized the political and social realities of HIV infection and the need for anonymous, confidential testing. Further debate is needed on mandatory testing of adolescents for military service and the Job Corp, since the results of a positive test are not coupled with counselling or provision of services. The Working Group opposed mandatory testing. A single counselling session before or after testing is insufficient to deal with the potential impact of testing on an adolescent's life [125].

As the possibility of treating asymptomatic HIV infected patients with medications to prevent *Pneumocystis carinii* pneumonia or to improve immunologic function increases and the approach to HIV infection changes to management, these guidelines will need to be reconsidered [126, 127]. In addition, knowledge of HIV status is becoming increasingly important in the treatment for infections such as tuberculosis and syphilis [128–131].

Physicians and other health care providers need to be in the lead of confronting the issues of HIV infection. Although vaccine efforts will continue, care must focus on education, prevention through risk reduction, and management of HIV infection.

REFERENCES

1. Reid R (ed.). Human papillomavirus. Obstet Gynecol Clin North Am 1987; 14:329.
2. Davis A, and Emans SJ. Human papilloma virus infection in the pediatric and adolescent patient. J Pediatr 1989; 115:1.
3. Reid R, Greenberg M, Jenson AB, Husain M, Willett J, et al. Sexually transmitted papillomaviral infections. I. The anatomic distribution and pathologic grade of neoplastic lesions associated with different viral types. Am J Obstet Gynecol 1987; 156:212.
4. Spitzer M, Krumholz BA, and Seltzer VL. The multicentric nature of disease related to human papillomavirus infection of the female lower genital tract. Obstet Gynecol 1989; 73:303.
5. Moscicki B. HPV infections: An old STD revisited. Contemp Pediatr 1989; 6:12.
6. Bergeron C, Ferenczy A, Shah KV, et al. Multicentric human papillomavirus infections of the female genital tract: Correlation of viral types with abnormal mitotic figures, colposcopic presentation, and location. Obstet Gynecol 1987; 69:736.
7. Rosenfeld W, Vermund S, Wentz S, et al. High prevalence rate of human papillomavirus infection and association with abnormal Papanicolaou smears in sexually active adolescents. Am J Dis Child 1989; 143: 1443.
8. Moscicki B, Palefsky J, Gonzales J, et al. Human papillomavirus (HPV) infection in adolescent females: Prevalence, risk factors, and cytology. (Abstract) Society for Adolescent Medicine, March, 1989.
9. Fife KH, Rogers RE, and Zwickl BW. Symptomatic and asymptomatic cervical infections with human papillomavirus during pregnancy. J Infect Dis 1987; 156:904.
10. Ritter DB, Kadish AS, Vermund SH, et al. Detection of human papillomavirus deoxyribonucleic acid in exfoliated cervicovaginal cells as a predictor of cervical neoplasia in a high-risk population. Am J Obstet Gynecol 1988; 159:1517.
11. Macnab JCM, Walkinshaw SA, Cordiner JW, et al. Human papillomavirus in clinically and histologically normal tissue of patients with genital cancer. N Engl J Med 1986; 315:1052.
12. Kurman RJ, Shiffman MH, Lancaster WD, et al. Analysis of individual human papillomavirus types in cervical neoplasia: A possible role for type 18 in rapid progression. Am J Obstet Gynecol 1988; 159:293.

13. Crum CP, Ikenberg H, Richart RM, et al. Human papillomavirus type 16 and early cervical neoplasia. N Engl J Med 1984; 310:880.
14. Lancaster WD, Castellano C, Santos C, et al. Human papillomavirus deoxyribonucleic acid in cervical carcinoma from primary and metastatic sites. Am J Obstet Gynecol 1986; 154:115.
15. Reeves WC, Brinton LA, Garcia M, et al. Human papillomavirus infection and cervical cancer in Latin America. N Engl J Med 1989; 320:1437.
16. Hillard GD, Massey FM, and O'Toole RVJ. Vulvar neoplasia in the young. Am J Obstet Gynecol 1980; 135:185.
17. Lister UM, and Ahinla O. Carcinoma of the vulva in childhood. Br J Obstet Gynecol 1972; 79:470.
18. Pfister H. Relationship of papillomaviruses to anogenital cancer. Obstet Gynecol Clin North Am 1987; 14:349.
19. Hellberg D, Nilsson S, Haley NJ, et al. Smoking and cervical intraepithelial neoplasia: Nicotine and cotinine in serum and cervical mucus in smokers and nonsmokers. Am J Obstet Gynecol 1988; 158:910.
20. Slattery ML, Robison LM, Schuman KL, et al. Cigarette smoking and exposure to passive smoke are risk factors for cervical cancer. JAMA 1989; 261:1593.
21. Halpert R, Fruchter RG, Sedlis A, et al. Human papillomavirus and lower genital neoplasia in renal transplant patients. Obstet Gynecol 1986; 68:251.
22. Sillman FH, and Sedlis A. Anogenital papillomavirus infection and neoplasia in immunodeficient women. Obstet Gynecol Clin North Am 1987; 14:437.
23. Witkin SS, Roth DM, and Ledger WJ. Papillomavirus infection and an allergic response to *Candida* in women with recurrent vaginitis (letter to the editor). JAMA 1989; 261:1584.
24. Bornstein J, Kaufman RH, Adam E, et al. Human papillomavirus associated with vaginal intraepithelial neoplasia in women exposed to diethylstilbestrol in utero. Obstet Gynecol 1987; 70:75.
25. Koss LG. The Papanicolaou test for cervical cancer detection: A triumph and a tragedy. JAMA 1989; 261:737.
26. Hein K, Schreiber K, Cohen MI, et al. Cervical cytology: The need for routine screening in the sexually active adolescent. J Pediatr 1977; 91:123.
27. Delke IM, Veridiano NP, Russell SH, et al. Abnormal cervical cytology in adolescents. J Pediatr 1981; 98:985.
28. Davis GL, Hernandez E, Davis JL, et al. Atypical squamous cells in Papanicolaou smears. Obstet Gynecol 1987; 69:43.
29. Noumoff JS. Atypia in cervical cytology as a risk factor for intraepithelial neoplasia. Am J Obstet Gynecol 1987; 156:628.
30. Sutton GP, Stehman FB, Ehrlich CE, et al. Human papillomavirus deoxyribonucleic acid in lesions of the female genital tract: Evidence for type 6/11 in squamous carcinoma of the vulva. Obstet Gynecol 1987; 70:564.
31. Nash JD, Burke TW, and Hoskins WJ. Biologic course of cervical human papillomavirus infection. Obstet Gynecol 1987; 69:160.
32. Nasiell K, Roger V, and Nasiell M. Behavior of mild cervical dysplasia during long-term follow-up. Obstet Gynecol 1986; 67:665.
33. Drake M, Medley G, and Mitchell H. Cytologic detection of human papillomavirus infection. Obstet Gynecol Clin North Am 1987; 14:431.
34. Reid R. Physical and surgical principles governing expertise with the carbon dioxide laser. Obstet Gynecol Clin North Am 1987; 14:515.

35. Follen MM, Levine RU, Carillo E, et al. Colposcopic correlates of cervical papillomavirus infection. Am J Obstet Gynecol 1987; 157:809.
36. Coppleson M. Colposcopic features of papillomaviral infection and premalignancy in the female lower genital tract. Obstet Gynecol Clin North Am 1987; 14:471.
37. Burk RD, Kadish AS, Calderin S, et al. Human papillomavirus infection of the cervix detected by cervicovaginal lavage and molecular hybridization: Correlation with biopsy results and Papanicolaou smear. Am J Obstet Gynecol 1986; 154:982.
38. Barrasso R, DeBrux J, Croissant O, et al. High prevalence of papillomavirus-associated penile intraepithelial neoplasia in sexual partners of women with cervical intraepithelial neoplasia. N Engl J Med 1987; 317:916.
39. Krebs HB, and Schneider V. Human papillomavirus-associated lesions of the penis: Colposcopy, cytology and histology. Obstet Gynecol 1987; 70:299.
40. Sand PK, Bower LW, Blischke SO, et al. Evaluation of male consorts of women with genital human papilloma virus infection. Obstet Gynecol 1986; 68:679.
41. Rosenberg SK, Greenberg MD, and Reid R. Sexually transmitted papillomaviral infections in men. Obstet Gynecol Clin North Am 1987; 14:495.
42. Sedlacek TV, Cunnane M, and Carpiniello V. Colposcopy in the diagnosis of penile condyloma. Am J Obstet Gynecol 1986; 154:494.
43. Ferenczy A. Laser treatment of patients with condylomata and squamous carcinoma precursors of the lower female genital tract. CA 1987; 37:334.
44. Riva JM, Sedlacek TV, Cunnane MF, et al. Extended carbon dioxide laser vaporization in the treatment of subclinical papillomavirus infection of the lower genital tract. Obstet Gynecol 1989; 73:25.
45. Ferenczy A, Mitao M, Nagai N, et al. Latent papillomavirus and recurring genital warts. N Engl J Med 1985; 313:784.
46. Garden JM, O'Banion MK, Shelnitz LS, et al. Papillomavirus in the vapor of carbon dioxide laser-treated verrucae. JAMA 1988, 259: 1199.
47. Krebs HB. Treatment of vaginal condylomata acuminata by weekly topical application of 5-fluorouracil. Obstet Gynecol 1987; 70:68.
48. Krebs HB. Prophylactic topical 5-fluorouracil following treatment of human papillomavirus–associated lesions of vulva and vagina. Obstet Gynecol 1986; 68:837.
49. Krebs HB. The use of topical 5-fluorouracil in the treatment of genital condylomas. Obstet Gynecol Clin North Am 1987; 14:559.
50. Trofatter KF. Interferon. Obstet Gynecol Clin North Am 1987; 14:569.
51. Friedman-Kien AE, Eron LJ, Conant M, et al. Natural interferon alfa for treatment of condylomata acuminata. JAMA 1988; 259:533.
52. Gross G. Interferon and genital warts (letter to the editor). JAMA 1988; 260:2066.
53. Gall SA, Hughes CE, Mounts P, et al. Efficacy of human lymphoblastoid interferon in the therapy of resistant condyloma acuminata. Obstet Gynecol 1986; 67:643.
54. Department of Health and Human Services. Alpha interferon for venereal warts. FDA Drug Bull 1988; 18:19.
55. Reid R. Human papillomaviral infection: The key to rational triage of cervical neoplasia. Obstet Gynecol Clin North Am 1987; 14:407.

56. Malviya VK, Deppe G, Pluszczynski R, et al. Trichloroacetic acid in the treatment of human papillomavirus infection of the cervix without associated dysplasia. Obstet Gynecol 1987; 70:72.
57. Falcone T, and Ferenczy A. Cervical intraepithelial neoplasia and condyloma: An analysis of diagnostic accuracy of posttreatment follow-up methods. Am J Obstet Gynecol 1986; 154:260.
58. Fife KH, Rogers RE, and Zwickl BW. Symptomatic and asymptomatic cervical infections with human papillomavirus during pregnancy. J Infect Dis 1987; 156:904.
59. Laraque D. Severe anogenital warts in a child with HIV infection (letter to the editor). N Engl J Med 1989; 320:1220.
60. Steinberg BM, Topp WC, Schneider PS, et al. Laryngeal papillomavirus infection during clinical remission. N Engl J Med 1983; 308:1261.
61. Bennett RS, and Powell KR. Human papillomaviruses: Association between laryngeal papillomas and genital warts. Pediatr Infect Dis J 1987; 6:229.
62. Kashima HK, and Shah K. Recurrent respiratory papillomatosis: Clinical overview and management principles. Obstet Gynecol Clin North Am 1987; 14:581.
63. Byrne JC, Tsao MS, Fraser RS, et al. Human papillomavirus-11 DNA in a patient with chronic laryngotracheo-bronchial papillomatosis and metastatic squamous-cell carcinoma of the lung. N Engl J Med 1987; 317:873.
64. Lee NK. Head and neck squamous cell carcinomas associated with human papillomaviruses and an increased incidence of cervical pathology. Otolaryngol Head Neck Surg 1988; 99:296.
65. Kirby P. Interferon and genital warts: Much potential, modest progress. JAMA 1988; 259:570.
66. Hein K. AIDS in adolescence. J Adolesc Health Care 1989; 10:10S-35S.
67. Falloon J, Eddy J, Wiener L, et al. Human immunodeficiency virus infection in children. J Pediatr 1989; 114:1.
68. Hein K. Commentary of adolescent acquired immunodeficiency syndrome: The next wave of the human immunodeficiency virus epidemic? J Pediatr 1989; 114:144.
69. CDC. AIDS and human immunodeficiency virus infection in the United States: 1988 update. MMWR 1989; 39(S-4):1.
70. MMWR. Revision of the CDC surveillance case definition for acquired immunodeficiency syndrome. JAMA 1987; 258:1143.
71. Levy JA. Human immunodeficiency viruses and the pathogenesis of AIDS. JAMA 1989; 261:2997.
72. Bolognesi DP. Prospects for prevention of and early intervention against HIV. JAMA 1989; 261:3007.
73. AAP Task Force on Pediatric AIDS. Pediatric guidelines for infection control of human immunodeficiency virus (acquired immunodeficiency virus) in hospitals, medical offices, schools, and other settings. Pediatrics 1988; 82:801.
74. Justice AC, Feinstein AR, and Wells CK. A new prognostic staging system for the acquired immunodeficiency syndrome. N Engl J Med 1989; 320:1388.
75. AAP Task Force on Pediatric AIDS. Infants and children with acquired immunodeficiency syndrome: Placement in adoption and foster care. Pediatrics 1989; 83:609.
76. CDC. Guidelines for prevention of transmission of human immunodeficiency virus and hepatitis B virus to health-care and public-safety workers. MMWR 1989; 38(S-6):1.

77. Francis DP, and Chin J. The prevention of acquired immunodeficiency syndrome in the United States: An objective strategy for medicine, public health, business, and the community. JAMA 1987; 257:1357.
78. Friedland GH, and Kelin RS. Transmission of the human immunodeficiency virus. N Engl J Med 1987; 317:1125.
79. AMA Board of Trustees. Prevention and control of acquired immunodeficiency syndrome: An interim report. JAMA 1987; 258:2097.
80. Haverkos HW, and Edelman R. The epidemiology of acquired immunodeficiency syndrome among heterosexuals. JAMA 1988; 260:1922.
81. Mann JM. AIDS: A global perspective (editorial). JAMA 1988; 319:302.
82. AAP Task Force on Pediatric AIDS, 1987–1988. Perinatal human immunodeficiency virus infection. Pediatrics 1988; 82:941.
83. Guinan ME, and Hardy A. Epidemiology of AIDS in women in the United States: 1981 through 1986. JAMA 1987; 257:2039.
84. Quinn TC, Glasser D, Cannon RO, et al. Human immunodeficiency virus infection among patients attending clinics for sexually transmitted diseases. N Engl J Med 1988; 318:197.
85. Kelen GD, Fritz S, Qaqish B, et al. Unrecognized human immunodeficiency virus infection in emergency department patients. N Engl J Med 1988; 318:1645.
86. Hoff R, Berardi VP, Weiblen BJ, et al. Seroprevalence of human immunodeficiency virus among childbearing women. N Engl J Med 1988; 318:525.
87. Novick LF, Berns D, Stricof R, et al. HIV seroprevalence in newborns in New York State. JAMA 1987; 261:1745.
88. Hahn RA, Onorato IM, Jones S, et al. Prevalence of HIV infection among intravenous drug users in the United States. JAMA 1989; 261:2677.
89. MMWR. Acquired immunodeficiency syndrome associated with intravenous-drug use—United States, 1988. JAMA 1989; 261:2314.
90. Chaisson RE, Bacchetti P, Osmond D, et al. Cocaine use and HIV infection in intravenous drug users in San Francisco. JAMA 1989; 261:561.
91. DesJarlais DC, Friedman SR, Novick DM, et al. HIV-1 infection among intravenous drug users in Manhattan, New York City, from 1977 through 1987. JAMA 1989; 216:1008.
92. Handsfield HH. Heterosexual transmission of human immunodeficiency virus (editorial). JAMA 1988; 260:1943.
93. Stamm WE, Handsfield HH, Rompalo AM, et al. The association between genital ulcer disease and acquisition of HIV infection in homosexual men. JAMA 1988; 260:1429.
94. Sorenson RE. Adolescent Sexuality in Contemporary America. New York: World Publishing, 1973.
95. Peterman TA, Cates W, and Curran JW. The challenge of human immunodeficiency virus (HIV) and acquired immunodeficiency syndrome (AIDS). Fertil Steril 1988; 49:571.
96. Gostin LO. Public health strategies for confronting AIDS: Legislative and regulatory policy in the United States. JAMA 1989; 261:1621.
97. Recommendations of the Work Group. AIDS testing and epidemiology for youth. J Adolesc Health Care 1989; 10(3S):52S.
98. Leads from the MMWR. Results from the National Adolescent Study Health Survey. JAMA 1989; 261:2025.
99. CDC. HIV-related beliefs, knowledge, and behaviors among high school students. MMWR 1988; 37:717.
100. Kenney AM, Guardado S, and Brown L. Sex education and AIDS educa-

tion in the schools: What states and large school districts are doing. Fam Plann Perspect 1989; 21:56.
101. Forrest JD, and Silverman J. What public school teachers teach about preventing pregnancy, AIDS and sexually transmitted diseases. Fam Plann Perspect 1989; 21:65.
102. CDC. HIV epidemic and AIDS: Trends in knowledge—United States, 1987 and 1988. MMWR 1989; 38:353.
103. Becker MH, and Joseph JG. AIDS and behavioral change to reduce risk: A review. Am J Public Health 1988; 78(4):394.
104. CDC. Coordinated community programs for HIV prevention among intravenous-drug users—California, Massachusetts. MMWR 1989; 38: 369.
105. Curtis JL, Crummey FC, Baker SN, et al. HIV screening and counseling for intravenous drug abuse patients: Staff and patient attitudes. JAMA 1989; 261:258.
106. Grace E, Emans SJ, and Woods ER. The impact of AIDS awareness on the adolescent female. Adolesc Pediatr Gynecol 1989; 2:40.
107. Nicholas SW, Sondheimer DL, Willoughby AD, et al. Human immunodeficiency virus infection in childhood, adolescence and pregnancy: A status report and national research agenda. Pediatrics 1989; 83:293.
108. U.S. Department of Health and Human Services. AIDS Prevention Guide. Atlanta, GA: Centers for Disease Control, 1989.
109. CDC. Guidelines for effective school health education to prevent the spread of AIDS. MMWR 1988; 37:(S-2):1.
110. Melton GB. Ethical and legal issues in research and intervention. J Adolesc Health Care 1989; 10:36S.
111. Keller SE, Schleifer SJ, Bartlett JA, et al. The sexual behavior of adolescents and risk of AIDS (letter). JAMA 1988; 260:3586.
112. Rickert VI, Jay MS, Gottlieb A, et al. Adolescents and AIDS: Female's attitudes and behaviors toward condom purchase and use. J Adolesc Health Care 1989; 10:313.
113. Rietmeijer CAM, Krebs JW, Foerino PM, et al. Condoms as physical and chemical barriers against human immunodeficiency virus. JAMA 1988; 259:1851.
114. Foster IM, and Bartlett J. Anti-HIV substances for rape victims (letter). JAMA 1989; 261:3407.
115. Brown LK, and Fritz GK. AIDS education in the schools: A literature review as a guide for curriculum planning. Clin Pediatr 1988; 27:311.
116. Hearst N, and Hulley SB. Preventing the heterosexual spread of AIDS: Are we giving our patients the best advice? JAMA 1988; 259:2428.
117. Ward JW, Holmberg SD, Allen JR, et al. Transmission of human immunodeficiency virus (HIV) by blood transfusions screened as negative for HIV antibody. N Engl J Med 1988; 318:473.
118. Cohen ND, Munoz A, Reitz BA, et al. Transmission of retroviruses by transfusion of screened blood in patients undergoing cardiac surgery. N Engl J Med 1989; 320:1172.
119. Overby KJ, Lo B, and Litt IF. Knowledge and concerns about acquired immunodeficiency syndrome and their relationship to behavior among adolescents with hemophilia. Pediatrics 1989; 83:204.
120. Landesman S, Minkoff H, Holman S, et al. Serosurvey of human immunodeficiency virus infection in parturients: Implications for human immunodeficiency virus testing programs of pregnant women. JAMA 1987; 258:2701.
121. Sachs BP, Tuomala R, and Frigoletto F. Acquired immunodeficiency

syndrome: Suggested protocol for counseling and screening in pregnancy. Obstet Gynecol 1987; 70:408.

122. Minkoff HL. Care of pregnant women infected with human immunodeficiency virus. JAMA 1987; 258:2714.

123. Selwyn PA, Carter PJ, Schoenbaum EE, et al. Knowledge of HIV antibody status and decisions to continue or terminate pregnancy among intravenous drug users. JAMA 1989; 261:3567.

124. Rogers MF, Ou CY, Rayfield M, et al. Use of the polymerase chain reaction for early detection of the proviral sequences of human immunodeficiency virus in infants born to seropositive mothers. N Engl J Med 1989; 320:1649.

125. Murzuk PM, Tierney H, Tardiff K, et al. Increased risk of suicide in persons with AIDS. JAMA 1988; 259:1333.

126. Rhame FS, and Maki DG. The case for wide use of testing for HIV infection. N Engl J Med 1989; 320:1248.

127. CDC. Guidelines for prophylaxis against *Pneumocystis carinii* pneumonia for persons infected with human immunodeficiency virus. MMWR 1989; 38(S-5):1.

128. Glatt AE, Chirgwin K, and Landesman SH. Treatment of infections associated with human immunodeficiency virus. N Engl J Med 1988; 318:1439.

129. Johns DR, Tierney M, and Felsenstein D. Alteration in the natural history of neurosyphilis by concurrent infection with the human immunodeficiency virus. N Engl J Med 1987; 316:1569.

130. Tramont EC. Syphilis in the AIDS era (editorial). N Engl J Med 1987; 316:1600.

131. CDC. Tuberculosis and human immunodeficiency virus infection: Recommendations of the Advisory Committee for the Elimination of Tuberculosis (ACET) MMWR 1989; 38:236.

SUGGESTED READING

Goodman E, and Cohall AT. Acquired immunodeficiency syndrome and adolescents: Knowledge, attitudes, beliefs, and behaviors in a New York City adolescent minority population. Pediatrics 1989; 84:36.

Kirby D, Harvey PD, Claussenis D, et al. A direct mailing to teenage males about condom use: Its impact on knowledge, attitudes and sexual behavior. Fam Plann Perspect 1989; 21:12.

Moscicki A-B, Winkler B, Irwin CE, et al. Differences in biologic maturation, sexual behavior, and sexually transmitted disease between adolescents with and without cervical intraepithelial neoplasia. J Pediatr 1989; 115:487.

Nuovo GJ, and Richart RM. Human papillomavirus: A review. In DR Mishell, TH Kirschbaum, CP Morrow (eds.), *The Year Book of Obstetrics and Gynecology*. Chicago: Year Book, 1989.

Vermund SH, Hein K, Gayle H, et al. Acquired immunodeficiency syndrome among adolescents. Am J Dis Child 1989; 143:1220.

12. In Utero Exposure to Diethylstilbestrol

From the mid 1940s to the early 1970s, diethylstilbestrol (DES) and other nonsteroidal estrogens were given to pregnant women with the hope of preventing miscarriage.

In 1946, Smith and associates [1] suggested the possible value of oral estrogen therapy as an agent to prevent repeated miscarriages, based on the assumption that this might increase efficiency of progesterone production from the placenta. Although in 1953 Dieckmann and colleagues [2] in Chicago questioned the efficacy of this compound in pregnancy, it was still used widely until the early 1970s when Herbst and co-workers [3] reported an association between maternal therapy with DES and the later development of clear cell adenocarcinoma of the vagina and cervix in female offspring. Several years later, Herbst and other investigators [4–8] demonstrated an association between maternal DES use and the presence in their offspring of vaginal adenosis, malformations of the cervix and vagina, and other abnormalities of the lower genital tract. In 1977, Kaufman and collaborators [9] described uterine malformations in DES-exposed women. Subsequent studies have shown an increased incidence of fetal wastage and premature births in women exposed to DES in utero, especially in women with malformations of the uterus [10–14].

PATIENT ASSESSMENT
The number of young women exposed to DES is estimated to range from at least several hundred thousand to perhaps several million. Although the association of DES and adenocarcinoma was reported in 1970 and 1971, some fetuses were exposed even as late as 1974. Since reliable histories are often difficult to obtain, adolescents born before 1974 who have abnormal vaginal bleeding should have a vaginal examination regardless of the history. The general physician needs to do the following:

1. Determine the maternal drug history on all patients.
2. Refer all patients with a known maternal history of any amount of DES or other nonsteroidal estrogen for gynecologic examination at menarche or at the age of 14 years.
3. Be available for counselling and for discussion of the importance of gynecologic follow-up.

Point number 3 is particularly important because it is not unusual for mothers to feel extremely guilty about having taken DES; some ask to have their daughters checked under some other pretext. The adolescent girl may express anger toward her mother for having made her body imperfect and for scheduling gynecologic examinations. It is much less destructive to a teenager to deal with these issues openly than to allow the doctor and mother to have a "secret."

Although mothers and daughters are usually seeking reassurance that the vagina and cervix are "normal," the high frequency of adenosis and uterine and cervical abnormalities indicates that reassurance is often not possible. However, a frank discussion of the facts, including the low risk of clear cell carcinoma and reassurance that the majority of DES-exposed patients enjoy normal reproductive lives, is helpful to mothers and daughters. It is useful to point out that, at the time, DES seemed to be the best therapy for what appeared to be a hopeless situation for the mother.

The gynecologic examination of the teenager exposed in utero to DES consists of the following:

1. Careful palpation of the vagina and cervix. Most tumors, even tiny ones, are palpable; some may be invisible to the naked eye if confined to the lamina propria and covered by intact normal or metaplastic squamous epithelium.
2. Speculum examination with visualization of the vagina and cervix. Cytologic sampling should include direct scrapings from the vagina, portio of the cervix, and endocervix; all slides should be examined as Papanicolaou (Pap) smears. Iodine staining with half-strength Lugol's solution (Schiller's test) and/or colposcopy with application of acetic acid is used to assess possible abnormalities.
3. Biopsy specimens taken as indicated by the results of the staining and/or colposcopy.

Although the colposcope, a binocular, low-power microscope, has been noted to detect more cases of adenosis (80–90%) than visual examination (<30%) or Schiller's stain (40–80%), the overall rate of abnormalities in DES-exposed young women may be even less in a nonreferred population. The colposcope appears to be most useful for following cases of large transformation zones and for directing the taking of biopsy specimens in cases where abnormal cells have been noted on Pap smears. The DES-exposed patient should be seen every 6 to 12 months by a gynecologist with expertise in following these young women.

Hysterosalpingograms are not recommended for routine screening but are important in the evaluation of DES daughters who have a history of infertility or fetal wastage.

CLEAR CELL ADENOCARCINOMA
Although sporadic cases of clear cell adenocarcinoma of the cervix and vagina had been reported prior to the 1960s, the incidence has risen dramatically since 1966 [3, 4, 15, 16]. More than 500 cases of clear cell carcinoma have been reported by the Registry for Research on Hormonal Transplacental Carcinogenesis]15]. The mean age of the patients at the time of diagnosis is 19 years, with a range of 7 to 34 years. After the age of 14 years, the age of occurrence rises sharply to an irregular plateau that extends from the ages of 17 to 21 years; thereafter, it declines rapidly. Ninety-one percent of cases have been diagnosed when the patient was between 15 and 27 years of age [15]. Approximately 60 percent of patients with clear cell adenocarcinoma have documented in utero exposure to DES or to a chemically related nonsteroidal estrogen, hexestrol and dienestrol; another 12 percent have been exposed to some other hormone or to an unidentified medication but the prenatal records have not been available. The majority of patients whose histories show no in utero exposure to DES or similar drugs have had cervical tumors, a finding consistent with the observation that clear cell adenocarcinoma of the cervix in young women was well recognized in the pre-DES era, whereas clear cell adenocarcinoma of the vagina was exceedingly rare.

It is estimated that the tumor develops in 0.014 to 0.14 percent of exposed females, with the most recent calculations being 1 in 1000 [15, 16]. If the risk of development is calculated, not for the exposed population, but rather for the entire U.S. female population, the highest risk is for daughters born in 1951 to 1953, when DES was most frequently prescribed. The rarity of this tumor had led investigators to suggest that DES is not a complete carcinogen and that some other factor is involved in the pathogenesis of clear cell adenocarcinoma of the vagina and cervix [15]. The risk is highest when the intrauterine exposure is begun early in pregnancy [17] and declines to very small values if the exposure began at the end of the seventeenth week or later. Other risk factors include a birth in the fall (winter conception) and a maternal history of at least one prior spontaneous abortion [17].

The tumor may involve any portion of the vagina or cervix, or both. Approximately 60 percent of the lesions are confined to the vagina; the remainder are limited to the cervix or involve both the cervix and the vagina. Most vaginal tumors arise from the anterior wall, usually the upper third, a location that corresponds to the most frequent sites of adenosis. Tumors vary in size from a microscopic focus to a size of more than 10 cm at the greatest diameter. Most are polypoid nodules, but some are flat or ulcerated with a granular surface.

Cells of clear cell adenocarcinoma can be detected cytologically; and occasionally, a suspicious or positive Pap smear may provide the first indication of an asymptomatic tumor. If circumvaginal and cervical

414 12. In Utero Exposure to Diethylstilbestrol

scrapings and endocervical aspirations are used, a high percentage of tumors should probably be detected. False-negative results do occur, however, because of the difficulty in distinguishing tumor cells from endocervical cells, the heavy overlay of polymorphonuclear leukocytes, and the possibility that some of the neoplasms may not shed cells or are covered with normal epithelium.

Tumor stage correlates well with survival. The 5-year survival of patients with stage I tumors is 87 percent, stage II 76 percent, stage III 30 percent, and virtually no survival with stage IV disease. In a series of 17 patients with clear cell adenocarcinoma (15 of 17 stage I) treated at Memorial Sloan Kettering Cancer Center, Jones and associates [18] observed that all were alive without evidence of disease 21 months to more than 10 years later, with radical surgery being the primary mode of therapy in 13 of 17. They noted that the tumors may metastasize to distant sites in the absence of pelvic disease, often years after the initial presentation, emphasizing the need for long-term surveillance. The overall 5-year survival of patients with clear cell carcinoma is better than squamous cell carcinoma of the cervix or vagina. The better prognosis may be the result of early detection of clear cell adenocarcinoma, since it occurs mainly in young patients exposed to DES, many of whom are receiving regular gynecologic examinations.

The possible risk to DES patients of dysplasia and squamous cell carcinoma has not been fully resolved. Two studies [16, 19] found no association, but a later large study by Robboy and colleagues [20] found that the incidence of dysplasia and carcinoma in situ was higher in women exposed to DES than those not exposed (15.7 versus 7.9 cases/1000 person-years of follow-up), with the higher rates in women with squamous metaplasia extending to the outer half of the cervix or onto the vagina. Interestingly, DES-exposed women were more likely to have had genital herpes (HSV), suggesting the potential role of HSV as a cofactor in oncogenesis. Exposed women have a wider transformation zone and greater extent of squamous metaplasia and thus have more epithelium exposed to HSV and more importantly to human papillomavirus (HPV). Indeed, Bornstein, Kaufman, and associates [21] have detected HPV types 6 or 16 in DES-exposed women who developed vaginal intraepithelial neoplasia while under surveillance. Earlier, Adam, Kaufman, and colleagues [22] had found a higher rate of antibodies to HSV-1 in DES-exposed women who developed cervical intraepithelial neoplasia (CIN). More studies are needed to elucidate risk factors in DES-exposed young women and the relationship to squamous cell carcinoma [23].

VAGINAL EPITHELIAL CHANGES
Early exposure to DES in utero is also associated with a risk of benign vaginal adenosis, known also by the term *vaginal epithelial changes*.

Exposure to DES appears to have interfered with normal differentiation and development of the cervix and vagina. Vaginal epithelial
changes encompass any mucosal change in the vagina that can be
observed microscopically with the colposcope, by iodine staining, or
by examining tissue sections. Changes found by colposcope include
alteration of the columnar epithelium, glands, cysts, white epithelium, leukoplakia, and punctation [3–7]. Changes found by microscopic examination of tissue include adenosis (columnar cells in the
vagina) and squamous metaplasia (usually in the form of glycogen-
poor squamous epithelium). The term *cervical epithelial changes* de-
notes similar changes in the cervix.

Vaginal epithelial changes, especially adenosis, are common findings in the DES-exposed female. In the pre-DES era, vaginal adenosis
was a medical rarity that was detected only occasionally in women,
usually in those in their thirties and forties. Not surprisingly, vaginal
epithelial changes were found more frequently in autopsy studies in
which the vagina was extensively examined microscopically. In about
4 percent of fetuses and infants who were unexposed or exposed only
to steroidal estrogens or progesterones, colposcopic and cytologic
examination at the time of autopsy revealed that the squamocolumnar junction lay in the vagina rather than in the cervix.

Vaginal epithelial changes should be suspected in any patient who
has a vaginal mucosa that contains red granular spots or patches,
does not stain with iodine solution, or is colposcopically abnormal.
The upper third of the vagina is usually involved and the anterior
walls are involved more frequently than the posterior walls. The glandular epithelium in 62 percent of biopsy specimens of vaginal
adenosis was found to consist of columnar cells resembling normal
endocervical mucosa. In the majority of biopsy specimens from cases
of vaginal epithelial changes, adenosis is replaced to various degrees
by metaplastic squamous cells; this suggests that the adenosis heals
as a result of squamous metaplasia, beginning as reserved cell proliferation and progressing through the stages of immature and mature
squamous metaplasia. Thus squamous metaplasia with replacement of the columnar epithelium is a normal event in these young
women [24].

Other changes associated with DES exposure are structural abnormalities of the vagina and cervix, including fibrous ridges, hoods (a
circular fold that partially covers the cervix), cock's comb (an irregular
peak on the anterior border of the cervix), hypoplasia of the cervix,
and pseudopolyp (Fig. 12-1). The incidence of structural anomalies of
the cervix and vagina may vary depending on the population studied,
with lower rates found among those identified by review of prenatal
records (25%) than those self-referred (43%) or physician referred
(49%) versus a rate in control subjects of 2 percent. The presence of

416

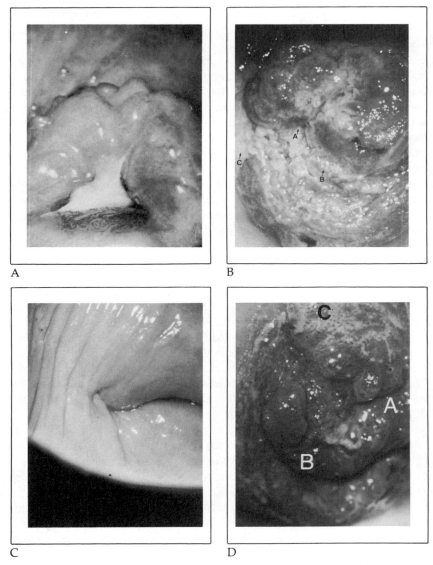

Figure 12-1. Colposcopic views of the cervix in patients exposed in utero to diethylstilbestrol (DES). A. Cock's comb appearance. B. Fibrous ridge (C) and extensive ectropion (B) partially obscuring the cervical os (A). C. Hypoplastic cervix flush to the vagina in a patient with cervical incompetence. D. Severely deformed cervix with extensive ectropion (A), annular ring (B), and early squamous metaplasia (C).

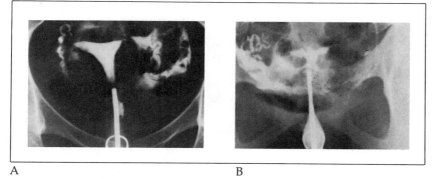

A   B

Figure 12-2. Uterotubograms. A. Normal uterine contour. B. Hypoplastic T-shaped uterus with notching in patient exposed in utero to DES.

anomalies is closely associated with the gestational week of first exposure and total dose [25]. The cervicovaginal hood regresses slowly over time, with complete regression described in 28 to 57 percent of women [13, 26].

UTERINE MALFORMATIONS AND PREGNANCY

A number of abnormalities of the uterus have been reported in DES-exposed women; these include T-shaped appearance of the endometrial cavity, constricting bands in the cavity, hypoplasia, and synechiae [9, 10, 14, 27]. These changes have been observed on hysterosalpingograms from DES-exposed patients (Figs. 12-2 and 12-3). Many studies have focused on fertility rates and reproductive outcome in DES patients [10–12, 14, 27–31] (Table 12-1). Herbst and co-workers [12] reported the outcome of the first complete pregnancy of DES daughters compared to that in nonexposed controls: full-term births occurred in 47 percent of DES daughters versus 85 percent of controls; premature births, 22 percent versus 7 percent; and premature nonviable pregnancies, miscarriages, and ectopic pregnancies, 31 percent versus 8 percent. However, 82 percent of DES-exposed daughters and 93 percent of the unexposed had at least one live offspring. Barnes and colleagues [11] also found an increased risk of unfavorable outcomes of pregnancy in DES-exposed women. Goldstein [30] found that several DES-exposed women experienced cervical incompetence during pregnancy, especially if the cervix was hypoplastic and flush to the vaginal wall.

The relationship between infertility and DES exposure has been more controversial and hampered by variable definitions of infertility [13, 28–30, 32] and the possible confounding factor that offspring of a mother with a fertility problem may be at risk of abnormal outcome independent of DES exposure. Barnes and colleagues [11, 29] did not

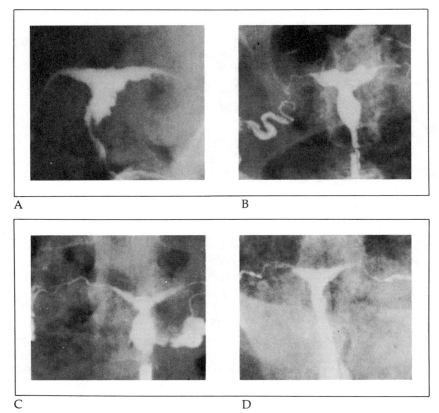

A   B

C   D

Figure 12-3. Uterotubograms in DES-exposed patients. A. Mild defect with
T-shaped uterus. B. Hypoplastic T-shaped uterus with more severe
notching. C. Y-shaped, hypoplastic uterus with large bulbous endocervical
canal predisposing to cervical incompetence. D. Markedly hypoplastic
uterus that sounds to only 2 inches.

find a lowered fertility rate. However, Kaufman and associates [14]
found that 36 percent of DES-exposed women had difficulty conceiv-
ing for a period of one or more years. Although the overall rate of
abnormal hysterosalpingogram between those unable to conceive
(73%) and those able to conceive (74%) were the same, two abnormalities were associated with the inability to conceive—constriction
of the upper uterine cavity (2.26-fold increase in infertility) and T-
shaped uterus associated with constriction of the upper uterine cavity
(2.63-fold increase in infertility risk). In a follow-up of daughters who
had participated in an evaluation of DES in the 1950s, Senekjian and
co-workers [32] reported primary infertility in 33 percent of DES-
exposed daughters and 14 percent in non-DES daughters. Abnormal

Table 12-1. Reproductive Outcome in 65 DES-Exposed Women

	No. of Patients	Percent
Patients who conceived	44	67.7
Pregnancies	76	
Therapeutic abortions	18	
Pregnancy failures	32	52.2*
Spontaneous abortions		
First trimester	17	29.3
Second trimester	9	15.5
Ectopic pregnancies	3	5.2
Premature deaths	3	5.2
Pregnancy successes	26	44.8

*Corrected for therapeutic abortion.

hysterosalpingograms were found in 46 percent of DES exposed and in none of the unexposed. Cervicovaginal ridges were detected more often in those with primary infertility at first examination. In this study, unlike one previously noted, 60 percent of exposed women and 83 percent of the unexposed women had a liveborn who survived. Twelve months after the diagnosis of primary infertility, 16 percent of the DES-exposed and 36 percent of the unexposed conceived. Tubal abnormalities were suggestive of old pelvic inflammatory disease in this study. DeCherney and associates [31] reported 16 women found by laparoscopy to have unique tubal morphology with foreshortened, convoluted tubes and "withered fimbria."

It is thus prudent to consider the DES-exposed pregnant patient high-risk and periodically to evaluate the cervix throughout the pregnancy. Cerclage is performed for the usual obstetric indications although many clinicians believe that pregnant DES patients with an abnormal uterus and short cervix should be cerclaged prophylactically. Ultrasound of the lower uterine segment and cervix coupled with periodic examinations may enhance the ability to detect cervical changes [33].

MALES
Although a number of genital abnormalities have been reported in DES-exposed sons, including epididymal cysts, testicular hypoplasia, cryptorchidism, microphallus, urethral stenosis, hypospadias, varicoceles, and pathologic semen [34, 35], a more recent study [36] found no increase in genitourinary abnormalities, infertility, or testicular cancer.

REFERENCES
 1. Smith OW, Smith GV, and Hurwitz D. Increased excretion of preg-
    nanediol in pregnancy from diethylstilbestrol with special reference to
    the prevention of late pregnancy accidents. Am J Obstet Gynecol 1946;
    51:411.
 2. Dieckmann WJ, Davis ME, Rynkiewicz LM, et al. Does the administra-
    tion of diethylstilbestrol during pregnancy have therapeutic value? Am J
    Obstet Gynecol 1953; 66:1062.
 3. Herbst A, Ulfelder H, and Poskanzer DC. Adenocarcinoma of the vagina.
    N Engl J Med 1971; 284:878.
 4. Herbst A, Robboy SJ, Scully RE, et al. Clear cell adenocarcinoma of the
    vagina and cervix: Analysis of 170 registry cases. Am J Obstet Gynecol
    1974; 119:713.
 5. Stafl A, Mattingly RF, Foley DV, et al. Clinical diagnosis of vaginal
    adenosis. Obstet Gynecol 1974; 43:118.
 6. Sherman AI, Goldrath M, Berlin A, et al. Cervical-vaginal adenosis
    after in utero exposure to synthetic estrogens. Obstet Gynecol 1974;
    44:531.
 7. Herbst A. A prospective comparison of exposed female offspring with
    unexposed controls. N Engl J Med 1975; 292:334.
 8. Burke L, and Antonioli D. Vaginal adenosis: correlation of colposcopic
    and pathologic findings. Obstet Gynecol 1974; 44:257.
 9. Kaufman RH, Binder GL, Gray PM, et al. Upper genital tract changes
    associated with exposure in utero to diethylstilbestrol. Am J Obstet Gy-
    necol 1977; 128:51.
10. Berger MJ, and Goldstein DP. Impaired reproductive performance in
    DES-exposed women. Obstet Gynecol 1980; 55:25.
11. Barnes AB, Colton T, Gundersen J, et al. Fertility and outcome of preg-
    nancy in women exposed in utero to diethylstilbestrol. N Engl J Med
    1980; 302:609.
12. Herbst AL, Hubby MM, Blough RR, et al. A comparison of pregnancy
    experience in DES-exposed and DES-unexposed daughters. J Reprod
    Med 1980; 24:62.
13. Herbst AL, Hubby MM, Azizi F, et al. Reproductive and gynecologic
    surgical experience in diethylstilbestrol-exposed daughters. Am J Obstet
    Gynecol 1981; 141:1019.
14. Kaufman RH, Adam E, Noller K, et al. Upper genital tract changes and
    infertility in diethylstilbestrol-exposed women. Am J Obstet Gynecol
    1986; 154:1312.
15. Melnick S, Cole P, Anderson D, et al. Rates and risks of diethylstilbestrol-
    related clear-cell adenocarcinoma of the vagina and cervix. N Engl J Med
    1987; 316:514.
16. Mattingly RE, and Stafl A. Cancer risk in diethylstilbestrol-exposed off-
    spring. Am J Obstet Gynecol 1976; 126:543.
17. Herbst AL, Anderson S, Hubby MM, et al. Risk factors for the develop-
    ment of diethylstilbestrol-associated clear cell adenocarcinoma: A case
    control study. Am J Obstet Gynecol 1988; 154:814.
18. Jones WB, Koulos JP, Saigo PE, et al. Clear-cell adenocarcinoma of the
    lower genital tract: Memorial Hospital 1974-1984. Obstet Gynecol 1987;
    70:573.
19. Robboy SR, Keh PC, Nickerson RJ, et al. Squamous cell dysplasia and
    carcinoma in situ of the cervix and vagina after prenatal exposure to
    diethylstilbestrol. Obstet Gynecol 1978; 51:528.

20. Robboy SJ, Noller KL, O'Brien P, et al. Increased incidence of cervical and vaginal dysplasia in 3,980 diethylstilbestrol-exposed young women. JAMA 1984; 252:2979.
21. Bornstein J, Kaufman RH, Adam E, et al. Human papillomavirus associated with vaginal intraepithelial neoplasia in women exposed to diethylstilbestrol in utero. Obstet Gynecol 1987; 70:75.
22. Adam E, Kaufman RH, Adler-Storthz K, et al. A prospective study of association of herpes simplex virus and human papillomavirus infection with cervical neoplasia in women exposed to diethylstilbestrol in utero. Int J Cancer 1985; 35:19.
23. MMWR. Report of the recommendations of the 1985 DES task force of the US Department of Health and Human Services. JAMA 1986; 255; 1849.
24. Frank AR, Krumholz BA, and Deutsch S. Regression of cervicovaginal abnormalities in DES-exposed women. A comparison of changes in sexually inactive women and the effects of the onset of sexual activity. J Reprod Med 1985; 30:400.
25. Jefferies JA, Robboy SJ, O'Brien PC, et al. Structural anomalies of the cervix and vagina in women enrolled in the Diethylstilbestrol Adenosis (DESAD) Project. Am J Obstet Gynecol 1984; 148:59.
26. Antonioli DA, Burke L, and Friedman EA. Natural history of diethylstilbestrol-associated genital tract lesions: cervical ectopy and cervicovaginal hood. Am J Obstet Gynecol 1980; 137:847.
27. Cohen AW, and Chhibber G. Obstetric complications of congenital anomalies of the paramesonephric ducts. Semin Reprod Endocrinol 1986; 4:1.
28. Berger MJ, and Alper MM. Intractable primary infertility in women exposed to diethylstilbestrol in utero. J Reprod Med 1986; 31:231.
29. Barnes AB. Menstrual history and fecundity of women exposed and unexposed in utero to diethylstilbestrol. J Reprod Med 1984; 29:651.
30. Goldstein DP. Incompetent cervix in offspring exposed to diethylstilbestrol in utero. Obstet Gynecol 1978; 52:735.
31. DeCherney AH, Cholst I, and Naftolin F. Structure and function of the fallopian tubes following exposure to DES during gestation. Fertil Steril 1981; 36:741.
32. Senekjian EK, Potkul RK, Frey K, et al. Infertility among daughters either exposed or not exposed to diethylstilbestrol. Am J Obstet Gynecol 1988; 158:493.
33. Michaels WH, Thompson HO, Schreiber FR, et al. Ultrasound surveillance of the cervix during pregnancy in diethylstilbestrol-exposed offspring. Obstet Gynecol 1989; 73:230.
34. Bibbo M, Gill WB, Azizi F, et al. Follow-up study of male and female offspring of DES-exposed mothers. Obstet Gynecol 1977; 49:1.
35. Gill WB, Schumacher GF, Bibbo M, et al. Association of diethylstilbestrol exposed in utero with cryptorchidism, testicular hypoplasia and semen abnormalities. J Urol 1979; 122:36.
36. Leary FJ, Resseguie LJ, Kurland LT, et al. Males exposed in utero to diethylstilbestrol. JAMA 1984; 252:2984.

13. Ovarian Masses

The scope of this book is not intended to include the histology and treatment of ovarian tumors in detail because most physicians will only infrequently encounter such lesions. Ovarian tumors are the most common genital neoplasm that occurs during childhood; however, overall ovarian tumors account for only about 1 percent of childhood tumors, and fortunately most are benign. However, ovarian cysts are very common in adolescents and appreciation of a conservative approach to the management of benign cysts is important.

DETECTION OF OVARIAN TUMORS
In the young child, an ovarian tumor is often discovered by the parent or physician as an asymptomatic abdominal mass or as increasing abdominal girth because of the abdominal location of the ovary. Chronic abdominal aching pain, either periumbilical or located in one lower quadrant, may be present. Acute severe pain, simulating appendicitis or peritonitis, may develop secondary to torsion, perforation, or infarction of a tumor or cyst. Patients may experience intermittent crampy pain, presumably because of partial torsion, which subsequently resolves without therapy or may be the warning sign of impending torsion and the need for emergency surgery. In some cases, torsion may occur with a normal adnexa. Nonspecific symptoms, including nausea, vomiting, a sense of abdominal fullness or bloating, and urinary frequency or retention, may signal the presence of a tumor. In the young child, a granulosa cell tumor or an ovarian cyst may secrete estrogen, causing precocious development and menses; in the adolescent, such tumors may be associated with hypermenorrhea and irregular menses. Certain conditions such as Peutz-Jeghers syndrome and basal cell nevus syndrome have an increased incidence of ovarian tumors [1–3].

The wide variety of symptoms caused by ovarian tumors suggests that abdominal palpation and bimanual vaginal-abdominal or recto-abdominal examination with the patient in the lithotomy position is important in any girl with nonspecific abdominal or pelvic complaints [4–7]. Ovarian tumors should always be considered in the differential diagnosis of abdominal masses; the list of other possibilities is long and includes mesenteric cysts, hydronephrosis, liver cysts, bowel reduplication, Wilms' tumor, neuroblastoma, urachal cysts, pelvic kidney, and hematometra. A large, thin-walled cyst may be confused with ascites. A firm midline tumor in the adolescent may simulate a pregnant uterus. A positive test for human chorionic gonadotropin (HCG) may be found in pregnancy (including ectopic pregnancy and miscarriage), in gestational trophoblastic neoplasia (choriocarcinoma, moles) and in some ovarian tumors containing germ cell elements. The size of the tumor is not indicative of its malignant potential. Exquisite tenderness suggests torsion or hemorrhage of the tumor or cyst but may also occur with appendicitis, pelvic inflammatory disease, ectopic pregnancy, endometriomas, and ruptured cysts.

Ultrasonography has revolutionized the management of patients with suspected ovarian masses, with the caveats noted on pp. 38–41. Not all tumors that are palpated will be visualized on ultrasound [8], and not all "masses" will turn out to be of significance. Nevertheless, ultrasound has continued to improve in the last few years, especially the use of vaginal probes for older patients. Selective use of other imaging modalities including computed tomography (CT) and magnetic resonance imaging (MRI) may further help to define lesions. The finding of a clear fluid–filled cyst on ultrasound has allowed for conservative management with observation in many adolescents with an asymptomatic pelvic mass. In contrast, the finding of a solid component or multiple septations in the mass has led to earlier operative intervention. The only problem with the now frequent use of ultrasound has been the overdiagnosis of "cysts" in adolescent girls who present to their physician with nonspecific abdominal symptoms and are found to have a 1- to 2-cm normal follicular cyst. Symptoms are often attributed to this normal finding, and the patient becomes convinced that she is suffering from a "cyst." It should also be noted that many 4- to 6-cm simple follicular cysts can be followed by pelvic examination without ultrasound. Repeated examination, however, may be problematic in adolescents.

Plain film radiograph of the abdomen may be useful to detect calcifications (teeth) in a benign cystic teratoma, the most common tumor in the young female. When a tumor is hormonally active, preoperative samples should be drawn for luteinizing hormone (LH), follicle-stimulating hormone (FSH), testosterone, dehydroepiandrosterone (DHA) and its sulfate (DHAS), androstenedione, and estradiol levels so that levels can be followed postoperatively. If a tumor is suspected to be malignant, serum should be saved preoperatively so that levels of potential tumor markers including HCG, alpha-fetoprotein (AFP), and carcinoembryonic antigen (Ca 125) can be measured later. It should be noted that a marker such as Ca 125 is more useful in older adult women. Other studies in the patient with suspected malignancy may include liver function tests, chest radiograph, liver and bone scans, and CT or MRI.

The nature of the intervention depends on the presentation. A patient with acute torsion or hemorrhage needs to be stabilized and laparotomy undertaken. In the patient with elective intervention, the approach depends on the suspected nature of the lesion. Surgical therapy should aim, whenever possible, at preservation of reproductive potential. Unless a malignancy is diagnosed on frozen section at the time of the procedure, conservative surgery should be undertaken with excision of the lesions and ovarian reconstruction or unilateral salpingo-oophorectomy. It is preferable to subject the patient to a second procedure after the final pathology specimens are reviewed than to perform unnecessary ablative procedures [5, 6]. If, however, malignancy is found or suspected, adequate staging is crucial with abdominal and pelvic exploration, peritoneal washings, and biopsies of suspicious areas as well as lymph nodes. Pathologic consultation may be invaluable in determining the exact diagnosis so that appropriate therapy can be undertaken postoperatively, especially since the advances in effective adjuvant chemotherapy for many ovarian tumors have improved the prognosis of many patients.

CATEGORIES OF OVARIAN TUMORS
The World Health Organization has classified ovarian tumors into nine major categories and 26 subtypes. An abbreviated version is shown in Table 13-1. In contrast to the adult experience in which epithelial tumors account for a significant proportion of tumors, they account for only 7 to 15 percent in girls less than 20 years old. A majority of nonneoplastic lesions are cysts and benign cystic teratomas (Table 13-2) [6]. The incidence of cysts and nonmalignant tumors in the community is probably even higher than indicated in most series because percentages are based on referred cases [6, 9]. Although the majority of lesions in childhood are benign, it is important for the clinician to make the diagnosis early to improve the prognosis for malignant lesions and to lessen the possibility of ovarian torsion and loss of an adnexa.

The staging of ovarian tumors has been defined by the International Federation of Gynecology and Obstetrics (FIGO) (Table 13-3) [10]; this classification is valuable to medical centers in defining appropriate surgery, radiotherapy (rarely indicated except for dysgerminomas), and chemotherapy. A brief discussion of treatment is found in each subsection and in the references [5, 6, 11–14].

OVARIAN CYSTS
Functional cysts (20–50% of ovarian tumors) are not true neoplasms but rather should be considered a variation of the normal physiologic process. More than one half of cysts are follicular cysts. As noted earlier, small follicular cysts frequently occur in the ovaries of healthy children and adolescents. More rarely, an atretic follicle may enlarge to 6 to 8 cm or more in diameter, producing a follicular cyst.

In neonates, large follicular cysts may occur secondary to in utero stimulation by maternal gonadotropins or persistent hypothalamic-pituitary activity. These cysts have been detected prenatally on

Table 13-1. International Histologic Classification of Ovarian Tumors

  I. Common Epithelial Tumors
     A. Serous tumor
     B. Mucinous tumor
     C. Endometrioid tumor
     D. Clear cell (mesonephroid) tumor
     E. Brenner tumor
     F. Mixed epithelial tumor
     G. Undifferentiated carcinoma
     H. Unclassified epithelial tumor
 II. Sex Cord Stromal Tumors
     A. Granulosa-stromal cell tumor
        1. Granulosa cell tumor
        2. Thecoma-fibroma group
     B. Androblastomas; Sertoli-Leydig (hilus) tumor
     C. Gynandroblastoma
     D. Unclassified
III. Lipid Cell Tumor
 IV. Germ Cell Tumor
     A. Dysgerminoma
     B. Endodermal sinus tumor
     C. Embryonal carcinoma
     D. Polyembryoma
     E. Choriocarcinoma
     F. Teratomas
        1. Immature
        2. Mature
           a. Solid
           b. Cystic
        3. Monodermal
  V. Gonadoblastoma
 VI. Soft Tissue Tumors Not Specific to Ovary
VII. Unclassified
VIII. Secondary (Metastatic) Tumors
 IX. Tumorlike Conditions
     A. Hyperplasia and hyperthecosis
     B. Cysts
     C. Endometriosis

routine obstetrical ultrasound. Because neonates have a shallow pelvis, the cysts are often displaced to the mid- or upper abdomen and are asymptomatic. Ultrasound reveals a clear fluid–filled cyst. Ovarian cysts usually regress within 3 to 6 months. If persistent, aspiration may be undertaken with ultrasound guidance. The symptoms of ovarian torsion should be explained to the caregivers [6, 15].

In prepubertal girls, a hormone-secreting cyst may cause sexual precocity, as is seen in association with the McCune-Albright syndrome. Cysts may also occur in patients with idiopathic central preco-

Table 13-2. Primary Ovarian Tumors
Treated at The Children's Hospital (1928–1982)

Kind	No.	(%)
Mature (benign) teratomas Cystic (76) Solid (2)	78	(47)
Common "epithelial" tumors Mucinous (12) Serous (14) Mixed (1)	27	(16)
Sex cord–stromal tumors Granulosa cell (10) Thecoma (2) Fibroma (1) Sertoli-Leydig (7) Unclassified (1)	21	(13)
Immature teratomas	17	(10)
Endodermal sinus tumor	14	(8)
Dysgerminoma	8	(5)
Choriocarcinoma*	1	(<1)
Total	166	

*Mixed malignant germ cell tumor with predominant element being choriocarcinoma.
Source: Lack EE, and Goldstein DP. Primary ovarian tumors in childhood and adolescence. Curr Prob Obstet Gynecol 1984; 8:1.

cious puberty and would be expected to resolve with the institution of gonadotropin releasing hormone (GnRH) analogue therapy (see Chap. 5). Another possible option may be the use of Depo-Provera suppression. If a child has a cystic mass without precocity, the cyst may well be a parovarian or mesothelial cyst which requires excision.

Cysts in the postmenarcheal adolescent may be asymptomatic or cause menstrual irregularities, pain, or, if large, urinary frequency, constipation, or pelvic heaviness. Cysts can rupture causing intra-abdominal hemorrhage. Torsion of a cyst causes acute pain, nausea, vomiting, and pallor, often followed by less severe localized pain. The white count may be elevated with a shift to the left. Examination reveals induration of the pelvic floor and a tender mass.

In most cases, follicular cysts, found on routine examination, resolve spontaneously in 1 to 2 months. If a cyst less than 6 cm is palpated in an asymptomatic patient and ultrasound or pelvic examination confirms a simple, fluid-filled cyst, the patient may be observed or preferably oral contraceptive pills prescribed for 6 to 8 weeks to suppress the hypothalamic-ovarian axis. Although reports of ovarian cysts on triphasic oral contraceptives are anecdotal, it is

Table 13-3. Staging of Carcinoma of the Ovary (FIGO)

Stage I   Tumor limited to the ovaries.
    Ia   Tumor limited to one ovary; no ascites. No tumor on the external surface; capsule intact.
    Ib   Tumor in both ovaries; no ascites. No tumor on the external surface; capsules intact.
    Ic   Tumor limited to one or both ovaries, but with tumor on the surface of one or both ovaries, or with capsule ruptured; or with ascites present containing malignant cells; or with positive peritoneal washings.
Stage II   Tumor in one or both ovaries with local pelvic extension.
    IIa   Extension and/or metastases to the uterus and/or tubes.
    IIb   Extension to other pelvic tissues.
    IIc   Tumor as either IIa or IIb but with tumor on the surface of one or both ovaries; or with capsule(s) ruptured; or with ascites present containing malignant cells; or with positive washings.
Stage III   Tumor involving one or both ovaries, with peritoneal implants outside the pelvis and/or positive retroperitoneal or inguinal nodes. Superficial liver metastasis qualifies as Stage III.
    IIIa   Tumor grossly limited to the true pelvis, with negative nodes but with histologically confirmed microscopic seeding of abdominal peritoneal surfaces.
    IIIb   Tumor of one or both ovaries with histologically confirmed implants of abdominal peritoneal surfaces, none exceeding 2 cm in diameter. Nodes are negative.
    IIIc   Abdominal implants greater than 2 cm in diameter and/or positive retroperitoneal or inguinal nodes.
Stage IV   Tumor in one or both ovaries with extra-abdominal metastases. Pleural effusion with positive cytology; parenchymal liver metastasis.

prudent to use monophasic pills for suppression of gonadotropin stimulation to the ovary. If the patient was already on a triphasic pill, switching to a monophasic (and perhaps one with 50 μg ethinyl estradiol for initial suppression) is recommended. The patient should be examined monthly or follow-up ultrasound performed. Similarly, patients found to have small follicular cysts at the time of appendectomy should not have needless ovarian surgery, since adhesions may form subsequently and cause chronic pelvic pain (see Chap. 8) [5, 16]. If a fluid-filled cyst is increasing in size, is greater than 6 cm, or is causing symptoms, the cyst may be aspirated through the laparoscope and the fluid sent for cytology. The patient is then placed on suppression with oral contraceptives. It should be noted that asymptomatic cysts of 6 to 10 cm may also spontaneously resolve and can be safely observed in some patients. If the cyst recurs or operative intervention is needed, the procedure should be conservative and preserve as much ovarian tissue as possible. Cystectomy with ovarian reconstruction should be used with microsurgical techniques to reduce periovarian adhesions.

Lutein cysts occur less commonly than follicular cysts and may reach 5 to 10 cm in diameter. Although such cysts are often asymptomatic, they may cause amenorrhea (secondary to the continued production of progesterone and estrogen) and profuse vaginal bleeding (as the cyst becomes atretic). Occasionally these cysts are responsible for crampy lower abdominal pain caused by torsion or hemorrhage of the cyst; in fact, rupture of the blood-filled cyst can precipitate an acute abdominal emergency. In the absence of pain or intraperitoneal bleeding, therapy with oral contraceptive pills and observation for 3 months are indicated. If hemorrhage or pain occurs or the cyst is large (> 6 cm) on initial examination, laparoscopy or laparotomy may be necessary.

Germ Cell Tumors

The most common ovarian tumor in childhood is the benign cystic teratoma, often termed the dermoid cyst. The malignant potential of teratomas is related to the histologic differentiation of the cells. Dermoid cysts are mature cystic teratomas and are benign in children (although malignant degeneration has been reported in a few adults). Dermoid cysts are bilateral in 10 to 25 percent of those found in adults and 0 to 9 percent of those reported in children (7% in a recent series at The Children's Hospital [6]). At our pediatric institution the average age of patients at presentation was 12 years (range 11 months to 24 years). Patients may present with abdominal pain or be asymptomatic. An adnexal mass is often palpated on physical examination. Plain x ray of the pelvis and abdomen may reveal calcification. Although ultrasound findings often point to the possibility of a dermoid cyst, these tumors can be missed by ultrasound. At the time of the initial ultrasound, the contralateral ovary should also be examined carefully to exclude bilateral disease. If the ultrasound of the apparently uninvolved ovary is negative preoperatively and careful inspection of this ovary is negative intraoperatively, routine bivalving of the opposite ovary is not necessary. Optimal treatment should preserve reproductive function. If the tumor is grossly compatible with a dermoid, it should be excised and the ovary reconstructed using microsurgical techniques to reduce periovarian adhesions. If the frozen sections are done because of clinical suspicion and the tumor is borderline, then oophorectomy is carried out.

The younger the patient, the more likely the occurrence of an immature germ-cell tumor—so-called immature teratoma. In our series of 17 girls, the average age was 13 years, with a range of 4 to 20 years

[6]. Patients presented with abdominal pain or enlargement, and a mass was palpable on abdominal or pelvic examination in all. Abdominal symptoms may occur acutely because of torsion or rupture of the tumor. These tumors are usually unilateral, although the opposite ovary may occasionally contain a mature teratoma. Levels of tumor markers such as AFP and HCG are usually negative but should be measured preoperatively; if a marker is present, it can be followed postoperatively and during chemotherapy to detect inadequate treatment and early recurrence. Tumor size and differentiation of the elements are factors in predicting survival. In a study published in 1976, Norris and co-workers [17] observed that 5-year survival was based on histologic grade of the pure immature teratomas: grade I—81 percent, grade II—60 percent, and grade III—30 percent. In the Air Force study of 1972 [18], all patients with tumors less than 10 cm at the greatest dimension survived regardless of stage or grade. The survival rate fell to 50 percent in patients whose tumors were greater than 10 cm. Of the patients diagnosed with immature teratoma at The Children's Hospital [6], 6 (35%) died of causes related to the tumor and another girl later developed an endodermal sinus tumor of the opposite ovary and died. Unilateral salpingo-oophorectomy appears adequate for treatment of stage Ia tumors. The prognosis for patients with higher stages has improved significantly in the last 15 years with the use of adjuvant chemotherapy [5, 6, 19, 20]. Gershenson's study [21] of 40 patients with malignant germ cell tumors reported that the majority had normal menstrual function and a reasonable probability of having normal reproductive outcomes.

Dysgerminoma is another common malignant ovarian tumor in children. In the Children's Hospital series, the average age of the patients was 14 years (range 6½ to 21 years). These tumors have the same histology as seminomas in males and indeed can occur in phenotypic females with abnormal karyotypes (XY) and abnormal gonads. Several tumors have also been reported in girls with Turner syndrome [22], one of whom had male-specific sequences of the Y chromosome detected by DNA probes [23]. The symptoms and signs are similar to those discussed for other germ cell tumors. Rarely (2%), pure dysgerminomas contain syncytiotrophoblastic cells and produce low levels of HCG. Many dysgerminomas are mixed with other cell types that may also produce HCG. Lactic dehydrogenase (LDH) is elevated in some patients with dysgerminoma, and the levels and the isoenzyme pattern (LDH-1 and LDH-2) may be useful in suggesting the diagnosis preoperatively, but data is needed on whether this enzyme has any useful role as a marker in post-operative follow-up [5, 24, 25]. Other tumor markers (AFP and carcinoembryonic antigen) should be measured, although they are usually negative. A conservative surgical approach with unilateral salpingo-oophorectomy is usually undertaken in young women with stage Ia tumors (< 10 cm, removed unruptured, without evidence of metastatic spread). Approximately 8 to 10 percent of dysgerminomas are bilateral. Since the spread of this tumor is usually lymphatic with early involvement of para-aortic lymph nodes, followed by mediastinal and supraclavicular nodes, para-aortic nodes should be palpated and biopsied to stage the patient. Staging is critical for determining therapy and prognosis for the girl. The 5-year survival rate for patients with dysgerminoma confined to one or both ovaries is excellent (80–96%), and two thirds of those with recurrences can be successfully treated later with radiation [5, 6, 26, 27]. Adjuvant chemotherapy appears promising to preserve reproductive potential. The 5-year survival of patients with dysgerminoma with extraovarian spread drops to 63 percent. Patients with advanced or bilateral disease should have abdominal hysterectomy, bilateral salpingo-oophorectomy, nodal biopsies, omental biopsy, and tumor debulking [5]. Depending on the center, postoperative radiotherapy and/or chemotherapy are used. Dysgerminomas with mixed elements of endodermal sinus tumor have an increased malignant potential and poorer prognosis.

Endodermal sinus tumors are rare but in our series ranked second in frequency among germ cells tumors [6]. The average age of patients was 10 years (range 18 months to 16 years). The duration of symptoms including abdominal pain was typically short (usually less than 2 weeks). Tumor markers such as AFP can be useful for following the course of therapy, and serum should be saved preoperatively. An unusual case of ataxia-telangiectasia and endodermal sinus tumor has been reported, emphasizing the occurrence of both conditions being associated with abnormal production of AFP [28]. Recent outcomes may be improved for patients with stage I tumor treated with unilateral salpingo-oophorectomy followed by aggressive chemotherapy [29]. Gale and co-workers had a survival rate of 50 percent [27].

Embryonal cell carcinoma is a highly malignant tumor and may produce precocious puberty in the child, and menstrual irregularity or hirsutism in the adolescent. AFP and HCG may be secreted by this tumor.

Primary ovarian choriocarcinoma of the ovary is a rare but aggressive tumor that may develop in the absence of a gestation. Similar to other choriocarcinomas, HCG can be used as a marker. Postoperative chemotherapy is used [5].

Mixed germ cell tumors consist of two or more germ cell tumors and usually have prognosis based on the "worst" cell element. Tumor markers should be measured, and postoperative chemotherapy selected on the basis of the elements found.

Common "Epithelial" (Coelomic) Tumors

Ten to twenty percent of ovarian tumors are cystadenomas, which are epithelial tumors filled with pseudomucinous (pseudomucinous cystadenoma) or cystic fluid (serous cystadenoma). Most of the tumors are diagnosed after menarche, and the youngest patient in our series was 11½ years old [6]. These tumors are usually benign, with about 7 percent being borderline and 4 percent malignant. Conservative surgery with unilateral salpingo-oophorectomy is appropriate for stage Ia borderline tumors involving only one ovary. Biopsy of the contralateral ovary (with serous cystadenomas and if the ovary appears suspicious in mucinous cystadenoma) and staging are important. Careful and prolonged follow-up is essential, since recurrences may appear many years later. Tumors of borderline malignancy have a more favorable prognosis than higher grade carcinomas. In the rare invasive tumor, patients with other than stage Ia should be managed similar to treatment in adult women.

Sex Cord Stromal Tumors

Tumors of sex cord stromal cell origin make up 10 to 20 percent of childhood ovarian tumors. Approximately one half are hormonally active. Juvenile granulosa cell tumors secrete estrogen and in the young child may therefore produce pseudoprecocious puberty with breast enlargement and vaginal bleeding. In 2 of 10 patients in our series, pubic hair and clitoral enlargement were also noted. In the adolescent, these tumors may cause menstrual irregularities, including hypermenorrhea. Juvenile granulosa cell tumors have a more favorable prognosis than the typical adult tumor [5, 6]. Since less than 5 percent of tumors are bilateral, unilateral salpingo-oophorectomy with appropriate staging is usually adequate, since almost all children have stage Ia tumors [6, 30]. Postoperatively, estrogen levels and vaginal maturation index should return to normal prepubertal levels in young girls. Serum inhibin levels appear promising as a marker to reflect the size of the tumor and the presence of recurrent disease in adult women. Prognosis is excellent, with 84 to 92 percent survival. More advanced disease may be treated with chemotherapy.

Thecomas-fibromas are rare in the pediatric age group. Only three patients have been treated at The Children's Hospital: one patient with a thecoma, polycystic ovarian syndrome, and androgen excess (the oligomenorrhea and androgen excess did not resolve postoperatively), one with Down's syndrome who presented with a Meigs' syndrome (ascites and pleural effusion with a benign thecoma), and one with a 1-cm fibroma discovered incidentally at the time of appendectomy.

Sertoli-Leydig cell tumors have been previously termed androblastoma or arrhenoblastoma. In our pediatric series, the average age at diagnosis was 13 years, with a range of 5 to 17 years. These tumors may secrete androgens and thus produce heterosexual precocity in young children and hirsutism or virilization in the adolescent. Two adolescents have been reported to have elevated levels of AFP, which initially suggested endodermal sinus tumors but returned to undetectable levels after surgery for Sertoli-Leydig cell tumors [31]. Prognosis is dependent on the stage and degree of differentiation of the tumor; most are low-grade malignant tumors. Unilateral salpingo-oophorectomy and staging are important; prognosis is usually good.

Gynandroblastoma is a rare ovarian tumor that consists of both male and female sex cord cells and may cause premature breast development in girls and either hyperestrogenism or hyperandrogenism in adolescents [32].

Sex cord tumors with annular tubules have been associated with Peutz-Jeghers syndrome (gastrointestinal polyposis and oral cutaneous pigmentation), a condition also associated with adenocarcinoma of the cervix [2, 33].

GONADOBLASTOMAS

Gonadoblastomas are rare tumors composed of germ cells and sex cord cells. They occur most frequently in patients with female phenotype and a Y line—male pseudohermaphroditism (46,XY) or mixed gonadal dysgenesis (e.g., 45,X/46,XY). Scully [34, 35] has regarded them as a type of "in situ" cancer from which malignant germ cell tumor such as dysgerminoma can develop. The frequency of a phenotypic female with a Y line developing a gonadoblastoma depends on the defect; for example, a patient with 46,XY gonadal dysgenesis has a probability of 25 to 35 percent, whereas a patient with 45,X/46,XY has a 15 to 25 percent incidence. The risk for these patients to develop a gonadoblastoma has led to the recommendation that these patients have prophylactic bilateral gonadectomy.

OTHER TUMORS

Lipid (lipoid) cell tumors are rare [36]. Wentz and co-workers [37] reported a 17-year-old adolescent with hirsutism and oligomenorrhea in association with a lipid cell tumor.

Fibrosarcomas and undifferentiated sarcomas are rare and rapidly fatal.

Lymphomas may occur as primary ovarian tumors [38], and other tumors may be metastatic to the ovary. Rarely, leukemia will relapse with ovarian enlargement simulating an ovarian tumor [6, 39].

REFERENCES
1. Southwick GJ, and Schwartz RA. The basal cell nevus syndrome: Disasters occurring among a series of 36 patients. Cancer 1979; 44:2294.

2. Young RH, Welch WR, Dickersin GR, et al. Ovarian sex cord tumor with annular tubules: Review of 74 cases including 27 with Peutz-Jeghers syndrome and four with adenoma malignum of the cervix. Cancer 1982; 50:1384.

3. Scully RE, Galdabini JJ, and McNeely BU (eds.). Case 14-1976. N Engl J Med 1976; 294:772.

4. Heald F. Ovarian tumors in adolescence. In F Heald (ed.), Adolescent Gynecology. Baltimore: Williams & Wilkins, 1966.

5. Kennedy AW. Ovarian neoplasms in childhood and adolescence. Semin Reprod Endocrin 1988; 6:79.

6. Lack EE, and Goldstein DP. Primary ovarian tumors in childhood and adolescence. Curr Prob Obstet Gynecol 1984; 8:1.

7. Abell MR. Ovarian neoplasms of childhood and adolescence. In A Blaustein (ed.), Pathology of the Female Genital Tract. New York, Springer-Verlag, 1977.

8. Laing FC, VanDalsem, VF, Marks WM, et al. Dermoid cysts of the ovary: their ultrasonographic appearances. Obstet Gynecol 1981; 57:99.

9. Diamond MP, Baxter JW, Peerman CG, et al. Occurrence of ovarian malignancy in childhood and adolescence: A community-wide evaluation. Obstet Gynecol 1988; 71:858.

10. Creasman WT. Changes in FIGO staging. Obstet Gynecol 1987; 70:138.

11. Carlson JA. Gynecologic neoplasms. In JP Lavery, and JS Sanfilippo (eds.), Pediatric and Adolescent Obstetrics and Gynecology. New York: Springer-Verlag, 1985.

12. Breen JL, Bonamo JF, and Maxson WS. Genital tract tumors in children. Pediatr Clin North Am 1981; 28:355.

13. Huffman JW, Dewhurst CJ, and Capraro VJ. The Gynecology of Childhood and Adolescence (2nd ed.). Philadelphia: W. B. Saunders, 1981.

14. Ein S, Darte JM, and Stephens CA. Cystic and solid ovarian tumors in children: a forty-five year review. J Pediatr Surg 1970; 5:148.

15. Starceski PJ, Lee PA, and Sieber WK. Bilateral ovarian pathology in infancy: assessment of pubertal and gonadal function. Adolesc Pediatr Gynecol 1988; 1:199.

16. Goldstein DP, deCholnoky C, Emans SJ, et al. Laparoscopy in the diagnosis and management of pelvic pain in adolescents. J Reprod Med 1980; 24:251.

17. Norris HJ, Zirkin HJ, and Benson WL. Immature (Malignant) teratoma of the ovary: A clinical and pathologic study of 58 cases. Cancer 1976; 2359.

18. Norris HJ, and Jensen RD. Relative frequency of ovarian neoplasms in children and adolescents. Cancer 1972; 30:713.

19. Pippitt CH Jr, Cain JM, Hakes TB, et al. Primary chemotherapy and the role of second-look laparotomy in non-dysgerminomatous germ cell malignancies of the ovary. Gynecol Oncol 1988; 31:268.

20. Sen DK, Sivanesaratnam V, Sivanathan R, et al. Immature teratoma of the ovary. Gynecol Oncol 1988; 30:321.

21. Gershenson DM. Menstrual and reproductive function after treatment with combination chemotherapy for malignant ovarian germ cell tumors. J Clin Oncol 1988; 6:270.

22. Sinisi AA, Perrone L, Quarto C, et al. Dysgerminoma in 45,X Turner syndrome: report of a case. Clin Endocrinol (Oxf) 1988; 28:187.

23. Shah KD, Kaffe S, Gilbert F, et al. Unilateral microscopic gonadoblastoma in a prepubertal Turner mosaic with Y chromosome material identified by restriction fragment analysis. Am J Clin Pathol 1988; 90:622.

24. Yoshimura T, Takemori K, Okazaki T, et al. Serum lactic dehydrogenase

and its isoenzymes in patients with ovarian dysgerminoma. Int J Gynaecol Obstet 1988; 27:459.

25. Schwartz PE, and Morris JM. Serum lactic dehydrogenase: a tumor marker for dysgerminoma. Obstet Gynecol 1988; 72:511.
26. LaPolla JP, Benda J, Vigliotti AP, et al. Dysgerminoma of the ovary. Obstet Gynecol 1987; 69:859.
27. Gale CL, Muram D, Thompson EE. Ovarian cancer in childhood. (Abstract). Presented at the North American Society for Pediatric and Adolescent Gynecology, January, 1990.
28. Pecorelli S, Sartori E, Favalli G, et al. Ataxia-telangiectasia and endodermal sinus tumor of the ovary: report of a case. Gynecol Oncol 1988; 29:240.
29. Athanikar N, Saikia TK, Ramkrishnan G, et al. Aggressive chemotherapy in endodermal sinus tumor. J Surg Oncol 1989; 40:17.
30. Zaloudek C, and Norris HJ. Granulosa tumors of the ovary in children: a clinical and pathologic study of 32 cases. Am J Surg Pathol 1982; 6:503.
31. Mann WJ, Chumas J, Rosenwaks Z, et al. Elevated serum α-fetoprotein associated with Sertoli-Leydig cell tumors of the ovary. Obstet Gynecol 1986; 67:141.
32. Simmons PS, Backes RJ, Kaufman GH, et al. Gynandroblastoma of the ovary in a young child. Adolesc Pediatr Gynecol 1988; 1:57.
33. Scully RE. Sex cord tumor with annular tubules: A distinctive ovarian tumor of the Peutz-Jeghers syndrome. Cancer 1970; 25:1107.
34. Scully RE. Tumors of the Ovary and Maldeveloped Gonads, Atlas of Tumor Pathology, Second Series, Fascicle 16. Washington, D.C., Armed Forces Institute of Pathology, 1979.
35. Scully RE. Gonadoblastoma. A review of 74 cases. Cancer 1970; 25:1340.
36. Hayes MC, and Scully RE. Ovarian steroid cell tumors (not otherwise specified): A clinicopathological analysis of 63 cases. Am J Surg Pathol 1987; 11:835.
37. Wentz AC, Gutai JP, Jones GS, et al. Ovarian hyperthecosis in the adolescent patient. J Pediatr 1976; 88:488.
38. Fox H, Langley FA, Govan AD, et al. Malignant lymphoma presenting as an ovarian tumour: A clinicopathological analysis of 34 cases. Br J Obstet Gynaecol 1988; 95:386.
39. Heaton DC, and Duff GB. Ovarian relapse in a young woman with acute lymphoblastic leukaemia. Am J Hematol 1989; 30:42.

14. The Breast: Examination and Lesions

Between the ages of 9 and 13 years, the majority of girls begin their adolescent breast development. Because breast development is often regarded as a sign of feminine sexuality, mother and teenagers may worry about minor asymmetry or "inadequate" development. It is often difficult for the teenager to accept small breasts as "normal." On the other hand, reassurance is in order only if the remainder of the examination and history excludes an endocrine disorder. Recent national publicity on breast cancer coupled with relatives and sometimes mothers of patients having breast cancer has made many adolescents exceptionally nervous about cystic breast changes and fibroadenomas. This concern may be used constructively to encourage patients to come for routine health assessments and to initiate monthly breast self-examination.

BREAST EXAMINATION
All patients should have a careful breast examination at the time of their annual physical examination regardless of whether specific complaints are mentioned. Teaching self-examination at the time of the annual physical often makes the adolescent feel at ease as the examiner palpates for any abnormalities [1, 2]. The patient is asked to lie supine with her arm under her head. Breast development should be recorded as Tanner stages B1 to B5 (see Chap. 4). If asymmetry or disorders of development are a concern, then exact measurement of the areola, glandular breast tissue, and overall breast size should be included at each examination (Fig. 14-1).

For example, one might record the following:

	Areola	Breast Gland	Overall
Right	2.5 cm	5 × 6 cm	9 cm
Left	2.4 cm	4 × 5 cm	8.5 cm

The first number in the breast gland figure is the upper to lower measurement; the second number is the right to left measurement. The overall size is the right to left measurement of the border of the fatty tissue of the breast mound.

The breast tissue should be carefully palpated in a straight line from the margin of the breast inward, clockwise around the breast (Fig. 14-2). The flat finger pads should be moved in a slightly rotatory fashion to feel abnormal masses. The breast can also be palpated by the examiner using a circular clockwise pattern or in vertical strips.

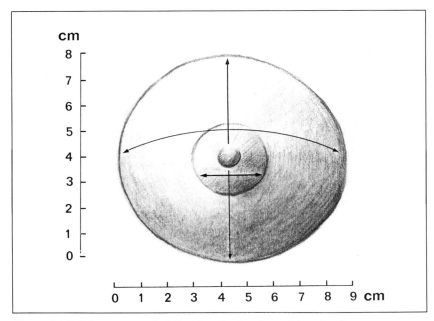

Figure 14-1. Measurement of the developing breast (see text).

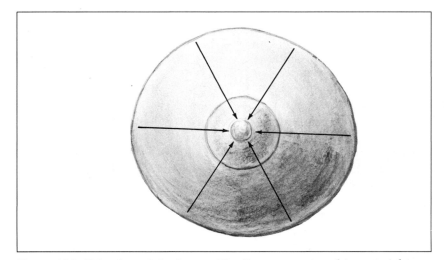

Figure 14-2. Palpation of the breast. The fingers are moved in a straight line inward going clockwise around the breast.

Normal glandular tissue has an irregular, granular surface (like "tapioca pudding"); a fibroadenoma feels firm, rubbery, or smooth. The areola should be compressed to assess any abnormal discharge.

During the examination, the teenager can be encouraged to learn routine self-examination, done at the end of each menstrual period. Instruction can include having the adolescent (1) look in the mirror for asymmetry while undressing for a shower, (2) examine the breasts while standing in the shower (soap on the hands facilitates the examination), and (3) reexamine the breasts that night supine (before going to sleep) with one hand behind the head and a small pillow under the shoulder. She should be shown how to begin at the outermost edge of her breast and press gently with the middle three finger pads in circular motions clockwise starting at 12 o'clock. The motion is repeated by moving inward an inch each circle, and proceeding clockwise around the breast tissue until the nipple is examined. A pamphlet such as "How to Examine Your Breasts" or "Special Touch" by the American Cancer Society should be available in the physician's office. It is particularly helpful for the patient to begin self-examination the night after a normal examination at the office visit so that she can be assured that the "lumps" she is feeling are normal glandular tissue.

Breast self-examination is also often taught in schools as part of health education classes. Although adolescents can become quite proficient in learning the necessary techniques, adolescents appear to practice self-examination only sporadically and often not at the end of menses, as is recommended [3]. Studies on the value of self-examination during adolescence toward promoting lifelong health habits or early detection of breast cancer have not been done [4]. In contrast to young adolescents, who are often uncomfortable with their body changes, older adolescent and young adult women are usually more interested in learning self-examination techniques, but even they require reinforcement at medical visits. Patients should be reassured that while cancer is extraordinarily unlikely in their age group, a new breast mass that does not disappear after a menstrual period or is associated with signs of infection should be evaluated by a physician. Adolescent women with previous radiation of the chest have an increased risk of second tumors including cancers of the breast [5,6, 7] and thus should be targeted as a group requiring early teaching of breast self-examination. The breasts also may be the site of metastases in adolescent cancer patients.

Breast tenderness is not usually a major complaint of healthy adolescents but may occur premenstrually, in association with fibrocystic changes or exercise, or importantly as a sign of early pregnancy. Thus the physician seeing adolescents must be prepared to do not only a breast assessment in girls complaining of mastalgia but also a pregnancy test. Although some case control studies have not demonstrated an association between caffeine and methylxanthines and benign breast disease [8, 9], many adolescents with cyclic breast discomfort do appear to benefit from wearing a comfortable supporting bra, a trial of elimination of substances such as coffee, tea, colas, and chocolate and perhaps a small dose of ibuprofen. Low-dose progestin-dominant oral contraceptives may offer relief to sexually active adolescents who also need birth control. With the active participation of many girls in sports, the bra industry has responded with the design of many new styles with smooth cups and support that are particularly helpful to girls with large breasts involved in activities such as jogging, basketball, and weight-lifting [10, 11].

PROBLEMS OF BREAST DEVELOPMENT

ASYMMETRY

Asymmetry of the breasts is a common complaint, especially from girls in the early stages of development. Since the breast bud may initially appear on one side as a tender, granular lump, mothers are often concerned about the possibility of a tumor.

The physician can play an important role in counselling the patient with true asymmetric breast development. The young adolescent needs to hear that many other adolescents and adult women have asymmetry; it should be pointed out that she may be unaware of the degree of asymmetry in other women because her observations are based on seeing fully clothed women.

It is helpful to let the 13- or 14-year-old girl know that most teenagers at the age of 18 or 19 years are coping well with the amount of breast asymmetry they have and that most decide not to have surgery. The physician should acknowledge that many younger adolescents (14 or 15 years old) are most anxious to have their body image equalized and "made normal" as quickly as possible without regard for the possible risks and long-term complications involved in augmentation mammoplasty. The young teenager can benefit from being told that the physician understands that the asymmetry may cause worries for her and that an annual examination is important to determine the degree of asymmetry and to help her to decide at the end of full growth (no further change in measurements) whether any consideration of intervention beyond simple bra pads is warranted for the asymmetry.

Since bathing suit fittings can be particularly difficult for girls with asymmetry, girls should be encouraged to try on a large number of styles that offer breast support before coming to a final decision. For many youngsters, the use of slightly padded bras also makes the asymmetry much less of a problem. A major difference in breast size

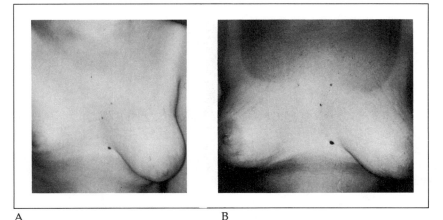

A   B

Figure 14-3. Sixteen-year-old girl with hypoplasia of the right breast. A. Preoperatively. B. After augmentation mammoplasty with a Cronin prosthesis. (Courtesy of Dr. George E. Gifford, The Children's Hospital, Boston.)

can be treated with a foam insert (available in department stores for mastectomy patients).

If asymmetry is still marked at age 15 to 18 years and serial measurements show no further increase in size of either breast, patients often wish to explore the option of mammoplasty. A plastic surgeon can discuss the risks and benefits. Potential long-term sequelae of implants are being studied. It is particularly important to select a plastic surgeon who is willing to discuss the options without pushing the patient inordinately in the direction of surgery. Success can be quite dramatic, as illustrated in Figure 14-3.

The possibility of a giant fibroadenoma enlarging one breast should always be considered during the physical examination. Such fibroadenomas are usually solitary but may blend into the normal breast tissue and be missed during palpation. The overlying skin is typically taut, and there is dilatation of the superficial veins.

HYPERTROPHY

Some adolescents develop very large breasts, which are associated with back pain, postural kyphosis, breast discomfort, shoulder soreness from bra straps, intertrigo, and psychological distress from teasing at school. Surgical reduction of the large breasts at the end of breast growth can give rewarding benefits to many girls. However, as is the case with augmentation mammoplasty, the adolescent needs to understand the results and risks of surgery, including infection, scars, and probable inability to breast-feed.

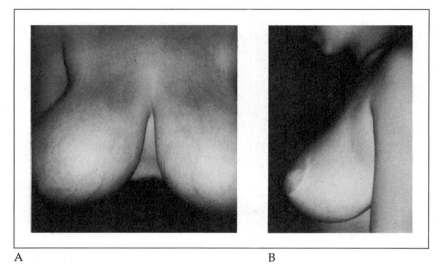

A   B

Figure 14-4. Nineteen-year-old-woman with virginal hypertrophy of both breasts, resulting in back pain and kyphosis. A. Preoperatively. B. After reduction mammoplasty. (Courtesy of Dr. George E. Gifford, The Children's Hospital, Boston.)

True virginal hypertrophy occurs rarely in adolescents and causes the breasts to continue to enlarge in size beyond normal; unilateral or segmental enlargement may occur. The differential diagnosis includes juvenile fibroadenomas and cystosarcoma phyllodes. Surgical reduction should be delayed if possible until growth has ceased (Fig. 14-4).

TUBEROUS BREASTS
Tuberous breasts are a variant of breast development in which the base of the breast is limited in size and the nipple/areola complex is overdeveloped, giving the appearance of a tuberous plant root. The glandular tissue may be totally within the distended, enlarged areolae. Plastic surgery may be undertaken for cosmetic reasons.

LACK OF DEVELOPMENT
Lack of development may be secondary to congenital absence of glandular tissue (amastia), a systemic disorder (e.g., malnutrition, Crohn's disease), radiation therapy, congenital adrenal hyperplasia (CAH), gonadal dysgenesis, hypogonadotropic hypogonadism, or rarely an intersex disorder or 17 α-hydroxylase deficiency. Amastia can be unilateral and associated with underdevelopment of the pectoral muscles (Poland's syndrome). The evaluation depends on the history and physical findings, discussed in Chapter 6. The finding of any evidence of androgen excess, such as mild enlargement of the

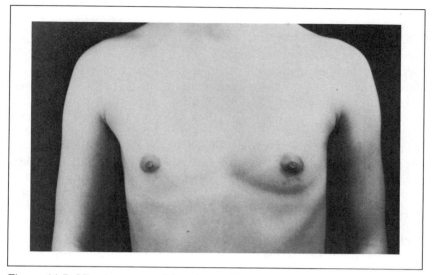

Figure 14-5. Nineteen-year-old patient who presented with irregular periods and lack of glandular tissue; late onset 21-hydroxylase deficiency adrenal hyperplasia (CAH) was diagnosed.

clitoris, hirsutism, or severe acne, should suggest a disorder such as congenital adrenal hyperplasia, an intersex disorder, polycystic ovary syndrome, or possibly an adrenal or ovarian tumor (see Chap. 7).

Figure 14-5 illustrates a 19-year-old patient who had irregular menses and lack of glandular breast development. Examination revealed normal pubic and axillary hair, mild clitoromegaly, and mild hirsutism. Adrenocorticotropic hormone (ACTH) testing was consistent with late onset 21-hydroxylase deficiency (CAH) (see Chap. 7). Suppression of adrenal androgens with dexamethasone resulted in regular menses and normal breast development.

Despite the need to consider endocrinologic problems, the physician should be aware that by far the majority of adolescents with small breasts, normal sexual hair, and regular menses are healthy young women and deserve reassurance. Sports bras, which tend to compress the breast further, can be avoided. With the current "oversized" sweater and sweatshirt look, fewer adolescents seem to be concerned about small breast size. This, of course, may change with styles that emphasize the "tank-top" look. Augmentation mammoplasty may be considered by some young women in their young adult years, and an understanding of the risks and benefits is essential. Athletes with small breasts are generally counselled to avoid augmentation mammoplasty until their careers are completed, since the change could potentially alter performance [10].

PREMATURE THELARCHE

A discussion of premature thelarche can be found in Chapter 5.

ACCESSORY NIPPLES OR BREASTS

Accessory nipples or breasts occur in 1 to 2 percent of healthy patients. In some cases, all three components of the breast—glandular tissue, areola, and nipple—are present. More commonly, only a small areola and nipple are found, usually along the embryologic milk line between the axillae and groin. The most common sites are medial and just inferior to the normal breast tissue and in the axilla. No therapy is usually undertaken unless at a later date the patient wishes to have the tissue removed for cosmetic reasons. Although studies have been conflicting on the association of supernumerary nipples and renal anomalies [12, 13] and further studies are needed, a reasonable approach is to perform renal ultrasonography in an infant with multiple congenital anomalies and supernumerary nipples.

Engorgement of accessory breasts is common during pregnancy and lactation. If no outlet is present, the breast tissue spontaneously involutes within several days to weeks after delivery.

NIPPLE DISCHARGE

Nipple discharge is unusual during the teen years. Occasionally, a small amount of yellow, clear serous material can be expressed in early adolescence. The more common clinical problem is galactorrhea, which occurs in adolescents following a pregnancy (full-term or after an abortion) or is associated with drug use (prescription and illicit), hypothyroidism, or prolactin-secreting tumors. The evaluation of galactorrhea and hyperprolactinemia is discussed on p. 171. Hyperprolactinemia has also been associated with mammary duct ectasia, a clinical syndrome of nipple discharge, nipple inversion, breast mass, and/or periareolar sepsis (nonpuerperal mastitis) [14]. In a study of 108 patients, Peters and Schuth [14] found that 27 percent of the patients had transiently elevated prolactin (42 ± 22 μg/liter) during the period of inflammation with return to normal within 4 weeks and that 20 percent of the patients had more severe hyperprolactinemia (78 ± 56 μg/liter), often associated with a previously undiagnosed prolactinoma. The authors suggested that the former group may have neurogenic hyperprolactinemia in response to the inflammation, whereas the latter group may be predisposed to the infection because nipple secretion might facilitate bacterial invasion. Nineteen of the patients in this study were between the ages of 12 and 20 years.

A blood-tinged discharge should prompt a search for an intraductal papilloma or, rarely, carcinoma. Occasionally, a periareolar gland of Montgomery will drain a small amount of clear to brownish fluid through an ectopic opening on the areola for several weeks. A small subareolar lump may be palpable. Usually no treatment is necessary and the discharge and lump resolve spontaneously [15]. If the cyst persists, however, excision is advisable.

PERIAREOLAR HAIR
Periareolar hair is not uncommon in the healthy adolescent. Cosmetic treatment (usually unnecessary) can be accomplished by cutting the hairs. Plucking or shaving may be uncomfortable and can lead to mastitis/cellulitis.

OTHER PROBLEMS
Joggers may experience sore or scaling nipples in response to friction. Lubrication of the nipple, a soft cotton bra without a seam in the cup, or Bandaids over the nipples in the girl with small breasts not using a bra are often curative [10]. Bicyclists may have difficulty with cold, painful nipples after several days of riding in the colder climates; a windbreaking jacket and increased insulation over the chest should be advised.

Overweight girls with large pendulous breasts may have local infections on the undersurface of the breast with agents such as *Candida*, which results in a bright red rash. Topical antifungal drugs are usually sufficient, although florid cases with axillary involvement as well have responded better to oral ketoconazole therapy.

BREAST MASSES
The majority of adolescents who present to the physician's office with a complaint of a "breast lump" have normal physiologic breast tissue or fibrocystic changes [16]. Adolescents typically have very dense breast tissue. Fibrocystic "changes" are characterized by diffuse cord-like thickening and lumps, which may become tender and enlarged prior to menses each month. Physical findings tend to change each month, so that suspected cysts can often be followed clinically. Love and colleagues [17] have questioned whether these findings should be characterized as a "disease," since the process occurs in 50 percent of women clinically and 90 percent histologically. Although a link between benign breast disease and methylxanthine consumption has not been demonstrated [8, 9], many clinicians do observe that breast symptoms or questionable lumps do improve when patients eliminate coffee, tea, cola, chocolate and street drugs for 2 to 3 months [18].

In contrast to the finding that most breast "lumps" seen in the office setting in adolescents are normal or simply fibrocystic changes, most breast masses that are surgically excised in this age group are fibroadenomas [2, 19, 20]. These lesions are typically firm or rubbery, are mobile, and usually have a clearly defined edge. They tend to be eccentric in position and occur more frequently in the lateral breast quadrants than the medial quadrants. The breast mass may remain unchanged or increase in size with subsequent menstrual cycles. Recurrent or multiple fibroadenomas may occur. Giant fibroadenomas may replace most of the breast tissue and, in fact, are often mistaken initially for normal tissue.

Cancer of the breast is extremely rare in children and adolescents [2, 19, 21–26]. In a series of 237 patients (10–20 years old) with breast lesions, Farrow and Ashikari [25] reported only 1 patient with primary breast carcinoma and 2 patients with sarcomas metastatic to breast tissue. In a retrospective review of surgically treated breast disease in 185 adolescents (11–17 years old) at the Mayo Clinic, 4 patients had malignant neoplasms (primary rhabdomyosarcoma, metastatic rhabdomyosarcoma, neuroblastoma, and non-Hodgkin's lymphoma) [20]. Primary lymphoma may present as a breast mass in adolescents [27]. Patients with previous radiation therapy to the chest have an increased risk of developing cancer of the breast at a young age and therefore require careful ongoing surveillance [5, 6, 7, 28]. Cystosarcoma phylloides is a rare primary tumor that is sometimes malignant [29].

A new entity, juvenile papillomatosis, is a rare breast tumor of young women first described in 1980. The results of 180 patients from the Juvenile Papillomatosis Registry were reported in 1985 [30]. The tumor features atypical papillary duct hyperplasia and multiple cysts. The mean age of the patients was 23 years with a range of 12 to 48 years. The localized tumor was often initially mistaken for a fibroadenoma. Twenty-eight percent of the patients had a relative with breast cancer, and seven percent had a first-degree relative with breast cancer. A small number of patients had breast cancer diagnosed concurrently with the juvenile papillomatosis, and several patients developed cancer at follow-up. Bilateral juvenile papillomatosis may especially increase the risk of later developing cancer. Thus careful surveillance is indicated in patients with this diagnosis found on excisional biopsy. Papillary hyperplasia without the cystic component of juvenile papillomatosis appears to be a more benign condition in young patients [31].

If the adolescent presents the complaint of a breast mass, palpation may make the diagnosis evident with such as fibrocystic changes or tenderness with overlying erythema consistent with a breast infection. Trauma may cause a breast mass, but examination immediately following a contusion may locate a preexisting lesion. If the differential diagnosis is a cyst or fibroadenoma, the lesion can be measured and the patient instructed to return after her next menstrual period. If the lesion has disappeared, then a cyst was probably present. If the lesion is still present and the patient is cooperative, a needle aspiration of the mass can be performed in the office using a 23-gauge needle on a 3-cc syringe. (A small amount of lidocaine can be used to infiltrate the skin with a 25-gauge needle.) A cyst can be aspirated, whereas a fibroadenoma gives a characteristic "gritty," solid sensation. Material obtained (even if just on the tip of the needle) may be smeared on a ground glass slide and sent in Papanicolaou fixative for cytology examination. If the mass collapses after aspiration, it is assumed to be a cyst, and the mass is reevaluated in 3 months. Ultrasound of the breast tissue can also be helpful in delineating a fibroadenoma from a cyst and can be used in localizing an abscess. Mammography should not be used to evaluate breast masses in the adolescent age group, since the breast tissue is very dense, the risk of the patient having carcinoma is negligible, and radiographic features have not influenced clinical management [32].

When aspiration of a persistent, discrete mass is not feasible or is nonproductive, or when masses are nonmobile and hard, enlarging, tender, or a source of considerable anxiety, the patient should have an excisional biopsy done. Unless there are underlying medical conditions, such as cardiac or pulmonary disease, an excisional biopsy can be done in an ambulatory setting under general or local anesthesia, depending on technical considerations and on the patient's preference and ability to cooperate. Since breast scars can be cosmetically deforming, the optimal incision for a lesion near the center of the breast is circumareolar. Curvilinear or semilunar incisions are superior to radial incisions in terms of wound healing and cosmetic results. Periareolar ectopic lobules, which often have clear or dark discharge from the areola (not the nipple), can be excised with a circumareolar incision.

In a review of 51 patients, aged 8 to 20 years, who underwent excision of breast masses at The Children's Hospital (Boston), 81.4 percent of the masses were fibroadenomas [2]. The pathology report on the remainder of the biopsy specimens showed fibrocystic disease, simple cysts, capillary hemangiomas, fat necrosis, adenomatous hyperplasia, and (in 1 patient) normal breast tissue. This is similar to the spectrum of breast disease reported by Daniel and Mathews [19], who found that fibroadenomas accounted for 94 percent of the breast tumors from adolescents 12 to 21 years of age.

Follow-up is particularly important in these cases because new cysts and fibroadenomas can occur.

CONTUSION
A contusion to the breast may result in a poorly defined, tender mass that resolves over several weeks. A mass from severe trauma may take several months to resolve, and occasionally, scar tissue remains

palpable indefinitely. Fat necrosis may also result from trauma, although the patient may not notice the growing lesion until several months later. Biopsy is frequently indicated in such circumstances. It should be remembered that the examination immediately following trauma to the breast may locate a preexisting lesion. A sharply delineated, nontender mass is probably unrelated to the recent injury.

INFECTION

Infection of the breast is seen chiefly in newborns and lactating women. In a review of neonatal mastitis at The Children's Hospital (Boston), Walsh and McIntosh [33] found that infections occurred in full-term infants 1 to 5 weeks of age with a sex ratio of 2:1 (females to males). All but a few cases were caused by *Staphylococcus aureus,* and most of the infants (10 of 17) treated since 1971 responded to appropriate beta-lactamase–resistant antibiotics without the need for incision and drainage. Infants with a persistent mass after treatment for an infection, or recurrent infections may have an underlying lesion such as a hemangioma, lymphangioma, or cystic hygroma.

Breast infections in adolescents are most common in lactating patients. Bacteria such as staphylococci and streptococci enter through cracks in the nipples; cellulitis is often associated with streptococci and abscesses with staphylococci. Nonlactating adolescents may also develop breast infections, usually beneath the areola or at the margin between the areola and the normal skin. The etiology of these infections is unclear, but they may occur because of duct ectasia or metaplasia of the duct epithelium. In addition, the adolescent may give a history of having recently shaved around the areola or having plucked a periareolar hair. Sexual play may also cause breast trauma. Subareolar inflammatory masses may occur secondary to rupture of an areolar gland. A recent report [14] of the association of hyperprolactinemia and mastitis warrants further study. The patient may present with a tender mass, or in the early stages of infection, with erythema and warmth of the skin adjacent to the areola. In agreement with our experience, Beach [18] has found that infections may be more extensive and deeper than initial superficial findings suggest. As in the neonate, staphylococci are the most common pathogens. Aspiration of the mass (with or without the aid of ultrasound) can help make the clinical and bacteriologic diagnosis. Mastitis associated with duct ectasia usually has a visible discharge, which can be gram-stained and cultured. If diagnosed early and the predominant feature is cellulitis, most cases will respond to oral antibiotics such as dicloxacillin or a cephalosporin given for 3 to 4 weeks. If the mass becomes fluctuant or if symptoms progress or fail to resolve, incision and drainage as an inpatient or in the ambulatory operating room setting are performed. Antibiotics should be continued postoperatively. Subareolar abscesses may become recurrent and require elective excision of the dilated milk ducts and associated inflammatory tissue [18, 21, 34, 35].

REFERENCES
1. Hein K, Dell R, and Cohen MI. Self-detection of a breast mass in adolescent females. J Adolesc Health Care 1982; 3:15.
2. Goldstein DP, and Miler V. Breast masses in adolescent females. Clin Pediatr 1982; 21:17.
3. Cromer BA, Frankel ME, and Keder LM. Compliance with breast self-examination instruction in healthy adolescents. J Adolesc Health Care 1989; 10:105.
4. O'Malley MS, and Fletcher SW. Screening for breast cancer with breast self-examination: A critical review. JAMA 1987; 257:2196.
5. Curtis RE, and Boice JD. Second cancers after radiotherapy for Hodgkin's disease (letter). N Engl J Med 1988; 319:244.
6. Tucker MA, Coleman CN, Cox RS, et al. Risk of second cancers after treatment for Hodgkin's disease. N Engl J Med 1988; 318:76.
7. Squire R, Bianchi A, and Jakate SM. Radiation-induced sarcoma of the breast in a female adolescent. Cancer 1988; 61:2444.
8. Lubin F, Ron E, Wax Y, et al. A case-control study of caffeine and methylxanthines in benign breast disease. JAMA 1985; 253:2388.
9. Shairer C, Brinton LA, and Hoover RN. Methylxanthines and benign breast disease. Am J Epidemiol 1986; 124:603.
10. Haycock CE. How I manage breast problems in athletes. Phys Sportsmed 1987; 15:89.
11. Gehlsen G, and Albohm M. Evaluation of sports bras. Phys Sportsmed 1980; 8:89.
12. Kenney RD, Flippo JL, and Black EB. Supernumerary nipples and renal anomalies in neonates. Am J Dis Child 1987; 141:987.
13. Hersh JH, Bloom AS, Cromer AO, et al. Does a supernumerary nipple/renal field defect exist? Am J Dis Child 1987; 141:989.
14. Peters F, and Schuth W. Hyperprolactinemia and nonpuerperal mastitis (duct ectasia). JAMA 1989; 261:1618.
15. Watkins F, Giacomantonio M, and Salisbury S. Nipple discharge and breast lump related to Montgomery's tubercles in adolescent females. J Pediatr Surg 1988; 23:718.
16. Diehl T, and Kaplan DW. Breast masses in adolescent females. J Adolesc Health Care 1985; 6:353.
17. Love SM, Gelman RS, and Silen W. Fibrocystic "disease" of the breast—a nondisease? N Engl J Med 1982; 307:1010.
18. Beach RK. Routine breast exams: A chance to reassure, guide, and protect. Contemp Pediatr 1987; 70:100.
19. Daniel W, and Mathews M. Tumors of the breast in adolescent females. Pediatrics 1968; 41:743.
20. Simmons PS, and Wold LE. Surgically treated breast disease in adolescent females: A retrospective review of 185 cases. Adolesc Pediatr Gynecol 1989; 2:95.
21. Ekland D, and Zeigler M. Abscess in the nonlactating breast. Arch Surg 1971; 107:398.
22. Sandison A, and Welker J. Diseases of the adolescent female breast. Br J Surg 1968; 55:443.

23. Oberman H, and Stephens P. Carcinoma of the breast in childhood. Cancer 1972; 30:470.
24. Simpson L, and Barson A. Breast tumors in infants and children. Can Med Assoc J 1969; 101:100.
25. Farrow J, and Ashikari H. Breast lesions in young girls. Surg Clin North Am 1969; 49:261.
26. Karl SR, Ballantine TV, and Zaino R. Juvenile secretory carcinoma of the breast. Br J Surg 1987; 74:214.
27. Dixon JM, Lumsden AB, Krajewski A, et al. Primary lymphoma of the breast. Br J Surg 1987; 74:214.
28. Ivins JC, Taylor WF, and Wold LE. Elective whole-lung irradiation in osteosarcoma treatment: Appearance of bilateral breast cancer in two long-term survivors. Skeletal Radiol 1987; 16:133.
29. Hart J, Layfield LJ, Trumbull WE, et al. Practical aspects in the diagnosis and management of cystosarcoma phyllodes. Arch Surg 1988; 123:1079.
30. Rosen PP, Holmes G, Lesser ML, et al. Juvenile papillomatosis and breast carcinoma. Cancer 1985; 55:1345.
31. Rosen PP. Papillary duct hyperplasia of the breast in children and young adults. Cancer 1985; 56:1611.
32. Williams SM, Kaplan PA, Petersen JC, et al. Mammography in women under age 30: Is there clinical benefit? Radiology 1986; 161:49.
33. Walsh M, and McIntosh K. Neonatal mastitis. Clin Pediatr 1986; 25:395.
34. Osuch JR. Benign lesions of the breast other than fibrocystic change. Obstet Gynecol Clin North Am 1987; 14:703.
35. Greydanus DE, Parks DS, and Farrell EG. Breast disorders in children and adolescents. Pediatr Clin North Am 1989; 36(3):601.

15. Contraception

Although many physicians caring for adolescents still feel ambivalent about providing sex education and contraceptive advice to their patients, it is clear that more teenagers are engaging in intercourse at earlier ages and often without any form of contraception. Fortunately, the percentage of sexually experienced 15- to 19-year-old girls appears to have plateaued in the 1980s. The increasing awareness of sexually transmitted diseases, especially acquired immunodeficiency syndrome (AIDS), has allowed more open discussion of adolescent sexuality. Sex education in schools and at home, peer counselling, and addressing the issue of the sexual messages in magazines and movies are needed to alleviate the problems associated with early premarital sexual intercourse. Thus, the adolescent should be asked about menses and sexual history at each visit to her health care provider. A teenager who is 14 or 15 years old will rarely make a specific request for contraceptives from her primary physician unless she knows that the topic can be discussed confidentially. Adolescents who become sexually active in their early teenage years are often involved in other risk-taking activities such as substance abuse and are especially likely to have an unplanned pregnancy or acquire a sexually transmitted disease [1]. A college student of 18 or 19 years of age is much more likely to seek gynecologic care on her own and deal with the issue of contraception. Lack of contraceptive services or the requirement for parental involvement will increase the number of unwanted pregnancies rather than decrease the number of sexually active adolescents.

Who should prescribe a contraceptive for the adolescent? This depends on whether the physician or nurse practitioner is familiar with routine pelvic examinations and knowledgeable about the indications and contraindications for using the various contraceptive methods. Above all, it is important that the physician be sympathetic to adolescents and that he or she not be prejudiced against certain birth control methods. The primary care physician needs to be familiar with the efficacy and side effects of the various methods even if the patient is referred to a gynecologist or family planning clinic.

Friends and family members remain the major source of referral for sexually active women 15 to 24 years old—friends the main source for clinics and families for private physicians [2]. The race, age at first visit, and income of the young woman all influence the choice of provider. Black, low-income, and younger women are more likely to select clinics. Adolescents often prefer clinics because of confidentiality, low cost, proximity, and not knowing the provider [3]. In the Zabin and Clark study [4] of family planning clinics, teenagers reported that they chose clinics because "it doesn't tell my parents," "the people there care about teens," "it is the closest," "my friends come to it," "it is the only one I know of." For black adolescents, the mother is often the source of the referral to the clinic. Unfortunately, the first visit to a family planning clinic is frequently because of a pregnancy scare. In Zabin and Clark's study, 36 percent of adolescents came for this reason.

The interval between first intercourse and clinic visit varies from 2 weeks to several years, with mean intervals of 9 to 23 months in different studies [2–7]. Surprisingly, in our study [8] the interval between intercourse and clinic visit to initiate oral contraceptives was not different between patients seen in an inner city adolescent clinic (10.7 months), a birth control clinic (8.5 months), and a suburban private practice of adolescent medicine (10.9 months). However, the suburban adolescents were much more likely to have used some type of contraceptive method (usually condoms) before making an appointment; 57 percent of inner city patients compared to 14 percent of suburban adolescents had never used a method before coming to the clinic.

A major challenge is to reach adolescent patients earlier, since pregnancy frequently occurs in the first 6 months of sexual activity. It may be possible to decrease the delay in obtaining contraceptives by offering community education programs for teenagers, enlisting the support of churches, developing relationships with youth groups, opening clinics during evening and weekend hours, and accepting teenagers as walk-in patients [9]. The latest effort has been to open school-based clinics. In a school-based program in Baltimore, Zabin and co-workers [10] found that the mean age of onset of sexual activity was in fact delayed, not increased, and that more students, especially younger boys and girls, had made visits to the clinic.

Sex education has become more acceptable in view of the tremendous concern about the spread of AIDS. Earlier studies have shown that adolescents who have had sex education courses are not more likely to become sexually active [11]. They are less likely to have been pregnant and more likely to use a method of contraception at first intercourse. Questionnaires show that adolescent behavior is often at variance with stated attitudes. For example, Zabin and co-workers [12] found that 83 percent of sexually experienced adolescents thought the best age for intercourse was older than the age at which they themselves experienced the event. Of adolescents who reported that they would have sexual intercourse only with a birth control method, 25 percent had used no method at last intercourse. Grace and colleagues [13], in questioning suburban patients about AIDS, found that concerned teenagers expressed a desire to change their sexual behavior in the *future* but were unwilling to alter *present* behavior, be more selective of partners, or use condoms. Peers were the only influence that appeared to alter behavior.

Since effective contraception involves the ability to think abstractly, plan ahead, and take action including visiting a clinic or doctor, young adolescents may not have reached the developmental stage where they can organize an effective plan. Risk taking and a sense of invulnerability are often a part of adolescence. In addition, the risks of contraception, especially the oral contraceptive, are often significantly overrated in the adolescent mind and in fact by the general public as well. Strategies to delay the onset of sexual activity, to make barrier contraceptives more acceptable to adolescents (especially inner city youths), to improve access to services, to tailor patient education, and to develop better long-acting contraception are needed [8]. In addition, overall changes are needed in the psychosocial environment of inner city youth, males need to be involved, and school-based day care and peer counselling are necessary to deal with the problem of early pregnancy in this country.

In providing good medical care to the sexually active adolescent, the physician should obtain a complete medical history and determine if there are any specific contraindications to the use of a particular form of birth control. If the patient has already practiced birth control, she may be more apt to comply with the method chosen. The degree to which one or both partners can take responsibility for avoiding an unwanted pregnancy should be assessed. Multiple partners, low evaluation of personal health, and feelings of hopelessness have been associated with noncompliance with oral contraceptives [14]. The future plans of the adolescent should be assessed, since those bound for college are more likely to be compliant with appropriate birth control measures [8, 15, 16]. In contrast, the 15-year-old adolescent who has dropped out of school and has no future plans may have ambivalent feelings about whether a pregnancy can give her adult status and help her to move out of her home. That adolescent may feel her life is controlled by external factors over which she has little control. Her motivation to avoid pregnancy may be minimal because the consequences are not seen in a negative light.

A large study of 209 adolescents at our institution found that compliance was quite different depending on the population served [8]. Three months after adolescents were given oral contraceptives, 48 percent of patients seen in an inner city adolescent clinic, 65 percent of patients seen in a birth control clinic in a mid-sized industrial city, and 84 percent of patients seen in a suburban private practice returned for their follow-up visit and continued to take the pill. Factors associated with compliance included older age, suburban residence, white race, health care in the suburban private practice, payment status, prior use of contraception, mother's lack of awareness of the oral contraceptives, married parents, older boyfriend, lack of worry about being pregnant, and satisfaction with pill use. Compliance at long-term follow-up (13.5 ± 3.7 months) was additionally associated with higher educational goals, father's higher educational level, and absence of side effects. Ten pregnancies occurred among noncompliant inner city patients. Furstenburg and associates [5] made similar observations in a study of compliance among family planning patients in which continuing use of contraception was associated with older age, white race, adolescents who had working parents with higher levels of education, being college bound, above-average grades, a steady sexual relationship, and satisfaction with the method chosen. An adolescent's view of the "cost" of a pregnancy in terms of the negative impact on her economic, psychosocial, and educational goals influences her continuing use of contraception. Accepting a form of birth control at her first visit to a family planning clinic is an important predictor of long-term compliance.

Before prescribing contraceptives, the physician should discuss the risks of being sexually active, including the emotional consequences, sexually transmitted diseases, and pregnancy. The possibility of parental involvement should be assessed with the adolescent, particularly since many adolescents can share the information with a parent, particularly her mother. Payment for the visit and laboratory tests and issues of confidentiality should be discussed early in the provision of contraceptive services. Involvement of the male partner is ideal but seldom achieved in current clinical practice.

Some states have passed laws that specifically allow minors to give their own informed consent for birth control. Although court decisions have allowed family planning clinics to dispense contraceptives without notifying the parents, the physician's decision about prescribing birth control may also be affected by the community or the patient's family. Gynecologists have been more willing to prescribe oral contraceptives to minors than pediatricians, probably in part because they see the consequences of nonuse [3].

The patient who does not share the information with her parents should at least think through with the physician what she would do if her parents found the contraceptive pills or device. In volatile situations, the physician should offer to be the mediator to help both sides come to a solution around responsible sexuality. The physician can facilitate communication by asking both the parent(s) and the daughter to come in for counselling at the end of the office day. Each health care provider has his or her own style of communication, but it is helpful to empathize with the parent(s) on problems caused by the change in sexual mores. At the same time the parent(s) should be congratulated on raising a daughter who is being responsible about birth control rather than becoming pregnant like so many of her

Table 15-1. Pregnancy Rates per 100 Woman-Years
of Use with Different Contraceptives

Type of Contraceptive	Pregnancy Rate
Oral contraceptives	
Combination	0.3–0.7
Minipill	1.5–3.0
IUDs	
Progestasert	2.1
Copper T380A	1.0
Condom and foam	2–10
Condom	2–20
Diaphragm and contraceptive cream	2.5–23
Cervical cap	6–17
Contraceptive sponge	13–28
Contraceptive foams and suppositories	3–30
Depo-Provera	0.4
Norplant	0.3–0.7

peers. Being a good listener and acknowledging how difficult it is to raise children are helpful. For the primary care physician, much miscommunication can be avoided if a simple explanation takes place when the girl is 11 or 12 years old. The parents can understand that a new phase of health is beginning, that the physician will share as much as possible, but that certain information about school, friends, drugs, and sex needs to remain confidential. The parents should be encouraged to call about any of their concerns. Most families welcome knowing that physicians and nurse practitioners are concerned about psychosocial and health issues far beyond simply completing sports physical forms.

The pregnancy rates of 100 women using different contraceptive devices for 1 year (100 woman-years of use) are listed in Table 15-1. Estimates for use-failure rates for a first year of contraception in fact may be 30 percent higher because of underreporting of abortions. For some teenagers, the pregnancy rate with the pill may climb to 9 to 12 pregnancies per 100 woman-years or even higher because of missed pills and misunderstanding the directions (Table 15-2). The teenager must feel that she has actively participated in the decision on the best method of contraception for her life-style; the dialogue between physician and patient is of supreme importance. For example, a patient will sometimes discontinue a form of contraception because she perceives that the health care provider is unhelpful, the time in the waiting room too long, or the pelvic examination distressing. Regardless of what the patient initially states as her preferred form of contraception, it is important for the physician to discuss all available

Table 15-2. Contraceptive Failure During The First 12 Months
of Use, by Method, Race, and Age (years) for Unmarried Women

Method	White		Nonwhite	
	<20	20–24	<20	20–24
Pill	9.3	5.9	18.1	11.7
Condom	13.3	22.5	22.3	36.3
Diaphragm	12.4	22.5	35.5	57.0
Spermicide	35.0	38.7	34.0	37.6

Source: Jones EF, Forrest JD. Contraceptive failure in the United States: Revised estimates from the 1982 National Survey of Family Growth. *Fam Plann Perspect* 1989; 21:103.

forms of birth control because method switching is common [17]. Writing the methods of contraception, the pregnancy rates, and the risks and benefits on a sheet of paper can help the patient make a rational choice.

Coitus interruptus (withdrawal) is practiced by a large number of adolescents who believe it to be a very effective form of contraception. Although it does have some efficacy, more effective forms of contraception should be strongly encouraged. The physician should also discuss abstinence and help patients to learn to say no when they are not ready for intercourse. Many excellent pamphlets are available from family planning agencies and the pharmaceutical firms that manufacture birth control pills; these materials allow patients to read factual information and contemplate their decision away from the medical clinic.

Since few women use the same form of contraception throughout their reproductive lives, it is important to emphasize to the young teenager that even if she chooses birth control pills initially, she may well make other choices in the future depending on her need for contraception, the frequency with which she is having intercourse, her age, parity, and her partner's preferences.

Although the mortality rate in young, sexually active women is slightly lower for barrier forms of contraception plus the selective use of induced abortion for unwanted pregnancies (Tables 15-3 and 15-4) [18], many teenagers find the possible risk of a pregnancy disturbing and a barrier method inconvenient. Many adolescents thus choose the more effective form of contraception—birth control pills. The pill is safest during the teens and twenties; it is important to remember that the risk from the pill is still substantially less than that of carrying a pregnancy to term. However, the pill offers no protection from acquiring a sexually transmitted disease.

It is also important for health care providers to address the needs of adolescents with chronic diseases, disabilities, and retardation. Ado-

Table 15-3. Cumulative Risk of Mortality from Birth-Related,
Method-Related, and Total Deaths Associated with
Control of Fertility per 100,000 Nonsterile Women,
by Fertility Control Method, According to Age-Group

Regimen	Age (years)		
	15–19	20–24	40–44
No control	35	37	141
Abortion	3	6	6
Pill/nonsmoker	3	3	160
Pill/smoker	12	18	588
IUD	6	6	10
Condom	6	8	2
Diaphragm/spermicide	10	6	14
Condom and abortion	<1	<1	<1
Rhythm	12	8	18

Source: Adapted from Ory, HW. Mortality associated with fertility and fertility control:
1983. *Fam Plann Perspect* 15:57, 1983.

lescents with chronic diseases, especially those with delayed development and undernutrition, are frequently assumed to be too sick to be sexually active or are infantilized by parents and health care providers. A discussion of sexuality and contraceptive methods is important for all adolescents. Many ill patients take chances because they falsely assume their disease has made them infertile. Patients with diseases such as Hodgkin's disease and patients requiring immunosuppression must be educated about their increased risks of persistent human papillomavirus (HPV) infection (see Chap. 11) and encouraged to use condoms with every sexual relationship. Permanent sterilization can be considered by young women with conditions such as severe heart

Table 15-4. Cumulative Number of Deaths Caused
or Averted per 100,000 Women Using Oral Contraceptives,
Then Having Two Wanted Children Followed by Tubal
Sterilization According to Age at First Birth in the United States

Age (years)	Smoker		Nonsmoker	
	Caused	Averted	Caused	Averted
20	40	111	31	111
25	65	110	41	110
30	121	108	68	108
35	244	106	133	106

Source: Adapted from Ory, HW. Mortality associated with fertility and fertility control:
1983. *Fam Plann Perspect* 15:57, 1983.

disease or cystic fibrosis, depending on the wishes of the patient. Patients with disabilities need sensitive counselling to help them through a pelvic examination, reassurance about their normal anatomy, and provision of contraception that meets their needs. Female barrier methods may not be possible for some.

Parents often bring in retarded adolescent girls for contraception. These patients, especially the mildly retarded girls, appear to be at increased risk of sexual assault or abuse. Thus depending on the environment, risk, and age of the adolescent, thoughtful discussion is needed about the choices of observation, prophylactic contraception with oral contraception or injectable progestins; or sterilization (depending on the needs of the patient and the legal issues involved). These adolescents can also benefit from education about hygiene, reproduction, contraception, and responsible sexuality.

ORAL CONTRACEPTIVE PILLS

Most teenagers choose oral contraceptive pills because of the low failure rate, the relief from dysmenorrhea, and the ease of use of a method that is not directly related to the episode of intercourse. Common pills and their hormone content are listed in Table 15-5. The majority of birth control pills are combination pills containing an estrogen and progestin. The so-called minipill contains only low-dose progestin.

The estrogen contained in the combination pills is either mestranol or ethinyl estradiol. Mestranol is converted in the liver to ethinyl estradiol; therefore, peak serum levels of ethinyl estradiol are lower and occur later after the ingestion of mestranol than after ingestion of the same dose of ethinyl estradiol. Some patients may have incomplete conversion of mestranol to ethinyl estradiol. All of the low-dose pills with 35 μg or less of estrogen contain ethinyl estradiol. The pills with 50 μg of estrogen have either mestranol or ethinyl estradiol. It is difficult to assess the exact potency of these two compounds in relation to each other because the progestin may potentiate or lessen the effects of a particular dose of the estrogen.

The progestins used in oral contraceptives are related to 19-carbon androgens, termed 19-nortestosterone derivatives, and include the estranes norethindrone, norethindrone acetate, norethynodrel, and ethynodiol diacetate and the gonane norgestrel. These progestins have varying qualities of being estrogenic, antiestrogenic, progestional (anabolic), and androgenic. Potencies are extremely controversial because of the varying tests used including animal models, delay of menses, and ability to induce glycogen vacuoles in human endometrium [19–22]. Generally, the estranes—norethindrone, norethindrone acetate, and ethynodiol diacetate—are considered fairly equipotent; norgestrel is estimated to be 5 to 10 times more potent,

459

Table 15-5. Oral Contraceptives Available in the United States

Drug	Estrogen	Dose (μg)	Progestin	Dose (mg)
Demulen 1/50	Ethinyl estradiol	50	Ethynodiol diacetate	1
Ovral	Ethinyl estradiol	50	Norgestrel	0.5
Ovcon 50	Ethinyl estradiol	50	Norethindrone	1
Norinyl 1 + 50	Mestranol	50	Norethindrone	1
Ortho-Novum 1/50	Mestranol	50	Norethindrone	1
Demulen 1/35	Ethinyl estradiol	35	Ethynodiol diacetate	1
Norinyl 1 + 35	Ethinyl estradiol	35	Norethindrone	1
Ortho-Novum 1/35	Ethinyl estradiol	35	Norethindrone	1
Brevicon	Ethinyl estradiol	35	Norethindrone	0.5
Modicon	Ethinyl estradiol	35	Norethindrone	0.5
Ovcon 35	Ethinyl estradiol	35	Norethindrone	0.4
Lo/Ovral	Ethinyl estradiol	30	Norgestrel	0.3
Loestrin 1.5/30	Ethinyl estradiol	30	Norethindrone acetate	1.5
Nordette	Ethinyl estradiol	30	Levonorgestrel	0.15
Loestrin 1/20	Ethinyl estradiol	20	Norethindrone acetate	1
Ortho-Novum 10/11	Ethinyl estradiol	35	Norethindrone	0.5 × 10 days 1.0 × 11 days
Ortho-Novum 7/7/7	Ethinyl estradiol	35	Norethindrone	0.5 × 7 days 0.75 × 7 days 1.0 × 7 days
Tri-Norinyl	Ethinyl estradiol	35	Norethindrone	0.5 × 7 days 1.0 × 9 days 0.5 × 5 days
Triphasil	Ethinyl estradiol	30	Levonorgestrel	0.05 × 6 days
Tri-Levlen		40		0.075 × 5 days
		30		0.125 × 10 days
Ovrette			Norgestrel	0.075
Nor-QD			Norethindrone	0.35
Micronor			Norethindrone	0.35

and levonorgestrel is 10 to 20 times more potent. Levonorgestrel has a longer half-life than norethindrone with no loss of drug with the first pass through the liver after absorption. Because of more sustained blood levels, levonorgestrel-containing pills are associated with less breakthrough bleeding. Other gonanes that may be used in future pills in the United States include desogestrel, norgestimate, and gestodene [23].

The combination pills prevent pregnancy by suppressing the ovarian-hypothalamic axis and thus inhibit ovulation. In addition, they alter the endometrium to make implantation unlikely, increase the viscosity of the endocervical mucus, and may have a direct effect on corpus luteum steroidogenesis. The low-dose pills have a less suppressive effect on the hypothalamic-pituitary axis, and thus a pregnancy may be more likely if pills are missed or forgotten.

Selection of the particular pill depends on the patient's needs and her response. Physicians should select a low-dose pill with 30 to

35 μg of ethinyl estradiol such as Norinyl 1 + 35, Ortho-Novum 1/35, Ortho-Novum 7/7/7, Tri-Norinyl, Triphasil, Tri-Levlen, TriMinulet, or Modicon. Some pills are more estrogen dominant and others more progestin dominant. A low-progestin pill such as Ovcon-35, Modicon, or Demulen 1/35 (or occasionally Demulen 1/50) would be more appropriate for adolescents with acne, hirsutism, or polycystic ovary syndrome. A more progestin-dominant pill is often helpful in patients with dysmenorrhea, hypermenorrhea, or previous breakthrough bleeding. The newer triphasic pills have the theoretical advantage of less total milligrams of contraceptive steroids per cycle than some monophasic pills. However, a pill such as Modicon still has less progestin than the triphasic Ortho-Novum 7/7/7. The current trend is to select pills low in both estrogen and progestin without having an excessive percentage of patients complain of breakthrough bleeding [24, 25, 26]. Although some adolescents may find the multicolored tablets confusing, most do well on the newer triphasic preparations [24]. The newest, Triphasil or Tri-Levlen, has the advantage of a start time on the first day of menses and an unusually low rate of breakthrough bleeding (6.9% of first cycle and 3.2% of total cycles) and amenorrhea (0.6% of cycles)[25]. Triphasil has less breakthrough bleeding in the first four cycles than Tri-Norinyl and Ortho-Novum 7/7/7. In a study of 317 women (18–34 years old) for a total of 4692 cycles with Triphasil, only one pregnancy occurred in a cycle in which four tablets were missed (0.28 pregnancies/100 woman-years of use); patients missed one or more tablets in 8.9 percent of the cycles [25]. A larger study of 3546 women found a use effectiveness of 0.33 pregnancies/100 woman-years [26]. In adolescents, compliance rates with triphasic pills and monophasic pills are similar at 3 months and 12 months [24].

The side effects and contraindications of oral contraceptives must be carefully understood before the pill is prescribed. Physicians are encouraged to read in detail the package insert that accompanies the pills to have a good understanding of the risks and potential problems and to become aware of the information that the patient will be reading prior to starting the pill. Counselling about risks and benefits should be documented in the medical record; many clinics use a standard informed consent form outlining any increased risks the individual may have (see Appendix 2). Although physicians are usually concerned about the serious but highly unlikely side effects from oral contraceptives, patients often have very different worries related to pill usage. In our contraceptive pill study [8], we found that inner city patients were concerned about weight gain (32%), blood clots (22%), birth defects (11%), and future fertility (10%); whereas suburban adolescents were almost exclusively worried about the possibility of weight gain (86%). Although birth defects and future fertility are not concerns for the physician as a medical consequence of prior oral contraceptive use, failure to address a patient's worries may lead to noncompliance. Our study as well as previous studies have found no significant weight gain associated with the use of low-dose oral contraceptives. In our study [8], the mean weight gain of 0.99 ± 3.3 kg of compliant oral contraceptive patients taking Norinyl $1+35$ was not statistically different from noncompliant adolescents. Similarly, Carpenter and associates [27] reported no significant difference between an oral contraceptive group and a control group in initial weight and weight after 1 year of use. Thus, care must be taken to address the worries of the individual adolescent when prescribing contraceptives. The statement "Some adolescents I see are worried about gaining weight" or "Some adolescents are worried about not being able to have children" helps initiate the dialogue between the adolescent and the health care provider. The safety of oral contraceptives in comparison with the risk of pregnancy needs to be stressed to the inner city adolescent; suburban teens should be informed that a low-dose oral contraceptive is rarely associated with weight gain.

Side Effects and Contraindications

Nausea, bloating, and weight gain
Although it is difficult to generalize because progestin and estrogen interact differently in each kind of pill, fluid retention and nausea are generally considered estrogenic side effects. Progestins can have an anabolic effect. Many patients will experience mild nausea for the first few days of taking birth control pills and sometimes for the first day of the subsequent one or two cycles. Generally, this mild nausea disappears without treatment, and most patients tolerate the low-dose pills that contain 30 to 35 µg of ethinyl estradiol quite well. However, if the nausea is persistent or bothersome to the patient, it is wise to reduce the amount of estrogen in the pill so that the patient will not discontinue her pills because of side effects. If the patient takes the pills one-half hour after dinner or with a snack at bedtime rather than in the morning, nausea is less likely to be a problem.

Weight gain is uncommonly caused by the low-dose pills; however, weight should be carefully checked at each visit. If weight gain occurs, diet (low salt), exercise, and a pill low in both estrogen and progestin usually solve the problem. Often an adolescent believes she has gained 5 to 10 pounds when in fact actual measurements show no change.

Breakthrough bleeding
Breakthrough bleeding is the occurrence of vaginal bleeding while the patient is taking hormone tablets. It occurs most frequently in the first one or two cycles, generally during the second week of the cycle; it

usually diminishes with subsequent cycles on the same pill. The patient should be told in advance about the possibility of breakthrough
bleeding so that she will not stop taking the pill because she is excessively concerned about this common side effect. Although there have
been attempts to attribute early-cycle spotting to estrogen deficiency
and late-cycle spotting to progestin deficiency, a direct correlation is
often not possible. Most patients with breakthrough bleeding for several days can be reassured that the bleeding will disappear with subsequent cycles. However, if the bleeding is particularly heavy or has
occurred because the patient has skipped or missed a pill, taking one
pill in the morning and another in the evening for several days until
the breakthrough bleeding stops is curative for the majority of patients. The additional pills should be drawn from a separate package
of pills so that the 21- or 28-day schedule is not disrupted. Another
method is to add 20 μg of ethinyl estradiol (or conjugated estrogen,
2.5 mg) daily for 7 days at the first sign of breakthrough bleeding [28],
but obtaining a second prescription for estrogen is likely to be difficult
for the adolescent patient. Other causes of bleeding should always be
considered including pregnancy (ectopic), neoplasia, and pelvic inflammatory disease (especially with *Chlamydia*).

If the breakthrough bleeding is a persistent problem after the first
three cycles or lasts an entire cycle, a change to a more progestin-
dominant pill or a triphasic pill (for example, *from* Brevicon *to* Tri-
Norinyl, Norinyl 1 + 35, or Triphasil) should be tried. Triphasil/
Tri-Levlen has less breakthrough bleeding than other triphasic pills.
If necessary, a higher dose estrogen pill can be used (for example,
changing *from* Norinyl 1 + 35 *to* Norinyl 1 + 50). Frequently after
several cycles of the higher dose pill, it is possible to resume a 35-μg
pill or a triphasic pill such as Triphasil/Tri-Levlen. It is important to
remember that breakthrough bleeding may be a sign of decreased
efficacy, especially if the patient is taking other medications, and a
backup method is advisable. If breakthrough bleeding occurs several
years after birth control pill therapy began, if it is not associated with
a missed pill and does not respond promptly to a change in dose, an
evaluation of the bleeding, including culturing for *Neisseria gonorrhoeae* and *Chlamydia trachomatis* and, often, obtaining an endometrial
biopsy specimen, should be undertaken.

Headaches
Because both migraine headaches and the use of birth control pills
appear to increase the risk of stroke (although not synergistically),
caution is obviously indicated when prescribing the birth control pill
for patients with migraine headaches. A low-dose pill may be prescribed for patients who do not wish to use other forms of contraception. The patients should be monitored closely for an increase in the

number or severity of headaches [29]. Although some patients do experience an increase in migraine headaches, others find that headaches are ameliorated, especially those with a prior increase in headaches premenstrually. A switch to the minipill or barrier contraceptive is important if symptoms increase. A prior history of migraine associated with ophthalmoplegia or hemiparesis is a contraindication to pill use.

Some patients without a history of migraine will develop headaches while taking the pill. The headaches should be evaluated to make sure that pill-induced hypertension does not account for the symptomatology. If the examination is normal, decreasing the estrogen content of the pill may alleviate symptoms. However, if headaches persist, changing to the minipill or another form of contraception may be the only solution.

Hypertension
The pill is not recommended for patients with hypertension. Approximately 1 to 5 percent of normotensive individuals will develop hypertension (a blood pressure greater than 140/90) within weeks to several months of starting the pill with the risk of hypertension increasing with age, parity, and obesity [30–34]. Noteworthy is a large study in black women that found no change in blood pressure [35].

The mechanism of development of the hypertension is still a matter of considerable controversy. The dosage of both the estrogen and the progestin in the pill may be related to the occurrence of hypertension. Oral contraceptive pills increase plasma renin substrate, renin activity, angiotensin, and aldosterone. Oral contraceptive users developing hypertension may have a predisposition to a hypertensive response to mineralocorticoids, a failure in feedback response, or an inadequate inactivation of angiotensin [36].

An elevated blood pressure usually returns to normal within 2 to 12 weeks after the pill is discontinued. Another form of contraception must be prescribed until the blood pressure returns to normal. If mild hypertension developed on a 35-μg pill, a pill lower in estrogen and progestin or the minipill is indicated; the patient's blood pressure must be monitored frequently. If hypertension recurs, the patient must use another form of contraception. The rare case of sustained hypertension that develops in a patient off the pill should be evaluated for underlying causes of hypertension.

Vascular thrombosis
The risk of developing deep vein thrombosis and pulmonary embolism has been estimated to be increased 2.8 to 4-fold for oral contraceptive users [37–41]. Nevertheless, the mortality caused by the pill is significantly less than that of carrying a pregnancy to term.

Some of the studies on thrombosis risk have been recently questioned because of the difficulty of making a clinical diagnosis of thrombophlebitis and case ascertainment [42]. The rate of false-positive clinical diagnosis varies from 25 to 83 percent. A recent large study (Puget Sound Study) of 37,807 woman-years of oral contraceptive use found 3 cases of venous thrombosis with a relative risk of 2.8 [43]. The Walnut Creek Study found no increase in thromboembolism [44]. The risk of thrombophlebitis appears to rise with increasing estrogen, and perhaps also progestin, dosage. Although the evidence is not conclusive, starting therapy with a low-dose pill is likely to reduce the possibility of thrombophlebitis. Because prior thrombophlebitis is a contraindication to the use of the pill, rigorous medical criteria should be used to determine whether a patient has thrombophlebitis. Newer methods of diagnosing thrombophlebitis include intravenous radiolabeled fibrinogen, ultrasound, and impedance plethysmography. Other factors influencing incidence rates are family history, low antithrombin III, obesity, chronic disease, and immobility [45–48].

Any adolescent on birth control pills who has significant pleuritic chest pain, hemoptysis, shortness of breath, or other symptoms suggestive of pulmonary embolism should have appropriate medical evaluation, including chest x-ray film, arterial blood gas measurement, ventilation-perfusion lung scan, and in suspected cases, angiography to confirm the diagnosis. Because two studies have found an increased risk of postoperative thromboembolism in women using oral contraceptives prior to major (especially abdominal) surgery [47, 49], current recommendations suggest that the pill should be discontinued 4 weeks before elective surgery. The possibility of an unplanned pregnancy must be weighed against the small likelihood of phlebitis in the adolescent. Higher risks are likely with prolonged bed rest and immobilization in plaster casts.

The pill is contraindicated in patients with cyanotic heart disease. Some clinicians now prescribe oral contraceptives to patients with sickle cell disease. Given the underlying risk of stroke in these women, more studies are needed to define the potential risks contrasted with needed benefits. The presence of varicose veins is no longer considered a contraindication to pill use.

An association between oral contraceptive use and stroke (including subarachnoid hemorrhage) has been reported by a number of studies. The Collaborative Group for the Study of Stroke in Young Women [39] estimated the risk of thrombotic stroke to be increased three- to fourfold, and hemorrhagic stroke twofold, by the use of oral contraceptives. These risks were further increased by hypertension, cigarette smoking, and age over 35 years [50]. In contrast, the Puget Sound Study found no increase in relative risk for cerebral vascular accident [43].

The data suggesting an association between myocardial infarction and use of oral contraceptives have been somewhat conflicting [43, 44, 51–56]. Although for women over the age of 30 years smoking and oral contraceptive use appear to increase the risk synergistically, the use of oral contraceptives alone in younger women appears to have a minimal, if any, effect on the incidence of myocardial infarction. The Walnut Creek Study found an increased incidence of acute myocardial infarction with oral contraceptives only in smokers over age 40 [44]. The Puget Sound Study found no cases of myocardial infarction among 36,807 woman-years of use [43]. A study of 119,061 women in the Nurses' Health Study found that past use of oral contraceptives did not increase the risk of subsequent cardiovascular disease [55].

Rare cases of mesenteric artery thrombosis and retinal artery thrombosis have been reported [57, 58].

Diabetes and Carbohydrate Metabolism
Early studies using middle-dose oral contraceptive pills suggested that these compounds impaired glucose tolerance. The 19-norprogestins ethynodiol diacetate and norethindrone given alone in moderate doses cause significant increases in blood glucose and insulin levels, but the most pronounced effect seems to occur with norgestrel [59, 60]. More recent studies using the lower dose formulations now available appear to show minimal, if any, impact [61–64]. Skouby and co-workers [65] found that lean nondiabetic women and women with previous gestational diabetes of normal weight without first-degree history of diabetes had unchanged glucose tolerance and insulin response to a glucose load during treatment with a low-dose triphasic oral contraceptive containing ethinyl estradiol and levo-norgestrel. A decrease in peripheral insulin sensitivity was more apparent in previous gestational diabetic women than in normal women but was not manifested by deterioration in glucose tolerance [61]. Contraceptives with 35 μg of ethinyl estradiol and 0.4 to 0.5 mg of norethindrone and the triphasic Ortho-Novum 7/7/7 have been shown to have no significant impact on glucose tolerance. More studies are needed to look at C-peptide and other indicators of carbohydrate metabolism.

Patients who are more than 30 percent overweight for height or who have a sibling or parent with diabetes have an increased risk for glucose intolerance. Although the benefits of screening have not been assessed, some physicians prefer to do a fasting blood glucose or 2-hour postprandial glucose in these patients before prescribing oral contraceptives. Such screening may be of more importance in the care of adults than adolescents. A difficult issue is the provision of contraceptive methods to the insulin-dependent diabetic. Barrier forms of contraception may seem preferable to the physician because of the association of premature atherosclerosis and diabetes and the increased risk of pill-related complications including thrombotic events, retinal artery problems, and possibly progressive retinopathy [66]. However, many adolescent and young adult diabetics need the effectiveness of oral contraception to prevent pregnancy or are unwilling to use barrier methods. Thus, the risks and benefits need to be discussed with each patient, and a pill low in progestin and estrogen should be selected [67]. Lipids should be drawn before initiating the oral contraceptive and periodically thereafter. Insulin requirements rarely change on low-dose pills. Because of continuing concern about levonorgestrel-containing pills, some centers prefer to start with pills which contain low doses of norethindrone both for diabetes and for patients with glucose intolerance.

Lipid Metabolism
There has been tremendous interest and concern about the role of oral contraceptives in altering plasma lipids [42, 68–78]. Much of the interpretation is difficult because of lack of knowledge as to whether changes have any impact on long-term morbidity. Conclusions about the association of high HDL (high-density-lipoprotein) cholesterol on the lower incidence of myocardial infarction are drawn from epidemiologic studies on men in their midlife, not from young women taking oral contraceptives. In addition, the benefit of altering HDL cholesterol in a supposedly beneficial direction has not been demonstrated. Because more than just triglycerides, cholesterol, and HDL cholesterol play a role in atherosclerosis, new interest has emerged in studying subfractions of HDL cholesterol as well as apolipoproteins [71–73, 76]. An elevated level of apolipoprotein B or depressed level of apolipoprotein A-1 (or a high ratio of apolipoprotein B/apolipoprotein A-1) has been associated with coronary heart disease.

Oral estrogens in high doses can increase liver synthesis and release of very low–density lipoproteins (VLDL), triglycerides, HDL cholesterol, and total cholesterol. Progestins are associated with a decline in HDL cholesterol and in the most antiatherogenic subfraction HDL_2. The balance of estrogen/progestin, the amount of contraceptive steroid, and the response of the individual patient determine the changes in lipid levels. Because of widely different protocols, including number and characteristics of subjects, duration of oral contraceptives, and the nature of lipoproteins studied, results must be interpreted with caution. For example, the ratios of HDL/total cholesterol and HDL/LDL cholesterol do not appear to change significantly with oral contraceptives containing less than 1 mg of norethindrone and 35 μg of ethinyl estradiol. Preliminary studies summarized by Gaspard [70] indicate an increase in both apolipoprotein A-1 and B. In a study of ethinyl estradiol, 30 μg, plus norgestrel,

0.3 mg, LDL cholesterol showed a borderline decrease, and the HDL cholesterol decreased about 10 percent with a moderate decrease in HDL_2 cholesterol. The ratios of HDL/total cholesterol, HDL/LDL cholesterol, and apolipoprotein A-1/apolipoprotein B were only slightly decreased. Krauss and associates [73] compared an oral contraceptive containing 0.4 mg of norethindrone and 35 μg of ethinyl estradiol with one containing 0.3 mg of norgestrel and 30 μg of ethinyl estradiol and reported that the norethindrone contraceptive increased HDL and total cholesterol; no changes occurred in the cholesterol/HDL cholesterol or LDL/HDL mass. In contrast, the norgestrel oral contraceptive showed no significant changes in the individual parameters of total cholesterol, HDL cholesterol, or total LDL, and a small but significant increase in the ratios of cholesterol/HDL cholesterol and LDL/HDL mass. The norgestrel but not the norethindrone hormone preparation was associated with increases in serum triglyceride and VLDL. None of the changes appeared to occur outside the normal range. A study of the Triphasil/Tri-Levlen preparations showed increases in total triglycerides and small increases in the apolipoproteins A, A-1, and A-2 with no changes in total cholesterol or HDL cholesterol [72]. It was concluded that if the assumption was correct that high LDL cholesterol and apolipoprotein B and low HDL cholesterol subfractions and apolipoprotein A were associated with an elevated risk of atherosclerosis, then the changes might be beneficial with the low-dose triphasic compounds. However, contrary to assumptions made on an epidemiologic basis in humans, studies in non-human primates suggested that even a progestin-dominant combination pill that lowered HDL cholesterol reduces the amount of arteriosclerosis [78]. The estrogen component appears to have a protective effect.

Given the problems of epidemiology, controlled studies, and extrapolation of risks to women, the most prudent course for the practitioners is to select a balanced contraceptive with a low dose of progestin and estrogen. For the individual patient with risk factors such as extreme obesity, family history of early cardiovascular disease or elevated cholesterol, or diabetes, screening serum lipids before and during pill use seems a reasonable plan. Instruction in low-cholesterol, high-fiber diets and exercise is a useful adjunct in the care of young women. Smoking should be discouraged in all adolescents.

An alternative method of contraception should be offered to patients with hyperlipidemia. Davidoff and associates [79] reported 2 patients with type IV hyperlipidemia who developed pancreatitis on the pill.

Changes in Laboratory Values
Miale and Kent [80] have compiled a list of 100 laboratory tests that are potentially altered by the ingestion of oral contraceptives. A long

list can also be found in the current *Contraceptive Technology* [19]. Among some of the effects noted are the following:

1. An increase in thyroxin (T4) and a decrease in resin triiodothyronine (resin T3) levels secondary to an increase in thyroid binding globulin. There is no change in free T4 or the clinical status of the patient.
2. Slightly increased levels of coagulation factors II, VIII, IX, X, and XII, increased Factor VII, and reduced antithrombin III activity. This tendency to hypercoagulability appears counterbalanced by an increase in fibrinolytic activity. The increase in clotting factors and decrease in antithrombin III occur to a lesser extent with 30-μg oral contraceptives than with 50-μg oral contraceptives [80–83]. Triphasic pills containing low-dose levonorgestrel may have less impact on the hemostatic system than older hormonal combinations. In fact, Farag and co-workers [48] have recently questioned whether the low-dose oral contraceptives have any impact on in vivo markers of hypercoagulability. However, patients with a family history of thromboembolism appeared predisposed to have a decrease in antithrombin III with oral contraceptive use and therefore may represent an at-risk group who would benefit from testing.
3. Decreased serum folate concentration occurs in some patients taking oral contraceptives. In our study [84], 37 percent of adolescents taking Norinyl 1 + 50 or Brevicon and 21 percent of controls had low serum folate level (less than 5.0 ng/ml). Low whole-blood folate values were seen in 33 percent of pill users and only 15 percent of controls; this was more likely to occur in white than black patients. However, nonusers were more likely to have low levels of ferritin than pill users, probably because of the diminished menstrual flow on the pill. Although the long-term use of the pill may rarely be associated with the development of megaloblastic anemia, in our study of adolescents there were no cases of megaloblastic anemia in spite of low folate levels and inadequate diets. More data on long-term pill use are needed.
4. Women who have reduced hepatic reserve because of an inherited or acquired defect may become jaundiced while taking oral contraceptives [85, 86]. Women with a history of recurrent cholestatic jaundice of pregnancy should not be given the pill. The pill is also contraindicated in patients with active hepatitis, and liver function tests should be checked prior to reinstituting the pill in such patients. Although a prior study suggested an association between the pill and admissions for gallbladder surgery, recent data have found no excess risk [87, 88]. However, the pill may accelerate gallbladder disease in women with susceptibility to this problem.

Collagen disease
Previously, the pill was contraindicated in patients with lupus ery-thematosus; however, low-dose pills are prescribed for some young adolescents with lupus when the risks of an unwanted pregnancy outweigh the increased risks of the pill [89]. Most patients with rheu-matoid arthritis will tolerate the pill well; however, occasionally, in-creased symptoms of the disease appear to be related to oral contra-ceptive therapy. Conflicting studies have shown either no effect or a protective effect of oral contraceptives on the development of rheu-matoid arthritis [90, 91].

Epilepsy
Although in the past epilepsy was considered a relative contraindica-tion to pill use, recent evidence has not demonstrated any increase in seizures with current formulations [92–94]. In fact, patients with a history of an increase in seizures in the premenstrual and/or men-strual phase of the cycle may benefit from oral contraceptive use.

The major problem with oral contraceptive use in epileptics is the potential for lowered efficacy of the pill and decreased anticonvulsant levels [95, 96]. Anticonvulsants such as phenobarbital, phenytoins, carbamezine, and primidone increase the metabolism of synthetic steroids by increasing conjugation in the gut and enzyme induction in the liver. In addition, these drugs increase the production of sex hormone binding globulin to which the progestin is bound [97]. The degree of induction is not predictable at the current time, although assays for contraceptive steroid levels may be commercially available in the future. The pregnancy rate for women on enzyme-inducing anticonvulsants is 3.1/100 woman-years of use [94]. Valproate has not been associated with oral contraceptive failure [98].

Generally, we initially prescribe a pill with 30 to 35 μg of ethinyl estradiol, informing the patient of the increased risk of pregnancy. A backup method such as condoms is suggested. Although not proved, the persistence of breakthrough bleeding in patients on anticonvul-sant therapy may imply lowered efficacy and the need to change to a pill with more estrogen (50 μg) and a more potent progestin. A barrier method should be used in cycles with breakthrough bleeding. Some clinicians reduce the pill-free interval from 7 days to 4 to 5 days with the hope of lowering the pregnancy risk; others advise prescribing only 50-μg oral contraceptive pills.

Drug Interactions
As noted, anticonvulsants and oral contraceptives have important drug interactions. In addition, the use of rifampicin also diminishes the efficacy of the pill [99–101]. Whether other antibiotics such as ampicillin or tetracycline alter efficacy is debatable, although a barrier

method should be advised, especially if breakthrough bleeding occurs [101]. Antidepressant levels should be monitored after initiating the pill; toxicity may occur because of increased bioavailability. The half-life of diazepam is prolonged with oral contraceptives [102]; the drugs apomorphine and meperidine have been noted to have increased central nervous system depression [19]. Mineral oil and oral contraceptive pills should not be taken at the same time. Asthmatics on theophylline preparations should have levels measured after starting oral contraceptives.

Oligomenorrhea or amenorrhea
Scanty or absent withdrawal flow, most commonly associated with progestin-dominant pills and the new low estrogen pills, may develop months or even several years after continuous use. If a patient becomes amenorrheic, she should continue taking her pills and the possibility of pregnancy should be evaluated promptly. A pregnancy test and physical examination will reassure the physician and patient that the diagnosis is pill amenorrhea. Menses may return spontaneously, or amenorrhea may persist. For persistent amenorrhea, a change to a more estrogenic pill by decreasing the amount or potency of progestin (e.g., Norinyl 1 + 35 to TriNorinyl or Brevicon; or Lo/Ovral to TriPhasil) or increasing the amount of estrogen (e.g., Norinyl 1 + 35 to Norinyl 1 + 50) may produce withdrawal flow. A small amount of supplemental estrogen (ethinyl estradiol, 20 µg or conjugated estrogens, 0.625–1.25 mg) can be added to the pills for 21 days for one to three cycles. Often normal cycles will persist even when the original lower dosage is resumed. Over the long term, it is best to try to find a pill with 30 to 35 µg of estrogen for the patient.

Patients with persistent amenorrhea (or very light spotting) can check basal body (oral) temperatures for 3 days during the 7-day hormone-free interval (on placebos). If no pills have been missed and the temperature is below 98°F, pill amenorrhea is likely and the pills can be continued. Temperatures above 98°F may imply a viral infection or incorrectly measured temperature, but a sensitive pregnancy test should be done. In adolescents with "pill amenorrhea," it is best to err on the side of too many pregnancy tests (e.g., monthly or every 2 months) because of the increased likelihood of missed pills and noncompliance. Patients on oral contraceptive therapy should be reassured that a 1- to 3-day light withdrawal flow is perfectly normal.

After discontinuation of the pill, 1 to 2 percent of patients develop post-pill amenorrhea [103–105]. Approximately 95 percent of these patients revert to regular periods within 12 to 18 months. It has been argued that such amenorrhea is perhaps no more common than in a control population [106]. Nevertheless, patients who have a history of oligomenorrhea or delayed menarche before starting oral contraceptives appear to have an increased risk of developing post-pill amenorrhea. As noted in Chapter 6, the cause of oligomenorrhea should be investigated in any patient so that the most appropriate form of contraception can be selected. For example, a patient with polycystic ovary syndrome and hirsutism may be appropriately treated with birth control pill suppression but will likely return to oligomenorrhea after the pill is discontinued. Patients who lose weight or engage in endurance sports while taking birth control pills appear to be more susceptible to post-pill amenorrhea. After discontinuing the pill, pill users have the same pregnancy and delivery rates as diaphragm users by 30 months in parous women and 42 months in nulliparous women [107].

Patients with amenorrhea of more than 6 months' duration following the cessation of birth control pill therapy or with galactorrhea or headaches should have a pelvic examination and serum levels of follicle-stimulating hormone (FSH), luteinizing hormone (LH), and prolactin measured. In adolescents, pregnancy must be an important consideration regardless of the number of weeks or months of amenorrhea.

Eye problems
Rarely, patients may develop dry eyes from lack of tearing or from corneal edema. Contact lens users should be warned about these possible effects; reduction of the estrogen dosage may be helpful. Optic nerve or retinal disease are contraindications to contraceptive pill therapy. The pill should be discontinued immediately if visual symptoms, especially transient loss of vision, occur since retinal thrombosis, optic neuritis, and ophthalmoplegic migraine may occasionally be associated with pill use.

Depression
Subjective symptoms such as depression, nervousness, or emotional lability appear to be associated with oral contraceptive use in some patients [108, 109]; however, evaluating these side effects is obviously difficult. Mood scales measured by the Minnesota Multiphasic Personality Inventory and several placebo-controlled studies have failed to document a dramatic increase in the occurrence of depression [110–112]. Although depression has been ascribed to a change in tryptophan metabolism and to reduced levels of serotonin in the cerebrospinal fluid [108, 113], other causes for the depression or emotional lability should be explored. A change to a different hormone preparation or discontinuing the pill may improve the subjective effects that the patient or physician feels are related to the pill. Supplementation with vitamin B_6 appears to lessen depression in some patients, but long-term effects are unknown.

Alopecia
Hair loss may be due to many stresses; therefore, it is difficult to establish the pill as a definite cause in most cases. In very rare instances, the pill may be a precipitating cause. A change to a more estrogenic pill may be helpful [58].

Pregnancy outcome
There is no increase in the incidence of congenital anomalies in patients who have previously taken birth control pills [114]. Whether the incidence of congenital anomalies (limb bud defect, congenital heart disease) is increased in women who have inadvertently taken pills during the first trimester of pregnancy is still a subject of controversy; if there is a risk, it is extremely low [114–120]. Nevertheless, hormonal pregnancy tests and oral contraceptive pills should be avoided during pregnancy.

Neoplasms
Although most studies to date, including Centers for Disease Control data on over 4700 women, have found no lifetime increase in breast cancer with the use of oral contraceptive pills [121–124], subgroup analysis of early and prolonged use is continuing to determine possible risk. After 2 years of continuous use, the pill may actually protect against benign breast lesions [125–127]. Although an increased incidence of cervical dysplasia and progression to carcinoma in situ has been reported in pill users, pill users may have higher rates of sexual activity, an increased number of partners, and an earlier age of beginning coitus [128–132]. The nonuse of a barrier method by the oral contraceptive user increases the likelihood of being infected with human papillomavirus (HPV; see Chap. 11). The immature cervix of the adolescent (likely to be a pill user) exposed to certain types of HPV increases the possibility of dysplasia. In addition, adolescents who are substance users, including tobacco, are more likely to be sexually active at an early age. Pill users are under increased surveillance with Papanicolaou smears because of the need for a prescription. Until all confounding variables are carefully examined, the risk, if any, of cervical dysplasia and cancer attributable to oral contraceptive use cannot be defined.

Although endometrial cancer has been associated with unopposed estrogen therapy in postmenopausal women [133, 134] and with the sequential birth control pills [135] (removed from the market in 1977), ever or current use of the combination pill reduces the incidence of endometrial cancer, probably because of the progestin. The protective effect increases with duration of use and lasts for at least 5 years after usage is stopped. For a duration of 2 years or longer of use there appears to be a 50 percent reduction in risk [136–139].

Benign ovarian cysts are less common in oral contraceptive users (see Chap. 13). Several studies have found a protective effect of oral contraceptives on the occurrence of ovarian cancer [140–142]. In the Centers for Disease Control study, oral contraceptive users had 0.6 the risk of epithelial ovarian cancer as nonusers [142]. The protective effect occurred with as little as 3 to 6 months of use and continued for 15 years after use ended.

Although the data have been interpreted in different ways, benign liver tumors may be increased by oral contraceptive therapy, especially in patients who have been taking the pill more than 5 years [139, 143, 144]. The risk of hepatocellular adenoma has been estimated to be between 1 and 2 per 100,000 users [145, 146]. However, in British studies, which included over a quarter of a million woman-years of use, no liver tumors were found [147]. The higher risk found for pills containing mestranol than those containing ethinyl estradiol has been attributed to the metabolism of this compound in the liver and to the percentage of the market occupied by these pills in the late 1960s and 1970s. A recent study at the Armed Forces Institute of Pathology suggested that the association of one type of hepatic tumor (fibrolamellar) occurs in the same age group that would be taking oral contraceptives, and thus an age-related bias in establishing an association may have occurred [148]. Patients with hepatocellular adenoma may have an abdominal mass, vague upper abdominal pain, or acute pain with circulatory collapse following hemorrhage.

Skin
The majority of pill users, especially those taking estrogen-dominant pills, note an improvement in acne. Patients taking the low-dose pills, especially those containing moderate doses of norgestrel or norethindrone acetate, may notice a mild exacerbation of acne. Acne usually improves with most pills, especially Brevicon, Modicon, Ovcon 35, and Triphasil/Tri-Levlen.

Chloasma has been noted in a small number of oral contraceptive users. It is more common in dark-skinned patients who are exposed to sunlight and taking higher dosage oral contraceptives [58].

It is unlikely there is any association of oral contraceptives and melanoma when the confounding factor of sun exposure is included in data analysis. More studies are needed; sunscreens should be advised for all patients.

Infections
Although oral contraceptives were thought earlier to be associated with an increased possibility of *Candida* vaginitis, more recent data have not confirmed this association.

Oral contraceptive usage lessens the risk of being hospitalized with pelvic inflammatory disease, but adolescent oral contraceptive users are at an increased risk of having *Chlamydial trachomatis* isolated from the cervix (see Chap. 10). The increased risk may be secondary to factors such as the non-use of barrier methods and the presence of a prominent and persistent cervical ectropion in adolescent pill users.

The ease of using oral contraceptives to prevent pregnancy may cause adolescents to forget about the equally important goal of preventing sexually transmitted diseases. Monogamous relationships and the use of condoms in addition to pills should be stressed to avoid exposure to HPV, human immunodeficiency virus (HIV), and other diseases. Education of adolescents is essential to prevent future morbidity and mortality.

PATIENT EVALUATION WHEN PRESCRIBING ORAL CONTRACEPTIVES
The long list of side effects, indications, and contraindications for birth control pills makes it mandatory that the physician take a complete medical history and perform a general physical examination, including blood pressure and breast and pelvic examinations, before prescribing the pill. Absolute contraindications include thromboembolic disease, cerebrovascular or coronary artery disease, breast cancer, estrogen-dependent neoplasia, undiagnosed genital bleeding (applicable primarily to older women), pregnancy, and liver tumors.

In adolescents, appropriate laboratory studies typically include urinalysis (or dipstick urine), hemoglobin level, Papanicolaou smear, endocervical tests for *Neisseria gonorrhoeae* and *C. trachomatis*, and serology for syphilis. The prevalence of these infections in sexually active adolescents in general and in a given adolescent population should be considered. All sexually active adolescents should be screened for *C. trachomatis* at least annually, more often if the patient is symptomatic or there is a change in partners. Screening for *N. gonorrhoeae* is more apt to be cost-effective in inner city patients, adolescents with multiple partners and early age of coitus, pregnant adolescents, symptomatic patients, and those with other sexually transmitted diseases. The incidence of *N. gonorrhoeae* is very low in college students and suburban adolescents in monogamous relationships. Similarly, a blood test for syphilis is indicated in high-risk patients and those with other sexually transmitted diseases. Vaginal washings or other sampling for HPV infection may soon be applicable to clinical practice. High-risk adolescents should be offered HIV testing; all adolescents should receive counselling on disease prevention and risk reduction, especially with regard to HPV and HIV (see Chap. 11).

Lipid levels (cholesterol, HDL cholesterol, triglycerides) should be done at minimum in patients who are obese or who have a family history of early arteriosclerotic heart disease or hypercholesterolemia. Indeed, as part of routine health care, probably all adolescents should have a determination of serum cholesterol at some point, preferably prior to initiating oral contraceptives. Patients should be counselled to stop smoking, although the risk from the pill and smoking is most striking after the late twenties.

For the patient with a history of regular menses and no particular indication for an estrogen- or progestin-dominant pill, selection of a pill containing 30 to 35 μg of estrogen is appropriate (e.g., Norinyl 1 + 35 or Ortho-Novum 1/35, Tri-Norinyl, Ortho-Novum 7/7/7, Brevicon or Modicon, Triphasil or Tri-Levlen). The possible occurrence of breakthrough bleeding for the first few cycles should be explained in detail, and the patient should be encouraged to call if any problems are worrying her. In a patient with borderline motivation or in whom prior discontinuance of the pill has been caused by breakthrough bleeding, a pill such as Norinyl 1 + 35, Ortho-Novum 1/35, Triphasil, Tri-Levlen, or Lo/Ovral, should be tried. A patient who has previously had nausea or bloating on the pill should be given a pill with less estrogen. Patients are instructed in possible side effects—headache, nausea, blood clots, and breakthrough bleeding. The acronym ACHES can be helpful to the patient and the physician for reviewing serious side effects: A—abdominal pain (severe); C—chest pain (severe), cough, shortness of breath; H—headache (severe), dizziness, weakness, numbness, speech problems; E—eye problems (vision loss or blurring); S—severe leg pain (calf or thigh) [19]. The patient should be instructed to read the package insert, and many centers use an informed consent form as an educational tool (Appendix 2). The benefits of the pill, including less iron-deficiency anemia, less dysmenorrhea, a lowered incidence of benign breast disease and uterine and ovarian cancers, less pelvic inflammatory disease, and increased bone density, should also be pointed out to the adolescent.

The patient should then be given a prescription or a 3-month supply of pills and asked to return to the clinic in 1 to 3 months to check weight, blood pressure, and side effects, the closer spacing helpful for high-risk patients. The patient who is older and who sought medical care specifically to obtain a contraceptive can be seen in 3 months and encouraged to call if any special problems arise. The younger teenager, or the teenager who has been having intercourse for months to years without adequate contraception, should be encouraged to return in 6 weeks or even sooner to continue the dialogue on contraceptive choices.

Most pills are available in 21- and 28-day packages; the latter have seven tablets that contain no hormones (these are placebos in all brands except Loestrin, which contain iron). The majority of teenagers do best using a 28-day pill, since it is easier to remember to take a pill every day rather than for 21 days and then not for 7 days. With the exception of Triphasil and Tri-Levlen, the patient is instructed to start on the Sunday following the first day of menses (unless menses starts on a Sunday, then the pills are started that day). An alternative method of starting is to commence pills on the fifth day of the menstrual cycle. This method is only possible for pills that do not have a Sunday start written on the packaging; in addition, pill switching is more difficult. For Tri-Levlen or Triphasil, pills are started on the first day of the menstrual cycle. Patients who are amenorrheic and have no possibility of early pregnancy should be given Provera to initiate withdrawal flow before starting oral contraceptives. The patient is instructed to take one pill daily at about the same time each day, preferably after dinner or at bedtime.

Adolescents frequently miss pills and thus should receive careful instructions on methods of dealing with this problem. If a pill is missed, the patient is instructed to take it as soon as she remembers; if two pills are missed in the first 2 weeks, then she is advised to take 2 pills on the day she remembers and 2 pills the next day. If 2 pills in a row are missed in the third week *or* 3 pills or more in a row in any week, Sunday starters take 1 pill per day until Sunday, throw away the unused portion of the rest of the current pack and start a new pack that day. The importance of a backup method (foam and condom, diaphragm, abstinence) for 7 days, preferably until the next cycle, should be stressed. The patient will likely experience breakthrough bleeding with missed pills. Written instructions (Appendix 1) can save phone calls; however, they are not a substitute for careful instruction in the office. The sheets should mainly serve as a guide for education of the patient, since many patients misplace these sheets soon after the visit.

The follow-up visit includes a blood pressure and weight check and questioning about what side effects were experienced. Not infrequently, the nausea and breakthrough bleeding that the patient experienced taking the first cycle of pills have disappeared by the third cycle. Adjustments in pill dosage can be made as suggested in the section on side effects. The adolescent is then seen at least every 6 months for renewal of the pill prescription, blood pressure and weight check, and breast and pelvic examinations. It is clear that patients with the potential for discontinuance should be seen more frequently to assess contraceptive compliance.

The Progestin-Only Minipill

For the patient who is unable to tolerate estrogen at any dosage, the minipill (progestin-only) may offer another option [149–152]. We have found it useful in patients with chronic disease such as cyanotic heart disease, those who have developed hypertension with the contraceptive pill, and lactating teens. The pregnancy rate is considerably higher (1.5–3.0 pregnancies/100 woman-years of use [up to 8/100 if pills are missed]) and may be unacceptable in some patients. The greatest disadvantage to the minipill is the irregular bleeding that many patients experience. The pill is taken every day at the same time, not cyclically as are the combination pills. It has several modes of action; foremost it alters cervical mucus, inhibiting sperm penetration. It also alters the endometrium in most women and in some patients blocks hypothalamic feedback mechanisms, thereby eliminating the midcycle LH surge (and ovulation). Since ovulation is not inhibited in many patients and pill failure is higher, pregnancy (especially ectopic) should be considered in patients with irregular bleeding or amenorrhea.

The thrombophlebitis risk has not been established but appears to be minimal. The coagulation changes associated with combination pills are not evident with the progestins in short-term studies. Hypertension is usually not a problem, but blood pressure should be monitored, especially in patients who previously developed hypertension on the combination pill. Carbohydrate and lipid metabolism are probably not affected in most patients, although Spellacy and associates [153] reported that 16 percent of women on norgestrel, 0.075 mg daily, had an abnormal glucose tolerance test after 18 months of use.

INTRAUTERINE DEVICES

Although, theoretically, the intrauterine device (IUD) is not as effective at preventing pregnancy as the birth control pill, it does offer the advantage that the side effects are limited principally to the female genital tract; it also does not require daily motivation to take a pill. It would then superficially appear to be the ideal form of contraception for adolescents, since pill failures are frequently related to discontinuance of or forgetting the pill. Unfortunately, the most serious side effect of the IUD—the risk of pelvic infection and possible future infertility—has sharply limited the use of this device in sexually active adolescents [154–158]. Adolescents who are most likely to be noncompliant with oral contraceptives and barrier methods are at highest risk of sexually transmitted infections such as N. *gonorrhoeae* and C. *trachomatis*.

Currently available IUDs are a progesterone impregnated IUD (Progestasert) and the new Copper T 380A [158–160]. The Progestasert must be replaced every 12 months; the Copper T380A is approved for 4 years of use. The pregnancy rate for Progestasert is 2.1 pregnancies/100 woman-years of use, and less than 2/100 for the Copper T380A. The exact mechanism of action of the IUD is unknown. The inert IUDs may prevent implantation by causing a low-grade endometritis. The contraceptive action of copper containing IUDs is probably secondary to the effect of the copper on various endometrial enzymes [161, 162]. The Progestasert releases small amounts of progesterone, which prevents pregnancy by local action on the endometrium and thickening cervical mucus [163].

IUDs are mostly useful for women over 30 years old, in stable monogamous relationships, who have had at least one child or preferably have completed childbearing [28]. Infection and its sequelae are the principal worry for IUD users. The newer IUDs have a much lower risk of pelvic inflammatory disease than the Dalkon Shield. The risk of pelvic inflammatory disease has been estimated to range from 1.6- to 3.1-fold greater for women using an IUD than for other sexually active women (the Dalkon Shield had a risk 4 to 5 times higher than other IUDs) [154, 155, 164–166]. Recent insertion within 4 months or reinsertion appears to increase the risk; women less than 25 years of age appear especially susceptible, perhaps because they are more likely to have more than one sexual partner [164]. A Swedish study [166] found a substantially higher risk (6.9) of pelvic inflammatory disease in nulliparous IUD users than in parous IUD users (1.7), but the U.S. Women's Health Study [167] did not confirm this difference. As is the case with age, such a difference may be related to the number of sexual partners. In fact, Kirshon and associates [168] did not find that current or past use of an IUD (Lippes Loop, Saf-T-Coil, and Copper 7) was associated with pelvic adhesions at the time of laparoscopic tubal sterilization. Most pelvic inflammatory disease diagnosed in patients with an IUD has the same bacterial flora seen in pelvic inflammatory disease not associated with IUD use (see Chap. 10); however, pelvic abscesses are more common in patients using an IUD. The patient presenting with PID should have the IUD removed and should be treated with the appropriate antibiotics.

Many patients experience increased vaginal discharge with the IUD in place, probably secondary to irritation from the string passing through the endocervical canal. Nevertheless, all cases of increased vaginal discharge should be evaluated for the possibility of infection. Other complications include heavy menses and irregular bleeding (with occasional anemia), dysmenorrhea, uterine perforation [169], loss of IUD strings and thus difficulty in removal, and pregnancy. If a pregnancy occurs with the device in situ, the IUD should be removed because there is a possible risk of septic abortion, which was first identified in association with the Dalkon Shield (subsequently removed from the market) [170]. Any patient who conceives with an IUD in place should be evaluated to exclude the possibility of an ectopic pregnancy. The risk of an extrauterine pregnancy occurring appears to be highest in patients using the Progestasert IUD. Since

IUDs are so effective in preventing intrauterine pregnancies, it is not surprising to find an excess of ectopic pregnancies among IUD users (3–4% in IUD users versus less than 1% among other women) [28]. Although bacteremia is rare with first insertions and removal of IUD, Murray and co-workers [171] have recently reported that 13 percent of 23 women who were having IUDs replaced had bacteremia 4 to 6 minutes after insertion of the new device. This finding is of importance in the care of patients with valvular heart disease at risk for bacterial endocarditis and immunosuppressed patients.

DIAPHRAGM
Because of the adverse publicity in the late 1970s about the pill and the IUD and concerns about sexually transmitted infections, an increasing number of young women switched to barrier forms of contraception in the 1980s. The diaphragm has become popular with older adolescents, especially those in their senior year of high school or in college. Young adolescents who are comfortable with their bodies can be taught to use a diaphragm effectively [172, 173]; however, the majority of the younger adolescents still prefer a hormonal form of contraception. Only an extremely motivated, mature adolescent who is able to cope with the increased risk of an unplanned pregnancy should rely on this form of contraception. Fisher and colleagues [173] reported that in a suburban-based adolescent clinic serving adolescent girls (13–20 years old), adolescents selecting diaphragms over the pill were better students, were of higher socioeconomic status, and had had fewer prior pregnancies. Continuous use for 12 months was reported by 43 percent of diaphragm users and 45 percent of pill users; however, regular use (diaphragm every intercourse, missing ≤1 pill/month) was reported by 36 percent of diaphragm users and 88 percent of pill users. Fifteen percent of those who initially selected a diaphragm and 18 percent of those who selected the pill became pregnant during the 12 months.

The diaphragm is fitted by the health care provider. There are four types of diaphragms available: the arcing spring, the coil spring, the flat spring, and the wide seal rim (Fig. 15-1). Diaphragms come in sizes between 55 and 95, but for most adolescents the sizes of 60 to 75 are most useful. Actual diaphragms rather than fitting rings should be used because the patient can then practice taking the diaphragm in and out before leaving the clinic.

The arcing spring ring provides firm pressure on the lateral vaginal walls and is therefore especially good for patients with poor vaginal tone, mild uterine prolapse, or marked uterine anteflexion or retroversion. The arcing spring diaphragm is useful for most adolescents because the diaphragm can be compressed to give a leading edge for

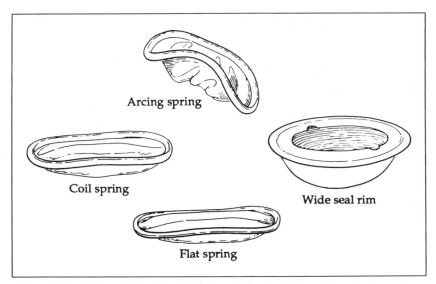

Figure 15-1. Types of diaphragms. (From Hatcher RA, et al., Contraceptive Technology, 1988–89. Atlanta: Irvington, 1988. By permission.)

ease of insertion. The allflex (Ortho) arcing diaphragm folds at any point along its rim and must be held in the center, whereas the Koroflex folds at two points and can be more easily held at the end.

The coil spring rim, which folds flat for insertion, can be used for most women with average vaginal tone and a normal pubic notch. Both the arcing spring and the coil spring are readily available by prescription in pharmacies.

The flat spring has a thin rim and is generally worn by nulliparous women with firm vaginal tone and a shallow arch behind the symphysis. This type of diaphragm may not be available in all pharmacies.

The wide seal rim (Milex) is currently distributed directly to physicians and clinics. The wide seal has a flexible flange on it to create a better seal and is available in arcing spring and coil spring. The arcing model folds in two places but has a light spring, which may make it useful for the adolescent who has experienced discomfort with other arcing spring diaphragms or who has had recurrent cystitis.

The size of the diaphragm is estimated by the examiner's placing a gloved index finger and middle finger in the vagina until they reach the posterior vaginal wall behind the cervix. The thumb is then placed on top of the index finger to mark the point at which the index finger touches the pubic bone. The fingers are removed in this position and the diaphragm size is determined by placing the tip of the middle finger against the rim and the opposite rim against the spot on the

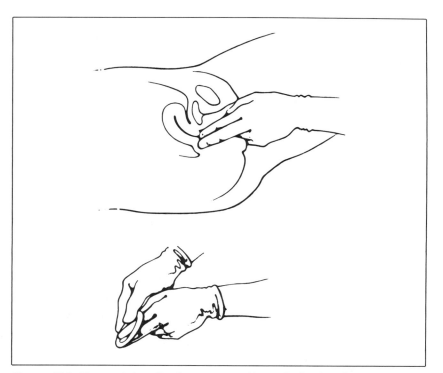

Figure 15-2. Determining diaphragm size. (From Ortho Diaphragms. Raritan, N.J.: Ortho Pharmaceutical Corp., 1981. By permission.)

index finger previously marked with the thumb (Fig. 15-2). The diaphragm should fit snugly, since vaginal size increases with sexual stimulation and coitus. Virginal patients who can be fitted because of having an adequate size introitus should have the size of the diaphragm checked after the first four to eight episodes of coitus. A too loose diaphragm will be displaced; a too large diaphragm can cause pressure and urinary tract infections.

The pregnancy rates reported with diaphragm use vary from 2.5 to 23 pregnancies/100 woman-years of use, with most studies reporting 10 to 18 pregnancies [19, 174]. The most common cause of failure in adolescents is nonuse. Other causes include an incorrect fit, a flawed device, and failure to insert additional spermicide with a second episode of intercourse. Occasional adolescents cannot be fitted with a diaphragm because of poor vaginal tone, congenital anomalies, uterine prolapse, or rectovaginal or vesicovaginal fistulas. Some patients develop an allergy to the rubber or the spermicide and can benefit from a change to different products.

An increased risk of urinary tract infections has been noted, with a 2-fold increase in risk in a case control study and a 2.5-fold increase in a retrospective study [175]. Vaginal colonization with *Escherichia coli* was significantly greater in diaphragm users. Thus, a change in diaphragm type or size, postcoital antibiotics, or a change to a different method of contraception may be necessary in adolescents with recurrent urinary tract infections associated with diaphragm use.

Other problems with the diaphragm include foul-smelling vaginal discharge associated with prolonged wearing of the diaphragm, pelvic discomfort, and vaginal ulceration from excessive rim pressure. Because of the rare association of diaphragm use and toxic shock syndrome (p. 330), patients should probably not leave a diaphragm in for more than 12 hours, should not use a diaphragm during menses (a condom should be used), and should learn about warning signs of the disease.

The diaphragm does have the benefit of offering some protection against sexually transmitted infections, probably in part because of the physical barrier effects of the diaphragm but also because of the antiviral and antibacterial properties of spermicides. The risk of pelvic inflammatory disease is less in diaphragm users than noncontraceptors and the same as pill users [176]; the risk of cervical neoplasia is less in diaphragm users than pill users and noncontraceptors [177].

The patient should be given careful instructions, preferably written, on the use and care of the diaphragm. Before a prescription is given, the patient should be shown how to feel for her cervix and should have an opportunity during the office visit to insert the diaphragm and remove it. Teaching aids such as the Ortho pelvic model and the Omni Health Communicator cassettes* are very helpful for the adolescent. Local Planned Parenthood clinics and diaphragm manufacturing companies can usually supply the physician with additional pamphlets and information sheets. A return appointment 2 to 3 weeks later to check for proper fit of the prescribed size allows the physician a chance to assess the patient's understanding and acceptance of this form of contraception.

The patient is given the following instructions:

1. Wash hands with soap and water.
2. Place 1 to 2 teaspoonsful of contraceptive jelly or cream inside the cup of the diaphragm and spread a small amount around the entire rim. The diaphragm can be inserted up to 6 hours prior to intercourse. If more than 6 hours has elapsed, an extra applicatorful of cream inserted into the vagina in front of the diaphragm provides added protection. (Many women routinely insert the diaphragm every night.) Never use Vaseline or petroleum products on the diaphragm.

*Omni, Education Division of Ortho Pharmaceuticals, Raritan, NJ 08869.

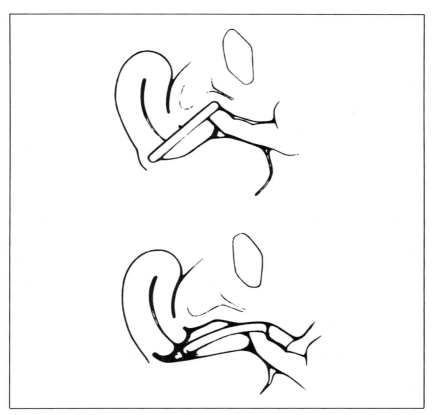

Figure 15-3. A technique for removal of the diaphragm. (From Ortho Diaphragms. Raritan, N.J.: Ortho Pharmaceutical Corp., 1981. By permission.)

3. After inserting the diaphragm, check the cervix to make sure that it is covered by the diaphragm.
4. Leave the diaphragm in place for at least 6 hours but not more than 12 hours after intercourse, and do not douche during the 6 hours after intercourse.
5. To remove the diaphragm, insert a forefinger up and over the top side of the diaphragm. Turn the palm of the hand downward and backward, hooking the finger firmly inside the top rim, breaking the suction. Pull the diaphragm down and out (Fig. 15-3).*
6. After removal, wash the diaphragm with Ivory soap and dry it thoroughly (dust it with corn starch, if desired, but do not use talcum or scented powders).
7. Before each use, hold the diaphragm up to the light and check for holes.

*Some companies recommend that the diaphragm be removed with the finger inside the top rim.

8. The diaphragm should be replaced at least every 2 years and at any time a small tear or "puckered" appearance near the rim is noted. If there is a weight change of 10 pounds or a pregnancy, a physician should be consulted to make sure that the diaphragm still fits.

CERVICAL CAP

A cervical cap is similar to a diaphragm except that it is made of rigid plastic and is designed to cover only the cervix. A small amount of spermicide is placed in the cap (about ⅓ full of a potent spermicide), and the cap is inserted onto the cervix; it is held in place by suction.

Although cervical caps have been available for a number of years and have been used for artificial insemination, the use of the cap as a contraceptive was not approved until 1988. The recently approved Prentif Cavity-Rim Cervical Cap is available in four sizes and is intended to be fitted for the individual patient. An instruction manual is listed in Additional Reading at the end of this chapter. One tenth to one third of women cannot be fitted, although the introduction of custom-molded caps may alleviate some of this problem in the future. Patients do better with using the cap if they feel comfortable with insertion of tampons and diaphragms into the vagina. Instructions on insertion and removal of the devices can be time-consuming. The Food and Drug Administration (FDA) has recommended that the device can be left in place for a maximum of 48 hours and that it should not be worn during menses. It should be left in place 8 hours after intercourse. It is not necessary to reapply spermicide with repeated intercourse, but the cap should be checked before and after intercourse (especially in the first month of use) to make sure it has not been dislodged. Use of additional spermicide in the vagina and/or use of a condom seems prudent in the first 2 months after fitting and with a new position or new partner.

The pregnancy rates are comparable to those of the diaphragm, with rates varying from 7.6 to 17 pregnancies/100 woman-years of use [178–183]. In a study of over 3400 women, Richwald and colleagues [179] estimated first year pregnancy rate to be 11.3 percent (8.3 percent and 3.8 percent for user and method failure). "Near perfect" users had half the pregnancy rate of others (6.1 versus 11.9 percent). During the National Institutes of Health (NIH) trials, 4 percent of cap users compared to 1.7 percent of diaphragm users experienced Papanicolaou smear changes from class I to III in the 3-month study period [183]. Conversion rates beyond this period were similar. Richwald's study [179] found only 2.7 percent converted from Class I to II and 0.2 percent from class I to III in 6 months. Further studies of this issue are needed. In the meantime, the cap is contraindicated in patients with abnormal Pap smears; Pap smears should be done at the time of fitting and 3 months later. Other problems with the cap include odor (which appears to be worse with the use of oil-based spermicides), dislodgement, vaginal discharge, partner discomfort, and difficulty with insertion or removal. One type of cap, the Vimule cap, was associated with vaginal lacerations during clinical trials and is not in use [184]. Contraindications to use of a cap include known or suspected uterine or cervical malignancy and current vaginal and cervical infections. Practitioners usually wait 6 to 8 weeks postpartum and 3 to 4 weeks post abortion to fit a cap. The patient should return for annual gynecologic examination, Pap smear, and cap fitting. Although a theoretic risk, no cases of toxic shock have been reported to date; however, postmarketing surveillance will be important to assess this risk.

CONTRACEPTIVE SPONGE

The contraceptive sponge Today, approved by the Food and Drug Administration in 1983, is a disposable polyurethane foam sponge impregnated with nonoxynol 9. The sponge's efficacy as a contraceptive is based on the release of spermicide, the barrier effect, and the absorption of semen. The dose of spermicide is 1 gm, which is significantly more than one application of other spermicide products (60–100 mg); thus, coitus can occur multiple times without addition of more spermicide within the recommended wearing period of 24 hours. The sponge can be inserted just before intercourse or in advance. It is very important that the sponge is moistened with 2 tablespoons of clean tap water and squeezed once before insertion. The concave side is inserted next to the cervix with the string out. The sponge must be left in place for 6 hours after the last intercourse. Problematic for adolescents are the need to be near a source of water at the time of insertion and the fact that removal can result in fragmentation of the device. Sponge users are more likely to discontinue this method because of allergic reactions (especially vaginal itching) than diaphragm users. One study in an extremely high-risk overseas population found that the sponge offered some protection against C. trachomatis and N. gonorrhoeae [185]. The risk of toxic shock has been estimated at 10 in 100,000 users; thus, adolescents selecting this device should not use it during the menses and should be educated about the warning signs. Pregnancy rates are reported between 13 and 26 pregnancies/100 woman-years of use [19, 186–188]. In one study [187], nulliparous patients had much lower rates of pregnancy (13.9 for the sponge and 12.8 for the diaphragm) than parous women (28.3 for the sponge and 13.4 for the diaphragm). A more recent study [188] that emphasized the importance of wetting the sponge found a pregnancy rate of 13.3 pregnancies/100 woman-years, with no difference between parous and nulliparous women. The advantage for the adolescent is that the sponge does not require a prescription or fitting and is less messy than the diaphragm. However, given the significant failure rate, condoms should be used in conjunction with all spermicides to increase the protection against pregnancy and sexually transmitted diseases.

FEMALE CONDOM
The introduction of a new barrier method, the female condom, offers an additional alternative for patients, especially in the era of heightened awareness of sexually transmitted diseases. WPC-333 (Wisconsin Pharmacal Company) is a loose fitting polyurethane sheath with 2 diaphragm-like flexible rings at either end. The inner ring covers the cervix (similar to a diaphragm) and the outer ring fits against the vulva. The device is disposable and is expected to be available over the counter in the 1990s. Similar devices are being tested in Europe.

SPERMICIDES
Spermicides include vaginal creams, jellies, foams, suppositories, and films. Spermicides are also important for the efficacy of the sponge, and spermicide-impregnated condoms have become increasingly popular because of the potential antiviral and, importantly, anti-HIV properties of spermicides in vitro [189]. These methods are important for the adolescent because they are available over the counter without the necessity of a health care visit. The pregnancy rates for spermicides alone have ranged from 3 to 30 pregnancies/100 woman-years of use; the lower rate can be achieved by educated, motivated women in their thirties who are given specific in-office demonstration of appropriate use and application (high in the vagina) of spermicides [19, 188–193]. Whenever possible, the adolescent should use the spermicide in combination with a diaphragm or condom.

The jellies, creams, and foams should be inserted no more than 30 minutes before intercourse and are effective within several minutes (foam immediately, but gels and creams need a few minutes to reach body temperature to melt). In contrast, the suppositories require 10 to 15 minutes to melt or effervesce. The suppositories appear more unpredictable in their dispersion, and many patients using the effervescing Encare Ovals notice extreme vaginal warmth and burning. However, the small size of the suppositories makes them attractive to adolescents. The newest form of spermicide is VCF (vaginal contraceptive film). The wax paper–like tissues come in a 2- by 2-inch flat package, with each film containing 72 mg of nonoxynol 9. The film should be inserted on the finger tip up into the vagina at least 5 minutes before intercourse and remains effective for 2 hours.

Although an early study suggested a possible association between spermicides and congenital anomalies [194], recent studies including FDA data have not proved any link [195–199]. Patients may have difficulty with odor and allergic reactions to the spermicides. During counselling, specific names of foams (Emko, Delfen), suppositories (Semicid, Intercept), and film (VCF) should be mentioned. A demonstration of how to fill the applicator with foam is useful. Individual one-dose applicators (Conceptrol) are convenient for adolescents but are also more expensive than the refillable applicators.

Our instructions to the teenage girl are the following:

1. Insert the contraceptive foam, suppository, or film high into the vagina so that it will cover the cervix. Use the foam 30 minutes or less *prior* to intercourse (not after intercourse).
2. Do not douche for at least 6 hours after intercourse.
3. Keep an extra condom with the contraceptive foam, since using the combination lessens the risk of failure.

CONDOMS

The advantage of the condom is that a teenager does not need a prescription to purchase them. The emergence of AIDS in the 1980s and recognition of the sequelae of many other sexually transmitted infections, especially *Chlamydia* and HPV infections, have resulted in increased interest in condoms, not only as a contraceptive but for prevention of the transmission of sexually transmitted diseases [200]. Although Americans have traditionally had low rates of condom usage compared to other developed nations, especially Japan, there is evidence that creative approaches in clinics, advertising, and marketing could improve usage. For example, educational efforts to improve the image of condom users and the provision of free condoms in drug stores and clinics and mail-in coupons has dramatically increased the usage in some urban settings. Men have become more actively involved in responsible contraception by such programs as "Condom Sense," MARCH (Men Acting Responsibly for Contraception and Health), and "Men Too" [19].

Adolescent girls frequently are not assertive about the use of condoms when the male rejects the notion. It is helpful for the health care provider to give the patient some ideas to bolster her self-esteem as well as some catchy phrases such as "If you don't use one, you can't use me," "My doctor says I must protect my cervix," and "You don't know how? Allow me." Sexually active adolescent girls should be encouraged to purchase condoms and keep them with their spermicide or oral contraceptive pills. Adolescents with chronic diseases that require treatment with immunosuppressive medications should receive additional education from their health care provider about avoiding exposure to HPV. Some condoms are now marketed exclusively for women and are shelved in pharmacies with other feminine hygiene products. Young women can be encouraged to place them on the man's penis to make the condom part of lovemaking. Many adolescents feel more comfortable purchasing contraceptive supplies from an unfamiliar pharmacy. It is clear that education of adolescents has increased knowledge about AIDS and condoms for the prevention of sexually transmitted diseases but may not have increased usage. Kegeles and associates [201] found that adolescents did not feel personally vulnerable to contracting diseases from their partners. Grace and co-workers [13] found that even adolescents with a personal history of a sexually transmitted infection were no more likely to use condoms than patients who had never had an infection. It is clear that we need more creative efforts to help adolescents delay the age of becoming sexually active and, once active, encourage responsible sexuality.

The pregnancy rate of condoms has varied in studies from 2 to 20 pregnancies/100 woman-years of use, with good usage resulting in pregnancy rates of 3 to 4 [19, 28, 190]. Condoms also provide significant protection against sexually transmitted diseases including *N. gonorrhoeae*, *C. trachomatis*, HIV, and cytomegalovirus. Depending on the location of the lesions, condoms also provide a barrier to herpes simplex and HPV. Because of the larger pores in natural condoms, the smaller particles of hepatitis B virus can pass through, and thus latex condoms are preferred for prevention of sexually transmitted diseases. Newer condoms that contain spermicides have the advantage of greater inactivation of sperm as well as antiviral properties. In vitro studies of condoms containing nonoxynol 9 have demonstrated that condoms offer an excellent physical barrier against HIV and that the addition of the spermicide prevented the detection of HIV even after rupture of the condom [189]. Epidemiologic studies have suggested that condoms are very effective in preventing AIDS transmission in patients who are consistent users. However, intercourse with an infected partner still poses a risk to the patient. The condom is also useful both in prevention and in the treatment of cervical dysplasia; consistent usage has been associated with significant regression of abnormalities. Pregnant teens should be encouraged to use condoms throughout pregnancy to prevent exposure to sexually transmitted infections.

Condoms may be lubricated or unlubricated, with the former being preferred by most adolescents. As mentioned previously, condoms also may be lubricated with spermicide, which increases the cost but also the protection. Although condoms may be used alone, it is preferable for adolescents to use both a vaginal spermicide and a condom. It is unknown whether thick condoms offer any more protection than thin condoms with vaginal intercourse, although thin condoms may be more likely to tear. Instruction is extremely important, with a demonstration if possible. Just the statement "Use condoms" may otherwise go unheeded. Condoms should not be exposed to excessive heat (i.e., in a wallet for more than 2 weeks or in a glove compartment).

The Center for Disease Control has made a number of suggestions including the following [200]:

1. Latex condoms are preferred because they offer greater protection against sexually transmitted diseases.
2. Condoms should be stored in a cool, dry place.
3. Condoms in damaged packages (brittle, sticky, discolored) should not be used.
4. Condoms should be put on before any genital contact. The tip of the condom should be held and the condom unrolled onto the erect penis, leaving space at the tip to collect semen, yet ensuring that no air is trapped in the tip.
5. Adequate lubrication should be used. Only water-based lubricants (such as K-Y Jelly, Surgilube) should be used, NOT petroleum-based lubricants such as Vaseline.
6. Use of condoms containing spermicide may offer greater protection although the use of a vaginal spermicide is likely to be even better.
7. If the condom breaks, it should be replaced. If ejaculation occurs after breakage, immediate application of a spermicide has been suggested although efficacy is unknown. Postcoital contraception (p. 492) should also be considered. It has been estimated that the risk of a broken condom is one per 161 acts of intercourse.
8. After ejaculation, the base of the condom should be held to prevent slippage. The penis should be withdrawn while still erect.

MEDROXYPROGESTERONE (DEPO-PROVERA)
Medroxyprogesterone acetate (Depo-Provera) is an injectable contraceptive that is, at the time of this writing, not approved as a contraceptive in the United States, although it is marketed for other indications. The American Academy of Pediatrics has endorsed the usefulness of this drug in certain limited situations (e.g., in some retarded teenagers). Sickle cell disease may be another indication. This drug has been used widely in developing countries but has been restricted here because of the rare occurrence of prolonged amenorrhea and extended time to the return of fertility, the occurrence of breast tumors in beagle dogs, possible teratogenity in the event of conception, and perceived lack of need [19, 202, 203]. A World Health Organization (WHO) study has not found an increase in breast or liver tumors in humans; Depo-Provera has a protective effect on ovarian and endometrial cancer [204]. The issue of teratogenity is unresolved but is unlikely to be a major problem because of the very effective contraception this drug offers.

Medroxyprogesterone, 150 mg intramuscularly every 3 months, suppresses the hypothalamic-ovarian axis and prevents the midcycle LH surge. In addition, it produces thinning and sometimes profound atrophy of the endometrium and increases the viscosity of the cervical mucus. The pregnancy rate of women given medroxyprogesterone is 0 to 0.4/100 woman-years.

The most important side effect is menstrual irregularities; patients often experience irregular spotting and, occasionally, very heavy periods during the first few months of therapy. The heavy bleeding usually responds to estrogen therapy so that a dilatation and curettage is rarely indicated. After 6 months (or 3 injections of medroxyprogesterone), most patients are amenorrheic. If desired, withdrawal menses can be produced by administering 0.04 mg of ethinyl estradiol for 7 to 10 days each month. A useful regimen for introducing Depo-Provera is oral medroxyprogesterone, 10 mg daily for 2–3 weeks (to ensure no adverse reactions to progestins), then Depo-Provera 150–200 mg IM every 2–3 weeks for 3 doses, 150 mg IM every 6 weeks for 2–3 doses, then 150 mg IM every 3 months (T. Elkins, personal communication). Side effects of medroxyprogesterone include headaches, nervousness, weight gain, nausea, vomiting, decreased glucose tolerance, and lowered HDL cholesterol. The risk of thromboembolic disease is probably not increased [203].

Because of the possible risk of delayed return of ovulatory cycles, the drug should not be prescribed for women who need a contraceptive to space their children. Data [202] indicate, however, that 82 percent of the 135 women studied became pregnant within 14 months of discontinuing medroxyprogesterone. This statistic can be compared with an 88 percent pregnancy rate 12 months after removal of an IUD and a 94 percent pregnancy rate 12 months after discontinuation of the pill.

Another injectable contraceptive used overseas is norethindrone enanthate (Noristerat), with pregnancy rates under 2/100 woman-years of use (two studies showing a rate of 0.4 and 0.6). Because a large WHO study showed a failure rate of 3.6 at 12 months with the pregnancies occurring 10 to 12 weeks following the last dose, the dosage was altered to 200 mg every 2 months for the first 6 months and then 200 mg every 90 days thereafter. Side effects are similar as those noted for Depo-Provera, although bleeding tends to be more regular [204–209]. Mean time to return of ovulation was 2.6 months for Noristerat compared to 5.5 months for Depo-Provera.

SUBDERMAL IMPLANTS

Norplant implants, which are nonbiodegradable Silastic implants slowly releasing levonorgestrel, are being marketed in a number of countries [19, 210–212]. The first Norplant system has six Silastic rods that are implanted through a small incision in a woman's upper or lower arm and are effective for 5 years; Norplant-2 has two Silastic rods that are effective for 3 years. The Norplant system releases approximately 39 μg of levonorgestrel each day, giving a blood level of 0.23 to 0.3 ng/ml. The pregnancy rate is 0.3 to 0.7 pregnancies/100 woman-years of use. Insertion should be performed in the immediate postabortal or postpartum period or within the first 7 days of the cycle. The main reason for discontinuation of Norplant is menstrual problems, chiefly frequent irregular bleeding. No unfavorable changes in carbohydrate metabolism, liver function, blood pressure, ectopic pregnancy, or total menstrual loss have been reported. Studies on lipids are conflicting, and further data need to be collected. It appears that the cholesterol/HDL cholesterol ratio is unchanged or only minimally decreased. Continuation rates are 60 to 90 percent at 1 year. Among those wishing a pregnancy, three quarters became pregnant within 1 year after discontinuing this method.

Several biodegradable implants are also in research and development. Capronor is a caprolactone polymer with levonorgestrel [213]. Alzamer is a polymer that undergoes hydrolytic erosion in contact with tissue and releases levonorgestrel or norethindrone for 4 to 6 months.

No studies have been carried out in adolescents, although the potential for effective contraception without the need for a daily action such as taking a pill is appealing. Whether adolescents will be willing to accept the possibility of a minor surgical procedure with the likelihood of more complicated consent procedures and the risk of discovery of the implant by a parent is at this point unknown. It may be most useful in teen mothers. More long-term data on safety would also be reassuring to the clinician.

NATURAL FAMILY PLANNING

The use of calendars, basal body temperature charts, cervical mucus awareness, and more recently hormonal testing have been used both for contraception and for facilitating the possibility of pregnancy in infertile couples [214, 215]. The advantages are the ease of the method and the fact that adolescents can be taught the method as a noncontroversial part of reproductive health. Some have felt that adolescents aware of their bodies are more likely to act in a sexually responsible manner. However, the major drawback is the high failure rate for pregnancies and the lack of protection against sexually transmitted diseases. Although the method does encourage communication between sexual partners, extensive records are required and sexual spontaneity is restricted. Calendar methods are less likely to help adolescents than adults because of the wider range of cycles seen in adolescents. It is hard to imagine that adolescents with their erratic schedules could take daily basal body temperatures. The Billings method of cervical mucus awareness is based on determining ovulation by the change of mucus to abundant slippery mucus. Secretions can be affected by coitus, vaginitis, cervicitis, and vaginal medications and spermicides. An unanswered question is whether the pregnancies that do occur are more likely to involve the fertilization of old ova and possibly increase the risk of congenital anomalies or miscarriage. Test kits that measure enzymes in cervical mucus may also be marketed soon. Most of the high-technology methods of hormonal assays are more appropriate for the treatment of infertile couples.

The pregnancy rates reported are variable and range from 6 to 38 pregnancies/100 woman-years of use, depending on the population studied and the method employed [19, 214–218].

POSTCOITAL CONTRACEPTION

High-dose estrogens have been shown to lower the risk of pregnancy significantly following unprotected intercourse. This form of therapy is used primarily in situations such as rape, first intercourse, or a broken condom. There is no doubt that more adolescents need to be made aware of the availability of postcoital contraception. High-dose estrogens were used in the past, including conjugated estrogens, 15 to 25 mg twice a day for 5 days, and ethinyl estradiol, 2.0 to 2.5 mg twice a day for 5 days. The Yuzpe regimen, which utilizes two tablets of Ovral (50 μg of ethinyl estradiol and 0.5 mg of norgestrel per tablet) within 72 hours (preferably within 24–48 hours) of unprotected intercourse followed by two tablets 12 hours later, is preferable at this time [219–222]. In general, a pregnancy test should be performed first, and the patient should be informed of the risks and benefits. The patient should be willing to have an abortion if she is already pregnant by a previous exposure, although the risks of four oral contraceptive tablets to an early embryo is minimal, if any. The hormones produce endometrial asynchrony, probably leading to insufficient nutrition of the blastocyst at the moment of implantation. A strong history of previous ectopic pregnancy may be a contraindication to this method.

Treatment with all of the high-dose estrogens can be associated with nausea and vomiting. Prochlorperazine (Compazine), 5 to 10 mg orally 2 hours prior to the second dose, may be important if the patient has difficulty with the first dose. Other possible side effects include fluid retention, headaches, dizziness, menstrual irregularities, and breast soreness. The patient is warned against having intercourse for the remainder of the cycle. Van Santen and Haspels [222] reported a pregnancy rate with the Yuzpe regimen of 1.5 percent versus an expected rate of 4.75 percent in one group of women and a rate of 0.5 percent versus an expected 5.5 percent in another group.

Schilling [221] found no pregnancies among a group of 115 college students treated with the doses of the Yuzpe regimen.

FUTURE DEVELOPMENTS IN CONTRACEPTION
Because of the side effects of birth control pills and the IUD and the lower efficacy of barrier methods, research continues for improved forms of contraception. Methods under development include vaginal rings that release progestin, luteinizing hormone releasing hormone analogues, vaccines, and a variety of potential methods for men [19, 223]. Studies are ongoing with RU 486 (mefepristone), a competitive progesterone antagonist that may be useful in the late follicular or midluteal phases as a contraceptive agent or in early pregnancy as an abortifacient [224]. This agent also has potential as a postcoital contraceptive.

REFERENCES
1. Zabin LS, Hard JB, Smith EA, et al. Substance abuse and its relation to sexual activity among inner city adolescents. J Adolesc Health Care 1986; 7:320.
2. Mosher WD, and Horn MC. First family planning visits by young women. Fam Plann Perspect 1988; 20:33.
3. Chamie M, Eisman S, Forrest JD, et al. Factors affecting adolescents' use of family planning clinic. Fam Plann Perspect 1982; 14:126.
4. Zabin LS, and Clark SD. Institutional factors affecting teenagers' choice and reasons for delay in attending a family planning clinic. Fam Plann Perspect 1983; 15:25.
5. Furstenberg FF, Shea J, Allison P, et al. Contraceptive continuation among adolescents attending family planning clinics. Fam Plann Perspect 1983; 15:211.
6. Zelnik M, Koenig MA, and Kim YJ. Sources of prescription contraceptives and subsequent pregnancy among young women. Fam Plann Perspect 1984; 16:6.
7. Zabin LS, Clark SD. Why they delay: A study of teenage family planning clinic patients. Fam Plann Perspect 1981; 13:205.
8. Emans SJ, Grace E, Woods ER, et al. Adolescents' compliance with the use of oral contraceptives. JAMA 1987; 257:3377.
9. Kisker EE. The effectiveness of family planning clinics in seeing adolescents. Fam Plann Perspect 1984; 16:212.
10. Zabin LS, Hirsch MD, and Smith EA. Evaluation of a pregnancy prevention program for urban teenagers. Fam Plann Perspect 1986; 18:119.
11. Zelnik M, Kim YJ. Sex education and its association with teenage sexual activity, pregnancy and contraceptive use. Fam Plann Perspect 1982; 14:117.
12. Zabin LS, Hirsch MB, and Smith EA, et al. Adolescent sexual attitude and behavior. Are they consistent? Fam Plann Perspect 1984; 16:181.
13. Grace E, Emans SJ, and Woods ER. The impact of AIDS awareness on the adolescent female. Pediatr Adolesc Gynecol 1989; 2:40.
14. Durant RH, Joy MS, and Linder CW, et al. Influence of psychosocial factors on adolescent compliance with oral contraceptives. J Adolesc Health Care 1984; 5:1.
15. Scher PW, Emans SJ, and Grace EM. Factors associated with compliance

to oral contraceptive use in an adolescent population. J Adolesc Health Care 1982; 3:120.

16. Litt IF. Know thyself: Adolescents' self assessment of compliance behavior. Pediatrics 1985; 75:693.

17. Hirsh MB, and Zelnik M. Contraceptive method switching among American female adolescents, 1979. J Adolesc Health Care 1985; 17:53.

18. Tietze C. New estimate of mortality associated with fertility control. Fam Plann Perspect 1977; 9:74.

19. Hatcher RA, Guest F, Stewart F, et al. Contraceptive Technology, 1988–89. Atlanta: Irvington, 1988.

20. Edgren RA, and Sturtevant FM. Potencies of oral contraceptives. Am J Obstet Gynecol 1976; 125:1029.

21. Dorflinger LJ. Relative potency of progestins used in oral contraceptives. Contraception 1985; 31:557.

22. Gilmer MD. Progestogen potency in oral contraceptive pills. Am J Obstet Gynecol 1987; 57:1040.

23. Runnebaum B, and Rabe T. New progestogens in oral contraceptives. Am J Obstet Gynecol 1987; 157:1059.

24. Woods ER, Grace E, Emans SJ, et al. Contraceptive compliance with a monophasic and triphasic pill (in press).

25. Hanson MS, Stewart GK, Bechtel RC, et al. Planned Parenthood experience with Triphasil. J Reprod Med 1987; 32:592.

26. Woutersz TB, Butler AJ, Cohen M, et al. A low dose triphasic oral contraceptive. Fertil Steril 1987; 47:425.

27. Carpenter S, and Neinstein LS. Weight gain in adolescent and young adult oral contraceptive users. J Adolesc Health Care 1986; 7:342.

28. Grimes DA. Reversible contraception for the 1980s. JAMA 1986; 255:69.

29. Nicolson DH, and Walsh FB. Oral contraceptives and neuroophthalamic disorders. J Reprod Med 1969; 3:37.

30. Greenblatt D, and Kochweser J. Oral contraceptives and hypertension. Obstet Gynecol 1974; 44:412.

31. Kunin CM, McCormack RC, and Abernathy JR. Oral contraceptives and blood pressure. Arch Intern Med 1969; 123:362.

32. Fisch IR, Freedman SH, and Myatt AV. Oral contraceptives, pregnancy and blood pressure. JAMA 1972; 22:1507.

33. Connell EB. Oral contraceptives: The current risk-benefit ratio. J Reprod Med 1984; 29:513.

34. Kols A, Rinehart W, Piotrow P, et al. Oral contraceptives in the 1980's. Popul Rep [A], 1982; No. 6.

35. Blumenstein BA, Douglas MB, and Hall WD. Blood pressure changes and oral contraceptive use: A study of 2,676 black women in the southeastern United States. Am J Epidemiol 1980; 112:539.

36. Tapia HR, Johnson CE, Strong CG. Effect of oral contraceptive therapy on renin-angiotensin system in normotensive and hypertensive women. Obstet Gynecol 1973; 41:643.

37. Inman W, Vessey MP, Westerholm B, et al. Thromboembolic disease and the steroidal content of oral contraceptive pills: A report to the committee on safety of drugs. Br Med J 1970; 2:203.

38. Boston Collaborative Drug Surveillance Program. Oral contraceptives and venous thromboembolic disease, surgically confirmed gallbladder disease and breast tumors. Lancet 1973; 1:1399.

39. Collaborative Group for the Study of Stroke in Young Women. Oral contraception and increased risk of cerebral ischemia or thrombosis. N Engl J Med 1973; 288:871.

40. Sartwell PE, Masi AT, Arthes FG, et al. Thromboembolism and oral contraceptives: An epidemiologic case-control study. Am J Epidemiol 1969; 90:365.
41. Meade TW. Update: Cardiovascular effects of oral contraception and hormonal replacement therapy. (Risks and mechanisms of cardiovascular events in users.) Am J Obstet Gynecol 1988; 158:1646.
42. Goldzieber JW. Hormonal contraception: Benefits versus risks. Am J Obstet Gynecol 1987; 157:1023.
43. Porter JB, Hunter JR, Jick H, et al. Oral contraceptives and nonfatal vascular disease. Obstet Gynecol 1985; 66:1.
44. Ramcharan S, Pellegrin FA, Ray RM, et al. The Walnut Creek contraceptive drug study: A prospective study of the side effects of oral contraceptives. J Reprod Med 1980; 25(suppl 6):345.
45. Jick H. Venous thromboembolism and ABO blood type. Lancet 1969; 1:539.
46. Vessey MP, and Doll R. Investigation of relations between the use of oral contraceptives and thromboembolic disease, a further report. Br Med J 1969; 2:651.
47. Vessey MP, Doll R, Fairbairn AS, et al. Postoperative thromboembolism and the use of oral contraceptives. Br Med J 1970; 3:123.
48. Farag AM, Bottoms SF, Mammen EF, et al. Oral contraceptives and the hemostatic system. Obstet Gynecol 1988; 71:584.
49. Greene GR, and Sartwell PE. Oral contraceptive use in patients with thromboembolism following surgery, trauma or infection. Am J Public Health 1972; 62:680.
50. Pettiti DB, and Wingerd J. Use of oral contraceptives, cigarette smoking, and risk of subarachnoid hemorrhage. Lancet 1978; 2:234.
51. Stadel B. Oral contraceptives and cardiovascular disease. N Engl J Med 1981; 305:672.
52. Rosenberg I, Armstrong B, and Jick H. Myocardial infarction and estrogen therapy in premenopausal women. N Engl J Med 1976; 294:1290.
53. Mann JL, Inman WH, and Thorogood M. Oral contraceptive use in older women and fatal myocardial infarction. Br Med J 1976; 2:445.
54. Jain AR. Cigarette smoking, use of oral contraceptives and myocardial infarction. Am J Obstet Gynecol 1976; 126:301.
55. Stampfer MJ, Willett WC, and Colditz GA. A prospective study of past use of oral contraceptive agents and risk of cardiovascular diseases. N Engl J Med 1988; 319:1313.
56. Goldbaum GM, Kendrick JS, Hogelin GC, et al. The relative impact of smoking and oral contraceptive use on women in the United States. JAMA 1987; 258:1339.
57. Hoyle M. Small bowel ischaemia and infarction in young women taking oral contraceptives and progestromal agents. Br J Surg 1977; 64:533.
58. Tyrer LB. Oral contraceptive practice. In Corson SL, Derman RJ, and Tyrer LB (eds.). Fertility Control. Boston: Little, Brown, 1985.
59. Perlman JA, Russell-Briefel R, Eczati T, et al. Oral glucose tolerance and the potency of contraceptive progestogens. J Chronic Dis 1985: 38:857.
60. Spellacy WN, Birksa, Buggie J, et al. Prospective studies of carbohydrate metabolism in "normal" women using norgestrel for 18 months. Fertil Steril 1981; 35:167.
61. Spellacy WN, Buhi WC, Birk SA. Carbohydrate metabolism with three months of low-estrogen contraceptive use. Am J Obstet Gynecol 1980; 138:151.
62. Skouby SO, Kühl C, Mølsted-Pedersen L, et al. Triphasic oral contracep-

tion: Metabolic effects in normal women and those with previous gestational diabetes. Am J Obstet Gynecol 1985; 153:495.

63. Skouby SO, Mølsted-Pedersen L, Kühl C, et al. Oral contraceptives in diabetic women: Metabolic effects of four compounds with different estrogen/progestogen profiles. Fertil Steril 1986; 46:858.

64. Skouby SO, Andersen O, Saurbrey N, et al. Oral contraception and insulin sensitivity: *In vivo* assessment in normal women and women with previous gestational diabetes. J Clin Endocrinol Metab 1987; 64:519.

65. Skouby SO, Andersen O, and Kühl C. Oral contraceptives and insulin receptor binding in normal women and those with previous gestational diabetes. Am J Obstet Gynecol 1986; 155:802.

66. Steel JM, and Duncan LJ. Serious complications of oral contraception in insulin dependent diabetes. Contraception 1978; 17:291.

67. Radberg T, Gustafson A, Skryten A, et al. Oral contraception in diabetic women: A cross-over study on serum and high density lipoprotein (HDL), lipids and diabetes control during progestogen and combined estrogen/progestogen contraception. Horm Metab Res 1982; 14:61.

68. Ginsburg KA, and Moghissi KS. Alternate delivery systems for contraceptive progestogens. Fertil Steril 1988; 49:16S.

69. Crook D, Godsland IF, and Wymann V. Oral contraceptives and coronary heart disease: Modulation of glucose tolerance and plasma lipid risk factors by progestins. Am J Obstet Gynecol 1988; 158:1612.

70. Gaspard UJ. Metabolic effects of oral contraceptives. Am J Obstet Gynecol 1987; 157:1029.

71. Burkman RT, Robinson JC, Kruszon-Moran D, et al. Lipid and lipoprotein changes associated with oral contraceptive use: A randomized clinic trial. Obstet Gynecol 1988; 71:33–38.

72. Marz W, Gross W, Gahn G, et al. A randomized cross over comparison of two low-dose contraceptives: Effects on serum lipids and lipoproteins. Am J Obstet Gynecol 1985; 153:287.

73. Krauss RM, Roy S, Mishell DR, et al. Effects of two low-dose oral contraceptives on serum lipids and lipoproteins: Differential changes in high-density lipoprotein subclasses. Am J Obstet Gynecol 1983; 145:446.

74. Powell MG, Hedlin AM, Cerskus I, et al. Effects of oral contraceptives on lipoprotein lipids: A prospective study. Obstet Gynecol 1984; 63:764.

75. Wahl P, Walden C, Knopp R, et al. Effect of estrogen/progestin potency on lipid/lipoprotein cholesterol. N Engl J Med 1983; 308:862.

76. Wynn V, and Niththyananthan R. The effect of progestins in combined oral contraceptives on serum lipids with special reference to high-density lipoproteins. Am J Obstet Gynecol 1982; 142:766.

77. Wallace RB, Tamir I, Heiss G, et al. Plasma lipids, lipoproteins, and blood pressure in female adolescents using oral contraceptives. J Pediatr 1979; 95:1055.

78. Adams MR, Clarkson TB, Koritnik DR, et al. Contraceptive steroids and coronary artery disease in cynomolgus macaques. Fertil Steril 1987; 47:1010.

79. Davidoff F, Tishler S, and Rosoff C. Hyperlipidemia and pancreatitis associated with oral contraceptive therapy. N Engl J Med 1973; 289:552.

80. Miale JB, and Kent JW. The effects of oral contraceptives on the results of laboratory tests. Am J Obstet Gynecol 1974; 120:264.

81. Bonnar J, Sabra A. Comparative data on the effects of low-dose oral contraceptives on coagulation: Update on Triphasic oral contraception. Excerpta Medica, 1983.

82. Notelovitz M, Zauner C, McKenzie L, et al. The effect of low-dose oral

contraceptives on cardiorespiratory function, coagulation, and lipids in exercising young women: A preliminary report. Am J Obstet Gynecol 1987; 156:591.

83. Bonnar J. Coagulation effects of oral contraception. Am J Obstet Gynecol 1987; 157:1042.
84. Grace EA, Emans SJ, and Drum D. Hematologic abnormalities in adolescents on birth control pills. J Pediatr 1982; 101:771–774.
85. Adlercreutz H, and Tenhunen C. Some aspects of the interaction between natural and synthetic female sex hormones and the liver. Am J Med 1970; 49:630.
86. Ockner RK, and Davidson CS. Hepatic effects of oral contraceptives. N Engl J Med 1967; 276:331.
87. Royal College of General Practitioners' Oral Contraception Study. Oral contraceptives and gallbladder disease. Lancet 1982; 2:957.
88. Layde PM, Vessey MP, and Yeates D. Risk factors for gall-bladder disease: A cohort study of young women attending family planning clinics. J Epidemiol Community Health 1982; 36:274.
89. Chapel T, and Burns R. Oral contraceptives and exacerbation of lupus erythematosus. Am J Obstet Gynecol 1971; 110:366.
90. Vandenbroucke JP, Witteman JCM, Valkenburg HA, et al. Noncontraceptive hormones and rheumatoid arthritis in perimenopausal and postmenopausal women. JAMA 1986; 255:1299.
91. Del Junco DJ, Annegers JF, Luthra HS, et al. Do oral contraceptives prevent rheumatoid arthritis? JAMA 1985; 254:1938.
92. Mattson RH, and Cramer JA. Epilepsy, sex hormones and antiepileptic drugs. Epilepsia 1985; 26(suppl 1):S40.
93. Dana-Haeri J, and Richers A. Effects of norethindrone on seizures associated with menstruation. Epilepsia 1983; 24:377.
94. Mattson RH, Cramer JA, Darney PD, et al. Use of oral contraceptives by women with epilepsy. JAMA 1986; 256:238–240.
95. Janz D, and Schmidt D. Anti-epileptic drugs and failure of oral contraceptives. Lancet 1974; 1:1113.
96. Laengner H, and Deterine K. Anti-epileptic drugs and failure of oral contraceptive drugs. Lancet 1974; 2:600.
97. Back DJ, Breckenridge AM, Crawford FE, et al. The effect of oral contraceptive steroids and enzyme inducing drugs on sex hormone binding globulin capacity in women. Br J Clin Pharmacol 1980; 9:115.
98. Crawford P, Chadwick D, Cleland P, et al. The lack of effect of sodium valproate on the pharmacokinetics of oral contraceptive steroids. Contraception 1986; 33:23.
99. Pettiti D. Oral contraceptive drug interactions. P P Med Digest 1981; 2:1.
100. Back DJ, Breckenridge AM, Crawford FE, et al. The effects on rifampicin on the pharmokinetics of ethinylestradiol in women. Contraception 1980; 21:135.
101. Szoka PR, and Edgren RA. Drug interactions with oral contraceptives: Compilation and analysis of an adverse experience report database. Fertil Steril 1988; 49:318.
102. Abernathy DR, Greenblatt DJ, Divoll M, et al. Impairment of diazepam metabolism by low-dose estrogen-containing oral-contraceptives steroids. N Engl J Med 1982; 306:791.
103. Evrard J, Buxton BH, Erickson D. Amenorrhea following oral contraception. Am J Obstet Gynecol 1976; 124:88.
104. Shearman RP. Prolonged secondary amenorrhea after oral contraceptive therapy: Natural and unnatural history. Lancet 1971; 2:64.

105. Shearman RP. Secondary amenorrhea after oral contraceptives: Treatment and follow-up. Contraception 1975; 2:123.
106. Hull MG. Normal fertility in women with post pill amenorrhea. Lancet 1981; 1:1329.
107. Vessey MP, Wright NH, McPherson K, et al. Fertility after stopping different methods of contraception. Br Med J 1978; 1:265.
108. Grant EC, and Pryse-Davies J. Effect of oral contraceptives on depressive mood changes. Br Med J 1968; 3:777.
109. Herzberg BN, Draper KC, Johnson AL, et al. Oral contraceptives, depression and libido. Br Med J 1971; 3:495.
110. Kutner SJ, and Brown WL. History of depression as a risk factor for depression with oral contraceptives and discontinuance: Types of oral contraceptives, depression and premenstrual symptoms. In Ramcharon S (ed.). The Walnut Creek Contraceptive Drug Study: A Prospective Study of the Side Effects of Oral Contraceptives. Bethesda, Maryland: U.S. Dept. H.E.W., 1976.
111. Barker CB, and Dightman CR. Side effects of oral contraceptives. Obstet Gynecol 1966; 28:373.
112. Goldzieher JW, Moses LE, Averkin C., et al. A placebo-controlled double-blind crossover investigation of the side-effects attributed to oral contraceptives. Fertil Steril 1971; 22:609.
113. Larsson-Cohn U. Oral contraceptives and vitamins: A review. Am J Obstet Gynecol 1975; 121:84.
114. Rothman KJ, and Louik C. Oral contraceptives and birth defects. N Engl J Med 1978; 299:522.
115. Vessey MP, Doll R, Peto R, et al. A long-term follow-up study of women using different forms of contraception: An interim report. J Biosoc Sci 1976; 8:373.
116. Royal College of General Practitioners. Oral Contraceptives and Health: An Interim Report. London: Pittman, 1974.
117. Heinonen OP, Slone D, Momson RR, et al. Cardiovascular birth defects and antenatal exposure to female sex hormones. N Engl J Med 1977; 296:67.
118. Janerich DT, Piper JM, and Glebatis DM. Oral contraceptives and congenital limb reduction defects. N Engl J Med 1974; 291:697.
119. Kricker A, Elliot JW, Forrest JM, et al. Congenital limb reduction deformities and use of oral contraceptives. Am J Obstet Gynecol 1986; 155:1072.
120. Lammer EJ, and Cordero JF. Exogenous sex hormone exposure and the risk for major malformations. JAMA 1986; 255:3128.
121. The Cancer and Steroid Hormone Study of the Centers for Disease Control and the National Institute of Child Health and Human Development. Oral-contraceptive use and the risk of breast cancer. N Engl J Med 1986; 315:405.
122. Oral contraceptive use and the risk of breast cancer in young women. MMWR 1984; 33:353.
123. Lipnick RJ, Buring JE, Hennekens CH, et al. Oral contraceptives and breast cancer: A prospective cohort study. JAMA 1986; 255:58.
124. Stadel BV, Rubin GL, Webster LA, et al. Oral contraceptives and breast cancer in young women. Lancet 1985; 2:970.
125. Sartwell P, Arthes FG, and Tonascia JA. Epidemiology of benign breast lesions. N Engl J Med 1973; 288:551.
126. Vessey MP, Doll R, and Sutton PM. Oral contraceptives and breast neoplasia: A retrospective study. Br Med J 1972; 3:719.

127. LiVolsi V, Stadel B, Kelsey J, et al. Fibrocystic breast disease in oral contraceptive users: Histopathological evaluation of epithelial atypia. N Engl J Med 1978; 299:381.
128. Brinton LA, Huggins GR, Lehman HF, et al. Longterm use of oral contraceptives and risk of invasive cervical cancer. Int J Cancer 6; 38:399.
129. Ebeling K, Nischan P, and Schindler C. Use of oral contraceptives and risk of invasive cervical cancer in previously screened women. Int J Cancer 1987; 39:427.
130. Valente PT, and Hanjani P. Endocervical neoplasia in long-term users of oral contraceptives: Clinical and pathologic observations. Obstet Gynecol 1986; 67:695.
131. Irwin KL, Rosero-Bixby L, Oberle MW, et al. Oral contraceptives and cervical cancer risk in Costa Rica: Detection bias or causal association? JAMA 1988; 259:59.
132. Swan S, and Brown W. Oral contraceptive use, sexual activity and cervical cancer. Am J Obstet Gynecol 1981; 139:52.
133. Ziel HK, and Finkle WD. Increased risk of endometrial carcinoma among users of conjugated estrogens. N Engl J Med 1975; 293:1167.
134. Shapiro S, Kaufman DW, Slone D, et al. Recent and past use of conjugated estrogens in relation to adenocarcinoma of the endometrium. N Engl J Med 1980; 303:485.
135. Kelley H, Miles PA, Buster JE, et al. Adenocarcinoma of the endometrium in women taking oral contraceptives. Obstet Gynecol 1976; 47:200.
136. Weiss NS, and Sayvetz TA. Incidence of endometrial cancer in relation to the use of oral contraceptives. N Engl J Med 1980; 302:551.
137. Kaufman DW, Shapiro S, Slone D, et al. Decreased risk of endometrial cancer among oral-contraceptive users. N Engl J Med 1980; 303:1045.
138. CDC. Oral contraceptive use and the risk of endometrial cancer. JAMA 1983; 249:1600.
139. Andrew WC. Principle of oral contraception. In Corson SL, Derman RJ, and Tyrer LB (eds.). Fertility Control. Boston: Little, Brown, 1985.
140. Cramer DW, et al. Factors affecting the association of oral contraceptives and ovarian cancer. N Engl J Med 1982; 307:1047.
141. The Cancer and Steroid Hormone Study of the Centers for Disease Control and the National Institute of Child Health and Human Development. The reduction in risk of ovarian cancer associated with oral-contraceptive use. N Engl J Med 1987; 316:650–655.
142. CDC. Oral contraceptive use and the risk of ovarian cancer. JAMA 1983; 249:1596.
143. Baum J, Bookstein JJ, Holtz F, et al. Possible association between benign hepatomas and oral contraceptives. Lancet 1973; 2:926.
144. Edmondson HA, Henderson B, and Benton B. Liver-cell adenomas associated with the use of oral contraceptives. N Engl J Med 1976; 294:470.
145. Rooks JB, Ory HW, and Ishak KG. Epidemiology of hepatocellular adenomas. JAMA 1979; 242:644.
146. Jick H, Herman R. Oral contraceptive induced benign liver tumors—the magnitude and the problem (Letter). JAMA 1978; 240:828.
147. Andrews W. Oral contraceptives. Clin Obstet Gynecol 1979; 6:3.
148. Goodman ZD, and Ishak KG. Hepatocellular carcinoma in women: Probable lack of etiologic association with oral contraceptive steroids. Hepatology 1982; 2:440.
149. Howie P. The progestogen-only pill. Br J Obstet Gynaecol 1985; 92:1001.
150. Graham S, and Frazer I. The progesterone-only mini-pill. Contraception 1982; 26:373.

151. Board JA. Continuous norethindrone, 0.35 mg, as an oral contraceptive agent. Am J Obstet Gynecol 1971; 109(4):531–535.
152. Vessey MP, Lawless M, Yeates D, et al. Progestin-only oral contraception: Findings in large prospective study with special reference to effectiveness. Br J Fam Plann 1985; 10:117–121.
153. Spellacy WN, Buhi WC, and Birk SA. Prospective studies of carbohydrate metabolism in "normal" women using norgestrel for 18 months. Fertil Steril 1979; 35:167.
154. Lee NC, Rubin GL, Ory HW, et al. Type of intrauterine device and the risk of pelvic inflammatory disease. Obstet Gynecol 1983; 62:1.
155. Kaufman DW, Watson J, Rosenberg L, et al. The effect of different types of intrauterine devices on the risk of pelvic inflammatory disease. JAMA 1983; 250:759.
156. Stadel BV, and Schlesselman S. Extent of surgery for pelvic inflammatory disease in relation to duration of intrauterine device use. Obstet Gynecol 1984; 63:171.
157. Daling JR, Weiss NS, Metch BJ, et al. Primary tubal infertility in relation to the use of an intrauterine device. N Engl J Med 1985; 312:937.
158. Cramer DW, Schiff I, Schoenbaum SC, et al. Tubal infertility and the intrauterine device. N Engl J Med 1985; 312:941.
159. Hutchings JE, Benson PJ, Perkin GW, et al. The IUD after 20 years: A review. Fam Plann Perspect 1985; 17:244.
160. Klitch M. The return of the IUD. Fam Plann Perspect 1988; 20:19.
161. Oster G, and Salgo M. The copper intrauterine device and its mode of action. N Engl J Med 1975; 293:432.
162. Levin H, Colombi DJ, and Bare WW. The Cu-7: A metallic copper intrauterine device. J Reprod Med 1974; 12:166.
163. Progestasert: A new intrauterine contraceptive device. Med Lett Drugs Ther 1976; 18:65.
164. Burkman RT, and the Women's Health Study. Association between intrauterine devices and pelvic inflammatory disease. Obstet Gynecol 1981; 57:269.
165. Osser S, Liedholm P, and Sjoberg N. Risk of PID among users of intrauterine devices, irrespective of previous pregnancy. Am J Obstet Gynecol 1980; 138:864.
166. Westrom L, Bengtsson L, and March PA. The risk of PID in women using IUDs compared to non-users. Lancet 1976; 3:221.
167. Ory HW, and the Women's Health Study. Ectopic pregnancy and intrauterine contraceptive device: New perspectives. Obstet Gynecol 1981; 57:269.
168. Kirshon B, Poindexter AN, and Spitz MR. Pelvic adhesions in intrauterine device users. Obstet Gynecol 1988; 71:251.
169. Heartwell SF, and Schlesselman S. Risk of uterine perforation among users of intrauterine devices. Obstet Gynecol 1983; 61:31.
170. Cates W, Ory HW, and Rochat RW. The IUD and spontaneous-abortion deaths. N Engl J Med 1976; 295:1155
171. Murray S, Hickey JB, and Houang E. Significant bacteremia associated with replacement of intrauterine contraceptive device. Am J Obstet Gynecol 1987; 156:698.
172. Lane MD, Arceo R, and Sobrero AJ. Successful use of the diaphragm and jelly by a young population: Report of a clinical study. Fam Plann Perspect 1976; 8:81.
173. Fisher M, Marks A, and Trieller K. Comparative analysis of the effec-

tiveness of the diaphragm and birth control pill during the first year of use among suburban adolescents. J Adolesc Health Care 1987; 8:393.

174. Wiley AT. The diaphragm. In Corson SL, Duman RJ, Tyrer LB (eds.). Fertility Control. Boston: Little, Brown, 1985.

175. Fihn SD, Lathan RH, Roberts P, et al. Association between diaphragm use and the urinary tract infection. JAMA 1985; 254:240.

176. Kelaghan J, Rubin GL, Ory HW, et al. Barrier method contraceptives and pelvic inflammatory disease. JAMA 1982; 248:184.

177. Sherris JD, Moore SH, and Fox G. New developments in vaginal contraception. Popul Rep [H] 1984; No. 7.

178. Tietze C, Lehfeldt H, and Liebmann HG. The effectiveness of the cervical cap as a contraceptive method. Am J Obstet Gynecol 1953; 66:904.

179. Richwald GA, Greenland S, Gerber M, et al. Effectiveness of the cavity-rim cervical cap: results of a large clinical study. Obstet Gynecol 1979; 74:143.

180. Koch JP. The Prentif cervical cap: Acceptability aspects and their implications for future cap design. Contraception 1982; 25:161.

181. Koch JP. The Prentif cervical cap: A contemporary study of its clinical safety and effectiveness. Contraception 1982; 25:135.

182. Eliot J, Anderson L, and Bernstein S. Progress report on a study of the cervical cap. J Reprod Med 1985; 30:753–759.

183. DHHS. Cervical cap approved for contraception. FDA Drug Bull 1988; 18:18.

184. Bernstein GS, Lilzer LH, Coulson AH, et al. Studies of cervical caps: I. Vaginal lesions associated with use of the Vimule cap. Contraception 1982; 26:443.

185. Rosenberg MJ, Rojanapithayakorn W, Feldblum PJ, et al. Effect of the contraceptive sponge on chlamydial infection, gonorrhea and candidiasis: A comparative clinical trial. JAMA 1987; 257:2308–2312.

186. Edelman DA, McIntyre SL, and Harper J. A comparative trial of the Today contraceptive sponge and diaphragm. Am J Obstet Gynecol 1984; 150:869.

187. McIntyre SL, and Higgins JE. Parity and use-effectiveness with the contraceptive sponge. Am J Obstet Gynecol 1986; 155:796.

188. Edelman DA, and North BB. Updated pregnancy rates for the Today sponge. Am J Obstet Gynecol 1987; 157:1164.

189. Rietmeijer CAM, Krebs JW, Foerino PM, et al. Condoms as physical and chemical barriers against human immunodeficiency virus. JAMA 1988; 259:1851.

190. Contraceptive failure in the United States: The impact of social, economic and demographic factors. Fam Plann Perspect 1982; 14:68.

191. Topical spermicides for contraception. Med Lett Drugs Ther 1980; 22:90.

192. Squire JJ, Berger GS, and Keith L. A retrospective clinical study of a vaginal contraceptive suppository. J Reprod Med 1977; 22:319.

193. Tyler LB, and Bradshaw LE. Barrier methods. Clin Obstet Gynecol 1979; 6:39.

194. Jick H, Walker AM, Rothman KJ, et al. Vaginal spermicides and congenital disorders. JAMA 1981; 245:1329.

195. Mills JL, Harley EE, Reed GF, et al. Are spermicides teratogenic? JAMA 1982; 248:2148.

196. Mills JL, Reed GF, Nugent RP, et al. Are there adverse effects of periconceptional spermicide use? Fertil Steril 1985; 43:442.

197. Harlap S, Shiono PH, Ramcharan S, et al. Chromosomal abnormalities

in the Kaiser-Permanente birth defects study with special reference to contraceptive use around the time of contraception. Teratology 1985; 31: 381.

198. Warburton D, Neugut RH, Lustenberger A, et al. Lack of association between spermicide use and trisomy. N Engl J Med 1987; 317:478.

199. Louik C, Mitchell AA, Werler MM, et al. Maternal exposure to spermicides in relation to certain birth defects. N Engl J Med 1987; 317:474.

200. CDC. Condoms for prevention of sexually transmitted diseases. MMWR 1988; 37:133–137.

201. Kegeles SM, Adler NE, and Irwin CE. Sexually active adolescents and condoms: Changes over one year in knowledge, attitudes and use. Am J Public Health 1988, 78:460.

202. Rosenfield AG. Injectable long-acting progestogen contraception: A neglected modality. Am J Obstet Gynecol 1974; 120:537.

203. Amatayakul K, Sirassomboom B, and Singkamani R. Effects of MPA in serum lipids, protein, glucose tolerance and liver function in Thai women. Contraception 1980; 21:283.

204. Liskin L, Blackburn R. Hormonal contraception: New long-acting methods. Popul Rep [K] 1987; (3): K57.

205. Rosenfield A. Injectable contraception. In Corson SL, Dermas RJ, Tyrer LB (eds.). Fertility Control. Boston: Little, Brown, 1985.

206. Howard G, Blair M, Chen JK, et al. A clinical trial of norethisterone oenanthate (Norigest) injected every two months. Contraception 1982; 25:333.

207. World Health Organization. Multinational comparative clinical evaluation of two long-acting injectable contraceptive steroids: Noresthisterone oenanthate and medroxyprogesterone acetate. Contraception 1977; 15:513.

208. World Health Organization. Multinational comparative trial of long-active injectable contraceptives: Norethisterone enanthate given in two dosage regimens and depot-medroxyprogesterone acetate. Final report. Contraception 1983; 28:1.

209. World Health Organization. A multicentered phase III comparative clinical trial of depot-medroxyprogesterone acetate given three-monthly at doses of 100 mg or 150 mg: Contraceptive efficacy and side effects. Contraception 1986; 34:223.

210. Sivin I, Diaz S, Holma P, et al. A four-year clinical study of Norplant implants. Stud Fam Plann 1983; 14:184.

211. Robertson DN, Diaz S, Alvarez-Sanchez F, et al. Contraception with long-acting subdermal implants: A five-year clinical trial with Silastic covered rod implants containing levonorgestrel. Contraception 1985; 31:351.

212. Segal S. A new delivery system for contraceptive steroids. Obstet Gynecol 1987; 157:1090.

213. Ory S, Hammond C, Yancy S, et al. The effect of a biodegradable contraceptive capsule (Capronor) containing levonorgestrel on gonadotropin, estrogen, and progesterone levels. Am J Obstet Gynecol 1983; 145:600.

214. Brown JB, Blackwell LF, Billings JJ, et al. Natural family planning. Am J Obstet Gynecol 1987; 157:1082.

215. Klaus H, Goebel J, Muraski B, et al. Use effectiveness and client satisfaction in six centers teaching the Billings Ovulation Method. Contraception 1979; 19:497.

216. Brown JS. Natural family planning: A review. Obstet Gynecol Surv 1982; 37:134.
217. Wade ME, McCarthy P, Braunstein GD, et al. A randomized prospective study of the use-effectiveness of two methods of natural family planning. Am J Obstet Gynecology 1981; 141:368.
218. Rice FJ, Lanctot CA, and Garcia-Deversa C. Effectiveness of the symptothermal method of natural family planning: An international study. Int J Fertil 1981; 26:222.
219. Yuzpe AA, Thurlow HJ, Ramzy I, et al. Postcoital contraception: A pilot study. J Reprod Med 1974; 13:53.
220. Yuzpe AA, and Lancee WJ. Ethinyl estradiol and dl-norgestrel as a postcoital contraceptive. Fertil Steril 1977; 28:932.
221. Schilling LH. An alternative to the use of high-dose estrogens for postcoital contraception. J Amer College Health Assoc 1979; 27:247.
222. Van Santen MR, and Haspels AA. Interception II: Postcoital low-dose estrogens and norgestrel combination in 633 women. Contraception 1985; 31:275.
223. Bergquist C, Nillins S, and Wide L. Inhibition of ovulation in women by intranasal treatment with luteinizing hormone–releasing hormone agonist. Contraception 1979; 19:497.
224. Nieman LK, Choat TM, Chrousos GP, et al. The progesterone antagonist RU 486: A potential new contraceptive agent. N Engl J Med 1987; 316:187.

SUGGESTED FURTHER READING
Mishell DR. Contraception. New Engl J Med 1989; 320:777.
Potts M. Birth control methods in the United States. Fam Plann Perspect 1988; 20:288.
DuRant RH, Sanders JM, Jay S, et al. Analysis of contraceptive behavior of sexually active female adolescents in the United States. J Pediatr 1988; 113:930.
Goldzieher JW. Hormonal Contraception: Pills, Injections and Implants. Dallas: Essential Medical Information Systems, Inc., 1989.
Gallagher DM, Richwald GA. Fitting the Cervical Cap: A Handbook for Clinicians. Los Gatos, CA (PO Box 38003-292): Cervical Cap Limited, 1989.
Chalker R. The Complete Cervical Cap Guide. New York: Harper and Row, 1987.

16. Teenage Pregnancy

The diagnosis and management of unplanned pregnancies among teenagers is a major issue for clinicians. The adolescent is faced with demands for premature heterosexual relationships in which intercourse is often defined as the major expression of love. The media, through both subtle and explicit advertisements, stories, and articles, have glorified sex, at the same time that school and other groups have withheld information on sexuality and birth control. Parents are frequently caught in the middle, unwilling to approve of the change in sexual mores and yet unable to provide the necessary discussion about issues of sexuality. Physicians need to address these issues in the office setting. In addition, many physicians are asked to be consultants to the community school system even though they may not be experienced in discussing teenage sexuality or sexually transmitted infections.

The number of sexually active adolescents has risen dramatically from the early 1970s to the 1980s, especially among white teenagers. The percent of never-married women age 15 to 19 years who had ever had sexual intercourse has been estimated to be 28 percent in 1974, 42 percent in 1982, and 49.5 percent in 1988 (25% of 15-year-old and 75% of 19-year-old women, both black and white, have experienced intercourse). Not surprisingly, with the increase in percentages of sexually active adolescents, 1 in 10 teens (15–19 years) becomes pregnant each year. A dramatic increase has occurred among white teenagers, but the pregnancy rate for nonwhite teens was twice as high as that for white teens in 1987. The earlier age of menarche, coupled with increased frequency of premarital intercourse, increases the risk of premarital pregnancy [1–3]. The percentage of out-of-wedlock births to women under 20 increased from 30.5 percent in 1970 to 54.1 percent in 1983.

Between 1974 and 1980, the pregnancy rate (number of live births plus induced abortions per 1000 women) for *all* teens increased, but the pregnancy rate for sexually experienced teens declined. From 1980 to 1983, the pregnancy rate declined among all teens and among sexually experienced teens. Birth rates declined between 1974 and 1983, with the decrease from 1974 to 1980 due primarily to the use of abortion, whereas the decrease from 1980 to 1983 was due to the decrease in the total number of teenage pregnancies [1]. An estimated 1,014,260 teens became pregnant in 1987 with 50% resulting in a birth, 36% in abortion, and 14% in miscarriage. Unfortunately, the number of pregnancies among the youngest group of adolescents (<15 years) has risen over the last decade. Although this group represents a very small percentage of the total pregnancies in the United

States, these girls are most likely to be from high-risk families of low socioeconomic status and to suffer the most adverse consequences from early childbearing [4–7]. Even among girls less than 15 years old, having a live birth is chosen more often than abortion (56% versus 44%). This is distinctly different from other developed countries; for example, in England and Wales 61 percent of this age group choose abortion, 86 percent in Norway, and 88 percent in Sweden [8].

The United States has one of the highest adolescent pregnancy rates among developed nations. In 1981, the adolescent pregnancy rate was 96/1000 in the United States compared to 14/1000 in the Netherlands. The consequences of early childbearing pose a significant problem because of the failure of many of these young patients to achieve adequate education and income. The ethnic makeup of the teen mothers depends on the demographics of the area. For example, teen prenatal clinics in the inner cities of the Northeast serve a large proportion of black adolescents, whereas clinics in San Diego and other parts of the southwestern U.S. serve a large percentage of Hispanic, primarily Mexican-American, teenagers. In the western United States, 75 percent of pregnant adolescents are white, Mexican-American or Native American. The significance of a pregnancy in a particular ethnic or socioeconomic group requires more research to target specific interventions. It should be remembered that pregnancy, especially pregnancy early in adolescence, carries a high risk of sexually transmitted infections, including *Neisseria gonorrhoeae*, *Chlamydia trachomatis*, human papillomavirus, HIV and syphilis.

Studies on teenage pregnancy are inextricably intertwined with social and economic factors, since factors associated with school-age pregnancy include minority status, low socioeconomic status, low educational and career aspirations, residence in a single parent home, and poor family relationships [6]. The presence of these confounding factors needs to be kept in mind as one reviews the literature on causes of pregnancy as well as outcome measures.

FACTORS IN TEENAGE PREGNANCY
Why do teenagers become pregnant? It is clearly difficult to generalize about all teenagers when unplanned pregnancy is such a common event. However, when dealing with the healthy patient, the health care provider needs to assess carefully what factors may have contributed to the pregnancy. In Zelnik and Kantner's [2] study of 15- to 19-year-olds with premarital pregnancy, only 18 percent expressed a desire for pregnancy in 1979, as opposed to 24 percent in 1971. Unfortunately, of those youngsters who did not want a pregnancy, only 32 percent used some form of contraception. In 1988 65% of

teens used a contraceptive at first intercourse but many still used no method at first or subsequent intercourse.

Adolescents frequently delay obtaining adequate contraception for a year or more after becoming sexually active. Denial of fertility is a common theme; statements such as, "I didn't think it would happen to me," or "I had sex for 2 years and didn't get pregnant," or "I never thought I would get pregnant," are frequently expressed. There may be an unexpected opportunity for sexual involvement when the use of contraception is not possible. Young teenagers are especially reluctant to destroy the spontaneity by planning ahead and acknowledging their own sexuality. To some, making an appointment at a family planning clinic to request contraceptives is tantamount to seeking sex; it also risks being discovered. Ignoring the question leaves the issue of sex unresolved, and the teenager retains the right not to have intercourse.

The maturation process during adolescence involves the formation of a stable self-image, a sexual identity, and a concept of self as separate from parents. This process does not occur in an orderly fashion; and thus the adolescent does not always see herself as a woman capable of fertility at the same time that she is in fact able to bear children and has become sexually mature. During early adolescence girls are particularly prone to impulsive action and have difficulty with long-range goals; part of the adolescent developmental process involves swings between irresponsibility and constraint, thoughtfulness and indulgence. Unfortunately, the consistency, responsibility, and planning necessary for effective contraceptive use are not always compatible with the stage of adolescent development in which the adolescent may have chosen to become sexually active.

The limitation in cognitive development in a young adolescent often makes it impossible for him or her to consider the feelings and values of the partner, that a pregnancy can result, and that contraception is necessary. Although for older adolescents risk-taking is less haphazard and acts and their consequences are more clearly connected, many continue to deny possible consequences of lack of contraceptive use. Often, the longer that an adolescent is sexually active without experiencing pregnancy, the more the risk-taking behavior is reinforced. Adolescents are usually unaware that with increasing gynecologic age, the chance of regular ovulatory cycles and thus fertility is greater.

The desire to avoid a pregnancy is an important motivating force. Adolescents who reject the idea of having children before marriage are three times less likely to become pregnant in the next 2 years. The "cost" of a pregnancy is much greater to the suburban white teenager with college aspirations than to the poor inner city adolescent who has dropped out of school. In the Rand Corporation study [9], single parenthood rates ranged from 1 in 1000 for white girls with high academic ability from upper income, intact families to 1 in 4 for black girls with low academic ability from poor, female-headed families. Risk factors for teen parenthood varied with the ethnic group; for example, decreased risk was found in whites with good parent-child communication, in blacks with good parental supervision, and in Hispanics with increased religiosity. The presence of problem behavior was a significant risk factor for Hispanics and whites to become pregnant. College plans reduced the likelihood of single parenthood in all groups, but most significantly for blacks [9].

Litt and her associates' study [10] at Stanford has suggested that adolescents who are most likely to adhere to a contraceptive program are those who made appointments specifically for the purpose of obtaining a contraceptive and who presumably thereby acknowledge their sexual identity. Use of effective contraception also seems to be related to an increase in sexual activity; increasing closeness of a relationship; increasing awareness of the risk of pregnancy, especially following a pregnancy scare; the influence of friends, family members, and physicians; and the discovery of a contraceptive program. Adolescents may stop using contraceptives if the program or the health providers do not meet the individual's needs. Moreover, adolescents who use contraception at the time of first intercourse are generally older and have higher academic aspirations than adolescents who have unprotected first intercourse.

Although the number of sexually active women using contraceptives has risen in the last decade, a significant percentage of adolescents still have never used contraceptives. Adolescents frequently overestimate the risk of oral contraceptives and therefore use less effective forms of birth control or no birth control [11–13]. Zelnick and colleagues [11] found that one of the major factors associated with a decreased risk of pregnancy among young women was the consistent use of a nonprescription method of contraception (or having been a virgin) prior to first use of a prescription method. Forty percent of white teenagers consistently used a nonprescription method before a prescription method compared to 24 percent of black adolescents. Forty-eight percent of black women had never used a nonprescription method before using a prescription method versus only 17 percent of white teenagers. Our study of inner city clinic patients compared to suburban adolescents found a similar contrast; 57 percent of inner city patients versus 14 percent of suburban adolescents had never used a method prior to obtaining a prescription for the pill [12]. Although the oral contraceptive pill is the first prescription method for 86 percent of whites and 92 percent of nonwhites, this method requires significant motivation for daily use [11].

Since teenagers frequently rely on having intercourse at a time in their cycle of low pregnancy risk, it is unfortunate that there still is a widespread lack of information about cyclic variation in fertility. Although Zelnik [14] found that 7 out of 10 never-married U.S. women, aged 15 to 19 years, reported having a sex education course in school, only 6 out of 10 who had had a course with information on the menstrual cycle claimed to know the period of greatest pregnancy risk. In fact, only 57 percent of these adolescents correctly identified the period of greatest risk. Fewer than 2 percent of the respondents had obtained this information from medical personnel; however, this group was more likely to identify correctly the period of greatest risk of pregnancy than those who obtained their information from other sources. Thus, it would be useful to include simple, factual information about the menstrual cycle in a program of meaningful, anticipatory guidance for adolescent patients.

It is also important to make sure the physician and the patient share a common set of words, since even intelligent young women may use a different terminology from that of the health care provider. For example, Sarrel and Sarrel [15] found 16 different definitions of intercourse, ranging from "when a man touches a woman" to "simultaneous orgasm which leads to pregnancy." The physician should emphasize the confidential nature of the doctor-patient relationship and provide access to birth control as a part of adolescent health care. Young men should also be encouraged by the health care provider to accept responsibility for the prevention of unwanted pregnancies and sexually transmitted infections.

Given the frequency of premarital pregnancy in adolescent girls, increased research on motivational issues and the impact of pregnancy at the various stages of adolescence is needed. Although the 13-year-old pregnant adolescent is distinctly different from the 18- or 19-year-old young woman who has completed high school, studies have tended to include such individuals in the category of "adolescent pregnancy." Some of the causes of adolescent pregnancy include nonuse of contraception because of denial of fertility and inability to plan ahead, lack of access to an acceptable clinic, death or loss of a family member, emotional deprivation in which the adolescent girl anticipates a nurturing figure in the child, and attempts to foster a relationship with a boyfriend. In a study by Nadelson and co-workers [16], 37 percent of young women in a maternity home agreed with the statement "sometimes I feel so lonely that I would like to have a baby." The urge to mother can also be an expression of the need to be mothered.

Other teenagers may believe that the baby will help establish a lasting relationship with a boyfriend; repeat pregnancies are more common when the boyfriend desires the pregnancy. The teenager who is threatened with punishment if she dares to become pregnant may feel compelled to rebel and test her mother's love. An occasional teenager will state with anger, "Well, I asked my mother for the pill and she refused, so this pregnancy is her fault." Pregnancy is often a plea for caring, and yet at the same time it represents an announcement by the adolescent that she has become an adult.

Contraceptive failure is frequently responsible for pregnancy. A teenager may forget her pills or discontinue them abruptly when a boyfriend insists, "The chemicals will mess up your body" or a newspaper article is entitled "The pill and cancer." An adolescent who is uncomfortable with her body and unable to use tampons or touch her external genitalia is unlikely to be a good candidate for the diaphragm, which she may be given by a contraceptive clinic that has a strong belief in barrier forms of contraception. A patient with a medical condition such as cystic fibrosis, diabetes mellitus, recurrent pelvic inflammatory disease (PID), delayed development, oligomenorrhea, or in utero diethylstilbestrol (DES) exposure may take more risks because of her belief that she is unlikely to get pregnant. Sexual encounters that do not result in pregnancy may reinforce risk taking. Variable cycles and unreliable methods are a key factor in unwanted pregnancies [17].

Among pregnant adolescents, feelings of despair and worthlessness and chronic failure in school appear to be more common in girls who choose to carry the pregnancy to term. Thus, depression and social isolation may be the causes as well as the consequences of early childbearing. Nadelson and associates' study [16] found that the group of teenagers who selected abortion was remarkably similar to a peer group of nonpregnant controls in that both focused on the importance of finishing school, the impracticality of caring for a child, and the need to take responsibility for one's actions. In contrast, those adolescents who elected to carry their pregnancy to term indicated that there was no real choice, that the decision had been passively made. This group was significantly less able to search for an active solution for an unplanned pregnancy. In contrast, Freeman and co-workers [18] did not find significant differences in personality factors, emotional distress, and social adjustment scores in urban black teens (<17 years) among never-pregnant, postabortion, and postpartum patients. However, self-esteem was highest in the never-pregnant group. Identifying adolescents at risk for future pregnancies is difficult. In a predominantly black population in North Carolina, Vernon and colleagues [19] found that a combination of three factors—(1) a family that would be pleased by a pregnancy, (2) a boyfriend listed as the girl's closest friend, and (3) four or more sisters—predicted a pregnancy in 57 percent of young women who became pregnant in the next year. The specificity of these factors, however, was only 67 percent.

It is clear that new approaches to sex education (see Chaps. 11 and 19) that look at motivational factors, in addition to contraceptive technology, will be important in the prevention of adolescent pregnancies. Good courses increase communication skills, improve the adolescent's sense of worth, and help him or her become more in touch with feelings and impulses. An adolescent may need help with peer pressure and sexual responsibility, including learning how to say, "No." Coupling education with the provision of concrete services has reduced pregnancy rates in several centers [20]. Involving parents in discussion groups and teaching them how to communicate with their adolescent can be extremely helpful.

An innovative program in St. Paul, Minnesota, in which a health clinic was opened within the high school has served as a model for other cities [21]. In a junior and senior high school served by the St. Paul Maternal and Infant Care Project, the pregnancy rate fell from 79 (in 1973) to 35 (in 1976) births per 1000. During the same period, the school dropout rate following delivery was reduced from 45 percent to 10 percent, and no repeat pregnancies occurred among the students who delivered while in the project and returned to school. Twelve-month contraceptive continuation rate was 86.4 per 100 women. Even when the program was transferred to the two high schools, it was readily accepted, and 25 percent of the students used the family planning service. The continuation rate of contraception was 92.8 percent at 12 months.

The excellent results were probably related to continuity of staff, personalized services, accessibility of free services, and the provision of educational and social services. The students were contacted by the nurse practitioner within 1 week after initiating contraception and then monthly to discuss any problems. Medical follow-up was arranged every 3 months. It is therefore apparent that efforts to lower the teenage pregnancy rate must include a multitude of factors that focus on the adolescent as well as the manner in which contraceptive services are delivered.

Many similar programs have been instituted throughout the United States, some within the school building, some across the street from a school. The most controversial part of each of these programs has been the provision of contraceptive services. Communities have found it hard to accept that teenagers are in need of services and have feared that provision of contraceptives would erode family values and promote more adolescents becoming sexually active. Program directors have found that enlisting the support of the community is crucial to the success of these programs. Clinics should be started with the aim of improving overall health of teens, not just reducing pregnancy rates. Offering comprehensive health services makes the clinic more attractive to students since many girls and boys might be unwilling to risk confidentiality by entering a clinic clearly designated as offering only birth control.

Zabin and colleagues [22] have recently reported on a school-based program that was carried out in a junior high and senior high school in inner-city Baltimore. The students were provided with sexuality and contraceptive education, individual and group counselling, and medical and contraceptive services over three school years. A social worker and a nurse-midwife or nurse practitioner made presentations in the classroom and were available in the school for counselling sessions. These same professionals provided services in a clinic across the street in the afternoon. Emphasis was placed on "the development of personal responsibility, goal-setting and communication with parents." Services were free. Significant changes in contraceptive and sexual knowledge occurred, and young men made significantly more visits to the clinic than had occurred before the intervention. For eighth grade boys the number attending the birth control clinic increased from 24 to 62 percent and for twelfth graders from 14 to 64 percent. Eighth grade girls increased attendance from 33 to 64 percent, and twelfth grade girls from 69 to 75 percent. Students at the two control schools that did not receive the intervention program did not see any change in the number of students using services. The mean age of first coitus was delayed slightly, not advanced as some opponents of school-based clinics have feared. Students were more likely to seek contraceptives before intercourse or during the early months of sexual activity than before the intervention. This program has demonstrated that school-based services could have a significant impact on students at reasonable cost [23, 24]. More studies are needed to assess school-based clinics using a variety of outcome measures [25]. Although some clinicians have rightly worried about clinics that are not open at night, weekends, or summers, practical solutions can be found, especially by using linkages with existing neighborhood services. In addition, creative solutions are needed to reach teenagers who do not attend school, a particularly high-risk group.

Another successful intervention program has been reported by Vincent and associates [26] in a South Carolina county. The educational program was designed to target parents, teachers, ministers, community leaders, and children enrolled in public school. An integrated curriculum of sex education was implemented in all grades from kindergarten to grade 12. The educational objectives included improved decision-making and communication skills, enhanced self-esteem, alignment of personal values with those of the family, church, and community, and increased knowledge of human reproduction and contraception. Further education occurred through churches and community groups, and the message was promoted in newspapers and radio. The estimated pregnancy rate for females 14 to 17 years old declined significantly during the intervention period (25/1000) in comparison to preintervention statistics (62/1000) and was markedly lower than similar counties in the area (49–59/1000).

Increased involvement of young people in sports also has the potential to improve self-esteem, and intervention projects are needed to target this area as well.

THE DIAGNOSIS OF PREGNANCY

Since the most common cause of secondary amenorrhea is pregnancy, any adolescent who is overdue for a period should have a urine screened for human chorionic gonadotropin (HCG). An adolescent who is 1 to 2 weeks late for a period and expresses concern about this should be seen by the physician to consider the diagnosis of pregnancy. If the teenager is not pregnant, she may well be sexually active and in need of contraceptive counselling. Some adolescents will express the fear that they may be pregnant; others may request appointments with the hope that the physician may accidentally discover the pregnancy. Often the patient's complaint is a minor stomachache, constipation, or headache, and the patient later admits to having missed her period only after being directly questioned. Other adolescents may not have thought of the possibility and may have dizziness, syncope, nausea, or urinary frequency. Occasionally, the patient will experience a light period in the first trimester and will, therefore, be falsely reassured she is not pregnant. It is important for primary care providers to have urine pregnancy tests available in the office (see Chap. 1).

Pregnancies are dated from the last menstrual period even though ovulation usually occurs at least 2 weeks later. Calculation of dates from the last menstrual period along with a pelvic examination is necessary so that the physician can discuss with the adolescent the possible options for the pregnancy. By rectal or vaginal examination, the 8-week uterus feels about the size of an orange; the 12-week uterus is approximately the size of a grapefruit. An abdominal examination with the patient supine helps in staging a later pregnancy; a 12-week uterus is just palpable at the symphysis pubis, a 20-week uterus at the level of the umbilicus, and a 16-week uterus midway between (Fig. 16-1).

Although adolescents can be quite inaccurate with dates of last menstrual period (LMP), other diagnoses need to be entertained if the uterus is small or large for dates. If the uterus is smaller than expected, possible diagnoses include false-positive pregnancy test (rare

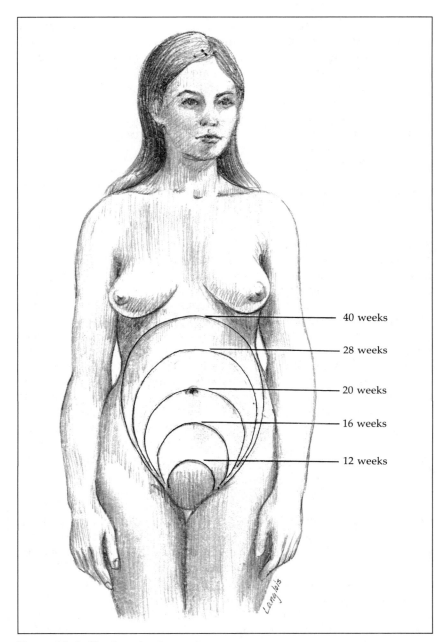

40 weeks

28 weeks

20 weeks

16 weeks

12 weeks

Figure 16–1. Uterine size in pregnancy.

with new sensitive tests unless a lab error) in a patient who is not pregnant, incomplete or missed abortion, molar or ectopic pregnancy. Ultrasonography (including the use of a vaginal probe) and serial quantitative HCG measures are important in making the diagnosis. A uterus felt to be larger than expected may be caused by inaccurate dates, leiomyomata, or molar pregnancy, or a corpus luteum cyst of pregnancy may be mistaken initially as part of the enlarged uterus in the poorly relaxed adolescent girl.

COUNSELLING THE PREGNANT ADOLESCENT

Counselling the pregnant teenager (and her family) is essential to alleviate the patient's anxiety and guilt and to reduce the long-term emotional sequelae. Unfortunately, there is no "good" alternative to an unwanted pregnancy. With both adoption and abortion, the teenager must ultimately work through the guilt and loss. The teenager who elects to keep her baby may be emotionally unprepared to cope with the demands of child care. Active participation of the teenager in the decision-making is essential.

When counselling pregnant teenagers, the physician will sense striking differences between the 11- to 14-year-old and the 17- to 18-year-old girl. The younger girl tends to have many sexual fantasies and to deny the pregnancy until quite late; it is not unusual to see a 12-year-old girl for her first visit 20 or even 26 weeks' pregnant. The young adolescent may be unable to take responsibility for her actions or even to connect pregnancy and motherhood. Since her decisions about what to do with the pregnancy may be related to angry feelings toward her parents that day, several visits may be necessary before a referral for abortion or obstetric care is made. Pregnancy in the very young also may be the first clue to an incestuous relationship within the family, and thus the counsellor needs to be sensitive in approaching the source of the pregnancy. Behavior such as running away and "acting out" may also be signs of disturbed family relationships and sexual abuse (see Chap. 17).

The 17- or 18-year-old girl is usually better able to appreciate the consequences of her action and to consider the choices available. The patient's needs, strengths, and defenses need to be assessed while formulating a plan [27, 28, 29].

The teenager not only has the final word on what decisions are to be made, but also it is she who must live with the decisions over a lifetime. Ambivalence about an unwanted pregnancy is a normal feeling and must be resolved as much as possible. To be fair to the teenager, the physician should be relatively unbiased about the ethics of abortion. If he or she is against abortion, then the patient should be referred to a pregnancy counselling service. Admittedly, it may be difficult to be unbiased about the prospect of a young adolescent keeping her baby, because problems with teenage marriages and single parenthood are so frequent.

The issue of parental consent and responsibility for the notification of a teenager's abortion is in considerable flux; currently, the issue is decided by the state legislatures.

Frequently, the teenager finds it easier to have the physician tell her mother the diagnosis. The majority of young to mid-adolescents benefit from the support parents, especially the mother, are able to provide. Effective counselling can then deal with the family issues that may have been important precipitants to the unplanned pregnancy. The parents may feel very guilty or very angry. It is important to state to the mother that if she expresses her demands for abortion or continuing the pregnancy too emphatically, she may push her daughter in the opposite direction. Since the teenager generally will continue to live with her parents, a solution acceptable to both parents and teenager needs to be evolved through counselling.

Many teenagers are unable to talk to their parents about the issue of an unwanted pregnancy, sometimes because of justified fear of physical or other abuse. Teenagers unable to involve their parents should be informed by their physician and counsellors of possible legal alternatives to parental consent provisions. It is important to discourage adolescents from delaying obtaining adequate medical intervention or from seeking abortions in nonmedical facilities because they fear parental reprisals.

ABORTION

If abortion is chosen, counselling the pregnant teenager enables her to withstand the sadness or trauma accompanying the procedures; her ability to cope with the abortion experience determines whether it becomes a source of maturation or guilt. Reassurance that her own choice is the primary factor in the hospital's or clinic's treatment provides an aura of trust for clarifying these issues.

Case intervention for healthy patients may be brief and effective and can support strengths formed from earlier life situations. For those less healthy, ongoing support may be required that focuses on self-determination. Counselling is often helpful to enable the adolescent to tolerate the delay between the time of the diagnosis and the actual abortion procedure. An immediately available abortion without any counselling may prevent some adolescents from accepting the reality of the pregnancy and working through the decision.

Physicians are often confronted with counselling the boyfriend as well; he may feel prematurely trapped by a relationship in which important decisions about a pregnancy may affect his life. Boyfriends are frequently called on to be strong and supportive at a time that

Table 16–1. Patient Interview Before an Abortion

Personal history
  Social situation and educational goals
  Self-esteem
  Medical problems
  Psychiatric history
Sexual history
  Information level
  Previous contraception
Relationship with partner, mother, and friends
  Who can be supportive?
Family attitudes
Current pregnancy
  Who wants this abortion?
  Ambivalence and fears about procedure
Postpregnancy
  Anticipation of feelings
  Contraception

---

they are working through their own feelings and guilt about the situation.

The interview that occurs before an abortion is crucial in laying the foundation for understanding the patient and providing for her future needs. Adolescents tend to be considerably more verbal before an abortion than following the procedure, when they may express a reluctance to talk about what has happened to them. An outline of the six most important parts of the interview are shown in Table 16-1. The personal history should include details of the patient's current social situation and educational goals. Clarifying the patient's educational plans before the unwanted pregnancy occurred allows the patient to put the pregnancy in perspective and assess its potential impact on her life's goals.

Assessment of the patient's self-esteem allows the physician some estimate of postabortion problems and contraceptive compliance. Freeman [30] reported that women with positive self-images have a high rate of contraceptive use, whereas those with dependent personalities and poor self-esteem had lower rates of use. Of those with poor self-esteem, abortion often signified giving up a child. Many of these women experienced depression following the abortion, although the majority had resolved these feelings by the 4-month follow-up period. A third group, with very poor self-esteem, anxiety, and avoidance of the issue, used birth control even less frequently; most expressed the feeling that the abortion was "too upsetting to think about." In this group, feelings of depression and anxiety persisted. Since an unwanted pregnancy can further the individual's feeling that "things just happen to me," it is important in the counselling process to foster the concept of decision-making and to stress the ability of the person to intervene in her own life.

The health care provider should also be aware of the girls' medical problems, because both patients with preexisting medical problems and patients with medical problems at the time of the abortion often have more difficulty in resolving the issue of abortion.

Assessing the patient's previous way of dealing with crisis and loss is important. The girl with anticipated difficulties may do better if the counsellor's concerns are shared with her. It is often less frightening to an adolescent, and potentially a relief to her, to understand the connection between her difficulty with acceptance of previous losses and the counsellor's concern about what the loss of this pregnancy through abortion means to her.

The level of information and the prior experience of the patient should be assessed, because fantasy and inaccurate information is still widespread even among the college population. As mentioned previously, pregnancy often results from the use of the less reliable methods of contraception [17, 31]. The nature of the current relationship with the male partner should be explored, and the patient should be encouraged to bring him in if she desires. Family attitude should be explored, since if it is strongly antiabortion, this may intensify the patient's sense of guilt. The actual details of how the unwanted pregnancy occurred are important in making plans for preventing repeat pregnancies.

It is essential to find out, "Who wants this abortion?" Adolescents sometimes have abortions to please their mothers and end up with another pregnancy very soon thereafter because they did not fully work through the decision themselves. Ambivalence about an unwanted pregnancy is universal and is related to the conflict between the positive aspects of conception and pregnancy versus the frustration and sadness about making a choice to terminate a pregnancy. Since ambivalence also occurs as part of the developmental process of adolescence, it is especially prominent in this age group and is more difficult to assess. Nonjudgmental support is critical if one is to effect resolution of the guilt that is frequently present. It is important that the adolescent reach the point of acceptance and comfort with her decision in order to minimize emotional sequela. The alternatives to abortion must be explored and carefully considered. It is often difficult to avoid interjecting personal values or feelings, but it is essential to work toward objectivity and tolerance.

Fears concerning the actual abortion procedure need to be explored, since this remains a significant issue for a high percentage of adolescents. A clear understanding of and attention to the nature of their fears and fantasies will reduce anxiety. Patients are often afraid to ask questions about pain, anesthesia, subsequent fertility, and about some of the details of the procedure. They often fantasize a more drastic procedure; perhaps this is related to guilt, feeling a need for punishment, or to previous experiences with doctors in hospitals. Thus, it is important that physicians keep abreast of the available resources and the procedures done within the community. The family physician or counsellor may be less threatening than the gynecologist who will actually be doing the procedure. The adolescent may feel freer communicating to a person whom she perceives as helpful, supportive, and understanding.

Feelings after the abortion and the need for contraceptives should be explored with the adolescent. For most, the overwhelming feeling postabortion is relief. However, feelings of depression may be apparent, especially in adolescents with low self-esteem. Introducing the topic of birth control after the pregnancy is essential, for many teenagers and parents feel that "it won't happen again." In our studies of adolescents who had received birth control pills, those with a prior abortion were not more compliant than those who had never experienced a pregnancy [32]. The likelihood of a repeat pregnancy should be emphasized.

In 1989, the Centers for Disease Control (CDC) reported the statistics of abortion surveillance in the United States in 1984 to 1985 and preliminary data on 1986 and 1987 [33–34]. In 1985, approximately 1,328,570 abortions were reported, a slight decrease from 1984. In 1987, 1,353,671 abortions were reported [34]. (It should be noted that not all abortions are reported, and thus the true number is probably closer to 1.5 million). In 1987, half of all abortions were performed at ≤8 weeks of gestation and approximately 90 percent were ≤12 weeks. Approximately 4 percent of legal abortions are performed between 16 and 20 weeks. Nearly all legal abortions were done with curettage (93% were performed using suction curettage); in 1.3 percent, intrauterine saline or prostaglandin instillation was used, a lower percentage than in 1984 [33–35].

Six percent of 18- to 19-year-olds had abortions compared to 3 percent of all women aged 14 to 44 years. Although the nonwhite abortion rate (number of abortions/1000 women) is about twice the rate for whites, teenage whites and nonwhites have about the same abortion ratio (number of abortions/100 live births and abortions). The highest abortion rates are found among unmarried women, women 40 years old and older, teenagers, and nonwhites. In 1983, approximately 411,000 teenagers aged 15 to 19 years and 16,350 teenagers less than 15 years had abortions [8, 33–36]. Abortions in teenagers less than 20 years old account for about 27 percent of the total abortions. Reasons for delay in seeking abortion services include young age, irregular menses, failure to recognize pregnancy symptoms, ambivalence about abortion, low educational level, and lacking awareness and availability of a clinic [37].

The death to case rate for abortion in 1983 was 0.7/100,000 and in 1985 0.5/100,000. In 1984, 14 deaths were reported, with 9 related to legally induced abortions (among an estimated 1.5 million abortions), 4 to spontaneous abortions, and 1 from an illegally induced abortion. Morbidity and mortality rise with increased gestational age so that the risk approximately doubles with each 2-week delay beyond 8 weeks. The death to case rate for legal abortion in 1972 to 1980 was 0.5/100,000 for ≤8 weeks, 1.3/100,000 for 9 to 10 weeks, and 2.1/100,000 for 11 to 12 weeks. Teenagers have lower rates of morbidity and mortality than older women at the same gestational age [38].

FIRST TRIMESTER ABORTION
The distinction between first and second trimester abortions is not as useful as previously because techniques have changed in the past decade and pregnancy is a continuum. In the first 12 weeks of gestation, the most commonly used method for abortion is suction curettage. Some clinicians use laminaria to facilitate dilatation of the cervix; these must be put in place 3 to 24 hours before the procedure and thus cause delay and an added procedure for patients. Clinicians currently follow their individual preferences, since controlled studies are conflicting. Use of laminaria may lessen the risk of cervical lacerations and uterine perforation, as these complications are most likely during the dilatation portion of the procedure. Other methods of augmenting dilatation are under investigation [39].

Preoperative evaluation in adolescents should include a history and physical examination. Laboratory testing should include a pregnancy test, Papanicolaou smear, cervical tests for *N. gonorrhoeae* and *C. trachomatis*, hematocrit, urinalysis, Rh determination, and in most adolescents a serology for syphilis. HIV counselling and testing may be a consideration. If cultures are done with sufficient time to obtain results before the procedure, treatment with antibiotics can be instituted for positive results. If cultures are done at the time of the procedure, many clinics prefer to give prophylactic tetracycline or doxycycline for 4 to 7 days in high-risk patients, including adolescents and those with a history of previous PID. In a recent study in Sweden [40] doxycycline, 400 mg, or placebo was given as a single oral dose 10 to 12 hours before first trimester abortion; 2.1 percent of doxycycline-treated patients and 6.2 percent of placebo patients developed PID (p < .01). As expected, a significant percentage of patients treated with such a large dose of doxycycline developed nausea and vomiting, although the authors felt the drug was well tolerated. Rh-negative adolescents should receive Rh_o immune globulin at the time of the abortion to prevent possible sensitization.

The procedure can be performed with general or local anesthesia in a hospital ambulatory operating room or a freestanding abortion clinic. Local anesthesia with paracervical block and intravenous sedation with valium and fentanyl are the common practice. Essential is a calm, sensitive clinician who can talk the patient through the procedure, which may be associated with uterine cramping. Many very young adolescents prefer general anesthesia, since the pelvic examination alone may be difficult. General anesthesia is associated with a two- to fourfold increase in the risk of death, compared to local anesthesia, and a higher rate of uterine perforation and hemorrhage, intra-abdominal hemorrhage, and cervical trauma [39]. Inhalation anesthetics relax the uterus, causing much larger blood loss; thus if general anesthesia is chosen for induction, intravenous drugs should be used during the procedure itself. However, local anesthesia is associated with higher rates of postoperative fever, perhaps due to more likelihood of retained products. At our hospital where we deliver abortion services only to very young adolescents, general anesthesia is generally used. The patient has her counselling and examination several days before the actual procedure, which is done in an ambulatory operating room. The adolescent is told that the abortion is like a "heavy period" and that she will continue to have her period for several days after the procedure. She is encouraged to start her birth control pills within 3 days or on the Sunday after the procedure.

Transcervical aspiration before 50 days is called menstrual extraction. With the advent of sensitive pregnancy tests, this procedure should no longer be performed on patients who are late for a menses but not pregnant. The earlier data suggested a higher rate of incomplete abortions for this procedure as compared to the usual suction aspiration later in the first trimester; this conclusion has been disputed as more experience with this technique has been gained.

Most abortions on adolescents involve the use of suction curettage with gentle dilatation of the cervix. The products of conception should always be carefully examined (and optimally sent to Pathology) to make sure that a pregnancy has been terminated and to rule out a molar gestation. Failure to detect fetal parts or villi should prompt the clinician to consider diagnoses such as ectopic pregnancy, false-positive pregnancy test (rare with the new kits), unrecognized early spontaneous abortion, uninterrupted intrauterine pregnancy, or uterine anomaly. Repeat pregnancy test, curettage, ultrasonography, and laparoscopy are tools for making the correct diagnosis.

Complications of first trimester abortion include excess blood loss resulting in transfusion in 0.6 percent, known perforation of the uterus in 0.2 percent, postabortion hematometra in 0.2 to 1.0 percent, cervical trauma in 0.18 to 0.96 percent, infection in 0.1 to 5.2 percent, retained products of conception in 0.61 percent, and failed abortion in 0.2 percent [39, 41, 42]. Immediately postprocedure oxytocic agents may decrease blood loss and are used primarily in second trimester abortions and with general anesthesia. Adolescents with retained products of conception usually complain of heavy bleeding and cramps, with or without fever, in the first week after the abortion and require repeat curettage. Pelvic infection following an abortion is a potentially serious problem because of the risks of subsequent infertility. Risk factors include late gestational age, endocervical infection with *N. gonorrhoeae* or *C. trachomatis*, and intra-amniotic instillations. Patients with infections typically complain of fever and bleeding 3 to 7 days after the abortion and have uterine tenderness and sometimes adnexal tenderness on examination. Antibiotics as indicated on page 364 for the treatment of PID should be instituted and recurettage performed. When an early pregnancy is terminated by menstrual extraction, it is especially important to consider the possibility of a failed abortion [43]. No matter what type of abortion is performed, the patient must be seen in a follow-up clinic to avoid missing a failed abortion.

The data on the long-term medical and psychological effects of first trimester abortion are reassuring [44, 45]. There is no conclusive evidence of an increase in miscarriages or adverse late pregnancy outcomes in patients with one previous induced abortion. The use of gentle cervical dilatation techniques in the past decade should lessen the previously noted increased risk of midtrimester spontaneous abortions [44]. Two or more induced abortions may increase slightly subsequent pregnancy loss [45]. There appears to be no change in the fertility or ectopic pregnancy rate in women who have had an induced abortion. Any change in ectopic pregnancy rate is likely to be confined to women who have had a postabortal infection. In a Danish study [46], postabortal pelvic infection was associated with a higher rate of spontaneous abortion, secondary infertility, dyspareunia, and chronic pelvic pain than uncomplicated abortion. Prophylactic antibiotics at the time of the abortion decreased the rates of later spontaneous abortion and dyspareunia.

A promising new approach to first trimester abortion is the synthetic progesterone antagonist RU-486. A single dose administered to women at less than 50 days from the LMP was effective and safe in causing abortion in most patients; efficacy was 100 percent with initial β-HCG level below 5000 mIU/ml compared to 81 percent at greater than 20,000 mIU/ml [47]. Overall 45 of 50 patients aborted, with only one of these requiring a curettage. The 5 patients who did not abort underwent a suction curettage without complications. The most serious side effect was bleeding, with the mean decrease in hemoglobin of 0.4 gm/100 ml and bleeding lasting up to 16 days in some patients. Only two patients had a drop greater than 3 gm/100 ml. Similar findings were reported by Couzinet and associates [48] in France with the recommendation that this drug be used only under close medical supervision because of the risk of bleeding. In one study [49], epostane, an inhibitor of 3 β-hydroxysteroid dehydrogenase, taken for 7 days, also appeared to be effective in inducing abortion in 84 percent of women between the fifth and eighth week of pregnancy but caused significant nausea in most.

SECOND TRIMESTER ABORTION
Second trimester abortions (≥13 weeks) account for only about 10 percent of abortions in the United States. These late abortions carry higher risks to the patient and have greater ethical and emotional consequences. Unfortunately, the political climate, the restriction of funding for poor patients, the lack of convenient access to first trimester abortion in some communities, and the legislation related to parental consent in some states may delay the adolescent's decision and may result in more late abortions. Age is a major factor in delay; in 1980, 25 percent of abortions performed on girls less than 15 years were midtrimester compared to 14 percent for 15- to 19-year-old adolescents and 7 percent for 30- to 34-year-old women [50, 51]. Another reason for delay is serious psychological problems resulting in denial of the pregnancy.

Techniques of performing second trimester abortions have significantly evolved over the past 15 years. Patients are no longer forced to wait from 13 to 16 weeks to take advantage of intra-amniotic instillation methods. Studies in the 1970s revealed that dilatation and evacuation (D and E) was significantly safer than intra-amniotic instillation. Currently D and E is the safest method for abortion from 13 to 16 weeks, and some surgeons use the technique up to 21 weeks. The risks of cervical injury are lessened if laminaria are used before dilatation. Stubblefield [50] recommends laminaria for all abortions beyond 13 weeks. New materials are under investigation for this purpose [52]. Most clinicians feel that intravenous sedation with local anesthesia is the safest for the patient to lessen the chance of uterine perforation. Ultrasound determination of gestational age is extremely useful in pregnancies over 13 weeks and should be done in all gestations over 20 weeks to prevent ethical, legal and medical complications. Intraoperative ultrasound, particularly in terminations later than 18 weeks, has proven invaluable to ensure that the uterine cavity is empty.

Beyond 16 weeks, a variety of techniques and combinations of these techniques are used to induce abortion including D and E, prostaglandins (systemic, vaginal, or intra-amniotic), urea, and saline. Placement of laminaria overnight followed by D and E can be used up to 21 weeks by an appropriately skilled surgeon. A combination of urea and prostaglandin appears to be particularly useful when D and E is not available. Although second trimester abortions make up only 10 percent of abortions, they accounted for half of the mortality from abortions between 1972 and 1981. Causes of death included infection (30%), amniotic fluid embolism, hemorrhage, disseminated intravascular coagulation, pulmonary embolism, and anesthetic complications. Potential problems encountered with these second trimester abortion methods include difficulties in the instillation, excessive bleeding, retained placenta, failed abortion, uterine rupture, and disseminated intravascular coagulation [50, 53, 54]. Cervical incompetence and later spontaneous losses may be associated with forceful dilatation of the cervix [53, 54]. Midtrimester abortion done by D and E is psychologically more trying to the physician, whereas instillation may be more traumatic psychologically to the patient.

Health care providers need to know in detail the medical procedures done in their community (including the availability and type of abortion done between 16 and 20 weeks) in order to do adequate counselling and to refer patients to appropriate centers. The telephone numbers and the fees (and types of insurance accepted) should be updated once a year.

FOLLOW-UP COUNSELLING

A phone contact by the primary care provider to the adolescent one day after the procedure is helpful to ask, "How did it go? How are you feeling?" and to make sure that the patient knows when to start her oral contraceptive pills (if that is the method chosen). Follow-up visits, 2 weeks postabortion and then at least every 3 months for a year, will allow the patient a chance to verbalize her feelings. Ambivalence about the pregnancy and abortion may recur. A teenager may discontinue her pills for several days when the ambivalent feelings emerge. The abortion date or due date itself may take on a magical quality for the teenager, and she may return 1 year after the abortion with psychosomatic complaints, depression, and, rarely, attempted suicide. It is very helpful if the patient's record gives some indication of the process by which the patient made her decision. Reminding her that she made the best decision she could at the time, taking into account her plans for school, a job, or college, often helps the patient resolve her feelings of ambivalence.

CONTINUING THE PREGNANCY TO TERM

The teenager who desires to continue the pregnancy to term should receive special prenatal care. Teenagers may appear in clinics very late in gestation or fail to make an appointment in a prenatal program because of inability to negotiate the secretaries and paperwork. Adolescents (aged 13–19 years) are at increased risk of delivering low-birth-weight babies [4–7, 55–57]; however, whether this problem can be attributed to age as opposed to socioeconomic and other factors has been disputed [58]. The risk for low-birth-weight infants seems especially prominent in adolescents less than 15 years old and in multiparous adolescents. McAnarney [55] has suggested that multiple maternal factors account for the findings of low birth weight (<2500 gm) and neonatal mortality, including poor nutrition, substance use (cigarettes, alcohol, and illicit drugs), and genital infections. Adolescents in the first 2 years postmenarche need more nutrients and are in competition for those needed by the developing fetus. Naeye [59] found that acetonuria of 2+ or greater was more than twice as frequent in very young mothers (5% of 10- to 14-year-olds compared to 2% of 17- to 32-year-olds), a sign of starvation and a marker for excessive perinatal mortality in undernourished gestations. Adequate maternal weight gain during adolescent pregnancies can markedly increase infant birth weight [60]. After adjusting for confounding variables, Scholl and co-workers [61] found that adolescent smokers had infants weighing 222 gm less than nonsmokers and were more than 3.1 times as likely to have a small-for-dates infant than nonsmokers. Substance abuse is common among pregnant adolescents and is associated with social and medical characteristics which contribute to poor outcomes [62]. Interventions need to help adolescents see the adverse fetal consequences of smoking and substance abuse. Close attention needs to be paid to the possibility of genital infections so that adequate treatment can be instituted. Condoms should be encouraged throughout pregnancy to prevent the acquisition of new infections including HPV, HIV, syphilis, gonorrhea, and chlamydia. Peer pressure, time constraints, and finances may lead to erratic eating habits. The short-term benefits of good nutrition, not just the impact on the health of the baby, need to be emphasized.

In a hospital-based cohort, Lieberman and colleagues [63] found that the best maternal predictors of giving birth to a premature infant were age less than 20, single marital status, receiving welfare, and not having graduated from high school. The presence of any one factor increased the risk of prematurity to 7.0 percent compared to 4.6 percent with no risk factors present. Although racial differences in the risk of prematurity are in part related to medical and socioeconomic factors, Kleinman and Kessel [64] have examined the 1983 national data and concluded that black race is associated with low birth weight. Prenatal care is especially important for blacks [59, 65, 66]. As Felice and co-workers [67, 68] have pointed out, ethnic differences between whites, blacks, and Hispanics are quite real and need further research rather than generalizing data to all adolescent pregnancies. In a study in California, lack of medical insurance seems to impact particularly on adverse outcomes for blacks and Latinos [69].

Many special programs have been developed in this country for pregnant teens to help prepare them for delivery, motherhood, and future family planning. The adolescent is seen for frequent visits by a multidisciplinary team, consisting of a doctor, nurse, social worker, and nutritionist. Informal discussion groups, often led by a nurse, help educate the adolescent in nutrition, basic physiology, types of anesthesia, fetal monitoring, breast- versus bottle-feeding, postpartum care, and use of contraceptives. In communities without such programs, a sympathetic nurse in the obstetrician's office or a nurse-midwife may fill a similar educational role. In general, adolescents who receive adequate prenatal care and support can have good obstetric outcomes and postpartum contraceptive compliance [68, 70]. Felice and co-workers [71] undertook a study of a high-risk group of inner city (93% black) pregnant adolescents served by a special multidisciplinary team and compared the outcomes to adolescents followed in the regular obstetrics clinic. Only 9.0 percent of infants born to mothers in the special clinic weighed less than 2500 gm as compared to 20.9 percent of infants in the regular clinic. Special clinics with peer counselling can also effectively promote breast-feeding, which is usually not accepted by teen mothers [72]. Adequate calcium should be provided to avoid compromising the bone mass of the teen. Felice and co-workers [67] have pointed out the need to target interventions to the ethnic population served. She found that Mexican-American adolescents were less likely to be cigarette smokers, were more likely to gain more than 12 kg, and delivered the heaviest babies. They were more likely to be married at conception and to breast-feed their babies than other ethnic groups.

Poverty, depression, and social isolation are frequent problems of the young parent. The young mother may have no access to day-care or babysitting and may have lost the social contacts she had in school. Teenagers who give birth while in school or soon after quitting school are far less likely to graduate from high school than those who delay childbearing to their twenties. Of those who did graduate, 40 percent obtain a GED, a credential that may not grant the same career opportunities as a high school diploma [73]. Even for young parents able to continue in school, extracurricular activities (especially sports) are often impossible. However, teenagers who do not continue in school can effectively postpone a second pregnancy if an intervention program provides close postpartum follow-up [74].

Many programs have focused on the adolescent's pregnancy and the immediate postpartum period when the needs are obviously long-term. In addition, the adolescent may lose the nurturing, supportive relationships that she has with clinic personnel when she delivers, and this loss may tend to promote recidivism. A number of innovative approaches have been tried to deal with these problems. The St. Paul Maternal and Infant Care Project [21] has had striking success in preventing the second pregnancy and in helping teenagers finish high school. Provision of medical and contraceptive services, infant day-care within the high school, and a multitude of social and nutritional services have made a dramatic impact. An intervention program in Syracuse included a family planning clinic across the street from the high school. Of the first 325 patients at a 4-year follow-up, only 59 became pregnant. Forty percent of those who finished high school went on to higher education. At follow-up, only 13 percent remained at home and on welfare [75]. PAGES (Pregnant Adolescent Group for Education and Support) is another new school-based program in Chicago, which combines educational and social support to help teens stay in school and deliver healthy babies [76]. At The Children's Hospital in Boston, we have a Young Parents Clinic, which provides contraceptive services and other medical and social services to the mother at the same time that she brings in her infant for well-child care. A provider with expertise in both adolescent and pediatric health provides medical care to the family. Outreach workers and visiting nurses fill an important educational role as well as helping the adolescent overcome barriers to making clinic appointments. In other settings, two practitioners can work together to optimize care for the adolescent mother and her child.

Since children of adolescent mothers are at particular risk of behavioral and cognitive difficulties, efforts need to be made to help mothers interact with their children [77]. McAnarney and colleagues [78] found that younger adolescent mothers tended to show less acceptance, sensitivity, and cooperation and more negative verbal communication with their 9- to 12-month-old infants than did older adolescent mothers.

The involvement of fathers in intervention programs has increased in the past decade. Many young fathers suffer negative psychosocial consequences including depression and social isolation [79]. They may quit school to try to provide financial support, an effort that is often counterproductive in the long run because of limited skills. Since many teenage fathers, especially blacks and Hispanics, tend to be involved with their children, inclusion in programs with job training would be ideal [80].

An adolescent's best hope for the future is to avoid repeated pregnancies, since closely spaced children appear to limit sharply the options for the future in terms of school achievement, independence from welfare, and other goals. In a follow-up study of women who were teen mothers in the 1960s, Furstenberg and associates [81] found that women who had more children in the 5 years after their first birth did less well in school, had lower aspirations, and came from more disadvantaged families. Women with better-educated parents who were more economically secure often were able to escape welfare, finish education, and find satisfying careers. Concrete services of education and job training are essential. Analyzing data from the National Survey of Family Growth, Ford [82] found that the probability of a second pregnancy to an adolescent mother in the year following a first birth to be 17 percent. Only 20 percent of adolescents planned the pregnancy; adolescents with incomes less than 150 percent of the poverty level had twice the risk of a second pregnancy than did adolescents whose incomes were above that level (21% versus 11%). Hispanic teen mothers are more likely to have a second birth and appear to be less knowledgeable about menstrual cycles and fertility. Longer-acting contraceptives, such as Norplant, may offer more effective options for delaying a second pregnancy.

There has been little attention given to the girl who chooses to give up her baby for adoption. The choice often allows the adolescent to continue her education and career plans. However, many may continue to experience depression and remorse and need help coping with the loss.

DISORDERS OF EARLY PREGNANCY

Adolescents can experience the same difficulties during early pregnancy as adults, including ectopic pregnancy; threatened, missed, or incomplete abortion; and molar pregnancy. The difference is that the adolescent may not have previously thought she was pregnant before presenting to the emergency ward with heavy bleeding, irregular menses, or pelvic pain. In addition, she may have a preexisting cervical infection with N. gonorrhoeae or C. trachomatis and may therefore be at increased risk for endometritis and salpingitis.

Wilcox and colleagues [83] have recently documented the risk of early pregnancy loss by collecting daily urine specimens on 221 healthy women attempting to conceive. They found that the total rate of pregnancy loss after implantation, including clinically recognized spontaneous abortions, was 31 percent. Twenty-two percent of the pregnancies ended before a pregnancy was detected clinically. Although this observation is important given the widespread use of very sensitive pregnancy tests, the possibility of an ectopic pregnancy always needs to be kept in mind.

The sharp rise in the incidence of ectopic pregnancy noted in the 1970s and 1980s has been attributed to a number of factors including the increased incidence of salpingitis, the use of intrauterine devices, the delay in childbearing to the thirties (an age with a higher rate of ectopic pregnancy), tubal surgery including tubal sterilization, the earlier detection of pregnancy with the use of sensitive urine and blood tests of HCG, and in one study the use of progestin-only birth control pills [84–90]. The rate should, however, be stated in relation to *all* pregnancies, not just live births, to take into account induced abortions. With the rising number of cases of sexually transmitted diseases and PID in adolescents, clinicians need to consider an ectopic pregnancy when evaluating adolescents with irregular bleeding and/or abdominal pain. In addition, girls may have more than one diagnosis—such as ectopic pregnancy and PID (as illustrated in Case 16 in Chap. 6)—at the time of presentation to the clinic. The youngest patient with ectopic pregnancy seen in our institution was 12 years old.

Mortality risks from ectopic pregnancy are higher for black women than white women, especially among teenagers and older women [91]. Blacks are less likely to seek prenatal care in the first trimester of pregnancy, when the diagnosis of an ectopic pregnancy might be raised. It is also likely that black women, especially black teenagers, have less adequate access to gynecologic services. Non-English-speaking patients, mentally retarded patients, and substance abusers are at increased risk of late diagnosis.

The classic history of ectopic pregnancy includes pelvic pain, amenorrhea, and vaginal bleeding. However, many patients do not have all or, in fact, any of these symptoms, in part because of earlier diagnosis with the use of ultrasonography and sensitive pregnancy tests. Adolescents may give vague histories of the timing of the LMP and may accept menstrual irregularity as a normal event. The data of previous large series of ectopic pregnancy may be of interest, although the clinician should realize that with earlier diagnosis the statistics are very different today. In two studies of symptoms of ectopic pregnancy, Kitchin and co-workers [92] found that 20 percent of their patients denied missing a period, and Helvacioglu and colleagues [93] found that 7 percent denied a skipped menses. Acute pelvic pain was reported in 96 to 99 percent of patients, a number higher than would be seen today. In the Kitchin study, 44 percent had pain of less than 24 hours' duration; 29 percent, 1 to 7 days; and 26 percent, for greater than 1 week. Nausea, vomiting, and fainting are reported by about one third of patients. Acute rupture with hemorrhage can cause shock and death. Fortunately, the risk of death from an ectopic pregnancy has declined in the last decade with earlier diagnosis and treatment, but this also means that fewer patients present with pain or other classic symptoms. A missed menstrual period or irregular spotting or bleeding is a frequent presentation now.

The physical examination may show helpful signs for the clinician but also may be nonspecific for other diagnoses. In acute, ruptured ectopic pregnancy, signs of intraperitoneal hemorrhage and shock are found. In unruptured ectopic pregnancy, findings are much more subtle. Abdominal tenderness and rebound tenderness may be found. Adnexal tenderness may prevent adequate assessment for the presence of a pelvic mass, which in fact may not be palpable with early diagnosis [92–94]. Bimanual examination should be performed gently in these patients. The uterus may be enlarged, simulating an early intrauterine pregnancy.

The HCG level is the mainstay of diagnosis in combination with ultrasonography and laparoscopy [95–98]. The clinician needs to decide if the pregnancy is ectopic or intrauterine and whether spontaneous abortion is occurring. The patient's desire for the pregnancy should be a factor in the approach to intervention, even though clinicians frequently assume that all adolescent pregnancies are unwanted. A sensitive urine test such as Hybritech's ICON can detect levels of HCG as low as 50 mIU/ml (the new kits to 20 mIU/ml). Only an extremely rare lesion without trophoblastic tissue or with apparent defects in HCG production would be expected to have no detectable HCG. A very early ectopic or intrauterine pregnancy can have a level of HCG less than 50 mIU/ml, but the likelihood of symptomatology is low. Quantitative serum tests should help the clinician to elucidate the diagnosis [98]. In order to rely on the results of the urine testing, the physician must feel comfortable that the urine belongs to the patient and has not been altered because of her fear of drug testing. In addition, molar pregnancies, gestational trophoblastic neoplasia, and some ovarian tumors also produce HCG.

The management of the unstable or shocky patient with a positive pregnancy test and ectopic pregnancy is clearly different from the evaluation of the stable or asymptomatic adolescent with a positive pregnancy test and vaginal bleeding. The unstable patient requires surgical intervention with immediate laparoscopy; a young woman in shock must be treated for the shock and taken to the operating room for laparotomy.

Most patients do not require immediate surgical intervention, and the treatment is guided by clinical assessment and measurement of quantitative HCG levels. During the evaluation, the patient needs to understand the nature of the differential diagnosis; she should receive careful instructions on warning signs of ectopic pregnancy and spontaneous abortion. Thus, if the adolescent presents with vaginal spotting or pain and has a positive pregnancy test, the possibility of an ectopic or threatened abortion needs to be determined. Serial HCG levels must be done in the same laboratory with the same reference preparation so that changes can be used to guide the clinician (see p. 37 for discussion of HCG and ultrasound). After an HCG of 100 mIU/ml, doubling time of HCG is approximately 2.3 days in early gestation. Mean doubling time is 1.6 days for 23 to 35 days of gestation, 2.0

days for 35 to 42 days of gestation, and 3.4 days for 41 to 50 days [99]. Because gestational age is unlikely to be known precisely, the clinician typically uses the lower limits of a 48 hour interval. Between 5 and 8 weeks, the HCG should increase by 66 percent at 48 hours and 114 percent in 72 hours; an increase of less than this increment should alert the clinician to the possibility of a failed intrauterine or ectopic pregnancy. A small number of normal pregnancies do have a lag in doubling.

Ultrasonography has proven a valuable tool in the diagnosis of normal and abnormal pregnancies. The so-called discriminatory zone is a key concept and depends on the medical center, the ultrasound equipment, the type of ultrasound (abdominal versus vaginal), and the radiologist. As noted on p. 37, a gestational sac can optimally be visualized by abdominal ultrasound using the latest scanning equipment at approximately 6000 mIU/ml of HCG (IRP) (5–6 weeks from LMP). Sometimes an ectopic pregnancy will be associated with a pseudodecidual reaction within the uterus which may mimic an intrauterine pregnancy. The location of a fetal heart (7–8 weeks from LMP) is conclusive evidence of an intrauterine pregnancy by ultrasound; it is extremely rare for intrauterine and ectopic pregnancies to coexist (1/30,000). Transvaginal ultrasound can detect an intrauterine pregnancy at a lower HCG level (around 1500 mIU/ml). An ectopic pregnancy may occasionally be visualized by sonography as a heart beat in the adnexa; a noncystic adnexal mass is suggestive of an ectopic pregnancy, but not conclusive. Communication with the ultrasonographer is critical in the care of the patient suspected of having an ectopic pregnancy.

Clinical management thus depends on the status of the patient, the levels of HCG, the desire to continue an intrauterine pregnancy, and the ultrasound results. In the *asymptomatic* adolescent who has *falling* HCG levels, the clinician should follow the HCG levels to 0 to make sure that whatever process (tubal pregnancy, missed abortion, abortion) has totally resolved. If the HCG results show a *constant* level or *subnormal increases*, the intervention depends in part on whether the pregnancy is desired. Another HCG may be required along with a repeat ultrasound done at the discriminatory zone if a normal pregnancy with initial slightly subnormal increases in HCG is suspected. If the HCG is above the discriminatory zone and no intrauterine gestational sac is seen on ultrasound, laparoscopy is undertaken. If the pregnancy is desired but the clinician suspects an ectopic pregnancy (noncystic adnexal mass or subnormal increases in HCG), laparoscopy is done first. If the pregnancy is *not* desired, a D and E is done first. If no villi from an intrauterine pregnancy are identified grossly or by pathology at the time of D and E, laparoscopy is performed.

Treatment of ectopic pregnancy should aim at timely intervention and preservation of future fertility. Salpingectomy, salpingostomy, and more recently laparoscopic salpingostomy have been used for the treatment of ectopic pregnancy. After salpingostomy, reapproximation of the fallopian tube is not necessary because healing will often occur with spontaneous closure resulting in less likelihood of kinking.

Several other approaches are under clinical investigation. Medical management with methotrexate-citrovorum factor has been safely used in small numbers of patients with HCG below 1500 mIU/ml; Sauer [100] reported a study of 21 patients with ectopic pregnancies of less than 3 cm, with intact serosa, and with no active bleeding. They concluded that ectopic pregnancies with formed fetal elements should not be treated medically. Two studies have also indicated that *some* ectopic pregnancies with no pain, of less than 2 cm, and with β-HCG of less than 1000 mIU/ml resolved spontaneously without surgery; however some of the patients entered into the trial required surgical treatment [101]. Thus, more studies are needed before clinicians alter current therapy with laparoscopy and surgical intervention in the care of adolescents. In all cases, HCG levels should be checked two weeks later to be sure that the levels have fallen to zero, and if not, followed to zero. Most patients have a negative titer by 12 days [98]. There is a small chance of regrowth of trophoblastic tissue with a procedure of less than a total salpingectomy. Methotrexate holds promise for the management of the rare persistent ectopic pregnancy.

Timely intervention has clearly improved the prognosis of patients as medical providers have had improved access to sensitive pregnancy testing and better ultrasonography. Other tests may also prove useful to the clinician considering the diagnosis of ectopic pregnancy. Serum progesterone levels under 15 ng/ml have been shown to be associated with ectopic pregnancy [102]. Also promising is rapid measurement of urinary pregnanediol glucuronide, which is low in abnormal pregnancies including ectopics [103]. The preservation of fertility is still difficult to achieve in all patients. Many young women are able to conceive but there is an increased risk (10 to 16 percent) of repeated ectopic pregnancy [104]. Adolescents with tubal disease sufficient to cause an ectopic pregnancy are at high risk of future tubal disease, and therefore total salpingectomy should be avoided, if possible, to leave open the options for future fertility repair. Salpingostomy is preferable to salpingectomy.

The treatment of the nonviable intrauterine pregnancy depends on several factors. As is the case with the management of ectopic pregnancies, the declining HCG levels must be from the same laboratory in order to establish that the pregnancy is nonviable. Patients without significant trophoblastic tissue and low levels of HCG can be followed without operative intervention, provided heavy bleeding does not occur and the HCG declines to zero. In spontaneous abortion the HCG is usually near zero by 19 days. In contrast, following elective first trimester abortion, patients will have a slower decline of HCG to zero because of high initial levels; HCG is detectable for 16 to 60 days after D and E with a mean of 30 days.

Two treatment options may be considered for the adolescent with a nonviable pregnancy, intrauterine products of conception, a closed cervix, and declining HCG levels: Observation or D and E. If observation is chosen, the patient must be followed closely and must be able to return promptly for curettage when she begins to pass tissue. The open os makes the procedure less risky, but adolescents may have difficulty arranging transportation to the hospital [98]. Early D and E avoids the adolescent's having to carry a nonviable pregnancy and having to come to the emergency ward for sudden bleeding. Importantly, the prime consideration in the adolescent with vaginal bleeding and pain 10 weeks after a missed period presenting with a positive pregnancy test is a spontaneous abortion, not an ectopic pregnancy. Many hospital emergency wards are now set up to offer immediate suction curettage. Cultures for *N. gonorrhoeae* and *C. trachomatis* should be done at the time of the examination, and consideration given to prescribing prophylactic antibiotics (doxycycline 100 mg twice daily for 7 days) following D and E.

The adolescent seen for "irregular bleeding" at follow-up after a spontaneous abortion, term pregnancy, or elective termination of pregnancy should always have a pregnancy test done at the appropriate interval when it would be expected to be negative. Irregular bleeding should not be assumed to be due to breakthrough bleeding from oral contraceptives. A positive pregnancy test should raise the possibility of a pregnancy (normal or abnormal) or a gestational neoplasia [98].

Clinicians caring for adolescent patients will be confronted with the medical and psychological issues of normal and abnormal pregnancies. Given the significant morbidity and mortality associated with ectopic pregnancy and the increase in incidence since the 1970s, physicians must be concerned about prevention of sexually transmitted infections. Lessening the occurrence of tubal disease in our adolescent population must remain a high priority for those providing medical care to this age group.

REFERENCES
1. Maciak BJ, Spitz AM, Strauss L, et al. Pregnancy and birth rates among sexually experienced US teenagers—1974, 1980, and 1983. JAMA 1987; 258:2069.
2. Zelnik M and Kantner JF. Sexual activity, contraceptive use and preg-

nancy among metropolitan-area teenagers, 1971–1979. Fam Plann Perspect 1980; 12:230.

3. Alan Guttmacher Institute. Teenage Pregnancy: The Problem That Hasn't Gone Away. New York: The Alan Guttmacher Institute, 1980.

4. Makinson C. The health consequences of teenage fertility. Fam Plann Perspect 1985; 17:132.

5. Zuckerman BS, Walker DK, Frank DA, et al. Adolescent pregnancy: Biobehavioral determinants of outcome. J Pediatr 1985; 105:857.

6. Spivak H, and Weitzman M. Social barriers faced by adolescent parents and their children. JAMA 1987; 258:1500.

7. McAnarney ER. Adolescent pregnancy and childbearing: New data, new challenges (Commentaries). Pediatrics 1985; 75:973.

8. Henshaw SK, Binkin NJ, Blaine E, and Smith JC. A portrait of American women who obtain abortions. Fam Plann Perspect 1985; 17:90.

9. Abrahamse AF, Morrison PA, Waite LJ, et al. Beyond Stereotypes: Who Becomes a Single Teenage Mother? R-3489-HHS-NICHD. Santa Monica, CA: Rand Corp., 1988.

10. Litt IF, Cuskey WR, and Rudd S. Identifying adolescents at risk for noncompliance with contraceptive therapy. J Pediatr 1980; 96:742.

11. Zelnik M, Koenig MA, and Kim YJ. Sources of prescription contraceptives and subsequent pregnancy among young women. Fam Plann Perspect 1984; 16:6.

12. Emans SJ, Grace E, Woods ER, et al. Adolescents' compliance with the use of oral contraceptives. JAMA 1987; 257:3377.

13. Grimes DA. Unplanned pregnancies in the United States. Obstet Gynecol 1986; 67:438.

14. Zelnik M. Sexual knowledge and knowledge of pregnancy risk among U.S. teenage women. Fam Plann Perspect 1979; 11:355.

15. Sarrel LJ, and Sarrel PM. Sexual Unfolding. Boston: Little, Brown, 1979.

16. Nadelson CC, Notman MT, and Gillon JW. Sexual knowledge and attitudes of adolescents: Relationship to contraceptive usage. Obstet Gynecol 1980; 55:340.

17. Cole JB, Beighton FC, and Jones IH. Contraceptive practice and unplanned pregnancy among single university students. Br Med J 1975; 4:217.

18. Freeman EW, Rickels K, Huggins GR, et al. Urban black adolescents who obtain contraceptive services before or after their first pregnancy. J Adolesc Health Care 1984; 5:183.

19. Vernon MEL, Green JA, and Frothington TE. Teenage pregnancy: A prospective study of self-esteem and other sociodemographic factors. Pediatrics 1983; 72:632.

20. Bran EA, Edwards L, Callicott T, et al. Strategies for prevention of pregnancy in adolescents. Adv Plann Parenthood 1979; 14:68.

21. Edwards LE, Steinman ME, Arnold KA, et al. Adolescent pregnancy prevention services in high school clinics. Fam Plann Perspect 1980; 12:6.

22. Zabin LS, Hirsch MB, Smith EA, et al. Evaluation of a pregnancy prevention program for urban teenagers. Fam Plann Perspect 1986; 18:119.

23. Zabin LS, Hirsch MB, Streett R, et al. The Baltimore pregnancy prevention program for urban teenagers: I. How did it work? Fam Plann Perspect 1988; 20:182.

24. Zabin LS, Hirsch MB, and Smith EA. The Baltimore pregnancy prevention program for urban teenagers: II. What did it cost? Fam Plann Perspect 1988; 20:188.

25. Dryfoos JG. School-based health clinics: Three years of experience. Fam Plann Perspect 1988; 20:193.
26. Vincent ML, Clearie AF, and Schluchter MD. Reducing adolescent pregnancy through school and community-based education. JAMA 1987; 257:3382.
27. Addelson F. Induced abortion: Source of guilt or growth. Am J Orthopsychiatry 1973; 43:815.
28. Nadelson C. Abortion counselling: Focus on adolescent pregnancy. Pediatrics 1974; 54:765.
29. Nadelson C. The pregnant teenager. Psychiatr Opinion 1975; 12:1.
30. Freeman EW. Influence of personality attribute on abortion experience. Am J Orthopsychiatry 1977; 47:503.
31. Bauman K. Selected aspects of the contraceptive practices of unmarried university students. Am J Obstet Gynecol 1970; 108:203.
32. Scher P, Emans SJ, and Grace E. Factors associated with compliance to oral contraceptive use in an adolescent population. J Adolesc Health Care 1982; 3:120.
33. CDC. Abortion surveillance, United States, 1984–85. MMWR 1989; 38:11.
34. CDC. Abortion surveillance: Preliminary Analysis—United States, 1986 and 1987. MMWR 1989; 38:662.
35. Henshaw SK. Trends in abortions, 1982–1984. Fam Plann Perspect 1986; 18:34.
36. Henshaw SK. Characteristics of U. S. women having abortions, 1982–1983. Fam Plann Perspect 1987; 19:5.
37. Grimes DA. Second-trimester abortions in the United States. Fam Plann Perspect 1984; 16:260.
38. Cates W, Schulz KF, and Grimes DA. The risks associated with teenage abortion. N Engl J Med 1983; 309:621.
39. Kaunitz AM, and Grimes DA. First-trimester abortion technology. In Corson SL, Derman RJ, and Tyrer LB (eds.). Fertility Control. Boston: Little, Brown, 1985.
40. Darj E, and Stralin EB. The prophylactic effect of doxycycline on postoperative infection rate after first-trimester abortion. Obstet Gynecol 1987; 70:755.
41. Cates W. Adolescent abortion in the United States. J Adolesc Health Care 1980; 1:18.
42. Burnhill MS, Armstead JW, Kessel E, et al. Computer-assisted evaluation of demographic trends and morbidity in first trimester vacuum aspiration. Adv Plann Parenthood 1978; 12:212.
43. Key TC, and Kreutner AK. Menstrual extraction in the adolescent. J Adolesc Health Care 1980; 1:127.
44. Harlap S, Shiono P, Ramcharan S, et al. A prospective study of spontaneous fetal losses after induced abortions. N Engl J Med 1979; 301:677.
45. Levin AA, Schoenbaum SC, Monson RR, et al. Association of induced abortion with subsequent pregnancy loss. JAMA 1980; 243:2495.
46. Heisterberg L, Hebjorn S, Andersen LF, and Petersen H. Sequelae of induced first-trimester abortion: A prospective study assessing the role of postabortal pelvic inflammatory disease and prophylactic antibiotics. Am J Obstet Gynecol 1986; 155:76.
47. Grimes DA, Mishell DR, Shoupe D, and Lacarra M. Early abortion with a single dose of the antiprogestin RU-486. Obstet Gynecol 1988; 158:1307.
48. Couzinet B, LeStrat N, Ulmann A, et al. Termination of early pregnancy

by the progesterone antagonist RU 486 (mifepristone). N Engl J Med 1986; 315:1565.

49. Crooij MJ, DeNooyer CCA, Rao BR, et al. Termination of early pregnancy by the 3 β-hydroxysteroid dehydrogenase inhibitor epostane. N Engl J Med 1988; 319:813.

50. Stubblefield PG. Induced abortion in the mid-trimester. In Corson SL, Derman RJ, Tyrer LB (eds.). Fertility Control. Boston: Little, Brown, 1985.

51. Brachen MD, and Kasl SV. Delay in seeking induced abortion: A review and theoretical analysis. Am J Obstet Gynecol 1975; 121:1008.

52. Blumenthal PD. Prospective comparison of dilapan and laminaria for pretreatment of the cervix in second-trimester induction abortion. Obstet Gynecol 1988; 72:243.

53. Benditt J. Second-trimester abortion in the United States. Fam Plann Perspect 1979; 11:358.

54. Grimes D, Schulz KF, Cates W, and Tyler CW. Midtrimester abortion by dilatation and evacuation. N Engl J Med 1977; 296:1141.

55. McAnarney ER. Young maternal age and adverse neonatal outcome. Am J Dis Child 1987; 141:1053.

56. Leppert PC, Namerow PB, and Barker D. Pregnancy outcomes among adolescent and older women receiving comprehensive prenatal care. J Adolesc Health Care 1986; 7:112.

57. Slap GB, and Schwartz JS. Risk factors for low birth weight to adolescent mothers. J Adolesc Health Care 1989; 10:267.

58. Zuckerman B, Alpert JJ, Dooling E, et al. Neonatal outcome: Is adolescent pregnancy a risk factor? Pediatrics 1983; 71:489.

59. Naeye RL. Teenaged and pre-teenaged pregnancies: Consequences of the fetal-maternal competition for nutrients. Pediatrics 1981; 67:146.

60. Scholl TO, Salmon RW, Miller LK, et al. Weight gain during adolescent pregnancy. J Adolesc Health Care 1988; 9:290.

61. Scholl TO, Salmon RW, and Miller L. Smoking and adolescent pregnancy outcome. J Adolesc Health Care 1986; 7:390.

62. Amaro H, Zuckerman B, and Cabral H. Drug use among adolescent mothers: Profile of risk. Pediatrics 1989; 84:144.

63. Lieberman E, Ryan KJ, Monson RR, et al. Risk factors accounting for racial differences in the rate of premature birth. N Engl J Med 1987; 317:743.

64. Kleinman JC, and Kessel SS. Racial differences in low birth weight: Trends and risk factors. N Engl J Med 1987; 317:749.

65. Murray JL, and Bernfield M. The differential effect of prenatal care on the incidence of low birth weight among blacks and whites in a prepaid health care plan. N Engl J Med 1988; 319:1385.

66. Gould JB, and LeRoy S. Socioeconomic status and low birth weight: A racial comparison. Pediatrics 1988; 82:896.

67. Felice ME, Shragg GP, James M, et al. Psychosocial aspects of Mexican-American, white and black teenage pregnancy. J Adolesc Health Care 1987; 8:330.

68. Felice ME, Shragg P, James M, et al. Clinical observations of Mexican-American, caucasian and black pregnant teenagers. J Adolesc Health Care 1986; 7:305.

69. Braveman P, Oliva G, Miller MG, et al. N Engl J Med 1989; 321:508.

70. McAnarney ER, Roghmann KJ, Adam BN, et al. Obstetric, neonatal and psychosocial outcome of pregnant adolescents. Pediatrics 1978; 61:199.

71. Felice ME, Granados JL, Ances IG, et al. The young pregnant teenager:

Impact of comprehensive prenatal care. J Adolesc Health Care 1981; 1:193.

72. Radius SM, and Joffe A. Understanding adolescent mothers' feelings about breast-feeding. J Adolesc Health Care 1988; 9:156.

73. Mott FL, and Marsiglio W. Early childbearing and completion of high school. Fam Plann Perspect 1985; 17:234.

74. Stevens-Simon C, Parsons J, and Montgomery C. What is the relationship between postpartum withdrawal from school and repeat pregnancy among adolescent mothers. J Adol Health Care 1986; 7:191.

75. Osofsky JD, and Osofsky HJ. Teenage pregnancy: Psychosocial considerations. Clin Obstet Gynecol 1978; 21:1161.

76. CDC. Pregnant adolescent group for education and support—Illinois. MMWR 1987; 36:549.

77. Elster AB, McAnarney ER, and Lamb ME. Parental behavior of adolescent mothers. Pediatrics 1983; 71:494.

78. McAnarney ER, Lawrence RA, Ricciuti HN, et al. Interactions of adolescent mothers and their 1-year-old children. Pediatrics 1986; 78:585.

79. Vaz R, Smolen P, and Miller C. Adolescent pregnancy: Involvement of the male partner. J Adolesc Health Care 1983; 4:246.

80. Rivara FP, Sweeney PJ, and Henderson BF. Black teenage fathers: What happens when the child is born? Pediatrics 1986; 78:151.

81. Furstenberg FF, Brooks-Gunn J, and Morgan SP. Adolescent mothers and their children in later life. Fam Plann Perspect 1987; 19:142.

82. Ford K. Second pregnancies among teenage mothers. Fam Plann Perspect 1983; 15:268.

83. Wilcox AJ, Weinberg CR, O'Connor JF, et al. Incidence of early loss of pregnancy. N Engl J Med 1988; 319:189.

84. Hollatt JG. Ectopic pregnancy associated with the intrauterine device: A study of seventy cases. Am J Obstet Gynecol 1976; 125:754.

85. Luikko P, Erkkola P, and Laakso L. Ectopic pregnancies during use of low-dose progestogens for oral contraceptives. Contraception 1977; 16:575.

86. Panayotou PP, Kaskarelis DB, Miettinen OS, et al. Induced abortion and ectopic pregnancies. Am J Obstet Gynecol 1972; 114:507.

87. Taylor RN. Ectopic pregnancy and reproductive technology. JAMA 1988; 259:1862.

88. Marchbanks RA, Annegers JF, Coulam CB, et al. Risk factors for ectopic pregnancy: A population-based study. JAMA 1988; 259:1823.

89. Sauer MV. New methods for diagnosis and management of ectopic pregnancy. Resident & Staff Physician 1987; 33:39.

90. CDC. Ectopic pregnancy—United States, 1970–1986. MMWR 1989; 38:1.

91. Atrash HK, Friede A, and Hogue CJ. Ectopic pregnancy mortality in the United States, 1980–1983. Obstet Gynecol 1987; 80:817.

92. Kitchin JD, Wein RM, Nunley WC, et al. Ectopic pregnancy: Current clinical trends. Am J Obstet Gynecol 1979; 134:870.

93. Helvacioglu A, Long EM, and Yang SL. Ectopic pregnancy. J Reprod Med 1979; 22:87.

94. Pauerstein CJ, and Spilman CH. The fallopian tube. Curr Concepts, 1980.

95. Kim DS, Chung SR, Park MI, et al. Comparative review of diagnostic accuracy in tubal pregnancy: A 14-year survey of 1040 cases. Obstet Gynecol 1987; 70:547.

96. DeCrespigny LC. Early diagnosis of pregnancy failure with transvaginal ultrasound. Am J Obstet Gynecol 1988; 159:408.

97. Leach RE, and Ory SJ. Modern management of ectopic pregnancy. J Reprod Med 1989; 34:324.
98. Davis AJ, O'Boyle EA, and Reindollar RH. Human chorionic gonadotropin in pediatric and adolescent gynecology. Adolesc and Pediatr Gynecol 1989; 2:207.
99. Pittaway DE, and Wentz AC. Evaluation of early pregnancy by serial chorionic gonadotropin determinations: A comparison of methods by receiver operating characteristic curve analysis. Fertil Steril 1985; 43:529.
100. Sauer MV. Nonsurgical management of unruptured ectopic pregnancy: An extended clinical trial. Fertil Steril 1987; 48:752.
101. Fernandez H, Rainhorm JD, Papiernik E, et al. Spontaneous resolution of ectopic pregnancy. Obstet Gynecol 1988; 71:717.
102. Yeko TR, Gorrill MJ, Hughes LH, et al. Timely diagnosis of early ectopic pregnancy using a single blood progesterone measurement. Fertil Steril 1987; 48:1048.
103. Sauer MV, Vermesh M, Anderson RE, et al. Rapid measurement of urinary pregnanediol glucuronide to diagnose ectopic pregnancy. Am J Obstet Gynecol 1988; 159:1531.
104. Hallott JG. Repeat ectopic pregnancy: A study of 123 consecutive cases. Am J Obstet Gynecol 1975; 122:520.

SUGGESTED READING

Hayes CD (ed.). Risking the Future: Adolescent Sexuality, Pregnancy, and Childbearing. Washington, DC: National Academy Press, 1987.
Jones EF, Forrest JD, Goldman N, et al. Teenage Pregnancy in Industrialized Countries. New Haven, CT: Yale University Press, 1986.
Burkman RT. Handbook of contraception and abortion. Boston: Little, Brown, 1989.
Lancaster JB, Hamburg BA (eds.). School-Age Pregnancy & Parenthood. Hawthorne, NY: Aldine de Gruyter, 1986.
McAnarney ER, and Hendee WR. Adolescent pregnancy and its consequences. JAMA 1989; 262:74.
McAnarney ER, and Hendee WR. The prevention of adolescent pregnancy. JAMA 1989; 262:78.
Furstenberg FF Jr, Brooks-Gunn J, and Chase-Lansdale L. Teenaged pregnancy and childbearing. Am Psychol 1989; 44:313.

17. Sexual Abuse

The past 15 years has witnessed an increasing awareness of the broad spectrum of problems that are seen under the term of "sexual abuse" [1–12]. The physician may be involved in the detection and diagnosis of sexual abuse cases and the management of the psychological sequelae.

Sexual abuse is generally defined as the involvement of developmentally immature children or adolescents in sexual activities that they do not fully comprehend, to which they are unable to give informed consent, or that violate taboos of family relationships. The term "sexual misuse" has also been coined to imply sexual stimulation inappropriate, not necessarily abusive, for the child's age and level of development [13]. Sexual abuse may include exhibitionism, fondling and manipulation, genital viewing, oral-genital contact, insertion of objects, or vaginal or rectal penetration. The contact may be a single event between the child and a stranger occurring with or without the use of force, or it may be the long-standing sexualized relationship between a father, stepfather, or known individual and a child and may involve repeated encounters over months to years. The sexual interaction may start with touching or fondling and progress over the course of months to vulvar coitus and penetration. In Orr's study of 100 sexually abused children, ages 1 to 15 years [14], the assailant was known to the child in 74 percent of cases, and in 50 percent of cases a relative was involved.

The formal definition of rape is the introduction of the penis within the genitalia of the victim by force, fear, or fraud. Even partial penetration or ejaculation of seminal fluid is sufficient to be called rape. The force used may be verbal threats as well as actual physical abuse. A child who is unconscious or intoxicated cannot give consent. Neither evidence of ejaculation nor laceration of the hymen is necessary for the allegation. Statutory rape is coitus with a female below the age of consent (in most states the age of 16 years). Sexual molestation is noncoital sexual contact without consent; it is generally covered under the same statutes as the crime of rape.

It is quite clear that the reported cases of sexual abuse probably represent the tip of the iceberg. Clinicians should ask questions that would reveal the possibility of sexual abuse at the routine physical examination, especially in children and adolescents with somatic complaints, nightmares, running away, "acting out," or pregnancy. After giving the adolescent reassurance about the confidential nature of the patient-doctor communication, the clinician can ask as part of the menstrual and sexual history, "Have you ever been forced into sexual involvement?" or "Have you ever felt someone older than you, even an adult in your family, made inappropriate sexual advances?" If the question brings dismay, the physician can proceed with the statement, "The reason I ask is that such sexual behavior does occur, and I want to help kids who have worries." Acknowledging that some youngsters may have felt embarrassed or unable to tell another person in the past can relieve anxiety.

The recognition of sexual abuse is frequently prompted by a child's disclosure to a parent, friend, teacher, or health professional. The disclosure may be purposeful or accidental. For example, a child may have told a peer about abuse, and the peer may subsequently tell her own mother, who reports the case. In most cases, the child does not anticipate the sequelae of the allegation. Sexual abuse may become evident during evaluation for somatic symptoms or behavioral difficulties.

The younger child with unexplained somatic symptoms or any evidence of genital infection, pain, or bleeding can be asked during the physical examination, "Has an adult or someone you know ever touched the vaginal area?" Girls with vaginal bleeding, foreign bodies in the vagina, condyloma acuminata, genital herpes, *Trichomonas*, *Chlamydia trachomatis*, or gonococcal vulvovaginitis need an especially careful history for sexual abuse, and the history is often best obtained without the parents present. Gonococcal infection in the prepubertal child necessitates culturing all possible contacts and identifying the source (see p. 351). Occasionally a pregnancy in a young adolescent is the first sign of long-standing incest.

Because physicians frequently feel uncomfortable about the diagnosis of incest or sexual abuse, even obvious problems are frequently overlooked, or the child is assumed to have "wild fantasies." It is well to remember that most children who disclose sexual abuse are telling the truth and that it is highly unlikely for a child to make up the concrete details of sexual involvement unless a sexually stimulating experience has occurred. Even if one encounters the rare circumstance in which the child has not had the sexual experience alleged, most likely something sexually stimulating has occurred that is unhealthy for the child's development. In cases of incest, there is a great deal of pressure from families to have the child retract the story to prevent disruption of the family unit and possible incarceration of the father. Thus, the physician must be prepared to support the youngster in her original story and proceed with an appropriate referral to a mental health facility capable of dealing with the issues of sexual abuse or to a sexual abuse team in a hospital setting.

In all cases of sexual abuse, it is extremely important that the patient be given sympathetic medical care. All patients with an episode of sexual abuse should be seen promptly by their primary care physician. If a sexual assault has occurred within hours or days, the physician will probably want to make use of an emergency ward setting or specially equipped clinic to collect the necessary forensic evidence in the event that prosecution is undertaken.

PATTERNS OF SEXUAL ABUSE

It is important for physicians to understand the various patterns of sexual misuse of children and to realize that all cases cannot be considered in the same way. Evaluation and treatment is quite different in the various forms of abuse [1]. Pedophilia is the preference of an adult for sexual contact with a child. Pedophilia may involve genital fondling, genital contact, or genital viewing. Some pedophilic adults may have a persistent pattern in which they do not find adults to be sexually desirable but rather feel compelled to interact sexually with children. Other pedophiles may have originally preferred peers or adult partners for sexual gratification but then regress and exhibit more primitive behavior. In this group, the offender is usually married, and then a situation develops that threatens the relationship. Overwhelmed by the stress, the man becomes sexually involved with a child, which often evokes feelings of guilt, shame, or embarrassment. This type of offender, in general, has a better prognosis for rehabilitation than the fixated offender.

Understanding the motivation and intent of the sexual contact and the means by which the offender obtains gratification is important in assessing a case. The offender may attempt to entice or entrap a youngster through the use of money, candy, or other bribes; the pedophile is attempting to gain sexual control over the child by developing a willing or consenting relationship without resorting to physical force. Very often the victim and offender know each other as neighbors or relatives. The involvement can continue over a long period of time or can involve a single episode. However, another offender may use intimidation or aggression or may attack or physically overpower the victim. The offender uses the child as an object of sexual relief and makes no attempt to engage the child in an emotional relationship. The exploitive situation makes the offender feel strong and in charge of the child. Although the majority of such offenders may not intend actual injury, the victim may end up harmed or with a hymenal laceration because she resists. A small group of sexual assault offenders actually derive pleasure in hurting the victim; children are at a considerable risk from this sort of individual.

In its broadest definition, incest means a sexual relationship between people who are related and cannot legally marry. It generally refers to relationships between members of the immediate nuclear family such as between father and daughter, mother and son, father and son, mother and daughter, or between siblings. Although sexual involvement between a stepparent and child is not traditional incest, it has many of the same psychodynamics and problems for management and treatment as do other forms of incest. Most referred cases of incest involve sexual offenses committed by the father against a child, usually the daughter. Mother-son incest is reported very infrequently; generally, either the mother or the son has major psychopathology or psychosis. Brother-sister incest is not frequently reported because of the assumption by many that it represents normal sexual play; however, it often occurs as an exploitive situation when the brother is considerably older than the sister. Incestuous relations may also include grandparents, uncles, and cousins. A sexual relationship between a stepfather and child or between a mother's boyfriend and child is sometimes called "functional parent incest."

There are some important differences between parent-child incest and pedophilia. The critical issue in a case of pedophilia is the dynamics of the adult; however, in every case of parental incest there is some form of major family dysfunction [15, 16, 17]. The husband frequently has a poor relationship with his wife; he may begin a relationship with the daughter as retaliation or in search of a relationship to fill his own needs for intimacy and to combat loneliness. Isolation and depression are frequently present. Although the child in such situations is sometimes described as seductive, the child obviously learns to adapt to the sexual expectations of the relationship. The mother may be involved in conscious or unconscious complicity, and by frequent absences from the home, she may allow a relationship to develop between the father and the daughter. The daughter may become "the little mother"; she may have responsibility for cooking the meals, doing laundry, and keeping the family together.

These incestuous relationships may start in the early childhood years and continue through to adolescence. Often, the daughter feels the threat of family disruption if she were to tell the secret. A crisis may occur if there is sudden disclosure of the situation when the child is in late puberty or adolescence; the youngster may begin to feel that her involvement is no longer age appropriate and may wish to have more meaningful relationships with her peer group. Although the mother usually denies knowledge of the incest, there is increasing clinical evidence that frequently the mother is aware of the special relationship but may not have intervened out of fear that the marriage would break up or that she would lose the husband's income. The child may also realize that the mother is not available as a protector. The youngster may actually derive some benefits from at least having a positive nurturing relationship with one parent (i.e., the father); however, it is a situation fraught with ambivalence and is highly anxiety provoking. The child is clearly being exploited.

An extraordinary number of families who are involved in incestuous situations will recount similar situations in their own childhood. Although incest is reported more frequently in chaotic families of lower socioeconomic status, it may be that such families are more likely to come to the attention of child-abuse workers because of their prior involvement with welfare and other social agencies. Clearly, incest occurs in higher socioeconomic groups; however, the secret may remain within the family for years, and it may only be disclosed when a young woman is in psychotherapy during her young adult years. Any disclosure of incestuous relationships should be taken seriously, and appropriate evaluation and treatment undertaken. Often the adults involved in the incest will show little remorse or shame and will typically deny or minimize the behavior.

PATIENT ASSESSMENT
Because of the legal implications, medical data should be carefully collected and recorded in all cases of alleged rape or sexual abuse [18]. It is important for the physician to understand the various patterns of sexual abuse in order to provide good medical care. The feelings aroused by such cases can be uncomfortable for the physician; reactions range from anger to fascination with the course of events. The clinician needs to make a careful assessment of the patient and to remain calm and nonjudgmental. The aim of the evaluation is to document what has happened, to obtain adequate medicolegal evidence, and to provide the patient with medical and psychological follow-up. The physician should avoid trying to decide whether rape actually occurred or if there is sufficient evidence for a verdict.

The timing and the extent of the physical examination depends on the history. Any child who has pain, vaginitis, bleeding, or dysuria or who has a history of trauma and any youngster in whom abuse has occurred within the past 72 hours should be seen immediately for an assessment and to document physical findings that may corroborate a sexual assault. Since children often have difficulty disclosing a full history of the nature of the abuse, a complete physical examination is always indicated. A standard protocol is available in most emergency rooms and should be followed so that samples can be passed directly to a police officer to maintain a legal "chain of evidence." Protocols with drawings of male and female genitalia are excellent for documenting abnormalities. Some states have protocols that are applicable for both child and adolescent acute assault victims; in others, the protocols are useful only in adult rape victims. The very extensive California protocol is reproduced in Appendix 4, and physicians may wish to use portions for their own protocols.

The patient who was abused weeks to months before seeking help should be interviewed as soon as is practical. The physical examination is done at the completion of the initial assessment, but samples for sperm are omitted.

SEXUALLY TRANSMITTED DISEASES AND SEXUAL ASSAULT

The risk of acquiring a sexually transmitted disease in the context of sexual abuse is often asked by parents and health care providers, especially with the increasing prevalence of herpes, human papillomavirus (HPV), and acquired immunodeficiency syndrome (AIDS). The estimate of the risk also determines which, if any, infections should be treated with prophylactic antibiotics at the time of the initial evaluation [19–25].

Jenny [26, 27] has recently reviewed the risk of sexually transmitted diseases (STDs) in children and adults with histories of sexual abuse. Importantly she has distinguished between infections noted at the initial evaluation and those found at follow-up visits. This distinction is particularly important in the care of adolescents, since adolescent assault victims who come to medical attention in hospital settings are more likely to be inner city, single, young women of lower socioeconomic and minority status, factors that also make the patient at higher risk of having a preexisting STD [24–28]. A review [26] of the studies of sexual assault victims has found *Neisseria gonorrhoeae* to be present in 2.4 to 12.0 percent of patients at initial evaluation; studies of patients negative at the initial visit have reported positive gonorrhea cultures in 2.6 to 2.9 percent of patients at follow-up. In children, a positive culture for gonorrhea has been reported in 0 to 26.7 percent, with a usual rate of 2 to 5 percent. As noted in Chapters 1 and 3, confirmation of *N. gonorrhoeae* in a reference laboratory is extremely important before undertaking a child abuse evaluation on the basis of preliminary culture results. Jenny [26] reported that 10.1 percent of women were positive for *C. trachomatis* at the initial visit; at follow-up, 1.5 percent of women with initially negative cultures who had not been given antibiotics were positive. *C. trachomatis* is found in 2 to 17 percent of girls, depending on the population studied. Bacterial vaginosis and *Trichomonas* were found in 5 to 25 percent of patients at follow-up examination. Bacterial vaginosis has been noted at follow-up in children with a history of acute vaginal assault. A single case report has associated a urinary tract infection with *Staphylococcus saprophyticus* in a 26-month-old with sexual abuse [29].

Jenny [26] has reported positive herpes simplex culture from 2.4 percent at initial visit and 0 at follow-up. The risk of syphilis appears to be exceedingly low, although in high-risk patients with other STDs the possibility needs to be considered, especially in view of the increased prevalence of syphilis. White and co-workers [23] have reported 6 of 108 (5.5%) children with positive serologies for syphilis in a high-risk group of children with a positive gonorrhea rate of 26.7 percent.

The risk of acquiring HPV is unknown, but we have seen adolescents with a single rape episode develop cervical dysplasia with HPV infection. The long-term risk to prepubertal children of infection with HPV is also unknown and needs further investigation with typing of the lesions and a number of years of observation (see Chaps. 3 and 11). The largest worry for patients and families is the risk of acquiring AIDS. Although the risk from a single contact is low, the majority of abuse situations involve multiple episodes. The acquisition of human immunodeficiency virus (HIV) from abuse is not a frequent occurrence at this time, but it is likely that this problem will increase with time as HIV infection spreads in the inner-city urban populations. Rarely, children have become infected after being injected with intravenous drugs using contaminated needles preceding the sexual abuse. Young males who have been sodomized would seem to be at particular risk of acquiring HIV infection.

Given the incubation time (see Chaps. 9–11) of the various infections, it is clear that initial cultures may miss many infections depending on the number of hours, days, or months the examination is done after sexual contact. Prepubertal children frequently come for examination weeks to months after the abusive episode(s), and thus a single set of cultures is adequate; in contrast, adolescents often come to medical attention shortly after the assault, and thus follow-up cultures and wet preparations for *Trichomonas* and bacterial vaginosis are necessary to detect infections acquired at the time of the assault. Since many infections are asymptomatic, cultures should be done on all victims. The best approach is to culture the pharynx, anal canal, and vagina (endocervix in adolescents) for *N. gonorrhoeae* and the vagina (endocervix in adolescents) for *C. trachomatis* and to examine the vaginal secretions for *Trichomonas* and clue cells (including a "whiff test," see p. 33). The significance of *Gardnerella vaginalis* is discussed on p. 69; culture for this organism is not helpful in the evaluation. Some centers also do cultures from the rectum and pharynx for *C. trachomatis;* more studies are needed on normal populations to use this as confirmatory evidence. Nonculture methods for *C. trachomatis* should not be used for abuse evaluations. Although the saline wet preparation is used to look for *Trichomonas*, both culture and direct slide test are more sensitive (see p. 314). Lesions suggestive of herpes simplex should be cultured for this virus.

A serologic test for syphilis can be done initially, and then 6 weeks later (8–12 weeks later if HIV tests are also to be drawn) if prophylactic antibiotics are not administered. If the child is seen more than 6 weeks after the abusive episode, a single serology is all that is necessary. Because of the low risk of acquiring this infection, some centers select patients for this blood test. A sample of serum can be frozen at the time of the initial visit so that if later testing is determined necessary and is positive for herpes, HIV, hepatitis B, or syphilis, confirmatory testing on the initial serum can be carried out to document lack of prior exposure. The low risk of HIV should be discussed with parents and child (if old enough) and the benefits and risks of testing made clear. High-risk situations include assault by an assailant who is HIV positive or known to be in a high-risk category, such as an intravenous drug user or a male homosexual. Acquisition of another STD may also place the patient in a higher risk category. Physicians need to be cognizant of the prevalence of HIV infections in their communities among adults as well as children (who have acquired the infection from their mothers). Patients and families may wish to make use of confidential anonymous counselling and testing centers. With 1989 technology for HIV testing (likely to improve in the future), follow-up HIV testing is optimal 3 to 6 months after the episode (repeated 12 months after the assault for negatives), and if positive, compared with the frozen serum saved from the initial visit. It is likely that prophylactic anti-HIV therapy (e.g., AZT) will become available for rape victims.

At the follow-up visit 2 weeks later, cultures for *N. gonorrhoeae* and *C. trachomatis* should be repeated if prophylactic antibiotics were not given and the examination was done shortly after the assault. Repeat wet preparations should be done for *Trichomonas* and bacterial vaginosis. At long-term follow-up, the patient should be examined for HPV infection, and Papanicolaou smears initiated in adolescents.

TESTS FOR SEMEN

Acid phosphatase tests may be negative during the first 3 hours and positive up to 48 hours [30, 31]. Acid phosphatase from vaginal sources or plant materials may give false-positive results, and thus the qualitative test is presumptive, not diagnostic, evidence of semen. Quantitative assays for acid phosphatase can be more definitive. The semen protein antigen p30 of prostatic origin is found in the semen of both normal and vasectomized men, but not in body fluids of women, and is thus more sensitive and specific than acid phosphatase [32]. P30 is undetectable in the vagina by 48 hours after intercourse. The newest test for semen, MHS-5, is an ELISA based on a monoclonal antibody to a seminal vesicle–specific antigen [33, 34, 35]. MHS-5 does not cross-react with other biologic fluids and appears to be stable on clothes for months. Swabs obtained during an evaluation should be immediately air-dried and then frozen or maintained in a dessicated chamber at ambient temperature. The use of both p30 and MHS-5 should provide a high level of confidence. Blood group antigens can also be evaluated by many forensic laboratories. It is likely that in the next few years DNA mapping of semen, blood, and other bodily fluids will become more widely accepted in forensic medicine and provide courts with precise identification of the perpetrators.

Data vary on the length of time that motile and nonmotile sperm may be found in the vagina or cervical mucus. Soules and co-workers [30] found, in adults with voluntary intercourse, that only 50 percent of the specimens examined had motile sperm 3 hours after intercourse, whereas at 72 hours nonmotile sperm could be detected on a fixed preparation in nearly 50 percent. All specimens contained whole sperm up to 18 hours after intercourse and sperm heads up to 24 hours. Since the staining technique in this study was very sensitive, the physician needs to know data from the police laboratory performing the test. Duenhoelter and associates [31] found motile sperm in 31.7 percent of the victims within 6 hours of the alleged sexual assault and in 18 percent of those examined 7 to 24 hours after the incident. However, the later group contained 3 patients in whom the sperm were detected in cervical mucus; sperm may remain motile longer in cervical mucus (up to 5 days). Nonmotile sperm may be present in the vagina for 3 to 5 days and in the endocervical canal for up to 17 days [8, 36]. It should be remembered that the absence of sperm should not be taken as evidence against a sexual assault; up to 50 percent of specimens obtained from victims of acute rape may have no motile sperm either because the offender has sexual dysfunction or oligospermia or because detection techniques are insensitive [37].

USE OF THE COLPOSCOPE

The use of the colposcope has been popularized by the courses and publications of Woodling and Heger [38, 39]. The advantages of the colposcope are that the hymen and vulva can be greatly magnified to detect small changes not easily visible with the naked eye and that photographs are easily taken at the time of the examination to provide future documentation. The latter prevents the need for repeated examinations when the presence of physical findings is disputed. The problem with the use of colposcopy has been that until recently normal genital anatomy in prepubertal girls has not been well defined. The problem has been compounded by the difficulty in assessing the strength of the association between a history of sexual abuse and variations in the hymenal appearance in individual cases, variations in the 50 states' statutory definition of sexual crimes, and misunderstanding among professionals providing examinations for victims of sexual abuse about the meaning of "penetration." Cross-sectional data and observations on genital anatomy have improved substantially in the past few years [9, 10, 40–43]. A study of 1131 newborn

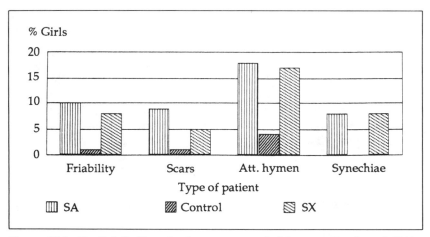

Figure 17-1. Genital findings in three groups of girls: sexually abused (SA), controls, and girls with other genital complaints (SX). Att = attenuated. (From Emans SJ, Woods ER, Flagg NT, et al. Genital findings in sexually abused, symptomatic and asymptomatic girls. Pediatrics 1987; 79:778. By permission.)

female infants found that all had hymens [44]. Longitudinal studies of girls should help define the changes in hymenal anatomy that may occur with age.

An atlas of photographs is being planned by a North American Society for Pediatric and Adolescent Gynecology (NASPAG) Task Force to aid physicians in assessing their own patients. The use of the colposcope had greatly increased physicians' knowledge of normal anatomy and fine-tuned visual skills. Knowledgeable physicians seeing a child for routine annual examination or assessing a genital problem may note changes suggestive of sexual abuse with unaided visual inspection or with magnification.

Some examples of the normal and abnormal hymenal and vulvar findings are shown in the color plates and in Chapters 1 and 3. The value of the medical examination in the determination of sexual abuse has been a subject of controversy. The percentage of children with a "normal" examination has varied from 16 to 85 percent depending on the case mix and age of patients, the definition of normal versus abnormal, and the examiners [7, 9, 38, 40].

In a recent study [9], we compared children presenting with a history of sexual abuse with children seen (1) for routine examinations and (2) for genital complaints. Girls with a history of sexual abuse were more likely to have scars, friability of the posterior forchette as the labia were separated, synechiae, and attenuated hymens than girls seen for routine examinations (Fig. 17-1). Hymenal transections or tears, condyloma, and/or abrasions occurred only among the sexually abused girls (in 9/119). Girls with a history of genital complaints had some findings similar to those girls with a history of sexual abuse. Vulvar erythema and friability of the posterior forchette can occur secondary to inflammation or sexual abuse; scars are the result of trauma. Since girls may take months to years to reveal a history of sexual abuse, it is very likely that some of the girls evaluated in our clinic for vaginitis had been abused but failed to give this history. The finding of a narrow, thin posterior rim of the hymen in children with vaginitis may suggest that some of these girls had been abused, or this particular anatomic variant may predispose a subset of girls to vaginal contamination and symptoms. In contrast, a narrow rim that has become rounded and scarred with attachment to the vagina results from sexual abuse. The significance of a labial adhesion in a child with a history of sexual abuse is controversial (see p. 88). Many normal children have labial adhesions, and yet it is possible that rubbing and irritation from abuse may also cause agglutination to occur. These adhesions have sometimes been mistaken for scars. The difference is usually evident with careful observation; if not, a short trial of estrogen-containing cream, which would lyse most labial adhesions but not scars, could be used. Another entity frequently confused with a scar in the posterior forchette is the white midline avascular line evident in some children. Conditions such as lichen sclerosus, failure of midline fusion from the anus to the posterior forchette, and ulcerating hemangioma have been confused with trauma from sexual abuse.

Children who have a history of sodomy frequently have no abnormal findings. Minor redness and hyperpigmentation and reflex anal dilatation are nonspecific findings that can have other etiologies. More specific findings include scars, sphincter tears and distortion of the anus (the latter can also occur with inflammatory bowel disease). Fissures can result from abuse and from constipation.

A discussion of various methods of measurement of the diameter of the hymenal orifice and the pitfalls of use of exact cutoff numbers without more normative data is on p. 6. The position of measurement (knee-chest versus supine) and the amount and duration of traction are very important in the amount of dilatation. The opening is larger in the knee-chest position than in the supine position using gentle separation only (not retraction). The type of hymen is also important; a posterior rim hymen has a larger orifice than a redundant hymen. The older the child and the more relaxed, the larger the opening. It is important to note that since the hymen is elastic, digital penetration is possible even if the *measured* diameter is only 5 mm. The passage of time, healing, variations in measurement technique, and error can lead to changing, especially decreasing, hymenal orifice diameters in serial examinations. A good rule of thumb is 1 mm for each year of age as the upper limits of normal (i.e., 8 mm for an 8-year-old). A 1-cm hymenal opening in a 4-year-old and a 1.5-cm opening in an 8-year-old are abnormal. The findings of an enlarged opening should be consistent with the rest of the total assessment of the child [45]. Importantly physicians should be comfortable with their own measurements in normal and sexually abused girls. Children with a history of vulvar or vaginal coitus are likely to have a larger opening than girls who have been fondled only.

Muram [46] published data on physical findings in 31 sexual assault victims (1–17 years old) based on offenders' confessions. Specific findings suggesting sexual abuse occurred in only 45 percent of the patients; findings occurred in 11 of 18 (61%) girls when the perpetrator confessed to penetration, compared to 3 of 13 (23%) when penetration was denied. Thus 7 of 18 (39%) in whom the perpetrator confessed to penetration had a normal examination or nonspecific findings.

ASSESSMENT OF THE PREPUBERTAL CHILD
The physician should take the history from the parents and the child separately if possible. If there was a forceful assault, the child may feel more comfortable being interviewed with the mother present. The interview should remain unhurried and calm, and a patient-doctor relationship should be established before questions are broached on the issue of the abuse. The physician should establish credibility with the child by showing interest and telling her that other children with similar problems have been helped. The clinician should remain nonjudgmental and not presuppose that the experience was bad or painful for the child. It may have been neutral or even pleasurable, and the child may not have experienced guilt or anger. In speaking with the child, the physician should use words that are familiar to the child; it is often helpful to repeat some of the questions during the actual physical examination to make sure the youngster understands what parts of the anatomy are being questioned. The history, written in the patient's words, should include such details as time, place, circumstances, others present, and resistance. Dating the time of the abuse may be easier by referring to a grade in school or a birthday. The child is asked to tell as much about the episode as she remembers. Leading questions should be avoided. Appropriate questions include, "How did it begin? What happened? Did anything change? Where? Where was everyone else? Why tell now? Has anybody told you to keep it a secret? Have you been hurt lately?" The child's exact statement should be recorded. It is important to remember that the first report is almost never the first incident. The interviewer should then ask open-ended questions to clarify the information: "And then what happened? What were you

wearing? What did the room look like?" Older children may be aware of whether ejaculation occurred. The physician should try to document whether vulvar, vaginal, or rectal penetration has occurred or whether there has been any evidence of oral contact. The child should be asked about any pain or injuries occurring at the time of the episode. Any symptoms that have occurred following the assault such as sore throat, dysuria, vaginal discharge or bleeding, rectal bleeding or pain, abdominal pain, nightmares, or changes in school performance should be recorded.

It is important to establish whether the relationship was prolonged and whether the child has been involved with more than one adult. The child should be asked if she received any gifts or remuneration from the adult and whether she knew the adult. It is important to know whether she told the parent of the event immediately after its occurrence. Often children have been threatened and sworn to secrecy. The clinician should make it clear to the child that the incident is not her fault. It is important to concentrate on what happened rather than "why" questions such as, "Why did you get in the car?" A young child may feel more comfortable using a doll, puppet, or picture and explaining how the doll feels about the incident. Hibbard and associates [47] reported that the presence of genitalia in a child's drawing can be associated with a history of sexual abuse. The child should be told what information needs to be shared, with whom, and why, and she needs a chance to ask her own questions both before and after the examination.

The child's history is an extraordinarily important part of the evaluation [48]. If the initial disclosure can be videotaped, the child may not have to relate the story over and over again. The validation of the story involves looking for behavioral clues, the occurrence of multiple episodes over time, a progression from fondling to penetration, an element of secrecy fostered by coercion, and explicit details of the abuse. Mental health workers with expertise in child sexual abuse can be extremely helpful in the evaluation of the child and her parents. The most problematic cases are those involving child custody disputes, especially visitation rights. In Paradise and co-workers' study [49], a custody dispute occurred in 39 percent of 31 sexual abuse complaints against a parent. Sexual abuse allegations were substantiated less frequently in cases involving parental conflict (67% versus 95%), but still a majority were substantiated. These disputes often involve very young children, so the issues are difficult to resolve.

Parents should be allowed to tell their own story separately from the child and to ventilate their feelings without traumatizing the child. In sexual abuse cases involving nonforceful misuse of a child by a stranger, parents may need more counselling and reassurance than the child. It is particularly important to help the parents to be supportive of their youngster and to help them realize that their child is not "ruined." The parental response may greatly influence the reaction of the child to the event [50]. The child needs to know that parental anger is toward the assailant and not toward her.

The physical examination of the young child should be done in a relaxed setting with the mother in the room. A nurse can help to collect the samples and reassure the child. The physician can put the child at ease by starting with a general physical examination. It is extremely important to elicit the cooperation of the child. The steps for an acute assault are outlined here, although most cases seen by the physician in the office will probably involve long-standing abuse by a known individual. Specimens should be collected so that the legal evidence is preserved if the family decides to press charges.

1. Description of the patient's general appearance and emotional state and condition of the clothing (neat, dishevelled, torn, blood-stained). She should be asked if she has changed clothes or bathed since the assault. If the clothing was worn at the time of the episode, the clothing should be placed in a paper bag. All debris observed during the gross examination of the patient, such as grass, sand, or hair fibers should be enclosed in a paper container.
2. General physical examination with notation of hematomas, bruises, edema, abrasions, lacerations, bite marks, and other evidence of struggle, such as hair or skin beneath the fingernails or scratches. The size and color of any hematomas should be recorded on a sketch of the child. Photographs should be taken of any contusions. After marking the location where the specimens were obtained, any area of dried secretions, such as saliva from bite marks, blood, or semen should be swabbed with a slightly moistened gauze pad or swabs and retained as evidence. A Wood's lamp can detect areas of semen by fluorescence.
3. Genital examination with careful inspection of the perineum noting bleeding, lacerations, condyloma accuminatum, and any evidence of dried secretions. The hymen and posterior forchette should be carefully examined using magnification of a hand lens, otoscope, or colposcope. Acute assaults may be accompanied by extensive hymenal and perineal lacerations or ecchymoses. Dried secretions are collected with a slightly moistened gauze pad. The size of the hymenal opening should be recorded as well as the position used. The vagina can be visualized in the knee-chest position, and any abnormal discharge, bleeding, or foreign bodies should be noted. One study has found that application of toluidine blue to the vulva of girls seen within 48 hours of abuse may aid in the detection of posterior forchette lacerations [51]; further data are needed.

Specimens to check for the presence of sperm and cultures for gonorrhea can be obtained with a soft plastic Clinitest eye dropper, a small French catheter gently inserted through the hymenal opening, a saline moistened Calgiswab, or a piece of intravenous tubing inside a catheter (see p. 16). We find the Calgiswab easiest in most situations. A vaginal culture for gonorrhea should be plated directly onto Thayer-Martin-Jembec media. A wet preparation should be done to look for motile sperm, trichomonads, and clue cells, and a "whiff" test should be done. Specimens should be streaked onto glass slides and allowed to air dry. A swab should be collected for sending to the police laboratory for semen testing (see p. 546). Any genital or anal discharge should be gram stained. Woodling and Kossoris [8] have suggested another method to obtain specimens from the prepubertal child; while the child is in a semireclining position on a bedpan, a rubber catheter is used to obtain vaginal washing. Such washings must be refrigerated or frozen immediately. Urine can be examined for white cells, trichomonads, and sperm.

A *culture* for *C. trachomatis* should be obtained by using a male urethral Dacron swab and gently scaping the vaginal wall. Nonculture methods such as direct smears and immunoassays should be avoided because of the possibility of a false-positive test. DNA probes for *Chlamydia* may be available in the near future, but studies done on prepubertal children are necessary before use can be recommended. Genital ulcers should be cultured for herpes simplex.

If a bleeding laceration cannot be properly assessed or the child has been too traumatized to cooperate with an examination, a brief examination under anesthesia is preferable to further trauma (see p. 15).

4. Inspection of the perianal area. If anal assault is suspected, specimens for detection of semen should be collected from the rectum. In all cases, a rectal culture for *N. gonorrhoeae* and, if possible, *C. trachomatis* should be done. Rectal sphincter tone should be assessed.
5. A throat swab should be plated for *N. gonorrhoeae* and possibly cultured for *C. trachomatis*. Oral swabs are obtained if oral-genital contact within 24 hours is suspected (see p. 560).
6. Blood drawn for a serologic test for syphilis (rapid plasma reagin [RPR] test).
7. Serum frozen to do future testing for HIV and hepatitis B.
8. Prophylaxis. In the asymptomatic child involved in chronic or prior abuse, cultures should be obtained and treatment given only if a positive culture is found. In the acute situation of sexual assault by a stranger, prophylaxis for gonorrhea and *Chlamydia* can be

554   17. Sexual Abuse

instituted (although the risk is low) by giving ceftriaxone 125mg
(children <45kg) to 250mg (>45kg) followed by erythromycin,
50 mg/kg/day for 7 days, or doxycycline if the patient is more than
9 years old. A short course of stool softeners may be prescribed for
sodomy cases and phenazopyridine (Pyridium) for girls with vulvar trauma and dysuria. Tetanus toxoid is given according to standard pediatric guidelines following acute injuries. In acute assaults, protocols for prophylactic anti-HIV therapies are likely to
become available. The child should be seen for medical follow-up
after the evaluation for the acute assault to assess healing of injuries, to document physical findings (if still present) noted in the
emergency ward, and to check the results of the initial cultures. If
no prophylactic antibiotics were given at the time of an acute assault, cultures for *N. gonorrhoeae* and *C. trachomatis* should be repeated at the follow-up visit. If, however, one to two weeks had
elapsed between the abusive incident and the initial evaluation,
cultures need not be repeated. Vaginal secretions should be examined for *Trichomonas* and bacterial vaginosis. Repeat serology for
syphilis and possibly HIV testing can be obtained at a follow-up
8 to 12 weeks later.

Most cases of sexual abuse in young children involve episodes that
occurred weeks to months before the actual examination. In such
cases, the examination should still include a general physical examination to look for signs of neglect or abuse and a genital examination
that includes inspection of the perineum, magnification of the hymen
and posterior forchette, visualization of the vagina in the knee-chest
position, measurement of the hymenal opening, and anal assessment. Cultures for gonorrhea and *Chlamydia* and wet preparations for
Trichomonas and clue cells should be obtained, and a serologic test for
syphilis may be done. In cases of long-standing abuse, genital fondling, oral-genital contact, or penile contact with either the vulva or
the abdomen constitute the type of sexual abuse; therefore, many
sexually abused prepubertal girls have a normal genital examination
or minimal signs of irritation and a small hymenal opening. In Rimsza
and Niggemann's study [7] of sexually abused children, genital fondling was reported as the only form of sexual contact in 30 of 52 (58%)
2- to 5-year-old children and in 24 of 63 (38%) 6- to 9-year-old children. The examination was normal in nearly one half of these patients. Thus, the finding of a normal examination should in no way
prevent the diagnosis of sexual abuse. Based on his work in Mem-
phis, Tennessee, Muram [52] has recently proposed the following
classifications of findings. Category 1 does not confirm or disprove a
history of sexual abuse.

Category 1. Normal-appearing genitalia.
Category 2. Nonspecific findings—Abnormalities of the genitalia that could have been caused by sexual abuse, but also often seen in girls who are not victims of sexual abuse (e.g., inflammation and scratching). These findings may be the sequelae of poor perineal hygiene or nonspecific infection. Included in this category are redness of the external genitalia, increased vascular pattern of the vestibular and labial mucosa, presence of purulent discharge from the vagina, small skin fissures or lacerations in the area of the posterior fourchette, and agglutination of the labia minora.
Category 3. Specific findings—The presence of one or more abnormalities strongly suggesting sexual abuse. Such findings include recent or healed lacerations of the hymen and vaginal mucosa, enlarged hymenal opening of 1 cm or more, procto-episiotomy (a laceration of the vaginal mucosa extending to the rectal mucosa), and indentations in the skin indicating teeth marks (bite marks). The category also includes patients with laboratory confirmation of a venereal disease.
Category 4. Definitive findings—Any presence of sperm.

At the conclusion of the examination it is extremely important to discuss with the child and parent(s) the clinical findings, since many assume the child is "damaged goods". Parents are greatly relieved to be told that their child is normal and healthy. Before the examination, parents often express extreme anxiety over the possible loss of virginity and reproductive potential and are greatly reassured by a careful discussion. When there has been an injury, the treatment and follow-up plan of care should be outlined. Most minor trauma heal without visible sequelae.

All cases of sexual abuse in children should be reported to the Child Protective Services. In our hospital, all children are seen for a psychological evaluation at the time of the history and physical examination. In intrafamilial situations, it is important to establish whether the child can be safely returned to the family environment; the alleged perpetrator should not be confronted in an intrafamilial situation until one is sure that the child is protected.

The need for long-term psychological support for the child depends on the individual case [3]. Both the child's stage of development and the nature of the encounter determine the impact on the child. In situations of one-time nonforceful exposure (fondling, touching), a careful history, genital examination, and reassurance for the family are important. Most of the follow-up counselling is directed to the parents, since, if they can remain unambiguously supportive, the impact on the child is usually minimal. In cases involving a caregiver and/or repetitive abuse, the child and family should receive counselling directed to their needs. Young children may have a high level of anxiety and be manifesting somatic and behavioral symptoms. The child may have difficulty separating from her mother and be exceptionally clinging. The child also may need to work through the loss of the individual babysitter, father, or uncle accused of sexually abusing her. Children may express anger not only toward the perpetrator but also toward the parent who in her mind "let it happen." Sorting out good and bad feelings toward the perpetrator, mother, and others involved is important. Reteaching "good and bad" touch is extremely important so children can hug and allow appropriate displays of affection. Children need to relearn the ability to trust; self-esteem needs to be fostered and increased. Allowing children to make choices can empower that child to realize that she can believe in herself and make wise choices in the future. Cases involving long-standing intrafamilial abuse are particularly problematic. The clinician needs a resource within the community prepared to deal creatively with these difficult situations. One successful program that treated more than 600 families is the Child Sexual Abuse Treatment Program of the Juvenile Probation Department of California. It demonstrated that well-organized programs can have a significant impact on cases of intrafamilial abuse with the coercion of court action and that, in most cases, the reestablishment of normal father-daughter relationships can be achieved [53]. Ninety-five percent of daughters returned home; this is in contrast to Kempe's program [4], which returned 20 to 30 percent to their homes.

The aim of incest treatment must be to stop the incest and to treat all the family members. The mother must be willing and able to protect her children, and both parents have to admit to the problem and have a desire to remedy it either by improving their marriage or divorcing. The best interest of the child and not the reuniting of the family must be first. The long-term outcome is not known, but clearly the inability of parents to provide the necessary protection for the child may cause long-term problems. The continuation of incest during adolescence appears to be particularly damaging and may result in conversion hysteria, promiscuity, phobias, suicide attempts, and psychosis.

The recent trend toward increased court involvement and prosecution has been useful in the resolution of some cases. Children can be helped through the court process by sensitive victim-witness advocates, district attorneys, and mental health professionals. Unfortunately, the long, drawn-out process and the need for the child to confront the defendant directly rather than by videotape have made the judicial process difficult for many [54, 55]. A not-guilty verdict can be devastating to the victim, who feels she has not been believed. On the other hand, a guilty verdict can be helpful in the child's recovery. Runyan and co-workers [56] reported that testimony in court helped the resolution of anxiety, but protracted criminal proceedings had the potential for an adverse effect. Psychotherapy should not await a court verdict but should be ongoing from the time of the disclosure.

The welfare of the child should be paramount. In addition, more attention needs to be focused on offenders, many of whom were previously sexually abused themselves.

Many cases of sexual misuse obviously never come to the attention of the physician. In a large survey of New England college students, Finkelhor [12] found that 15 percent of young women and 10 percent of young men reported some type of sexual experience (usually fondling or touching with siblings) during childhood. One quarter of these incidences could be classified as exploitive because they involved force or age discrepancy. Reactions to the experience were mixed, but the women often felt bad, especially if the experience had involved an older sibling and had occurred before they were 9 years old. Few had ever told anyone about the episode. In a survey of junior high school students, physical and/or sexual abuse was reported by 18.3 percent of students and was associated with running away, considering hurting oneself, suicide attempts, and the use of drugs, marijuana, cigarettes, and laxatives [57]. Causation versus association cannot be determined in such a study. More data needs to be gathered on the long-term effects of abuse to offer effective intervention. Since sexual misuse reported to the physician represents the tip of the iceberg, the clinician must be aware of the problem and be willing to entertain the possibility that misuse may be responsible for a variety of both physical and psychological symptoms in children.

ASSESSMENT OF THE ADOLESCENT

In contrast to the pattern of sexual abuse in prepubertal children, sexual abuse during adolescence is more likely to be a one-time assault by a stranger and involve vaginal intercourse. Thus a rape kit is more likely to be necessary for this evaluation. However, even among adolescents the rape may involve an acquaintance or someone the teenager had seen in her neighborhood or school and who was assumed to be a safe individual. In these cases, the adolescent may accept a ride with that individual and then later be forced into a sexual relationship, often involving intercourse. Risk-taking behaviors such as alcohol and drug use and hitchhiking may make certain adolescents more vulnerable [28]. In other cases, the developmental changes that take place during adolescence may make a long-standing incestuous relationship intolerable; the adolescent may then respond with a sudden disclosure, may seek medical care for somatic symptoms such as abdominal pain or headache, or become involved in impulsive behavior such as running away. A pregnancy may be the first sign of a previous rape or chronic sexual abuse. It is, therefore, important to ask adolescents not only whether they have ever had sexual relations but also whether they have ever been forced into a sexual relationship.

558 17. Sexual Abuse

In recording the history of the adolescent with alleged sexual assault, the clinician should follow a similar outline as is described in the section Assessment of the Prepubertal Child. It is important to record the date of the visit, sources of the history, who brought in the patient, and who knows of the current situation. The date, time, and place of the sexual assault(s) should be recorded. In acute situations, the patient should be asked if she has bathed, douched, or urinated since the assault. Menstrual and contraceptive history should be obtained. The physician should not try to decide whether rape or seduction has occurred on the basis of the patient's emotional response to the trauma, for clearly some patients will be tearful, tense, and hysterical, and others will appear controlled or subdued. Questions should focus on what happened and whether vaginal, rectal, or oral penetration occurred (terms understood by the patient should be used). These questions may need to be repeated during the examination when the adolescent is more familiar with the anatomic terms. The patient should be asked if she is aware of any other injuries or symptoms following the attack. A rape protocol should be used to collect evidence. It is extremely helpful if a nurse, preferably an experienced rape-victim counsellor, can be assigned to the adolescent throughout the 2- to 4-hour stay in the emergency ward and can be present during the history taking, physical examination, and police interviews. The rape-victim counsellor can provide to the patient information on the details of the physical examination and be an ally to the patient. A number of general hospitals now have a rotating system of nurses who have had special training in rape counselling and who are available on an on-call basis to provide such support for the victim. The police officer should not be present during the medical evaluation.

After the history is obtained, the patient should be told of the need for a thorough physical examination to assess injury and to collect laboratory specimens. Each part of the examination should be discussed in advance, and the patient should be given a sense of control over the tempo of the examination. She should be told that the examination is important but that the examiner can stop if the patient wishes and finish at another appointment. Pictures or the plastic Ortho model can be used to familiarize the adolescent with the type of examination. The following assessment applies to the acute sexual assault. When there is a history of an ongoing incestuous relationship in which intercourse has occurred longer ago than 5 days before the physical examination, the search for motile sperm is omitted (see previous section for discussion of semen tests).

The physical examination should include the following seven steps:

1. A description should be recorded of the patient's general appearance, emotional state, and especially the condition of the clothing.

Any clothing that might provide evidence in a legal case should be included in the rape-evidence clothing bag.

2. A general physical examination should note any evidence of bruises, scratches, or lacerations. As noted in the section Assessment of the Prepubertal Child, debris and dried secretions should be properly collected. The Tanner stage of sexual development should be noted. If the history indicates any attempt of the patient to scratch or fight her assailant, fingernail scrapings should be obtained with a wooden applicator stick and saved in an envelope. Head hair combings and a head hair standard (clipped close to the scalp) are included in many rape kits.

3. The pelvic examination should include a careful inspection of the perineum, noting any evidence of bleeding or lacerations. A gauze pad or cotton swab lightly moistened with nonbacteriostatic sterile saline should be used to wipe the vulva. The location of any dried secretions should be marked on a sketch. A collection paper should be placed under the buttocks of the patient and the pubic hair combed toward the paper to collect any debris. The debris should be placed in the collection envelope. If any foreign hairs are noted, 8 to 25 pubic hairs of the patient should be cut near the surface of the skin and included in a separate envelope. Soules and associates [30] found no hair transfer in 15 patients studied after intercourse.

The hymenal border can be examined for tears by running a saline-moistened cotton-tipped applicator around the edges. A hand lens or colposcope can aid in the evaluation. The size of the hymenal ring should be noted in millimeters and as Q-tip size, one-finger breadth, or two-finger breadth. Vaginal swabs for semen can be obtained by gently inserting a cotton-tipped applicator through the hymenal ring. In most protocols the swabs are then smeared on two dry slides (frosted at one end so that the patient's name and date can be recorded) and allowed to air dry. The swabs are protected in a test tube, and saved for transport to a police laboratory. At the police laboratory the swabs and slides can be examined using specific semen tests, including in some cases DNA mapping. A moistened cotton-tipped applicator can be used to obtain further vaginal samples to look for the presence of motile sperm, trichomonads, and clue cells. A "whiff test" is also done on this specimen. Any genital discharge should be gram-stained. Genital ulcers suggestive of genital herpes should be cultured with a cotton swab and appropriate media.

In most pubertal adolescent girls, a gentle vaginal examination can be done with a water-moistened (Huffman) speculum. If the hymen is too tight, cultures for C. trachomatis and N. gonorrhoeae can be obtained from the vagina (although these samples are less satisfactory). It is extremely important to examine the teenager gently so that the examination does not represent a further trauma. With the speculum in place, the vagina is inspected for injury and the presence of semen or vaginal discharge, and endocervical cultures are obtained. A purulent endocervical discharge should be gram-stained to look for white cells and gram-negative intracellular diplococci. If cervical smears are also taken to check for motile sperm, the wet and dry smears should be appropriately marked.

4. The anus should be inspected and any discharge swabbed and gram-stained. Specimens for sperm should be obtained if there is a history of rectal assault within 24 hours. Perianal swabs are collected using cotton swabs lightly moistened with saline; anorectal swabs are not moistened prior to collection. A culture for *N. gonorrhoeae* (and *C. trachomatis*) is obtained. Anoscopy should be done if rectal bleeding is present or the rectal examination reveals hematest-positive stool. A bimanual recto-abdominal or recto-vaginal-abdominal examination should be done gently to make sure that there is no tenderness and no enlargement of the uterus to suggest infection or pregnancy. Rectal sphincter tone should be assessed, since patients subjected to chronic rectal sexual abuse may have reflex relaxation.

5. If oral-genital contact has occurred, specimens from the girl's mouth should be obtained. A throat swab should be plated for *N. gonorrhoeae* and, if possible, for *C. trachomatis*. Oral swabs are obtained for detection of semen and other foreign matter if oral-genital contact occurred within 24 hours. Dry swabs are wiped on the areas between the lips and gums and along the tooth and gum lines. A saliva sample is also obtained for secretor status (even if no oral contact occurred).

6. Blood should be drawn for a serologic test for syphilis (rapid plasma reagin [RPR] or VDRL) and serum frozen to do future testing for HIV and hepatitis B, if indicated. A blood sample is also frequently included in rape kits for the police laboratory to do ABO blood typing of the victim.

7. A sensitive urine pregnancy test (such as ICON) should be done to detect a pre-existing pregnancy.

If the patient was unconscious during the assault, samples should be obtained from vagina, rectum, and mouth.

All laboratory specimens for the pathology laboratory or the police should be delivered personally by the doctor or nurse involved in the case, and properly signed receipts should be obtained. Use of a rape-evidence kit or rape protocol does not imply that the family or patient must push for prosecution; however, reporting the rape and using a protocol to collect the evidence ensures that the evidence has been appropriately handled and will be admissible in court if prosecution is to occur. Under the stress of the crisis, many families may have difficulty deciding whether prosecution will be sought; it, therefore, behooves the physician to obtain evidence that is medically and legally appropriate.

In cases of acute rape, the decision to prescribe antibiotics should be individualized and based on the risks as noted on page 544 of acquiring a sexually transmitted disease. The benefits of prophylactic treatment for syphilis, gonorrhea, and *Chlamydia* should be discussed with the patient. In asymptomatic adolescents with long-standing incestuous relationships, the physician should wait for the cultures and blood tests before initiating treatment (unless the perpetrator is known to be infected). For adolescent victims of acute assault, we prefer to give antibiotics. However, the patient needs to be informed that not all organisms are covered and follow-up is essential. For therapy, single-dose ceftriaxone (250 mg IM) is followed by 7 days of tetracycline, doxycycline, or erythromycin (see p. 347). If the initial RPR is negative, a follow-up serologic test for syphilis is necessary if spectinomycin is chosen as an alternative for gonococcal prophylaxis or no prophylaxis is given. Tetanus toxoid should be given following standard pediatric guidelines for injuries, and when available, anti-HIV prophylaxis discussed with the patient.

"Morning-after" estrogen therapy should be offered to the post-pubertal adolescent who was raped less than 72 hours (preferably less than 48 hours) before being treated. It is important that the patient understand that the medicine should not be used if there is the possibility of a preexisting pregnancy; she should feel ready to have an abortion if she discovers several weeks later that she was in fact pregnant at the time of the estrogen administration. Morning-after therapy is discussed on page 492. A sensitive (urine or blood) pregnancy test should be done before medication is given.

A current telephone number should be verified, and a follow-up appointment should be given for 2 weeks later. A repeat pelvic examination is done to assess healing of injuries and to look for *Trichomonas* and bacterial vaginosis. It should be remembered that absence of injuries does not preclude the possibility of rape. In Cartwright and colleagues' study [58] from Tennessee of sexual assault victims over age 10, 40 percent sustained nongenital and 16 percent genital injuries. Repeat cultures for *N. gonorrhoeae* and *Chlamydia* should be done if initial cultures were positive (and treated), or if prophylaxis was not given. A sensitive pregnancy test should be done 2 to 3 weeks after the rape, regardless of whether pregnancy prophylaxis was given. Testing for HIV and hepatitis B can be performed at 8 to 12 weeks post-assault and, if positive, compared with the serum frozen from the initial visit. If HIV testing is negative, it can be repeated 12 months post-assault. The patient should be reassured that her genital anatomy is normal. Patients greatly benefit from drawings to show them the range of hymenal size. The virginal adolescent who has had a forced episode of sexual intercourse may feel considerably relieved to understand that her introitus is not very different from some adolescents who have not had intercourse. She needs to be reassured that the assault in no way changes her ability to have normal sexual intercourse in the future or to have normal, healthy children. We have seen older teenagers who had unprotected intercourse because they felt that a rape, which occurred when they were 12 or 13 years old, markedly diminished their reproductive potential.

The extent of the counselling in the aftermath of a sexual assault depends on the initial encounter. For example, in the situation of an isolated episode of exhibitionism or nonforceful genital fondling by a stranger or neighbor, counselling should help integrate the event with a strongly positive view of the future. A case of a long-standing incestuous relationship requires proper reporting to the Children's Protective Services and a long-term treatment program. If the young adolescent has been trained to be a sexual object and to give and receive sexual pleasure in order to get approval, the outcome is often poor; such girls are often provocative in foster home settings. Cases of acute sexual assault during adolescence require that the physician discuss the possibility of prosecution and suggest the need for long-term counselling.

The availability of counselling should be stressed to the teenager [3]. Even if she seems nonverbal or appears to be coping well, the counsellor can often play an educational and supportive role in the initial interviews. The patient needs reassurance about her intactness and her femininity. She may need the opportunity to tell and retell her story to a caring, sympathetic person. Ideally, an experienced counsellor should be available at the time the rape is reported and should be willing to follow up the patient by telephone or home visits. It is not unusual for a patient to have somatic reactions in the first several weeks following a rape—muscle soreness, headache, fatigue, stomach pain, dysuria, sleep disturbances, and nightmares. Most rape victims express an extreme fear of physical violence and death. Many older women move and change their telephone numbers [59].

In the course of counselling, it is important to acknowledge to the patient that she may feel vulnerable and helpless and that the rape incident may interfere in the short term with her ability to form trusting relationships, especially with men. It is not unusual for women to experience extreme shame, guilt, and loss of self-esteem after a rape, and to insist that they might have somehow avoided the incident.

Self-blame may, however, have an adaptive value for the victim as she identifies factors of the assault that she could control, thus permitting her to feel in greater control of situations in the future. The response of parents, doctors, and friends often fosters this guilt in the victim and forces her to regard the rape as a sexual act rather than the violent crime she perceived.

The physician should work with the parents to help them support their daughter. Even when the daughter has been a victim of forced rape, parents may feel that the style of dress, the acceptance of a ride, or other behavior meant the youngster was "asking for it." The physician should make it clear to the parents that the teenager will deal with the crisis considerably better if she has their support.

Also, parents and boyfriends may respond by being overprotective at a time when the teenager is striving for independence; her sense of adequacy is thus further questioned. The young adolescent is often reluctant to return to school because of the fear that peer groups "will whisper behind her back." Stating this as a problem and suggesting that some of this behavior may be related to the feeling, "I'm glad it did not happen to me, but I wonder what it was like," may relieve the patient of some of her anxiety. Preventive measures, such as avoiding walking alone or hitchhiking, can be emphasized in such a way that the patient does not feel that she shares the blame for the incident.

It is difficult to predict the long-term sequelae of a rape because victims cope with stress in many different ways. However, it is clear that later sexual disturbances are common when the first sexual experience occurs in the context of violence and degradation. The other issues that tend to emerge later include (1) mistrust of men, (2) phobic reactions, and (3) neurotic symptoms of anxiety and depression precipitated by events that remind the victim of the original episode [60].

Despite the need to work through these issues both at the time of crisis and in later years, the teenager often expresses reluctance to continue follow-up care, because repeated encounters with the hospital setting remind her of the original incident. Thus, the initial counseling interviews should assess the patient's strengths in coping with stress and emphasize the availability of follow-up or referral. Telephone contact should be continued if at all possible. Involving a friend or relative whom the patient views as supportive is often helpful. The emphasis must be on working through the long-term problems that confront the rape victim and not merely on dealing with the immediate crisis measured in days or weeks.

In general, responsibility for reporting the incident to law enforcement officials belongs to the patient and her parents (if the patient is less than 18 years old). Although improvements are in sight, prosecution may intensify the guilt and shame of the victim. Questions such as, "What were you doing out late?", or "What did you expect?", or "Why didn't you struggle?", may force the patient to feel that she was somehow responsible for the rape. On the other hand, unless rapes are reported and prosecuted, the prevention of further violence is jeopardized. A counsellor for the victim should ideally accompany the teenager through the legal process and explain the involvement of prosecutors, judges, and courts.

SEXUAL ABUSE PREVENTION
With the recognition by health care professionals and educators of the widespread problem of sexual abuse, a number of efforts have been made in the area of prevention. Jenny and associates [11] have out-lines a protocol for pediatric visits (Table 17-1). The American Academy of Pediatrics (AAP) has published a brochure in consultation with the National Committee for Prevention of Child Abuse entitled *Child Sexual Abuse: What It Is and How to Prevent It.* The pamphlet outlines simple steps for suspecting abuse, dealing with a disclosure, and prevention. The AAP encourages parents to make sure their schools have prevention programs for students and teachers, to dis-cuss the subject with their children, to teach their children about body parts and be good listeners, and to know with whom their children are spending time. Young children should have sufficient knowledge of their bodies to know what types of behavior from adults to avoid or report. Children need to know that they can refuse the demands for physical closeness, even from friends or relatives. Children should be told early to avoid accepting rides with strangers or candy or money for close relationships. Reality dictates that children understand what are threats from others.

Programs have been initiated in many communities to help young women deal with rape prevention. Since rape commonly occurs among college students and other young women who have recently moved to a new location where environmental cues may not be so apparent, prevention programs stress the need for young women to learn about safe versus unsafe areas, to walk in a purposeful way, and to be constantly aware of dark corners and people who may be walking near them. If a threatening situation arises, women are in-structed to run toward traffic areas or lighted areas where other peo-ple are present. If self-defense measures are used initially, the women should then run as soon as possible. Women living alone may wish to change their mailboxes to read Mr. and Mrs. Smith instead of Sue Smith or S. Smith.

Although this chapter has dealt only with girls, because of focus of this book is gynecology, boys, too, may be subject to intrafamilial and stranger homosexual and heterosexual abuse; they need the same type of education and meaningful medical care during childhood [61].

Table 17-1. Protocol for Sex Education and Abuse Prevention in Well-Child Care

Age	Developmental Issues	Prevention Plan
Newborns	Complete dependency	Discuss choosing day-care and baby sitter
6 mo	Discovery of pleasant feelings associated with genitals	Talk about normalcy of infant genital exploration and self-stimulation
18 mo	Beginning of language development	Encourage parents to teach children normal anatomic terms for body parts
2½–4 yr	Establishment of gender identity	Identify children with sex role confusion
3–5 yr	Increasing independence of child, beginning of oedipal stage, recognition of sexual differences	Encourage parents to give child permission to say "no" to advances, teach children about "private places", reassure parents about normalcy of sexual curiosity and play, encourage parents to give their children straightforward answers about sex
5–8 yr	Developing increasing independence and accomplishments, beginning school	Discuss safety away from home, encourage parents to teach children safe behaviors, reinforce self-protective behaviors and difference between good touch and bad touch, encourage children to talk about frightening experiences
8–12 yr	Developing sexuality, the time of highest incidence of child sexual abuse	Parental planning for sex education for their children, reinforce personal safety education
13–18 yr	Development of adult identity, increasing independence from family, beginning of normal sexual experimentation	Discuss personal safety and risk taking behavior including alcohol and drug abuse, discuss sexuality, birth control and sexually transmitted diseases

Source: Jenny C, Sutherland SE, Sandahl BB. Developmental approach to preventing the sexual abuse of children. *Pediatrics* 1987; 78:1034.

REFERENCES
1. Burgess AW, Groth AN, Holmstrom LL, et al. Sexual Assault of Children and Adolescents. Lexington, MA: Lexington Books, 1978.
2. Finkelhor D. Sexually Victimized Children. New York: The Free Press, 1979.
3. Sgroi S. Handbook of Clinical Interventions in Child Sexual Abuse. Lexington, MA: Lexington Books, 1984.
4. Kempe CH. Sexual abuse, another hidden pediatric problem. Pediatrics 1978; 62:382.
5. Sarles RM. Incest. Pediatr Rev 1980; 2:51.
6. Tilelli JA, Turek D, and Jaffe AC. Sexual abuse in children. N Engl J Med 1980; 302:319.
7. Rimsza MR, and Niggemann EH. Medical evaluation of sexually abused children: A review of 311 cases. Pediatrics 1982; 69:8.
8. Woodling B, and Kossoris P. Sexual abuse: Rape, molestation, and incest. Pediatr Clin North Am 1981; 28:481.
9. Emans SJ, Woods ER, Flagg NT, et al. Genital findings in sexually abused, symptomatic and asymptomatic girls. Pediatrics 1987; 79:778.
10. Herman-Giddens ME, and Frothingham TC. Prepubertal female genitalia: Examination for evidence of sexual abuse. Pediatrics 1987; 80:203.
11. Jenny C, Sutherland SE, and Sandahl BB. Developmental approach to preventing the sexual abuse of children. Pediatrics 1987; 78:1034.
12. Finkelhor D. Sex among sibships: A survey on prevalence, rarity, and effects. Arch Sex Behav 1980; 3:171.
13. Brant RS, and Tisza VB. The sexually misused child. Am J Orthopsychiatry 1977; 47:80.
14. Orr DP, and Prietto SV. Emergency management of sexually abused children. Am J Dis Child 1979; 33:628.
15. Rosenfeld AA. Endogamic incest and the victim-perpetrator model. Am J Dis Child 1979; 133:406.
16. Rosenfeld AA. The clinical management of incest and sexual abuse of children. JAMA 1979; 242:1761.
17. Herman JL. Father-Daughter Incest. Cambridge, MA: Harvard University Press, 1981.
18. Schetsky DH, and Green AH. Child Sexual Abuse: A Handbook for Health Care and Legal Professionals. New York: Brunner/Mazel, 1988.
19. Fuster CD, and Neinstein LS. Vaginal Chlamydia trachomatis prevalence in sexually abused prepubertal girls. Pediatrics 1987; 79:235.
20. Glaser JB, Hammerschlag MR, and McCormack WM. Sexually transmitted disease in victims of sexual abuse. N Engl J Med 1986; 313:625.
21. Hammerschlag MR, Cummings M, Doraiswamy B, Cox P, et al. Nonspecific vaginitis following sexual abuse. Pediatrics 1985; 75:1028.
22. Ingram DL, White ST, Occhiuti AC, et al. Childhood vaginal infections: Associations of Chlamydia trachomatis with sexual contact. Pediatr Infect Dis 1986; 5:226.
23. White ST, Loda FA, and Ingram DL. Sexually transmitted diseases in sexually abused children. Pediatrics 1983; 72:16.
24. Jones JG, Jamauchi T, and Lambert B. Trichomonas vaginalis infestation in sexually abused girls. Am J Dis Child 1985; 139:846.
25. Dattel BJ, Landers DV, Coulter K, et al. Isolation of Chlamydia trachomatis from sexually abused female adolescents. Obstet Gynecol 1988; 72:240.
26. Jenny C. Sexual assault and STD. In Holmes KK, Mårdh P-A, Sparling PF, et al. (eds.). Sexually Transmitted Diseases (2nd ed.). New York: McGraw-Hill, 1990.
27. Jenny C. Child sexual abuse and STD. In Holmes KK, Mardh P-A, Sparl-

ing PF, et al. (eds.). Sexually Transmitted Diseases (2nd ed.). New York: McGraw-Hill, 1990.

28. Jenny C. Adolescent risk-taking behavior and the occurrence of sexual assault. Am J Dis Child 1988; 142:770.

29. Goldenring JM.*Staphylococcus saprophyticus* urinary tract infection in a sexually abused child. Pediatr Infect Dis 1988; 7:73.

30. Soules MR, Pollard AA, Brown KM, et al. The forensic laboratory evaluation of evidence in alleged rape. Am J Obstet Gynecol 1978; 130:142.

31. Duenhoelter JH, Stone IC, Santos-Ramos R, et al. Detection of seminal fluid constituents after alleged sexual assault. J Forensic Sci 1978; 4:824.

32. Graves HC, Sensabaugh GF, and Blake ET. Postcoital detection of a male-specific semen protein. N Engl J Med 1985; 312:330.

33. Evans RJ, and Herr JC. Immunohistochemical localization of the MHS-5 antigen in principal cells of human seminal vesicle epithelium. Anat Rec 1986; 214:372.

34. Herr JC, and Woodward MP. An enzyme-linked immunosorbent assay (ELISA) for human semen identification based on a biotinylated monoclonal antibody to a seminal vesicle–specific antigen. J Forensic Sci 1987; 32:346.

35. Herr JC, Summers TA, and McGee RS. Characterization of a monoclonal antibody to a conserved epitope on human seminal vesicle–specific peptides: A novel probe/marker system for semen identification. Biol Reprod 1986; 35:773.

36. Dahlke MC, Cooke C, Cunnanne M, et al. Identification of semen in 500 patients seen because of rape. Am J Clin Pathol 1977; 68:740.

37. Groth AN, and Burgess AW. Sexual dysfunction during rape. N Engl J Med 1977; 297:764.

38. Woodling BA, and Heger A. The use of the colposcope in the diagnosis of sexual abuse in the pediatric age group. Child Abuse Negl 1986; 10:111.

39. Woodling BA. Medical Examination of the Sexually Abused Child. Ventura, CA: New Horizons Medical Associates Production, 1985.

40. Enos FW, Conrath TB, and Byer JC. Forensic evaluation of the sexually abused child. Pediatrics 1986; 78:385.

41. Teixeira W. Hymenal colposcopic examination in sexual abuse. Am J Forensic Med Pathol 1980; 2:209.

42. Pokorny SF. Configuration of the prepubertal hymen. Am J Obstet Gynecol 1987; 157:950.

43. Pokorny SF, and Kozinetz CA. Configuration and other anatomic detail of the prepubertal hymen. Adolesc Pediatr Gynecol 1988; 1:97.

44. Jenny C, Kuhns ML, and Abrahams F. Hymens in newborn female infants. Pediatrics 1987, 80:399.

45. Paradise JE. Predictive accuracy and the diagnosis of sexual abuse: A big issue about a little tissue. Child Abuse Negl 1989; 13:169.

46. Muram D. Child sexual abuse: Relationship between genital findings and sexual acts. Child Abuse Neglect 1989; 13:211.

47. Hibbard RA, Roghmann K, and Hoekelman RA. Genitalia in children's drawings: An association with sexual abuse. Pediatrics 1987; 79:129.

48. Myers JEB. Role of physician in preserving verbal evidence of child abuse. J Pediatr 1986; 109:409.

49. Paradise JE, Rostain AL, Nathanson M. Substantiation of sexual abuse charges when parents dispute custody or visitation. Pediatrics 1988; 81:835.

50. DeJong AR. Maternal responses to the sexual abuse of their children. Pediatrics 1988; 81:14.

51. McCauley J, Gorman RL, and Guzinski G. Toluidine blue in the detection

of perineal lacerations in pediatric and adolescent sexual abuse victims. Pediatrics 1986; 78:1039.
52. Muram D. Classification of genital findings in prepubertal girls who are victims of sexual abuse. Adolesc Pediatr Gynecol 1988; 1:151.
53. Giaretto H, Giarretto A, and Sgroi SM. Coordinated Community Treatment of Incest. Lexington, MA: Lexington Books, 1978.
54. Landwirth J. Children as witnesses in child sexual abuse trials. Pediatrics 1987; 60:585.
55. Berliner L, Barbieri MK. The testimony of the child victim of sexual assault. J Soc Issues 1984; 40:125.
56. Runyan DK, Everson MD, Edelsohn GA, et al. Impact of legal intervention on sexually abused children. Pediatrics 1988; 113:647.
57. Hibbard RA, Brack CJ, Rauch S, et al. Abuse, feelings, and health behaviors in a student population. Am J Dis Child 1988; 142:326.
58. Cartwright PS. Factors that correlate with injury sustained by survivors of sexual assault. Obstet Gynecol 1987; 70:44.
59. Burgess A, and Holmstrom L. Rape trauma syndrome. Am J Psychiatry 1974; 131:981.
60. Notman M, and Nadelson C. The rape victim: Psychodynamic considerations. Am J Psychiatry 1976; 133:408.
61. Spencer MJ, and Dunklee P. Sexual abuse of boys. Pediatrics 1986; 78:133.

SUGGESTED READING
Finkel M. Anogenital trauma in sexually abused children. Pediatrics 1989; 84:317.
Muram D. Anal and perianal abnormalities in prepubertal victims of sexual abuse. Am J Obstet Gynecol 1989; 161:278.
McCann J, Voris J, Simon M, et al. Comparison of genital examination techniques in prepubertal girls. Pediatrics 1990; 85:182.
McCann J, Voris J, Simon M, et al. Perianal findings in prepubertal children selected for non-abuse: a descriptive study. Child Abuse Negl 1989; 13:179.
Muram D. Child sexual abuse—genital tract findings in prepubertal girls. I. The unaided medical examination. Am J Obstet Gynecol 1989; 160:328.
Muram D, Elias S. Child sexual abuse—genital tract findings in prepubertal girls. II. Comparison of colposcopic and unaided examinations. Am J Obstet Gynecol 1989; 160:333.

18. Legal Issues in Pediatric and Adolescent Gynecology

Richard Bourne, J.D.

This chapter focuses on legal issues in pediatric and adolescent gynecology. The legal complexity of these issues is compounded by social, psychological, and moral questions such as the morality of teenage sex; the perceived need for parents to be aware of the behavior of children; the authority to consent to medical intervention; the point at which life begins; the desirability of preventing birth through contraception, abortion, or sterilization; and issues of quality of life.

THE NATURE AND SOURCES OF LAW

Law emanates from both the state and federal levels of government. In the medical area, state law is generally the more important source of legal guidelines and constraints. It is important to remember that unlike federal law, state law varies by jurisdiction. Therefore, it is necessary to know the laws of the state in which you practice before making treatment decisions. It is equally important to understand that when state and federal law conflict, federal law under the doctrine of preemption usually takes precedence. Thus, for example, if the federal government permits abortions and state law does not, the federal law controls.

Both state and federal law have similar sources. The United States Constitution, of course, is interpreted by the federal courts, including the U.S. Supreme Court, while state courts interpret the state constitutions. Constitutional rights may differ between the state and federal level, with state rights being either broader or more narrow when compared with the federal constitution.

Law that is made or interpreted by judges is called *case law*. Judges, in deciding a particular case, are guided by legal precedents. The process of using decisions of prior courts to decide a case is called *stare decisis*. Much legal debate exists as to whether the proper function of judges is to interpret narrowly existing case law and statutes or actually to create law in response to a matter before them. Those who oppose "judicial legislation" argue that courts have as their sole responsibility the interpretation of legislative action, that is, the action of elected representatives.

Laws promulgated by the legislature are called *statutes* and usually appear in bound volumes under various chapters and sections. Generally when one wishes to clarify the law in a certain area, the first step is to find out whether there is a statute dealing with the issues.

In addition to constitutional law, case law, and statutes are laws promulgated by the executive branch of government called *executive orders*. There are also laws created by state or federal agencies called *regulations*. State agencies such as a department of public health or a department of mental health and federal agencies such as the Federal Trade Commission enact regulations that serve to clarify and interpret statutes. These regulations of executive agencies have the force and effect of law.

A final distinction of importance is that between civil and criminal law. Civil law involves such actions as medical malpractice where a plaintiff, the alleged victim, brings suit against a defendant, the alleged wrongdoer, seeking monetary damages for harmful acts. In civil actions, the burden of proof is on the plaintiff, who must prove his or her case by a preponderance of the evidence, that is, more evidence showing that the plaintiff has been wronged than evidence legally exculpating the defendant. In a criminal case, the state acts as the prosecutor and must prove criminal wrongdoing beyond a reasonable doubt. While the primary purpose of a civil suit is to recover damages for an injured plaintiff, the primary purpose of criminal action is to punish a guilty defendant. Such punishment, of course, can range from a fine to death.

CONSENT TO MEDICAL CARE
The general rule regarding consent to medical care is that anyone who has reached the age of majority, usually 18 or 21 years, may consent to treatment. If a patient is under the age of majority, a parent or legal guardian must usually consent to medical intervention. Every legal rule, however, has exceptions. In the case of an emergency, for example, consent is implied, and neither a parent, legal guardian, nor patient need explicitly authorize the medical care. It is important, however, to document that an emergency existed and what efforts were made to notify the parents of a minor patient.

It is also necessary to determine how state law defines an emergency. For example, in Massachusetts an emergency is defined as the following: "When delay in treatment will endanger the life, limb or mental well being of the patient" [1]. The definition of emergency may vary from state to state, but generally involves the same concept.

In addition to the emergency exception, minors are legally capable of consenting to their own health care if they are emancipated. Emancipation generally has two statutory definitions. The first is a minor fulfilling an adult status. If a patient, for example, is a member of the armed forces, is a parent of a child, is married, widowed, or divorced, or is living separately from and is financially independent of parents, he or she may consent to intervention without informing the parent or guardian.

The second basis of emancipation is where the minor's health may be endangered and the state wishes to encourage the minor to seek help despite possible parental resistance. Such areas where a minor may consent to treatment under state law include pregnancy, diseases dangerous to the public health, and alcohol or drug dependency. Reasoning that getting treatment is more important than obtaining parental consent, the state in these areas encourages the minor to seek intervention on his or her own authority by allowing treatment without parental consent. Unlike minors fulfilling an adult status, who generally may consent to any kind of medical care, minors in the second category generally may only consent to treatment for the specific condition creating emancipation.

The separate concept of mature minor, moreover, has received increasing judicial approval. Courts have recognized that there may be situations not otherwise controlled by statute where it is in the best interest of the minor not to notify parents of the intended medical treatment. If the minor is able to give informed consent to the intended treatment, the mature minor rule may apply.

The initial determination of whether a minor is mature or not usually rests with the treating physician, who assesses the nature of the procedure, its likely benefit, and the capacity of the particular minor to understand fully what the medical procedure involves. Thus, in a situation where a minor is not emancipated, it may still be possible to enter into a provider-patient relationship with the minor and without parental consent on the basis of the provider's assessment that the minor is mature.

Generally the caregiver will not be held liable for providing medical treatment without parental consent if the caregiver relies in good faith upon the minor's reasonable representation that he or she is emancipated. Consents obtained from emancipated and mature minors, and any interventions resulting from such consents, moreover, are confidential. Parents should not be informed unless the minor agrees. Such agreement should be documented in the patient's medical record.

Some states require physicians treating minors to inform the parent if the minor's condition is endangering of life or limb. Under such circumstances, the situation should be discussed with the minor before informing the parent, and this discussion should be documented in the patient's record. Under circumstances not endangering to life or limb, no information should be shared with the parent without the consent of the minor patient, and billings should not be mailed to parents if they undermine or are likely to undermine the confidentiality of the relationship.

Obtaining informed consent is a process that involves four distinct steps. The first step, which has already been discussed, is determining who has the authority to consent. The second step is determining whether the person with the authority to consent is competent to consent.

Legally, a person is presumed competent until demonstrated otherwise. Thus, for example, parents of a mentally retarded patient who has reached the age of majority do not automatically become their child's legal guardian. They must be appointed by a court, and without such judicial appointment, they do not have the legal authority to consent to their child's treatment. The provider should be cautious about providing treatment if there is any question regarding a person's capacity to understand the nature and consequences of a proposed procedure. Such reasons may include mental retardation, inebriation, or drug usage.

The third step in obtaining informed consent involves providing the person who has the authority to consent with all the material information necessary for a reasonable person to make an informed decision. Generally speaking, the patient or parent/guardian must be informed of the nature of the patient's condition, the nature and probability of the risks, the benefits to be reasonably expected, the inability of the treater to predict results, the reversibility of the procedure, the likely result of no treatment, and the alternatives to the proposed treatment including the risks and benefits of such alternatives. The provider should keep in mind that the more elective a proposed treatment, the more necessary it is to disclose all risks.

The final step in the informed consent process is obtaining the agreement of the person with the authority to consent. The person with legal authority to consent should sign the consent form agreeing to any interventions after such interventions have been fully communicated and understood. It is important to note that merely obtaining the signature of the person with authority to consent, without going through the other steps in the process, does not constitute informed consent. It is advisable, therefore, to make a note in the medical record documenting the informed consent process.

Finally, it is necessary for the practitioner to be aware of special situations where the general rules of consent may not apply. Such situations include a child's being in the custody of the state or a divorce situation where one parent may have physical care of a child but both parents may have legal custody or decision-making responsibility. Other special situations may include abortion, sterilization, management of child abuse cases, and consent to HIV testing, to be discussed subsequently.

CONFIDENTIALITY OF PATIENT INFORMATION

As a general rule, medical records and communications between providers and patients and their families are confidential and should not be released without the authorization of the patient/guardian or a proper judicial order. Even though parents usually have access to medical information of their minor children, certain situations may mandate a denial of access. As indicated previously, mature minors and emancipated minors who consent to treatment need not reveal either the consent or the treatment to their parents. Later sections will discuss other exceptions to parental notification, including the prescription of contraceptives to unemancipated minors.

Physicians and other care providers should learn whether statutory or common law privileges protect the confidentiality of a patient relationship. In some jurisdictions, for example, statutory privileges exist between psychotherapists and patients, physicians and patients, and social workers and clients. These privileges prevent professionals from revealing any information about their patients without specific authorization. Case law may further prohibit a professional's ability to disclose information without written consent.

SEXUAL ABUSE

Reporting statutes exist in every state that require various professionals to report sexual abuse to state agencies, usually a department of social services or its equivalent. Physicians, nurses, and other medical professionals are mandated reporters. The standard employed for determining whether the state agency should be notified is reasonable belief or suspicion that a child has suffered sexual abuse. Knowledge of incest or sexual abuse is not required because very rarely is a professional certain that sexual abuse has occurred. Symptoms such as fear of men, nightmares and sleep disturbances, stomachaches, and headaches are symptomatic, but not diagnostic of sexual exploitation and may require reporting.

From a legal point of view, if a mandated reporter has concerns about sexual abuse of a patient, it is generally safer to file a report than to withhold filing. Most states, for example, have an immunity provision protecting from suit or liability those professionals who file a report that is later proved erroneous. On the other hand, there are sanctions for mandated reporters who fail to fulfill their statutory responsibility to report.

After child abuse reports are received by state agencies, the agency must investigate the allegedly abusive family to determine whether a child is at risk. Assuming that a report is corroborated, the state agency has an obligation to monitor the child's safety, to provide services that may protect a child from future harm, and in certain circumstances, to refer the case for possible criminal prosecution or to remove the child from biologic parents for placement in foster care. Most states waive any privileges that otherwise may exist between the professional and patient in order to encourage reporting; in other words, the confidentiality that usually exists within a relationship is waived by law in the case of child abuse.

In addition to mandatory reporting statutes, states may have other legislation relevant to the management of sexual abuse. For example, statutes often exist that allow a physician serving in a hospital or health center to prevent a child from being removed by his or her caretaker if the child is in imminent and serious danger because of abuse and neglect. Legislation may also exist that allows professionals to petition juvenile or family courts if they feel that parental unfitness is causing harm to a child. Under such circumstances, the courts may remove legal custody from biologic parents and place it in the state and may order that such children be placed in foster care or other more secure environment.

Finally, because sexual abuse is more often criminally prosecuted than physical abuse, physicians and medical personnel may need to testify as expert or fact witnesses in prosecutions of alleged abusers. Because of this, it is imperative for physicians to keep complete and accurate records of any examinations conducted on children who have been victimized. Before testifying, the professional should make certain that no privileges exist that impede communication without the consent of patient or parent and should thoroughly review all records in order to become as knowledgeable as possible about the case. It should be understood that cases of child sexual abuse are very difficult to prosecute successfully because of the child's age and frequent lack of tangible evidence. In criminal matters, the state must prove a defendant guilty beyond a reasonable doubt, and this standard is difficult to reach in sexual abuse cases.

CONTRACEPTION

The provision of contraception to minors raises two legal issues, consent and the need for parental notification. In regard to consent, in 1977 the U.S. Supreme Court in *Carey* v. *Population Serv. Int'l* invalidated a New York statute that prohibited the distribution or sale of contraceptives to minors under the age of 16 [2]. The court ruled that the New York law violated the privacy rights of minors, which included the right to make procreative decisions. Such decisions, of course, should be based on informed consent, and a medical practitioner should review state law to ascertain whether additional requirements need to be met before contraceptives are prescribed.

Even if unemancipated minors can obtain contraceptives without parental consent, state law may require a provider to notify parents of the provision of contraceptives. In 1980, a U.S. Appeals Court in the case of *Doe* v. *Irwin* found that parents did not have a right to notification when minors voluntarily sought contraceptive devices from publicly operated family planning centers [3]. This decision finds support in more recent cases that find it is not in the best interest of the minor to breach a confidential relationship between the minor and the family planning service.

STERILIZATION

The sterilization of minors is almost exclusively a matter of state law. Because sterilization, if successful, ends the minor's reproductive capability, it is strictly regulated or prohibited outright. In some states, a mentally retarded child or adult may be sterilized but only after a formal proceeding to ensure protection of the incompetent's best interest. In other states, there is no legal basis for performing sterilization procedures on incompetents. The general rule is that neither courts nor a guardian can authorize voluntary sterilization of minors without specific statutory authority.

A private hospital may prohibit its medical staff from performing voluntary sterilization. Some states, moreover, have so-called conscience clauses that allow individual physicians or nurses to refuse participation in sterilization or abortion procedures if such procedures are performed in the facility in which they work.

ABORTIONS

In 1973, the U.S. Supreme Court in *Roe* v. *Wade* held that the "fundamental right" of privacy included the right of abortion. It then developed a trimester system which made the woman's health and viability of the fetus key decision points. In the first trimester of pregnancy, the abortion decision is primarily between a woman and her physician. In the second trimester, the state has an increasing interest in the woman's health and can regulate the conditions under which an abortion is performed. In the third trimester, because the fetus is viable and can generally survive separate and apart from its mother, the state develops a "compelling interest" in the life of the fetus and can prohibit abortions except if the mother's life or health is endangered [4].

In the recent case of *Webster* v. *Reproductive Health Services* the Court upheld a Missouri statute requiring doctors to test for fetal viability on any fetus thought to be at least 20 weeks old and forbidding public facilities and employees (doctors, nurses and other health care providers) from performing abortions other than those to save the life of the mother. Though not specifically overruling the Roe decision, Chief Justice Rehnquist, writing for a plurality of the Court, attacked its trimester structure as "unsound" and "unworkable". He said there is "no reason why the state's compelling interest in protecting potential human life should not extend throughout pregnancy rather than coming into existence only at the point of viability" [5]. While the Roe case functioned to keep states from restricting most abortions, the Webster decision will allow states much greater license to regulate and curtail abortions.

Prior to Webster, the Supreme Court had consistently struck down regulations and procedures that inhibit a woman's access to abortion. Impermissible restrictions include requirements that all second trimester abortions be performed in a hospital, that minors obtain either parental or judicial consent for abortions, and that women wait a minimum of 24 hours after signing a consent form before an abortion can occur. The Seventh Circuit U.S. Court of Appeals, for example, struck down an Illinois statute imposing a 24-hour waiting period on minors seeking abortion [6].

Generally, statutes requiring parental consent as a precondition to abortion have been struck down. In the case of *Planned Parenthood of Cent. Mo. v. Danforth*, the U.S. Supreme Court held unconstitutional a statute requiring parental consent to abortions for unmarried women under age 18 [7]. Some states, however, have enacted legislation allowing minors seeking abortions to apply for judicial consent as an alternative to parental consent. In the Massachusetts case of *Bellotti v. Baird* the court ruled that the state must provide a pregnant minor with a timely and confidential opportunity to show she is mature and informed enough to make her own abortion decision in consultation with her physician [8]. If the court finds the minor not sufficiently mature to give consent, it must authorize an abortion if this is found to be in her best interest. If state legislation contains these two provisions, then according to the *Baird* case, requiring parental consent would not constitute the absolute and arbitrary veto that was found unconstitutional in *Danforth*.

In addition to the issue of parental consent for a minor's abortion is the question of parental notification. In *H.L. v. Matheson* the U.S. Supreme Court upheld a Utah statute that required physicians to "notify if possible" the parents or guardian of an unmarried minor who sought an abortion [9]. The Supreme Court stated that the statute served an important state interest in protecting family integrity, safeguarding adolescents, and providing parents the opportunity to supply essential psychological and medical information to their child's physician. Although most parental notification statutes have been found constitutional, those that require more than simple notification have been struck down. For example, in *Hodgson v. Minnesota*, the U.S. Court of Appeals for the Eighth Circuit ruled that a judicial consent alternative must be an option in abortion statutes that require parental notification [10]. The court wished to ensure that the notice requirement was not unduly burdensome to the pregnant minor attempting to obtain an abortion. To ensure that the parental notification requirement is not unduly burdensome, the minor must be given the option of an alternative court procedure in which she can show her maturity or that performance of an abortion is in her best interest.

SEXUALLY TRANSMITTED DISEASES

States commonly require that health care professionals report cases of venereal disease or diseases dangerous to the public health to a state or local board of health. For example, in Massachusetts a physician treating a patient with acquired immunodeficiency syndrome (AIDS) must report the fact of AIDS to the local board of health. Gonorrhea and syphilis, on the other hand, are reported directly to the state Department of Public Health. As indicated earlier, a minor who believes that he or she is suffering from a sexually transmitted disease usually can consent to treatment without the authorization of a parent or guardian.

HIV AND AIDS

The statutes on human immunodeficiency virus (HIV) and AIDS are of recent origin and, like other laws, vary by state. Four important issues that arise are testing, confidentiality, universal precautions, and documentation. To test for the presence of HIV antibody, voluntary and informed consent of the patient and/or parent/guardian usually is required. As a matter of public policy, many states prohibit mandatory, coerced, or secret testing of individual patients for AIDS.

Many states, moreover, require that HIV testing and test results be maintained in confidence. In these states, the fact of and the results of such testing cannot be disclosed without the subject's written informed consent. This confidentiality requirement may conflict with the professional's perceived duty to warn a party who may be exposed to HIV or AIDS. For example, a teenager who has used drugs and tests positive on an HIV test may request that her boyfriend not be informed about test results. The physician may feel strongly that the boyfriend is entitled to the test information so that he also may be tested, receive medical and psychiatric intervention, and take prophylactic action regarding other sexual partners. The health care provider should learn whether a state confidentiality statute exists for HIV or AIDS.

The Occupational Safety and Health Administration of the Department of Labor requires the implementation of universal precautions in health care settings. Use of universal precautions makes mandatory testing less necessary to protect hospital staff. If professionals assume that blood and body fluids of all patients need be avoided, the rationale for universal mandatory testing becomes less salient.

Though health care providers need to maintain the confidentiality of HIV testing and results, it is necessary to document the fact and results of testing in hospital and private patient records. Documentation is necessary so that professionals can provide the best and most appropriate care for a patient. The confidentiality concern is not met by failing to record medical information. It is fulfilled by giving access only to those who have a clinical or administrative need to know.

SUMMARY

Minors are generally not capable of consenting to their own health care. In an emergency situation, however, consent of a parent or a guardian is not required. Furthermore, if a minor is mature (close to the age of majority and capable of reasonable decision making), he or she may consent to care without parental involvement if the mature minor doctrine is recognized by the state courts. If the minor is emancipated under state statute (has an adult status or a condition that is health endangering such as pregnancy, venereal disease, or drug dependency), the teen is empowered to consent to treatment.

Parents generally have access to the medical and other information of their children. However, if a statutory privilege exists such as between social worker and client or psychotherapist and patient, or if common law requires that a physician not disclose patient data, the confidential relationship between the professional and minor must be maintained. Confidentiality also must be respected if the minor is defined as mature or emancipated.

All 50 states have child abuse reporting statutes that require professionals to report cases of incest and sexual abuse to government agencies. State law may also allow or require professionals to obtain restraining orders to protect victims of sexual exploitation who are in imminent and serious danger. Legislation may also exist that allows minors to be placed in the temporary custody of the state for their protection.

The U.S. Supreme Court has upheld the right of minors to make procreative decisions and has forbidden states from prohibiting the distribution of contraceptives to them. In terms of notification, a U.S. Court of Appeals has ruled that parents have no constitutional right to be advised when a public facility distributes contraceptives to their children.

In the case of Peck v. Califano, it was held that sterilization of persons under 21 years of age may not lawfully be funded with federal monies [11]. This decision supports social policy restricting a minor's access to sterilization.

The U.S. Supreme Court decisions in Roe and Doe essentially permit abortions to occur during the first two trimesters of pregnancy. States may not promulgate regulations or procedures that restrict the constitutionally protected right of privacy unless a compelling state interest overrides that right [4, 12]. Generally, statutes requiring parental consent as a precondition to an abortion have been struck down by courts. Some states, however, have passed laws allowing minors seeking abortions to apply for the consent of a judge as an alternative to parental consent.

Certain sexually transmitted diseases must be reported to local or state public health agencies. HIV testing generally requires the voluntary informed and written consent of the patient and/or parent/guardian. The testing itself and test results usually are confidential, but a duty to warn may exist if someone is in danger of contagion. Universal precautions as specified by the federal Center for Disease Control should be followed, and HIV or AIDS testing and treatment should be properly documented in a medical record.

REFERENCES
1. M.G.L. C112, sec 12F.
2. Carey v. Population Serv. Int'l, 431 U.S. 678, 97 S. Ct. 2010 (1977).
3. Doe v. Irwin, 615 F. 2d 1162 (6th Cir. 1980).
4. Roe v. Wade, 410 U.S. 113, 93 S. Ct. 705 (1973).
5. Webster v. Reproductive Health Services, 109 S. Ct. 3040 (1989).
6. Zbarez v. Hartigan, 763 F. 2d 1532 (7th Cir. 1985).
7. Planned Parenthood of Cent. Mo. v. Danforth, 428 U.S. 52, 96 S. Ct. 2831 (1976).
8. Bellotti v. Baird, 443 U.S. 622, 99 S. Ct. 3035 (1979).
9. H.L. v. Matheson, 450 U.S. 398, 1101 S. Ct. 1164 (1981).
10. Hodgson v. Minnesota, 827 F. 2d 1191 (8th Cir. 1987).
11. Peck v. Califano, 454 F. Supp. 484 (1977).
12. Doe v. Bolton, 410 U.S. 179, 93 S. Ct. 739 (1973).

19. Sex Education

Robert P. Masland, Jr.

Without doubt sex education remains a cloudy issue in the United States, even though the need for competent, sensitive teaching of this material has never been so important. Our children are entering their adolescent years faced with the responsibility of making informed decisions regarding behavior that can and does affect their immediate health and, ultimately for some, whether they live or die. Sex education is much more than providing specific information about sexual intimacy, birth control, and the prevention of sexually transmitted diseases. That this information is essential is self-evident. To prevent an unwanted pregnancy requires one of two things—abstinence or birth control—and birth control being something more specific than the unreliable practice of coitus interruptus or the rhythm method. To prevent a sexually transmitted disease, either abstinence or the proper use of a condom is required. There is nothing fancy or difficult to comprehend about straightforward factual information. Of equal and perhaps even greater importance is sex education that includes attention to attitudes, moral and social values, and religion as well as cultural, ethnic, and family backgrounds. To be successful and to reach out to all young people in the community, the program must be designed to present information that is both factual and attitudinal as well as approved by the majority of sponsoring adults.

My bias, based on experience, as to the most appropriate setting for a sex education program is the school. Of course the school is not the only place for this program. The cornerstone for sex education may well be in the home, even though surveys and personal recollection provide convincing evidence that although attitudes are discussed and implied, it is the rare and occasional parent who is able to impart factual information with accuracy and composure. Learning about sex from friends and siblings continues to be the source of information for adolescents. Through the media, young people supplement their peer/street knowledge in a much more sophisticated fashion than was true 20 years ago. Sexual intercourse is depicted in graphic fashion in films as well as television. It would be silly to think that adolescents are naive as to the physical aspect of human sexuality.

The term *sex education* always seems to imply young adolescent females must be given information (warning!) about sexual behavior that could lead to an unwanted pregnancy. Similar education for the adolescent males in the past has placed undue emphasis on sexually transmitted disease (Army and Navy training films for example) while at the same time almost totally neglecting the responsibility that males must share with females for behavior that could result in pregnancy. Both males and females must have similar and equal instruction regarding pregnancy and sexually transmitted diseases, accompanied by an opportunity to express feelings and attitudes engendered by the material presented. Meetings can be single sex or mixed depending on the needs of the young people at that particular time in their lives. Younger adolescents may be more comfortable with the single-sex setting, whereas the older boys and girls will welcome a format that enables them to express ideas and concerns in a mixed group. To facilitate the discussion, it is important to have one or two adults present, preferably an adult of the same sex for the single-sex groups and a female/male couple for the mixed, older boys and girls. With the assistance of the adults, structure can be provided as well as direction as to topics that should be considered beyond the areas that are most comfortable. For example, teen pregnancy will be easier to talk about than homophobia or sexual harassment. Since 1972 when many previously single-sex independent schools decided to become coeducational, I have worked with many of these schools setting up programs along with the faculty and the full support of the heads and trustees. The format is exactly as described. Rather than using the somewhat bold label sex education and knowing that many issues will be addressed about behavior beyond the usual sex information, two titles have been particularly successful and are in place at the majority of the schools that have the program. They are Human Relations and Sexuality (HR&S) and Human Relations and Development (HR&D).

In these schools, which are located principally in New England, the programs are offered as an elective. If well done, an elective course can easily become popular, which means that many students will clamor to be included. Then, in effect, the so-called elective becomes a standard course in the curriculum. Typically, the enrollment in the course is by grade and age. The course is offered as a semester or term course at two levels—one group ninth and tenth grades and the other group eleventh and twelfth grades. Although the groupings may seem to be arbitrary without acknowledging degrees of awareness and sensitivity in the high school adolescent population, nevertheless the groups as arranged have worked well. Indeed, the level of sophisticated discussion can often be surprising for the leaders in the ninth/tenth grade groups, whereas the paucity of accurate sexual information in the eleventh/twelfth grade groups can be both alarming and distressing. The course enrollment is 12 to 16 students. Classes are usually held in late afternoon or early evening for 2 hours once a week during a term (fall, winter, or spring). Students are encouraged to take the course at both levels before graduation. The students in this particular population are, by and large, advantaged and goal oriented. It is, therefore, not surprising to learn that the courses have been successful. The positive response from the students and faculty is further reinforced by parental approval. Could such an approach be adopted and prove useful in the public and parochial schools? Indeed, in the public sector as well as in parochial and independent schools with middle school classes, parents and faculty should seriously consider a similar program for grades 6 through 8. What is required is the support and understanding of the parents and school authorities that the classes are being conducted in a dignified and thoughtful manner, with attitudes and standards of behavior sharing the stage with specific sexuality information. Too many times adults can sabotage well-meaning efforts to introduce sex education into the curriculum, fearing that the material presented will promote sexual activity. Although the following fact is rarely if ever accepted by adults who are opposed to sex education in the schools, children will learn about sex outside the home and schools, so why not attempt to educate at home and in the schools to counterbalance what is all too often inaccurate and inappropriate information?

Surveys and reports of adolescent behavior patterns after completing a sex education course in school tend to be negative when looking at pregnancy rates and incidence of sexually transmitted diseases. Since the courses reviewed vary in content and manner of presentation, it is understandable that the outcome could lead one to believe that sex education in the schools is of little value and should be considered expendable. Rather than be discouraged by negative outcome reports, we should do more to strengthen the existing courses in content, discussion, counselling, and access to professionals in health maintenance and prevention who will reinforce the need for responsible behavior when sexually active. The stakes are too high in today's society to abandon sex education.

PARENTS AND SEX EDUCATION
Although parents may not be actively providing sex education for their children in the home, they can and do furnish models of behavior. Affection, respect, and love between father and mother are unmistakable signals that are picked up by children of all ages. A man or woman raising a child or children without a partner for the child to observe poses some problems. Most single parents make a considerable effort to involve people of the opposite sex in family activities to provide appropriate role models. It is expected that children will learn a great deal about how to behave as an adult by observing adult behavior. It is not uniformly true that a strong, caring marriage will lead to offspring who will develop similar relationships, but it does help! Many children have overcome impossible family conditions, survived, and become adolescents and adults capable of considerate, responsible sexual behavior; but it does seem to be less hazardous for a child who grows up in a supportive family atmosphere. A home

where information can be exchanged without rancor or fear of retribution is the preferred setting for dealing with the ultimate questions of young people: What does it mean to be a woman? What does it mean to be a man?

In either case, the physician can be helpful to parents and adolescents, particularly when the adolescent is already sexually active or is on the verge of being sexually active. Physician-patient confidentiality is always maintained when sexuality issues are discussed with the adolescent. The physician should indicate to the adolescent that it might be in order to include one or both parents in the decision-making process. This advice is given with no assurance that it will be heeded. Adolescents do not live in a vacuum; there are adults who care about them as well as for them.

Adolescents require guidelines, a point of reference if you will, either to accept or rebel against. In the area of sexual behavior, it is important for parents to answer questions with facts when known and always with a statement of personal opinion. A parental opinion must be expressed on sexual matters as a benchmark for children to recall. Children can and will obtain sexual information outside the home; more often than not, this information is a mixture of truth, half-truth, and myths. Such information must be reviewed with adults who have a rapport with the young person, and the preferred adults are the parents. The physician must be available as a backup for the parents or to take over when the parents are lacking in information that the child must have in addition to parental feelings. There are many highly competent counsellors available for young people in addition to parents and physicians; teachers, psychologists, guidance counsellors, clergy, and social workers are key people to whom adolescents may turn when perplexed by sexual issues.

Decisions must be made by the adolescent in all areas of life, but most particularly with regard to interaction with members of the same and opposite sex. Points of view, which may be quite different, can be exchanged between adult and adolescent. In the home, with parent and child locked in emotional conflict, there may be little room for discussion of the highly charged subject of sexual activity. Parents are traditionally more comfortable in the posture that defines clearly to the child an irrevocable position. The inflexible, "thou shalt not" parent is all too familiar. No discussion necessary; case dismissed! At the opposite pole we find confused parents, unable to make decisions for themselves or for their children. In this instance, the result may be a home filled with doubts, permissiveness, and irresponsibility. Vacillation by adults on many issues can and does lead to exploitation by the adolescent. When the parent and adolescent are no longer able to communicate in a reasonable fashion, then it is appropriate to seek professional help. With support from a professional, one can hope to resolve the parent-adolescent conflict.

THE PHYSICIAN AS COUNSELLOR

Ample opportunity must be provided for the adolescent to state the problem when meeting with the physician. The physician must be willing to listen with minimum interruption. If the adolescent's story does not include information concerning sexual activity, then it is proper for the physician to ask questions in this area.

The adolescent's story may lead the physician to ask questions concerning a variety of sexual issues. For example, there may be tension at home relating to the parents' disapproval of the daughter's boyfriend. In her conversation with the physician, the girl may not wish to reveal her primary concern, which may be questions concerning birth control. If sexual activity is suspected by the physician, then the question should be clearly asked so that the adolescent realizes that specific information is required and available. The physician must stress the confidentiality of the doctor-patient relationship.

The physician who listens, asks the appropriate questions, and provides medical information in a confidential manner will have little difficulty dealing with adolescent sexuality problems. One cannot dictate the physician's personal preferences, but one can be certain that the manner in which this information is presented may well reflect the physician's attitude. The physician may not be in agreement with the adolescent's life-style, but to be an effective counsellor for adolescents, one must not act in a judgmental manner.

Homosexual feelings often surface during adolescence. It is normal for boys and girls to have close friends of the same sex, not only in early adolescence but throughout adolescence and adult life. Should the friendship become a physical relationship, there may be anxiety expressed by the adolescent boy or girl. If the physician is comfortable dealing with the subject of homosexuality, at least in the preliminary stage of evaluating whether the problem is a serious one for the patient, then the physician must ask the right questions and provide both answers and recommendations. It may be necessary for the physician to refer the patient for a psychiatric consultation. When a psychiatric consultation is requested, the patient must know that the reason for the referral is that a psychiatrist knows a great deal more about the subject of homosexuality than the physician and therefore is the ideal person to deal with the anxieties provoked in some individuals.

The boy who is unsure of himself, and certainly there are many boys in this category, may turn away from heterosexual interests. The boy who shies away from girls because he fears that he would be inadequate in a sexual encounter may find himself drifting into homosexual liaisons. It may be a new situation for physicians to see boys withdrawing from heterosexual activity, and it is well worth remembering when evaluating young male patients.

SEX EDUCATION IN THE COMMUNITY AND SCHOOLS

Education in adolescent behavior, including sexuality, for parents and children can be achieved only with the approval and support of the adult community. The physician with interest and training in the developmental problems of children and youth should be a voice in the community for information and instruction in adolescent behavior. Although elective courses in human sexuality are available in most medical schools, these courses are not given high priority in student education. As a consequence, only a small number of physicians can be considered reasonably knowledgeable in the field of sexuality. It is not that the practicing physician lacks information regarding the physical aspects of sex, but rather that physicians have not been sensitized to the specific emotional needs of young people and their parents when this information is dispensed.

For the interested physician who wishes additional training in the area of sexuality, there are postgraduate courses, textbooks, and clinics devoted to this subject. A good beginning would be to contact SIECUS (Sex Information and Educational Council of the United States*); through this organization the physician will receive a list of recommended reading material, both at the professional and the parent-patient level. Reading material is noted at the close of this chapter.

When a community looks to the medical profession for guidance in developing a program for sex education, it is essential that two issues be met head on: the content of the program and the necessity of having both young people and parents on the committee that develops the curriculum. It is essential that the program include a thorough discussion of the biologic growth and development of boys and girls during adolescence. The wide range of normal biologic growth must be covered so that boys and girls at different stages of development will understand that the body differences during early adolescence are to be expected and, therefore, can be understood as a normal variant. One cannot begin too early to provide information about human sexuality for children in preparation for the important decisions that adolescents must make about sexual behavior.

SUGGESTED READING

Hayes CD (Ed). *Risking the Future*, Vol I. Washington, DC: National Academy Press, 1987.

Lancaster JB, Hamburg BA. *School Age Pregnancy and Parenthood*. New York: Aldine DeGroyter, 1986.

Masters WH, Johnson VE. *Sex and Human Loving*. Boston: Little, Brown, 1986.

Masland RP Jr. *What Teenagers Want to Know about Sex*. Boston: Little, Brown, 1988.

*SIECUS, 1855 Broadway, New York, N.Y. 10023.

Appendix 1. Instruction Sheet for Taking 28-Day Oral Contraceptive Pills*

1. The name of your birth control pill is _____.
2. If you are taking pills for the first time, take the first pill of your first package on the Sunday following the first day of your next period, even if you have stopped bleeding before that day. If your period begins on Sunday, start taking the pills on the same day.

If menstrual flow starts on	Tablet taking begins on
Monday Tuesday Wednesday Thursday Friday Saturday	Following Sunday
Sunday	*that* Sunday

3. Take one pill every day without fail. As soon as you finish your last pill in the package, the next day start the first pill in a new package. This means that you will be taking the pills even during the days you are having a period.
4. Always take the pill at approximately the same time each day. The best time is ½ hour after a good meal or snack, or at bedtime, but whatever schedule you set up, you should stick to it.
5. *If you forget pills:*
   A. If you forget 1 pill—take the pill you forgot as soon as you remember, then take your regular pill for that day at the time you usually take your pill.
   B. If you forget 2 pills in a row in the first 2 weeks—take 2 pills on the day you remember and 2 pills the next day. Take 1 pill per day until the pack is finished. Use a back-up method (foam and condom, diaphragm) for at least 7 days.
      If you miss 2 pills in a row in the third week *or* you miss 3 pills or more in a row at any time—Sunday starter: Keep taking a pill every day until Sunday. On Sunday throw away the unused portion of the pack and start a new pack. Use a back-up method for at least 7 days. Non-Sunday starters: Throw out the rest of the current pack. Start a new pack the same day. Use a back-up method for at least 7 days.

6. Your period will appear normally sometime during your last week of pills in each package.

*From The Adolescent Clinic, The Children's Hospital, Boston.

7. *Extra Bleeding While Taking the 21 Hormone Tablets*
Breakthrough bleeding is very common in the first 3 months of taking birth control pills. The bleeding usually occurs during the second week of taking the hormone tablets and may be light (spotting for a few days) or heavy (like a normal menstrual period).

If light bleeding persists for more than 5 days or heavy bleeding lasts for more than 2 days, take 2 hormone tablets each day (one in the morning and one in the evening). The extra tablet needed each day should be drawn from an EXTRA package of pills. You should continue taking 2 tablets per day until you have stopped bleeding for one day. Normally you will need to take the extra medicine for 2 or 3 days. If you have questions, call 735-7181 or at night page the Adolescent Fellow on call 735-6369.

8. *If you purchase your pills in 3-month supplies, you must keep the pharmacy label from the first package and bring it with you when you go to the pharmacy to get refills. This label has your prescription number on it.*

9. If you have any problems or questions, please call us. The number is 735-7181.

10. While you are on the pills, you have to be re-examined every 6 months unless told otherwise by the doctor. The number you should call to make an appointment to see a doctor in the Adolescents' Unit is 735-7181. If you have a scheduled appointment, please keep it. If you are unable to keep the appointment, please call and cancel at least 24 hours in advance.

Appendix 2. Informed Consent for Oral Contraceptives*

Patient should check each space to indicate that she has read and understood each statement.

I have discussed the methods of birth control and have chosen to take the birth control pill. _____

I understand the Pill is very effective birth control but occasionally women might get pregnant taking it. I know there is less chance of this happening if I take the Pill correctly and do not skip or miss taking any. I understand I should not begin to take the Pill if I am pregnant. _____

I understand that Pill users have a slightly greater chance than non-users of developing certain serious problems that may become fatal in rare cases, including:
    blood clots
    stroke
    heart attack (to women age 35 and older)
    liver tumors _____

I understand that the chances of developing serious health problems increase with age, and when certain other health risk factors are present such as:
    smoking more than 15 cigarettes a day
    age 35 or older
    high blood pressure
    high levels of blood cholesterol
    diabetes _____

I understand that I should not use the Pill if I have had, now have, or develop in the future:
    blood clots
    inflammation in the veins (phlebitis) _____

I understand that some minor reactions to the Pill may include:
    nausea, vomiting
    breast tenderness
    weight gain or loss
    spotting between periods
    headaches _____

I know when taking the Pill I should watch for these danger signals:
    A - abdominal pain
    C - chest pain or shortness of breath
    H - headaches that are severe
    E - eye problems such as blurring or double vision
    S - severe depression
    S - severe leg pain/swelling

and report them immediately to The Children's Hospital (nurse or physician) _____

*From The Children's Hospital, Boston.

I understand that I need regular check-ups while taking the Pill including a physical, pelvic, and lab tests.   _____

I understand that I should do a monthly self-breast exam (SBE) (and I understand how to do this examination)   _____

I understand that there may be less protection from pregnancy when the Pill is taken with some drugs, including drugs to control seizures and certain antibiotics. I understand that I should talk to my doctor about taking any other medicine with the Pill.   _____

I understand that in addition to its benefit as a method of birth control, some women experience the following benefits from using the Pill:

   decreased menstrual cramps and blood loss
   predictable, regular menstrual cycles
   less iron deficiency anemia
   less acne
   some protection from non-cancerous tumors and ovarian cysts
   some protection from ovarian and uterine lining cancer
   decreased risk of infection of the pelvis, uterus, or tubes (P.I.D.)
   fewer ectopic pregnancies   _____

I understand that if I see a doctor for any reason, I should tell him/her that I am on the Pill.   _____

I understand that the Pill does not protect me from getting STDs (sexually transmitted diseases) and it is recommended that condoms be used to do this.   _____

I know that if I have any questions or problems a provider is available to me by phone (735-7181) or in the Emergency Room.   _____

Signature _____   Date _____

Witness _____

Appendix 3. Patient Handout for Calcium Intake*

Where to find your calcium

1,200 milligrams of calcium are recommended each day if you are between 11 and 18 years old. This amount increases to 1,600 milligrams per day for girls who are pregnant or breastfeeding.[1]

	Calcium (milligrams)[2,3]	Calories[2,3]
Buttermilk: 1 cup	285	100
Cheese:		
American, pasteurized process, 1 ounce	174	105
Cheddar, 1 ounce	204	115
Cheese spread, American, pasteurized process, 1 ounce	159	80
Cottage, creamed, large curd, 1 cup	135	235
Cottage, low fat (2%), 1 cup	155	205
Monterey Jack, 1 ounce	212	106
Mozzarella, part skim, low moisture, 1 ounce	207	80
Muenster, 1 ounce	203	105
Swiss, 1 ounce	272	105
Cocoa, made with whole milk, 1 cup	298	225
Ice Cream, vanilla:		
Hardened (about 11% fat), 1 cup	176	270
Hardened (about 16% fat), 1 cup	151	350
Ice Milk, vanilla:		
Hardened (about 4% fat), 1 cup	176	185
Soft serve (about 3% fat), 1 cup	274	225
Milk:		
Whole, 1 cup	291	150
Low fat (2%), 1 cup	297	120
Low fat (1%), 1 cup	300	100
Skim, 1 cup	302	85
Chocolate, low fat (2%), 1 cup	284	180
Milkshake, thick		
Chocolate, 10 ounces	374	335
Vanilla, 10 ounces	413	315
Pudding: Chocolate, regular (cooked), 1 cup	292	300
Yogurt:		
Coffee and vanilla, low fat, 8-ounce container	389	194
Fruit, low fat, 8-ounce container	345	230
Plain, low fat, 8-ounce container	415	145

*From The National Dairy Board, *Why Your Doctor Says Calcium Is So Important*

Appendix 4. Sexual Abuse Protocol of the State of California

D. OBTAIN PATIENT HISTORY. RECORDER SHOULD ALLOW PATIENT OR OTHER PERSON PROVIDING HISTORY TO DESCRIBE INCIDENT(S) TO THE EXTENT POSSIBLE AND RECORD THE ACTS AND SYMPTOMS DESCRIBED BELOW. DETERMINE AND USE TERMS FAMILIAR TO THE PATIENT. FOLLOW-UP QUESTIONS MAY BE NECESSARY TO ENSURE THAT ALL ITEMS ARE COVERED.

1. Name of person providing history	Relationship to child	Address	City	County	State	Phone (W) (H)

2. Chief complaint(s) of person providing history

3. Chief complaint(s) in child's own words

4. ☐ Less than 72 hours since incident(s) took place Date/time/location	☐ Over 72 hours since incident(s) took place Date(s) or time frame/location

5. Identity of alleged perpetrator(s), if known	Age	Sex	Race	Relationship to child

6. Acts described by patient and/or other historian

	Described by patient			Described by historian		
	Yes	No	Unk	Yes	No	Unk
Vaginal contact						
Penis						
Finger						
Foreign object						
Describe the object						
Anal contact						
Penis						
Finger						
Foreign object						
Describe the object						
Oral copulation of genitals						
of victim by assailant						
of assailant by victim						
Oral copulation of anus						
of victim by assailant						
of assailant by victim						
Masturbation						
of victim by assailant						
of assailant by victim						
other						
Did ejaculation occur outside a body orifice?						
If yes, describe the location on the body:						
Foam, jelly, or condom used (circle)						
Lubricant used						
Fondling, licking or kissing (circle)						
If yes, describe the location on the body:						
Other acts:						

Was force used upon patient?
If yes, describe:

7. Post-assault hygiene/activity ( ) Not applicable if over 72 hours

	Described by patient			Described by historian		
	Yes	No	Unk	Yes	No	Unk
Urinated						
Defecated						
Genital wipe/wash						
Bath/shower						
Douche						
Removed/inserted tampon						
Brushed teeth						
Oral gargle/swish						
Changed clothing						

8. Symptoms described by patient and/or other historian

	Described by patient			Described by historian		
	Yes	No	Unk	Yes	No	Unk
Physical symptoms						
Abdominal/pelvic pain						
Vulvar discomfort or pain						
Dysuria						
Urinary tract infections						
Enuresis (daytime or nighttime)						
Vaginal itching						
Vaginal discharge						
Describe color, odor and amount below.						
Vaginal bleeding						
Rectal pain						
Rectal bleeding						
Rectal discharge						
Constipation						
Incontinent of stool (daytime or nighttime)						
Lapse of consciousness						
Vomiting						
Physical injuries, pain, or tenderness. Describe below.						
Behavioral/emotional symptoms						
Sleep disturbances						
Eating disorders						
School						
Sexual acting out						
Fear						
Anger						
Depression						
Other symptoms						

Additional information:

HOSPITAL IDENTIFICATION INFORMATION

CCJP 925   —2—   86 96690

E. OBTAIN PERTINENT PAST MEDICAL HISTORY

1. Menarche age ( ) N/A	Date of last menstrual period ( ) N/A	Use of tampons ( ) Yes ( ) No ( ) N/A	History of Vaginitis ( ) Yes ( ) No ( ) N/A

2. Note pre-existing physical injuries ( ) N/A

3. Pertinent medical history of anal-genital injuries, surgeries, diagnostic procedures, or medical treatment? ( ) Yes ( ) No If yes, describe

4. Previous history of child abuse? ( ) Yes ( ) No ( ) Unknown. If known, describe

F. CONDUCT A GENERAL PHYSICAL EXAM AND RECORD FINDINGS. COLLECT AND PRESERVE EVIDENCE FOR EVIDENTIAL EXAM.

1. Blood pressure	Pulse	Temperature	Respiration	Include percentiles for children under six
				Height Weight

2. Record general physical condition noting any abnormality   ( ) Within normal limits

* Record injuries and findings on diagrams: erythema, abrasions, bruises (detail shape), contusions, induration, lacerations, fractures, bites, and burns.
* Record size and appearance of injuries. Note swelling and areas of tenderness.
* Examine for evidence of physical neglect.
* Take a GC culture from the oropharynx as a base line. Take other STD cultures as indicated. Provide prophylaxis.
  IF EXAMINED WITHIN 72 HOURS OF ALLEGED INCIDENT(S):
* Note condition of clothing upon arrival (rips, tears, or foreign materials) if applicable. Use space below to record observations.
* Collect outer and underclothing if worn during or immediately after the incident.
* If applicable, collect fingernail scrapings.
* Collect dried and moist secretions, stains, and foreign materials from the body including the head, hair, and scalp. Identify location on diagrams.
* Scan the entire body with a Wood's Lamp. Swab each suspicious substance or fluorescent area with a separate swab. Label Wood's Lamp findings "W.L."
* Examine the oral cavity for injury and the area around the mouth for seminal fluid. Note frenulum trauma. If indicated by history: Swab the area around the mouth. Collect 2 swabs from the oral cavity up to 6 hours post-assault for seminal fluid. Prepare two dry mount slides.
* Collect saliva and head hair reference samples at the time of the exam if required by crime lab and if there is a need to compare them to a suspect.
* Record specimens collected on Section 7.

HOSPITAL IDENTIFICATION INFORMATION

OCJP 925   -3-   86 96698

Optional: Take photographs of genitals before and after exam.

Record injuries and findings on anal-genital diagrams: abrasions, erythema, bruises, tears/transections, scars, distortions or adhesions, etc. Use anal-genital chart on next page to record additional descriptive information.

3. External genitalia
* Examine the external genitalia and perianal area including inner thighs for injury.
* For boys, take a GC culture from the urethra. Take other STD cultures as indicated. Provide prophylaxis.
    IF EXAMINED WITHIN 72 HOURS OF INCIDENT:
* Collect dried and moist secretions and foreign materials. Identify location on diagrams.
* Pubertal children: Cut matted pubic hair. Comb pubic hair to collect foreign materials. Collect pubic hair reference samples at time of exam if required by crime lab and if there is a need to compare them to a suspect.
* Scan area with Wood's Lamp. Swab each suspicious substance or fluorescent area. Label Wood's Lamp findings "W.L."
* For boys, collect 2 penile swabs if indicated. Collect one swab from the urethral meatus and one swab from the glans and shaft. Take a GC culture from the urethra. Take other STD cultures as indicated. Provide prophylaxis.
* Record specimens collected on Section 7.
4. Vagina
* Examine for injury and foreign materials.
* Pre-pubertal girls with intact hymen/normal vaginal orifice: No speculum exam necessary.
* Pre-pubertal girls with non-intact hymen and/or enlarged vaginal orifice: Only conduct a speculum exam if major trauma is suspected and use pediatric speculum.
* Take a GC culture from the vaginal introitus in pre-pubertal girls with intact hymen/normal vaginal orifice; from the vagina in pre-pubertal girls with non-intact hymen and/or enlarged vaginal orifice; and, the endocervix in adolescents. Take other STD cultures as indicated. Provide prophylaxis.
* Obtain pregnancy test (blood or urine) from pubertal girls.
    IF EXAMINED WITHIN 72 HOURS OF INCIDENT:
* Pre-pubertal girls with intact hymen/normal vaginal orifice: Collect 2 swabs from the vulva.
* Adolescents or pre-pubertal girls with non-intact hymen and/or enlarged vaginal orifice: Collect 3 swabs from vaginal pool. Prepare 1 wet mount and 2 dry mount slides. Examine wet mount for sperm and trichomonas.
* Record specimens collected on Section 7.
5. Anus and rectum
* Examine the buttocks, perianal skin, and anal folds for injury.
* Conduct an anoscopic or proctoscopic exam if rectal injury is suspected.
* Take a GC culture from the rectum. Take other STD cultures as indicated. Provide prophylaxis.
* Take blood for syphilis serology. Provide prophylaxis.
    IF EXAMINED WITHIN 72 HOURS OF ALLEGED INCIDENT:
* Collect dried and moist secretions and foreign materials. Foreign materials may include lubricants and fecal matter.
* If indicated by history and/or findings: Collect 2 rectal swabs and prepare 2 dry mount slides. Avoid contaminating rectal swabs by cleaning the perianal area and relaxing the anus using the lateral or knee-chest position prior to insertion of swabs.
* Record specimens collected on Section 7.

DRAW SHAPE OF ANUS AND ANY LESIONS ON GENITALIA, PERINEUM, AND BUTTOCKS

DRAW SHAPE OF HYMEN AND ANUS AND ANY LESIONS ON GENITALIA, PERINEUM, OR BUTTOCKS

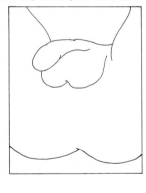

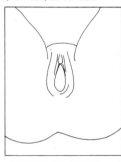

HOSPITAL IDENTIFICATION INFORMATION

6. Anal-genital chart

Female/Male General	WNL	ABN	Describe
Tanner stage			
Breast 1 2 3 4 5	☐	☐	_____
Genitals 1 2 3 4 5	☐	☐	_____
Inguinal adenopathy	☐	☐	_____
			_____
Medial aspect of thighs	☐	☐	_____
			_____
Perineum	☐	☐	_____
			_____

	Yes	No	
Vulvovaginal/urethral discharge	☐	☐	_____
			_____
Condyloma acuminata	☐	☐	_____

Female	WNL	ABN	Describe
Labia majora	☐	☐	_____
			_____
Clitoris	☐	☐	_____
			_____
Labia minora	☐	☐	_____
			_____
Periurethral tissue/ urethral meatus	☐	☐	_____
			_____
Perihymenal tissue (vestibule)	☐	☐	_____
			_____
Hymen	☐	☐	_____
Record diameter of hymen and check measurement used:			_____
☐ Horizontal			_____
☐ Vertical			_____
Posteriour fourchette	☐	☐	_____
			_____
Fossa Navicularis	☐	☐	_____
			_____
Vagina	☐	☐	_____
			_____
Other			_____

Exam position used:
☐ Supine
☐ Knee chest

Male	WNL	ABN	Describe
Penis	☐	☐	_____
Circumcised ☐ Yes ☐ No			
Urethral Meatus	☐	☐	_____
			_____
Scrotum	☐	☐	_____
			_____
Testes	☐	☐	_____
			_____

Female/Male Anus	WNL	ABN	Describe
Buttocks	☐	☐	_____
			_____
Perianal skin	☐	☐	_____
			_____
Anal verge/ folds/rugae	☐	☐	_____
			_____
Tone	☐	☐	_____

Anal spasm
☐ Yes ☐ No
Anal laxity
☐ Yes ☐ No
Note presence of stool in rectal ampulla
☐ Yes ☐ No
Method of exam for anal tone (discretion of examiner)
☐ Observation
☐ Digital exam
Exam position used:
☐ Supine
☐ Prone
☐ Lateral recumbent
Anoscopic exam
☐ Yes ☐ No ☐ N/A
Proctoscopic exam
☐ Yes ☐ No ☐ N/A
Genital exam done with:
Direct visualization   ☐
Colposcope   ☐
Hand held magnifier   ☐

HOSPITAL IDENTIFICATION INFORMATION

7. Record evidential and specimens collected.

FOR EVIDENTIAL EXAMS CONDUCTED WITHIN 72 HOURS OF ALLEGED INCIDENT

ALL SWABS AND SLIDES MUST BE AIR DRIED PRIOR TO PACKAGING (PENAL CODE § 13823.11). AIR DRY UNDER A STREAM OF COOL AIR FOR 60 MINUTES. Swabs and slides must be individually labeled, coded to show which slides were prepared from which swabs, and time taken. All containers (tubes, bindles, envelopes) for individual items must be labeled with the name of the patient, contents, location of body where taken, and name of hospital. Package small containers in a larger envelope and record chain of custody. See the State of California Medical Protocol for Examination of Sexual Assault and Child Sexual Abuse Victims published by the state Office of Criminal Justice Planning, 1130 K Street, Sacramento, California 95814 (916) 324-9100 for additional information.

SPECIMENS FOR PRESENCE OF SEMEN, SPERM MOTILITY, AND TYPING TO CRIME LAB

	Swabs	Dry Mount Slides	Yes	No	N/A	Taken by	Time
Oral							
Vaginal							
Rectal							
Vulvar							
Penile							

Vaginal wet mount slide examined for spermatozoa and trichomonas, dried, and submitted to crime lab			
Motile sperm observed			
Non-motile sperm observed			

OTHER EVIDENCE TO CRIME LAB

	Yes	No	N/A	Taken by
Clothing				
Fingernail scrapings				
Foreign materials on body				
Blood				
Dried secretions				
Fiber/loose hair				
Vegetation				
Dirt/gravel/glass				
Matted pubic hair cuttings				
Pubic hair combings				
Comb				
Swabs of bite marks				
Control swabs				
Photographs				
Area of body _____				
Type of camera _____				
Other _____				

REFERENCE SAMPLES AND TOXICOLOGY SCREENS TO CRIME LAB

Reference samples can be collected at the time of the exam or at a later date according to crime lab policies if there is a need to compare them to a suspect. Toxicology screens should be collected at the time of the exam upon the recommendation of the physical examiner, law enforcement officer, or child protective services.

Reference samples	Yes	No	N/A	Taken by
Blood typing (yellow top tube)				
Saliva				
Head hair				
Pubic hair				
Toxicology screens				
Blood/alcohol toxicology (grey top tube)				
Urine toxicology				

OCJP 925

CLINICAL EVIDENCE TO HOSPITAL LAB

	Yes	No	N/A	Taken by
Syphilis serology (red top tube)				
STD culture				
Oral				
Vaginal				
Rectal				
Penile				
Pregnancy test				
Blood (red top tube) or urine				

PERSONNEL INVOLVED (print)	PHONE
History taken by:	
Physical examination performed by:	
Specimens labeled and sealed by:	
Assisting nurse:	
Family assessment taken by: ( ) N/A ( ) Report attached	
Additional narrative prepared by physician: ( ) N/A ( ) Report attached	

FINDINGS AND FOLLOW-UP

Report of child sexual abuse, exam reveals:

☐ PHYSICAL FINDINGS   ☐ NO PHYSICAL FINDINGS
  ☐ Exam consistent with history   ☐ Exam consistent with history
  ☐ Exam inconsistent with history   ☐ Exam inconsistent with history

SUMMARY OF PHYSICAL FINDINGS:
☐ Oral trauma   ☐ Genital trauma
☐ Perineal trauma   ☐ Anal trauma
☐ Hymenal trauma
☐ Other findings consistent/inconsistent (circle one) with history as follows:

_____
_____
_____

Follow-up arranged: ( ) Yes ( ) No
Child released to: _____

PHYSICAL EXAMINER

Print name of examiner

Signature of examiner

License number of examiner

LAW ENFORCEMENT/CHILD PROTECTIVE SERVICES

I have received the indicated items of evidence and the original of this report.

Law enforcement officer or child protective services

Agency	ID number	Date

HOSPITAL IDENTIFICATION INFORMATION

– 6 –

86 96698

Appendix 5. Sexuality: Additional Information Sources

Physicians interested in providing reading materials for their patients should consult their public library and peruse the books available for parents, children, and adolescents to become familiar with the content. It is useful to order many different pamphlets and read them before selecting several to have available in the office. The pamphlets are for different age groups, different levels of sophistication, and often have different messages on the important issues of sexuality, contraception, and abortion. The following is a partial list and more extensive lists can be obtained from local Planned Parenthood clinics, SIECUS, and the American Academy of Pediatrics. Physicians working with developmentally disabled patients will find the SIECUS bibliographies especially helpful. The addresses for obtaining these materials as well as other sources are found at the end of this section. Many of the pharmaceutical firms that make contraceptives and medications for vaginitis also have free pamphlets available.

FOR CHILDREN UNDER 10
Aho JJ, Petras JW. *Learning About Sex. A Guide for Children and Their Parents.* New York: Holt, Rinehart, and Winston, 1978.
Andry A, Schepp S. *How Babies are Made.* Boston: Little, Brown, 1984.
Gordon S, Gordon J. *Did the Sun Shine Before You Were Born?* Syracuse: Ed-U-Press, 1982.
Gruenberg S. *The Wonderful Story of How You Were Born.* New York: Doubleday, 1970.
May J. *How We Are Born.* Chicago: Follett, 1969.
Mayle P. *Where Did I Come From?* New Jersey: Lyle Stuart, 1973.
Portal C. *The Beauty of Birth.* New York: Knopf, 1971.
Ratner M, Chamlins S. *Straight Talk: Sexuality Education for Parents and Kids 4–7.* Planned Parenthood of Westchester, New York, 1985.
Showers D, Showers K. *Before You Were a Baby.* New York: Crowell, 1968.
Stein S. *Making Babies.* New York: Walker, 1974.

FOR PRETEENS AND YOUNG TEENAGERS
McCoy K, Wibblesman C. *Growing and Changing: A Handbook for Preteens.* New York: Perigee Books, 1986.
Madaras L. *Lynda Madaras' Growing-up Guide for Girls.* New York: Newmarket Press, 1986.
Madaras L. *What's Happening to My Body: Book for Girls.* New York: Newmarket Press, 1986.
Johnson EW. *People, Love, Sex, and Families: Answers to Questions Preteens Ask.* New York: Walker, 1985.
Johnson EW. *Love and Sex in Plain Language.* New York: Bantam, 1985.
Gardner-Loulan J, Lopez B, Quackenbush M. *Period.* San Francisco: Volcano Press, 1981.

Mayle P. *What's Happening to Me?* New Jersey: Lyle Stuart, 1975.
Cole J. *Asking about Sex and Growing Up.* New York: Morrow Junior Books, 1988.

PAMPHLETS
American College of Obstetricians and Gynecologists (ACOG):
  Growing Up
Planned Parenthood Federation of America (PPFA):
  About Menstruation
  Having Your Period: Do You Know the Facts About Menstruation?
  That Growing Feeling: Facts of Life for Teens and Pre-Teens
Network Publications:
  Growing Older: Facts and Feelings
RAJ Publications:
  The Perils of Puberty
  The Problem with Puberty
  This is You

FOR MIDDLE TO OLDER TEENAGERS
AND SEXUALLY ACTIVE TEENAGERS
Boston Children's Hospital with Robert Masland. *What Teenagers Want to Know About Sex.* Boston: Little, Brown, 1988.
McCoy K, Wibblesman C. *The New Teenage Body Book.* Los Angeles: The Body Press, 1987.
Bell R, Boston Women's Health Book Collective. *Changing Bodies, Changing Lives.* New York: Random House, 1988.
Boston Women's Health Book Collective. *The New Our Bodies, Ourselves.* New York: Simon and Schuster, 1984.
Breitman P, Knutson K, Reed P. *How to Persuade Your Lover to Use a Condom . . . And Why You Should.* Rocklin, CA: Prima Publishing, 1987.

PAMPHLETS
American Academy of Pediatrics (AAP):
  Making the Right Choice—Facts Young People Need to Know About Avoiding Pregnancy
ACOG:
  Being A Teenager: You and Your Sexuality
  Oral Contraceptives
  The Facts: What You Need to Know About Contraceptives to Make the Right Choice
PPFA:
  Sexuality Alphabet
  Teen Sex? It's Okay to Say: No Way
  What Teens Want to Know But Don't Know How to Ask
  Pelvic Exam: Your Key to Good Health
  Guide to Birth Control: Seven Accepted Methods of Contraception
  Condom: What Is It For, How It Works
Network Publications:
  Deciding About Sex . . . The Choice to Abstain
  Birth Control Facts
  Are You Kidding Yourself?
  The Condom
  The Diaphragm

Foam and Vaginal Suppositories
The Birth Control Pill
The Contraceptive Sponge
Talking with Your Parents About Birth Control
STD Facts
Genital Warts
Chlamydia
Herpes
RAJ Publications:
Choices
Roses Have Thorns (about STD's)
Teen Sax
So You Don't Want to Be a Sex Object
This Is You
Private Line:
"No" and Other Methods of Birth Control
Landers A. *Sex and the Teenager.* (Teen, c/o Ann Landers, Box 11562, Chicago, IL 60611–0562).

AIDS
Hein K, DiGeronimo TM, Editors of Consumer Books. *AIDS: Trading Fears for Facts.* New York: Consumer Reports Books, 1989.
Madaras L. *Lynda Madaras Talk to Teens About AIDS.* New York: Newmarket Press, 1988.

PAMPHLETS
Network Publications:
Teens and AIDS: Why Risk It?
Talking with Your Partner about Safer Sex
Condom and STD
Talking with Your Teenager About AIDS

FOR PARENTS
Wattleton F, Newcomer S. *How to Talk with Your Child About Sexuality.* New York: PPFA and Doubleday, 1986.
Cassell C. *Straight From the Heart: How to Talk to Your Teenager About Love and Sex.* New York: Simon and Schuster, 1987.
Gordon S, Gordon J. *Raising a Child Conservatively in a Sexually Permissive World.* New York: Simon and Schuster, 1986.
Bernstein A. *The Flight of the Stork.* New York: Delacorte, 1978.
Lewis H. *Sex Education Begins at Home: How to Raise Sexually Healthy Children.* Norwalk, CT: Appleton-Century-Crofts, 1983.
Lewis HR, Lewis ME. *The Parent's Guide to Teenage Sex and Pregnancy.* New York: St. Martin's, 1980.
Calderone M, Johnson EW. *The Family Book About Sexuality.* New York: Bantam, 1983.
Calderone M. *Talking with Your Child About Sex: Questions and Answers for Children from Birth to Puberty.* New York: Random House, 1982.
Gochros J. *What to Say After You Clear Your Throat.* Kailua, HA: Press Pacifica, 1980.
Flowers JV, Horsman J, Schwartz B. *Raising Your Child to be a Sexually Healthy Adult.* Englewood Cliffs, NJ: Prentice-Hall, 1982.

PAMPHLETS:
ACOG:
  Teaching Your Child About Sexuality
The National PTA:
  How to Talk to Your Preteen and Teen About Sex: A Guide for Parents
PPFA:
  How to Talk to Your Teenager About the Facts of Life
Planned Parenthood of Syracuse:
  Sex Education at Home. A Guide for Parents
Planned Parenthood of Santa Cruz:
  Saying Goodbye to the Birds and the Bees and Telling the Real Story: A Guide for Parents
Planned Parenthood of Southeastern Pennsylvania:
  Love, Sex, and Birth Control for the Mentally Handicapped: A Guide for Parents
Gordon S, Dickman I. *Sex Education. The Parents' Role.* Public Affairs Pamphlet No. 549.
Changes and Choices. Your Children and Sex. DHEW No. HSA 80-5647.

ADDRESSES FOR PAMPHLETS
American Academy of Pediatrics
Division of Publications
141 Northwest Point Blvd.
P.O. Box 927
Elk Grove Village, IL 60009-0927

American College of Obstetricians and Gynecologists
Distribution Center
409 12th Street, SW
Washington, DC 20024-2188

The National PTA
700 Rush Street
Chicago, Il 60611-2571

Network Publications
ETR Associates
P.O. Box 1830
Santa Cruz, CA 96061-1830

Planned Parenthood Alameda/San Francisco
815 Eddy Street
San Francisco, CA 94109

Planned Parenthood Center of Syracuse, Inc.
1120 East Genesee Street
Syracuse, NY 13210-1994

Planned Parenthood Federation of America, Inc.
810 Seventh Avenue
New York, N.Y. 10019

Public Affairs Committee, Inc.
381 Park Avenue South
New York, N.Y. 10016–8884

RAJ Publications
P.O. 15720
Lakewood, CO 80215

Tambrands Inc.
1 Marcus Avenue
Lake Success, NY 11042

Private Line
P.O. Box 131
Kenilworth, IL 60043

Planned Parenthood of Santa Cruz County
Education Department Publications
212 Laurel Street
Santa Cruz, CA 95060

Planned Parenthood of Southeastern Pennsylvania
1220 Sansom Street
Philadelphia, PA 19107

BIBLIOGRAPHIES

Sex Information and Education Council of the U.S. (SIECUS). Publications Department, 32 Washington Place, Suite 52. New York, N.Y. 10003 (bibliographies available for $2.50 each plus 15% postage and handling).

AIDS and Safer Sex Education (1988)
Bibliography of Religious Publications on Sex Education and Sexuality (1987)
Child Sexual Abuse and Prevention (1986)
Human Sexuality: A Bibliography for Everyone (1987)
Publications for Professionals (1989)
Sexuality and Family Life Education: An Annotated Bibliography of Curricula for Sale (1985)
Sexuality Education Pamphlets (1986)
Sexuality and the Developmentally Disabled (1988)

American Academy of Pediatrics, 141 Northwest Point Blvd, P.O. Box 927, Elk Grove Village, IL 60009 (1-800-433-9016). Sex Education for Adolescents (bibliography of sex education materials for children, adolescents, and parents).

U.S. Department of Health, Education and Welfare, Public Health Service, Health Services Administration, Bureau of Community Health Services, 5600 Fishers Lane, Rockville, MD 20857.

Index

semen tests in, 546–547
vulvovaginitis in, 68–70, 77, 351–352
legal definitions of, 539
as legal issue, 573–574
prevention of, 564, 565t
sexually transmitted disease and, 544–546
syphilis in, 544–546
Trichomonas in, 69, 544–546
Sexual development, delayed, 182–189.
See also Puberty, delayed.
case studies on, 184–189, 185f–188f
differential diagnosis in, 183f, 183–184
therapy in, 176–184
Sexual molestation, 539. *See also* Sexual abuse.
Sexuality
discussion of, in prepubertal years, 1
sex education, 398–402, 581–586
sourcebooks for, 599–603
Sexually transmitted disease, as legal issue, 577. *See individual infections.*
Shigella, in prepubertal vulvovaginitis, 68
Skin disorders
acne and hirsutism, 254
in oral contraceptive use, 473
in prepubertal vulvovaginitis, 71
Soap, in prepubertal vulvovaginitis, 67, 75
Sodomy, of child, 549
Span, arm, 109, 110
Specula, in adolescent examination, 23, 24f
Spermicides, 486–487
Spironolactone, in idiopathic hirsutism, 265
Staphylococcus aureus, in prepubertal vulvovaginitis, 67–68
Stein-Leventhal syndrome, 212. *See also* Polycystic ovary syndrome.
Sterilization, as legal issue, 575
Steroids. *See* Sex steroids.
Straddle injury, vaginal bleeding in, 82–83
Strawberry cervix, 25, 313
Streptococcus pyogenes, in prepubertal vaginitis, 67–68, 71–72
Stress
amenorrhea due to, 151, 162, 208–209
hirsutism due to, 245
Stress fracture, in athletic amenorrhea, 170
Stroke, and oral contraceptives, 464
Subdermal implants, contraceptive, 490–491
Swyer's syndrome, 59
Syphilis, 371–377
diagnosis in pregnancy of, 372–373
follow-up in, 377
incidence of, 371

screening for, 371–372
in sexual abuse, 544–546
stages of, 373
treatment of, 373–377
in congenital disease, 376–377
HIV infection and, 375
in latent disease, 374–375
in neurosyphilis, 375
in pregnancy, 375–376
in primary, secondary disease or contact, 374
vulvar ulcer in, 328

T4 levels, in oral contraceptive use, 468
Tampon
retained, 224, 321
toxic shock syndrome and, 333
Tanner stage
of breast development, 100, 101f 102f
at menarche, 102f, 110–111, 111f, 112t
of pubic hair development, 101, 101f, 102f
Teratoma
benign cystic, 429
immature, 429–430
Testicular feminization, 51, 198–199
case, 199
Testis
cryptorchidism of, 62–64
embryogenesis, 48–51, 49f, 60f
unilateral absence of, 64
Testis determining factor (TDF), 48
Testosterone
in adrenal and ovarian tumors, 138, 206, 207, 258
in androgen insensitivity, 198, 199
bound vs. free, 246
defects in synthesis of, 59
fetal, 50
in hirsutism, 245–246, 258, 266f
at puberty, 104f
Thalassemia, 163
Thecoma-fibroma, 432
Thelarche
delayed, in athlete, 169
normal pattern, 100, 101f, 102f
premature, 125, 140–142
Thrombosis, vascular, in oral contraceptive use, 463–465
Thyroid
disorders and anovulation, 223t
hypothyroidism and
amenorrhea in, 216, 217f
delayed puberty in, 162–163
hyperprolactinemia, 173
precocious puberty in, 126
thyroiditis and oophoritis, 160
Torsion, ovarian, acute pelvic pain in, 275–276, 423
Toxic shock syndrome, 330–333
causes of, 330–331